(9–1)

$$S^2_{\text{Pooled}} = \frac{df_1}{df_{\text{Total}}}(S^2_1) + \frac{df_2}{df_{\text{Total}}}(S^2_2)$$

The pooled estimate of the population variance is the degrees of freedom in the first sample divided by the total degrees of freedom (from both samples) multiplied by the population variance estimate based on the first sample, plus the degrees of freedom in the second sample divided by the total degrees of freedom multiplied by the population variance estimate based on the second sample.

(9–2)

$$S^2_{M_1} = \frac{S^2_{\text{Pooled}}}{N_1}$$

The variance of the distribution of means for the first population (based on an estimated population variance) is the pooled estimate of the population variance divided by the number of participants in the sample from the first population.

(9–4)

$$S^2_{\text{Difference}} = S^2_{M_1} + S^2_{M_2}$$

The variance of the distribution of differences between means is the variance of the distribution of means for the first population (based on an estimated population variance) plus the variance of the distribution of means for the second population (based on an estimated population variance).

(9–7)

$$t = \frac{M_1 - M_2}{S_{\text{Difference}}}$$

The t score in a t test for independent means is the difference between the two sample means divided by the standard deviation of the distribution of differences between means.

(10–1)

$$S^2_{\text{Within}} = \frac{S^2_1 + S^2_2 + \cdots + S^2_{\text{Last}}}{N_{\text{Groups}}}$$

The within-groups population variance estimate is the sum of the population variance estimates based on each sample, divided by the number of groups.

(10–2)

$$S^2_M = \frac{\Sigma(M - GM)^2}{df_{\text{Between}}}$$

The estimated variance of the distribution of means is the sum of each sample mean's squared deviation from the grand mean, divided by the degrees of freedom for the between-groups population variance estimate.

(10–4)

$$S^2_{\text{Between}} = (S^2_M)(n)$$

The between-groups population variance estimate is the estimated variance of the distribution of means multiplied by the number of scores in each group.

(10–5)

$$F = \frac{S^2_{\text{Between}}}{S^2_{\text{Within}}}$$

The F ratio is the between-groups population variance estimate divided by the within-groups population variance estimate.

(11–1)

$$\chi^2 = \Sigma \frac{(O - E)^2}{E}$$

Chi-square is the sum, over all the categories or cells, of the squared difference between observed and expected frequencies divided by the expected frequency.

(11–3)

$$E = \left(\frac{R}{N}\right)(C)$$

A cell's expected frequency is the number in its row divided by the total number of people, multiplied by the number in its column.

Statistics
for the Behavioral
and Social Sciences

Statistics for the Behavioral and Social Sciences

A Brief Course

Fourth Edition

Arthur Aron
Elaine N. Aron
State University of New York at Stony Brook

Elliot J. Coups
Fox Chase Cancer Center

PEARSON

Prentice
Hall

Upper Saddle River, New Jersey 07458

Library of Congress Cataloging-in-Publication Data

Aron, Arthur.
  Statistics for the behavioral and social sciences : a brief course / Arthur Aron, Elaine N. Aron,
Elliot J. Coups.—4th ed.
      p. cm.
  Includes bibliographical references and index.
  ISBN-13: 978–0–13–156278–3
  ISBN-10: 0–13–156278–9
  1. Social sciences—Statistical methods.   2. Social sciences—Data processing.   I. Aron, Elaine.
II. Coups, Elliot J.   III. Title.
  HA29.A745 2007
  300.1′5195—dc22

                                                                    2007003551

Executive Editor: Jeff Marshall
Editor-in-Chief: Leah Jewell
Project Manager (Editorial): LeeAnn Doherty
Editorial Assistant: Jennifer Puma
Director, Media and Assessment: Shannon Gattens
Media Project Manager: Richard Virginia
Marketing Manager: Jeanette Moyer
Marketing Assistant: Laura Kennedy
Assistant Managing Editor: Maureen Richardson
Project Manager (Production): Kathy Sleys
Manufacturing Buyer: Sherry Lewis
Interior Design: L. P. Zeidenstein
Cover Design: Bruce Kenselaar
Cover Illustration/Photo: Robert Harding World Imagery
Production Editor: Bruce Hobart
Full-Service Project Management: Pine Tree Composition
Printer/Binder: Edwards Brothers
Cover Printer: Coral Graphics

Credits and acknowledgments borrowed from other sources and reproduced, with permission, in this textbook appear on appropriate page within text (or on page xvi).

Pearson Prentice Hall™ is a trademark of Pearson Education, Inc.
Pearson® is a registered trademark of Pearson plc
Prentice Hall® is a registered trademark of Pearson Education, Inc.

Pearson Education Ltd.
Pearson Education Australia PTY, Ltd.
Pearson Education Singapore, Pte. Ltd.
Pearson Education North Asia Ltd.
Pearson Education, Canada, Ltd.
Pearson Educación de Mexico, S.A. de C.V.
Pearson Education—Japan
Pearson Education Malaysia, Pte. Ltd.
Pearson Education, Upper Saddle River, NJ

10 9 8 7 6 5 4 3
ISBN-13: 978-0-13-156278-3
ISBN-10:   0-13-156278-9

Brief Contents

Contents   vii

Preface to the Instructor   xi

Introduction to the Student   xvii

Chapter 1   Displaying the Order in a Group of Numbers Using Tables
and Graphs   1

Chapter 2   The Mean, Variance, Standard Deviation, and Z Scores   32

Chapter 3   Correlation and Prediction   66

Chapter 4   Some Key Ingredients for Inferential Statistics: The Normal
Curve, Sample versus Population, and Probability   120

Chapter 5   Introduction to Hypothesis Testing   145

Chapter 6   Hypothesis Tests with Means of Samples   172

Chapter 7   Making Sense of Statistical Significance: Effect Size
and Statistical Power   203

Chapter 8   Introduction to the t Test: Single Sample
and Dependent Means   234

Chapter 9   The t Test for Independent Means   275

Chapter 10   Introduction to the Analysis of Variance   311

Chapter 11   Chi-Square Tests and Strategies When Population
Distributions Are Not Normal   359

Chapter 12   Applying Statistical Methods
in Your Own Research Project   412

Appendix A: Tables   425

Appendix B: Answers to Set I Practice Problems   435

Glossary   455

Glossary of Symbols   463

References   465

Index   469

Web Chapter W1: Overview of the Logic and Language
of Behavioral and Social Sciences Research
(available at http://www.prenhall.com/aron)

Web Chapter W2: Making Sense of Advanced Statistical Procedures
in Research Articles
(available at http://www.prenhall.com/aron)

Contents

Preface to the Instructor   xi

Introduction to the Student   xvii

Chapter 1   Displaying the Order in a Group of Numbers Using Tables and Graphs   1
The Two Branches of Statistical Methods   2
Box 1-1: Math Anxiety, Statistics Anxiety, and You: A Message for Those of You Who Are Truly Worried about This Course   3
Some Basic Concepts   4
Kinds of Variables   5
Frequency Tables   6
Frequency Graphs   10
Shapes of Frequency Distributions   16
Box 1-2: Gender, Ethnicity, and Math Performance   19
Frequency Tables, Histograms, and Frequency Polygons in Research Articles   21
Summary   22
Key Terms   23
Example Worked-Out Problems   23
Practice Problems   25
Using SPSS   29

Chapter 2   The Mean, Variance, Standard Deviation, and *Z* Scores   32
Representative Values   33
Variability   39
Z Scores   46
Box 2-1: The Psychology of Statistics and the Tyranny of the Mean   48
Mean, Variance, Standard Deviation, and *Z* Scores in Research Articles   52
Summary   55
Key Terms   55
Example Worked-Out Problems   55
Practice Problems   58
Using SPSS   61

Chapter 3   Correlation and Prediction   66
Graphing Correlations: The Scatter Diagram   68
Patterns of Correlation   71
The Correlation Coefficient   76
Box 3-1: Galton: Gentleman Genius   81
Issues in Interpreting the Correlation Coefficient   84
Prediction   87
Prediction Using Raw Scores   91
The Correlation Coefficient and Proportion of Variance Accounted for   92
Correlation and Prediction in Research Articles   93
Advanced Topic: Multiple Regression and Multiple Correlation   95
Advanced Topic: Multiple Correlation and Multiple Regression in Research Articles   98
Summary   99

Key Terms   100
Example Worked-Out Problems   101
Practice Problems   104
Using SPSS   113
Appendix: Hypothesis Tests and Power for the Correlation Coefficient   117

Chapter 4   Some Key Ingredients for Inferential Statistics: The Normal Curve, Sample Versus Population, and Probability   120
The Normal Curve   121
Sample and Population   130
Probability   133
Box 4-1: Surveys, Polls, and 1948's Costly "Free Sample"   134
Normal Curves, Samples and Populations, and Probabilities
   in Research Articles   138
Summary   139
Key Terms   139
Example Worked-Out Problems   140
Practice Problems   142

Chapter 5   Introduction to Hypothesis Testing   145
A Hypothesis-Testing Example   146
The Core Logic of Hypothesis Testing   147
The Hypothesis-Testing Process   148
One-Tailed and Two-Tailed Hypothesis Tests   154
Box 5-1: To Be or Not to Be—But Can Not Being Be? The Problem of Whether
      and When to Accept the Null Hypothesis   157
Decision Errors   159
Hypothesis Tests as Reported in Research Articles   162
Summary   163
Key Terms   164
Example Worked-Out Problems   164
Practice Problems   166

Chapter 6   Hypothesis Tests with Means of Samples   172
The Distribution of Means   173
Hypothesis Testing with a Distribution of Means: The Z Test   182
Hypothesis Tests about Means of Samples (Z Tests) in Research Articles   186
Box 6-1: More about Polls: Sampling Errors and Errors in Thinking
      about Samples   186
Advanced Topic: Estimation and Confidence Intervals   188
Advanced Topic: Confidence Intervals in Research Articles   192
Summary   193
Key Terms   194
Example Worked-Out Problems   194
Practice Problems   197

Chapter 7   Making Sense of Statistical Significance: Effect Size and Statistical Power   203
Effect Size   203
Statistical Power   210
Box 7-1: Effect Sizes for Relaxation and Meditation: A Restful Meta-Analysis   211
Box 7-2: Jacob Cohen, the Ultimate New Yorker: Funny, Pushy, Brilliant,
      and Kind   215
What Determines the Power of a Study?   215
The Role of Power When Planning a Study   222
The Role of Power When Interpreting the Results of a Study   225
Effect Size and Power in Research Articles   228

Summary   229
Key Terms   230
Example Worked-Out Problems   230
Practice Problems   231

Chapter 8   Introduction to the *t* Test: Single Sample and Dependent Means   234
The *t* Test for a Single Sample   235
Box 8-1: William S. Gosset, alias "Student": Not a Mathematician, but a Practical Man   236
The *t* Test for Dependent Means   246
Assumptions of the *t* Test for a Single Sample and *t* Test for Dependent Means   255
Effect Size and Power for the *t* test for Dependent Means   256
Single-Sample *t* Tests and Dependent Means *t* Tests in Research Articles   260
Summary   261
Key Terms   262
Example Worked-Out Problems   262
Practice Problems   266
Using SPSS   272

Chapter 9   The *t* Test for Independent Means   275
The Distribution of Differences between Means   276
Hypothesis Testing with a *t* Test for Independent Means   283
Assumptions of the *t* Test for Independent Means   290
Effect Size and Power for the *t* Test for Independent Means   291
Box 9-1: Two Women Make a Point about Gender and Statistics   293
Review and Comparison of the Three Kinds of *t* Tests   295
The *t* Test for Independent Means in Research Articles   296
Summary   296
Key Terms   297
Example Worked-Out Problems   297
Practice Problems   301
Using SPSS   307

Chapter 10   Introduction to the Analysis of Variance   311
Basic Logic of the Analysis of Variance   312
Box 10-1: Sir Ronald Fisher, Caustic Genius at Statistics   318
Carrying Out an Analysis of Variance   319
Hypothesis Testing with the Analysis of Variance   327
Assumptions in the Analysis of Variance   328
Comparing Each Group to Each Other Group   329
Effect Size and Power for the Analysis of Variance   331
Factorial Analysis of Variance   334
Recognizing and Interpreting Interaction Effects   338
Analyses of Variance in Research Articles   344
Summary   345
Key Terms   346
Example Worked-Out Problems   346
Practice Problems   348
Using SPSS   356

Chapter 11   Chi-Square Tests and Strategies When Population Distributions Are Not Normal   359
Chi-Square Tests   360
Box 11-1: Karl Pearson: Inventor of Chi-Square and Center of Controversy   360

The Chi-Square Statistic and the Chi-Square Test for Goodness of Fit   362
The Chi-Square Test for Independence   367
Assumptions for the Chi-Square Tests   376
Effect Size and Power for the Chi-Square Tests for Independence   376
Strategies for Hypothesis Testing When Population Distributions
     Are Not Normal   379
Data Transformations   382
Rank-Order Tests   387
Comparison of Methods   389
Chi-Square Tests, Data Transformations, and Rank-Order Tests
     in Research Articles   391
Summary   393
Key Terms   394
Example Worked-Out Problems   395
Practice Problems   399
Using SPSS   405

**Chapter 12   Applying Statistical Methods in Your Own
                    Research Project   412**
Designing Your Study: Selecting a Statistical Test   413
Figuring Power and Needed Sample Size   416
Box 12-1: The Golden Age of Statistics: Four Guys Around London   417
Conducting the Study   417
Data Screening   418
Carrying Out the Major Analyses   421
Writing Up Your Results   421
In Closing   422
Summary   422
Key Terms   423

Appendixes   425

A: Tables   425

B: Answers to Set I Practice Problems   435

Glossary   455

Glossary of Symbols   463

References   465

Index   469

**Web Chapter W1: Overview of the Logic and Language
                         of Behavioral and Social Sciences Research
                         (available at http://www.prenhall.com/aron)**

**Web Chapter W2: Making Sense of Advanced Statistical Procedures
                         in Research Articles
                         (available at http://www.prenhall.com/aron)**

Preface to the Instructor

The heart of this book was written over a summer in a small apartment near the Place Saint Ferdinand, having been outlined in nearby cafes and on walks in the Bois de Boulogne. It is based on our many years of experience teaching, researching, and writing. We believe that this book is as different from the conventional lot of statistics books as Paris is from Pompeii, yet still comfortable and stimulating to the long-suffering community of statistics instructors.

Our approach was developed over decades of successful teaching—successful not only in the sense that students have consistently rated the course (a statistics course, remember) as a highlight of their undergraduate years, but also in the sense that students come back to us later saying, "I was light-years ahead of my fellow graduate students because of your course," or "Even though I don't do research, your course has really helped me understand statistics that I read about in my field."

In this fourth edition of this *Brief Course* we have tried to maintain those things about the book that have been especially appreciated, while reworking the text to take into account the feedback we have received, our own teaching experiences, and advances and changes in the field. However, before turning to what's new in the fourth edition, we want to reiterate some comments we made in the first edition about how this book from the beginning has been quite different from other statistics texts.

What We Have Done Differently

Different as this book is, it has from the start also done what the best of the statistics texts of the last few years have been already doing well: emphasizing the intuitive, deemphasizing the mathematical, and explaining everything in direct, simple language. But what we have done always has gone beyond these books in ten key respects.

1. *The definitional formulas are brought to center stage* because they provide a concise symbolic summary of the logic of each particular procedure. All our explanations, examples, practice problems, and test bank items are based on these definitional formulas. (The amount of data to be processed in our practice problems and test items are reduced appropriately to keep computations manageable.)

Why this approach? Amazingly, in an era where even our graduate students were born long after data analysis was routinely done by computer, statistics texts have failed to adjust to technologic reality. What is important is not that the students learn to calculate a correlation coefficient by hand with a large data set—programs like SPSS can do this in an instant with just a few mouse clicks. What is important is that students work problems in a way that keeps them constantly aware of the underlying logic of what they are doing. Consider the population variance—the average of the squared deviations from the mean. This concept is immediately clear from the definitional formula (once the student is used to the symbols): The population variance $= [\Sigma(X - M)^2]/N$. Repeatedly working problems using this formula ingrains the meaning in the student's mind. In contrast, the usual computational version of this formula only obscures this meaning: The population variance $= [\Sigma X^2 - (\Sigma X)^2/N]/N$. Repeatedly working problems using this formula does nothing but teach the student the difference between ΣX^2 and $(\Sigma X)^2$!

Teaching computational formulas today is an anachronism—at least forty years out of date! Researchers do their statistics on computers, and the use of statistical software makes the understanding of the basic principles, as they are symbolically expressed in the definitional formula, more important than ever. Students still need to work lots of problems by hand to learn the material. But they need to work them using the definitional formulas that reinforce the concepts, not using the antiquated computational formulas that obscure them. Not since the era when Eisenhower was U.S. president have those computational formulas made some sense as time-savers for researchers who had to work with large data sets by hand. But they were always poor teaching tools. (Because some instructors may feel naked without them, we still provide the computational formulas, usually in a brief footnote, at the point in the chapter where they would traditionally have been introduced.)

2. ***Each procedure is taught both verbally and numerically—and usually visually as well.*** In fact, when we introduce *every* formula, it has attached to it a concise statement of the formula in words. Typically, each example lays out the procedures in worked-out formulas, in words (often with a list of steps), and usually illustrated with an easy-to-grasp figure. Practice problems and test bank items, in turn, require the student to calculate results, write a short explanation in layperson's language of what they have done, and make a sketch (for example, of the distributions involved in a *t* test). The chapter material completely prepares the student for these kinds of practice problems and test questions.

It is our repeated experience that these different ways of expressing an idea are crucial for permanently establishing a concept in a student's mind. Many students in the behavioral and social sciences are more at ease with words than with numbers. In fact, some have a positive fear of all mathematics. Writing the formula in words and providing the lay-language explanation gives them an opportunity to do what they do best.

3. A main goal of any introductory statistics course in the behavioral and social sciences is to ***prepare students to read research articles.*** The way a procedure such as a *t* test or chi-square is described in a research article is often quite different from what the student expects from the standard textbook discussions. Therefore, as this book teaches a statistical method, it also gives examples of how that method is reported in journal articles. And we don't just leave it there. The practice problems and test bank items also include excerpts from journal articles for the student to explain.

4. The book is ***unusually up-to-date.*** For some reason, most introductory statistics textbooks read as if they were written in the 1950s. The basics are still the basics, but statisticians and researchers think far more subtly about those basics now. Today, the basics are undergirded by a new appreciation of issues like effect size, power, the accumulation of results through meta-analysis, the critical role of models, and a whole host of new orientations arising from the central role of the computer in statistical analyses. We are much engaged in the latest developments in statistical theory and application, and this book reflects that engagement. For example, we devote an entire early chapter to effect size and power and then return to these topics as we teach each technique. Furthermore, we discuss how to handle situations in which assumptions are violated, and we cover data transformations (this widely used approach is easily accessible to introductory students but is rarely mentioned in current introductory texts).

5. We ***capitalize on the students' motivations.*** We do this in two ways. First, our examples, while attempting to represent the diversity of behavioral and social science research, emphasize topics or populations that students seem to find most interesting. The very first example is from a real study in which students in their first week of an introductory statistics class rate how much stress they feel they are under. Also, our examples continually emphasize the usefulness of statistical methods and ideas as tools in the research process, never allowing students to feel that what they are learning is theory for the sake of theory.

Second, we have worked to make the book extremely straightforward and systematic in its explanation of basic concepts so that students can have frequent "aha!" experiences. Such experiences bolster self-confidence and motivate further learning. It is quite inspiring to *us* to see even fairly modest students glow from having mastered some concept like negative correlation or the distinction between failing to reject the null hypothesis and supporting the null hypothesis. At the same time, we do not constantly remind them how greatly oversimplified we have made things, as some books do.

6. *We emphasize statistical methods as a living, growing field of research.* Each chapter includes a "box" about famous statisticians or interesting sidelights. The goal is for students to see statistical methods as human efforts to make sense out of the jumble of numbers generated by a research study; to see that statistics are not "given" by nature, not infallible, not perfect descriptions of the events they try to describe, but rather constitute a language that is constantly improving through the careful thought of those who use it. We hope that this orientation will help them maintain a questioning, alert attitude as students and later as professionals.

7. *We include a Web Chapter (available at http://www.prenhall.com/aron) that looks at advanced procedures* without actually teaching them in detail. It explains in simple terms how to make sense out of these statistics when they are encountered in research articles. Most research articles today use methods such as hierarchical multiple regression, factor analysis, structural equation modeling, analysis of covariance, or multivariate analysis of variance. Students completing the ordinary introductory statistics course are ill-equipped to comprehend most of the articles they must read to prepare a paper or study a course topic in further depth. This chapter makes use of the basics that students have just learned (along with extensive excerpts from current research articles) to give a rudimentary understanding of these advanced procedures. This chapter also serves as a reference guide that students can print out to use in the future when reading such articles.

8. We have written an *Instructor's Manual that really helps teach the course.* The manual begins with a chapter summarizing what we have gleaned from our own teaching experience and the research literature on effectiveness in college teaching. The next chapter discusses alternative organizations of the course, including tables of possible schedules and a sample syllabus. Then each chapter, corresponding to the text chapters, provides full lecture outlines and *additional worked-out examples not found in the text* (in a form suitable for copying onto student handouts). These worked-out examples are especially useful to new instructors or those using our book for the first time, since creating good examples is one of the most difficult parts of preparing statistics lectures.

9. Our *Test Bank section of the Instructor's Manual makes preparing good exams easy.* We supply approximately 40 multiple-choice, 25 fill-in, and 10 to 12 problem/essay questions for each chapter. Considering that the emphasis of the course is so conceptual, the multiple-choice questions will be particularly useful for those of you who do not have the resources to grade essays. This supplement also includes computational answers to each textbook chapter's Set II practice problems. (The text provides answers to the Set I practice problems at the back of the book, including at least one example answer to an essay-type question for each chapter.)

10. The accompanying *Study Guide and SPSS Workbook* focuses on mastering concepts and also includes instructions and examples for working problems using statistical software. Most study guides focus on plugging numbers into formulas and memorizing rules (which is consistent with the emphasis of the textbooks they accompany). For each chapter, our *Study Guide and SPSS Workbook* provides learning objectives, a detailed chapter outline, the chapter's formulas (with all symbols defined), and summaries of steps of conducting each procedure covered in the chapter, plus a set of self-tests, including multiple-choice, fill-in, and problem/essay questions.

Also, our *Study Guide and SPSS Workbook* goes beyond the brief SPSS sections in each text chapter to provide the needed support for teaching students to become comfortable with this program and carrying out analyses on the computer. First, there is a special appendix on getting started with SPSS. Then, in each chapter corresponding to the text chapters, there is a section showing in detail how to carry out the chapter's procedures with SPSS. (These sections include step-by-step instructions, examples, and illustrations of how each menu and each output appears on the screen.) There are also special activities for using the computer to strengthen understanding. As far as we know, no other statistics textbook package provides this much depth of explanation.

About this *Brief Course*

We have been thrilled by the enthusiastic response of instructors and students to the four editions of our *Statistics for Psychology* (Aron & Aron, 1994, 1999, 2003; Aron, Aron, & Coups, 2006), as well as the positive comments of reviewers, including most encouraging evaluations in *Contemporary Psychology* (Bourgeois, 1997) and *Psychology Learning and Teaching* (Shevlin, 2005).

This *Brief Course* was our answer to the many requests we received from instructors and students for a textbook using our approach that is (a) more general in its focus than psychology alone and (b) shorter, to accommodate less comprehensive courses. Of course, we tried to retain all the qualities that endeared the original to our readers. At the same time, the *Brief Course* was not a cosmetic revision. The broadening of focus meant using examples from the entire range of behavioral and social sciences, from anthropology to political science. Most important, the broadening informed the relative emphasis (and inclusion) of different topics and the tenor of the discussion of these topics. The shortening was also dramatic: This *Brief Course* is substantially briefer than the original, making it quite feasible to cover the whole book even in a quarter-length course.

Influences on the Fourth Edition

We did the revision for the fourth edition in New York. We hope that this has not resulted in a loss of whatever romance the first edition gained from being written in Paris.

This revision is enriched by what we learned teaching with the first three editions and by what we learned from the many instructors and students who have written to us about their experiences using the book. This revision is also informed by our own use of statistical methods. The last several years have been quite productive for all of us in our own research programs. Our recent research endeavors have focused on diverse topics in personality, social, and health psychology, including the social neuroscience of romantic attraction, childhood roots of adult experience, and health behaviors among cancer survivors. Our research collaborations have helped us to keep in touch with how the best researchers are using statistics.

Specific Changes in the Fourth Edition

With each new edition we have strived to improve the writing, update content, and make adjustments based on our experience teaching and the wonderful input we have received from instructors using the text. In the third edition, we also focused extensively on adding important pedagogical features including "How Are You Doing?" self-tests throughout the chapters, tripling the number of practice problems, providing worked out computational problems as examples just prior to each chapter's practice problems, and as each new formula is introduced, including a boxed concise statement of the formula in words.

With the third edition, we also developed a unique web page available to instructors who adopt the book and their students: http://www.prenhall.com/aron. The web page provides a variety of study aids for each chapter, including learning objectives, quiz questions, a list of relevant and interesting websites, a chapter review, and downloadable PowerPoint slides. In addition, the website for this fourth edition includes two Web Chapters, one on the basics of research methods (Web Chapter W1) and one that helps students to make sense of advanced statistical procedures in research articles (Web Chapter W2). (As you may recognize, this latter web chapter was Chapter 12 in the third edition of the book.)

In this fourth edition, we of course have continued to focus on simplifying exposition and have done our usual updating of content, examples, boxes, and so on, plus making a host of minor adjustments to make the book more effective. And we have added further pedagogical aids, such as separating out some sections as "Advanced Topics," adding essay outlines before the Practice Problems section, including definitions of key terms in the margin, and introducing most chapters with an engaging example that we carry out throughout the chapter. Another major new feature is a section at the end of many chapters showing how to carry out the chapter's procedures using SPSS statistical software. We have also added a new final chapter that gives students practical advice and tips on how to apply the statistical methods they learned in the course to their own research projects. This chapter covers topics such as entering the data into the computer, screening the data, selecting an appropriate statistical test, and writing up the results. We hope that this chapter will help students to cross the bridge from a sound conceptual understanding of statistics to applying that understanding to real-world data analysis situations.

Keep in Touch

Our goal is to do whatever we can to help you make your course a success. If you have any questions or suggestions, please send us an e-mail (**Arthur.Aron@ sunysb.edu** will do for all of us). Also, if you should find an error somewhere, for everyone's benefit, please let us know right away. When errors have come up in the past, we have usually been able to fix them in the very next printing.

Acknowledgments

First and foremost, we are grateful to our students through the years, who have shaped our approach to teaching by rewarding us with their appreciation for what we have done well, as well as their various means of extinguishing what we have done not so well. We also much appreciate all those instructors who have sent us their ideas and encouragement.

We remain grateful to all of those who helped us with the first three editions of this book, as well as to those who helped with the first four editions of the larger book. For their very helpful input on the development of this fourth edition of the

Brief Course, we want to thank David E. Tanner, California State University, Fresno; Ben D. Jee, University of Illinois at Chicago; Pamela Auburn, University of Houston Downtown; George Johanson, Ohio University; Amy R. Pearce, Arkansas State University; and Dennis Jowaisas, Oklahoma City University. We are extremely grateful to Jeff Marshall of Prentice Hall for his good ideas for improving the book and for superbly leading us through the long revision process. We also particularly want to acknowledge Marie Thomas (California State University, San Marcos) for identifying many crucial final changes to the text.

Arthur Aron

Elaine N. Aron

Elliot J. Coups

Credits

Data in tables 3–13, 3–14, 8–8, 8–9, 9–4, 9–5, 10–8, 10–9, 11–7, 11–8, and 11–9 are based on tables in Cohen, J. (1988). *Statistical power analysis for the behavioral sciences* (2nd ed.). Copyright © 1988 by Lawrence Erlbaum Associates, Inc. Reprinted by permission.

Introduction to the Student

The goal of this book is to help you *understand* statistics. We emphasize meaning and concepts, not just symbols and numbers.

This emphasis plays to your strength. Many behavioral and social science students are not lovers of mathematics but are keenly attuned to ideas. And we want to underscore the following, based on our collective many decades of experience in teaching: *We have never had a student who could do well in other college courses who could not also do well in this course.* (However, we will admit that doing well in this course may require more work than doing well in others.)

In this introduction, we discuss why you are taking this course and how you can gain the most from it.

Why Learn Statistics, Other Than to Fulfill a Requirement?

1. *Understanding statistics is crucial to being able to read research articles.* In most of the behavioral and social sciences, nearly every course you take will emphasize the results of research studies, and these usually include statistics. If you do not understand the basic logic of statistics—if you cannot make sense of the jargon, the tables, and the graphs that are at the heart of any research report—your reading of research will be very superficial. (We also recommend that you take a course on how to design and evaluate good research. In this book, we focus on the statistical methods for making sense of the data collected through research. However, we have included a downloadable Web Chapter—available at http://www.prenhall.com/ aron—that provides an overiew of the logic and language of behavioral and social sciences research.)

2. *Understanding statistics is crucial to doing your own research.* Many students eventually go on to graduate school. Graduate study in the behavioral and social sciences almost always involves *doing* research. In fact, learning to do research on your own is often the entire focus of graduate school, and doing research almost always involves statistics. This course gives you a solid foundation in the statistics you need for doing research. Further, by mastering the basic logic and ways of thinking about statistics, you will be unusually well prepared for the advanced courses, which focus on the nitty-gritty of analyzing research results.

Many universities also offer opportunities for undergraduates to do research. The main focus of this book is understanding statistics, not using statistics. Still, you will learn the basics you need to analyze the results of the kinds of research you are likely to do. And in the final chapter you will learn some practical advice and tips for using what you learn in this book for analyzing the results of your own research. The website for the book (http://www.prenhall.com/aron) also has a downloadable Web Chapter that will help you to make sense of advanced statistical procedures that you may come across in research articles.

3. *Understanding statistics develops your analytic and critical thinking.* Behavioral and social science students are often most interested in people and in improving things in the practical world. This does not mean that you avoid abstractions. In fact, the students we know are exhilarated most by the almost philosophical levels of abstraction where the secrets of human experience so often seem to hide. Yet even this kind of abstraction often is grasped only superficially at first, as slogans instead of useful knowledge. Of all the courses you are likely to take in the behavioral and social sciences, this course will probably do the most to help you learn to think precisely, to evaluate information, and to apply logical analysis at a very high level.

How to Gain the Most from This Course

There are five things we can advise:

1. *Keep your attention on the concepts.* Treat this course less like a math course and more like a course in logic. When you read a section of a chapter, your attention should be on grasping the principles. When working the exercises, think about why you are doing each step. If you simply try to memorize how to come up with the right numbers, you will have learned very little of use in your future studies—nor will you do very well on the tests in this course.

2. *Be sure you know each concept before you go on to the next.* Statistics is cumulative. Each new concept is built on the last one. There are short "How Are You Doing?" self-tests at the end of each main chapter section. Be sure you do them. And if you are having trouble answering a question—or even if you can answer it but aren't sure you really understand it—*stop.* Reread the section, rethink it, ask for help. Do whatever you need to do to grasp it. Don't go on to the next section until you are completely confident you have gotten this one. If you are not sure, and you've already done the "How Are You Doing?" questions, take a look at the "Example Worked-Out Problems" toward the end of the chapter, or try working a practice problem on this material from the end of the chapter. The answers to the Set I practice problems are given toward the end of the book, so you will be able to check your work.

Having to read the material in this book over and over does not mean that you are stupid. Most students have to read each chapter several times. And each reading in statistics is usually much slower than that in other textbooks. Statistics reading has to be pored over with clear, calm attention for it to sink in. Allow plenty of time for this kind of reading and rereading.

3. *Keep up.* Again, statistics is cumulative. If you fall behind in your reading or miss lectures, the lectures you then attend will be almost meaningless. It will get harder and harder to catch up.

4. *Study especially intensely in the first half of the course.* It is especially important to master the material thoroughly at the start of the course. Everything else you learn in statistics is built on what you learn at the start. Yet the beginning of the semester is often when students study least.

If you have mastered the first half of the course—not just learned the general idea, but really know it—the second half will be easier. If you have not mastered the first half, the second half will be close to impossible.

5. *Help each other.* There is no better way to solidify and deepen your understanding of statistics than to try to explain it to someone having a harder time. (Of course, this explaining has to be done with patience and respect.) For those of you who are having a harder time, there is no better way to work through the difficult parts than by learning from another student who has just mastered the material.

Thus, we strongly urge you to form study groups with one to three other students. It is best if your group includes some who expect this material to come easily and some who don't. Those who learn statistics easily will get the very most from helping others who have to struggle with it—the latter will tax the former's supposed understanding enormously. Those who fear trouble ahead, you need to work with those who do not—the blind leading the blind is no way to learn. Pick group members who live near you so that it is easy for you to get together. Also, meet often—between each class, if possible.

A Final Note

Believe it or not, we love teaching statistics. Time and again, we have had the wonderful experience of having beaming students come to us to say, "Professor, I got a 90% on this exam. I can't believe it! Me, a 90 on a statistics exam!" Or the student who tells us, "This is actually fun. Don't tell anyone, but I'm actually enjoying . . . statistics, of all things!" We hope you will have these kinds of experiences in this course.

Arthur Aron

Elaine N. Aron

Elliot J. Coups

Statistics
for the Behavioral
and Social Sciences

CHAPTER 1

Displaying the Order in a Group of Numbers Using Tables and Graphs

CHAPTER OUTLINE

- The Two Branches of Statistical Methods
- Some Basic Concepts
- Kinds of Variables
- Frequency Tables
- Frequency Graphs
- Shapes of Frequency Distributions
- Frequency Tables, Histograms, and Frequency Polygons in Research Articles
- Summary
- Key Terms
- Example Worked-Out Problems
- Practice Problems
- Using SPSS

Welcome to *Statistics for the Behavioral and Social Sciences: A Brief Course.* We imagine you to be as unique as the other students we have known who have taken this course. Some of you are highly scientific sorts; others are more intuitive. Some of you are fond of math; others are less so, or even afraid of it. Whatever your style, we welcome you. We want to assure you that if you give this book some special attention (perhaps a little more than most other textbooks require), you *will* learn statistics. The approach used in this book has successfully taught all sorts of students before you, including people who had taken statistics previously and done poorly. With this book, and your instructor's help, you will learn statistics and learn it well.

Given that you *can* learn statistics, you still have to decide if you want to make the effort it will require. Why would you want to do that, except to meet a requirement of your major? (Not a very energizing motive.) First, you will be far better equipped to read research articles in your major. Second, you'll be on your way to being able

statistics   A branch of mathematics that focuses on the organization, analysis, and interpretation of a group of numbers.

descriptive statistics   Procedures for summarizing a group of scores or otherwise making them more comprehensible.

inferential statistics   Procedures for drawing conclusions based on the scores collected in a research study but going beyond them.

to do your own research if you so choose. Third, you will improve both your reasoning and your intuition. Fourth, each time you finally grasp something you were struggling with, you will feel great.

Formally, **statistics** is a branch of mathematics that focuses on the organization, analysis, and interpretation of a group of numbers. But what is statistics, really? Think of statistics as a tool that extends a basic thinking process that every human employs: You observe a thing; you wonder what it means or what caused it; you have an insight or make an intuitive guess; you observe again, but now in detail, or you try making some little changes in the process to test your intuition. Then you face the eternal problem: Was your hunch confirmed or not? What are the chances that what you observed this second time will happen again and again so that you can announce your insight to the world as something probably true? Statistics is a method of pursuing truth. At the very least, statistics can tell you the likelihood that your hunch is true in this time and place, with these sorts of people. (The truths of statistics also depend on how carefully you have collected your information, but good research design is another topic altogether.) This pursuit of truth, or at least of future likelihood, is the essence of science. It is also the essence of human evolution and survival. Think of the first research questions: What will the mammoths do next spring? What will happen if I eat this root? It is easy to see how the accurate have survived. You are among them. Because your ancestors exercised brains as well as brawn, you are here. Do those who come after you the same favor: Think carefully about outcomes. Statistics is one good way to do that.

Behavioral and social scientists usually use a computer and statistical software to carry out statistical procedures, such as the ones you will learn in this book. However, the best way to develop a solid understanding of statistics is to learn how to do the procedures by hand (with the help of a calculator). In order to minimize the amount of figuring you have to do, we use relatively small groups of numbers in each chapter's practice problems. We hope that this will also allow you to focus more on the underlying principles and logic of each statistical procedure, rather than on the mathematics of the particular practice problem you are working on (such as subtracting 3 from 7 and then dividing the result by 2 to give an answer of 2). (See the *Introduction to the Student* on pp. xv-xvii for more information on the goals of this book.) Having said that, we also recognize the importance of learning how to do statistical procedures on a computer, as you most likely would when conducting research. So, at the end of relevant chapters, there is a section called *Using SPSS* (see also the *Student's Study Guide and SPSS Workbook* that accompanies this text for a guide to getting started with SPSS). SPSS statistical software is commonly used by behavioral and social scientists to carry out statistical analyses. Check with your instructor to see if you have access to SPSS at your institution.

The Two Branches of Statistical Methods

There are two main branches of statistical methods:

1. **Descriptive statistics:** Behavioral and social scientists use descriptive statistics to summarize and make understandable—to describe—a group of numbers from a research study.
2. **Inferential statistics:** Behavioral and social scientists use inferential statistics to draw conclusions and inferences that are based on the numbers from a research study, but go beyond these numbers.

BOX 1–1   **Math Anxiety, Statistics Anxiety, and You: A Message for Those of You Who Are Truly Worried about This Course**

Let's face it: Many of you dread this course, even to the point of having a full-blown case of "statistics anxiety" (Zeidner, 1991). If you become tense the minute you see numbers, we need to talk about that right now.

First, this course is a chance for a fresh start with digits. Your past performance in (or avoidance of) geometry, trigonometry, calculus, or similar horrors need not influence in any way how well you comprehend statistics. This is largely a different subject.

Second, if your worry persists, you need to decide where it is coming from. Math or statistics anxiety, test anxiety, general anxiety, and general low self-confidence each seems to play its own role in students' difficulties with math courses (Cooper & Robinson, 1989; Dwinell & Higbee, 1991).

Is your problem mainly math/statistics anxiety? There are wonderful books and websites to help you. Do a search, or try *http://www.mathanxiety.net* or *http://www.mathpower.com*. We highly recommend Sheila Tobias's *Overcoming Math Anxiety* (1995) or *Succeed With Math: Every Student's Guide to Conquering Math Anxiety* (1987). Tobias, a former math avoider herself, suggests that your goal be "math mental health," which she defines as "the willingness to learn the math you need when you need it" (1995, p. 12). (Could it be that this course in statistics is one of those times?)

Tobias explains that math mental health is usually lost in elementary school, when you are called to the blackboard, your mind goes blank, and you are unable to produce the one right answer to an arithmetic problem. What confidence remained probably faded during timed tests, which you did not realize were difficult for everyone except the most proficient few.

Tobias says that students who are good at math are not necessarily smarter than the rest of us, but they really know their strengths and weaknesses, their styles of thinking and feeling around a problem. They do not judge themselves harshly for mistakes. In particular, they do not expect to understand things instantly. Allowing yourself to be a "slow learner" does not mean that you are less intelligent. It shows that you are growing in math mental health.

Is your problem test anxiety? Then you need to learn to handle anxiety better. Test taking requires the use of the thinking part of our brain, the prefrontal cortex. When we are anxious, we naturally "downshift" to more basic, instinctual brain systems. And that ruins our thinking abil-

ity. Anxiety produces arousal, and one of the best understood relationships in psychology is between arousal and performance. Whereas moderate arousal helps performance, too much or too little dramatically reduces performance. Things you have learned become harder to recall. Your mind starts to race, and this creates more anxiety, more arousal, and so on. Because during a test you may be fearing that you are "no good and never will be," it is important to rethink beforehand any poor grades you may have received in the past—most likely these reflected your problems with tests more than your abilities.

There are many ways to reduce anxiety and arousal in general, such as learning to breathe properly and to take a quick break to relax deeply. Your counseling center should be able to help you or direct you to some good books on the subject. Again, there are also many websites about reducing anxiety.

Test anxiety specifically is first reduced by overpreparing for a few tests, so that you go in with the certainty that you cannot possibly fail, no matter how aroused you become. The best time to begin applying this tactic is the first test of this course: There will be no old material to review, success will not depend on having understood previous material, and it will help you do better throughout the course. (You also might enlist the sympathy of your instructor or teaching assistant. Bring in a list of what you have studied, state why you are being so exacting, and ask if you have missed anything.) Your preparation must be ridiculously thorough, but only for a few exams. After these successes, your test anxiety should decline.

Also, create a practice test situation as similar to a real test as possible, making a special effort to duplicate the aspects that bother you most. If feeling rushed is the troubling part, once you think you are well prepared, set yourself a time limit for solving some homework problems. Make yourself write out answers fully and legibly. This may be part of what makes you feel slow during a test. If the presence of others bothers you, the sound of their scurrying pencils while yours is frozen in midair, do your practice test with others in your course. Even make it an explicit contest to see who can finish first.

Is your problem a general lack of confidence? Is there something else in your life causing you to worry or feel bad about yourself? Then we suggest that it is time you tried your friendly college counseling center.

Last, could you be highly sensitive? A final word about anxiety and arousal. About 15 to 20 percent of humans (and all higher animals) seem to be born with a temperament trait that has been seen traditionally as shyness, hesitancy, or introversion (Eysenck, 1981; Kagan, 1994). But this shyness or hesitancy seems actually due to a preference to observe and an ability to notice subtle stimulation and process information deeply (Aron, 1996; Aron & Aron, 1997). This often causes highly sensitive persons (HSPs) to be very intuitive or even gifted. But it also means they are more easily overaroused by high levels of stimulation, like tests.

You might want to find out if you are an HSP (at *http://www.hsperson.com*). If you are, appreciate the trait's assets and make some allowances for its one disadvantage, this tendency to become easily overaroused. It has to affect your performance on tests. What matters is what you actually know, which is probably quite a bit. This simple act of self-acceptance—that you are *not* less smart but *are* more sensitive—may in itself help ease your arousal when trying to express your statistical knowledge.

So good luck to all of you. We wish you the best while taking this course and in your lives.

---

variable   Characteristic that can have different values.

value   Number or category that a score can have.

score   Particular person's value on a variable.

In this chapter and the next two, we focus on descriptive statistics. This topic is important in its own right, but it also prepares you to understand inferential statistics. Inferential statistics are the focus of the remainder of the book.

In this chapter, we introduce you to some basic concepts, then you learn to use tables and graphs to describe a group of numbers. The purpose of descriptive statistics is to make a group of numbers easy to understand. As you will see, tables and graphs help a great deal.

Some Basic Concepts

Variables, Values, and Scores

As part of a larger study (Aron, Paris, & Aron, 1995), researchers gave a questionnaire to 151 students in an introductory statistics class during the first week of class. One question asked was, "How stressed have you been in the last 2½ weeks, on a scale of 0 to 10, with 0 being *not at all stressed* and 10 being *as stressed as possible?*" (How would *you* answer?) In this study, the researchers used a survey to examine students' level of stress. Other methods that researchers use to study stress include measuring stress-related hormones in human blood or by conducting controlled laboratory studies with animals.

In the current example, level of stress is a **variable,** which can have **values** from 0 to 10, and the value of any particular person's answer is the person's **score.** If you had answered 6, your score would be 6; it would have a value of 6 on the variable called level of stress.

More formally, a variable is a condition or characteristic that can have different values. In short, it can *vary.* In our example, the variable is level of stress. It can have values of 0 through 10. Height is a variable, social class is a variable, score on a creativity test is a variable, number of people absent from work on a given day is a variable, dosage of a medication is a variable, political party preference is a variable, and class size is a variable.

A value is just a number, such as 4, −81, or 367.12. A value can also be a category, such as male or female or the country you live in (Canada, the United States, Australia, and so forth).

Finally, on any variable, each person has a particular number or score that is that person's value on the variable. For example, your score on the stress variable might have a value of 6. Another student's score might have a value of 8. We often use the

Table 1–1 Some Basic Terminology		
Term	**Definition**	**Examples**
Variable	Condition or characteristic that can have different values	Stress level, age, gender, religion
Value	Number or category	0, 1, 2, 3, 4, 25, 85, female, Catholic
Score	A particular person's value on a variable	0, 1, 2, 3, 4, 25, 85, female, Catholic

numeric variable   Variable whose values are numbers (as opposed to a nominal variable).

equal-interval variable   A variable in which the numbers stand for about equal amounts of what is being measured.

rank-order variable   Numeric variable in which the values are ranks, such as class standing or place finished in a race; also called *ordinal variable.*

nominal variable   Variable with values that are categories (that is, they are names rather than numbers); same as *categorical variable.*

word *score* for a particular person's value on a variable. This is because much behavioral and social science research involves scores on some type of test.

Behavioral and social science research is about variables, values, and scores (see Table 1–1). We will be using these terms throughout the book. The formal definitions are a bit abstract. In practice, you will find that what we mean when we use these words is usually obvious.

Kinds of Variables

Most of the variables behavioral and social scientists use are like those in the stress ratings example. The scores are numbers that tell you how much there is of the thing being measured. In the stress ratings example, the higher the number, the more stress. We call this kind of variable a **numeric variable.** (Numeric variables also are called *quantitative variables.*)

Behavioral and social scientists use two main kinds of numeric variables. The kind of variable used most often is a variable in which the numbers stand for about equal amounts of what is being measured. This is called an **equal-interval variable.** Take grade point average (GPA). This is a roughly equal-interval variable. For example, the difference between a GPA of 2.5 and 2.8 means about as much of a difference as the difference between that of 3.0 and 3.3 (both are a difference of .3 of a GPA). Most behavioral and social scientists also consider scales like the 0 to 10 stress ratings as roughly equal interval. So, for example, a difference between stress ratings of 4 and 6 means about as much difference in degree of stress as a difference between 7 and 9.

The other kind of numeric variable social scientists often use is where the numbers only stand for relative rankings. This is called a **rank-order variable.** (Rank-order variables are also called *ordinal variables.*) An example is rank in one's graduating class. Notice that with a rank-order variable, the difference between one number and the next does not always mean the same amount of the underlying thing being measured. For example, the difference between being second and third in your graduating class could be a very unlike amount of difference in underlying GPA than the difference between being eighth and ninth. There is somewhat less information in the rank-order variable. It is less precise. However, behavioral and social scientists often use rank-order variables because they are the only information available.

There is also a kind of variable that is not about numbers at all, but which refers just to names or categories. This is called a **nominal variable.** The term *nominal* comes from the idea that its values are names. (Nominal variables are also called *categorical variables* because their values are categories.) For example, for the nominal variable gender, the values are female and male. A person's "score" on the variable gender is one of these two values. Similarly, hair color has values, such as brown, black, and so forth.

level of measurement Type of underlying numerical information provided by a measure, such as equal-interval, rank-order, and nominal (categorical).

Table 1–2 Levels of Measurement

Level	Definition	Example
Equal-interval	Numeric variable in which differences between values correspond to differences in the underlying thing being measured	Stress level, age
Rank-order	Numeric variable in which values correspond to the relative position of things measured	Class standing, position finished in a race
Nominal	Variable in which the values are categories	Gender, religion

These different kinds of variables are based on different **levels of measurement** (see Table 1–2). Researchers sometimes have to decide whether they will measure a particular variable using an equal-interval scale, a rank-order scale, or a nominal scale. The level of measurement selected affects the type of statistics that can be used with a variable. In this book, we focus mostly on numeric equal-interval variables. However, rank-order and nominal variables also are fairly common in the behavioral and social sciences. We discuss some statistical procedures specifically designed for using rank-order and nominal variables in Chapter 11.

How are you doing?

1. A father rates his daughter as a 2 on a 7-point scale (from 1 to 7) of crankiness. In this example, (a) what is the variable, (b) what is the particular score, and (c) what is the range of possible values?
2. What is the difference between a numeric and a nominal variable?
3. Name the kind of variable for each of the following variables: (a) a person's nationality (Mexican, French, Japanese, etc.), (b) a person's score on a standardized IQ test, (c) a person's place on a waiting list (first in line, second in line, etc.).

Answers

1. (a) crankiness, (b) 2, (c) 1 to 7.
2. A numeric variable has values that are numbers that tell you the degree or extent of what the variable measures; a nominal variable has values that are different categories and have no particular numeric order.
3. (a) nominal, (b) equal-interval, (c) rank-order.

Frequency Tables

An Example

Let's return to the stress rating example. Recall that in this study, students in an introductory statistics class during the first week of the course answered the question "How stressed have you been in the last 2½ weeks, on a scale of 0 to 10, with 0 being *not at all stressed* and 10 being *as stressed as possible?*" In the actual study, there were scores from 151 students. To ease the learning for this example, we are going to use a representative subset of scores from 30 of these 151 students (this will also save you time if you want to try it for yourself). The 30 students' scores (their ratings on the scale) are:

8, 7, 4, 10, 8, 6, 8, 9, 9, 7, 3, 7, 6, 5, 0, 9, 10, 7, 7, 3, 6, 7, 5, 2, 1, 6, 7, 10, 8, 8.

Looking through all these scores gives some sense of the overall tendencies. But this is hardly an accurate method. One solution is to make a table showing how many students used each of the 11 values the ratings can have (0, 1, 2, and so on, through 10). We have done this in Table 1–3. We also figured the percentage each value's frequency is of the total number of scores. Tables like this sometimes give only the raw-number frequencies and not the percentages, or only the percentages and not the raw-number frequencies.[1]

Table 1–3 is called a **frequency table** because it shows how frequently (how many times) each rating number was used. A frequency table makes the pattern of numbers easy to see. In this example, you can see that most of the students rated their stress around 7 or 8, with few rating it very low.

How to Make a Frequency Table

There are four steps for making a frequency table.

❶ **Make a list of each possible value down the left edge of a page, starting from the highest and ending with the lowest.** In the stress rating results, the list goes from 10, the highest possible rating, down through 0, the lowest possible rating. Note that even if one of the ratings between 10 and 0 had not been used, you would still include that value in the listing, showing it as having a frequency of 0. For example, if no one in the class had given a stress rating of 2, you would still include 2 as one of the values on the frequency table.

❷ **Go one by one through the scores, making a mark for each next to its value on your list.** This is shown in Figure 1–1.

❸ **Make a table showing how many times each value on your list was used.** To do this, add up the number of marks beside each value.

❹ **Figure the percentage of scores for each value.** To do this, take the frequency for that value, divide it by the total number of scores, and multiply by 100. You usually will need to round off the percentage. As a rough guideline, with fewer

Table 1–3	Frequency Table of Number of Students Rating Each Value of the Stress Scale	
Stress Rating	**Frequency**	**Percent**
10	3	10.0
9	3	10.0
8	5	16.7
7	7	23.3
6	4	13.3
5	2	6.7
4	1	3.3
3	2	6.7
2	1	3.3
1	1	3.3
0	1	3.3

Source: Data based on Aron, Paris, and Aron (1995).

TIP FOR SUCCESS

When doing Step ❷, cross off each score as you mark it on the list. This should help you to avoid mistakes, which are common in this step.

frequency table Listing of the number of individuals having each of the different values for a particular variable.

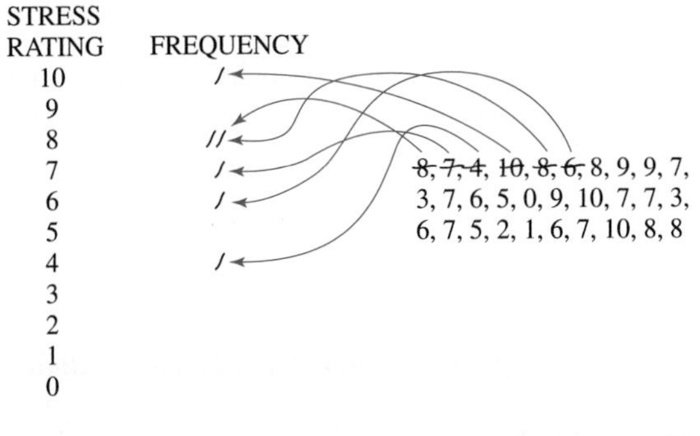

Figure 1–1 Making a frequency table for the stress ratings scores. (Data based on Aron, Paris, and Aron, 1995.)

---

[1]In addition, some frequency tables include, for each value, the total number of scores with that value and all values preceding it. These are called *cumulative frequencies* because they tell how many scores are accumulated up to this point on the table. If percentages are used, cumulative percentages also may be included. Cumulative percentages would give, for each value, the percentage of scores up to and including that value. The cumulative percentage for any given value (or for a score that has that value) is also called a *percentile*. Cumulative frequencies and cumulative percentages help you see where a particular score falls in the overall group of scores.

than 10 values, round to the nearest whole percentage; with 10 or more values, round to one decimal place. Note that because of the rounding, your percentages will not usually add up to exactly 100% (but it should be close).

Frequency Tables For Nominal Variables

The above steps assume you are using numeric variables, the most common situation. However, you can also use a frequency table to show the number of scores in each value (or category) of a nominal variable. For example, researchers (Aron, Aron, & Smollan, 1992) asked 208 students to name the closest person in their life. As shown in Table 1–4, 33 students selected a family member, 76 a nonromantic friend, 92 a romantic partner, and 7 selected some other person. As you can see in Table 1–4, the values listed on the left-hand side of the frequency table are the values (the categories) of the variable.

Table 1-4 Frequency Table for a Nominal Variable: Closest Person in Life for 208 Students

Closest Person	Frequency	Percent
Family member	33	15.9
Nonromantic friend	76	36.5
Romantic partner	92	44.2
Other	7	3.4

Source: Data from Aron, Aron, and Smollan (1992).

Another Example

McLaughlin-Volpe, Aron, and Reis (2001) had 94 first- and second-year university students keep a diary of their social interactions for a week during the regular semester. Each time a student had a social interaction lasting 10 minutes or longer, the student would fill out a card. The card included questions about who were the other people in the interaction and about various aspects of the conversation. Excluding family and work situations, the number of social interactions of 10 minutes or longer over a week for these 94 students were as follows:

> 48, 15, 33, 3, 21, 19, 17, 16, 44, 25, 30, 3, 5, 9, 35, 32, 26, 13, 14, 14, 47, 47, 29, 18, 11, 5, 19, 24, 17, 6, 25, 8, 18, 29, 1, 18, 22, 3, 22, 29, 2, 6, 10, 29, 10, 21, 38, 41, 16, 17, 8, 40, 8, 10, 18, 7, 4, 4, 8, 11, 3, 23, 10, 19, 21, 13, 12, 10, 4, 17, 11, 21, 9, 8, 7, 5, 3, 22, 14, 25, 4, 11, 10, 18, 1, 28, 27, 19, 24, 35, 9, 30, 8, 26

Now, let's follow our four steps for making a frequency table.

❶ **Make a list of each possible value down the left edge of a page, starting from the highest and ending with the lowest.** In this study, the highest number of interactions could be any number. However, the highest actual number in this group was 48, so we can use 48 as the highest value. The lowest possible number of interactions is 0. Thus, the first step is to list these values down a page. (It might be good to use several columns so that you can have all the scores on a single page.)

❷ **Go one by one through the scores, making a mark for each next to its value on your list.** Figure 1–2 shows this.

❸ **Make a table showing how many times each value on your list was used.** Table 1–5 is the result.

❹ **Figure the percentage of scores for each value.** We have *not* done so in this example because with so many categories, it would not help much for seeing the pattern of scores. However, if you want to check your understanding of this step, the first three percentages would be 1.1%, 2.1%, and 0.0%. (These are the percentages for frequencies of 1, 2, and 0, rounded to one decimal place.)

48 - /	31 -	15 - /
47 - //	30 - //	14 - ///
46 -	29 - ////	13 - //
45 -	28 - /	12 - /
44 - /	27 - /	11 - ////
43 -	26 - //	10 - ⊬⊬⊬ /
42 -	25 - ///	9 - ///
41 - /	24 - //	8 - ⊬⊬⊬ /
40 - /	23 - /	7 - //
39 -	22 - ///	6 - //
38 - /	21 - ////	5 - ///
37 -	20 -	4 - ////
36 -	19 - ////	3 - ⊬⊬⊬
35 - //	18 - ⊬⊬⊬	2 - /
34 -	17 - ////	1 - //
33 - /	16 - //	0 -
32 - /		

Figure 1-2 Making a frequency table of students' social interactions over a week. (Data from McLaughlin-Volpe et al., 2001.)

TIP FOR SUCCESS

Be sure to check your work by adding up the frequencies for all of the scores. This sum should equal the total number of scores you started with.

Table 1-5 Frequency Table for Number of Social Interactions During a Week for 94 College Students

Score	Frequency	Score	Frequency	Score	Frequency
48	1	31	0	15	1
47	2	30	2	14	3
46	0	29	4	13	2
45	0	28	1	12	1
44	1	27	1	11	4
43	0	26	2	10	6
42	0	25	3	9	3
41	1	24	2	8	6
40	1	23	1	7	2
39	0	22	3	6	2
38	1	21	4	5	3
37	0	20	0	4	4
36	0	19	4	3	5
35	2	18	5	2	1
34	0	17	4	1	2
33	1	16	2	0	0
32	1				

Source: Data from McLaughlin-Volpe et al. (2001).

interval In a grouped frequency table, the range of values that are grouped together. (For example, if the interval size was 10, one of the intervals might be from 10 to 19.)

grouped frequency table Frequency table in which the number of individuals (frequency) is given for each interval of values.

Table 1-6 Grouped Frequency Table for Stress Ratings

Stress Rating Interval	Frequency	Percent
10–11	3	10.0
8–9	8	26.7
6–7	11	36.7
4–5	3	10.0
2–3	3	10.0
0–1	2	6.7

Source: Data based on Aron, Paris, and Aron (1995).

Grouped Frequency Tables

Sometimes there are so many possible values that a frequency table is too awkward to give a simple picture of the scores. The last example was a bit like that, wasn't it? The solution is to make groupings of values that include all values within a certain range. For example, consider our stress example. Instead of having a separate frequency figure for the students who rated their stress as 8 and another for those who rated it as 9, you could have a combined category of 8 and 9. This combined category is a range of values that includes these two values. A combined category like this is called an **interval.** This particular interval of 8 and 9 has a frequency of 41 (the sum of the 26 scores with a value of 8 and the 15 scores with a value of 9).

A frequency table that uses intervals is called a **grouped frequency table.** Table 1–6 is a grouped frequency table for the stress ratings example. (However, in this example, the full frequency table has only 11 different values. Thus, a grouped frequency table was not really necessary.) Table 1–7 is a grouped frequency table for the 94 students' numbers of social interactions over a week.

A grouped frequency table can make information even more directly understandable than an ordinary frequency table can. Of course, the greater understandability of a grouped frequency table is at a cost. You lose information about the breakdown of frequencies within each interval.

When setting up a grouped frequency table, it makes a big difference how many intervals you use. There are guidelines to help researchers with this, but in practice it is done automatically by the researcher's computer (see the *Using SPSS* section at the end of the chapter for instructions on how to create frequency tables using statistical

Table 1-7 Grouped Frequency Table for Number of Social Interactions during a Week for 94 College Students

Interval	Frequency	Percent
45–49	3	3.2
40–44	3	3.2
35–39	3	3.2
30–34	4	4.3
25–29	11	11.7
20–24	10	10.6
15–19	16	17.0
10–14	16	17.0
5–9	16	17.0
0–4	12	12.8

Source: Data from McLaughlin-Volpe et al. (2001).

histogram   Barlike graph of a frequency distribution in which the values are plotted along the horizontal axis and the height of each bar is the frequency of that value; the bars are usually placed next to each other without spaces, giving the appearance of a city skyline.

software). Thus, we will not focus on it in this book. However, should you have to make a grouped frequency table on your own, the key is to experiment with the interval size until you come up with an interval size that is a round number (such as 2, 3, 5, or 10) and that creates about 5 to 15 intervals. Then, when actually setting up the table, be sure you set the start of each interval to a multiple of the interval size and the top end of each interval to the number that is just below the start of the next interval. For example, Table 1–5 uses six intervals with an interval size of 2. The intervals are 0–1, 2–3, 4–5, 6–7, 8–9, and 10–11. Note that each interval starts with a multiple of 2 (0, 2, 4, 6, 8, 10) and the top end of each interval (1, 3, 5, 7, 9) is the number just below the start of the next interval (2, 4, 6, 8, 10). Table 1–6 uses 10 intervals with an interval size of 5. The intervals are 0–4, 5–9, 10–14, 15–19, and so on, with a final interval of 45–49. Note that each interval starts with a multiple of 5 (0, 5, 10, 15, and so on) and the top end of each interval (4, 9, 14, 19, and so on) is the number just below the start of the next interval (5, 10, 15, 20, and so on).

How are you doing?

1. What is a frequency table?
2. Why would a researcher want to make a frequency table?
3. Make a frequency table for the following scores: 5, 7, 4, 5, 6, 5, 4
4. What does a grouped frequency table group?

Answers

1. A systematic listing of the number of scores (the frequency) of each value in the group studied.
2. It makes it easy to see the pattern in a large group of scores.
3.

Value	Frequency	Percent
7	1	14
6	1	14
5	3	43
4	2	29

4. It groups together the frequencies of adjacent values into intervals.

Frequency Graphs

A graph is another good way to make a large group of scores easy to understand. "A picture is worth a thousand words"—and sometimes a thousand numbers. A straightforward approach is to make a graph of the frequency table. There are two main kinds of such graphs: histograms and frequency polygons.

Histograms

One kind of graph of the information in a frequency table is a kind of bar chart called a **histogram.** In a histogram, the height of each bar is the frequency of each value in the frequency table. Ordinarily, in a histogram all the bars are put next to each other with no space in between. The result is that a histogram looks a bit like a city skyline. Figure 1–3 shows two histograms based on the stress ratings example, one based on

(a) Frequency Table

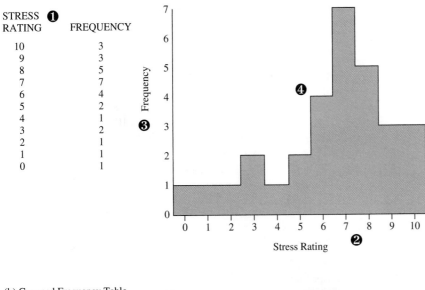

STRESS RATING ❶	FREQUENCY
10	3
9	3
8	5
7	7
6	4
5	2
4	1
3	2
2	1
1	1
0	1

(b) Grouped Frequency Table

STRESS RATING INTERVAL ❶	FREQUENCY
10 – 11	3
8 – 9	8
6 – 7	11
4 – 5	3
2 – 3	3
0 – 1	2

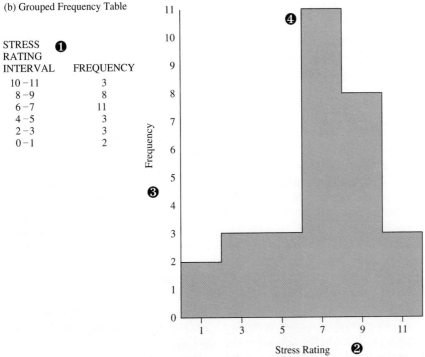

Figure 1-3 Four steps in making a histograms based on (a) a frequency table and (b) a grouped frequency table for the stress ratings example. (Data based on Aron, Paris, and Aron, 1995.) ❶ Make a frequency table. ❷ Put the values along the bottom of the page. ❸ Make a scale of frequencies along the left edge of the page. ❹ Make a bar for each value.

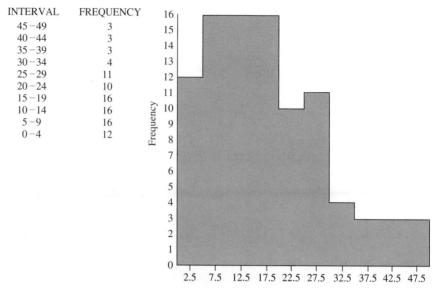

INTERVAL	FREQUENCY
45–49	3
40–44	3
35–39	3
30–34	4
25–29	11
20–24	10
15–19	16
10–14	16
5–9	16
0–4	12

Figure 1–4   Histogram for number of social interactions during a week for 94 college students, based on grouped frequencies. (Data from McLaughlin-Volpe et al., 2001.)

the ordinary frequency table and one based on the grouped frequency table. Figure 1–4 shows a histogram based on the grouped frequency table for the example of the numbers of students' social interactions in a week.

How to Make a Histogram   There are four steps for making a histogram.

❶ **Make a frequency table (or grouped frequency table).**
❷ **Put the values along the bottom of the page.** The numbers should go from left to right, from lowest to highest. If you are making a histogram from a grouped frequency table, the values you put along the bottom of the page are the interval midpoints. The midpoint of an interval is halfway between the start of that interval and the start of the next highest interval. So, in Figure 1–4, the midpoint for the 0–4 interval is 2.5, because 2.5 is halfway between 0 (the start of the interval) and 5 (the start of the next highest interval). For the 5–9 interval, the midpoint is 7.5, since 7.5 is halfway between 5 (the start of the interval) and 10 (the start of the next highest interval). Do this for each interval. When you get to the last interval, you find the midpoint between the start of the interval and the start of what would be the next highest interval. So, in Figure 1–4, the midpoint for the 45–49 interval is halfway between 45 (the start of the interval) and 50 (the start of what would be the next interval), which is 47.5.
❸ **Make a scale of frequencies along the left edge of the page.** The scale should go from 0 at the bottom to the highest frequency for any value.
❹ **Make a bar for each value.** The height of each bar is the frequency of the value it is placed over. For each bar, make sure that the middle of the bar is above its value.

When you have a nominal variable, the histogram is called a bar graph. Since the values of a nominal variable are not in any particular order, you leave a space in between the bars. Figure 1–5 shows a bar graph based on the frequency table in Table 1–4.

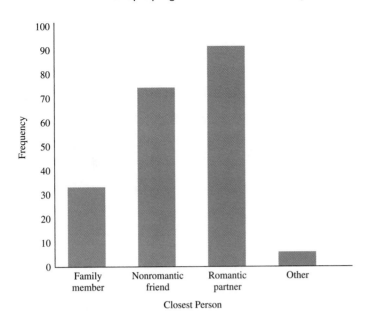

frequency polygon Line graph of a distribution in which the values are plotted along the horizontal axis and the height of each point is the frequency of that value; the line begins and ends at the horizontal axis, and the graph resembles a mountainous skyline.

Figure 1-5 Bar graph for the closest person in life for 208 students (see Table 1–4). (Data from Aron et al., 1995.)

Frequency Polygons

Another way to graph the information in a frequency table is to make a special kind of line graph called a **frequency polygon.** In a frequency polygon, the line moves from point to point. The height of each point shows the number of scores that have that value. This creates a kind of mountain-peak skyline. Figure 1–6 shows the frequency polygon for the frequency table in the stress ratings example.

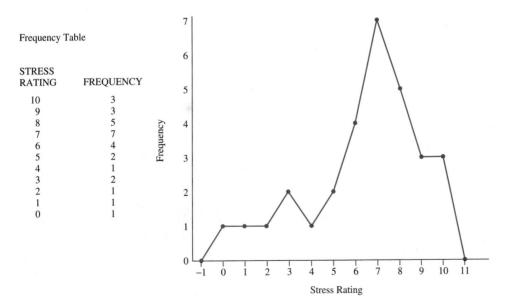

Frequency Table

STRESS RATING	FREQUENCY
10	3
9	3
8	5
7	7
6	4
5	2
4	1
3	2
2	1
1	1
0	1

Figure 1-6 Frequency polygon based on a frequency table for the stress ratings example. (Data based on Aron et al., 1995.)

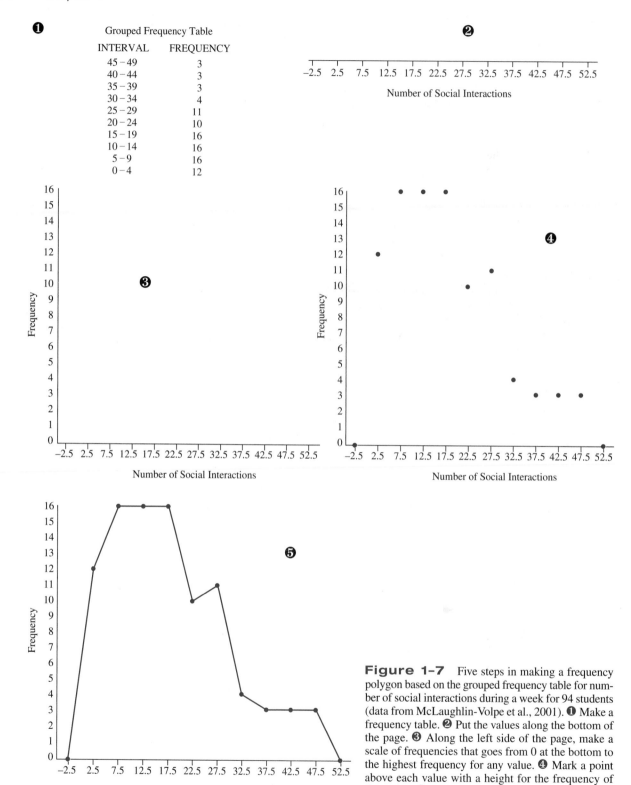

Figure 1-7 Five steps in making a frequency polygon based on the grouped frequency table for number of social interactions during a week for 94 students (data from McLaughlin-Volpe et al., 2001). ❶ Make a frequency table. ❷ Put the values along the bottom of the page. ❸ Along the left side of the page, make a scale of frequencies that goes from 0 at the bottom to the highest frequency for any value. ❹ Mark a point above each value with a height for the frequency of that value. ❺ Connect the points with lines.

How to Make a Frequency Polygon   There are five steps for making a frequency polygon.

❶ **Make a frequency table (or grouped frequency table).**
❷ **Put the values along the bottom of the page.** Be sure to include one extra value above and one extra value below the values that actually have scores in them. You need the extra value so that the line starts and ends along the baseline of the graph, at zero frequency. This creates a closed or "polygon" figure.
❸ **Along the left of the page, make a scale of frequencies that goes from 0 at the bottom to the highest frequency for any value.**
❹ **Mark a point above each value with a height for the frequency of that value.**
❺ **Connect the points with lines.**

Figure 1–7 shows the five steps for making a frequency polygon based on the grouped frequency table for the students' social interactions example.

How are you doing?

1. Why do researchers make frequency graphs?
2. When making a histogram from a frequency table, (a) what goes along the bottom, (b) what goes along the left edge, and (c) what goes above each value?
3. Based on the frequency table below, make (a) a histogram and (b) a frequency polygon.

Value	Frequency
5	2
4	5
3	8
2	4
1	3

4. How are histograms and frequency polygons (a) similar and (b) different?
5. Why does a frequency polygon include an extra value at the start and end along the bottom?

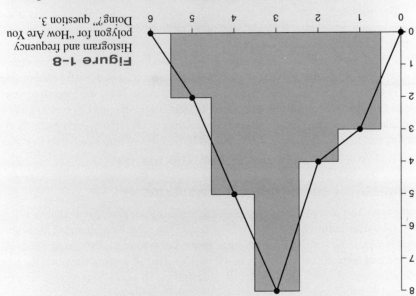

Figure 1–8
Histogram and frequency polygon for "How Are You Doing?" question 3.

frequency distribution   Pattern of frequencies over the various values; what a frequency table, histogram, or frequency polygon describes.

unimodal distribution   Frequency distribution with one value clearly having a larger frequency than any other.

bimodal distribution   Frequency distribution with two approximately equal frequencies, each clearly larger than any of the others.

multimodal distribution   Frequency distribution with two or more high frequencies separated by a lower frequency; a bimodal distribution is the special case of two high frequencies.

rectangular distribution   Frequency distribution in which all values have approximately the same frequency.

symmetrical distribution   Distribution in which the pattern of frequencies on the left and right side are mirror images of each other.

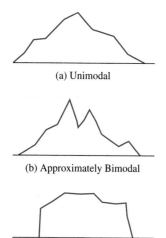

(a) Unimodal

(b) Approximately Bimodal

(c) Approximately Rectangular

Figure 1-9   Examples of (a) unimodal, (b) approximately bimodal, and (c) approximately rectangular frequency polygons.

Answers

1. To show the pattern visually in a frequency table.
2. (a) The values, from lowest to highest; (b) the frequencies from 0 at the bottom to the highest frequency of any value at the top; (c) a bar with a height of the frequency for that value.
3. See Figure 1–8.
4. (a) Both show the frequency table visually, with heights for each value for the frequency of that value. (b) A histogram uses bars; a frequency polygon is a line graph.
5. The extra values make the line start and end at zero frequency so that the line and the bottom of the graph together make a closed figure (a polygon).

Shapes of Frequency Distributions

A frequency table, histogram, or frequency polygon describes a **frequency distribution.** That is, these show the pattern or shape of how the frequencies are spread out, or "distributed." Behavioral and social scientists also describe this shape in words. Describing the shape of a distribution is important both for the descriptive statistics we focus on in this chapter and also for the inferential statistics you will learn in later chapters.

Unimodal and Bimodal Frequency Distributions

One important aspect of a distribution's shape is whether it has only one main high point (one high "tower" in the histogram or one main "peak" in the frequency polygon). For example, in the stress ratings study, the most frequent score is a 7, giving a graph with only one very high area. This is called a **unimodal distribution.** If a distribution has two fairly equal high points, it is called a **bimodal distribution.** Any distribution with two or more high points is called a **multimodal distribution.** Finally, if all the values have about the same frequency, it is called a **rectangular distribution.** These frequency distributions are shown in Figure 1–9.

The information we collect in behavioral and social science research is usually approximately unimodal. Bimodal and other multimodal distributions occasionally turn up. A bimodal example would be the distribution of the ages of people in a toddler's play area in a park, who are mostly either toddlers with ages of around 2 to 4 or caretakers with ages of 20 to 40 or so (with few people aged 5–19 years or above 40). Thus, if you made a frequency distribution of these ages, the large frequencies would be at the values for low ages (2 to 4) and for higher ages (20 to 40 or so). An example of a rectangular distribution is the number of children at each grade level attending an elementary school. There would be about the same number in first grade, second grade, and so on. Figure 1–10 shows these examples.

Symmetrical and Skewed Distributions

Look again at the frequency graphs of the stress rating example (Figures 1–3 and 1–6). The distribution is lopsided, with more scores near the high end. This is somewhat unusual. Most things we measure in the behavioral and social sciences have about equal numbers on both sides of the middle. That is, most of the time, the scores follow an approximately **symmetrical distribution** (if you fold the graph of a symmetrical distribution in half, the two halves look the same).

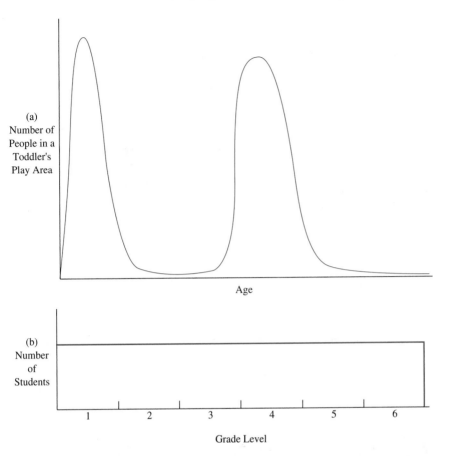

Figure 1–10   Fictional examples of distributions that are not unimodal: (a) A bimodal distribution showing the possible frequencies for people of different ages in a toddler's play area. (b) A rectangular distribution showing the possible frequencies of students at different grade levels in an elementary school.

A distribution that clearly is not symmetrical is called a **skewed distribution.** The stress ratings distribution is an example of a skewed distribution. A skewed distribution has one side that is long and spread out, somewhat like a tail. The side with *fewer* scores (the side that looks more like a tail) describes the direction of the skew. Thus a distribution with fewer scores left of the peak, like our stress ratings example, is *skewed to the left*. The other example we have examined in this chapter, the distributions of students' numbers of interactions in a week, is *skewed to the right*. Figure 1–11 shows examples of approximately symmetrical and skewed distributions.

TIP FOR SUCCESS

You may be interested to know that the word *skew* comes from the French *queue,* which means line or tail. This should help you remember that the direction of the skew (to the left or right) is the side that has the long line or tail.

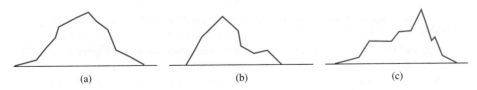

Figure 1–11   Examples of frequency polygons of distributions that are (a) approximately symmetrical, (b) skewed to the right (positively skewed), and (c) skewed to the left (negatively skewed).

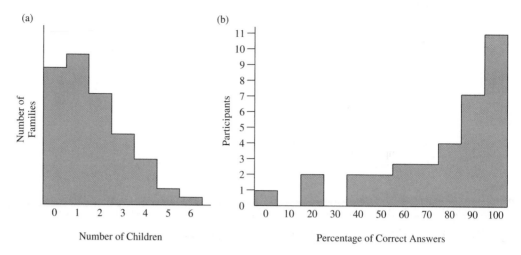

Figure 1–12 (a) A distribution skewed to the right due to a floor effect: fictional distribution of the number of children in families. (b) A distribution skewed to the left due to a ceiling effect: fictional distribution of adults' scores on a multiplication table test.

floor effect Situation in which many scores pile up at the low end of a distribution (creating skewness) because it is not possible to have any lower score.

ceiling effect Situation in which many scores pile up at the high end of a distribution (creating skewness) because it is not possible to have a higher score.

heavy-tailed distribution Distribution that differs from a normal curve by being too spread out so that a histogram of the distribution would have too many scores at each of the two extremes ("tails").

light-tailed distribution Distribution that differs from a normal curve by being too peaked or pinched so that a histogram of the distribution would have too few scores at each of the two extremes ("tails").

normal curve Specific, mathematically defined, bell-shaped frequency distribution that is symmetrical and unimodal; distributions observed in nature and in research commonly approximate it.

A distribution that is skewed to the right is also called *positively skewed.* A distribution skewed to the left is also called *negatively skewed.*

Strongly skewed distributions come up in the behavioral and social sciences mainly when what is being measured has some lower or upper limit. For example, a family cannot have fewer than zero children. This kind of situation in which many scores pile up at the low end because it is impossible to have a lower score is called a **floor effect.** A skewed distribution caused by a lower limit is shown in Figure 1–12a.

A skewed distribution caused by an upper limit is shown in Figure 1–12b. This is a distribution of adults' scores on a multiplication table test. This distribution is strongly skewed to the left. Most of the scores pile up at the right, the high end (a perfect score). This is an example of a **ceiling effect.** The stress ratings example also shows a mild ceiling effect. This is because many students had high levels of stress, the maximum rating was 10, and people often do not like to use ratings right at the maximum.

Normal, Heavy-Tailed, and Light-Tailed Distributions

Behavioral and social scientists also describe a distribution in terms of whether its tails are particularly "heavy" (thick, with many scores in them) or "light" (thin, with few scores in them). These are called **heavy-tailed distributions** and **light-tailed distributions.** (This aspect of the shape of a distribution is also called *kurtosis.*) The standard of comparison is a bell-shaped curve. In behavioral and social science research and in nature generally, distributions often are quite similar to this bell-shaped standard, called the **normal curve.** We discuss this curve in some detail in later chapters. For now, however, the important thing is that the normal curve is a unimodal, symmetrical curve with average tails—the sort of bell shape shown in Figure 1–13a. The stress ratings example in this chapter is very roughly like a normal curve, except that it is somewhat skewed to the left. In our experience, most distributions that result from behavioral and social science research are actually closer to the normal curve than this example.

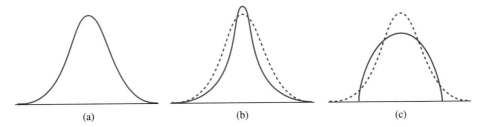

Figure 1-13 Examples of (a) normal, (b) heavy-tailed, and (c) light-tailed distributions. The normal distribution is shown as a dashed line in (b) and (c). (Adapted from DeCarlo, 1997.)

BOX 1-2   Gender, Ethnicity, and Math Performance

From time to time, someone tries to argue that because some groups of people score better on math tests and make careers out of mathematics, this means that these groups have some genetic advantage in math (or statistics). Other groups are said or implied to be innately inferior at math. The issue comes up about gender and also racial and ethnic groups, and of course in arguments about overall intelligence as well as math. There's no evidence for such genetic differences that can't be refuted (a must-see article: Block, 1995). But the stereotypes persist.

The impact of these stereotypes has been well established in research by Steele and his colleagues (1997), who have done numerous studies on what they call "stereotype threat," which occurs when a negative stereotype about a group you belong to becomes relevant to you because of the situation you are in, like taking a math test, and provides an explanation for how you will behave. A typical experiment creating stereotype threat (Spencer, Steele, & Quinn, 1999) involved women taking a difficult math test. Half were told that men generally do better on the test and the other half that women generally do equally well. When told that women do worse, the women did indeed score substantially lower. In the other condition there was no difference. (In fact, in two separate studies, men performed a little worse when they were told there was no gender difference, as if they had lost some of their confidence.)

The same results occur when African Americans are given parts of the Graduate Record Exam—they do fine on the test when they are told no racial differences in the scores have been found and do worse when they are told such differences have been found (Steele, 1997).

These results certainly argue against there being any inherent differences in ability in these groups. But that is

nothing new. Many lines of research indicate that prejudices, not genetics, are the probable cause of differences in test scores between groups. For example, the same difference of 15 IQ points between a dominant and minority group has been found all over the world, even when there is no genetic difference between the groups, and in cases where opportunities for a group have changed, as when they emigrate, differences have rapidly disappeared (Block, 1995).

If groups such as women and African Americans are not inherently inferior in any area of intellectual endeavor, but perform worse on tests, what might be the reasons? The usual explanation is that they have internalized the "superior" group's prejudices. Steele thinks the problem might not be so internal but may have to do with the situation. The stigmatized groups perform worse when they know that's what is expected—when they experience the threat of being stereotyped.

What Can You Do for Yourself?

So, do you feel you belong to a group that is expected to do worse at math? (This includes white males who feel they are among the "math dumbbells.") What can you do to get out from under the shadow of "stereotype threat" as you take this course?

First, care about learning statistics. Don't discount it to save your self-esteem and separate yourself from the rest of the class. Fight for your right to know this subject. What a triumph for those who hold the prejudice if you give up! Consider these words from the former president of the Mathematics Association of America:

The paradox of our times is that as mathematics becomes increasingly powerful, only the powerful seem to benefit from it. The ability to think mathematically—broadly interpreted—is absolutely crucial to advancement in virtually every career. Confidence in dealing with data, skepticism in analyzing arguments, persistence in penetrating complex problems, and literacy in communicating about technical matters are the enabling arts offered by the new mathematical sciences. (Steen, 1987, p. xviii)

Second, once you care about succeeding at statistics, realize you are going to be affected by stereotype threat. Think of it as a stereotype-induced form of test anxiety and work on it that way (see Box 1–1).

Third, in yourself, root out the effects of that stereotype as much as you can. It takes some effort. That's why we are spending time on it here. Research on stereotypes shows that they can be activated without our awareness (Fiske, 1998), even when we are otherwise low in prejudice or a member of the stereotyped group.

Some Points To Think About

- Women: Every bit of evidence for thinking that men are genetically better at math can and has been well disputed. For example, yes, the very top performers tend to be male, but the differences are slight, and the lowest performers are not more likely to be female, as would probably be the case if there were a genetic difference. Tobias (1982) cites numerous studies providing nongenetic explanations for why women might not make it to the very top in math. For example, in a study of students identified by a math talent search, it was found that few parents arranged for their daughters to be coached before the talent exams. Sons were almost invariably coached. In another study, parents of mathematically gifted girls were not even aware of their daughters' abilities, whereas parents of boys invariably were. In general, girls tend to avoid higher math classes, according to Tobias, because parents, peers, and even teachers often advise them against pursuing too much math. So even though women are earning more PhDs in math than ever before, it is not surprising that math is the field with the highest dropout rate for women.
- We checked the grades in our own introductory statistics classes and simply found no reliable difference for gender. More generally, Schram (1996) analyzed re-

sults of 13 independent studies of performance in college statistics and found an overall average difference of almost exactly zero (the slight direction of difference favored females). It has never even occurred to us to look for racial or ethnic differences, as they are so obviously not present.

- Persons of color: Keep in mind that only 7 percent of the genetic variation in humans is between races (Block, 1995). Mostly, we are all the same.
- Associate with people who have a positive attitude about you and your group. Watch for subtle signs of prejudice and reject it. For example, Steele found that the grades of African Americans in a large midwestern university rose substantially when they were enrolled in a transition-to-college program emphasizing that they were the cream of the crop and much was expected of them, while African American students at the same school who were enrolled in a "remedial program for minorities" received considerable attention, but their grades improved very little and many more of them dropped out of school. Steele argues that the very idea of a remedial program exposed those students to a subtle stereotype threat.
- Work hard during this course. If you are stuck, get help. If you work at it, you can do it. This is not about genetics. Think about a study cited by Tobias (1995) comparing students in Asia and the United States on an international mathematics test. The U.S. students were thoroughly outperformed, but more important was why: Interviews revealed that Asian students saw math as an ability fairly equally distributed among people and thought that differences in performance were due to hard work. Contrarily, U.S. students thought some people are just born better at math, so hard work matters little.

In short, our culture's belief that "math just comes naturally to some people" is false and harmful. It especially harms students whose real problem is due to gender or racial stereotypes or difficulty with English. But once you vow to undo the harm done to you, you can overcome effects of prejudice. Doing well in this course may even be more satisfying for you than for others. And it will certainly be a fine thing that you have modeled that achievement for others in your group.

Figures 1–13b and 1–13c show examples of heavy-tailed and light-tailed distributions, with the normal distribution shown as a dashed line. Distributions that have tails that are heavier (thicker) or lighter (thinner) than a normal curve also tend to have a different shape in the middle. Those with heavy tails are usually more peaked than the normal curve (see Figure 1–13b). It is as if the normal curve got pinched in the middle and some of it went up into a sharp peak and the rest spread out into thick tails. Those with light tails are usually flatter than the normal curve (see Figure 1–13c). It is as if the tails and the top of the curve both got sucked in to right near the middle on both sides. (An extreme case of a light-tailed distribution would be a rectangular distribution.)

How are you doing?

1. Describe the difference between a unimodal and multimodal distribution in terms of (a) a frequency graph and (b) a frequency table.
2. What does it mean to say that a distribution is skewed to the left?
3. What kind of skew is created by (a) a floor effect and (b) a ceiling effect?
4. When a distribution is described as heavy-tailed or light-tailed, what is it being compared to?

Answers

1. (a) A unimodal distribution has one main high point; a multimodal distribution has more than one main high point. (b) A unimodal distribution has one value with a higher frequency than all the other frequencies; a multimodal distribution has more than one value with large frequencies compared to the values around it.
2. Fewer scores have low values than have high values.
3. (a) Skewed to the right; (b) skewed to the left.
4. The normal curve.

Frequency Tables, Histograms, and Frequency Polygons in Research Articles

Frequency tables, histograms, and frequency polygons are not usually included in research articles. However, they are commonly used by researchers as a first step in more elaborate statistical procedures, particularly when the distribution seems to deviate from normal. The shapes of distributions (normal, skewed, and so on) are occasionally described in words. (In the second half of Chapter 11, we will consider some examples where distributions are not normally distributed.) When frequency tables are included in research articles they are often used to summarize the characteristics of the people in the study. For example, Bolognesi and colleagues (2006) conducted a study in Italy to test whether having doctors provide a new type of physical activity counseling to their overweight patients helped the patients to lose weight. The researchers randomly assigned patients to one of two groups: an experimental group that received the new type of physical activity counseling and a control group that received the regular type of counseling. Table 1–8 is a frequency table showing the characteristics of the full sample, the control group, and the experimental group. It gives the frequencies and percentages for three variables: age group, gender, and education. The table shows, for example, that few of the study participants were aged 21–30 and only a small number of participants had a college degree. (Incidentally, the results of the study showed that patients in the experimental group lost more weight than patients in the control group.)

Table 1-8 Demographics by Group

Variable	Entire Sample		Control		Experimental	
	n	%	*n*	%	*n*	%
Age						
21–30	8	8.3	3	6.3	5	10.4
31–40	18	18.8	7	14.6	11	22.9
41–50	26	27.1	14	29.2	12	25.0
51–60	29	30.2	14	29.2	15	31.3
61–70	15	15.6	10	20.8	5	10.4
Gender[a]						
Male	45	46.9	18	37.5	27	56.3
Female	51	53.1	30	62.5	21	43.8
Education						
Primary	27	28.1	16	33.3	11	22.9
Junior high	36	37.5	18	37.5	18	37.5
High school	29	30.2	12	25.0	17	35.4
University degree	4	4.2	2	4.2	2	4.2

[a]More men and fewer women were in the experimental group compared to the control group (p < .05).
Source: Bolognesi, M., Nigg, C.R., Massarini, M., & Lippke, S. (2006). Reducing obesity indicators through brief physical activity counseling (PACE) in Italian Primary care settings. *Annals of Behavioral Medicine, 31,* 179–185. Copyright © 2006 by Lawrence Erlbaum Associates. Reprinted by permission of the publisher.

Summary

1. Behavioral and social scientists use descriptive statistics to describe—to summarize and make understandable—a group of numbers from a research study.
2. A value is a number or category; a variable is a characteristic that can have different values; a score is a particular person's value on the variable.
3. Most variables in the behavioral and social sciences are numeric with approximately equal intervals. However, some numeric variables are rank-order (where the values are ranks), and some variables are not numeric at all, but are nominal (where the values are categories).
4. A frequency table organizes the scores into a table in which each of the possible values is listed from highest to lowest, along with its frequency (number of scores that have that value and percentage).
5. When there are many different values, a grouped frequency table will be more useful. It is like an ordinary frequency table except that the frequencies are given for intervals that include a range of values.
6. The pattern of frequencies in a distribution can be shown visually with a histogram (or bar graph), in which the height of each bar is the frequency for a particular value and there are no spaces between the bars. An alternative is a frequency polygon, in which a line connects dots, the height of each of which is the frequency for a particular value.

7. The general shape of a histogram or frequency polygon can be unimodal (having a single peak), bimodal, multimodal (including bimodal), or rectangular (having no peak); it can be symmetrical or skewed (having a long tail) to the right or the left; and compared to the bell-shaped normal curve, it can be light-tailed or heavy-tailed.
8. Frequency tables rarely appear in research articles, but when they do they often summarize the characteristics of the people in the study. Histograms and frequency polygons almost never appear in articles, though the shapes of distributions (normal, skewed, and so on) occasionally are described in words.

Key Terms

statistics (p. 2)
descriptive statistics (p. 2)
inferential statistics (p. 2)
variable (p. 4)
value (p. 4)
score (p. 4)
numeric variable (p. 5)
equal-interval variable (p. 5)
rank-order variable (p. 5)
nominal variable (p. 5)
level of measurement (p. 6)
frequency table (p. 7)
interval (p. 9)
grouped frequency table (p. 9)
histogram (p. 10)
frequency polygon (p. 13)
frequency distribution (p. 16)
unimodal distribution (p. 16)
bimodal distribution (p. 16)
multimodal distribution (p. 16)
rectangular distribution (p. 16)
symmetrical distribution (p. 16)
skewed distribution (p. 17)
floor effect (p. 18)
ceiling effect (p. 18)
heavy-tailed distribution (p. 18)
light-tailed distribution (p. 18)
normal curve (p. 18)

Example Worked-Out Problems

Ten first-year students rated their interest in graduate school on a scale from 1 = *no interest* at all to 6 = *high interest.* Their scores were as follows: 2, 4, 5, 5, 1, 3, 6, 3, 6, 6.

Making a Frequency Table

See Figure 1–14.

❶ Interest in Graduate School	❸ Frequency	❹ Percent	❷
6	3	30	///
5	2	20	//
4	1	10	/
3	2	20	//
2	1	10	/
1	1	10	/

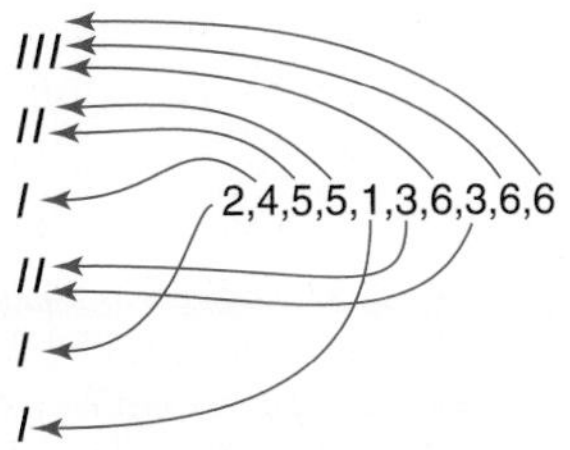

Figure 1–14 Answer to Example Worked-Out Problem for making a frequency table. ❶ Make a list of each possible value down the left edge of a page, starting from the highest and ending with the lowest. ❷ Go one by one through the scores, making a mark for each next to its value on your list. ❸ Make a table showing how many times each value on your list is used. ❹ Figure the percentage of scores for each value.

Making a Histogram

See Figure 1–15.

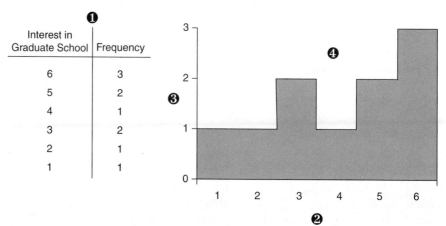

Figure 1-15 Answer to Example Worked-Out Problem for making a histogram. ❶ Make a frequency table. ❷ Put the values along the bottom of the page (from left to right, from lowest to highest). ❸ Make a scale of frequencies along the left edge of the page (going from 0 at the bottom to the highest frequency for any value). ❹ Make a bar for each value (with a height for the frequency of that value).

Making a Frequency Polygon

See Figure 1–16.

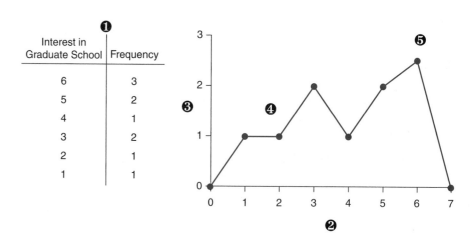

Figure 1-16 Answer to Worked-Out Problem for making a frequency polygon. ❶ Make a frequency table. ❷ Put the values along the bottom of the page (from left to right, starting one value below the lowest value and ending one value above the highest value). ❸ Along the left edge of the page, make a scale of frequencies that goes from 0 at the bottom to the highest frequency for any value. ❹ Mark a point above each value with a height for the frequency of that value. ❺ Connect the points with lines.

Practice Problems

These problems involve tabulation and making graphs. Most real-life statistics problems are done on a computer with special statistical software. Even if you have such software, do these problems by hand to ingrain the method in your mind. To learn how to use a computer to solve statistics problems like those in this chapter, refer to the *Using SPSS* section at the end of this chapter and the *Student's Study Guide and SPSS Workbook* that accompanies this text.

All data are fictional unless an actual citation is given.

Set I (for answers, see pp. 435-437)

1. A client rates her satisfaction with her vocational counselor as a "3" on a 4-point scale from 1 = *not at all satisfied* to 4 = *very satisfied*. What are the (a) variable, (b) possible values, and (c) score?

2. You fill out a survey question that asks you to give the likelihood that you will vote in an upcoming election. The question uses a 5-point response scale from 1 = *not at all likely* to 5 = *very likely* and you answer "5." What are the (a) variable, (b) possible values, and (c) score?

3. Name the kind of variable for each of the following: (a) ethnic group to which a person belongs, (b) number of times a mouse makes a wrong turn in a laboratory maze, and (c) position one finishes in a race.

4. A particular block in a suburban neighborhood has 20 households. The number of children in these households is as follows: 2, 4, 2, 1, 0, 3, 6, 0, 1, 1, 2, 3, 2, 0, 1, 2, 1, 0, 2, 2.

   Make (a) a frequency table, (b) a histogram, and (c) a frequency polygon. Then (d) describe the general shape of the distribution.

5. Fifty students were asked how many hours they had studied this weekend. Here are their answers:

   11, 2, 0, 13, 5, 7, 1, 8, 12, 11, 7, 8, 9, 10, 7, 4, 6, 10, 4, 7, 8, 6, 7, 10, 7, 3, 11, 18, 2, 9, 7, 3, 8, 7, 3, 13, 9, 8, 7, 7, 10, 4, 15, 3, 5, 6, 9, 7, 10, 6

   Make (a) a frequency table, (b) a histogram, and (c) a frequency polygon. Then (d) describe the general shape of the distribution.

6. Following are the speeds of 40 cars clocked by radar on a particular road in a 35-mph zone on a particular afternoon:

   30, 36, 42, 36, 30, 52, 36, 34, 36, 33, 30, 32, 35, 32, 37, 34, 36, 31, 35, 20, 24, 46, 23, 31, 32, 45, 34, 37, 28, 40, 34, 38, 40, 52, 31, 33, 15, 27, 36, 40

   Make (a) a frequency table, (b) a histogram, and (c) a frequency polygon. Then (d) describe the general shape of the distribution.

7. These are the scores on a measure of sensitivity to smell taken by 25 chefs attending a national conference:

   96, 83, 59, 64, 73, 74, 80, 68, 87, 67, 64, 92, 76, 71, 68, 50, 85, 75, 81, 70, 76, 91, 69, 83, 75

   Make (a) a frequency table and (b) histogram. (c) Make a grouped frequency table using intervals of 50–59, 60–69, 70–79, 80–89, and 90–99. Based on the grouped frequency table, (d) make a histogram and (e) describe the general shape of the distribution.

8. Below are the number of minutes it took each of a group of 34 10-year-olds to do a series of abstract puzzles:

24, 83, 36, 22, 81, 39, 60, 62, 38, 66, 38, 36, 45, 20, 20, 67, 41, 87, 41, 82, 35, 82, 28, 80, 80, 68, 40, 27, 43, 80, 31, 89, 83, 24

Make (a) a frequency table and (b) a frequency polygon. (c) Make a grouped frequency table using intervals of 20–29, 30–39, 40–49, 50–59, 60–69, 70–79, and 80–89. Based on the grouped frequency table, (d) make a histogram and (e) describe the general shape of the distribution.

9. Describe the shapes of the three distributions illustrated.

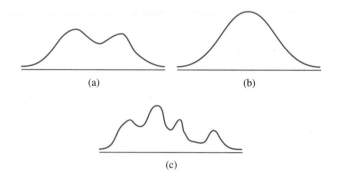

      (a)   (b)

(c)

10. Explain to a person who has never had a course in statistics what is meant by (a) a symmetrical unimodal distribution and (b) a negatively skewed unimodal distribution. (Be sure to include in your first answer an explanation of what is meant by a distribution.)

11. What is a ceiling effect?

12. McKee and Ptacek (2001) asked 90 college students about a time they had "delivered bad news" to someone. Table 1–9 (their Table 1) shows the results for the type of bad news given. (a) Using this table as an example, explain the idea of a frequency table to a person who has never had a course in statistics. (b) Explain the general meaning of the pattern of results.

Table 1-9   Descriptive Statistics for the Type of News Given

Category	Frequency	Percentage
1. Relationship with family	19	21.1
2. School	1	1.1
3. Job/work	6	6.7
4. Relationship with actual/potential girlfriend/boyfriend	17	18.9
5. Personal health	1	1.1
6. Finance	1	1.1
7. Relationship with friends	21	23.3
8. Health of family member/friend	23	25.6
9. Other	1	1.1

Set II

13. A participant in a research study is given 50 words to remember and later asked to recall as many as he can of those 50 words. This participant recalls 17. What is the (a) variable, (b) possible values, and (c) score?

14. Explain and give an example for each of the following types of variables: (a) equal-interval, (b) rank-order, and (c) nominal.

15. Here are the number of children in each of 30 classrooms in a particular elementary school.

> 24, 20, 35, 25, 25, 22, 26, 28, 38, 15, 25, 21, 24, 25, 25, 24, 25,
> 20, 32, 25, 22, 26, 26, 28, 24, 22, 26, 21, 25, 24

Make (a) a frequency table, and (b) a histogram. Then (c) describe the general shape of the distribution.

16. Pick a book and page number of your choice (select a page with at least 30 lines; *do not pick a textbook or any book with tables or illustrations*). Make a list of the number of words on each line; use that list as your data set. Make (a) a frequency table, (b) a histogram, and (c) a frequency polygon. Then (d) describe the general shape of the distribution. (Be sure to give the name, author, publisher, and year of the book you used, along with the page number, with your answer.)

17. An organizational researcher asks 20 employees in a particular company to rate their job satisfaction on a 5-point scale from 1 = *very unsatisfied* to 5 = *very satisfied*. The ratings were as follows:

> 3, 2, 3, 4, 1, 3, 3, 4, 5, 2, 3, 5, 2, 3, 3, 4, 1, 3, 2, 4

Make (a) a frequency table, (b) a histogram, and (c) a frequency polygon. Then (d) describe the general shape of the distribution.

18. A researcher asked 15 college students how many times they "fell in love" before they were 11 years old. The numbers of times were as follows:

> 2, 0, 6, 0, 3, 1, 0, 4, 9, 0, 5, 6, 1, 0, 2

Make (a) a frequency table, (b) a histogram, and (c) a frequency polygon. Then (d) describe the general shape of the distribution.

19. Here are the number of holiday gifts purchased by 25 families randomly interviewed at a local mall at the end of the holiday season:

> 22, 18, 22, 26, 19, 14, 23, 27, 2, 18, 28, 28, 11, 16, 34, 28, 13,
> 21, 32, 17, 6, 29, 23, 22, 19

Make (a) a frequency table and (b) a frequency polygon. (c) Make a grouped frequency table using intervals of 0–4, 5–9, 10–14, 15–19, 20–24, 25–29, and 30–34. Based on the grouped frequency table, (d) make a histogram and (e) describe the general shape of the distribution.

20. Explain to a person who has never taken a course in statistics the meaning of (a) a grouped frequency table and (b) a frequency polygon.

21. Nownes (2000) surveyed representatives of interest groups who were registered as lobbyists of three U.S. state legislatures. One of the issues he studied was whether interest groups are in competition with each other. Table 1–10 (Nownes's Table 1) shows the results for one such question. (a) Using this table as an example, explain the idea of a frequency table to a person who has never had a course in statistics. (b) Explain the general meaning of the pattern of results.

Table 1-10 Competition for Members and Other Resources

| Answer | Question: How much competition does this group face from other groups with similar goals for members and other resources? | |
	Percentage	Number
No competition	20	118
Some competition	58	342
A lot of competition	22	131
Total	100	591

Note: There were no statistically significant differences between states. For full results of significance tests, contact the author.
Source: Nownes, A. J. (2001). Policy conflict and the structure of interest communities. *American Politics Quarterly, 28,* 316. Copyright © 2001. Reprinted by permission of Sage Publications, Inc.

22. Mouradian (2001) surveyed college students selected from a screening session to include two groups: (a) "Perpetrators"—students who reported at least one violent act (hitting, shoving, etc.) against their partner in their current or most recent relationship—and (b) "Comparisons"—students who did not report any such uses of violence in any of their last three relationships. At the actual testing session, the students first read a description of an aggressive behavior such as "Throw something at his or her partner" or "Say something to upset his or her partner." They then were asked to write "as many examples of circumstances of situations as [they could] in which a person might engage in behaviors or acts of this sort with or toward their significant other." Table 1–11 (Mouradian's Table 3) shows the "Dominant Category of Explanation" (the category a participant used most) for females and males, broken down by comparisons and perpetrators. (a) Using this table as an example, explain the idea of a frequency table to a person who has

Table 1-11 Dominant Category of Explanation for Intimate Aggression by Gender and Perpetrator Status

	Group							
	Female				Male			
	Comparisons ($n = 36$)		Perpetrators ($n = 33$)		Comparisons ($n = 32$)		Perpetrators ($n = 25$)	
Category	f	%	f	%	f	%	f	%
Self-defense	2	6	3	9	3	9	1	4
Control motives	8	22	9	27	9	28	3	12
Expressive aggression	4	11	3	9	3	9	8	32
Face/self-esteem preservation	1	3	2	6	2	6	3	12
Exculpatory explanations	5	14	3	9	3	9	3	12
Rejection of perpetrator or act	12	33	6	18	10	31	7	28
Prosocial/acceptable explanations	0	0	0	0	0	0	0	0
Tied categories	4	11	7	21	2	6	0	0

Note: f = frequency. % = percentage of respondents in a given group who provided a particular category of explanation.
Source: Mouradian, V. E. (2001). Applying schema theory to intimate aggression: Individual and gender differences in representation of contexts and goals. *Journal of Applied Social Psychology, 31,* 376–408. Copyright © 2001 by Blackwell Publishing. Reprinted by permission of the publisher.

never had a course in statistics. (b) Explain the general meaning of the pattern of results.

23. Draw an example of each of the following distributions: (a) symmetrical, (b) rectangular, and (c) skewed to the right.

24. Give an example of something having these distribution shapes: (a) bimodal, (b) approximately rectangular, and (c) positively skewed. Do not use an example given in this book or in class.

Using SPSS

The ✐ in the steps below indicates a mouse click. (We used SPSS version 13.0 to carry out these analyses. The steps and output may be slightly different for other versions of SPSS.)

Creating a Frequency Table

❶ Enter the scores from your distribution in one column of the data window.

❷ ✐ *Analyze.*

❸ ✐ *Descriptive statistics.*

❹ ✐ *Frequencies.*

❺ ✐ on the variable you want to make a frequency table of and then ✐ the arrow.

❻ Optional: To get the values listed from highest to lowest (as you learned in this chapter), ✐ *Format,* ✐ *Descending values,* ✐ *Continue.*

❼ ✐ *OK.*

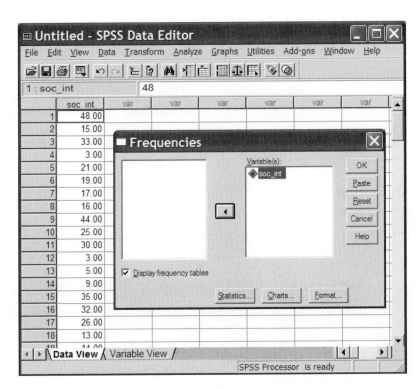

Figure 1–17   SPSS data window and frequencies window for the social interactions example. (Data from McLaughlin-Volpe et al., 2001.)

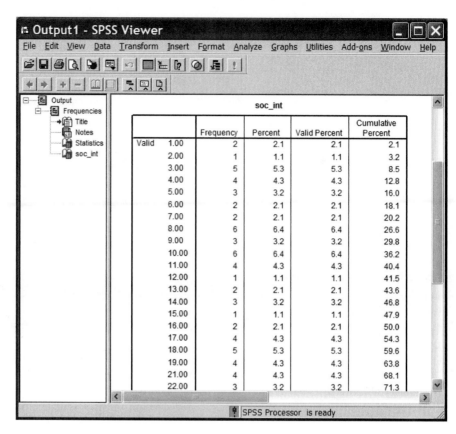

Figure 1–18 SPSS frequency table for the social interactions example. (Data from McLaughlin-Volpe et al., 2001.)

Practice the steps above by creating a frequency table for the social interactions example in this chapter. After Step ❺, your screen should look like Figure 1–17. Your output window (which will appear after you ✑ *OK* in Step ❼) should look like Figure 1–18. As you will see, SPSS automatically produces a column with the cumulative percent for each value (see footnote 1, p. 7).

Creating a Histogram

❶ Enter the scores from your distribution in one column of the data window.

❷ ✑ *Analyze.*

❸ ✑ *Descriptive statistics.*

❹ ✑ *Frequencies.*

❺ ✑ on the variable you want to make a frequency table of and then ✑ the arrow.

❻ ✑ *Charts,* ✑ *Histograms,* ✑ *Continue.*

❼ Optional: To instruct SPSS *not* to produce a frequency table, ✑ the box labeled *Display frequency tables* (this *un*checks the box).

❽ ✑ *OK.*

Practice the steps above by creating a histogram for the social interactions example in this chapter. Your output window should look like Figure 1–19.

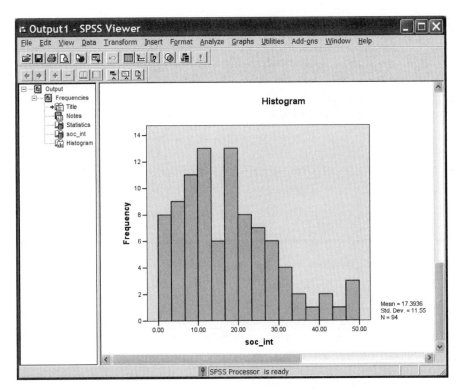

Figure 1–19 SPSS histogram for the social interactions example. (Data from McLaughlin-Volpe et al., 2001).

CHAPTER 2

The Mean, Variance, Standard Deviation, and *Z* Scores

CHAPTER OUTLINE

- Representative Values
- Variability
- *Z* Scores
- Mean, Variance, Standard Deviation, and *Z* Scores in Research Articles
- Summary
- Key Terms
- Example Worked-Out Problems
- Practice Problems
- Using SPSS

As we noted in Chapter 1, the purpose of descriptive statistics is to make a group of scores understandable. We looked at some ways of getting that understanding through tables and graphs. In this chapter, we consider the main statistical techniques for describing a group of scores with numbers. First, you can describe a group of scores in terms of a *representative* (or *typical*) *value*. A representative value gives the *central tendency* of a group of scores. A representative value is an efficient way to describe a group of scores (and there may be hundreds or even thousands of scores). The main representative value we focus on is the *mean*. Next, we focus on ways of describing how spread out the numbers are in a group of scores. In other words, we consider the amount of variation, or *variability*, among the scores. The two measures of variability you will learn about are called the *variance* and *standard deviation*. Finally, we show you how to describe a particular score in terms of how much that score varies from the average. To do this, you will learn how to combine the mean and standard deviation to create a *Z score*.

In this chapter, for the first time in this book, you use statistical formulas. Such formulas are not designed to confuse you. Hopefully, you will come to see that they actually simplify things and provide a very efficient way of describing statistical procedures. Still, to be sure you grasp the meaning of such formulas, whenever we present formulas in this book, we always also give the "translation" in ordinary English.

Representative Values

The representative value of a group of scores (a distribution) refers to the middle of the group of scores. You will learn about three representative values: the *mean, mode, and median*. Each uses its own method to come up with a single number describing the middle of a group of scores. We start with the mean, the most commonly used measure of the representative value of a group of scores. Understanding the mean is also an important foundation for much of what you learn in later chapters.

The Mean

Usually, the best measure of the representative value of a group of scores is the ordinary average, the sum of all the scores divided by the number of scores. In statistics, this is called the **mean**. Suppose that a political scientist does a study on years of experience in elected office. As part of this research, the political scientist finds out the number of years served by mayors of the 10 largest cities in a particular region. The numbers of years served were as follows:

7, 8, 8, 7, 3, 1, 6, 9, 3, 8

The mean of these 10 scores is 6 (the sum of 60 years served divided by 10 mayors). That is, on average, these 10 mayors had served 6 years in office. The information for the 10 mayors is thus summarized by this single number, 6.

You can think of the mean as a kind of balancing point for the distribution of scores. Try it by visualizing a board balanced over a log, like a rudimentary seesaw. On the board, imagine piles of blocks set along the board according to their values, one for each score in the distribution. (This is a little like a histogram made of blocks.) The mean would be the point on the board where the weight of the blocks on each side would balance exactly. Figure 2–1 shows this for our 10 mayors.

Mathematically, you can think of the mean as the point at which the total distance to all the scores above that point equals the total distance to all of the scores below that point. Let's first figure the total distance from the mean to all of the scores above the mean for the mayors' example shown in Figure 2–1. There are two scores of 7, each of which is 1 unit above 6 (the mean). There are three scores of 8, each of which is 2 units above 6. And, there is one score of 9, which is 3 units above 6. This gives a total

mean (*M*) Arithmetic average of a group of scores; sum of the scores divided by the number of scores.

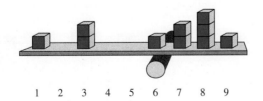

1   2   3   4   5   6   7   8   9

Figure 2-1 Mean of the distribution of the numbers of years in office for 10 mayors, illustrated using blocks on a board balanced on a log.

M   Mean.

Σ   Sum of; add up all the scores following.

distance of 11 units (1 + 1 + 2 + 2 + 2 + 3) from the mean to all of the scores above the mean. Now, let's look at the scores below the mean. There are two scores of 3, each of which is 3 units below 6 (the mean). And, there is one score of 1, which is 5 units below 6. This gives a total distance of 11 units (3 + 3 + 5) from the mean to all of the scores below the mean. As we would expect, the total distance from the mean to the scores above the mean is the same as the total distance from the mean to the scores below the mean. The scores above the mean balance out the scores below the mean (and vice versa).

Some other examples are shown in Figure 2–2. Notice that there doesn't have to be a block right at the balance point. That is, the mean doesn't have to be a score actually in the distribution. The mean is the average of the scores, the balance point. The mean can be a decimal number, even if all the scores in the distribution have to be whole numbers (a mean of 2.3 children, for example). For each distribution in Figure 2–2, the total distance from the mean to the scores above the mean is the same as the total distance from the mean to the scores below the mean. (By the way, this analogy to blocks on a board, in reality, would work out precisely only if the board had no weight of its own.)

Formula for the Mean and Statistical Symbols.   The rule for figuring the mean is to add up all the scores and divide by the number of scores. Here is how this can be written as a formula:

> The mean is the sum of the scores divided by the number of scores.

(2-1)

$$M = \frac{\Sigma X}{N}$$

M is a symbol for the mean. An alternative symbol, $\overline{X}$ ("*X*-bar"), is sometimes used. However, *M* is most commonly used in research publications. In fact, you should know that there is not a general agreement for many of the symbols used in statistics. (In this book, we generally use the symbols most widely found in research publications.)

Σ, the capital Greek letter "sigma," is the symbol for "sum of." It means "add up all the numbers" for whatever follows. It is the most common special arithmetic symbol used in statistics.

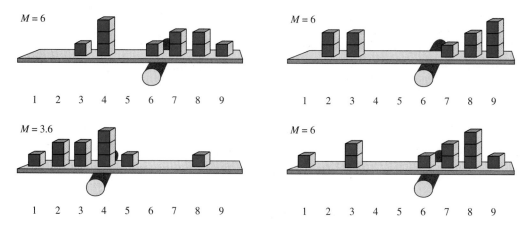

Figure 2-2   Means of various distributions illustrated with blocks on a board balanced on a log.

X stands for the scores in the distribution of the variable *X*. We could have picked any letter. However, if there is only one variable, it is usually called *X*. In later chapters we use formulas with more than one variable. In those formulas, we use a second letter along with *X* (usually *Y*) or subscripts (such as X_1 and X_2).

ΣX is "the sum of *X*." That is, this tells you to add up all the scores in the distribution of the variable *X*. Suppose *X* is the number of years in office in our example of 10 mayors: ΣX is $7 + 8 + 8 + 7 + 3 + 1 + 6 + 9 + 3 + 8$, which is 60.

N stands for number—the number of scores in a distribution. In our example, there are 10 scores. Thus, *N* equals 10.

Overall, the formula says to divide the sum of all the scores for the variable *X* by the total number of scores, *N*. In our example, this tells us that we divide 60 by 10. Put in terms of the formula,

$$M = \frac{\Sigma X}{N} = \frac{60}{10} = 6$$

> **X** Scores in the distribution of the variable *X*.
>
> **N** Number of scores in a distribution.

Additional Examples of Figuring the Mean.   Consider the examples from Chapter 1. The stress ratings of the 30 students in the first week of their statistics class (based on Aron et al., 1995) were:

8, 7, 4, 10, 8, 6, 8, 9, 9, 7, 3, 7, 6, 5, 0, 9, 10, 7, 7, 3, 6, 7, 5, 2, 1, 6, 7, 10, 8, 8.

In Chapter 1 we summarized all these scores into a frequency table (Table 1–3). You can now summarize all this information as a single number by figuring the mean. You figure the mean by adding up all the stress ratings and dividing by the number of stress ratings. That is, you add up the 30 stress ratings: $8 + 7 + 4 + 10 + 8 + 6 + 8 + 9 + 9 + 7 + 3 + 7 + 6 + 5 + 0 + 9 + 10 + 7 + 7 + 3 + 6 + 7 + 5 + 2 + 1 + 6 + 7 + 10 + 8 + 8$, for a total of 193. Then you divide this total by the number of scores, 30. In terms of the formula,

$$M = \frac{\Sigma X}{N} = \frac{193}{30} = 6.43$$

This tells you that the average rating was 6.43 (after rounding off). This is clearly higher than the middle of the 0–10 scale. You can also see this on a graph. Think again of the histogram as a pile of blocks on a board and the mean of 6.43 as the point where the board balances on a fulcrum (see Figure 2–3). This single representative value simplifies the information in the 30 stress scores.

Similarly, consider the Chapter 1 example of students' social interactions (McLaughlin-Volpe et al., 2001). The actual number of interactions over a week for the 94 students are listed on page 8. In Chapter 1, we organized the original scores into a frequency table (see Table 1–5). We can now take those same 94 scores, add them up, and divide by 94 to figure the mean:

$$M = \frac{\Sigma X}{N} = \frac{1635}{94} = 17.39$$

This tells us that during this week these students had an average of 17.39 social interactions. Figure 2–4 shows the mean of 17.39 as the balance point for the 94 social interaction scores.

> **TIP FOR SUCCESS**
>
> When an answer is not a whole number, we suggest that you use two more decimal places in the answer than for the original numbers. In this example, the original numbers did not use decimals, so we rounded the answer to two decimal places.

Steps for Figuring the Mean.   You figure the mean in two steps.

❶ **Add up all the scores.** That is, figure ΣX.
❷ **Divide this sum by the number of scores.** That is, divide ΣX by *N*.

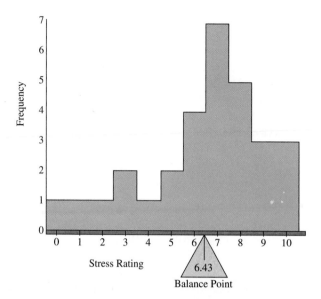

Figure 2–3 Analogy of blocks on a board balanced on a fulcrum showing the mean for 30 statistics students' ratings of their stress level. (Data based on Aron, Paris, and Aron, 1995.)

mode   Value with the greatest frequency in a distribution.

The Mode

The **mode** is another measure of the representative (or typical) value in a group of scores. The mode is the most common single value in a distribution. In our mayors' example, the mode is 8. This is because there are three mayors with 8 years served in office and no other number of years served in office with as many mayors. Another

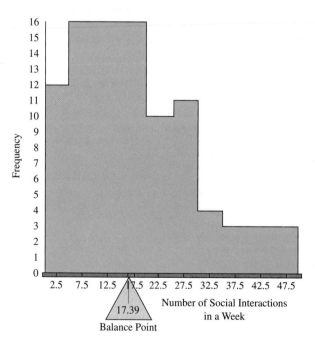

Figure 2–4 Analogy of blocks on a board balanced on a fulcrum illustrating the mean for number of social interactions during a week for 94 college students. (Data from McLaughlin-Volpe et al., 2001.)

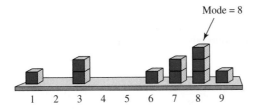

Figure 2–5   The mode as the high point in a distribution's histogram, using the example of the number of years in office served by 10 mayors.

way to think of the mode is that it is the value with the largest frequency in a frequency table, the high point or peak of a distribution's frequency polygon or histogram (as shown in Figure 2–5).

In a perfectly symmetrical unimodal distribution, the mode is the same as the mean. However, what happens when the mode and the mean are not the same? In that situation the mode is usually not a very good representative value for scores in the distribution. In fact, sometimes researchers compare the mode to the mean in order to show that the distribution is *not* perfectly symmetrical and unimodal. Also, the mode can be a particularly poor representative value because it does not reflect many aspects of the distribution. For example, you can change some of the scores in a distribution without affecting the mode—but this is not true of the mean, which is affected by any changes in the distribution (see Figure 2–6).

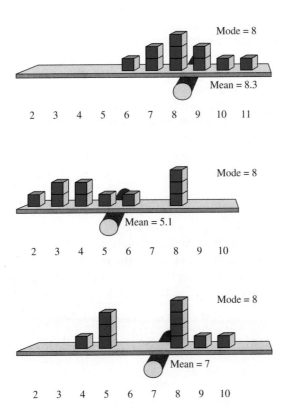

Figure 2–6   The effect on the mean and on the mode of changing some scores, using the example of the number of years in office served by 10 mayors.

median   Middle score when all the scores in a distribution are arranged from highest to lowest.

outlier   Score with an extreme value (very high or very low) in relation to the other scores in the distribution.

On the other hand, the mode *is* the usual way of describing the representative value for a nominal variable. For example, if you know the religions of a particular group of people, the mode tells you which religion is the most frequent. However, when it comes to the numerical variables that are most common in behavioral and social science research, the mode is rarely used.

The Median

Another different measure of the representative value of a group of scores is the **median.** If you line up all the scores from highest to lowest, the middle score is the median. As shown in Figure 2–7, if you line up the numbers of years in office from highest to lowest, the fifth and sixth scores (the two middle ones) are both 7s. Either way, the median is 7 years.

When you have an even number of scores, the median will be between two scores. In that situation, the median is the average (the mean) of the two scores.

Sometimes, the median is better than the mean as a representative value for a group of scores. This happens when there are a few extreme scores that would strongly affect the mean but would not affect the median. For example, suppose that among the 100 families on a banana plantation in Central America, 99 families have an annual income of $100 and 1 family (the owner's) has an annual income of $90,100. The mean family income on this plantation would be $1,000 ($99 \times 100 = 9,900$; $9,900 + 90,100 = 100,000$; $100,000/100 = 1,000$). No family has an income even close to $1,000, so this number is completely misleading. The median income in this example would be $100—an income much more representative of whomever you would meet if you walked up to someone randomly on the plantation.

As this example illustrates, behavioral and social scientists use the median as a descriptive statistic mainly in situations where there are a few extreme scores that would make the mean unrepresentative of most of the scores. An extreme score like this is called an **outlier.** (In this example, the outlier was much higher than the other scores, but in other cases an outlier may be much lower than the other scores in the distribution.) There are also times when the median is used as part of more complex statistical methods. However, unless there are extreme scores, behavioral and social scientists almost always use the mean as the measure of the representative value of a group of scores. In fact, as you will learn, the mean is a fundamental building block for most other statistical techniques.

Steps for Finding the Median.   Finding the median can be summarized as three steps.

❶ **Line up all the scores from highest to lowest.**
❷ **Figure how many scores there are to the middle score, by adding 1 to the number of scores and dividing by 2.** For example, with 29 scores, adding 1 and dividing by 2 gives you 15. The 15th score is the middle score. If there are 50

Figure 2–7   The median is the middle score when scores are lined up from highest to lowest, using the example of the number of years in office served by 10 mayors.

scores, adding 1 and dividing by 2 gives you 25.5. There are no half scores, so the 25th and 26th scores (the scores either side of 25.5) are the middle scores.

❸ **Count up to the middle score or scores.** If you have one middle score, this is the median. If you have two middle scores, the median is the average (the mean) of these two scores.

How are you doing?

1. Name and define three measures of the representative value of a group of scores.
2. Write the formula for the mean and define each of the symbols.
3. Figure the mean of the following scores: 2, 8, 3, 6, and 6.
4. For the following scores, find (a) the mode and (b) the median: 5, 4, 2, 8, 2.

Answers

1. The mean is the ordinary average—the sum of the scores divided by the number of scores. The mode is the most frequent score in a distribution. The median is the middle score—that is, if you line the scores up from highest to lowest, it is the score halfway along.
2. $M = (\Sigma X)/N$. M is the mean; Σ is the symbol for "sum of"—add up all the scores that follow; X is for the variable whose scores you are adding up; N is the number of scores.
3. $M = (\Sigma X)/N = (2 + 8 + 3 + 6 + 6)/5 = 5$.
4. (a) 2, (b) 4.

Variability

Researchers also want to know how spread out the scores are in a distribution. This shows the amount of variability in the distribution. For example, suppose you were asked, "How old are the students in your statistics class?" At a city-based university with many returning and part-time students, the mean age might be 38. You could answer, "The average age of the students in my class is 38." However, this would not tell the whole story. You could, for example, have a mean of 38 because every student in the class was exactly 38 years old. If this is the case, the scores in the distribution are not spread out at all. In other words, there is no variability among the scores. Or, you could have a mean of 38 because exactly half the class was 18 and the other half was 58. In this situation, the distribution is much more spread out. There is considerable variability among the scores.

You can think of the variability of a distribution as the amount of spread of the scores around the mean. Distributions with the same mean can have very different amounts of spread around the mean; Figure 2–8a shows histograms for three different frequency distributions with the same mean but different amounts of spread around the mean. Also, distributions with different means can have the same amount of spread around the mean. Figure 2–8b shows three different frequency distributions with different means but the same amount of spread. So, while the mean provides a representative value of a group of scores, it doesn't tell you about the variability (or spread) of the scores. You will now learn about two measures of the variability of a group of scores: the *variance* and *standard deviation.*

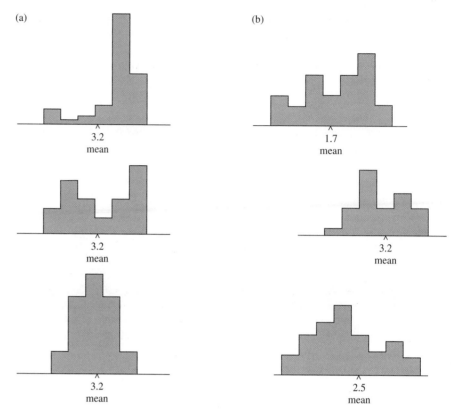

(a)

3.2
mean

3.2
mean

3.2
mean

(b)

1.7
mean

3.2
mean

2.5
mean

Figure 2–8 Examples of distributions with (a) the same mean but different amounts of spread and (b) different means but the same amount of spread.

variance Measure of how spread out a set of scores are; average of the squared deviations from the mean.

deviation score Score minus the mean.

squared deviation score Square of the difference between a score and the mean.

sum of squared deviations Total over all the scores of each score's squared difference from the mean.

The Variance

The **variance** of a group of scores tells you how spread out the scores are around the mean.[1] To be precise, the variance is the average of each score's squared difference from the mean.

Here are the four steps to figure the variance.

❶ **Subtract the mean from each score.** This gives each score's **deviation score.** The deviation score is how far away the actual score is from the mean.

❷ **Square each of these deviation scores** (multiply each by itself). This gives each score's **squared deviation score.**

❸ **Add up the squared deviation scores.** This total is called the **sum of squared deviations.**

❹ **Divide the sum of squared deviations by the number of scores.** This gives the average (the mean) of the squared deviations, called the variance.

---

[1]This section focuses on the variance and standard deviation as measures of spread (or variation). There is also another way to describe the spread of a group of scores, the *range*—the highest score minus the lowest score. Suppose that for a particular class of students the highest score on a midterm is 98 and the lowest score on the midterm is 60; the range is 38 (that is, 98 − 60 = 38). Researchers rarely use the range because it is a very crude way of describing the spread. It is crude because it considers only two scores from the group of scores and does not take into account how clumped together the scores are within the range.

This procedure may seem a bit awkward or hard to remember at first, but it works quite well. Suppose one distribution is more spread out than another. The more spread-out distribution has a larger variance because being spread out makes the deviation scores bigger. If the deviation scores are bigger, the squared deviation scores also are bigger. Thus, the average of the squared deviation scores (the variance) is bigger.

In the example of the class in which everyone was exactly 38 years old, the variance would be exactly 0. That is, there would be no variance (which makes sense, as there is no variability among the ages). (In terms of the numbers, each person's deviation score would be $38 - 38 = 0$; 0 squared is 0. The average of a bunch of zeros is 0.) By contrast, the class of half 18-year-olds and half 58-year-olds would have a rather large variance of 400. (The 18-year-olds would each have deviation scores of $18 - 38 = -20$. The 58-year-olds would have deviation scores of $58 - 38 = 20$. All the squared deviation scores, which are -20 squared or 20 squared, would come out to 400. The average of all 400s is 400.)

The variance is extremely important in many statistical procedures you will learn about later. However, the variance is rarely used as a descriptive statistic. This is because the variance is based on *squared* deviation scores, which do not give a very easy-to-understand sense of how spread out the actual, nonsquared scores are. For example, it is clear that a class with a variance of 400 has a more spread-out distribution than one whose variance is 10. However, the number 400 does not give an obvious insight into the actual variation among the ages, none of which are anywhere near 400.

The Standard Deviation

The most widely used way of *describing* the spread of a group of scores is the **standard deviation.** The standard deviation is directly related to the variance and is figured by taking the square root of the variance. There are two steps to figure the standard deviation.

❶ **Figure the variance.**
❷ **Take the square root.** The standard deviation is the *positive* square root of the variance. (Any number has both a positive and a negative square root. For example, the square root of 9 is both $+3$ and -3.)

If the variance of a distribution is 400, the standard deviation is 20. If the variance is 9, the standard deviation is 3.

The variance is about squared deviations from the mean. Therefore, its square root, the standard deviation, is about direct, ordinary, nonsquared deviations from the mean. *Roughly speaking, the standard deviation is the average amount that scores differ from the mean.* For example, consider a class where the ages have a standard deviation of 20 years. This would tell you that the ages are spread out, on average, about 20 years in each direction from the mean. Knowing the standard deviation gives you a general sense of the degree of spread.

The standard deviation usually is not *exactly* the average amount that scores differ from the mean. To be precise, the standard deviation is the square root of the average of the scores' squared deviations from the mean. This squaring, averaging, and then taking the square root usually gives a slightly different result from simply averaging the scores' deviations from the mean. Still, the result of this approach has technical advantages to outweigh this slight disadvantage of giving only an approximate description of the average variation from the mean.

standard deviation   Square root of the average of the squared deviations from the mean; the most common descriptive statistic for variation; approximately the average amount that scores in a distribution vary from the mean.

SD² Variance.

SD Standard deviation.

> The variance is the sum of the squared deviations of the scores from the mean, divided by the number of scores.

Formulas for the Variance and the Standard Deviation. We have seen that the variance is the average squared deviation from the mean. Here is the formula for the variance

(2-2)

$$SD^2 = \frac{\sum(X - M)^2}{N}$$

SD^2 is the symbol for the variance. (In Chapter 8 you learn another symbol, S^2. This other symbol is for a slightly different kind of variance.) SD is short for *standard deviation.* The symbol SD^2 emphasizes that the variance is the standard deviation squared.

The top part of the formula is the *sum of squared deviations.* X is for each score and M is the mean. Thus, $X - M$ is the score minus the mean, the deviation score. The ^{2} tells you to square each deviation score. Finally, the sum sign (Σ) tells you to add together all these squared deviation scores. The bottom part of the formula tells you to divide the sum of squared deviation scores by N, the number of scores.

The standard deviation is the square root of the variance. So, if you already know the variance, the formula is

> The standard deviation is the square root of the variance.

(2-3)

$$SD = \sqrt{SD^2}$$

TIP FOR SUCCESS

A common error when figuring the standard deviation is to jump straight from the sum of squared deviations to the standard deviation (by taking the square root of the sum of squared deviations). Remember, before finding the standard deviation, you first have to figure the variance (by dividing the sum of squared deviations by the number of scores, N). Then take the square root of the variance to find the standard deviation.)

TIP FOR SUCCESS

Always check that your answers make *intuitive sense.* For example, looking at the scores for the mayors' example, a standard deviation—which, roughly speaking, represents the average amount the scores vary from the mean—of 2.57 makes sense. If your answer had been 21.23, however, it would mean that, on average, the number of years in office varied by more than 20 years from the mean of 6. Looking at the scores, that just couldn't be true.

Examples of Figuring the Variance and the Standard Deviation. Table 2–1 shows the figuring for the variance and standard deviation for our mayors' example. (The table assumes we already have figured out the mean to be 6 years in office.) Usually, it is easiest to do your figuring using a calculator, especially one with a square root

Table 2-1 Figuring of Variance and Standard Deviation in the Example of Number of Years Served by 10 Mayors

Score (Number of Years Served)	−	Mean score (Mean Number of Years Served)	=	Deviation score	Squared Deviation score
7		6		1	1
8		6		2	4
8		6		2	4
7		6		1	1
3		6		−3	9
1		6		−5	25
6		6		0	0
9		6		3	9
3		6		−3	9
8		6		2	4
				Σ: 0	66

Variance = $SD^2 = \dfrac{\Sigma(X - M)^2}{N} = \dfrac{66}{10} = 6.60$

Standard deviation = $SD = \sqrt{SD^2} = \sqrt{6.60} = 2.57$

Table 2-2 Figuring the Variance and Standard Deviation for Number of Social Interactions during a Week for 94 College Students

Number of Interactions	−	Mean Number of Interactions	=	Deviation Score	Squared Deviation Score
48		17.39		30.61	936.97
15		17.39		−2.39	5.71
33		17.39		15.61	243.67
3		17.39		−14.39	207.07
21		17.39		3.61	13.03
.		.		.	.
.		.		.	.
.		.		.	.
35		17.39		17.61	310.11
9		17.39		−8.39	70.39
30		17.39		12.61	159.01
8		17.39		−9.39	88.17
26		17.39		8.61	74.13
				Σ: 0.00	12,406.44

$$\text{Variance} = SD^2 = \frac{\Sigma(X - M)^2}{N} = \frac{12{,}406.44}{94} = 131.98$$

$$\text{Standard deviation} = \sqrt{SD^2} = \sqrt{131.98} = 11.49$$

Source: Data from McLaughlin-Volpe et al. (2001).

computational formula Equation mathematically equivalent to the definitional formula. It is easier to use for figuring by hand, but does not directly show the meaning of the procedure.

TIP FOR SUCCESS

Notice in Table 2–1 that the deviation scores (shown in the third column) add up to 0. The sum of the deviation scores is *always* 0 (or very close to 0, allowing for rounding error). This is because, as you learned earlier in the chapter, the mean is the balancing point of a distribution (where the total distance from the mean to the scores above the mean is the same as the total distance from the mean to the scores below the mean). So, to check your figuring, always sum the deviation scores. If they do not add up to 0, do your figuring again!

key. The standard deviation of 2.57 tells you that roughly speaking, on average, the number of years the mayors were in office varied by about 2½ from the mean of 6.

Table 2–2 shows the figuring for the variance and standard deviation for the example of students' numbers of social interactions during a week (McLaughlin-Volpe et al., 2001). To save space, the table shows only the first few and last few scores. Roughly speaking, this result indicates that a student's number of social interactions in a week varies from the mean (of 17.39) by an average of 11.49 interactions. This can also be shown on a histogram (see Figure 2–9).

Measures of variability, such as the variance and standard deviation, are heavily influenced by the presence of one or more outliers (extreme values) in a distribution. The scores in the mayors' example were 7, 8, 8, 7, 3, 1, 6, 9, 3, 8, and we figured the standard deviation of the scores to be 2.57. Now imagine that one additional mayor is added to the study who has been in office for 21 years. The standard deviation of the scores would now be 4.96, which is almost double the size of the standard deviation without this additional single score.

TIP FOR SUCCESS:

When figuring the variance and standard deviation, lay your working out as shown in Tables 2–1 and 2–2. This will help to ensure that you follow all of the steps and end up with the correct answers.

Computational and Definitional Formulas. In actual research situations, behavioral and social scientists must often figure the variance and the standard deviation for distributions with a great many scores, often involving decimals or large numbers. This can make the whole process quite time-consuming, even with a calculator. To deal with this problem, over the years researchers have developed a various shortcuts to simplify the figuring. A shortcut formula of this type is called a **computational formula.** The traditional computational formula for the variance of the kind we are discussing in this chapter is

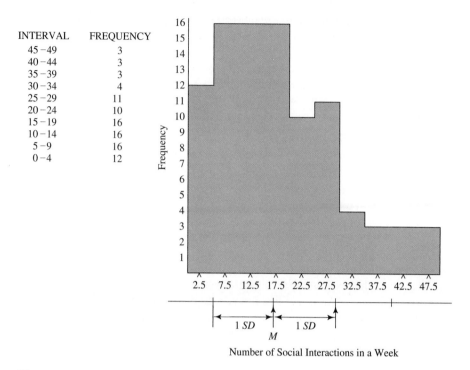

INTERVAL	FREQUENCY
45–49	3
40–44	3
35–39	3
30–34	4
25–29	11
20–24	10
15–19	16
10–14	16
5–9	16
0–4	12

Figure 2–9   The standard deviation as the distance along the base of a histogram, using the example of number of social interactions in a week. (Data from McLaughlin-Volpe et al., 2001)

> The variance is the sum of the squared scores minus the re-sult of taking the sum of all the scores, squaring this sum and dividing by the number of scores, then taking this whole difference and dividing it by the number of scores.

definitional formula   Equation for a statistical procedure directly showing the meaning of the procedure.

$$SD^2 = \frac{\sum X^2 - \left(\left(\sum X\right)^2/N\right)}{N} \qquad (2\text{-}4)$$

ΣX^2 means that you square each score and then take the sum of these squared scores. However, $(\Sigma X)^2$ means that you add up all the scores first and then take the square of this sum. This formula is easier to use if you are figuring the variance for a lot of numbers by hand because you do not have to first find the deviation score for each score.

However, these days computational formulas are mainly of historical interest. They are used by researchers only when computers are not readily available to do the figuring. In fact, today, even many hand calculators are set up so that you need only enter the scores and press a button or two to get the variance and the standard deviation.

In this book we give a few computational formulas, just so you will have them if you someday do a research project with a lot of numbers and you don't have access to statistical software. However, we recommend *not* using the computational formulas when you are learning statistics. The problem is that the computational formulas tend to make it harder to understand the *meaning* of what you are figuring. It is much better to use the regular formulas we give when doing the practice problems. These are the formulas designed to help you strengthen your understanding of what the figuring *means.* These usual formulas we give are called **definitional formulas.**

The purpose of this book is to help you understand statistical procedures, not to turn you into a computer by having you memorize computational formulas you will rarely, if ever, use. To simplify the actual figuring, however, our practice problems generally use small groups of whole numbers. For students who have access to a computer and statistics software, the *Using SPSS* sections at the end of relevant chapters and the *Study Guide and SPSS Workbook* accompanying this textbook are designed to give you experience doing statistics as behavioral and social scientists normally would, working with standard statistics programs on a computer.

The Importance of Variability in Behavioral and Social Sciences Research

So far, we have focused on the variance and standard deviation as measures of the variability in a group of scores. More generally, variability is an important topic in behavioral and social sciences research, as much of that research focuses on explaining variability. We will use an example to show what we mean by "explaining variability." As you might imagine, different students experience different levels of stress with regard to learning statistics: Some students experience little stress; for other students, learning statistics can be a source of great stress. So, in this example, explaining variability means identifying the factors that explain why students differ in the amount of stress they experience. Perhaps how much experience students have had with math explains some of the variability in stress. That is, according to this explanation, the differences (variability) among students in amount of stress are partially due to the differences (variability) among students in the amount of experience they have had with math. Thus, the variation in math experience patially explains, or accounts for, the variation in stress. Perhaps the degree to which students generally experience stress in their lives also partly explains differences among students' stress with regard to learning statistics. Much of the rest of this book focuses on procedures for evaluating and testing whether variation on some specific factor (or factors) explains the variability in some variable of interest.

The Variance as the Sum of Squared Deviations Divided by $N - 1$

Researchers often use a slightly different kind of variance. We have defined the variance as the average of the squared deviation scores. Using that definition, you divide the sum of squared deviation scores by the number of scores. But you learn in Chapter 8 that for many purposes it is better to define the variance as the sum of squared deviation scores *divided by 1 less than the number of scores*. That is, for those purposes, the variance is the sum of squared deviations divided by $N - 1$. (As you learn in Chapter 8, you use this $N - 1$ approach when you have scores from a particular group of people and you want to estimate what the variance would be for the larger group of people these individuals represent.)

The variances and standard deviations given in research articles are usually figured using the $N - 1$ approach. Also, when calculators or computers give the variance or the standard deviation automatically, they are usually figured in this way (for example, see the *Using SPSS* section at the end of this chapter). But don't worry. The approach you are learning in this chapter of dividing by N is entirely correct for our purpose here, which is to use descriptive statistics to describe the variation in a particular group of scores. It is also entirely correct for the material covered in the rest of this chapter (Z scores of the kind we are using), and for the material you learn in Chapters 3 through 7. We mention this $N - 1$ approach now only so you will not be confused when you read about variance or standard deviation in other places or if your calculator or a computer program gives a surprising result. To keep things simple, we wait to discuss the $N - 1$ approach until it is needed, starting in Chapter 8.

How are you doing?

1. (a) Define the variance. (b) Describe what it tells you about a distribution and how this is different from what the mean tells you.
2. (a) Define the standard deviation, (b) describe its relation to the variance, and (c) explain what it tells you approximately about a group of scores.
3. Give the full formula for the variance and indicate what each of the symbols mean.
4. Figure the (a) variance and (b) standard deviation for the following scores: 2, 4, 3, and 7 ($M = 4$).
5. Explain the difference between a definitional and a computational formula.
6. What is the difference between the formula for the variance you learned in this chapter and the formula that is usually used to figure the variance in research articles?

Answers

1. (a) The variance is the average of the squared deviations of each score from the mean. (b) The variance tells you about how spread out the scores are (that is, their variability), while the mean tells you the representative value of the distribution.
2. (a) The standard deviation is the square root of the average of the squared deviations from the mean. (b) The standard deviation is the square root of the variance. (c) The standard deviation tells you approximately the average amount that scores differ from the mean.
3. $SD^2 = [\Sigma(X - M)^2]/N$. SD^2 is the variance. Σ means the sum of what follows. X is for the scores for the variable being studied. M is the mean of the scores. N is the number of scores.
4. (a) $SD^2 = [\Sigma(X - M)^2]/N = [(2 - 4)^2 + (4 - 4)^2 + (3 - 4)^2 + (7 - 4)^2]/4 = 14/4 = 3.5$.
   (b) $SD = \sqrt{SD^2} = \sqrt{3.5} = 1.87$.
5. A definitional formula is the standard formula that is in the straightforward form that shows the meaning of what the formula is figuring. A computational formula is a mathematically equivalent variation of the definitional formula that is easier to use if figuring by hand with a lot of scores, but it tends not to show the underlying meaning.
6. The formula for the variance in this chapter divides the sum of squared deviations by N (the number of scores). The variance in research articles is usually figured by dividing the sum of squared deviations by $N - 1$ (one less than the number of scores).

Z Scores

So far in this chapter you have learned about describing a group of scores in terms of a representative score and variation. In this section, you learn how to describe a particular score in terms of where it fits into the overall group of scores. That is, you learn how to use the mean and standard deviation to create a Z score; a Z score describes a score in terms of how much it is above or below the average.

    Suppose you are told that a student, Jerome, is asked the question "To what extent are you a morning person?" Jerome answers "5" on a 7-point scale, where 1 = *not at all* and 7 = *extremely.* Now suppose that we do not know anything about how other

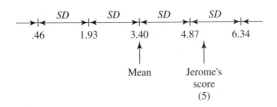

Figure 2-10 showing SD intervals at .46, 1.93, 3.40, 4.87, 6.34 with Mean at 3.40 and Jerome's score (5) at 4.87.

Figure 2–10 Score of one student, Jerome, in relation to the overall distribution on the measure of the extent to which students are morning people.

students answer this question. In this situation, it is hard to tell whether Jerome is more or less of a morning person in relation to other students. However, suppose that we know for students in general, the mean is 3.40 and the standard deviation is 1.47. (These values are the actual mean and standard deviation that we found for this question in a large sample of statistics students from 8 different colleges across the United States and Canada.) With this knowledge, we can see that Jerome is more of a morning person than is typical among students. We can also see that the amount Jerome is above the average (1.60 units more than average) is a bit more than students typically vary from the average. This is all shown in Figure 2–10.

What Is a Z Score?

A Z score makes use of the mean and standard deviation to describe a particular score. A **Z score** is the number of standard deviations the actual score is above or below the mean. If the actual score is above the mean, the Z score is positive. If the actual score is below the mean, the Z score is negative. The standard deviation now becomes a kind of yardstick, a unit of measure in its own right.

In our example, Jerome has a score of 5, which is 1.60 units above the mean of 3.40 (that is, $5 - 3.40 = 1.60$). One standard deviation is 1.47 units, so Jerome's score is a little more than 1 standard deviation above the mean. To be precise, Jerome's Z score is +1.09 (which means his score of 5 is 1.09 standard deviations above the mean). Another student, Maxine, had a score of 2. Her score is 1.40 units below the mean. Therefore, her score is a little less than one standard deviation below the mean (a Z score of −.95). So, Maxine's score is below the average by about as much as students typically vary from the average.

Z scores have many practical uses. They also are part of many of the statistical procedures you learn later in this book. It is important that you become very familiar with them.

Z Scores as a Scale

Figure 2–11 shows a scale of Z scores lined up against a scale of raw scores for our example of the degree to which students are morning people. A **raw score** is an ordinary score as opposed to a Z score. The two scales are something like a ruler with inches lined up on one side and centimeters on the other.

Z score: −2, −1, 0, +1, +2; Raw score: .46, 1.93, 3.40, 4.87, 6.34

Figure 2–11 Scales of Z scores and raw scores for the example of the extent to which students are morning people.

BOX 2–1   **The Psychology of Statistics and the Tyranny of the Mean**

Looking in the behavioral and social science research journals, you would think that statistical methods are their sole tool and language, but there have also been rebellions against the reign of statistics. We are most familiar with this issue in psychology, where one of the most unexpected oppositions came from the leader of behaviorism, the school of psychology most dedicated to keeping the field strictly scientific.

Behaviorism opposed the study of inner states because inner events are impossible to observe objectively. (Today most research psychologists attempt to measure inner events indirectly but objectively.) Behaviorism's most famous advocate, B. F. Skinner, was quite opposed to statistics. He was constantly pointing to the information lost by averaging the results of a number of cases. For instance, Skinner (1956) cited the example of three overeating mice—one naturally obese, one poisoned with gold, and one whose hypothalamus had been altered. Each had a different curve for learning to press a bar for food. If these learning curves had been summed or merged statistically, the result would have represented no actual eating habits of any real mouse at all. As Skinner said, "These three individual curves contain more information than could probably ever be generated with measures requiring statistical treatment" (p. 232).

A different voice of caution was raised by another school of psychology, humanistic psychology, which began in the 1950s as a "third force" in reaction to Freudian psychoanalysis and behaviorism. The point of humanistic psychology was that human consciousness should be studied intact, as a whole, as it is experienced by individuals, and it can never be fully explained by reducing it to numbers (any more than it can be reduced to words). Each individual's experience is unique.

Today, the rebellion is led in psychology by qualitative research methodologies (e.g., McCracken, 1988), an approach that is much more prominent in other behavioral and social sciences. The qualitative research methods were developed mainly in anthropology and can involve long interviews or observations of a few individuals. The mind of the researcher is the main tool because, according to this approach, only that mind can find the important relationships among the many categories of events arising in the respondent's speech. Many who favor qualitative methods argue for a blend: First, discover the important categories through a qualitative approach. Then, determine their incidence in the larger population through quantitative methods.

Finally, Carl Jung, founder of Jungian psychology, sometimes spoke of the "statistical mood" and its effect on a person's feeling of uniqueness. The Jungian analyst Marie Louise von Franz (1979) wrote about Jung's thoughts on this subject: When we walk down a street and observe the hundreds of blank faces and begin to feel diminished, or even so overwhelmed by overpopulation that we are glad that humans don't live forever, this is the statistical mood. Yet, there is at least as much irregularity to life as ordinariness. As she puts it,

> The fact that this table does not levitate, but remains where it is, is only because the billions and billions and billions of electrons which constitute the table tend statistically to behave like that. But each electron in itself could do something else. (pp. IV–17)

Likewise, when we are in love, we feel that the other person is unique and wonderful. Yet in a statistical mood, we realize that the other person is ordinary, like many others.

Jung did not cherish individual uniqueness just to be romantic about it, however. He held that the important contributions to culture tend to come from people thinking at least a little independently or creatively, and their independence is damaged by this statistical mood.

Furthermore, von Franz (1979) argues that a statistical mood is damaging to love and life. In particular, feeling the importance of our single action makes immoral acts—war and killing, for example—less possible. We cannot count the dead as numbers but must treat them as persons with emotions and purposes, like ourselves.

Suppose that a developmental specialist observed 3-year-old Peter in a standardized laboratory situation playing with other children of the same age. During the observation, the specialist counted the number of times Peter spoke to the other children. The result, over several observations, is that Peter spoke to other children about 8 times per hour of play. Without any standard of comparison, it would be hard to draw any conclusions from this. Let's assume, however, that it was known from pre-

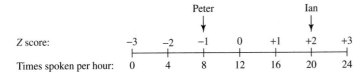

Figure 2–12   Number of times each hour that two children spoke, shown as raw scores and Z scores.

vious research that under similar conditions the mean number of times children speak is 12, with a standard deviation of 4. Clearly, Peter spoke less often than other children in general, but not extremely less often. Peter would have a Z score of -1 ($M =$ 12 and $SD = 4$, thus a score of 8 is 1 SD below M), as shown in Figure 2–12.

Suppose Ian was observed speaking to other children 20 times in an hour. Ian would clearly be unusually talkative, with a Z score of +2 (see Figure 2–12). Ian would speak not merely more than the average but more by twice as much as children tend to vary from the average!

Z Scores as Providing a Generalized Standard of Comparison

Another advantage of Z scores is that scores on completely different variables can be made into Z scores and compared. With Z scores, the mean is always 0 and the standard deviation is always 1. Suppose the same children in our example were also measured on a test of language skill. In this situation, we could directly compare the Z scores on language skill to the Z scores on speaking to other children. Let's say Peter had a score of 100 on the language skill test. If the mean on that test was 82 and the standard deviation was 6, then Peter is much better than average at language skill, with a Z score of +3. Thus, it seems unlikely that Peter's less-than-usual amount of speaking to other children is due to poorer-than-usual language skill (see Figure 2–13).

Notice in this latest example that by using Z scores, we can directly compare the results of both the specialist's observation of the amount of talking and the language skill test. This is almost as wonderful as being able to compare apples and oranges! Converting a number to a Z score is a bit like converting the words for measurement in various obscure languages into one language that everyone can understand—inches, cubits, and zinqles (we made up that last one), for example, into centimeters. It is a very valuable tool.

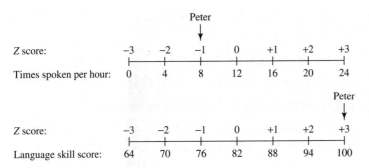

Figure 2–13   Scales of Z scores and raw scores for number of times spoken per hour and language skill, showing the first child's score on each.

Formula to Change a Raw Score to a Z Score

As we have seen, a Z score is the number of standard deviations the raw score is above or below the mean. To figure a Z score, subtract the mean from the raw score, giving the deviation score. Then, divide the deviation score by the standard deviation. The formula is

> A Z score is the raw score minus the mean, divided by the standard deviation.

$$Z = \frac{X - M}{SD} \qquad \text{(2-5)}$$

For example, using the formula for Peter, the child who spoke to other children 8 times in an hour (where the mean number of times children speak is 12 and the standard deviation is 4),

$$Z = \frac{8 - 12}{4} = \frac{-4}{4} = -1$$

Steps to Change a Raw Score to a Z Score

❶ **Figure the deviation score: Subtract the mean from the raw score.**
❷ **Figure the Z score: Divide the deviation score by the standard deviation.**

Using these steps for Peter, the child who spoke with other children 8 times in an hour,

❶ **Figure the deviation score: Subtract the mean from the raw score.** $8 - 12 = -4$.
❷ **Figure the Z score: Divide the deviation score by the standard deviation.** $-4/4 = -1$.

Formula to Change a Z Score to a Raw Score

To change a Z score to a raw score, the process is reversed: You multiply the Z score by the standard deviation and then add the mean. The formula is

> The raw score is the Z score multiplied by the standard deviation, plus the mean.

$$X = (Z)(SD) + M \qquad \text{(2-6)}$$

Suppose a child has a Z score of 1.5 on the number of times spoken with another child during an hour. This child is 1.5 standard deviations above the mean. Because the standard deviation in this example is 4 raw score units (times spoken), the child is 6 raw score units above the mean. The mean is 12. Thus, 6 units above this is 18. Using the formula,

$$X = (Z)(SD) + M = (1.5)(4) + 12 = 6 + 12 = 18$$

Steps to Change a Z Score to a Raw Score

❶ **Figure the deviation score: Multiply the Z score by the standard deviation.**
❷ **Figure the raw score: Add the mean to the deviation score.**

Using these steps for the child with a Z score of 1.5 on the number of times spoken with another child during an hour:

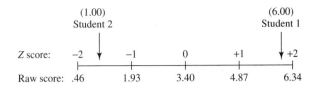

Figure 2-14   Scales of Z scores and raw scores for the example of the extent to which students are morning people, showing the scores of two sample students.

❶ **Figure the deviation score: Multiply the Z score by the standard deviation.** $1.5 \times 4 = 6$.

❷ **Figure the raw score: Add the mean to the deviation score.** $6 + 12 = 18$.

Additional Examples of Changing Z Scores to Raw Scores and Vice Versa

Consider again the example in which students were asked the extent to which they were a morning person. Using a scale from 1 (*not at all*) to 7 (*extremely*), the mean was 3.40 and the standard deviation was 1.47. Suppose a student's raw score is 6. That student is well above the mean. Specifically, using the formula,

$$Z = \frac{X - M}{SD} = \frac{6 - 3.40}{1.47} = \frac{2.60}{1.47} = 1.77$$

That is, the student's raw score is 1.77 standard deviations above the mean (see Figure 2–14, Student 1). Using the 7-point scale (from 1 = *not at all* to 7 = *extremely*), to what extent are *you* a morning person? Now figure the Z score for your raw score.

Another student has a Z score of −1.63, a score well below the mean. (This student is much less of a morning person than is typically the case for students.) You can find the exact raw score for this student using the formula,

$$X = (Z)(SD) + M = (-1.63)(1.47) + 3.40 = -2.40 + 3.40 = 1.00$$

That is, the student's raw score is 1.00 (see Figure 2–14, Student 2).

Let's also consider some examples from the study of students' stress ratings. The mean stress rating of the 30 statistics students (using a 0–10 scale) was 6.43, and the standard deviation was 2.56. Figure 2–15 shows the raw score and Z score scales. Suppose a student's stress raw score is 10. That student is well above the mean. Specifically, using the formula,

$$Z = \frac{X - M}{SD} = \frac{10 - 6.43}{2.56} = \frac{3.57}{2.56} = 1.39$$

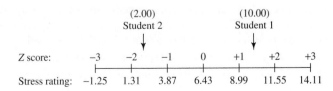

Figure 2-15   Scales of Z scores and raw scores for 30 statistics students' ratings of their stress level, showing the scores of two sample students. (Data based on Aron et al., 1995.)

That is, the student's stress level is 1.39 standard deviations above the mean (see Figure 2–15, Student 1). On a scale of 0–10, how stressed have *you* been in the last 2½ weeks? Figure the Z score for your raw stress score.

Another student has a Z score of −1.73, a stress level well below the mean. You can find the exact raw stress score for this student using the formula,

$$X = (Z)(SD) + M = (-1.73)(2.56) + 6.43 = -4.43 + 6.43 = 2.00.$$

That is, the student's raw stress score is 2.00 (see Figure 2–15, Student 2).

How are you doing?

1. What is a Z score (that is, how is it related to a raw score)?
2. Write the formula for changing a raw score to a Z score and define each of the symbols.
3. For a particular group of scores, M = 20 and SD = 5. Give the Z score for (a) 30, (b) 15, (c) 20, and (d) 22.5.
4. Write the formula for changing a Z score to a raw score and define each of the symbols.
5. For a particular group of scores, M = 10 and SD = 2. Give the raw score for a Z score of (a) +2, (b) +.5, (c) 0, and (d) −3.
6. Suppose a person has a Z score for overall health of +2 and a Z score for overall sense of humor of +1. What does it mean to say that this person is healthier than she is funny?

Answers

1. A Z score is the number of standard deviations a raw score is above or below the mean.
2. $Z = (X - M)/SD$. Z is the Z score; X is the raw score; M is the mean; SD is the standard deviation.
3. (a) $Z = (X - M)/SD = (30 - 20)/5 = 2$; (b) −1; (c) 0; (d) +.5
4. $X = (Z)(SD) + M$. X is the raw score; Z is the Z score; SD is the standard deviation; M is the mean.
5. (a) $X = (Z)(SD) + M = (2)(2) + 10 = 4 + 10 = 14$; (b) 11; (c) 10; (d) 4.
6. This person is more above the average (in terms of how much people typically vary from average in health) than this person is above the average (in terms of how much people typically vary from the average in humor).

Mean, Variance, Standard Deviation, and Z Scores in Research Articles

The mean and the standard deviation (and occasionally, the variance) are commonly reported in research articles. The median and the mode are less often reported in research articles. Z scores are rarely reported in research articles. Sometimes the mean and standard deviation are included in the text of an article. For example, our fictional political scientist, in a research article about the mayors of this region, would write, "At the time of the study, the mean number of years in office for the 10 mayors in this region was 6.0 (SD = 2.57)." Means and standard deviations are also often listed in tables, especially if a study includes several groups or several different variables. For example, Misra and Castillo (2004) conducted a study comparing the academic stress experienced by American and international students at two universities in the United States. The students completed questionnaire measures that asked how often they experience each of five sources of "academic stressors": change, conflict, frustration, pressure, and self-imposed. The students also indicated how often they use each of four types of reactions to academic stressors: emotional, cognitive, behavioral, and physiological. All of the measures used a 5-point scale from 1 = *never* to 5 = *most of the time*. Table 2–3 (reproduced from Misra & Castillo's [2004] article) shows the means and standard deviations for each type of academic stressor and each type of reaction to stressors, separated out for male and female American and international students. As noted at the bottom of the table, the standard deviations are the numbers in the parentheses (a common approach in such tables). As you can see, the table provides a useful summary of the descriptive results of the study.

A particularly interesting example is shown in Table 2–4 (reproduced from Norcross, Kohout, & Wicherski, 2005). The table shows the application and enrollment statistics for psychology doctoral programs, broken down by area of psychology and year (1973, 1979, 1992, and 2003). The table does not give standard deviations, but it does give both means and medians. For example, in 2003 the mean number of applicants to doctoral counseling psychology programs was 71.0, but the median was only 59. This suggests that there were some programs with very high numbers of applicants that skewed the distribution. In fact, you can see from the table that in almost every case, and for both applications and enrollments, the means are typically higher than the medians. You may also be struck by just how competitive it is to get into doctoral programs in many areas of psychology. It is our experience that one of the factors that makes a lot of difference is doing well in statistics courses!

Table 2-3 Mean Academic Stressors and Reactions to Stressors by Gender and Status

	American Students			International Students		
Variable	**Males**	**Females**	**Total**	**Males**	**Females**	**Total**
Stressor						
Change	2.61 (0.72)	2.60 (0.72)	2.60 (0.72)	2.53 (1.21)	2.64 (1.01)	2.59 (1.10)
Conflict	3.14 (0.59)	3.06 (0.62)	3.08 (0.61)	2.75 (0.71)	2.52 (0.71)	2.64 (0.74)
Frustration	2.71 (0.49)	2.72 (0.53)	2.72 (0.52)	2.60 (0.67)	2.44 (0.62)	2.51 (0.64)
Pressure	3.61 (0.65)	3.68 (0.60)	3.66 (0.62)	3.16 (0.79)	3.34 (0.86)	3.26 (0.83)
Self-imposed	3.62 (0.52)	3.77 (0.55)	3.72 (0.55)	2.93 (0.79)	3.02 (0.74)	2.98 (0.76)
Reaction						
Emotional	2.73 (0.91)	2.90 (1.08)	2.86 (1.04)	2.53 (0.86)	2.82 (0.95)	2.68 (0.93)
Cognitive	2.77 (1.01)	2.92 (0.97)	2.88 (0.98)	3.28 (1.11)	3.13 (1.07)	3.21 (1.10)
Behavioral	2.00 (0.65)	2.12 (0.72)	2.09 (0.71)	1.59 (0.51)	1.81 (0.48)	1.71 (0.50)
Physiological	1.81 (0.59)	2.07 (0.75)	2.00 (0.72)	1.86 (0.57)	2.07 (0.49)	1.97 (0.53)

Note: Standard deviations are in parentheses. Academic stressors and reactions to stressors: 1 = *never,* 5 = *most of the time.*
Source: Misra, R., & Castillo, L. G. (2004). Academic stress among college students: Comparison of American and international students. *International Journal of Stress Management, 11,* 132–148. Copyright © 2004 by the Educational Publishing Foundation (American Psychological Association). Reprinted with permission.

Table 2-4 Application and Enrollment Statistics by Area and Year: Doctoral Programs

Program	N of programs				Applications								Enrollments			
					M				Mdn				M		Mdn	
	1973	1979	1992	2003	1973	1979	1992	2003	1973	1979	1992	2003	1992	2003	1992	2003
Clinical	105	130	225	216	314.4	252.6	191.1	142.0	290	234	168	126	12.0	15.4	8	8
Clinical neuro				20				72.3				37		10.7		6
Community	4	2	5	13	90.5		24.4	23.5	60		23	21	3.2	3.3	2	3
Counseling	29	43	62	66	133.4	90.9	120.2	71.0	120	84	110	59	7.3	6.8	6	7
Health			7	13			40.7	71.2			30	56	4.4	6.7	5	4
School	30	39	56	57	78.5	54.0	31.3	38.7	53	34	32	31	5.4	6.9	5	5
Other health service provider subfield				52				83.5				48		9.2		7
Cognitive			47	104			24.6	30.1			22	22	2.6	3.4	2	3
Developmental	56	72	97	111	54.1	38.9	27.6	25.5	41	30	24	22	2.8	3.4	2	2
Educational	23	28	30	35	67.8	39.7	20.0	19.7	34	26	12	13	6.0	4.9	4	4
Experimental	118	127	78	40	56.2	33.2	31.3	26.7	42	25	26	17	4.4	4.1	3	3
I/O	20	25	49	60	39.9	54.7	66.2	46.9	37	48	70	41	4.9	4.7	4	4
Neuroscience				53				22.0				16		2.8		2
Personality	23	15	10	18	42.5	24.7	12.3	47.8	33	17	6	31	1.0	2.8	1	2
Psychobiological/physiological				18				21.1				17		2.4		2
Quantitative	40	43	76	17	33.2	29.3	20.0	11.2	29	24	20	11	3.9	1.9	2	1
Social	58	72	59	85	46.7	30.9	47.1	43.1	40	24	37	35	3.3	3.2	3	3
Other fields	60	47	288	101	61.6	74.1	26.6	26.0	27	25	15	17	3.3	3.8	2	3
Total	566	645	1,089	1,079	106.1	85.2	69.4	59.6			31	33	5.6	6.7	4	4

Note. The academic years correspond to the 1975–1976, 1981–1982, 1994, and 2005 editions of *Graduate Study in Psychology*, respectively. Clinical neuro = clinical neuropsychology; I/O = industrial–organizational.

Source: Norcross, J. C., Haanych, J. M. & Terranova, R. D. (2005). Graduate study in Psychology: 1992–1993. *American Psychologist, 51*, 631–643. Copyright © 2005 by American Psychological Association.

Summary

1. The mean is the most commonly used way of describing the representative value of a group of scores. The mean is the ordinary average—the sum of the scores divided by the number of scores. In symbols, $M = (\Sigma X)/N$.
2. Other, less frequently used ways of describing the representative value of a group of scores are the mode (the most common single value) and the median (the value of the middle score if all the scores were lined up from highest to lowest).
3. The variation among a group of scores can be described by the variance—the average of the squared deviations of each score from the mean. In symbols, $SD^2 = [\Sigma(X - M)^2]/N$.
4. The variation among a group of scores can also be described by the standard deviation. The standard deviation is the square root of the variance. In symbols, $SD = \sqrt{SD^2}$. It can be best understood as approximately the average amount that scores differ from the mean.
5. A Z score is the number of standard deviations a raw score is above or below the mean. Among other uses, with Z scores you can compare scores on variables that have different scales.
6. Means and standard deviations are often given in research articles in the text or in tables. Z scores rarely are reported in research articles.

Key Terms

mean (M) (p. 33)
Σ (sum of) (p. 34)
X (scores in the distribution of the variable X) (p. 35)
N (the number of scores) (p. 35)
mode (p. 36)

median (p. 38)
outlier (p. 38)
variance (SD^2) (p. 40)
deviation score (p. 40)
squared deviation score (p. 40)
sum of squared deviations (p. 40)

standard deviation (SD) (p. 41)
computational formula (p. 43)
definitional formula (p. 44)
Z score (p. 47)
raw score (p. 47)

Example Worked-Out Problems

Figuring the Mean

Find the mean for the following scores: 8, 6, 6, 9, 6, 5, 6, 2.

Answer

You can figure the mean using the formula or the steps.
    Using the formula: $M = (\Sigma X)/N = 48/8 = 6$.
    Using the steps:

❶ **Add up all the scores.** $8 + 6 + 6 + 9 + 6 + 5 + 6 + 2 = 48$.
❷ **Divide this sum by the number of scores.** $48/8 = 6$.

Finding the Median

Find the median for the following scores: 1, 7, 4, 2, 3, 6, 2, 9, 7.

Answer

❶ **Line up all the scores from highest to lowest.** 9, 7, 7, 6, 4, 3, 2, 2, 1.
❷ **Figure how many scores there are to the middle score by adding 1 to the number of scores and dividing by 2.** There are 9 scores, so the middle score is 9 plus 1, divided by 2, which comes out to 5. The middle score is the fifth score.
❸ **Count up to the middle score or scores.** The fifth score is a 4, so the median is 4.

Figuring the Sum of Squared Deviations and the Variance

Find the sum of squared deviations and the variance for the following scores: 8, 6, 6, 9, 6, 5, 6, 2. (These are the same scores used above for the mean. $M = 6$.)

Answer

You can figure the sum of squared deviations and the variance using the formulas or the steps.

Using the formulas:

$$\text{Sum of squared deviations} = \Sigma(X - M)^2 = (8 - 6)^2 + (6 - 6)^2 + (6 - 6)^2 +$$
$$(9 - 6)^2 + (6 - 6)^2 + (5 - 6)^2 + (6 - 6)^2 + (2 - 6)^2$$
$$= 2^2 + 0^2 + 0^2 + 3^2 + 0^2 + -1^2 + 0^2 + -4^2$$
$$= 4 + 0 + 0 + 9 + 0 + 1 + 0 + 16 = 30.$$
$$SD^2 = [\Sigma(X - M)^2]/N = 30/8 = 3.75.$$

Table 2–5 shows the figuring, using the following steps:

❶ **Subtract the mean from each score.** This gives deviation scores of 2, 0, 0, 3, 0, −1, 0, −4.
❷ **Square each of these deviation scores.** This gives squared deviation scores of 4, 0, 0, 9, 0, 1, 0, 16.
❸ **Add up the squared deviation scores.** $4 + 0 + 0 + 9 + 0 + 1 + 0 + 16 = 30$. This is the sum of squared deviations.
❹ **Divide the sum of squared deviations by the number of scores.** The sum of squared deviations, 30, divided by the number of scores, 8, gives a variance of 3.75.

Table 2-5 Figuring for Example Worked-Out Problem for the Sum of Squared Deviations and Variance Using Steps

Score	Mean	❶ Deviation	❷ Squared Deviation
8	6	2	4
6	6	0	0
6	6	0	0
9	6	3	9
6	6	0	0
5	6	−1	1
6	6	0	0
2	6	−4	16
			$\Sigma = 30$ ❸

❹ Variance = 30/8 = 3.75

Figuring the Standard Deviation

Find the standard deviation for the following scores: 8, 6, 6, 9, 6, 5, 6, 2. (These are the same scores used above for the mean, sum of squared deviations, and variance. SD^2 = 3.75.)

Answer

You can figure the standard deviation using the formula or the steps.
    Using the formula: $SD = \sqrt{SD^2} = \sqrt{3.75} = 1.94$.
    Using the steps:

❶ **Figure the variance.** The variance (from above) is 3.75.
❷ **Take the square root.** The square root of 3.75 is 1.94.

Changing a Raw Score to a Z Score

A distribution has a mean of 80 and a standard deviation of 20. Find the Z score for a raw score of 65.

Answer

You can change a raw score to a Z score using the formula or the steps.
    Using the formula: $Z = (X - M)/SD = (65 - 80)/20 = -15/20 = -.75$.
    Using the steps:

❶ **Figure the deviation score: Subtract the mean from the raw score.** $65 - 80 = -15$.
❷ **Figure the Z score: Divide the deviation score by the standard deviation.** $-15/20 = -.75$.

Changing a Z Score to a Raw Score

A distribution has a mean of 200 and a standard deviation of 50. A person has a Z score of 1.26. What is the person's raw score?

Answer

You can change a Z score to a raw score using the formula or the steps.
    Using the formula: $X = (Z)(SD) + M = (1.26)(50) + 200 = 63 + 200 = 263$.
    Using the steps:

❶ **Figure the deviation score: Multiply the Z score by the standard deviation.** $1.26 \times 50 = 63$.
❷ **Figure the raw score: Add the mean to the deviation score.** $63 + 200 = 263$.

Outline for Writing Essays on Finding the Mean, Variance, and Standard Deviation

1. Explain that the mean is a type of representative value of a group of scores. Mention that the mean is the ordinary average, the sum of the scores divided by the number of scores.
2. Explain that the variance and standard deviation both measure the amount of variability (or spread) among a group of scores.
3. The variance is the the average of each score's squared difference from the mean. Describe the steps for figuring the variance.

4. Roughly speaking, the standard deviation is the average amount that scores differ from the mean. Explain that the standard deviation is directly related to the variance and is figured by taking the square root of the variance.

Outline for Writing Essays Involving Z Scores

1. If required by the problem, explain the mean, variance, and standard deviation as shown above.
2. Describe the basic idea of a Z score as a way of describing where a particular score fits into an overall group of scores. Specifically, a Z score shows the number of standard deviations a score is above or below the mean.
3. Explain the steps for figuring a Z score from a raw score (an ordinary score).
4. Mention that changing raw scores to Z scores puts scores on different variables onto the same scale, which makes it easier to make comparisons between the scores on the variables.

Practice Problems

These problems involve figuring. Most real-life statistics problems are done on a computer with special statistical software. Even if you have such software, do these problems by hand to ingrain the method in your mind. To learn how to use a computer to solve statistics problems like those in this chapter, refer to the *Using SPSS* section at the end of this chapter and the *Student's Study Guide and SPSS Workbook* that accompanies this text.

All data are fictional unless an actual citation is given.

Set I (for answers, see p. 437)

1. For the following scores, find the (a) mean, (b) median, (c) sum of squared deviations, (d) variance, and (e) standard deviation:

   32, 28, 24, 28, 28, 31, 35, 29, 26

2. For the following scores, find the (a) mean, (b) median, (c) sum of squared deviations, (d) variance, and (e) standard deviation:

   6, 1, 4, 2, 3, 4, 6, 6

3. Here are the noon temperatures (in degrees Celsius) in a particular Canadian city on December 26 for the 10 years from 1997 through 2006: $-5, -4, -1, -1, 0,$ $-8, -5, -9, -13,$ and -24. Describe the representative (typical) temperature and the amount of variation to a person who has never had a course in statistics. Give three ways of describing the representative temperature and two ways of describing its variation, explaining the differences and how you figured each. (You will learn more if you try to write your own answer first, before reading our answer at the back of the book.)

4. A researcher is studying the amygdala (a part of the brain involved in emotion). Six participants in a particular fMRI (brain scan) study are measured for the increase in activation of their amygdala while they are viewing pictures of violent scenes. The activation increases are .43, .32, .64, .21, .29, and .51. Figure the (a) mean and (b) standard deviation for these six activation increases. (c) Explain what you have done and what the results mean to a person who has never had a course in statistics.

5. On a measure of concern for the environment, the mean is 79 and the standard deviation is 12 (scores on the measure can vary from 0 to 150). What are the Z scores for each of the following raw scores? (a) 91, (b) 68, and (c) 103.
6. If the mean of a measure is −11.46 and the standard deviation is 2.28, what are the Z scores for each of the following raw scores? (a) −13.12, (b) −7.26, and (c) −11.23.
7. If the mean of a measure is 145 and the standard deviation is 19, what are the raw scores for each of the following Z scores? (a) 0, (b) 1.43, (c) −2.54.
8. Six months after a divorce, the former wife and husband each take a test that measures divorce adjustment. The wife's score is 63, and the husband's score is 59. Overall, the mean score for divorced women on this test is 60 ($SD = 6$); the mean score for divorced men is 55 ($SD = 4$). Which of the two has adjusted better to the divorce in relation to other divorced people of their own gender? Explain your answer to a person who has never had a course in statistics.
9. A researcher studied the number of nights students reported having too little sleep over a 4-week period. In an article describing the results of the study, the researcher reports: "The mean number of nights of too little sleep was 6.84 ($SD = 3.18$)." Explain these results to a person who has never had a course in statistics.
10. In a study by Gonzaga, Keltner, Londahl, and Smith (2001), romantic couples answered questions about how much they loved their partner and also were videotaped while revealing something about themselves to their partner. The videotapes were later rated by trained judges for various signs of affiliation. Table 2–6 (reproduced from their Table 2) shows some of the results. Explain to a person who has never had a course in statistics the results for self-reported love for the partner and for the number of seconds "leaning toward the partner."

Set II

11. (a) Describe and explain the difference between the mean, median, and mode. (b) Make up an example (not in the book or in your lectures) in which the median would be the preferred measure of the representative value of a group of scores.

Table 2-6   Mean Levels of Emotions and Cue Display in Study 1

Indicator	Women (n = 60)		Men (n = 60)	
	M	SD	M	SD
Emotion reports				
Self-reported love	5.02	2.16	5.11	2.08
Partner-estimated love	4.85	2.13	4.58	2.20
Affiliation-cue display				
Affirmative head nods	1.28	2.89	1.21	1.91
Duchenne smiles	4.45	5.24	5.78	5.59
Leaning toward partner	32.27	20.36	31.36	21.08
Gesticulation	0.13	0.40	0.25	0.77

Note: Emotions are rated on a scale of 0 (*none*) to 8 (*extreme*). Cue displays are shown as mean seconds displayed per 60 s.
Source: Gonzaga, G. C., Keltner, D., Londahl, E. A., & Smith, M. D. (2001). Love and the commitment problem in romantic relations and friendship. *Journal of Personality and Social Psychology, 81*, 247–262. Copyright © 2001 by The American Psychological Association. Reprinted with permission.

12. (a) Describe the variance and standard deviation. (b) Explain why the standard deviation is more often used as a descriptive statistic.

13. For the following scores, find the (a) mean, (b) median, (c) sum of squared deviations, (d) variance, and (e) standard deviation.

$$2, 2, 0, 5, 1, 4, 1, 3, 0, 0, 1, 4, 4, 0, 1, 4, 3, 4, 2, 1, 0$$

14. For the following scores, find the (a) mean, (b) median, (c) sum of squared deviations, (d) variance, and (e) standard deviation.

$$1,112; 1,245; 1,361; 1,372; 1,472$$

15. For the following scores, find the (a) mean, (b) median, (c) sum of squared deviations, (d) variance, and (e) standard deviation.

$$3.0, 3.4, 2.6, 3.3, 3.5, 3.2$$

16. For the following scores, find the (a) mean, (b) median, (c) sum of squared deviations, (d) variance, and (e) standard deviation.

$$8, -5, 7, -10, 5$$

17. Make up three sets of scores: (a) one with the mean greater than the median, (b) one with the median and the mean the same, and (c) one with the mode greater than the median. (Each madeup set of scores should include at least 5 scores.)

18. A researcher interested in political behavior measured the square footage of the desks in the official office of four U.S. governors and of four chief executive officers (CEOs) of major U.S. corporations. The figures for the governors were 44, 36, 52, and 40 square feet. The figures for the CEOs were 32, 60, 48, and 36 square feet. (a) Figure the mean and the standard deviation for the governors and for the CEOs. (b) Explain what you have done to a person who has never had a course in statistics. (c) Note the ways in which the means and standard deviations differ, and speculate on the possible meaning of these differences, presuming that they are representative of U.S. governors and large U.S. corporations' CEOs in general.

19. A developmental specialist studies the number of words seven infants have learned at a particular age. The numbers are 10, 12, 8, 0, 3, 40, and 18. Figure the (a) mean, (b) median, and (c) standard deviation for the number of words learned by these seven infants. (d) Explain what you have done and what the results mean to a person who has never had a course in statistics.

20. On a measure of artistic ability, the mean for college students in New Zealand is 150 and the standard deviation is 25. Give the Z scores for New Zealand college students who score (a) 100, (b) 120, (c) 140, and (d) 160. Give the raw scores for persons whose Z scores on this test are (e) -1, (f) $-.8$, (g) $-.2$, and (h) $+1.38$.

21. On a standard measure of peer influence among adolescents, the mean is 300 and the standard deviation is 20. Give the Z scores for adolescents who score (a) 340, (b) 310, and (c) 260. Give the raw scores for adolescents whose Z scores on this measure are (d) 2.4, (e) 1.5, (f) 0, and (g) -4.5.

22. A person scores 81 on a test of verbal ability and 6.4 on a test of math ability. For the verbal ability test, the mean for people in general is 50 and the standard deviation is 20. For the math ability test, the mean for people in general is 0 and the standard deviation is 5. Which is this person's stronger ability, verbal or math? Explain your answer to a person who has never had a course in statistics.

23. A study involves measuring the number of days absent from work for 216 employees of a large company during the preceding year. As part of the results, the researcher reports, "The number of days absent during the preceding year ($M = 9.21$; $SD = 7.34$) was . . ." Explain the material in parentheses to a person who has never had a course in statistics.

Table 2-7	Descriptive Statistics for News Coverage Variables Aggregated by Month. *New York Times Index*, January 1981–November 1992.			
	Mean	**Standard Deviation**	**Range**	**Total**
Total Front-Page Articles	5.84	4.10	0–22	835
Positive Front-Page Articles	1.64	1.33	0–6	261
Negative Front-Page Articles	1.83	1.92	0–11	234

Source: New York Times Index.
From Goidel, R. K., & Langley. R. E. (1995). Media coverage of the economy and aggregate economic evaluations: Uncovering evidence of indirect media effects. *Political Research Quarterly, 48*, 313–328. Copyright © 1995 by the University of Utah. Reprinted by permission of Sage Publications, Inc.

24. Goidel and Langley (1995) studied the positivity and negativity of newspaper accounts of economic events in the period just before the 1992 U.S. Presidential election. Table 2–7, reproduced from their report, describes the numbers of front-page articles on economic news in the *New York Times* for the 23 months preceding the election. Explain the results in the Mean and Standard Deviation columns to a person who has never had a course in statistics. (Be sure to explain some specific numbers as well as the general principle.)

Using SPSS

The ✑ in the steps below indicates a mouse click. (We used SPSS version 13.0 to carry out these analyses. The steps and output may be slightly different for other versions of SPSS.)

Finding the Mean, Mode, and Median

❶ Enter the scores from your distribution in one column of the data window.
❷ ✑ *Analyze.*
❸ ✑ *Descriptive statistics.*
❹ ✑ *Frequencies.*
❺ ✑ on the variable for which you want to find the mean, mode, and median, and then ✑ the arrow.
❻ ✑ *Statistics.*
❼ ✑ *Mean,* ✑ *Median,* ✑ *Mode,* ✑ *Continue.*
❽ Optional: To instruct SPSS *not* to produce a frequency table, ✑ the box labeled *Display frequency tables* (this *un*checks the box).
❾ ✑ *OK.*

Practice the steps above by finding the mean, mode, and median for the mayors' example at the start of the chapter. (The scores in that example are: 7, 8, 8, 7, 3, 1, 6, 9, 3, 8.) Your output window should look like Figure 2–16. (If you instructed SPSS not to show the frequency table, your output will only show the mean, median, and mode.)

Finding the Variance and Standard Deviation

As we mentioned earlier in the chapter, most calculators and computer software—including SPSS—calculate the variance and standard deviation using a formula that involves dividing by $N - 1$ instead of N. So, if you request the variance and standard

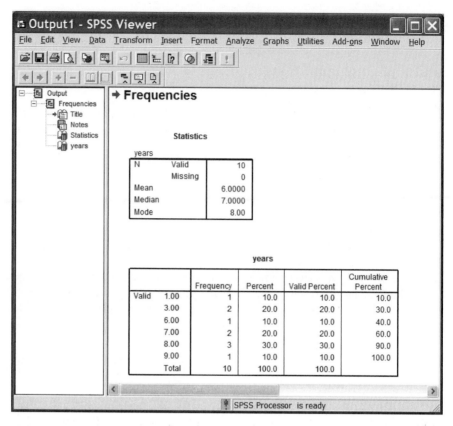

Figure 2-16 Using SPSS to find the mean, median, and mode for the example of the number of years served in office by city mayors.

deviation directly from SPSS (for example, by clicking *variance* and *std. deviation* in Step ❼ above), the answers provided by SPSS will be different than the answers in this chapter.[2] The steps below show you how to use SPSS to figure the variance and standard deviation using the dividing by N method you learned in this chapter. It is easier to learn these steps using actual numbers, so we will use the mayors' example again.

❶ Enter the scores from your distribution in one column of the data window. We will call this variable "years."

❷ Find the mean of the scores by following the steps shown above for Finding the Mean, Mode, and Median. The mean of the years variable is 6.

❸ You are now going to create a new variable that shows each score's squared deviation from the mean. ✐ *Transform,* ✐ *Compute.* You can call the new variable any name that you want, but we will call it "sqdev" (for "squared deviation"). So, write *sqdev* in the box labeled *Target Variable.* You are now going to tell SPSS how to figure this new variable called sqdev. In the box labeled *Numeric Ex-*

---

[2]Note that if you request the variance from SPSS, you can convert it to the variance as we figure it in this chapter by multiplying the variance from SPSS by $N - 1$ (that is, the number of scores minus 1) and then dividing the result by N (the number of scores). Taking the square root of the resulting value will give you the standard deviation (using the formula you learned in this chapter). We use a slightly longer approach to figuring the variance and standard deviation in order to show you how to create new variables in SPSS.

pression, write *(years − 6) * (years − 6).* (The asterisk is how you show *multiply* in SPSS.) As you can see, this formula takes each score's deviation score and multiplies it by itself to give the squared deviation score. Your Compute Variable window should look like Figure 2–17. ✎ *OK.* You will see that a new variable called *sqdev* has been added to the data window (see Figure 2–18). The scores are the squared deviations of each score from the mean.

❹ As you learned in this chapter, the variance is figured by dividing the sum of the squared deviations by the number of scores. This is the same as taking the mean of the squared deviation scores. So, to find the variance of the years scores, follow the steps shown earlier to find the mean of the *sqdev* variable. This comes out to 6.60, so the variance of the years scores is 6.60.

❺ To find the standard deviation, use a calculator to find the square root of 6.60, which is 2.57.

If you were conducting an actual research study, you would most likely request the variance and standard deviation directly from SPSS. However, for our purposes in this chapter (describing the variation in a group of scores), the steps we outlined above are entirely appropriate. Also, following this procedure will further engrain the principles in your mind, and also teaches you how to create new variables in SPSS.

Changing Raw Scores to Z Scores

It is easier to learn these steps using actual numbers, so we will use the mayors' example again.

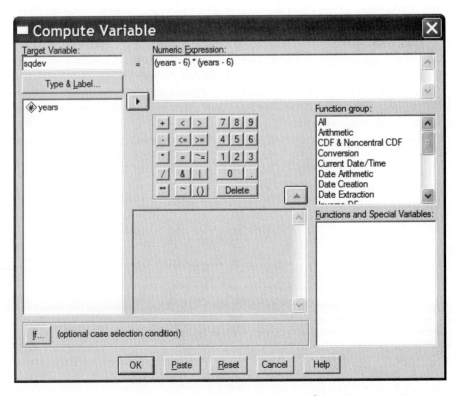

Figure 2–17   SPSS compute variable window for Step ❸ of finding the variance and standard deviation for the example of the number of years served in office by city mayors.

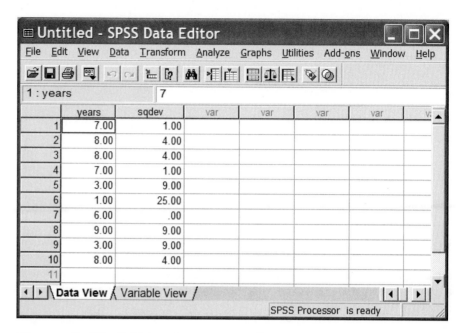

Figure 2–18   SPSS data window after Step ❸ of finding the variance and standard deviation for the example of the number of years served in office by city mayors.

❶ Enter the scores from your distribution in one column of the data window (the scores are 7, 8, 8, 7, 3, 1, 6, 9, 3, 8). We will call this variable "years."

❷ Find the mean and standard deviation of the scores using the steps above for Finding the Mean, Mode, and Median, and Finding the Variance and Standard Deviation. The mean is 6 and the standard deviation is 2.57.

❸ You are now going to create a new variable that shows the Z score for each raw score. ✑ *Transform,* ✑ *Compute.* You can call the new variable any name that you want, but we will call it "zyears." So, write *zyears* in the box labeled *Target Variable.* In the box labeled *Numeric Expression,* write *(years - 6)/2.57.* As you can see, this formula creates a deviation score (by subtracting the mean from the raw score) and divides the deviation score by the standard deviation. ✑ *OK.* You will see that a new variable called *zyears* has been added to the data window. The scores for this *zyears* variable are the Z scores for the years variable. Your data window should now look like Figure 2–19.[3]

---

[3]You can also request the Z scores directly from SPSS. However, SPSS figures the standard deviation based on the dividing by $N - 1$ formula for the variance. Thus, the Z scores figured directly by SPSS will be different from the Z scores as you learned to figure them. Here are the steps for figuring Z scores directly from SPSS: ❶ Enter the scores from your distribution in one column of the data window. ❷ ✑ *Analyze,* ✑ *Descriptive statistics,* ✑ *Descriptives.* ❸ ✑ on the variable for which you want to find the Z scores, and then ✑ the arrow. ❹ ✑ the box labeled *Save standardized values as variables* (this checks the box). ❺ ✑ *OK.* A new variable is added to the data window. The values for this variable are the Z scores for your variable. (You can ignore the output window, which by default will show descriptive statistics for your variable.)

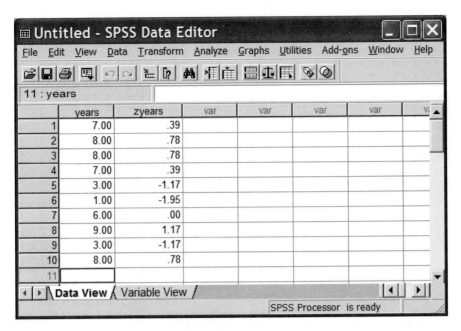

Figure 2–19   Using SPSS to change raw scores to *Z* scores for the example of the number of years served in office by city mayors.

CHAPTER 3

Correlation and Prediction

CHAPTER OUTLINE

- Graphing Correlations: The Scatter Diagram
- Patterns of Correlation
- The Correlation Coefficient
- Issues in Interpreting the Correlation Coefficient
- Prediction
- The Correlation Coefficient and Proportion of Variance Accounted For
- Correlation and Prediction in Research Articles
- Summary
- Key Terms
- Example Worked-Out Problems
- Practice Problems
- Using SPSS
- Appendix: Hypothesis Tests and Power for the Correlation Coefficient

TIP FOR SUCCESS

Before beginning this chapter, be sure you have mastered the material in Chapter 2 on mean, standard deviation, and Z scores.

So far, in Chapters 1 and 2, you have learned about descriptive statistics for a single variable. In Chapter 1, you learned how to use tables and graphs to describe a group of numbers. In Chapter 2, you learned some statistics for describing a group of scores with numbers (such as the mean, variance, standard deviation, and Z scores). We now move on to look at some descriptive statistics for the relationship between two or more variables. To give you an idea of what we mean, let's consider some common real-world examples. Among students, there is a relationship between high school grades and college grades. It isn't a perfect relationship, but generally speaking, students with better high school grades tend to get better grades in college. Similarly, there is a relationship between parents' heights and the adult height of their children. Taller parents tend to give birth to children who grow up to be taller than the children of shorter parents. Again, the relationship isn't perfect, but the general pattern is clear. Now we'll look at an example in detail.

One hundred thirteen married people in the small college town of Santa Cruz, California, responded to a questionnaire in the local newspaper about their marriage. (This was part of a larger study reported by Aron, Norman, Aron, McKenna, & Heyman, 2000.) As part of the questionnaire, they answered the question, "How exciting are the things you do together with your partner?" using a scale from 1 "Not exciting at all" to 5 "Extremely exciting." The questionnaire also included a standard measure of marital satisfaction (that included items such as "In general, how often do you think that things between you and your partner are going well?").

The researchers were interested in finding out the relationship between doing exciting things with a marital partner and the level of marital satisfaction people reported. In other words, they wanted to look at the relationship between two groups of scores: the group of scores for doing exciting things and the group of scores for marital satisfaction. As shown in Figure 3–1, the relationship between these two groups of scores can be shown very clearly using a graph. The horizontal axis is for people's answers to the question, "How exciting are the things you do together with your partner?" The vertical axis is for the marital satisfaction scores. Each person's score on the two variables is shown as a dot.

The overall pattern is that the dots go from the lower left to the upper right. That is, lower scores on the variable "doing exciting activities with your partner" more often go with lower scores on the variable "marital satisfaction," and higher with higher. So, in general, this graph shows that the more that people did exciting activities with their partner, the more satisfied they were in their marriage. Even though

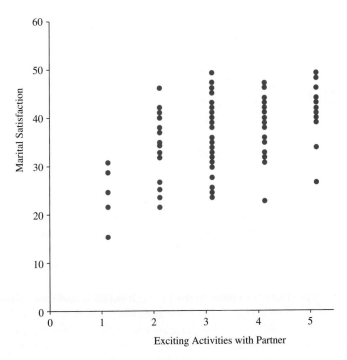

Figure 3-1   Scatter diagram showing the correlation for 113 married individuals between doing exciting activities with their partner and their marital satisfaction. (Data from Aron et al., 2000)

correlation Association between scores on two variables.

scatter diagram Graph showing the relationship between two variables: the values of one variable are along the horizontal axis and the values of the other variable are along the vertical axis; each score is shown as a dot in this two-dimensional space.

the pattern is far from one to one, you can see a general trend. This general pattern is of high scores on one variable going with high scores on the other variable, low scores going with low scores, and moderate with moderate. This is an example of a **correlation.**

A correlation describes the relationship between two variables, specifically the relationship between *two equal-interval numeric variables.* As you learned in Chapter 1, the difference between values for equal-interval numeric variables correspond to differences in the underlying thing being measured. (Most behavioral and social scientists consider scales like a 1 to 10 rating scale as approximately equal-interval scales.) In addition to the correlations we mentioned at the start of the chapter (between students' high school grades and college grades, and between parents' heights and the adult height of their children), there are countless other examples of correlations: In children, there is a correlation between age and coordination skills; among students, there is a correlation between amount of time studying and amount learned; in the marketplace, we often assume that a correlation exists between price and quality—that high prices go with high quality and low with low.

This chapter explores correlation, including how to describe it graphically, different types of correlations, how to figure the *correlation coefficient* (which describes the degree of correlation), issues about how to interpret a correlation coefficient, and how you can use correlation to predict the score on one variable from knowledge of a person's score on another correlated variable (such as predicting college grades from high school grades).

Graphing Correlations: the Scatter Diagram

Figure 3–1 shows the correlation between exciting activities and marital satisfaction. This kind of diagram is an example of a **scatter diagram** (also called a *scatterplot* or *scattergram*). A scatter diagram shows you at a glance the pattern of the relationship between two variables.

How to Make a Scatter Diagram

There are three steps to making a scatter diagram.

❶ **Draw the axes and decide which variable goes on which axis.** Often, it doesn't matter which variable goes on which axis. However, sometimes the researchers are thinking of one of the variables as predicting or causing the other. In that case, the variable that is doing the predicting goes on the horizontal axis and the variable that is being predicted about goes on the vertical axis. In Figure 3–1, we put exciting activities on the horizontal axis and marital satisfaction on the vertical axis. This was because the study was based on a theory that how much people do exciting activities predicts their marital satisfaction. (We will have more to say about prediction later in the chapter.)

❷ **Determine the range of values to use for each variable and mark them on the axes.** Your numbers should go from low to high on each axis, starting from where the axes meet. Usually, your low value on each axis is 0. However, you can use a higher value to start each axis if the lowest value your measure can possibly have in the group you are studying is a lot higher than 0. For example, if a variable is age and you are studying college students, you might start that axis with 16 or 17, rather than 0.

The axis should continue to the highest value your measure can possibly have. When there is no obvious highest possible value, make the axis go to a value that is as high as people ordinarily score in the group of people of interest for your study.

In Figure 3–1, the horizontal axis is for the question about exciting activities, which was answered on a scale of 1 to 5. We start the axis at 0, because this is standard, even though the lowest possible score on the scale is 1. We went up to 5, because that is the highest possible value on the scale. Similarly, the vertical axis goes from 0 to 60, since the highest possible score on marital satisfaction was 60. (There were 10 marital satisfaction items, each answered on a 1 to 6 scale.) Note also that scatter diagrams are usually made roughly square, with the horizontal and vertical axes being about the same length (a 1:1 ratio).

❸ **Mark a dot for each pair of scores.** Find the place on the horizontal axis for the first pair of scores on the horizontal-axis variable. Next, move up to the height for the score for the first pair of scores on the vertical-axis variable. Then mark a clear dot. Continue this process for the remaining people. Sometimes the same pair of scores occurs twice (or more times). This means that the dots for these people would go in the same place. When this happens, you can put a second dot as near as possible to the first—touching, if possible—but making it clear that there are in fact two dots in the one place. Alternatively, you can put the number 2 in that place.

An Example. Suppose a researcher is studying the relation of sleep to mood. As an initial test, the researcher asks six students in her morning seminar two questions:

1. How many hours did you sleep last night?
2. How happy do you feel right now on a scale from 0 "Not at all happy" to 8 "Extremely happy"?

The (fictional) results are shown in Table 3–1. (In practice, a much larger group would be used in this kind of research. We are using an example with just six to keep things simple for learning. In fact, we have done a real version of this study. Results of the real study are similar to what we show here, except not as strong as the ones we made up to make the pattern clear for learning.)

Table 3-1	Hours Slept Last Night and Happy Mood Example (Fictional Data)

Hours Slept	Happy Mood
7	4
5	2
8	7
6	2
6	3
10	6

❶ **Draw the axes and decide which variable goes on which axis.** Because sleep comes before mood in this study, it makes most sense to think of sleep as the predictor. (However, it is certainly possible that people who are in general in a good mood are able to get more sleep.) Thus, as shown in Figure 3–2a, we put hours slept on the horizontal axis and happy mood on the vertical axis.

❷ **Determine the range of values to use for each variable and mark them on the axes.** For the horizontal axis, we start at 0 as usual (and the minimum amount of sleep possible is 0 hours). We do not know the maximum possible, but let us assume that students rarely sleep more than 12 hours. The vertical axis goes from 0 to 8, the lowest and highest scores possible on the happiness question (see Figure 3–2b.)

❸ **Mark a dot for each pair of scores.** For the first student, the number of hours slept last night was 7. Move across to 7 on the horizontal axis. The happy mood rating for the first student was 4, so move up to the point across from the 4 on the vertical axis. Place a dot at this point, as shown in Figure 3–2c. Do the same for each of the other five students. The result should look like Figure 3–2d.

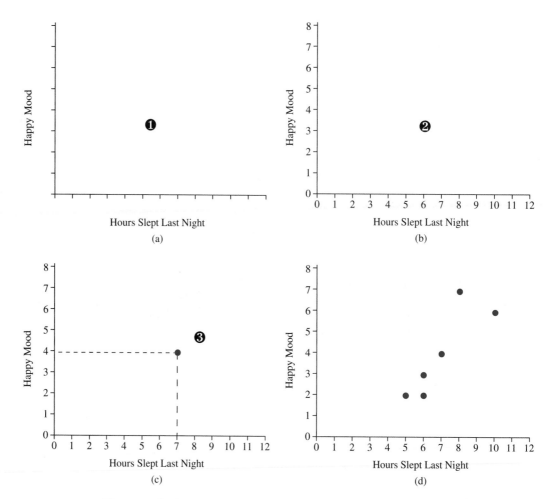

Figure 3–2   Steps for making a scatter diagram. (a) ❶ Draw the axes and decide which variable goes on which axis—the predictor variable (Hours Slept Last Night) on the horizontal axis, the other (Happy Mood) on the vertical axis. (b) ❷ Determine the range of values to use for each variable and mark them on the axes. (c) ❸ Mark a dot for the pair of scores for the first student. (d) ❸ continued: Mark dots for the remaining pairs of scores.

How are you doing?

1. What does a scatter diagram show, and what does it consist of?
2. (a) When it is the kind of study in which one variable can be thought of as predicting another variable, which variable goes on the horizontal axis? (b) Which on the vertical axis?
3. Make a scatter diagram for the scores shown below for four people who were each tested on two variables, *X* and *Y*. *X* is the variable we are predicting from; it can have scores ranging from 0 to 6. *Y* is the variable being predicted; it can have scores from 0 to 7.

Person	X	Y
A	3	4
B	6	7
C	1	2
D	4	6

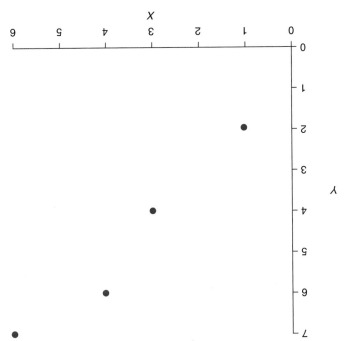

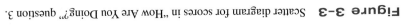

Figure 3–3   Scatter diagram for scores in "How Are You Doing?" question 3.

linear correlation   Relationship between two variables that shows up on a scatter diagram as the dots roughly following a straight line.

curvilinear correlation   Relationship between two variables that shows up on a scatter diagram as dots following a systematic pattern that is not a straight line; any association between two variables other than a linear correlation.

Answers

1. A scatter diagram is a graph that shows the relation between two variables. One axis is for one variable; the other axis, for the other variable. The graph has a dot for each pair of scores. The dot for each pair is placed above the score for that pair on the horizontal axis and directly across from the score for that pair on the vertical axis.
2. (a) The variable that is doing the predicting. (b) The variable that is being predicted.
3. See Figure 3–3.

Patterns of Correlation

Linear and Curvilinear Correlations

In each example so far, the pattern in the scatter diagram very roughly approximates a straight line. Thus, each is an example of a **linear correlation.** In the scatter diagram for the study of exciting activities and marital satisfaction (Figure 3–1), you could draw a line showing the general trend of the dots, as we have done in Figure 3–4. Similarly, you could draw such a line in the happy mood and sleep study example, as shown in Figure 3–5. Notice that the scores do not all fall right on the line, far from it in fact. Notice, however, that the line does describe the general tendency of the scores.

Sometimes, however, the general relationship between two variables does not follow a straight line at all, but instead follows the more complex pattern of a **curvilinear correlation.** Consider, for example, the relationship between a person's

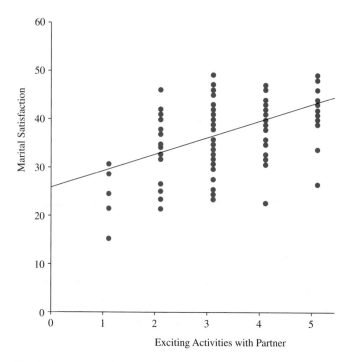

Figure 3-4 The scatter diagram of Figure 3–1 with a line drawn in to show the general trend. (Data from Aron et al., 2000)

level of kindness and the degree to which that person is desired by others as a potential romantic partner. There is evidence suggesting that, up to a point, a greater level of kindness increases a person's desirability as a romantic partner. However, beyond that point, additional kindness does little to increase desirability (Li et al., 2002). This particular curvilinear pattern is shown in Figure 3–6. Notice that the line you could draw to describe this pattern is *not* a straight line. There are many different curvilin-

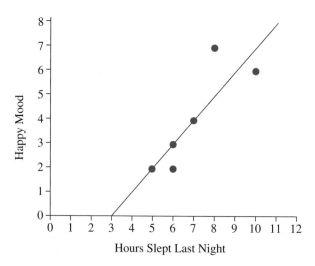

Figure 3-5 The scatter diagram of Figure 3–2d with a line drawn in to show the general trend.

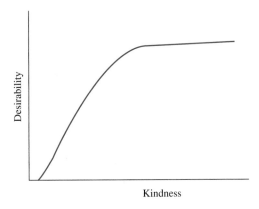

Figure 3-6   Example of a curvilinear relationship: Desirability and kindness.

ear patterns. For example, the pattern can look like the letter u, the letter v, the letter c, or in fact any systematic pattern that is not a straight line.

   The usual way of figuring the correlation (the one you learn shortly in this chapter) gives the degree of *linear* correlation. If the true pattern of association is curvilinear, figuring the correlation in the usual way could show little or no correlation. Thus, it is important to look at scatter diagrams to identify these richer relationships rather than automatically figuring correlations in the usual way, assuming that the only relationship is a straight line.

no correlation   No systematic relationship between two variables.

No Correlation

It is also possible for two variables to be essentially unrelated to each other. For example, if you were to do a study of income and shoe size, your results might appear as shown in Figure 3–7. The dots are spread everywhere, and there is no line, straight or otherwise, that is any reasonable representation of a trend. There is simply **no correlation.**

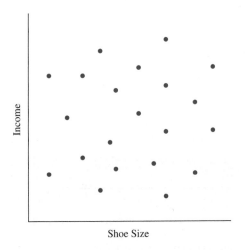

Figure 3-7   Two variables with no association with each other: income and shoe size (fictional data).

positive correlation Relationship between two variables in which high scores on one go with high scores on the other, mediums with mediums, and lows with lows; on a scatter diagram, the dots roughly follow a straight line sloping up and to the right.

negative correlation Relationship between two variables in which high scores on one go with low scores on the other, mediums with mediums, and lows with highs; on a scatter diagram, the dots roughly follow a straight line sloping down and to the right.

Positive and Negative Linear Correlations

In the examples so far of linear correlations, such as exciting activities and marital satisfaction, high scores generally go with high scores, lows with lows, and mediums with mediums. This situation is called a **positive correlation.** (One reason for the term "positive" is that in geometry, the slope of a line is positive when it goes up and to the right on a graph like this. Notice that in Figures 3–4 and 3–5 the positive correlation is shown by a line that goes up and to the right.)

Sometimes, however, high scores tend to go with low scores and lows with highs. This is called a **negative correlation.** For example, in the newspaper survey about marriage, the researchers also asked about boredom with the relationship. Not surprisingly, the more bored a person was, the *lower* was the person's marital satisfaction. Similarly, the less bored a person was, the higher the marital satisfaction. That is, high scores on one variable went with low scores on the other. This is shown in Figure 3–8, where we also put in a line to emphasize the general trend. You can see that as it goes from left to right, it slopes slightly downward. (Compare this to the result for the relation of exciting activities and marital satisfaction shown in Figure 3–4, which slopes upward.)

Another study (Mirvis & Lawler, 1977) also illustrates a negative correlation. That study found that absenteeism from work had a negative linear correlation with job satisfaction. That is, the higher the level of job satisfaction, the lower the level of absenteeism. Put another way, the lower the level of job satisfaction, the higher the absenteeism.

Strength of the Correlation. What we mean by the *strength of the correlation* is how much there is a clear pattern of some particular relationship between two variables. For example, we saw that a positive linear correlation is when high scores go with highs, mediums with mediums, lows with lows. The strength of such a correlation, then, is how much highs go with highs, and so on. Similarly, the strength of a neg-

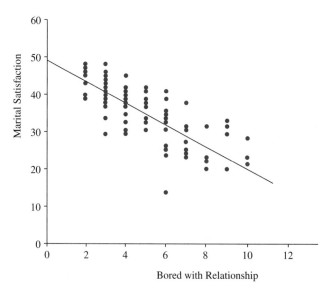

Figure 3–8 Scatter diagram with the line drawn in to show the general trend for a negative correlation between two variables: Greater boredom with the relationship goes with lower marital satisfaction. (Data from Aron et al., 2000.)

ative linear correlation is how much highs on one variable go with lows on the other, and so forth.

Importance of Identifying the Pattern of Correlation

The procedure you learn in the next main section is for figuring the direction and strength of linear correlation. As we suggested earlier, the best approach to such a problem is *first* to make a scatter diagram and use it to identify the pattern of correlation. If the pattern is curvilinear, then you would not go on to figure the linear correlation. This is important because figuring the linear correlation when the true correlation is curvilinear would be misleading. (For example, you might conclude that there is little or no correlation when in fact it is large, just not linear.) You should assume that the correlation is linear, unless the scatter diagram shows a curvilinear correlation. We say this because when the linear correlation is small, the dots will fall far from a straight line. In such situations, it can sometimes be hard to imagine a straight line that roughly shows the pattern of dots.

If the correlation appears to be linear, it is also important to "eyeball" the scatter diagram a bit more. The idea is to note the direction (positive or negative) of the linear correlation and also to make a rough guess as to the strength of correlation. There is a "small" (or "weak") correlation when you can barely tell there is a correlation at all—the dots fall far from a straight line. There is a "large" (or "strong") correlation if the dots fall very close to a straight line. The correlation is "moderate" if the pattern of dots is somewhere between a small and a large correlation. Some examples of scatter diagrams with varying directions and strengths of correlation are shown in Figure 3–9. Using a scatter diagram to examine the direction and approximate strength of correlation is important because it lets you check to see whether you have made a major mistake when you then do the figuring you learn in the next section.

How are you doing?

1. What is the difference between a linear and curvilinear correlation in terms of how they appear in a scatter diagram?
2. What does it mean to say that two variables have no correlation?
3. What is the difference between a positive and negative linear correlation? Answer this question in terms of (a) the patterns in a scatter diagram and (b) what those patterns tell you about the relationship between the two variables.
4. For each of the scatter diagrams shown in Figure 3–10, say whether the pattern is roughly linear, curvilinear, or no correlation. If the pattern is roughly linear, also say if it is positive or negative, and whether it is large, moderate, or small.
5. Give two reasons why it is important to identify the pattern of correlation in a scatter diagram before proceeding to figure the linear correlation.

Answers

1. In a linear correlation, the pattern of dots roughly follow a straight line (although with a small correlation, the dots will be spread widely around a straight line); in a curvilinear correlation, there is a clear systematic pattern to the dots, but it is not a straight line.
2. There is no pattern of relationship between the two variables.

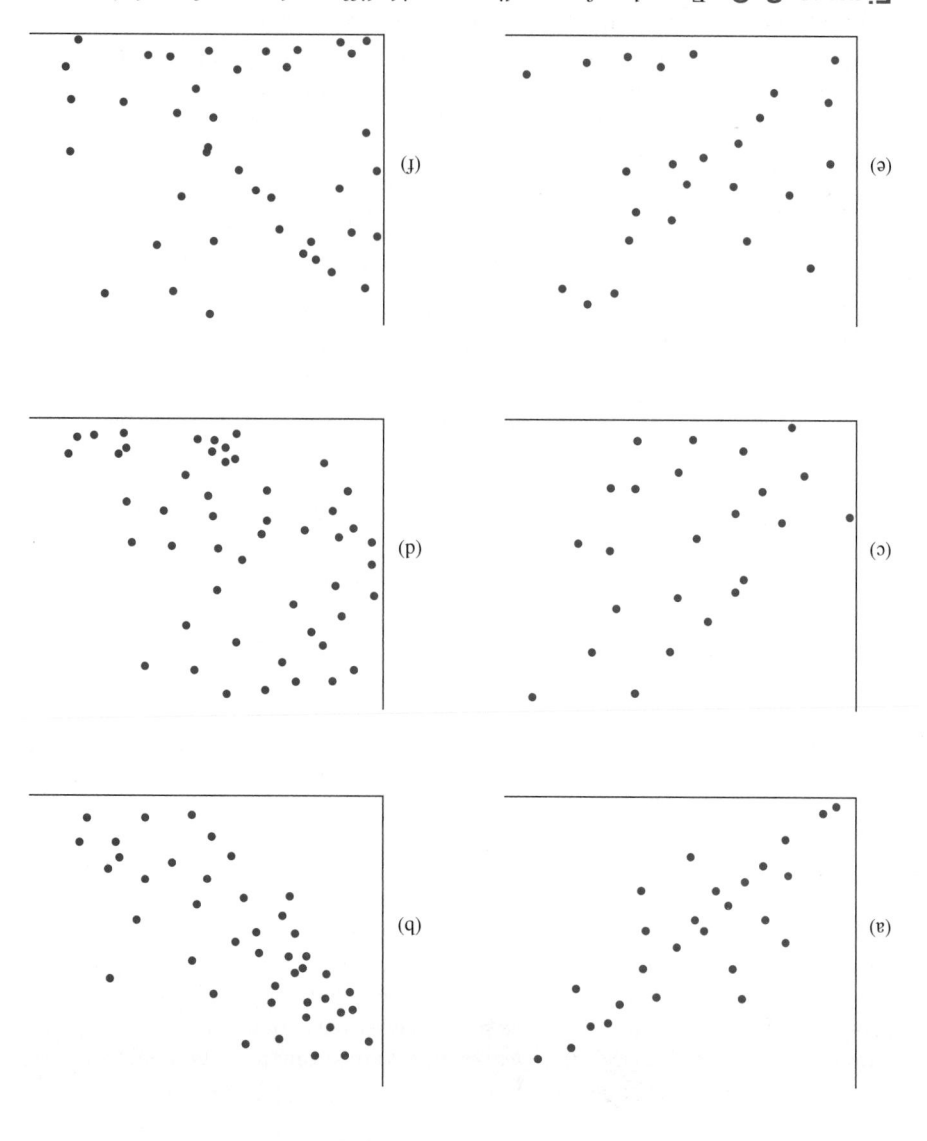

Figure 3-9 Examples of scatter diagrams with different degrees of correlation.

3. (a) In a scatter diagram for a positive linear correlation, the line that roughly describes the pattern of dots goes up and to the right; in a negative linear correlation, the line goes down and to the right. (b) In a positive linear correlation, the basic pattern is that high scores on one variable go with high scores on the other, mediums go with mediums, and lows go with lows; in a negative linear correlation, high scores on one variable generally go with low scores on the other, mediums go with mediums, and lows go with highs.

4. (a) linear, negative, large; (b) curvilinear; (c) linear, positive, large; (d) no correlation.

5. Identifying whether it is linear tells you whether it is appropriate to use the standard procedures for figuring a linear correlation. If it is linear, identifying the direction and approximate strength of correlation before doing the figuring lets you check the results of your figuring when you are done.

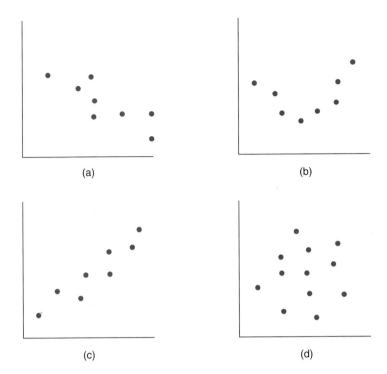

Figure 3–10   Scatter diagrams for "How Are You Doing?" question 4.

The Correlation Coefficient

Looking at a scatter diagram gives a *rough idea* of the type and strength of relationship between two variables. But it is not a very precise approach. What you need is a number that gives the *exact correlation* (in terms of its direction and strength). For example, we saw that a positive linear correlation is when high scores go with highs, mediums with mediums, lows with lows. The exact correlation tells us precisely how much highs go with highs, and so on. As you just learned, in terms of a scatter diagram, a large linear correlation means that the dots fall close to a straight line (the line sloping up or down depending on whether the linear correlation is positive or negative). A *perfect linear correlation* means all the dots fall *exactly* on the straight line.

Logic of Figuring the Exact Linear Correlation

The first thing you need to figure the linear correlation is some way to gauge what is a high score and what is a low score—and how high a high score is and how low a low score is. This means comparing scores on different variables in a consistent way. As we saw in Chapter 2, you can solve this problem of comparing apples and oranges by using Z scores.

To review, a Z score is the number of standard deviations a score is from the mean. Whatever the range of values of the variable, if you change your raw scores to Z scores, a raw score that is high (that is, above the mean of the scores on that variable) will always have a positive Z score. Similarly, a raw score that is low (below the mean) will always have a negative Z score. Further, regardless of the particular measure used, Z scores tell you in a very standard way just how high or low each score is. A Z score of 1 is always exactly 1 standard deviation above the mean, and a Z score of 2 is twice as many standard deviations above the mean. Z scores on one variable are directly comparable to Z scores on another variable.

cross-product of *Z* scores The result of multiplying a person's *Z* score on one variable by the person's *Z* score on another variable.

perfect correlation Relation between two variables that shows up on a scatter diagram as the dots exactly following a straight line; correlation of $r = 1$ or $r = -1$; situation in which each person's *Z* score on one variable is exactly the same as that person's *Z* score on the other variable.

There is an additional reason why *Z* scores are so useful when figuring the exact correlation. It has to do with what happens if you multiply a score on one variable by a score on the other variable, which is called a *cross-product.* When using *Z* scores, this is called a **cross-product of *Z* scores.** If you multiply a high *Z* score by a high *Z* score, you will always get a positive cross-product. This is because no matter what the variable, scores above the mean are positive *Z* scores, and a positive multiplied by a positive is a positive. Furthermore—and here is where it gets interesting—if you multiply a low *Z* score by a low *Z* score, you also always get a positive cross-product. This is because no matter what the variable, scores below the mean are negative *Z* scores, and a negative multiplied by a negative gives a positive.

If highs on one variable go with highs on the other, and lows on one go with lows on the other, the cross-products of *Z* scores always will be positive. Considering a whole distribution of scores, suppose you take each person's *Z* score on one variable and multiply it by that person's *Z* score on the other variable. The result of doing this when highs go with highs and lows with lows is that the multiplications all come out positive. If you add up these cross-products of *Z* scores, which are all positive, for all the people in the study, you will end up with a big positive number.

On the other hand, with a negative correlation, highs go with lows and lows with highs. In terms of *Z* scores, this would mean positives with negatives and negatives with positives. Multiplied out, that gives all negative cross-products. If you add all these negative cross-products together, you get a large negative number.

Finally, suppose there is no linear correlation. In this situation, for some people highs on one variable would go with highs on the other variable (and some lows would go with lows), making positive cross-products. For other people, highs on one variable would go with lows on the other variable (and some lows would go with highs), making negative cross-products. Adding up these cross-products for all the people in the study would result in the positive cross-products and the negative cross-products cancelling each other out, giving a result of 0.

In each situation, we changed all the scores to *Z* scores, multiplied each person's two *Z* scores by each other, and added up these cross-products. The result was a *large positive number* if there was a *positive linear correlation,* a *large negative number* if there was a *negative linear correlation,* and a *number near 0* if there was *no linear correlation.*

However, you are still left with the problem of figuring the *strength* of a positive or negative correlation. The larger the number, the bigger the correlation. But how large is large, and how large is not very large? You can't judge the strength of correlation from the sum of the cross-products alone, because it gets bigger just by adding the cross-products of more people together. (That is, a study with 100 people would have a larger sum of cross-products than the same study with only 25 people.) The solution is to divide this sum of the cross-products by the number of people in the study. That is, you figure the *average of the cross-products of Z scores.* It turns out that because of the nature of *Z* scores, this average can never be more than +1, which would be a positive linear **perfect correlation.** It can never be less than −1, which would be a negative linear perfect correlation. In the situation of no linear correlation, the average of the cross-products of *Z* scores is 0.

For a positive linear correlation that is not perfect, which is the usual situation, the average of the cross-products of *Z* scores is between 0 and +1. To put it another way, if the general trend of the dots is upward and to the right, but they do not fall exactly on a single straight line, this number is between 0 and +1. The same rule holds for negative correlations: They fall between 0 and −1.

The Correlation Coefficient

The average of the cross-products of Z scores is called the **correlation coefficient (r)**. It is also called the *Pearson correlation coefficient* (or the *Pearson product–moment correlation coefficient,* to be very traditional). It is named after Karl Pearson (whom you will meet in Box 11–1). Pearson, along with Francis Galton (see Box 3–1), played a major role in developing the correlation coefficient. The correlation coefficient is abbreviated by the letter **r,** which is short for *regression,* an idea closely related to correlation. (We discuss regression later in the chapter.)

The sign (+ or −) of a correlation coefficient tells you the general trend, in terms of whether the scores go up and to the right (a positive correlation) or down and to the right (a negative correlation). The actual value of the correlation coefficient—from a low of 0 to a high of 1, ignoring the sign of the correlation coefficient—tells you the strength of the linear correlation. So, a correlation coefficient of +.85 is a stronger linear correlation than a correlation of +.42. Similarly, a correlation of −.90 is a stronger linear correlation than +.85 (since .90 is bigger than .85). Another way of thinking of this is that in a scatter diagram, the closer the dots are to falling on a single straight line, the stronger the linear correlation. Figure 3–11 shows the scatter diagrams from Figure 3–9, with the correlation coefficient shown for each scatter diagram.

correlation coefficient (r) Measure of the degree of linear correlation between two variables, ranging from −1 (a perfect negative linear correlation) through 0 (no correlation) to +1 (a perfect positive linear correlation); average of the cross-products of Z scores of two variables.

r Correlation coefficient.

Z_X Z score for variable X.

Z_Y Z score for variable Y.

Formula for the Correlation Coefficient

The correlation coefficient, as we have seen, is the average of the cross-products of Z scores. Put as a formula,

$$r = \frac{\sum Z_X Z_Y}{N}$$

(3-1)

r is the correlation coefficient. Z_X is the Z score for each person on the X variable and Z_Y is the Z score for each person on the Y variable. $Z_X Z_Y$ is Z_X multiplied by Z_Y (the cross-product of the Z scores) for each person and $\sum Z_X Z_Y$ is the sum of the cross-products of Z scores over all the people in the study. N is the number of people in the study.[1]

> The correlation coefficient is the sum, over all the people in the study, of the product of each person's two Z scores, then divided by the number of people.

Steps for Figuring the Correlation Coefficient

Here are the four steps for figuring the correlation coefficient.

❶ **Change all scores to Z scores.** This requires figuring the mean and the standard deviation of each variable, then changing each raw score to a Z score (using the method from Chapter 2).

---

[1]There is also a "computational" version of this formula, which is mathematically equivalent and thus gives the same result:

$$r = \frac{N\sum(XY) - \sum X \sum Y}{\sqrt{N\sum X^2 - (\sum X)^2}\sqrt{N\sum Y^2 - (\sum Y)^2}}$$

(3-2)

This formula is easier to use when figuring by hand when you have a large number of people in the study, because you don't have to first figure all the Z scores. However, as we emphasized in Chapter 2, researchers rarely use computational formulas like this any more because most of the actual figuring is done by a computer. As a student learning statistics, it is better to use the definitional Formula (3–1). This is because when solving problems using the definitional formula, you are strengthening your understanding of what the correlation coefficient means. In all examples in this chapter, we use the definitional formula and we urge you to use it in doing the chapter's practice problems.

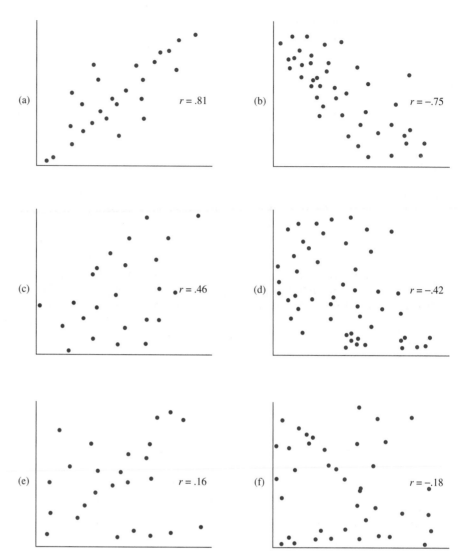

Figure 3–11 Examples of scatter diagrams and correlation coefficients for different degrees of correlation.

❷ **Figure the cross-product of the Z scores for each person.** That is, for each person, multiply the person's Z score on one variable by the person's Z score on the other variable.

❸ **Add up the cross-products of the Z scores.**

❹ **Divide by the number of people in the study.**

An Example

Let us try these steps with the sleep and mood example.

❶ **Change all scores to Z scores.** Starting with the number of hours slept last night, the mean is 7 (sum of 42 divided by 6 students), and the standard deviation is 1.63 (sum of squared deviations, 16, divided by 6 students, for a variance of 2.67, the square root of which is 1.63). For the first student, then, a number of hours slept of 7 is the same as the mean of 7, and 0 divided by 1.63 is .00. Thus the first

BOX 3–1   Galton: Gentleman Genius

Corbiss/Bettman

Francis Galton is credited with inventing the correlation coefficient. (Karl Pearson worked out the formulas, but Pearson was a student of Galton and gave Galton all the credit.) Statistics at this time (around the end of the nineteenth century) was a tight little British club. In fact, most of science was an only slightly larger club. Galton also was influenced greatly by his own cousin, Charles Darwin.

Galton was a typical, eccentric, independently wealthy gentleman scientist. Aside from his work in statistics, he possessed a medical degree, had explored "darkest Africa," invented glasses for reading underwater, experimented with stereoscopic maps, dabbled in meteorology and anthropology, and wrote a paper about receiving intelligible signals from the stars.

Above all, Galton was a compulsive counter. Some of his counts are rather infamous. Once while attending a lecture, he counted the fidgets of an audience per minute, looking for variations with the boringness of the subject matter. While twice having his picture painted, he counted the artist's brushstrokes per hour, concluding that each portrait required an average of 20,000 strokes. While walking the streets of various towns in the British Isles, he classified the beauty of the female inhabitants by fingering a recording device in his pocket to register "good," "medium," or "bad."

Galton's consuming interest, however, was the counting of geniuses, criminals, and other types in families. He wanted to understand how each type was produced so that science could improve the human race by encouraging governments to enforce eugenics—selective breeding for intelligence, proper moral behavior, and other qualities—to be determined, of course, by the eugenicists. (Eugenics has since been generally discredited.) The concept of correlation came directly from his first simple efforts in this area, the study of the relation of the height of children to their parents.

You can learn more about Galton on the following Web page: http://www-history.mcs.st-andrews.ac.uk/Biographies/Galton.html

Sources: Peters (1987), Salsburg (2001), Tankard (1984).

score is a Z score of .00. We figured the rest of the Z scores in the same way and you can see them in the appropriate columns in Table 3–2.

❷ **Figure the cross-product of the Z scores for each person.** For the first student, multiply .00 by .00. This gives .00. The cross-products for all the students are shown in the last column of Table 3–2.

❸ **Add up the cross-products of the Z scores.** Adding up all the cross-products of Z scores, as shown in Table 3–2, gives a sum of 5.09.

❹ **Divide by the number of people in the study.** Dividing 5.09 by 6 (the number of students in the study) gives a result of .848, which rounds off to .85. This is the correlation coefficient.

In terms of the correlation coefficient formula,

$$r = \frac{\sum Z_X Z_Y}{N} = \frac{5.09}{6} = .85.$$

TIP FOR SUCCESS

When figuring the cross-products of the Z scores, pay careful attention to the sign of each Z score. As you know, a negative score multiplied by a negative score gives a positive score. Mistakes in this step are common, so do your figuring carefully!

Because this correlation coefficient is positive and near 1, the highest possible value, this is a *very strong positive linear correlation.*

An Example of Graphing and Figuring a Correlation

In this example, we put together the steps of making a scatter diagram and computing the correlation coefficient.

Table 3-2 Figuring the Correlation Coefficient for the Sleep and Mood Study (Fictional Data)

Number of Hours Slept (X)				Happy Mood (Y)				Cross-Products
Deviation		Dev Squared	Z Scores	Deviation		Dev Squared	Z Scores	
X	X − M	(X − M)²	Z_X	Y	Y − M	(Y − M)²	Z_Y	$Z_X Z_Y$
7	0	0	0	4	0	0	0	0
5	−2	4	−1.23	2	−2	4	−1.04	1.28
8	1	1	.61	7	3	9	1.56	.95
6	−1	1	−.61	2	−2	4	−1.04	.63
6	−1	1	−.61	3	−1	1	−.52	.32
10	3	9	1.84	6	2	4	1.04	1.91
Σ = 42		Σ (X − M)² = 16		Σ = 24		Σ (Y − M)² = 22		$\Sigma Z_X Z_Y$ = 5.09
M = 7		SD² = 16/6 = 2.67		M = 4		SD² = 22/6 = 3.67		r = 5.09/6 = .85
		SD = 1.63				SD = 1.92		

Suppose that an educational researcher knows the average class size and average achievement test score from the five elementary schools in a particular small school district, as shown in Table 3–3. (Again, it would be very rare in actual research practice to do a study or figure a correlation with only five cases. We have kept the numbers low here to make it easier for you to follow the steps of the example.) The question he then asks is, what is the relationship between these two variables?

The first thing he must do is to make a scatter diagram. This requires three steps.

❶ **Draw the axes and decide which variable goes on which axis.** Because it seems more reasonable to think of class size as affecting achievement test scores rather than the other way around, we will draw the axes with class size along the bottom.

❷ **Determine the range of values to use for each variable and mark them on the axes.** We will assume that the achievement test scores go from 0 to 100. Class size has to be at least 1 and in this example we guessed that it would be unlikely to be more than 50.

❸ **Mark a dot for each pair of scores.** The completed scatter diagram is shown in Figure 3–12.

As you learned earlier in the chapter, before figuring the correlation coefficient it is a good idea to look at the scatter diagram to be sure that the pattern is not curvi-

Table 3-3 Average Class Size and Achievement Test Scores in Five Elementary Schools (Fictional Data)

Elementary School	Class Size	Achievement Test Score
Main Street	25	80
Casat	14	98
Harland	33	50
Shady Grove	28	82
Jefferson	20	90

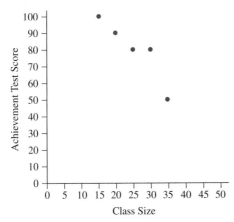

Figure 3-12   Scatter diagram for the scores in Table 3–3.

linear. In this example, the pattern of dots does not appear to be curvilinear (in fact, it is roughly a straight line), so you can assume that the pattern is linear. It is also wise to make a rough estimate of the direction and strength of correlation. This serves as a check against making a major mistake in figuring. In this example, the basic pattern is one in which the dots go down and to the right fairly consistently. This suggests a strong negative correlation. Now we can proceed to figure the correlation coefficient, following the usual steps.

❶ **Change all scores to Z scores.** The mean for class size is 24, and the standard deviation is 6.54. The Z score for the first class size, of 25, is .15. That is, $(25 - 24)/6.54 = .15$. All of the Z scores are shown in the appropriate columns of Table 3–4.

❷ **Figure the cross-product of the Z scores for each person.** For the first cross-product, multiply .15 by 0, which is 0. The second is -1.53 multiplied by 1.10, which is -1.68. All of the cross-products of Z scores are shown in the last column of Table 3–4.

❸ **Add up the cross-products of the Z scores.** The total is -4.52.

❹ **Divide by the number of people in the study.** The sum of the cross-products of Z scores (-4.52) divided by the number of schools (5) is $-.90$. That is, $r = -.90$.

Table 3-4   Figuring the Correlation Coefficient for Average Class Size and Achievement Test Scores in Five Elementary Schools (Fictional Data)

School	Class Size		Achievement Test Score		Cross-Products
	X	Z_X ❶	Y	Z_Y ❶	$Z_X Z_Y$ ❷
Main Street	25	.15	80	.00	.00
Casat	14	-1.53	98	1.10	-1.68
Harland	33	1.38	50	-1.84	-2.54
Shady Grove	28	.61	82	.12	.07
Jefferson	20	$-.61$	90	.61	$-.37$
Σ:	120		400		-4.52 ❸
M:	24		80		$r = -.90$ ❹
	$SD = \sqrt{214/5} = 6.54$		$\sqrt{1,328/5} = 16.30$		

In terms of the correlation coefficient formula,

$$r = \frac{\sum Z_X Z_Y}{N} = \frac{-4.52}{5} = -.90.$$

This correlation coefficient of $-.90$ agrees well with our original estimate of a strong negative correlation.

How are you doing?

1. Give two reasons why we use Z scores for figuring the exact linear correlation between two variables, thinking of correlation as how much highs go with highs and lows go with lows (or vice versa for negative correlations).
2. When figuring the correlation coefficient, why do you divide the sum of cross-products of Z scores by the number of people in the study?
3. Write the formula for the correlation coefficient and define each of the symbols.
4. Figure the correlation coefficient for the Z scores shown below for three people who were each tested on two variables, X and Y.

Person	Z_X	Z_Y
K	.5	$-.7$
L	-1.4	$-.8$
M	.9	1.5

Answers

1. First, Z scores put both variables on the same scale of measurement so that a high or low score (and how much it is high or low) means the same thing for both variables. Second, high Z scores are positive and low Z scores are neg-ative. Thus, if highs go with highs and lows go with lows, the cross-products will all be positive. Similarly, with a negative correlation where highs go with lows and lows with highs, the cross-products will all be negative.
2. Otherwise, the more people in the study, the bigger the sum of the cross-products, even if the strength of correlation is the same. Dividing by the num-ber of people corrects for this.
3. $r = (\sum Z_X Z_Y)/N$. r is the correlation coefficient. $\sum$ is the symbol for sum of—add up all the scores that follow (in this formula, you add up all the cross-products that follow). Z_X is the Z score for each person's raw score on one of the vari-ables (the one labeled X) and Z_Y is the Z score for each person's raw score on the other variable (labeled Y). N is the number of people in the study.
4. $r = (\sum Z_X Z_Y)/N = [(.5)(-.7) + (-1.4)(-.8) + (.9)(1.5)]/3 = [-.35 + 1.12 + 1.35]/3 = 2.12/3 = .71$.

Issues in Interpreting the Correlation Coefficient

There are some subtle cautions in interpreting a correlation coefficient.

Causality and Correlation

If two variables have a clear linear correlation, we normally assume that there is some-thing causing them to go together. However, you can't know the **direction of causal-ity** (what is causing what) just from the fact that the two variables are correlated.

direction of causality Path of causal effect; if X is thought to cause Y, then the direction of causality is from X to Y.

Three Possible Directions of Causality

Consider the example with which we started the chapter, the correlation between doing exciting activities with your partner and satisfaction with the relationship. There are three possible directions of causality for these two variables:

1. It could be that doing exciting activities together causes the partners to be more satisfied with their relationship.
2. It could also be that people who are more satisfied with their relationship choose to do more exciting activities together.
3. Another possibility is that something like having less pressure (versus more pressure) at work makes people happier in their marriage and also gives them more time and energy to do exciting activities with their partner.

These three possible directions of causality are shown in Figure 3–13a.

The principle is that for any correlation between variables X and Y, there are at least three possible directions of causality:

1. X could be causing Y.
2. Y could be causing X.
3. Some third factor could be causing both X and Y.

These three possible directions of causality are shown in Figure 3–13b.

It is also possible (and often likely) that there is more than one direction of causality making two variables correlated.

Ruling Out Some Possible Directions of Causality

Sometimes you can rule out one or more of these possible directions of causality based on additional knowledge of the situation. For example, the correlation between high school grades and college grades cannot be due to college grades causing high school grades—causality doesn't go backward in time. But we still do not know whether the high school grades somehow caused the college grades (for example, by giving the students greater confidence), or some third factor, such as a tendency to study hard, makes for good grades in both high school and college.

In the behavioral and social sciences, one major strategy to rule out at least one direction of causality is to do studies where people are measured at two different

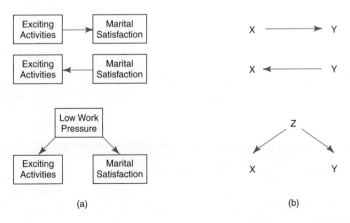

(a)   (b)

Figure 3–13   Three possible directions of causality (shown with arrows) for a correlation for (a) the exciting activities and marital satisfaction example and (b) the general principle for any two variables X and Y.

longitudinal study A study where people are measured at two or more points in time.

true experiment A study in which participants are randomly assigned (say, by flipping a coin) to a particular level of a variable and then measured on another variable.

statistically significant Conclusion that the results of a study would be unlikely if in fact there were no association in the larger group you want to know about.

points in time. This is called a **longitudinal study.** (For example, we might measure a couple's level of exciting activities at one time and then examine the quality of their marriage a year later.)

Another major way we can rule out alternative directions of causality is by conducting a **true experiment.** In a true experiment, participants are randomly assigned (say, by flipping a coin) to a particular level of a variable and then measured on another variable. For example, Aron et al. (2000) followed up their survey studies of married couples with a series of true experiments. Married couples came to their laboratory, spent 10 minutes doing a structured activity together, and then filled out a marital satisfaction questionnaire. What made this a true experiment is that half of the couples were randomly assigned (by flipping a coin) to do an activity that was exciting and the other half did an activity that was pleasant but not particularly exciting. The finding was that when those who had done the exciting activities filled out the marital satisfaction questionnaires, they reported substantially higher levels of marital satisfaction than did those who had done the pleasant but not exciting activities. As a result of this experiment, we can be confident that at least under these kinds of conditions, there is a direction of causality from the activities to marital satisfaction.

The main point to remember from all this is that just knowing that two variables are correlated, by itself, does not tell you anything about the direction of causality between them. *Understanding this principle is perhaps the single most important indication of sophistication in understanding behavioral and social science research!*

The Statistical Significance of a Correlation Coefficient

The correlation coefficient by itself is a descriptive statistic. It describes the direction (positive or negative) and strength of linear correlation in the particular group of people studied. However, when doing research, you often are more interested in a particular group of scores as representing some larger group that you have not studied directly. For example, the researcher studying sleep and mood tested only six individuals. But the researcher's intention in such a study is that the scores from these six people would tell us something about sleep and mood for people more generally. (In practice, you would want a much larger group than six for this purpose. We used small numbers of people in our examples to make them easier to learn from.)

There is a problem, however, in studying only some of the people in the larger group you want to know about. It is possible that, by chance, the ones you pick to study happen to be just those people for whom highs happen to go with highs and lows with lows—even though, had you studied all the people in the larger population, there might really be no correlation.

We say that a correlation is **statistically significant** if it is unlikely that you could have gotten a correlation as big as you did if in fact the overall group had no correlation. Specifically, you figure out whether that likelihood is less than some small degree of probability (p), such as .05 (5%) or .01 (1%). If the probability is that small, we say that the correlation is "statistically significant" with "$p < .05$" or "$p < .01$" (spoken as "p less than point oh five" or "p less than point oh one").

The method and logic of figuring *statistical significance* is the main focus of this book, starting with Chapter 4. We would be jumping ahead to try to explain it fully now. However, by the time you complete the later chapters, the details will be quite clear. (The needed details for applying the general principles of statistical significance you learn in those chapters to figuring statistical significance of a correlation coefficient is in the Appendix to this chapter. But we suggest that you leave this Appendix at least until you have completed Chapter 8.) We bring up this topic now only to give you a general idea of what is being talked about if you see mentions of statistical significance, $p < .05$ or some such phrase, when reading a research article that reports correlation coefficients.

How are you doing?

1. If anxiety and depression are correlated, what are three possible directions of causality that might explain this correlation?
2. A researcher randomly assigns participants to eat either zero or four cookies and then asks them how full they feel. The number of cookies eaten and feeling full are highly correlated. What directions of causality can and cannot be ruled out?
3. What does it mean to say that a particular correlation coefficient is statistically significant?

Answers

1. Being depressed can cause a person to be anxious; being anxious can cause a person to be depressed; some third variable (such as some aspect of heredity or childhood traumas) could be causing both anxiety and depression.
2. Eating more cookies can cause participants to feel full. Feeling full cannot have caused participants to have eaten more cookies, because how many cookies were eaten was determined randomly. Third variables can't cause both, because how many cookies were eaten was determined randomly.
3. The probability is very low of getting a correlation this big between these two variables in the group of people studied if in fact there is no correlation between these two variables for people in general.

Prediction

Building on what you have already learned about correlations in this chapter, we now consider one of their major practical applications—making predictions. Behavioral and social scientists of various kinds are called on to make informed (and precise) guesses about such things as how well a particular job applicant is likely to perform if hired, how much a reading program is likely to help a particular third grader, how likely a particular patient is to attempt to commit suicide, or how likely a potential parolee is to commit a violent crime if released.

Statistical prediction also plays a major part in helping behavioral and social scientists understand how various factors affect outcomes of interest. For example, what are the factors in people who marry that predict whether they will be happy and together ten years later; what are the factors in childhood that predict depression and anxiety in adulthood; what are the circumstances of learning something that predict good or poor memory for it years later; or what are the various kinds of support from friends and family that predict how quickly or poorly someone recovers from a serious accident.

We first consider procedures for making predictions about one variable, such as college GPA, based on information about another variable, such as SAT scores. Then, in an Advanced Topic section, we introduce situations in which predictions about one variable, such as college GPA, are made based on information about two or more other variables, such as using both SAT scores and high school GPA.

TIP FOR SUCCESS

Be sure you have fully mastered the material on correlation before reading this part of the chapter.

predictor variable (usually *X*) In prediction, variable that is used to predict scores of individuals on another variable.

criterion variable (usually *Y*) In prediction, a variable that is predicted.

prediction model Formula for making predictions; that is, formula for predicting a person's score on a criterion variable based on the person's score on one or more predictor variables.

standardized regression coefficient (beta, β) Regression coefficient in a prediction model using *Z* scores.

β standardized regression coefficient.

Predictor (*X*) and Criterion (*Y*) Variables

With correlation it does not matter much which variable is which. But with prediction you have to decide which variable is being *predicted from* and which variable is being *predicted to.* The variable being predicted from is called the **predictor variable.** The variable being predicted to is called the **criterion variable.** In equations the predictor variable is usually labeled *X,* the criterion variable, *Y.* That is, *X* predicts *Y.* In the example we just considered, SAT scores would be the predictor variable or *X* and college GPA would be the criterion variable or *Y* (see Table 3–5).

Prediction Using *Z* Scores

It is easier to learn about prediction if we first consider prediction using *Z* scores. (We will get to prediction using ordinary scores shortly.)

The Prediction Model

The **prediction model,** or *prediction rule,* to make predictions with *Z* scores is as follows: A person's predicted *Z* score on the criterion variable is found by multiplying a particular number, called a **standardized regression coefficient,** by that person's *Z* score on the predictor variable. The standardized regression coefficient is symbolized by the Greek letter **beta (β).**

Beta (β) is called a standardized regression *coefficient* because a coefficient is a number you multiply by another number. It is called a standardized *regression* coefficient because the statistical method for prediction is sometimes called regression (for reasons we discuss later in the chapter). Finally, it is called a *standardized* regression coefficient because you are working with *Z* scores, which are also called *standard scores.*

Formula for the Prediction Model Using Z Scores. Here is the formula for the prediction model using *Z* scores (also known as the *Z*-score prediction model):

> A person's predicted *Z* score on the criterion variable is the standardized regression coefficient multiplied by that person's *Z* score on the predictor variable.

$$\text{Predicted } Z_Y = (\beta)(Z_X) \tag{3-3}$$

In this formula, Predicted Z_Y is the predicted value of the particular person's *Z* score on the criterion variable *Y.* (The predicted value of a score often is written with a hat symbol. Thus $\hat{Z}_Y$ means Predicted Z_Y.) β is the standardized regression coefficient. Z_X is the particular person's *Z* score on the predictor variable *X.* Thus, $(\beta)(Z_X)$ means multiplying the standardized regression coefficient by the person's *Z* score on the predictor variable.

For example, suppose that at your school the standardized regression coefficient (β) is .30 for predicting college GPA at graduation from SAT at admission. So, the *Z*-score prediction model for predicting college GPA from high school SAT score is:

$$\text{Predicted } Z_Y = (.30)(Z_X)$$

Table 3-5 Predictor and Criterion Variables		
	Variable Predicted From	**Variable Predicted To**
Name	**Predictor variable**	**Criterion variable**
Symbol	*X*	*Y*
Example	SAT scores	College GPA

A person applying to your school has an SAT score that is 2 standard deviations above the mean (that is, a Z score of +2). The predicted Z score for this person's GPA would be .30 multiplied by 2, which is .60. That is, this person's predicted Z score for his or her college GPA is .60 standard deviations above the mean. In terms of the prediction model (Formula 3-3),

$$\text{Predicted } Z_Y = (\beta)(Z_X) = (.30)(2) = .60$$

Steps for the Prediction Model Using Z Scores.   Here are the steps for the prediction model using Z scores.

❶ **Determine the standardized regression coefficient (β).**
❷ **Multiply the standardized regression coefficient (β) by the person's Z score on the predictor variable.**

We can illustrate the steps using the same example as above for predicting college GPA of a person at your school with an entering SAT 2 standard deviations above the mean.

❶ **Determine the standardized regression coefficient (β).** In the example, it was .30.
❷ **Multiply the standardized regression coefficient (β) by the person's Z score on the predictor variable.** In the example, the person's Z score on the predictor variable is +2. Multiplying .30 by 2 gives .60. Thus, .60 is the person's predicted Z score on the criterion variable (college GPA).

The Standardized Regression Coefficient (β)

It can be proved mathematically that the best number to use for the standardized regression coefficient (β) when predicting one variable from another is the correlation coefficient. That is, when predicting one variable from another using Z scores, $\beta = r$.

An Example.   Consider again the sleep and mood example from earlier in the chapter. In this example, six students had a correlation of .85 between number of hours slept the night before and happy mood that day. Because the correlation is .85, the standardized regression coefficient (β) is also .85. That is, $r = .85$ thus $\beta = .85$. This means that the model for predicting a person's Z score for happy mood is to multiply .85 by the person's Z score for the number of hours slept the night before.

Suppose you were thinking about staying up so late one night you would get only 4 hours' sleep. This would be a Z score of -1.84 on numbers of hours slept—that is, nearly 2 standard deviations less sleep than the mean. (We changed 4 hours to a Z score using the mean and standard deviation for the scores in this example and applying the procedure you learned in Chapter 2 for changing raw scores to Z scores: $Z = (X - M)/SD$.) We could then predict your Z score on happy mood the next day by multiplying .85 by -1.84. The result comes out to -1.56. This means that based on the results of our little study, if you sleep only 4 hours tonight, tomorrow we would expect you to have a happy mood that is more than one and a half standard deviations below the mean (that is, you would be very unhappy). In terms of the formula,

$$\text{Predicted } Z_Y = (\beta)(Z_X) = (.85)(-1.84) = -1.56$$

In terms of the steps,

❶ **Determine the standardized regression coefficient (β).** Because the correlation coefficient is .85, the standardized regression coefficient (β) is also .85.

❷ **Multiply the standardized regression coefficient (β) by the person's Z score on the predictor variable.** Your Z score on the predictor variable is −1.84. Multiplying .85 by −1.84 gives a predicted Z score on happy mood of −1.56.

By contrast, if you planned to get 9 hours' sleep, the prediction model would predict that tomorrow you would have a Z score for happy mood of .85 multiplied by 1.23 (the Z score when the number of hours slept is 9), which is +1.05. You would be somewhat happier than the average. In terms of the formula,

$$\text{Predicted } Z_Y = (\beta)(Z_X) = (.85)(1.23) = 1.05$$

(Incidentally, it is not a good idea to make predictions that involve values of the predictor variable very far from those in the original study. For example, you should not conclude that sleeping 20 hours would make you extremely happy the next day!)

Why Prediction Is Also Called Regression

Behavioral and social scientists often call this kind of prediction *regression*. Regression means, literally, going back or returning. We use the term *regression* here because in the usual situation in which there is less than a perfect correlation between two variables, the criterion variable Z score is some fraction of the predictor variable Z score. This fraction is β (the standardized regression coefficient). In our sleep and mood example, β = .85, thus the fraction is 85/100. This means that a person's predicted Z score on the criterion variable is 85/100 of the person's Z score on the predictor variable. As a result, the predicted Z score on the criterion variable is closer to the mean of 0 than is the Z score on the predictor variable. (In our sleep and mood example, when the Z score on the predictor variable was 1.23, the Z score predicted for the criterion variable was 1.05, a number closer to 0 than 1.23.) That is, the Z score on the criterion variable *regresses,* or goes back, toward a Z of 0.

How are you doing?

1. In words, what is the prediction model using Z scores?
2. Why does the standardized regression coefficient have this name? That is, explain the meaning of each of the three words that make up the term: standardized, regression, and coefficient.
3. Write the formula for the prediction model using Z scores, and define each of the symbols.
4. Figure the predicted Z score on the criterion variable (Y) in each of the following situations:

Situation	r	Z_X
a	.20	1.20
b	.50	2.00
c	.80	1.20

Answers

1. A person's predicted Z score on the variable being predicted about (the criterion variable) is the standardized regression coefficient (β) multiplied by the person's Z score on the variable being predicted from (the predictor variable).

4. a. $(.20)(1.20) = .24$.
   b. $(.50)(2.00) = 1.00$.
   c. $(.80)(1.20) = .96$.

3. Predicted $Z_Y = (\beta)(Z_X)$. Predicted Z_Y is the predicted Z score on the criterion variable. β is the standardized regression coefficient. Z_X is the Z score on the predictor variable.

2. It is called *standardized* because you are predicting with Z scores, which are also called standard scores. It is called a *regression* coefficient because it is used in prediction, which is also called regression. (Prediction is also called regression because the result of the prediction process is a predicted score on the criterion variable that is closer to the mean—goes back toward the mean—than is the score on the predictor variable.) It is called a *coefficient* because it is a number you multiply by another number.

Prediction Using Raw Scores

Based on what you have learned, you can now also make predictions involving raw scores. To do this, change the raw score on the predictor variable to a Z score, make the prediction using the prediction model with Z scores, and then change the predicted Z score on the criterion variable to a raw score.

Steps of Raw-Score Prediction

❶ **Change the person's raw score on the predictor variable to a Z score.** That is, change X to Z_X. Based on Formula (2-1) from Chapter 2, $Z_X = (X - M_X)/SD_X$.

❷ **Multiply the standardized regression coefficient (β) by the person's Z score on the predictor variable.** That is, multiply β (which is the same as r) by Z_X. This gives the predicted Z score on the criterion variable. This is Formula (3-3):

$$\text{Predicted } Z_Y = (\beta)(Z_X)$$

❸ **Change the person's predicted Z score on the criterion variable to a raw score.**[2] That is, change the Predicted Z_Y to Predicted Y. Based on Formula (2-6) from Chapter 2,

$$\text{Predicted } Y = (SD_Y)(\text{Predicted } Z_Y) + M_Y$$

An Example.   Recall our example from the sleep and mood study in which we wanted to predict your mood the next day if you sleep 4 hours the night before. In this example, the mean for sleep was 7 and the standard deviation was 1.63; for happy

---

[2]In practice, if you are going to make predictions for many different people, you would use a *raw-score prediction formula* that allows you to just plug in a particular person's raw score on the predictor variable and then solve directly to get the person's predicted raw score on the criterion variable. What the raw score prediction formula amounts to is taking the usual Z-score prediction formula, but substituting for the Z scores the formula for getting a Z score from a raw score. If you know the mean and standard deviation for both variables and the correlation coefficient, this whole thing can then be reduced algebraically to give the raw-score prediction formula. This raw-score prediction formula is of the form Predicted $Y = a + (b)(X)$ where a is called the *regression constant* (because this number that is added into the prediction does not change regardless of the value of X) and b is called the *raw-score regression coefficient* (because it is the number multiplied by the raw-score value of X and then added to a to get the predicted value of Y). You will sometimes see these terms referred to in research reports. However, since the logic of regression and its relation to correlation is most directly appreciated from the Z-score prediction formula, that is our emphasis in this introductory text.

Table 3-6 Steps, Formulas, and Example of Raw-Score Prediction

Step	Formula	Example
❶	$Z_x = (X - M_x)/SD_x$	$Z_x = (9 - 7)/1.63 = 1.23$
❷	Predicted $Z_y = (\beta)(Z_x)$	Predicted $Z_y = (.85)(1.23) = 1.05$
❸	Predicted $Y = (SD_y)(\text{Predicted } Z_y) + M_y$	Predicted $Y = (1.92)(1.05) + 4 = 6.02$

Proportion of variance accounted for (r^2) Measure of association between variables used when comparing associations found in different studies or with different variables; correlation coefficient squared; the proportion of the total variance in one variable that can be explained by the other variable.

r^2 Proportion of variance accounted for.

mood, the mean was 4 and the standard deviation was 1.92. The correlation between sleep and mood was .85.

❶ **Change the person's raw score on the predictor variable to a Z score.** $Z_x = (X - M_x)/SD_x = (4 - 7)/1.63 = -3/1.63 = -1.84$. That is, as we saw earlier, the Z score for 4 hours' sleep is -1.84.

❷ **Multiply the standardized regression coefficient (β) by the person's Z score on the predictor variable.** Predicted $Z_y = (\beta)(Z_x) = (.85)(-1.84) = -1.56$. That is, as we also saw earlier, your predicted Z score for mood if you sleep only 4 hours is -1.56.

❸ **Change the person's predicted Z score on the criterion variable to a raw score.** Predicted $Y = (SD_y)(\text{Predicted } Z_y) + M_y = (1.92)(-1.56) + 4 = -3.00 + 4 = 1.00$. In other words, using the prediction model based on the study of 6 students, we would predict that if you sleep only 4 hours tonight, tomorrow you will not be happy at all!

Table 3–6 shows these steps worked out for sleeping 9 hours tonight.

The Correlation Coefficient and the Proportion of Variance Accounted for

A correlation coefficient tells you the strength of a linear relationship. As you learned earlier in the chapter, bigger rs (values farther from 0) mean a stronger correlation. So, an r of .40 is a stronger correlation than an r of .20. However, an r of .40 is *more than* twice as strong as an r of .20. To compare correlations with each other, you have to square each correlation (that is, you use r^2 instead of r). For example, a correlation of .20 is equivalent to an r^2 of .04, and a correlation of .40 is equivalent to an r^2 of .16. Therefore, a correlation of .20 actually means a relationship between X and Y that is only one-quarter as strong as a correlation of .40.

The correlation squared is called the **proportion of variance accounted for (r^2)**. It is given this name because in the context of correlation it represents the proportion of the total variance in one variable (i.e., its total variability) that can be explained by the other variable.[3]

---

[3]The reason r^2 is called proportion of variance accounted for can be understood as follows: Suppose you used the prediction formula to predict each person's score on Y. Unless the correlation between X and Y was perfect (1.0), the variance of those predicted Y scores would be smaller than the variance of the original Y scores. There is less variance in the predicted Y scores because these predicted scores are on average closer to the mean than are the original scores. (We discussed this in the section on why prediction is called regression.) However, the more accurate the prediction, the more the predicted scores are like the actual scores. Thus, the more accurate the prediction, the closer the variance of the predicted scores is to the variance of the actual scores. Now suppose you divide the variance of the predicted Y scores by the variance of the original Y scores. The result of this division is the proportion of variance in the actual scores "accounted for" by the variance in the predicted scores. This proportion turns out (for reasons beyond what we can cover in this book) to be r^2.

How are you doing?

1. Explain the principle behind prediction using raw scores.
2. List the steps of making predictions using raw scores.
3. For a variable X, the mean is 10 and the standard deviation is 3. For a variable Y, the mean is 100 and the standard deviation is 10. The correlation of X and Y is .60. (a) Predict the score on Y for a person who has a score on X of 16. (b) Predict the score on Y for a person who has a score on X of 7. (c) Give the proportion of variance accounted for (r^2).
4. For a variable X, the mean is 20 and the standard deviation is 5. For a variable Y, the mean is 6 and the standard deviation is 2. The correlation of X and Y is .80. (a) Predict the score on Y for a person who has a score on X of 20. (b) Predict the score on Y for a person who has a score on X of 25. (c) Give the proportion of variance accounted for (r^2).

Answers

1. The principle is that you first change the raw score you are predicting from to a Z score, then make the prediction using the prediction model with Z scores, then change the predicted Z score to a predicted raw score.
2. ❶ Change the person's raw score on the predictor variable to a Z score. ❷ Multiply the standardized regression coefficient (β) by the person's Z score on the predictor variable. ❸ Change the person's predicted Z score on the criterion variable to a raw score.
3. (a) $Z_X = (X - M_X)/SD_X = (16 - 10)/3 = 6/3 = 2.$
   Predicted $Z_Y = (\beta)(Z_X) = (.60)(2) = 1.20$
   Predicted $Y = (SD_Y)(\text{Predicted } Z_Y) + M_Y = (10)(1.20) + 100 = 12 + 100 = 112.$
   (b) $Z_X = (X - M_X)/SD_X = (7 - 10)/3 = -3/3 = -1.$
   Predicted $Z_Y = (\beta)(Z_X) = (.60)(-1) = -.60.$
   Predicted $Y = (SD_Y)(\text{Predicted } Z_Y) + M_Y = (10)(-.60) + 100 = -6 + 100 = 94.$
   (c) $r^2 = .60^2 = .36.$
4. (a) $Z_X = (X - M_X)/SD_X = (20 - 20)/5 = 0/5 = 0.$
   Predicted $Z_Y = (\beta)(Z_X) = (.80)(0) = 0.$
   Predicted $Y = (SD_Y)(\text{Predicted } Z_Y) + M_Y = (2)(0) + 6 = 0 + 6 = 6.$
   (b) $Z_X = (X - M_X)/SD_X = (25 - 20)/5 = 5/5 = 1.$
   Predicted $Z_Y = (\beta)(Z_X) = (.80)(1) = .80.$
   Predicted $Y = (SD_Y)(\text{Predicted } Z_Y) + M_Y = (2)(.80) + 6 = 1.60 + 6 = 7.60.$
   (c) $r^2 = .80^2 = .64.$

Correlation and Prediction in Research Articles

Scatter diagrams are occasionally reported in research articles. For example, Elsesser and colleagues (2004) conducted a study of stress reactions in a sample of 37 people who had recently experienced a traumatic event (such as having a car accident or being the victim of a robbery). For each trauma victim, the researchers measured the number of symptoms of acute stress disorder (such as being unable to report important aspects of the trauma, having dreams or recurrent thoughts about the trauma, and feeling anxious), which is a disorder that can be brought on by the experience of a traumatic event. They also showed the trauma victims a series of trauma-relevant pictures while monitoring their heart rate. The researchers figured each person's heart rate re-

correlation matrix   Common way of reporting the correlation coefficients among several variables in a research article; table in which the variables are named on the top and along the side and the correlations among them are all shown (only half of the resulting square, above or below the diagonal, is usually filled in, the other half being redundant).

action to the pictures by subtracting their heart rate while viewing the pictures from their heart rate prior to seeing the pictures. As shown in Figure 3–14, Elsesser et al. (2004) used a scatter diagram to describe the relationship between acute stress disorder symptoms and the heart rate reaction to trauma-relevant pictures. There was a clear tendency for a strong, positive linear correlation (with a correlation coefficient of $r = .60$). The scatter diagram suggests that the more symptoms of acute stress disorder, the greater the increase in heart rate when viewing the trauma-relevant pictures. Of course, this is a correlational result, so it is possible that something about heart rate reactions to trauma-relevant stimuli triggers symptoms of acute stress disorder, or that some other factor, such as general life stress, causes both heart rate reactions and symptoms of acute stress disorder.

Correlation coefficients are very commonly reported in research articles, both in the text of articles and in tables. The result with which we started the chapter would be described as follows: There was a positive correlation ($r = .51$) between excitement of activities done with partner and marital satisfaction. (Usually the "significance level" of the correlation will also be reported—in this example it would be $r = .51, p < .05$.)

Tables of correlations are common when several variables are involved. Usually, the table is set up so that each variable is listed down the left and also across the top. The correlation of each pair of variables is shown inside the table. This is called a **correlation matrix.**

Table 3–7 is a correlation matrix from a study by Baldwin and colleagues (2006) that examined the associations among feelings of shame, guilt, and self-efficacy in a sample of 194 college students. Self-efficacy refers to people's beliefs about their ability to be successful at various things they may try to do. (For example, the students indicated how much they agreed with statements such as "When I make plans, I am

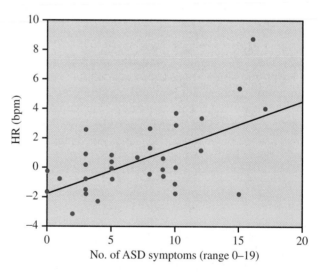

Figure 3–14   Scatterplot of number of acute stress disorder (ASD) symptoms and amplitude of the heart-rate (HR) reaction (Second 5) to the trauma-relevant picture in recent trauma victims ($r = .60$). The HR reaction increased with number of ASD symptoms. bpm = beats per minute. (*Source:* Elsesser, K., Sartory, G., & Tackenberg, A. (2004). Attention, heart rate, and startle response during exposure to trauma-relevant pictures: A comparison of recent trauma victims and patients with posttraumatic stress disorder. *Journal of Abnormal Psychology, 113,* 289–301. Copyright © 2004 by the American Psychological Association. Reprinted by permission.)

Table 3-7 Correlations Among Shame, Guilt, and Self-Efficacy Subscales

	1	2	3	4	5
1. Shame					
2. Guilt	.34**				
3. General Self-efficacy	−.29**	.12			
4. Social Self-efficacy	−.18*	−.06	.47**		
5. Total Self-efficacy	−.29**	.07	.94**	.74**	

Note. $*p < .01$; $**p < .001$. For all correlations, n is between 184 and 190.

Source: Baldwin, K. M., Baldwin, J. R., & Ewald, T. (2006). The relationship among shame, guilt, and self-efficacy. *American Journal of Psychotherapy, 60,* 1–21. Copyright © 2006 by The Association for the Advancement of Psychotherapy. Reprinted by permission of the publisher.

certain I can make them work".) Table 3–7 shows the correlations among the questionnaire measures of shame, guilt, general self-efficacy, social self-efficacy, and total self-efficacy (general self-efficacy plus social self-efficacy).

This example shows several features that are typical of the way correlation matrixes are laid out. First, notice that the correlation of a variable with itself is not given. In this example, they are just left blank; sometimes, a short line is put in instead. Also notice that only the lower triangle is filled in. This is because the upper triangle would contain exactly the same information. For example, the correlation of shame with social self-efficacy (which is −.18) has to be the same as the correlation of guilt with shame. (Thus, there is no point in putting −.18 again in the upper part of the table.) Another shortcut saves space across the page: The names of the variables are listed only on the side of the table, with the numbers for them put across the top.

Looking at this example, among other results, you can see that there is a moderate positive correlation ($r = .34$) between feelings of shame and guilt and a moderate negative correlation ($r = −.29$) between shame and general self-efficacy. The asterisks—* and **—after some of the correlation coefficients tell you that those correlations are statistically significant. As noted at the bottom of the table, one asterisk (*) means that the correlation coefficient is significant at $p < .01$ and two asterisks (**) means it is statistically significant at $p < .001$.

It is rare for prediction models in research articles to focus on predicting a criterion variable from a single predictor variable. Instead, when prediction models are given in research articles, they are usually for *multiple regression* in which scores on a criterion variable are predicted from *two or more* predictor variables (see the Advanced Topic section below).

multiple correlation Correlation of a criterion variable with two or more predictor variables.

multiple regression Procedure for predicting scores on a criterion variable from scores on two or more predictor variables.

Advanced Topic: Multiple Regression and Multiple Correlation

So far, we have predicted a person's score on a criterion variable using the person's score on a single predictor variable. Suppose you could use more than one predictor variable? For example, in predicting happy mood, all you had to work with was the number of hours slept the night before. Suppose you also knew how well the person slept or how many dreams the person had. With this added information, you might be able to make a much more accurate prediction of mood.

The association between a criterion variable and two or more predictor variables is called **multiple correlation** Making predictions in this situation is called **multiple regression.**

We explore these topics only briefly because the details are beyond the level of an introductory book. However, multiple regression and correlation are frequently used in research articles in the behavioral and social sciences, so it is valuable for you to have a general understanding of them.

Multiple Regression Prediction Models

The predicted Z score for the criterion variable is the standardized regression coefficient for the first predictor variable multiplied by the person's Z score on the first predictor variable, plus the standardized regression coefficient for the second predictor variable multiplied by the person's Z score on the second predictor variable, plus the standardized regression coefficient for the third predictor variable multiplied by the person's Z score on the third predictor variable.

In multiple regression, each predictor variable has its own regression coefficient. The predicted Z score of the criterion variable is found by multiplying the Z score for each predictor variable by its standardized regression coefficient and then adding up the results. For example, here is the Z-score multiple regression formula with three predictor variables

$$\text{(3-4)} \qquad \text{Predicted } Z_Y = (\beta_1)(Z_{X_1}) + (\beta_2)(Z_{X_2}) + (\beta_3)(Z_{X_3})$$

Predicted Z_Y is the person's predicted score on the criterion variable. β_1 is the standardized regression coefficient for the first predictor variable; β_2 and β_3 are the standardized regression coefficients for the second and third predictor variables. Z_{X_1} is the person's Z score for the first predictor variable; Z_{X_2} and Z_{X_3} are the person's Z scores for the second and third predictor variables. $(\beta_1)(Z_{X_1})$ means multiplying β_1 by Z_{X_1} and so forth.

For example, in the sleep and mood study, a multiple regression model for predicting happy mood (Y) using the predictor variables of number of hours slept, which we could now call X_1, and also a rating of how well you slept (X_2) and number of dreams during the night (X_3) might turn out to be as follows:

$$\text{Predicted } Z_Y = (.53)(Z_{X_1}) + (.28)(Z_{X_2}) + (.03)(Z_{X_3})$$

Suppose you were asked to predict the mood of a student who had a Z score of -1.82 for number of hours slept, a Z score of 2.34 for how well she slept, and a Z score of .94 for number of dreams during the night. That is, the student did not sleep very long, slept very well, and had a few more dreams than average. You would figure the predicted Z score for happy mood by multiplying .53 by the number-of-hours slept Z score, multiplying .28 by the how-well-slept Z score, and multiplying .03 by the number-of-dreams Z score, then adding up the results:

$$\text{Predicted } Z_Y = (.53)(-1.82) + (.28)(2.34) + (.03)(.94)$$
$$= -.96 + .66 + .03 = -.27$$

Thus, under these conditions, you would predict a happy mood Z score of $-.27$. This means a happy mood about one-quarter of a standard deviation below the mean. You can see that how well the student slept partially offset getting fewer hours' sleep. Given the very low standardized regression coefficient (β_3) for dreams in this model, once you have take into account the number of hours slept and how well you slept, number of dreams (no matter how many or how few) would in general make very little difference in mood the next day.

In general terms, the size of the standardized regression coefficient for a predictor variable shows the amount of influence that variable has when predicting a score on the criterion variable. The larger the standardized regression coefficient for a predictor variable, the more influence that variable has when predicting a score on the criterion variable.

An Important Difference between Multiple Regression and Prediction Using One Predictor Variable

There is one particularly important difference between multiple regression and prediction when using only one predictor variable. In prediction when using one predictor variable, $\beta = r$. That is, the standardized regression coefficient is the same as the correlation coefficient. But in multiple regression, the standardized regression coefficient (β) for a predictor variable is *not* the same as the ordinary correlation coefficient (r) of that predictor with the criterion variable.

In multiple regression, a β will usually be closer to 0 than r. The reason is that part of what makes any one predictor successful in predicting the criterion will usually overlap with what makes the other predictors successful in predicting the criterion variable. In multiple regression, the standardized regression coefficient is about the unique, distinctive contribution of the predictor variable, excluding any overlap with other predictor variables.

Consider the sleep and mood example. When we were predicting mood using just the number of hours slept, β was the same as the correlation coefficient of .85. Now, with multiple regression, the β for number of hours slept is only .53. It is less because part of what makes number of hours slept predict mood overlaps with what makes sleeping well predict mood (in this fictional example, people who sleep more hours usually sleep well).

In multiple regression, the overall correlation between the criterion variable and all the predictor variables is called the **multiple correlation coefficient** and is symbolized as R. However, because of the usual overlap among the predictor variables, the multiple correlation (R) is usually smaller than the sum of the individual rs of each predictor variable with the criterion variable. In multiple regression, the proportion of variance in the criterion variable accounted for by all the predictor variables taken together is the multiple correlation coefficient squared, R^2.

multiple correlation coefficient (R) Measure of degree of multiple correlation; positive square root of the proportion of variance accounted for in a multiple regression analysis.

R Multiple correlation coefficient.

How are you doing?

1. What is multiple regression?
2. Write the multiple regression prediction model with two predictors, and define each of the symbols.
3. In a multiple regression model, the standardized regression coefficient for the first predictor variable is .40 and for the second predictor variable is .70. What is the predicted criterion variable Z score for (a) a person with a Z score of +1 on the first predictor variable and a Z score of +2 on the second predictor variable, and (b) a person with a Z score of +2 on the first predictor variable and a Z score of +1 on the second predictor variable?
4. In multiple regression, why are the standardized regression coefficients for each predictor variable often smaller than the ordinary correlation coefficient of that predictor variable with the criterion variable?

Answers

1. The procedure for predicting a criterion variable from a prediction rule that includes more than one predictor variable.
2. Predicted $Z_Y = (\beta_1)(Z_{X_1}) + (\beta_2)(Z_{X_2})$
   Predicted Z_Y is the person's predicted score on the criterion variable. β_1 is the standardized regression coefficient for the first predictor variable. β_2 is

the standardized regression coefficient for the second predictor variable. Z_{X_1} is the person's Z score for the first predictor variable, and Z_{X_2} is the person's Z score for the second predictor variable.

3. (a) Predicted $Z_Y = (.40)(Z_{X_1}) + (.70)(Z_{X_2}) = (.40)(1) + (.70)(2) = .40 + 1.40$ = 1.80.

(b) Predicted $Z_Y = (.40)(Z_{X_1}) + (.70)(Z_{X_2}) = (.40)(2) + (.70)(1) = .80 + .70$ = 1.50.

4. In multiple regression, a predictor variable's association with the criterion variable usually overlaps with the other predictor variables' association with the criterion variable. Thus, the unique association of a predictor variable with the criterion variable (the standardized regression coefficient) is usually smaller than the ordinary correlation of the predictor variable with the criterion variable.

Advanced Topic: Multiple Correlation and Multiple Regression in Research Articles

Multiple correlation results are only occasionally reported in behavioral and social science research articles. However, multiple regression results are quite common and are often reported in tables. Buboltz and colleagues (2003) conducted a study of the relationship between various aspects of college students' family relationships and students' level of "psychological reactance." "Reactance" in this study referred to a tendency to have an extreme reaction when your behavior is restricted in some way. Buboltz et al. used a multiple regression model to predict psychological reactance from three family characteristics: conflict, cohesion, and expressiveness. Each of these three characteristics represents a different dimension of the relationship among family members. The standardized regression coefficients for this multiple regression model are shown in Table 3–8 (in the β column). You can see that family conflict had a negative standardized regression coefficient ($\beta = -0.23$) and the standardized regression coefficients were both positive for family cohesion ($\beta = 0.22$) and family expressiveness ($\beta = 0.10$). You can also see that the standardized regression coefficients for conflict and cohesion were larger than the standardized regression coefficient for expressiveness. This tells you that family conflict and family cohesion were more important unique predictors of psychological reactance than family expressiveness.

Table 3–8 Summary of Regression Analysis Assessing the Unique Effects of Each Relationship Dimension Predicting Psychological Reactance

Relationship Dimension	B	SE B	β
Conflict	−1.71	0.49	−0.23***
Cohesion	1.46	0.45	0.22***
Expressiveness	0.90	0.52	0.10

Note: Beta coefficients for each predictor are over and above the other predictors.
*$p < .05$, **$p < .01$, ***$p < .001$.
Source: Buboltz, W. C., Jr., Johnson, P., & Woller, K. M. P. (2003). Psychological reactance in college students: Family-of-origin predictors. *Journal of Counseling and Development, 81,* 311–317. Copyright © 2003 by Copyright © ACA. Reprinted by permission. No further reproduction authorized without written permission of the American Counseling Association.

The table also includes the raw-score (unstandardized) regression coefficients (labeled with a capital B here). Finally, for each B, it gives what is called its standard error ($SE\ B$). These have to do with how accurately you can apply to the general population the coefficients they found in the particular sample used in this study. You will have a better understanding of the standard error after Chapter 6.

Summary

1. When two variables are associated in a clear pattern, for example, when high scores on one consistently go with high scores on the other, and lows on one go with lows on the other, the two variables are correlated.

2. A scatter diagram shows the relationship between two variables. The lowest to highest possible values of one variable (the one you are predicting from, if they are distinguishable) are marked on the horizontal axis. The lowest to highest possible values of the other variable are marked on the vertical axis. Each individual's pair of scores is shown as a dot.

3. When the dots in the scatter diagram generally follow a straight line, this is called a linear correlation. In a curvilinear correlation, the dots follow a line pattern other than a simple straight line. No correlation exists when the dots do not follow any kind of line. In a positive linear correlation, the line goes upward to the right (so that low scores tend to go with lows and highs with highs). In a negative linear correlation, the line goes downward to the right (so that low scores generally go with highs and highs with lows).

4. The correlation coefficient (r) gives the direction and strength of linear correlation. It is the average of the cross-products of Z scores. The correlation coefficient is highly positive when there is a strong positive linear correlation. This is because positive Z scores are multiplied by positive, and negative Z scores by negative. The correlation coefficient is highly negative when there is a strong negative linear correlation. This is because positive Z scores are multiplied by negative and negative Z scores by positive. The coefficient is 0 when there is no linear correlation. This is because positive Z scores are sometimes multiplied by positive and sometimes by negative Z scores and negative Z scores are sometimes multiplied by negative and sometimes by positive. Thus, positive and negative cross-products cancel each other out.

5. The maximum positive value of r is $+1$. $r = +1$ when there is a perfect positive linear correlation. The maximum negative value of r is -1. $r = -1$ when there is a perfect negative linear correlation.

6. The actual value of the correlation coefficient—from a low of 0 to a high of 1, ignoring the sign of the correlation coefficient—tells you the strength of the linear correlation. The closer a correlation coefficient is to 1, the stronger the linear correlation.

7. Correlation does not tell you the direction of causation. If two variables, X and Y, are correlated, this could be because X is causing Y, Y is causing X, or a third factor is causing both X and Y.

8. A correlation figured using scores from a particular group of people is often intended to apply to people in general. A correlation is statistically significant when statistical procedures (taught later in this book) make it highly unlikely that you would get a correlation as big as the one found with the group of people studied, if in fact there were no correlation between these two variables among people in general.

9. Prediction (or regression) makes predictions about scores on a criterion variable based on scores on a predictor variable. The prediction model for predicting a person's Z score on the criterion variable is to multiply the standardized regression coefficient (β) by the person's Z score on the predictor variable. The best number to use for the standardized regression coefficient in this situation is the correlation coefficient (r).

10. Predictions with raw scores can be made by changing a person's score on the predictor variable to a Z score, multiplying it by the standardized regression coefficient (β) and then changing the predicted criterion variable Z score to a raw score.

11. Comparisons of the strength of linear correlation are considered most accurate in terms of the correlation coefficient squared (r^2), the proportion of variance accounted for.

12. Correlational results are usually presented in research articles either in the text with the value of r (and sometimes the significance level) or in a special table (a correlation matrix) showing the correlations among several variables. Results of prediction in which a criterion variable is predicted from a single variable are rarely described directly in research articles.

13. ADVANCED TOPIC: In multiple regression, a criterion variable is predicted from two or more predictor variables. In a multiple regression model, each predictor variable is multiplied by its own standardized regression coefficient, and the results are added up to make the prediction. However, because the predictor variables overlap in their influence on the criterion variable, each of the regression coefficients generally is smaller than the variable's correlation coefficient with the criterion variable. The multiple correlation coefficient (R) is the overall degree of association between the criterion variable and the predictor variables taken together. The multiple correlation coefficient squared (R^2) is the proportion of variance in the criterion variable accounted for by all the predictor variables taken together. Multiple regressions are commonly reported in articles, often in a table that includes the regression coefficients.

Key Terms

correlation (p. 68)
scatter diagram (p. 68)
linear correlation (p. 71)
curvilinear correlation (p. 71)
no correlation (p. 73)
positive correlation (p. 74)
negative correlation (p. 74)
cross-product of Z scores (p. 77)
perfect correlation (p. 78)
correlation coefficient (r) (p. 79)
Z_X (p. 79)

Z_Y (p. 79)
direction of causality (p. 84)
longitudinal study (p. 86)
true experiment (p. 86)
statistically significant (p. 86)
predictor variable (p. 88)
criterion variable (p. 88)
prediction model (p. 88)
standardized regression coefficient (β) (p. 88)

proportion of variance accounted for (r^2) (p. 92)
correlation matrix (p. 94)
multiple correlation (p. 95)
multiple regression (p. 95)
multiple correlation coefficient (R) (p. 97)
R (p. 97)

Example Worked-Out Problems

Making a Scatter Diagram and Describing the General Pattern of Association

Based on the number of hours studied and the test score for the five students shown below, make a scatter diagram and describe in words the general pattern of association.

Student	Hours Studied	Test Score
A	0	52
B	10	92
C	6	75
D	8	71
E	6	64

Answer

The steps of solving the problem are described below; Figure 3–15 shows the scatter diagram with markers for each step.

❶ **Draw the axes and decide which variable goes on which axis.** Since studying comes before the test score, we will draw the axes with number of hours studied along the bottom.

❷ **Determine the range of values to use for each variable and mark them on the axes.** We will assume that the test scores go from 0 to 100. We do not know the maximum possible for the number of hours studied, but let us assume a maximum of 10 in this example.

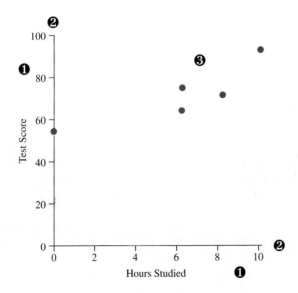

Figure 3–15 Scatter diagram for scores in Example Worked-Out Problem. ❶ Draw the axes and decide which variable goes on which axis. ❷ Determine the range of values to use for each variable and mark them on the axes. ❸ Mark a dot for each pair of scores.

❸ **Mark a dot for each pair of scores.** For example, to mark the dot for student D, you go across to 8 and up to 71.

The general pattern is roughly linear. Its direction is positive (it goes up and to the right, with more hours studied going with larger test scores and vice versa). It is a quite strong correlation, since the dots all fall fairly close to a straight line—it should be fairly close to +1. In words, it is a strong, linear, positive correlation.

Figuring the Correlation Coefficient

Figure the correlation coefficient for the hours studied and test score example given above.

Answer

You can figure the correlation using either the formula or the steps. The basic figuring is shown in Table 3–9 with markers for each of the steps.

Using the formula,

$$r = (\Sigma Z_X Z_Y)/N = 4.49/5 = .90.$$

Using the steps,

❶ **Change all scores to Z scores.** For example, the mean for hours studied is 6, and the standard deviation is 3.35; thus, the Z score for student A, who studied for 0 hours, is $(0 - 6)/3.35 = -1.79$.
❷ **Figure the cross-product of the Z scores for each person.** For example, for student A, the cross-product is -1.79 multiplied by -1.43 which is 2.56; for student B, it is 1.19 multiplied by 1.61, which equals 1.92.
❸ **Add up the cross-products of the Z scores.** The total is 4.49.
❹ **Divide by the number of people in the study.** The sum (4.49) divided by 5 is .90; that is, $r = .90$.

Outline for Writing Essays on the Logic and Figuring of a Correlation Coefficient

1. Explain how and why you created a scatter diagram to show the pattern of relationship between the two variables. Explain the meaning of the term *correlation*. Mention the type of correlation (e.g., linear; positive or negative; small, moderate, or strong) shown by the scatter diagram.

Table 3-9 Figuring Correlation Coefficient for Answer to Example Worked-Out Problem

Hours Studied		Test Score		Cross-Products
X	Z_x ❶	Y	Z_y ❶	$Z_x Z_y$ ❷
0	−1.79	52	−1.43	2.56
10	1.19	92	1.61	1.92
6	.00	75	.32	.00
8	.60	71	.02	.01
6	.00	64	−.52	.00
Σ: 30		354		4.49 ❸
M: 6		70.8		$r = 4.49/5 = .90$ ❹
SD: $\sqrt{56/5} = 3.35$		$\sqrt{866.8/5} = 13.17$		

2. Explain the idea that a correlation coefficient provides an indication of the direction and strength of linear correlation between two variables.
3. Outline and explain the steps for figuring the correlation coefficient. Be sure to mention that the first step involves changing all of the scores to Z scores. (If required by the question, explain the meaning of Z scores, mean, and standard deviation.) Describe how to figure the cross-products of the Z scores. Explain why the cross-products of the Z scores will tend to be positive if the correlation is positive and will tend to be negative if the correlation is negative. Mention that the correlation coefficient is figured by taking the mean of the cross-products of the Z scores. Explain what the value of the correlation coefficient means in terms of the direction and strength of linear correlation.
4. Be sure to discuss the direction and strength of correlation of your particular result.

Prediction Using Z Scores

Based on the data shown below (which are the same data used for an example earlier in the chapter), predict the Z scores for achievement for schools that have class sizes with Z scores of $-2, -1, 0, +1, +2$.

Elementary School	Class Size	Achievement Test Score
Main Street	25	80
Casat	14	98
Harland	33	50
Shady Grove	28	82
Jefferson	20	90
M	24	80
SD	6.54	16.30

$r = -.90$

Answer

This can be done using either the formula or the steps. Using the formula Predicted $Z_Y = (\beta)(Z_X)$, the Z-score prediction model for this problem is,

$$\begin{aligned} \text{Predicted } Z_Y &= (-.90)(Z_X) = (-.90)(-2) = 1.80. \\ &\quad (-.90)(-1) = .90. \\ &\quad (-.90)(0) = 0. \\ &\quad (-.90)(+1) = -.90. \\ &\quad (-.90)(+2) = -1.80. \end{aligned}$$

Using the steps,

❶ **Determine the standardized regression coefficient (β).** The correlation coefficient is $-.90$. Thus, $\beta = -.90$.
❷ **Multiply the standardized regression coefficient by the person's Z score on the predictor variable.** $-.90 \times -2 = 1.80$; $-.90 \times -1 = .90$; $-.90 \times 0 = 0$; $-.90 \times 1 = -.90$; $-.90 \times 2 = -1.80$.

Prediction Using Raw Scores

Using the data from the example above on class size and achievement test score, predict the raw scores for achievement for a school that has a class size of 27.

Answer

Using the steps,

❶ **Change the person's raw score on the predictor variable to a Z score (note that in this example, we have a school's raw score).** $Z_X = (X - M_X)/SD_X = (27 - 24)/6.54 = 3/6.54 = .46$.

❷ **Multiply the standardized regression coefficient (β) by the person's predictor variable Z score.** Predicted $Z_Y = (\beta)(Z_X) = (-.90)(.46) = -.41$. That is, the predicted Z score for this school is $-.41$.

❸ **Change the person's predicted Z score on the criterion variable to a raw score.** Predicted $Y = (SD_Y)(\text{Predicted } Z_Y) + M_Y = (16.30)(-.41) + 80 = -6.68 + 80 = 73.32$. In other words, using the prediction model based on the study of 5 schools, we would predict that a school with an average class size of 27 students will have an average achievement test score of 73.32.

Advanced Topic: Multiple Regression Predictions

A (fictional) researcher studied the talkativeness of children in families with a mother, father, and one grandparent. The researcher found that the child's talkativeness score depended on the quality of the child's relationship with each of these people. The multiple regression prediction model using Z scores is as follows:

Predicted talkativeness Z score of the child = (.32)(Z mother) + (.21)(Z father) + (.11)(Z grandparent)

Predict a child's talkativeness Z score who had Z scores for relationship quality of .48 with mother, $-.63$ with father, and 1.25 with grandparent.

Answer

Predicted talkativeness Z score of the child = (.32)(Z mother) + (.21)(Z father) + (.11)(Z grandparent) = (.32)(.48) + (.21)(-.63) + (.11)(1.25) = .15 + -.13 + .14 = .16.

Practice Problems

These problems involve figuring. Most real-life statistics problems are done on a computer with special statistical software. Even if you have such software, do these problems by hand to ingrain the method in your mind. To learn how to use a computer to solve statistics problems like those in this chapter, refer to the *Using SPSS* section at the end of this chapter and the *Student's Study Guide and SPSS Workbook* that accompanies this text.

All data are fictional unless an actual citation is given.

Set I (for answers, see pp. 437–440)

1. For each of the following scatter diagrams, indicate whether the pattern is linear, curvilinear, or no correlation; if it is linear, indicate whether it is positive or negative and approximately how strong the correlation is (strong, moderate, small).

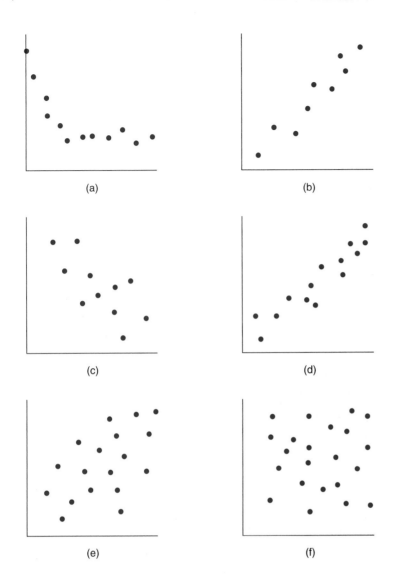

(a)

(b)

(c)

(d)

(e)

(f)

2. The following have been prepared so that data sets B through D are slightly modified versions of data set A. Make scatter diagrams and figure the correlation coefficients for each data set.

Data Set A		Data Set B		Data Set C		Data Set D	
X	Y	X	Y	X	Y	X	Y
1	1	1	1	1	5	1	1
2	2	2	2	2	2	2	4
3	3	3	3	3	3	3	3
4	4	4	5	4	4	4	2
5	5	5	4	5	1	5	5

3. A researcher is interested in whether a new drug affects the development of a cold. Eight people are tested: Four take the drug and four do not. (Those who take it are rated 1; those who don't, 0.) Whether they get a cold (rated 1) or not

(0) is recorded. Four possible results are shown. Figure the correlation coefficient for each possibility (A, B, C, and D).

Possibility A		Possibility B		Possibility C		Possibility D	
Take Drug	Get Cold	Take Drug	Get Cold	Take Drug	Get Cold	Take Drug	Get Cold
0	1	0	1	0	1	0	1
0	1	0	1	0	1	0	1
0	1	0	1	0	0	0	1
0	1	0	0	0	0	0	0
1	0	1	1	1	1	1	0
1	0	1	0	1	1	1	0
1	0	1	0	1	0	1	0
1	0	1	0	1	0	1	0

For problems 4 and 5, (a) make a scatter diagram of the raw scores; (b) describe in words the general pattern of correlation, if any; and (c) figure the correlation coefficient. In these problems, the mean, standard deviation, and Z scores for each variable are given to save you some figuring.

4. The Louvre Museum is interested in the relation of the age of a painting to public interest in it. The number of people stopping to look at each of ten randomly selected paintings is observed over a week. The results are as shown:

Painting Title	Approximate Age (Years) ($M = 253.40$, $SD = 152.74$)		Number of People Stopping to Look ($M = 88.20$, $SD = 29.13$)	
	X	Z_X	Y	Z_Y
The Entombment	465	1.39	68	−.69
Mys Mar Ste Catherine	515	1.71	71	−.59
The Bathers	240	−.09	123	1.19
The Toilette	107	−.96	112	.82
Portrait of Castiglione	376	.80	48	−1.38
Charles I of England	355	.67	84	−.14
Crispin and Scapin	140	−.75	66	−.76
Nude in the Sun	115	−.91	148	2.05
The Balcony	122	−.86	71	−.59
The Circus	99	−1.01	91	.10

5. A schoolteacher thought that he had observed that students who dressed more neatly were generally better students. To test this idea, the teacher had a friend rate each of the students for neatness of dress. Following are the ratings for neatness, along with each student's score on a standardized school achievement test.

Child	Neatness Rating ($M = 19.60$, $SD = 3.07$)		Achievement Test ($M = 63.10$, $SD = 4.70$)	
	X	Z_X	Y	Z_Y
Janet	18	−.52	60	−.66
Gareth	24	1.43	58	−1.09
Grove	14	−1.82	70	1.47
Kevin	19	−.20	58	−1.09

Joshua	20	.13	66	.62
Nicole	23	1.11	68	1.04
Susan	20	.13	65	.40
Drew	22	.78	68	1.04
Marie	15	−1.50	56	−1.51
Chad	21	.46	62	−.23

For problems 6 and 7, do the following: (a) Make a scatter diagram of the raw scores; (b) describe in words the general pattern of correlation, if any; (c) figure the correlation coefficient; (d) explain the logic of what you have done, writing as if you are speaking to someone who has never had a statistics course (but who does understand the mean, standard deviation, and Z scores); (e) give three logically possible directions of causality, saying for each whether it is a reasonable direction in light of the variables involved (and why); (f) make raw score predictions on the criterion variable for persons with Z scores on the predictor variable of −2, −1, 0, +1, +2; and (g) give the proportion of variance accounted for (r^2).

6. Four young children were monitored closely over a period of several weeks to measure how much they watched violent television programs and their amount of violent behavior toward their playmates. (For part (f), assume that hours watching violent television is the predictor variable.) The results were as follows:

Child's Code Number	Weekly Viewing of Violent TV (hours)	Number of Violent or Aggressive Acts toward Playmates
G3368	14	9
R8904	8	6
C9890	6	1
L8722	12	8

7. A political scientist studied the relation between the number of town-hall meetings held by the four candidates for mayor in a small town and the percentage of people in the town who could name each candidate. (For part (f), assume that the number of town-hall meetings is the predictor variable.) Here are the results:

Mayor Candidate	Number of Town-Hall Meetings	Percentage of People Who Can Name Candidate
A	4	70
B	5	94
C	2	36
D	1	48

8. Chapman, Hobfoll, and Ritter (1997) interviewed 68 inner-city pregnant women and their husbands (or boyfriends) twice during their pregnancy, once between 3 and 6 months into the pregnancy and again between 6 and 9 months into the pregnancy. Table 3–10 shows the correlations among several of their measures. ("Zero-Order Correlations" means the same thing as ordinary correlations.) Most important in this table are the correlations among women's reports of their own stress, men's reports of their partners' stress, women's perception of their partners' support at the first and at the second interviews, and women's depression at the first and at the second interviews.

Table 3-10 Zero-Order Correlations for Study Variables

Variable	1	2	3	4	5	6	7	8	9	10
1. Women's report of stress	—									
2. Men's report of women's stress	.17	—								
3. Partner Support 1	−.28*	−.18	—							
4. Partner Support 2	−.27*	−.18	.44***	—						
5. Depressed Mood 1	.23*	.10	−.34**	−.17	—					
6. Depressed Mood 2	.50***	.14	−.42***	−.41***	.55***	—				
7. Women's age	.06	.16	.04	−.24*	−.35*	−.09	—			
8. Women's ethnicity	−.19	−.09	−.16	−.14	.11	.13	−.02	—		
9. Women's marital status	−.18	.01	.12	.24*	−.04	−.20	.05	−.34**	—	
10. Parity	.19	.13	−.11	−.17	.10	.16	.26*	.31*	−.12	—

*$p < .05$, **$p < .01$, ***$p < .001$.
Source: Chapman, H. A., Hobfoll, S. E., & Ritter, C. (1997). Partners' stress underestimations lead to women's distress: A study of pregnant inner-city women. *Journal of Personality and Social Psychology, 73,* 418–425. Copyright © 1997 by the American Psychological Association. Reprinted by permission.

Explain the results on these measures as if you were writing to a person who has never had a course in statistics. Specifically, (a) explain what is meant by a correlation coefficient using one of the correlations as an example; (b) study the table and then comment on the patterns of results in terms of which variables are relatively strongly correlated and which are not very strongly correlated; and (c) comment on the limitations of making conclusions about direction of causality based on these data, using a specific correlation as an example (noting at least one plausible alternative causal direction and why that alternative is plausible).

9. A researcher working with hockey players found that knowledge of fitness training principles correlates .40 with number of injuries received over the subsequent year. The researcher now plans to test all new athletes for their knowledge of fitness training principles and use this information to predict the number of injuries they are likely to receive. Indicate the (a) predictor variable, (b) criterion variable, and (c) standardized regression coefficient. (d) Write the Z-score prediction model. Indicate the predicted Z scores for number of injuries for athletes whose Z scores on the principles of fitness training test are (e) −2, (f) −1, (g) 0, (h) +1, and (i) +2.

10. ADVANCED TOPIC: Gunn, Biglan, Smolkowski, and Ary (2000) studied reading in a group of Hispanic and non-Hispanic third graders. As part of this study, they did an analysis predicting reading comprehension (called "passage comprehension") from three more specific measures of reading ability: "Letter-Word Identification" (ability to read irregular words), "Word Attack" (ability to use phonic and structural analysis), and "Oral Reading Fluency" (correct words per minute). The results are shown in Table 3–11. Explain the results as if you were writing to a person who understands correlation but has never learned anything about regression or multiple regression analysis. (Ignore the columns for *t, p, F,* and *p.* These have to do with statistical significance.)

11. ADVANCED TOPIC: Based on Table 3–11 (from Gunn et al., 2000), (a) determine the Z score multiple regression formula, and (b) calculate the predicted pas-

Table 3-11   Multiple Regression Predicting Comprehension from Decoding Skill and Oral Reading Fluency

Variable	Beta	t	p	R^2	F	p
Passage Comprehension raw score						
Letter-Word Identification	−.227	−2.78	.006			
Word Attack	.299	3.75	.001			
Oral Reading Fluency—	.671	9.97	.001			
Correct words per minute				.534	57.70	.001

Source: Gunn, B., Biglan, A., Smolkowski, K., & Ary, D. (2000). The efficacy of supplemental instruction in decoding skills for Hispanic and non-Hispanic students in early elementary school. *Journal of Special Education, 34,* 90–103. Copyright © 2000 by PRO-ED, Inc. Reprinted by permission.

sage comprehension Z score for each of the following third graders (figures are Z scores):

Third Grader	Letter-Word Identification	Word Attack	Oral Reading Fluency
A	1	1	1
B	0	0	0
C	−1	−1	−1
D	1	0	0
E	0	1	0
F	0	0	1
G	3	1	1
H	1	3	1
I	3	1	3

Set II

12. For each of the scatter diagrams on p. 110, indicate whether the pattern is linear, curvilinear, or no correlation; if it is linear, indicate whether it is positive or negative and approximately how strong the correlation is (strong, moderate, small).

13. Make up a scatter diagram with 10 dots for each of the following situations: (a) perfect positive linear correlation, (b) strong but not perfect positive linear correlation, (c) weak positive linear correlation, (d) strong but not perfect negative linear correlation, (e) no correlation, (f) clear curvilinear correlation.

    For problems 14 and 15, (a) make a scatter diagram of the raw scores; (b) describe in words the general pattern of correlation, if any; and (c) figure the correlation coefficient.

14. A researcher studying people in their 80s was interested in the relation between number of very close friends and overall health (on a scale from 0 to 100). The scores for six research participants are shown on the following page.

Research Participant	Number of Friends	Overall Health
A	2	41
B	4	72
C	0	37
D	3	84
E	2	52
F	1	49

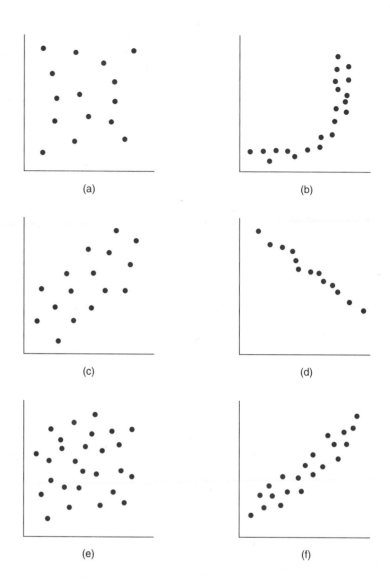

15. In a study of people first getting acquainted with each other, researchers reasoned the amount of self-disclosure of one's partner (on a scale from 1 to 30) and one's liking for one's partner (on a scale from 1 to 10). The Z scores for the variables are given to save you some figuring. Here are the results:

Partner's Self-Disclosure		Liking for Partner	
Actual Score	Z Score	Actual Score	Z Score
18	.37	8	1.10
17	.17	9	1.47
20	.80	6	.37
8	−1.72	1	−1.47
13	−.67	7	.74
24	1.63	1	−1.47
11	−1.09	3	−.74
12	−.88	5	.0
18	.38	7	.74
21	1.00	3	−.74

For problems 16 and 17, (a) make a scatter diagram of the raw scores; (b) describe in words the general pattern of correlation, if any; (c) figure the correlation coefficient; (d) explain the logic of what you have done, writing as if you are speaking to someone who has never had a statistics course (but who does understand the mean, standard deviation, and Z scores); (e) give three logically possible directions of causality, saying for each whether it is a reasonable direction in light of the variables involved (and why); (f) make raw score predictions on the criterion variable for persons with Z scores on the predictor variable of -2, -1, 0, $+1$, $+2$, and (g) give the proportion of variance accounted for (r^2).

16. Four research participants take a test of manual dexterity (high scores mean better dexterity) and an anxiety test (high scores mean more anxiety). (For part (f), assume that dexterity is the predictor variable.) The scores are as follows:

Person	Dexterity	Anxiety
A	1	10
B	1	8
C	2	4
D	4	-2

17. Five college students were asked about how important a goal it is to them to have a family and about how important a goal it is for them to be highly successful in their work. Each variable was measured on a scale from 0 "Not at all important goal" to 10 "Very important goal." (For part (f), assume that the family goal is the predictor variable.) The scores are as follows:

Student	Family Goal	Work Goal
A	7	5
B	6	4
C	8	2
D	3	9
E	4	1

18. As part of a larger study, Speed and Gangestad (1997) collected ratings and nominations on a number of characteristics for 66 fraternity men from their fellow fraternity members. The following paragraph is taken from their "Results" section:

> ... men's romantic popularity significantly correlated with several characteristics: best dressed ($r = .48$), most physically attractive ($r = .47$), most outgoing ($r = .47$), most self-confident ($r = .44$), best trendsetters ($r = .38$), funniest ($r = .37$), most satisfied ($r = .32$), and most independent ($r = .28$). Unexpectedly, however, men's potential for financial success did not significantly correlate with romantic popularity ($r = .10$). (p. 931)

Explain these results as if you were writing to a person who has never had a course in statistics. Specifically, (a) explain what is meant by a correlation coefficient using one of the correlations as an example; (b) explain in a general way what is meant by "significantly" and "not significantly," referring to at least one specific example; and (c) speculate on the meaning of the pattern of results, taking into account the issue of direction of causality.

19. Gable and Lutz (2000) studied 65 children, 3 to 10 years old, and their parents. One of their results was: "Parental control of child eating showed a negative association with children's participation in extracurricular activities ($r = .34$; $p < .01$)" (p. 296). Another result was: "Parents who held less appropriate beliefs

about children's nutrition reported that their children watched more hours of television per day ($r = .36$; $p < .01$)" (p. 296).

Explain these results as if you were writing to a person who has never had a course in statistics. Be sure to comment on possible directions of causality for each result.

20. Arbitrarily select eight people, each from a different page of the telephone directory. Do each of the following: (a) make a scatter diagram for the relation between the number of letters in each person's first and last name, (b) figure the correlation coefficient for the relation between the number of letters in each person's first and last name, (c) describe the result in words, and (d) suggest a possible interpretation for your results.

21. A researcher studying adjustment to the job of new employees found a correlation of .30 between amount of employees' education and rating by job supervisors two months later. The researcher now plans to use amount of education to predict supervisors' later ratings of employees. Indicate the (a) predictor variable, (b) criterion variable, and (c) the standardized regression coefficient (β). (d) Write the Z-score prediction model. Give the predicted Z scores for supervisor ratings for employees with amount of education Z scores of (e) -1.5, (f) -1, (g) $-.5$, (h) 0, (i) $+.5$, (j) $+1$, and (k) $+1.5$.

22. Ask five other students of the same gender as yourself (each from different families) to give you their own height and also their mother's height. Based on the numbers these five people give you, (a) figure the correlation coefficient, and (b) determine the Z-score prediction model for predicting a person's height from his or her mother's height. Finally, based on your prediction model, predict the height of a person of your gender whose mother's height is (c) 5 feet, (d) 5 feet 6 inches, and (e) 6 feet. (Note: Either convert inches to decimals of feet or do the whole problem using inches.)

23. ADVANCED TOPIC: Researchers studying criminal justice issues have long been interested in what influences people's attitudes about punishment of criminal offenders. Graham, Weiner, and Zucker (1997) took advantage of the very public trial of U.S. football star O. J. Simpson to test some basic issues in this area. In the first few days after Simpson was accused of having murdered his ex-wife, the researchers asked people a series of questions about the case. The researchers were mainly interested in the responses of the 177 individuals who believed Simpson was probably guilty, particularly their belief about retribution—how much they agreed or disagreed with the statement, "The punishment should make O. J. suffer as he made others suffer." The researchers were interested in a number of possible influences on this belief. These included "control" (how much control they believed Simpson had over his actions at the time of the crime), "responsibility" (how much they believed he was responsible for the crime), "anger" they felt toward him, "sympathy" they felt for him, "stability" (how much they believed his actions represented a stable versus temporary way of behaving), and "expectancy" (if they thought he would commit such a crime again). Graham and her colleagues reported:

> . . . Table [3–12] reveals partial support for our hypotheses. As expected, the strongest predictors of the retributive goal of making Simpson suffer were inferences about responsibility and the moral emotions of anger and sympathy. Stability and expectancy . . . were relatively weak [predictors]. (p. 337)

Explain these results as if you were writing to a person who understands correlation but has never had any exposure to prediction or multiple regression analysis. (Refer only to the retribution part of the table. You may ignore the *t* column, which is about statistical significance of the results.)

Table 3-12 Multiple Regressions Predicting Punishment Goals from the Attributional Variables, Study 1

	Punishment Goal							
	Retribution		Rehabilation		Protection		Deterrence	
Predictors	β	t	β	t	β	t	β	t
Control	−.05	<1	−.05	<1	−.03	<1	.15	1.90
Responsibility	.17	2.07*	−.00	<1	−.04	<1	.19	2.15*
Anger	.30	4.04***	.11	1.54	−.03	<1	−.04	<1
Sympathy	−.30	−3.68***	.39	5.18***	−.07	<1	−.13	−1.54
Stability	−.01	<1	−.34	−4.85***	−.19	2.33*	.04	<1
Expectancy	−.10	−1.33	−.06	<1	−.27	3.36***	.08	1.04
R^2		.27		.37		.17		.18

Note: β = standardized regression coefficient.
*$p < .05$; ***$p < .001$.
Source: Graham, S., Weiner. B., & Zucker, G. S. (1997). An attributional analysis of punishment goals and public reactions to O. J. Simpson. *Personality and Social Psychology Bulletin.* 23, 331–346. Copyright © 1997 by the Society for Personality and Social Psychology, Inc. Reprinted by permission of Sage Publications, Inc.

24. ADVANCED TOPIC: Based on Table 3–12 from problem 23, (a) write out the Z-score multiple regression formula for predicting retribution, and (b) figure the predicted Z score for retribution for persons A through J, whose Z scores on each predictor variable are shown below.

	Predictor Variable					
Person	Control	Responsibility	Anger	Sympathy	Stability	Expectancy
A	1	0	0	0	0	0
B	0	1	0	0	0	0
C	0	0	1	0	0	0
D	0	0	0	1	0	0
E	0	0	0	0	1	0
F	0	0	0	0	0	1
G	1	1	1	0	0	0
H	0	0	1	1	0	0
I	1	1	1	1	1	1
J	−1	−1	−1	−1	−1	−1

Using SPSS

The ✑ in the steps below indicates a mouse click. (We used SPSS version 13.0 for Windows to carry out these analyses. The steps and output may be slightly different for other versions of SPSS.)

In the steps below for the scatter diagram, correlation coefficient, and prediction, we will use the example of the sleep and happy mood study. The scores for that study are shown in Table 3–1, the scatter diagram is shown in Figure 3–2, and the figuring for the correlation coefficient is shown in Table 3–2.

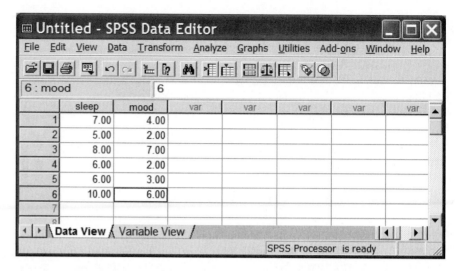

Figure 3–16   SPSS data editor window for the fictional study of the relationship between hours slept last night and mood.

Creating a Scatter Diagram

❶ Enter the scores into SPSS. Enter the scores as shown in Figure 3–16.

❷ ✐ *Graphs.*

❸ ✐ *Scatter/Dot.* A box will appear that allows you to select different types of scatter diagrams (or *scatterplots,* as SPSS calls them). You want the "Simple scatter" diagram. This is selected as the default type of scatter diagram, so you just need to ✐ *Define.*

❹ ✐ the variable called "mood" and then ✐ the arrow next to the box labeled "Y axis." This tells SPSS that the scores for the "mood" variable should go on the vertical (or Y) axis of the scatter diagram. ✐ the variable called "sleep" and then ✐ the arrow next to the box labeled "X axis." This tells SPSS that the scores for the "sleep" variable should go on the horizontal (or X) axis of the scatter diagram.

❺ ✐ *OK.* Your SPSS output window should look like Figure 3–17.

Finding the Correlation Coefficient

❶ Enter the scores into SPSS. Enter the scores as shown in Figure 3–16.

❷ ✐ *Analyze.*

❸ ✐ *Correlate.*

❹ ✐ *Bivariate.*

❺ ✐ on the variable called "mood" and then ✐ the arrow next to the box labeled "Variables." ✐ on the variable called "sleep" and then ✐ the arrow next to the box labeled "Variables." This tells SPSS to figure the correlation between the "mood" and "sleep" variables. (If you wanted to find the correlation between each of several variables, you would put all of them into the "Variables" box.) Notice that by default SPSS will carry out a Pearson correlation (the type of correlation you have learned in this chapter), will automatically give the significance level (using a two-tailed test), and will flag statistically significant correlations using the .05 significance level.

❻ ✐ *OK.* Your SPSS output window should look like Figure 3–18.

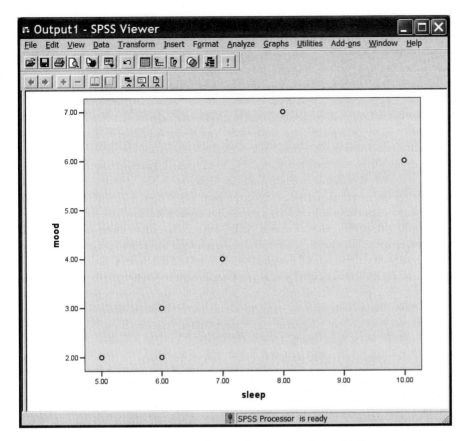

Figure 3–17   An SPSS scatter diagram showing the relationship between hours slept last night and mood (fictional data).

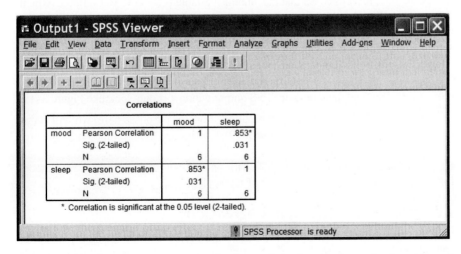

Figure 3–18   SPSS output window for the correlation between hours slept last night and mood (fictional data).

The table shown in Figure 3–18 is a small correlation matrix (there are only two variables). (If you were interested in the correlations among more than two variables—which is often the case in behavioral and social sciences research—SPSS would produce a larger correlation matrix.) The correlation matrix shows the correlation coefficient ("Pearson Correlation"), the exact significance level of the correlation coefficient ["Sig. (2-tailed)"], and the number of people in the correlation analysis ("N"). Note that two of the cells of the correlation matrix show a correlation coefficient of exactly 1. You can ignore these cells, as they simply show that each variable is perfectly correlated with itself. (In larger correlation matrixes all of the cells on the diagonal from the top left to the bottom right of the table will have a correlation coefficient of 1.) You will also notice that the remaining two cells provide identical information. This is because the table shows the correlation between sleep and mood and also between mood and sleep (which are, of course, identical correlations). So you can look at either one. (In a larger correlation matrix, you need only look either at all of the correlations above the diagonal that goes from top left to bottom right or at all of the correlations below that diagonal.) The correlation coefficient is .853 (which is usually rounded to two decimal places in research articles). The significance level of .031 is less than our .05 cutoff, which means that it is a statistically significant correlation. The asterisk (*) by the correlation of .853 also shows that it is statistically significant (at the .05 significance level, as shown by the note under the table).

Prediction with a Single Predictor Variable

In actual research, prediction is most often done using raw scores (as opposed to Z scores). However, as you will learn below, even if you do prediction with raw scores, the output provided by SPSS allows you to determine the Z score prediction model (or prediction rule).

❶ Enter the scores into SPSS. Enter the scores as shown in Figure 3–16.

❷ ✑ *Analyze.*

❸ ✑ *Regression.*

❹ ✑ *Linear.* This tells SPSS that you are figuring a *linear* prediction rule (as opposed to any one of a number of other prediction rules).

❺ ✑ the variable called "mood" and then ✑ the arrow next to the box labeled "Dependent." This tells SPSS that the "mood" variable is the criterion variable (which is also called the *dependent variable* in prediction, because it "depends" on the predictor variable's score). ✑ the variable called "sleep" and then ✑ the arrow next to the box labeled "Independent(s)." This tells SPSS that the "sleep" variable is the predictor variable (which is also called the *independent variable* in prediction).

❻ ✑ *OK.* The final table in your SPSS output window should look like Figure 3–19.

SPSS provided four tables in the output. For our purposes here, we will focus only on the final table (shown in Figure 3–19), which gives the information for the prediction model. Most important for us, the table gives the standardized regression coefficient (labeled "Beta"), which is .853. This tells us that the Z score prediction model for predicting mood from the number of hours slept is: $Z_{mood} = (.853)(Z_{hours\ slept})$.

Advanced Topic: Multiple Regression

If you were conducting a multiple regression, you would put all of the predictor variables in the "Independent(s)" box in Step ❺ above. In the SPSS output, the standardized regression coefficient for each predictor would be listed in the "Beta" column. Examination of these standardized regression coefficients would tell you the unique

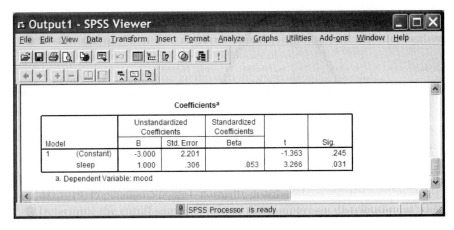

Figure 3–19   SPSS output window for predicting mood from hours slept last night (fictional data).

influence that each predictor has for predicting the criterion variable. (As you learned earlier in the chapter, the larger the standardized regression coefficient for a predictor variable, the more influence that variable has when predicting a score on the criterion variable.)

Appendix: Hypothesis Tests and Power for the Correlation Coefficient

This material is for students who have already completed at least through Chapter 8 and are now returning to this chapter.

Significance of a Correlation Coefficient

Hypothesis testing of a correlation coefficient follows the usual steps of hypothesis testing. However, there are four important points to note.

1. Usually, the null hypothesis is that the correlation in a population like that studied is no different from a population in which the true correlation is 0.
2. If the data meet assumptions (explained below), the comparison distribution is a t distribution with degrees of freedom equal to the number of people minus 2.
3. You figure the correlation coefficient's score on that t distribution using the formula

$$t = \frac{(r)\left(\sqrt{N - 2}\right)}{\sqrt{1 - r^2}} \tag{3-5}$$

> The t score is the correlation coefficient multiplied by the square root of 2 less than the number of people in the study, divided by the square root of 1 minus the correlation coefficient squared.

4. Note that significance tests of a correlation, like a t test, can be either one-tailed or two-tailed. A one-tailed test means that the researcher has predicted the sign (positive or negative) of the correlation.

Assumptions for the significance test of a correlation coefficient are that (a) the populations for both variables are normally distributed, and (b) in the population, the distribution of each variable at each point of the other variable has about equal variance. However, as with the t test and analysis of variance (Chapter 10), moderate violations of these assumptions are not fatal.

An Example

Here is an example using the sleep and mood study example. Let's suppose that the researchers predicted a positive correlation between sleep and mood, to be tested at the .05 level.

❶ **Restate the question as a research hypothesis and a null hypothesis about the populations.** There are two populations:

Population 1: People like those in this study.

Population 2: People for whom there is no correlation between number of hours slept the night before and mood the next day.

The null hypothesis is that the two populations have the same correlation. The research hypothesis is that Population 1 has a higher correlation than Population 2. (That is, the prediction is for a population correlation greater than 0.)

❷ **Determine the characteristics of the comparison distribution.** Assuming we meet the assumptions (in practice, it would be hard to tell with only 6 people in the study), the comparison distribution is a t distribution with $df = 4$. (That is, $df = N - 2 = 6 - 2 = 4$.)

❸ **Determine the cutoff sample score on the comparison distribution at which the null hypothesis should be rejected.** The t table (Table A–2 in the Appendix) shows that for a one-tailed test at the .05 level, with 4 degrees of freedom, you need a t of at least 2.132.

❹ **Determine your sample's score on the comparison distribution.** We figured a correlation of $r = .85$. Applying the formula to find the equivalent t, we get

$$t = \frac{(r)\left(\sqrt{N-2}\right)}{\sqrt{1-r^2}} = \frac{(.85)\left(\sqrt{6-2}\right)}{\sqrt{1-.85^2}} = \frac{(.85)(2)}{.53} = 3.21.$$

❺ **Decide whether to reject the null hypothesis.** The t score of 3.21 for our sample correlation is more extreme than the minimum needed t score of 2.132.

Table 3-13	Approximate Power of Studies Using the Correlation Coefficient (r) for Testing Hypotheses at the .05 Level of Significance		
		Effect Size	
	Small ($r = .10$)	**Medium** ($r = .30$)	**Large** ($r = .50$)
Two-tailed Total *N:* 10	.06	.13	.33
20	.07	.25	.64
30	.08	.37	.83
40	.09	.48	.92
50	.11	.57	.97
100	.17	.86	*
One-tailed Total *N:* 10	.08	.22	.46
20	.11	.37	.75
30	.13	.50	.90
40	.15	.60	.96
50	.17	.69	.98
100	.26	.92	*

*Power is nearly 1.

Table 3-14	Approximate Number of Participants Needed for 80% Power for a Study Using the Correlation Coefficient (r) for Testing a Hypothesis at the .05 Significance Level		
	Effect Size		
	Small ($r = .10$)	**Medium** ($r = .30$)	**Large** ($r = .50$)
Two-tailed	783	85	28
One-tailed	617	68	22

Thus, you can reject the null hypothesis, and the research hypothesis is supported.

Effect Size and Power

The correlation coefficient itself is a measure of effect size. (Thus, in the example, effect size is $r = .85$.) Cohen's (1988) conventions for the correlation coefficient are .10 for a small effect size, .30 for a medium effect size, and .50 for a large effect size. You can find the power for a correlation using a power table, a power software package, or an Internet power calculator. Table 3–13 gives the approximate power, and Table 3–14 gives minimum sample size for 80% power at the .05 level of significance. (More complete tables are provided in Cohen, 1988, pp. 84–95, 101–102.) For example, the power for a study with an expected medium effect size ($r = .30$), two-tailed, with 50 participants, is .57 (which is below the standard desired level of at least .80 power). This means that even if the research hypothesis is in fact true and has a medium effect size (that is, even if the two variables are correlated at $r = .30$ in the population), there is only a 57% chance that the study will produce a significant correlation.

CHAPTER 4

Some Key Ingredients for Inferential Statistics

The Normal Curve, Sample versus Population, and Probability

CHAPTER OUTLINE

- The Normal Curve
- Sample and Population
- Probability
- Normal Curves, Samples and Populations, and Probabilities in Research Articles
- Summary
- Key Terms
- Example Worked-Out Problems
- Practice Problems

Ordinarily, behavioral and social scientists do a research study to test some theoretical principle or the effectiveness of some practical procedure. For example, an educational researcher might compare reading speeds of students taught with two different methods to examine a theory of teaching. A sociologist might examine the effectiveness of a program of neighborhood meetings intended to promote water conservation. Such studies are carried out with a particular group of research participants. But the researchers usually want to make more general conclusions about the theoretical principle or procedure being studied—conclusions that go beyond the particular group of research participants studied. To do this, researchers use inferential statistics.

This chapter and Chapters 5, 6, and 7 introduce inferential statistics. In this chapter, we consider three topics: the normal curve, sample versus population, and probability. This is a relatively short chapter, preparing the way for the next ones, which are more demanding.

The Normal Curve

As we noted in Chapter 1, the graphs of many of the distributions of variables that behavioral and social scientists study (as well as many other distributions in nature) follow a unimodal, roughly symmetrical, bell-shaped distribution. These bell-shaped histograms or frequency polygons approximate a precise and important distribution called the **normal distribution** or, more simply, the **normal curve.** The normal curve is a mathematical (or theoretical) distribution. Researchers often compare the actual distributions of the variables they are studying (that is, the distributions they find in research studies) to the normal curve. They don't expect the distributions of their variables to match the normal curve *perfectly* (since the normal curve is a theoretical distribution), but researchers often check whether their variables *approximately* follow a normal curve. An example of the normal curve is shown in Figure 4–1.

normal distribution   Frequency distribution following a normal curve.

normal curve   Specific, mathematically defined, bell-shaped frequency distribution that is symmetrical and unimodal; distributions observed in nature and in research commonly approximate it.

Why the Normal Curve Is So Common in Nature

Take, for example, the number of different letters a particular person can remember accurately on various testings (with different random letters each time). On some testings, the number of letters remembered may be high, on others low, and on most somewhere in between. That is, the number of different letters a person can recall on various testings probably approximately follows a normal curve. Suppose that the person has a basic ability to recall, say, seven letters in this kind of memory task. Nevertheless, on any particular testing, the actual number recalled will be affected by various influences—noisiness of the room, the person's mood at the moment, a combination of random letters unwittingly confused with a familiar name, and so on.

These various influences add up to make the person recall more than seven on some testings and less than seven on others. However, the particular combination of such influences that come up at any testing is essentially random. Thus, on most testings, positive and negative influences should cancel out. The chances are not very good of all the negative influences happening to come together on a testing when none of the positive influences show up. Thus, in general, the person remembers a middle amount, an amount in which all the opposing influences cancel each other out. Very high or very low scores are much less common.

This creates a unimodal distribution with most of the scores near the middle and fewer at the extremes. It also creates a distribution that is symmetrical, because the number of letters recalled is as likely to be above as below the middle. Being a unimodal symmetrical curve does not guarantee that it will be a normal curve; it could be too flat or too pointed. However, it can be shown mathematically that in the long run, if the influences are truly random and the number of different influences being combined is large, a precise normal curve results. Mathematical statisticians call this principle the *central limit theorem.*

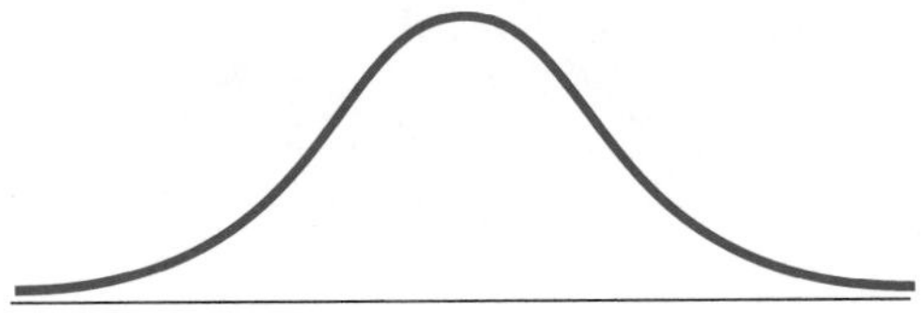

Figure 4–1   A normal curve.

The Normal Curve and the Percentage of Scores between the Mean and 1 and 2 Standard Deviations from the Mean

The shape of the normal curve is standard. Thus, there is a known percentage of scores above or below any particular point. For example, exactly 50 percent of the scores in a normal curve are below the mean, because in any symmetrical distribution, half the scores are below the mean. More interestingly, as shown in Figure 4–2, approximately 34 percent of the scores are always between the mean and 1 standard deviation from the mean. (Notice, incidentally, that in Figure 4–2 the 1 standard deviation point on the normal curve is at the place the curve starts going more out than down.)

Consider IQ scores. On many widely used intelligence tests, the mean IQ is 100, the standard deviation is 16, and the distribution of IQs is roughly normal (see Figure 4–3). Knowing about the normal curve and the percentage of scores between the mean and 1 standard deviation above the mean tells you that about 34 percent of people have IQs between 100, the mean IQ, and 116, the IQ score that is 1 standard deviation above the mean. Similarly, because the normal curve is symmetrical, about 34 percent of people have IQs between 100 and 84 (the score that is 1 standard deviation below the mean), and 68% (34% + 34%) have IQs between 84 and 116.

There are many fewer scores between 1 and 2 standard deviations from the mean than there are between the mean and 1 standard deviation from the mean. It turns out that about 14 percent of the scores are between 1 and 2 standard deviations above the mean (see Figure 4–2). (Similarly, about 14 percent of the scores are between 1 and 2 standard deviations below the mean.) Thus, about 14 percent of people have IQs between 116 (1 standard deviation above the mean) and 132 (2 standard deviations above the mean).

You will find it very useful to remember the 34 percent and 14 percent figures. These figures tell you the percentage of people above and below any particular score whenever you know that score's number of standard deviations above or below the mean. You can also reverse this approach and figure out a person's number of standard deviations from the mean from a percentage. Suppose a laboratory test showed that a particular archaeological sample of ceramics was in the top 2 percent of all the samples in the excavation for containing iron, and it is known that the distribution of iron in such samples is roughly normal. In this situation, the sample must have a level of iron that is at least 2 standard deviations above the mean level of iron. This is because a total of 50 percent of the scores are above the mean. There are 34 percent between the mean and 1 standard deviation above the mean and another 14 percent between 1 and 2 standard deviations above the mean. That leaves 2 percent of scores (that is, 50% – 34% – 14% = 2%) that are 2 standard deviations or more above the mean.

Remember from Chapter 2 that a *Z* score is the number of standard deviations a score is above or below the mean—which is just what we are talking about here. Thus, if you knew the mean and the standard deviation of the iron concentrations in the

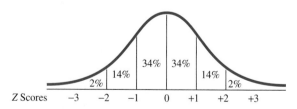

Figure 4–2 Normal curve with approximate percentages of scores between the mean and 1 and 2 standard deviations above and below the mean.

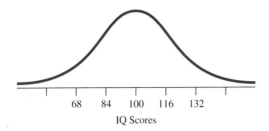

Figure 4–3 Distribution of IQ scores on many standard intelligence tests (with a mean of 100 and a standard deviation of 16).

samples, you could figure out the raw score (the actual level of iron in this sample) that is equivalent to being 2 standard deviations above the mean. You would do this using the methods of changing Z scores (in this case, a Z score of +2) to raw scores and vice versa that you learned in Chapter 2, which are

$$X = (Z)(SD) + M \text{ and } Z = (X - M)/SD$$

The Normal Curve Table and Z Scores

The 50%, 34%, and 14% figures are important practical rules for working with a group of scores that follows a normal distribution. However, in many research and applied situations, behavioral and social scientists need more accurate information. Because the normal curve is a precise mathematical curve, you can figure the *exact percentage* of scores between any two points on the normal curve (not just those that happen to be right at 1 or 2 standard deviations from the mean). For example, exactly 68.59 percent of scores have a Z score between +.62 and -1.68; exactly 2.81 percent of scores have a Z score between +.79 and +.89, and so forth.

You can figure these percentages using calculus, based on the formula for the normal curve (which you can look up in a mathematical statistics text). However, you can also do this much more simply (which you are probably glad to know!). Statisticians have worked out tables for the normal curve that give the percentage of scores between the mean (a Z score of 0) and any other Z score (as well as the percentage of scores in the tail for any Z score).

We have included such a **normal curve table** in the Appendix (Table A–1, pp. 425–426). Table 4–1 shows the first part of the full table. The first column in the table lists the Z score. The second column, labeled "% Mean to Z," gives the percentage of scores between the mean and that Z score. The shaded area in the curve at the top of the column gives a visual reminder of the meaning of the percentages in the column. The third column, labeled "% in Tail," gives the percentage of scores in the tail for that Z score. The shaded tail area in the curve at the top of the column shows the meaning of the percentages in the column. Notice that the table lists only positive Z scores. This is because the normal curve is perfectly symmetrical. Thus, the percentage of scores between the mean and, say, a Z of +.98 (which is 33.65%) is exactly the same as the percentage of scores between the mean and a Z of $-.98$ (again, 33.65%); and the percentage of scores in the tail for a Z score of +1.77 (3.84%) is the same as the percentage of scores in the tail for a Z score of -1.77 (again, 3.84%). Notice that for each Z score, the "% Mean to Z" value and the "% in Tail" value sum to 50.00. This is because exactly 50 percent of the scores are above the mean for a normal curve. For example, for the Z score of .57, the % Mean to Z value is 21.57 percent and the % in Tail value is 28.43 percent, and 21.56% + 28.43% = 50.00%.

normal curve table Table showing percentages of scores associated with the normal curve; the table usually includes percentages of scores between the mean and various numbers of standard deviations above the mean and percentages of scores more positive than various numbers of standard deviations above the mean.

TIP FOR SUCCESS
Remember that negative Z scores are scores below the mean and positive Z scores are scores above the mean.

Suppose you want to know the percentage of scores between the mean and a *Z* score of .64. You just look up .64 in the "*Z*" column of the table and the "% Mean to *Z*" column tells you that 23.89 percent of the scores in a normal curve are between the mean and this *Z* score. These values are highlighted in Table 4–1.

You can also reverse the process and use the table to find the *Z* score for a particular percentage of scores. For example, imagine that 30 percent of ninth-grade students had a creativity score higher than Janice's. Assuming that creativity scores follow a normal curve, you can figure out her *Z* score as follows: If 30 percent of students scored higher than her, then 30 percent of the scores are in the tail above her score. This is shown in Figure 4–4. So, you would look at the "% in Tail" column of the table until you found the percentage that was closest to 30 percent. In this example, the closest is 30.15 percent. Finally, you would look at the "*Z*" column to the left of this percentage, which lists a *Z* score of .52 (these values of 30.15% and .52 are highlighted in Table 4–1). Thus, Janice's *Z* score for her level of creativity is .52. If you

Table 4–1 Normal Curve Areas: Percentage of the Normal Curve Between the Mean and the *Z* Scores Shown and Percentage of Scores in the Tail for the *Z* Scores Shown. (First part of table only: full table is Table A-1 in the Appendix. Highlighted values are examples from the text.)

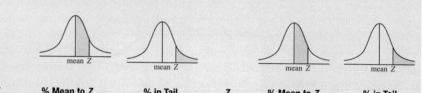

Z	% Mean to Z	% in Tail	Z	% Mean to Z	% in Tail
.00	.00	50.00	.45	17.36	32.64
.01	.40	49.60	.46	17.72	32.28
.02	.80	49.20	.47	18.08	31.92
.03	1.20	48.80	.48	18.44	31.56
.04	1.60	48.40	.49	18.79	31.21
.05	1.99	48.01	.50	19.15	30.85
.06	2.39	47.61	.51	19.50	30.50
.07	2.79	47.21	.52	19.85	30.15
.08	3.19	46.81	.53	20.19	29.81
.09	3.59	46.41	.54	20.54	29.46
.10	3.98	46.02	.55	20.88	29.12
.11	4.38	45.62	.56	21.23	28.77
.12	4.78	45.22	.57	21.57	28.43
.13	5.17	44.83	.58	21.90	28.10
.14	5.57	44.43	.59	22.24	27.76
.15	5.96	44.04	.60	22.57	27.43
.16	6.36	43.64	.61	22.91	27.09
.17	6.75	43.25	.62	23.24	26.76
.18	7.14	42.86	.63	23.57	26.43
.19	7.53	42.47	.64	23.89	26.11
.20	7.93	42.07	.65	24.22	25.78
.21	8.32	41.68	.66	24.54	25.46

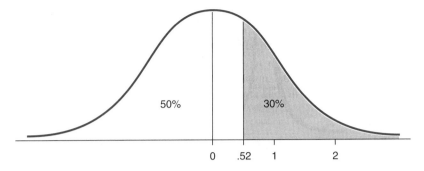

Figure 4-4 Distribution of creativity test scores showing area for top 30% and Z score where this area begins.

know the mean and standard deviation for ninth-grade students' creativity scores, you can figure out Janice's actual raw score on the test by changing her Z score of .52 to a raw score using the usual formula, $X = (Z)(SD) + (M)$.

Steps for Figuring the Percentage of Scores above or below a Particular Raw Score or *Z* Score Using the Normal Curve Table

Here are the five steps for figuring percentage of scores.

❶ **If you are beginning with a raw score, first change it to a Z score.** Use the usual formula, $Z = (X - M)/SD$.

❷ **Draw a picture of the normal curve, where the Z score falls on it, and shade in the area for which you are finding the percentage.** (When marking where the Z score falls on the normal curve, be sure to put it in the right place above or below the mean according to whether it is a positive or negative Z score.)

❸ **Make a rough estimate of the shaded area's percentage based on the 50%–34%–14% percentages.** You don't need to be very exact—it is enough just to estimate a range in which the shaded area has to fall, figuring it is between two particular whole Z scores.

❹ **Find the exact percentage using the normal curve table, adding 50% if necessary.** Look up the Z score in the "Z" column of Table A–1 and find the percentage in the "% Mean to Z" column or "% in Tail" next to it. If you want the percent of scores between the mean and this Z score, the percentage in the table is your final answer. However, sometimes you need to add 50% to the percentage in the table. You need to do this if the Z score is positive and you want the total percent below this Z score, or if the Z score is negative and you want the total percent above this Z score.

   You don't need to memorize these rules. It is much easier to make a picture for the problem and reason out whether the percentage you have from the table is correct as is, or if you need to add 50%.

❺ **Check that your exact percentage is within the range of your rough estimate from Step ❸.**

Examples

Here are two examples using IQ scores where $M = 100$ and $SD = 16$.

   Example 1: If a person has an IQ of 125, what percentage of people have higher IQs?

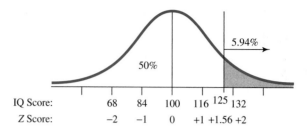

Figure 4-5 Distribution of IQ scores showing percentage of scores above an IQ score of 125 (shaded area).

❶ **If you are beginning with a raw score, first change it to a Z score.** Using the usual formula, $Z = (X - M)/SD$, $Z = (125 - 100)/16 = +1.56$.

❷ **Draw a picture of the normal curve, where the Z score falls on it, and shade in the area for which you are finding the percentage.** This is shown in Figure 4–5 (along with the exact percentages figured later).

❸ **Make a rough estimate of the shaded area's percentage based on the 50%–34%–14% percentages.** If the shaded area started at a Z score of 1, it would have 16% above it. If it started at a Z score of 2, it would have only 2% above it. So, with a Z score of 1.56, it has to be somewhere between 16% and 2%.

❹ **Find the exact percentage using the normal curve table, adding 50% if necessary.** In Table A–1, 1.56 in the "*Z*" column goes with 5.94 in the "% in Tail" column. Thus, 5.94% of people have IQ scores higher than 125. This is the answer to our problem. (There is no need to add 50% to the percentage.)

❺ **Check that your exact percentage is within the range of your rough estimate from Step ❸.** Our result, 5.94%, is within the 16% to 2% range we estimated.

Example 2: If a person has an IQ of 95, what percentage of people have higher IQs than this person?

❶ **If you are beginning with a raw score, first change it to a Z score.** Using the usual formula, $Z = (95 - 100)/16 = -.31$.

❷ **Draw a picture of the normal curve, where the Z score falls on it, and shade in the area for which you are finding the percentage.** This is shown in Figure 4–6 (along with the exact percentages figured later).

❸ **Make a rough estimate of the shaded area's percentage based on the 50%–34%–14% percentages.** You know that 34% of the scores are between the mean and a Z score of −1. Also, 50% of the curve is above the mean. Thus, this Z score of −.31 has to have between 50% and 84% of scores above it.

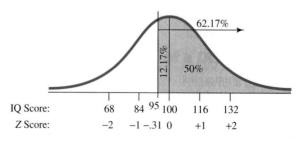

Figure 4-6 Distribution of IQ scores showing percentage of scores above an IQ score of 95 (shaded area.)

❹ **Find the exact percentage using the normal curve table, adding 50% if necessary.** The table shows that 12.17% of scores are between the mean and a Z score of .31. Thus, the percentage of scores above a Z score of −.31 is the 12.17% between the Z score and the mean plus the 50% above the mean, which is 62.17%.

❺ **Check that your exact percentage is within the range of your rough estimate from Step ❸.** Our result of 62.17% is within the 50% to 84% range.

Figuring Z Scores and Raw Scores from Percentages Using the Normal Curve Table

Going from a percentage to a Z score or raw score is similar to going from a Z score or raw score to a percentage. However, you reverse the procedure for the part of figuring the exact percentage. Also, any necessary changes from a Z score to a raw score are done at the end.

Here are the five steps.

❶ **Draw a picture of the normal curve and shade in the approximate area for your percentage using the 50%–34%–14% percentages.**

❷ **Make a rough estimate of the Z score where the shaded area stops.**

❸ **Find the exact Z score using the normal curve table (subtracting 50% from your percentage if necessary before looking up the Z score).** Looking at your picture, figure out the percentage in the shaded tail, or the percentage between the mean and where the shading stops. For example, if your percentage is the bottom 35%, then the percentage in the shaded tail is 35%. Figuring the percentage between the mean and where the shading stops will sometimes involve subtracting 50% from the percentage in the problem. For example, if your percentage is the top 72%, then the percentage from the mean to where that shading stops is 22% (that is, 72% − 50% = 22%).

Once you have the percentage, look up the closest percentage in the appropriate column of the normal curve table ("% Mean to Z" or "% in Tail") and find the Z score for that percentage. That Z will be your answer—except it may be negative. The best way to tell if it is positive or negative is by looking at your picture.

❹ **Check that your exact Z score is within the range of your rough estimate from Step ❷.**

❺ **If you want to find a raw score, change it from the Z score.** Use the usual formula, $X = (Z)(SD) + M$.

Examples

Here are three examples. Once again, we will use IQ for our examples, where $M = 100$ and $SD = 16$.

Example 1: What IQ score would a person need to be in the top 5%?

❶ **Draw a picture of the normal curve and shade in the approximate area for your percentage using the 50%–34%–14% percentages.** We wanted the top 5%. Thus, the shading has to begin above (to the right of) 1 *SD* (there are 16% of scores above 1 *SD*). However, it cannot start above 2 *SD* because only 2% of all the scores are above 2 *SD*. But 5% is a lot closer to 2% than to 16%. Thus, you would start shading a small way to the left of the 2 *SD* point. This is shown in Figure 4–7.

❷ **Make a rough estimate of the Z score where the shaded area stops.** The Z score has to be between +1 and +2.

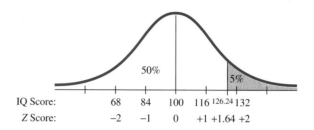

IQ Score: 68   84   100   116   126.24 132

Z Score: −2   −1   0   +1 +1.64 +2

Figure 4–7   Finding the Z score and IQ raw score for where the top 5% starts.

❸ **Find the exact Z score using the normal curve table (subtracting 50% from your percentage if necessary before looking up the Z score).** We want the top 5%, so we can use the "% in Tail" column of the normal curve table. Looking in that column, the closest percentage to 5% is 5.05% (or you could use 4.95%). This goes with a Z score of 1.64 in the "Z" column.

❹ **Check that your exact Z score is within the range of your rough estimate from Step ❷.** As we estimated, +1.64 is between +1 and +2 (and closer to 2).

❺ **If you want to find a raw score, change it from the Z score.** Using the formula, $X = (Z)(SD) + M = (1.64)(16) + 100 = 126.24$. In sum, to be in the top 5%, a person would need an IQ of at least 126.24.

Example 2: What IQ score would a person need to be in the top 55%?

❶ **Draw a picture of the normal curve and shade in the approximate area for your percentage using the 50%–34%–14% percentages.** You want the top 55%. There are 50% of scores above the mean. So, the shading has to begin below (to the left of) the mean. There are 34% of scores between the mean and 1 *SD* below the mean, so the score is between the mean and 1 *SD* below the mean. You would shade the area to the right of that point. This is shown in Figure 4–8.

❷ **Make a rough estimate of the Z score where the shaded area stops.** The Z score has to be between 0 and −1.

❸ **Find the exact Z score using the normal curve table (subtracting 50% from your percentage if necessary before looking up the Z score).** Being in the top 55% means that 5% of people have IQs between this IQ and the mean (that is, 55% − 50% = 5%). In the normal curve table, the closest percentage to 5% in the "% Mean to Z" column is 5.17%, which goes with a Z score of .13. Because you are below the mean, this becomes −.13.

❹ **Check that your exact Z score is within the range of your rough estimate from Step ❷.** As we estimated, −.13 is between 0 and −1.

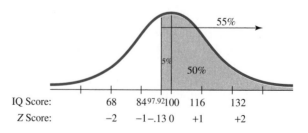

IQ Score: 68   84 97.92 100   116   132

Z Score: −2   −1 −.13 0   +1   +2

Figure 4–8   Finding the IQ score for where the top 55% start.

❺ **If you want to find a raw score, change it from the Z score.** Using the usual formula, $X = (-.13)(16) + 100 = 97.92$. So, to be in the top 55% on IQ, a person needs an IQ score of 97.92 or higher.

Example 3: What range of IQ scores includes the 95% of people in the middle range of IQ scores?

This kind of problem, of finding the middle percentage, may seem odd. However, it is actually a very common situation used in procedures you will learn in later chapters. Think of this kind of problem in terms of finding the scores that go with the upper and lower ends of this percentage. Thus, in this example, you are trying to find the points where the bottom 2.5% ends and the top 2.5% begins (which, out of 100%, leaves the middle 95%).

❶ **Draw a picture of the normal curve, and shade in the approximate area for your percentage using the 50%–34%–14% percentages.** Let's start with the point where the top 2.5% begins. This has to be higher than 1 *SD* (there are 16% of scores higher than 1 *SD*). However, it cannot start above 2 *SD* because there are only 2% of scores above 2 *SD*. But 2.5% is very close to 2%. Thus, the top 2.5% starts just to the left of the 2 *SD* point. Similarly, the point where the bottom 2.5% comes in is just to the right of -2 *SD*. The result of all this is that we will shade in the area starting just above -2 *SD* and continue shading up to just below $+2$ *SD*. This is shown in Figure 4–9.

❷ **Make a rough estimate of the Z score where the shaded area stops.** You can see from the picture that the Z score for where the shaded area stops above the mean is just below $+2$. Similarly, the Z score for where the shaded area stops below the mean is just above -2.

❸ **Find the exact Z score using the normal curve table (subtracting 50% from your percentage if necessary before looking up the Z score).** Being in the top 2.5% means that 2.5% of the IQ scores are in the upper tail. In the normal curve table, the closest percentage to 2.5% in the "% in Tail" column is exactly 2.50%, which goes with a Z score of $+1.96$. The normal curve is symmetrical. Thus, the Z score for the lower tail is -1.96.

❹ **Check that your exact Z score is within the range of your rough estimate from Step ❷.** As we estimated, $+1.96$ is between $+1$ and $+2$ and is very close to $+2$, and -1.96 is between -1 and -2 and very close to -2.

❺ **If you want to find a raw score, change it from the Z score.** For the high end, using the usual formula, $X = (1.96)(16) + 100 = 131.36$. For the low end, $X = (-1.96)(16) + 100 = 68.64$. In sum, the middle 95% of IQ scores run from 68.64 to 131.36.

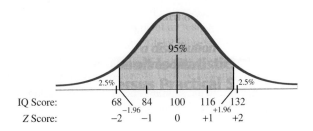

Figure 4-9   Finding the IQ scores for where the middle 95% of scores begin and end.

How are you doing?

1. Why is the normal curve (or at least a curve that is symmetrical and unimodal) so common in nature?
2. Without using a normal curve table, about what percentage of scores on a normal curve are (a) above the mean, (b) between the mean and 1 *SD* above the mean, (c) between 1 and 2 *SD*s above the mean, (d) below the mean, (e) between the mean and 1 *SD* below the mean, and (f) between 1 and 2 *SD*s below the mean?
3. Without using a normal curve table, about what percentage of scores on a normal curve are (a) between the mean and 2 *SD*s above the mean, (b) below 1 *SD* above the mean, (c) above 2 *SD*s below the mean?
4. Without using a normal curve table, about what *Z* score would a person have who is at the start of the top (a) 50%, (b) 16%, (c) 84%, (d) 2%?
5. Using the normal curve table, what percentage of scores are (a) between the mean and a *Z* score of 2.14, (b) above 2.14, (c) below 2.14?
6. Using the normal curve table, what *Z* score would you have if (a) 20% are above you, (b) 80% are below you?

Answers

1. It is common because any particular score is the result of the random combination of many effects, some of which make the score larger and some of which make the score smaller. Thus, on average these effects balance out to produce scores near the middle, with relatively few scores at each extreme, because it is unlikely for most of the increasing or decreasing effects to come out in the same direction.
2. (a) 50%, (b) 34%, (c) 14%, (d) 50%, (e) 34%, (f) 14%.
3. (a) 48%, (b) 84%, (c) 98%.
4. (a) 0, (b) 1, (c) −1, (d) 2.
5. (a) 48.38%, (b) 1.62%, (c) 98.38%.
6. (a) .84, (b) .84.

---

population Entire group of people to which a researcher intends the results of a study to apply; the larger group to which inferences are made on the basis of the particular set of people (sample) studied.

sample Scores of the particular group of people studied; usually considered to be representative of the scores in some larger population.

Sample and Population

We are going to introduce you to some important ideas by thinking of beans. Suppose you are cooking a pot of beans and taste a spoonful to see if they are done. In this example, the pot of beans is a **population,** the entire set of things of interest. The spoonful is a **sample,** the part of the population about which you actually have information. This is shown in Figure 4–10a. Figures 4–10b and 4–10c are other ways of showing the relation of a sample to a population.

In behavioral and social science research, we typically study samples not of beans but of individuals to make inferences about some larger group. A sample might consist of 50 Canadian women who participate in a particular experiment; but the population might be intended to be all Canadian women. In an opinion survey, 1,000 people might be selected from the voting-age population and asked for whom they plan to vote. The opinions of these 1,000 people are the sample. The opinions of the larger voting public, to which the pollsters hope to apply their results, is the population (see Figure 4–11).[1]

---

[1]Strictly speaking, *population* and *sample* refer to scores (numbers or measurements), not to the people who have those scores. In the first example, the sample is really the scores of the 50 Canadian women, not the 50 women themselves, and the population is really what the *scores* would be if all Canadian women were tested.

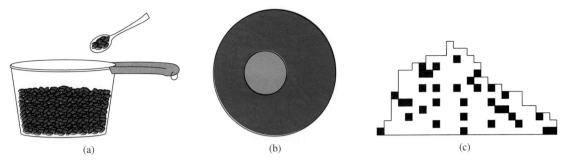

Figure 4–10 Populations and samples: In (a), the entire pot of beans is the population and the spoonful is a sample. In (b), the entire larger circle is the population and the circle within it is the sample. In (c), the histogram is of the population and the particular shaded scores together make up the sample.

Why Samples Instead of Populations Are Studied

If you want to know something about a population, your results would be most accurate if you could study the *entire population* rather than a *subgroup* from that population. However, in most research situations this is not practical. More important, the whole point of research is usually to be able to make generalizations or predictions about events beyond our reach. We would not call it research if you tested three particular cars to see which gets better gas mileage—unless you hoped to say something about the gas mileage of those models of cars in general. In other words, a researcher might do an experiment on the effect of a particular new method of teaching geography using 40 eighth-grade students as participants in the experiment. But the purpose of the experiment is not to find out how these *particular 40 students* respond to the experimental condition. Rather, the purpose is to learn something about how *eighth-grade students in general* respond to the new method of teaching geography.

The strategy in almost all behavioral and social science research is to study a sample of individuals who are believed to be representative of the general population (or of some particular population of interest). More realistically, researchers try to study people who do not differ from the general population in any systematic way that should matter for that topic of research.

The sample is what is studied, and the population is an unknown that researchers draw conclusions about on the basis of the sample. Most of what you learn in the rest of this book is about the important work of drawing conclusions about populations based on information from samples.

Methods of Sampling

Usually, the ideal method of picking out a sample to study is called **random selection.** The researcher starts with a complete list of the population and randomly selects some of them to study. An example of a random method of selection would be to put each name on a table tennis ball, put all the balls into a big hopper, shake it up, and have a blindfolded person select as many as are needed. (In practice, most researchers use a computer-generated list of random numbers.)

It is important not to confuse truly random selection with what might be called **haphazard selection;** for example, just taking whoever is available or happens to be first on a list. When using haphazard selection, it is surprisingly easy accidentally to pick a group of people to study that is really quite different from the population as a whole. Consider a survey of attitudes about your statistics instructor. Suppose you

random selection Method for selecting a sample that uses truly random procedures (usually meaning that each person in the population has an equal chance of being selected); one procedure is for the researcher to begin with a complete list of all the people in the population and select a group of them to study using a table of random numbers.

haphazard selection Procedure of selecting a sample of individuals to study by taking whoever is available or happens to be first on a list.

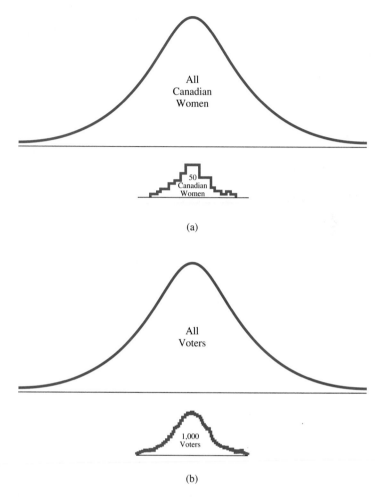

Figure 4-11   Additional examples of populations and samples. In (a), the population is the scores of all Canadian women and the sample is the scores of the 50 particular Canadian women studied. In (b), the population is the voting preferences of the entire voting-age population and the sample is the voting preferences of the 1,000 voting-age people who were surveyed.

give your questionnaire only to other students sitting near you in class. Such a survey would be affected by all the things that influence where students choose to sit, some of which have to do with just what you are studying—how much they like the instructor or the class. (Thus, asking students who sit near you would likely result in opinions more like your own than a truly random sample would.)

Unfortunately, it is often impractical or impossible to study a truly random sample. One problem is that we do not usually have a complete list of the full population. Another problem is that not everyone a researcher approaches agrees to participate in the study. Yet another problem is the cost and difficulty of tracking down people who live in remote places. For these and other reasons as well, behavioral and social scientists use various approximations to truly random samples that are more practical. However, researchers are consistently careful to rule out, as much as possible in advance, any systematic influence on who gets selected. Once the study has begun, researchers are constantly on the alert for any ways in which the sample may be systematically different from the population. For example, in much experimental research in education and psychology, it is common to use volunteer college students as the participants in the study. This is done for practical reasons and because often the topics studied in these experiments (for example, how short-term memory works) are thought to be relatively consistent across different types of people. Yet even in these cases, researchers avoid, for example, selecting people with a special interest in their research topic. Such researchers are also very aware that their results may not apply beyond college students, volunteers, people from their region, and so forth.

Statistical Terminology for Samples and Populations

The mean, variance, and standard deviation of a population are called **population parameters.** A population parameter usually is unknown and can only be estimated from what you know about a sample taken from that population. You do not taste all the beans, just the spoonful. "The beans are done" is an inference about the whole pot.

In this book, when referring to the population mean, standard deviation, or variance, even in formulas, we use the word "Population"[2] before the M, SD^2, or SD. The mean, variance, and standard deviation you figure for the scores in a sample are called **sample statistics.** A sample statistic is figured from known information. Sample statistics are what we have been calculating all along. Sample statistics use the symbols we have been using all along: M, SD^2, and SD.

population parameter Actual value of the mean, standard deviation, and so on, for the population (usually population parameters are not known, though often they are estimated based on information in samples).

sample statistic Descriptive statistic, such as the mean or standard deviation, figured from the scores in a particular group of people studied.

How are you doing?

1. Explain the difference between the population and a sample for a research study.
2. Why do behavioral and social scientists usually study samples and not populations?
3. Explain the difference between random sampling and haphazard sampling.
4. Explain the difference between a population parameter and a sample statistic.

Answers

1. The population is the entire group to which results of a study are intended to apply. The sample is the particular, smaller group of individuals actually studied.
2. It is not practical in most cases to study the entire population.
3. In random sampling, the sample is chosen from among the population using a completely random method, so that any particular individual has an equal chance of being included in the sample. In haphazard sampling, the researcher selects individuals who are easily available or are convenient to study.
4. A population parameter is about the population (such as the mean of all the scores in the population); a sample statistic is about a particular sample (such as the mean of the scores of the people in the sample).

Probability

The purpose of most research in the behavioral and social sciences is to examine the truth of a theory or the effectiveness of a procedure. But scientific research of any kind can only make that truth or effectiveness seem more or less likely; it cannot give

---

[2]In statistics writing, it is common to use Greek letters for population parameters. For example, the population mean is μ ("mu") and the population standard deviation is σ (lower case "sigma") However, we have not used these symbols in this text, wanting to make it easier for students to grasp the formulas without also having to deal with Greek letters.

BOX 4–1   **Surveys, Polls, and 1948's Costly "Free Sample"**

It is time to make you a more informed reader of polls in the media. Usually the results of properly done public polls will be accompanied, somewhere in fine print, by a statement like "From a telephone poll of 1,000 American adults taken on June 4 and 5. Sampling error ± 3%." What does all this mean?

The Gallup poll is as good an example as any (Gallup, 1972; see also *http://www.galluppoll.com*), and there is no better place to begin than 1948, when all three of the major polling organizations—Gallup, Crossley (for Hearst papers), and Roper (for *Fortune*)—wrongly predicted Thomas Dewey's victory over Harry Truman for the U.S. presidency. Yet Gallup's prediction was based on 50,000 interviews and Roper's on 15,000. By contrast, to predict George H. W. Bush's 1988 victory, Gallup used only 4,089. Since 1952, the pollsters have never used more than 8,144—but with very small error and no outright mistakes. What has changed?

The method used before 1948, and never repeated since, was called "quota sampling." Interviewers were assigned a fixed number of persons to interview, with strict quotas to fill in all the categories that seemed important, such as residence, sex, age, race, and economic status. Within these specifics, however, they were free to interview whomever they liked. Republicans generally tended to be easier to interview. They were more likely to have telephones and permanent addresses and to live in better houses and better neighborhoods. In 1948, the election was very close, and the Republican bias produced the embarrassing mistake that changed survey methods forever.

Since 1948, all survey organizations have used what is called a "probability method." Simple random sampling is the purest case of the probability method, but simple random sampling for a survey about a U.S. presidential election would require drawing names from a list of all the eligible voters in the nation—a lot of people. Each person selected would have to be found, in diversely scattered locales. So instead, "multistage cluster sampling" is used. The United States is divided into seven size-of-community groupings, from large cities to rural open country; these groupings are divided into seven geographic regions (New England, Middle Atlantic, and so on), after which smaller equal-sized groups are zoned, and then city blocks are drawn from the zones, with the probability of selection being proportional to the size of the population or number of dwelling units. Finally, an interviewer is given a randomly selected starting point on the map and is required to follow a given direction, taking households in sequence.

Actually, telephoning is often the favored method for polling today. Phone surveys cost about one-third of door-to-door polls. Since most people now own phones, this method is less biased than in Truman's time. Phoning also allows computers to randomly dial phone numbers and, unlike telephone directories, this method calls unlisted numbers. However, survey organizations in the United States are not allowed to call cell phone numbers. Thus, the 8% of U.S. households that use a cell phone for all calls and do not have a home phone are not included in telephone opinion polls. Most survey organizations consider the current cell-phone-only rate to be low enough not to cause large biases in poll results (especially since the demographic characteristics of individuals without a home phone suggest that they are less likely to vote than individuals who live in households with a home phone). However, anticipated future increases in the cell-phone-only rate will likely make this an important issue for opinion polls. Survey organizations will need to consider additional polling methods, perhaps using the Internet and email.

Whether by telephone or face to face, there will be about 35% nonrespondents after three attempts. This creates yet another bias, dealt with through questions about how much time a person spends at home, so that a slight extra weight can be given to the responses of those reached but usually at home less, to make up for those missed entirely.

Now you know quite a bit about opinion polls, but we have left two important questions unanswered: Why are only about 1,000 included in a poll meant to describe all U.S. adults, and what does the term *sampling error* mean? For these answers, you must wait for Chapter 6 (Box 6–1).

---

us the luxury of knowing for certain. Probability is very important in science. In particular, probability is very important in *inferential statistics,* the methods behavioral and social scientists use to go from results of research studies to conclusions about theories or applied procedures.

Probability has been studied for centuries by mathematicians and philosophers. Yet even today, the topic is full of controversy. Fortunately, however, you need to know only a few key ideas to understand and carry out the inferential statistical procedures you learn in this book.[3] These few key points are not very difficult—indeed, some students find them obvious.

In statistics, we usually define **probability** as the expected relative frequency of a particular outcome. An **outcome** is the result of an experiment (or just about any situation in which the result is not known in advance, such as a coin coming up heads or it raining tomorrow). *Frequency* is how many times something happens. The *relative frequency* is the number of times something happens relative to the number of times it could have happened. That is, relative frequency is the proportion of times it happens. (A coin might come up heads 8 times out of 12 flips, for a relative frequency of 8/12, or 2/3.) **Expected relative frequency** is what you expect to get in the long run, if you repeated the experiment many times. (In the case of a coin, in the long run you expect to get 1/2 heads.) This is called the **long-run relative-frequency interpretation of probability.**

probability   Expected relative frequency of a particular outcome; the proportion of successful outcomes to all outcomes.

outcome   Term used in discussing probability for the result of an experiment (or almost any event, such as a coin coming up heads or it raining tomorrow).

expected relative frequency   In figuring probabilities, number of successful outcomes divided by the number of total outcomes you would expect to get if you repeated an experiment a large number of times.

long-run relative-frequency interpretation of probability   Understanding of probability as the proportion of a particular outcome that you would get if the experiment were repeated many times.

Figuring Probabilities

Probabilities are usually figured as the proportion of successful possible outcomes, the number of possible successful outcomes divided by the number of *all* possible outcomes. That is,

$$\text{Probability} = \frac{\text{Possible successful outcomes}}{\text{All possible outcomes}}$$

Consider the probability of getting heads when flipping a coin. There is one possible successful outcome (getting heads) out of two possible outcomes (getting heads or getting tails). This makes a probability of 1/2, or .5. In a throw of a single die, the probability of a 2 (or any other particular side of the die) is 1/6, or .17. This is because there is one possible successful outcome out of six possible outcomes of any kind. The probability of throwing a die and getting a number 3 or lower is 3/6, or .5. There are three possible successful outcomes (a 1, a 2, or a 3) out of six possible outcomes.

Now consider a slightly more complicated example. Suppose a class has 200 people in it, and 30 are seniors. If you were to pick someone from the class at random, the probability of picking a senior would be 30/200, or .15. This is because there are 30 possible successful outcomes (getting a senior) out of 200 possible outcomes.

Steps for Figuring Probabilities

There are three steps for figuring probabilities.

❶ **Determine the number of possible successful outcomes.**
❷ **Determine the number of all possible outcomes.**
❸ **Divide the number of possible successful outcomes (Step ❶) by the number of all possible outcomes (Step ❷).**

Applying these three steps to the probability of getting a number 3 or lower on a throw of a die,

---

[3]There are, of course, many probability topics that are not related to statistics and other topics related to statistics that are not important for the kinds of statistics used in the social and behavioral sciences. For example, computing joint and conditional probabilities, which is covered in many statistics books, is not covered here because it is rarely seen in published research in the social and behavioral sciences and is not necessary for an intuitive grasp of the logic of the major inferential statistical methods covered in this book.

p   Probability.

❶ **Determine the number of possible successful outcomes.** There are three outcomes of 3 or lower—a 1, 2, or 3.
❷ **Determine the number of possible outcomes.** There are six possible outcomes in the throw of a die—a 1, 2, 3, 4, 5, or 6.
❸ **Divide the number of possible successful outcomes (Step ❶) by the number of all possible outcomes (Step ❷). 3/6 = .5.**

Range of Probabilities

A probability is a proportion, the number of possible successful outcomes to the total number of possible outcomes. A proportion cannot be less than 0 or greater than 1. In terms of percentages, proportions range from 0% to 100%. Something that has no chance of happening has a probability of 0, and something that is certain to happen has a probability of 1. Notice that when the probability of an event is 0, the event is completely *impossible;* it cannot happen. But when the probability of an event is low, say .05 (5%) or even .01 (1%), the event is *improbable* or *unlikely,* but not impossible.

"p" for Probability

Probability usually is symbolized by the letter ***p.*** The actual probability number is usually given as a decimal, though sometimes fractions are used. A 50–50 chance is usually written as $p = .5$, but it could also be written as $p = 1/2$ or $p = 50\%$. It is also common to see a probability written as being less than some number using the "less than" sign. For example, $p < .05$ means "the probability is less than .05."

Probability, *Z* Scores, and the Normal Distribution

So far, we have mainly discussed probabilities of specific events that might or might not happen. We also can talk about a range of events that might or might not happen. The throw of a die coming out 3 or lower is an example (it includes the range 1, 2, and 3). Another example is the probability of selecting someone on a city street who is between the ages of 30 and 40.

If you think of probability in terms of proportion of scores, probability fits in well with frequency distributions (see Chapter 1). In the frequency distribution shown in Figure 4–12, 3 of the total of 50 people scored 9 or 10. If you were selecting people from this group of 50 at random, there would be 3 chances (possible successful

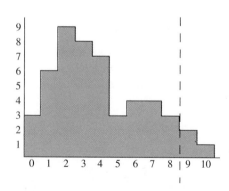

Figure 4–12   Frequency distribution (shown as a histogram) of 50 people in which $p = .06$ (3/50) of randomly selecting a person with a score of 9 or 10.

outcomes) out of 50 (all possible outcomes) of selecting one that was 9 or 10, so $p = 3/50 = .06$.

You can also think of the normal distribution as a probability distribution. With a normal curve, the percentage of scores between any two Z scores is known. The percentage of scores between any two Z scores is the same as the probability of selecting a score between those two Z scores. As you saw earlier in this chapter, approximately 34% of scores are between the mean and 1 standard deviation from the mean. You should therefore not be surprised to learn that the probability of a score being between the mean and a Z score of +1 (1 standard deviation above the mean) is .34 (that is, $p = .34$).

In one of the earlier examples in the normal curve section of this chapter, we figured that 95% of the scores in a normal curve are between a Z score of +1.96 and a Z score of -1.96 (see Figure 4–9). Thus, if you were to select a score at random from a distribution that follows a normal curve, the probability of selecting a score *between* Z scores of +1.96 and -1.96 is .95 (that is, a 95% chance). This is a very high probability. Also, the probability of selecting a score from such a distribution that is either *greater* than a Z score of +1.96 or *less than* a Z score of -1.96 is .05 (that is, a 5% chance). This is a very low probability. It helps to think about this visually. So, if you look back to Figure 4–9 on page 129, the .05 probability of selecting a score that is either *greater* than a Z score of +1.96 or *less than* a Z score of -1.96 is represented by the unshaded tail areas in the figure. The probability of a score being in the tail of a normal curve is a topic you will learn more about in the next chapter.

Probability, Samples, and Populations.   Probability is also relevant to samples and populations. You will learn more about this topic in Chapters 5 and 6, but we will use an example to give you a sense of the role of probability in samples and populations. Imagine you are told that a sample of one person has a score of 4 on a certain measure. However, you do not know whether this person is from a population of women or a population of men. You are told that a population of women has scores on this measure that are normally distributed with a mean of 10 and a standard deviation of 3. How likely do you think it is that your sample of 1 person comes from this population of women? From your knowledge of the normal curve (see Figure 4–2), you know there are very few scores as low as 4 in a normal distribution that has a mean of 10 and a standard deviation of 3. So, there is a very low likelihood that this person comes from the population of women. Now, what if the sample person had a score of 9? In this case, there is a much greater likelihood that this person comes from the population of women, as there are many scores of 9 in that population. This kind of reasoning provides an introduction to the process of *hypothesis testing* that is the focus of the remainder of the book.

How are you doing?

1. The probability of an event is defined as the expected relative frequency of a particular outcome. Explain what is meant by (a) relative frequency and (b) outcome.
2. Suppose you have 400 pennies in a jar and 40 of them are more than 9 years old. You then mix up the pennies and pull one out. (a) What is the probability of getting one that is more than 9 years old? In this problem, (b) what is the number of possible successful outcomes? and (c) what is the number of all possible outcomes?

3. Suppose people's scores on a particular measure are normally distributed with a mean of 50 and a standard deviation of 10. If you were to pick a person completely at random, what is the probability you would pick someone with a score on this measure higher than 60?
4. What is meant by $p < .01$?

Normal Curves, Samples and Populations, and Probabilities in Research Articles

You need to understand the topics we covered in this chapter to learn what comes next. However, the topics of this chapter are rarely mentioned directly in research articles (except articles *about* methods or statistics). Sometimes you will see the normal curve mentioned, usually when a researcher is describing the pattern of scores on a particular variable. (We talk more about this and give some examples from research articles in Chapter 11, where we consider circumstances in which the scores do not follow a normal curve.)

Probability is also rarely discussed directly, except in relation to statistical significance, a topic we mentioned briefly in Chapter 3. In almost any article you look at, the Results section will have many descriptions of various methods associated with statistical significance, followed by something like "$p < .05$" or "$p < .01$." The p refers to probability, but the probability of what? That is the main topic of our discussion of statistical significance in Chapter 5.

Finally, you will sometimes see a brief mention of the method of selecting the sample from the population. For example, Viswanath and colleagues (2006) used data from the U.S. National Cancer Institute (NCI) Health Information National Trends Survey (HINTS) to examine differences in knowledge about cancer across individuals from varying socioeconomic and racial/ethnic groups. Their report was published in the *Journal of Health Communication.* They described the method of their study as follows:

> The data from this study come from the NCI HINTS, based on a random-digit-dial (RDD) sample of all working telephones in the United States. One adult was selected at random within each household using the most recent birthday method in the case of more than three adults in a given household. . . . Vigorous efforts were made to increase response rates through advanced letters and $2 incentives to selected households. (p. 4)

Whenever possible, researchers report the proportion of individuals approached for the study who actually participated in the study. This is called the *response rate.* Viswanath and colleagues noted that "The final sample size was 6,369, yielding a response rate of 55%. . . ." (p. 4).

Researchers sometimes also check whether their sample is similar to the population as a whole, based on any information they may have about the overall population. For example, Schuster and colleagues (2001) conducted a national survey of stress reactions of U.S. adults after the September 11, 2001, terrorist attacks. In this study, the researchers compared their sample to 2001 census records and reported that the "sample slightly overrepresented women, non-Hispanic whites, and persons with higher levels of education and income" (p. 1507). Schuster and colleagues went on to note that overrepresentation of these groups "is typical of samples selected by means of random-digit dialing" (pp. 1507–1508).

Summary

1. The scores on many variables in behavioral and social science research approximately follow a bell-shaped, symmetrical, unimodal distribution called the *normal curve* (or *normal distribution*). Because the shape of this curve follows an exact mathematical formula, there is a specific percentage of scores between any two points on a normal curve.

2. A useful working rule for normal curves is that 50% of the scores are above the mean, 34% are between the mean and 1 standard deviation above the mean, and 14% are between 1 and 2 standard deviations above the mean.

3. A normal curve table gives the percentage of scores between the mean and any particular Z score, and the percentage of scores in the tail for any Z score. Using this table, and knowing that the curve is symmetrical and that 50% of the scores are above the mean, you can figure the percentage of scores above or below any particular Z score. You can also use the table to figure the Z score for the point where a particular percentage of scores begins or ends.

4. A *sample* is an individual or group that is studied—usually as representative of a larger group or *population* that cannot be studied in its entirety. Ideally, the sample is selected from a population using a strictly random procedure. The mean, variance, and so forth of a sample are called *sample statistics*. When of a population, they are called *population parameters*.

5. Most behavioral and social scientists consider the probability of an event to be its expected relative frequency. Probability is figured as the proportion of successful outcomes to total possible outcomes. It is symbolized by *p* and has a range from 0 (event is impossible) to 1 (event is certain). The normal curve provides a way to know the probabilities of scores' being within particular ranges of values.

6. Research articles rarely discuss normal curves (except briefly when the variable being studied seems not to follow a normal curve) or probability (except in relation to statistical significance). Procedures of sampling are sometimes described, particularly when the study is a survey, and the representativeness of a sample may also be discussed.

Key Terms

normal distribution (p. 121)
normal curve (p. 121)
normal curve table (p. 123)
population (p. 130)
sample (p. 130)

random selection (p. 131)
haphazard selection (p. 131)
population parameters (p. 133)
sample statistic (p. 133)
probability (*p*) (p. 135)

outcome (p. 135)
expected relative frequency (p. 135)
long-run relative-frequency interpretation of probability (p. 135)

Example Worked-Out Problems

Figuring the Percentage above or below a Particular Raw Score or *Z* Score

Suppose a test of sensitivity to violence is known to have a mean of 20, a standard deviation of 3, and to follow a normal curve. What percentage of people have scores above 24?

Answer

❶ **If you are beginning with a raw score, first change it to a *Z* score.** Using the usual formula, $Z = (X - M)/SD$, $Z = (24 - 20)/3 = 1.33$.

❷ **Draw a picture of the normal curve, where the *Z* score falls on it, and shade in the area for which you are finding the percentage.** This is shown in Figure 4–13.

❸ **Make a rough estimate of the shaded area's percentage based on the 50%–34%–14% percentages.** If the shaded area started at a *Z* score of 1, it would include 16%. If it started at a *Z* score of 2, it would include only 2%. So with a *Z* score of 1.33, it has to be somewhere between 16% and 2%.

❹ **Find the exact percentage using the normal curve table, adding 50% if necessary.** In Table A–1 (in the Appendix), 1.33 in the "*Z*" column goes with 9.18% in the "% in Tail" column. This is the answer to our problem: 9.18% of people have a higher score than 24 on the sensitivity to violence measure. (There is no need to add 50% to the percentage.)

❺ **Check that your exact percentage is within the range of your rough estimate from Step ❸.** Our result, 9.18%, is within the 16% to 2% range estimated.

Note: If the problem involves *Z* scores that are all 0, 1, or 2 (or −1 or −2), you can work the problem using the 50%−34%−14% figures and without using the normal curve table. However, you should still draw a figure and shade in the appropriate area.

Figuring *Z* Scores and Raw Scores from Percentages

Consider the same situation: A test of sensitivity to violence is known to have a mean of 20, a standard deviation of 3, and to follow a normal curve. What is the minimum score a person needs to be in the top 75%?

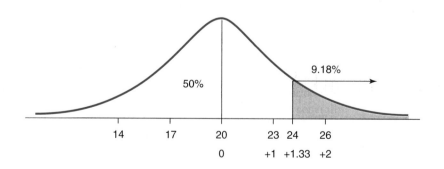

Figure 4–13 Distribution of sensitivity to violence scores showing percentage of scores above a score of 24 (shaded area).

Answer

❶ **Draw a picture of the normal curve and shade in the approximate area for your percentage using the 50%–34%–14% percentages.** The shading has to begin between the mean and 1 *SD* below the mean. (There are 50% above the mean and 84% above 1 *SD* below the mean.) This is shown in Figure 4–14.

❷ **Make a rough estimate of the *Z* score where the shaded area stops.** The *Z* score has to be between 0 and −1.

❸ **Find the exact *Z* score using the normal curve table (subtracting 50% from your percentage if necessary before looking it up).** Since 50% of people have IQs above the mean, for the top 75% you need to include the 25% below the mean (that is, 75% − 50% = 25%). Looking in the "% Mean to *Z*" column of the normal curve table, the closest figure to 25% is 24.86, which goes with a *Z* of .67. Since we are interested in below the mean, we want −.67.

❹ **Check that your exact *Z* score is similar to your rough estimate from Step ❷.** −.67 is between 0 and −1.

❺ **If you want to find a raw score, change it from the *Z* score.** Using the usual formula, $X = (Z)(SD) + M$, $X = (−.67)(3) + 20 = −2.01 + 20 = 17.99$. That is, to be in the top 75%, a person would need to have a score on this test of at least 18.

Note: If the problem instructs you not to use a normal curve table, you should be able to work the problem using the 50%–34%–14% figures. However, you should still draw a figure and shade in the appropriate area.

Outline for Writing Essays on the Logic and Computations for Figuring a Percentage from a *Z* Score and Vice Versa

1. Note that the normal curve is a mathematical (or theoretical) distribution, describe its shape (be sure to include a diagram of the normal curve), and mention that many variables in nature and in the behavioral and social sciences approximately follow a normal curve.

2. If necessary (that is, if required by the question), explain the mean and standard deviation (using the points in the essay outline in Chapter 2).

3. Describe the link between the normal curve and the percentage of scores between the mean and any *Z* score. Be sure to include a description of the normal curve table and show how it is used.

4. Briefly describe the steps required to figure a percentage from a *Z* score or vice versa (as required by the question). Be sure to draw a diagram of the normal curve

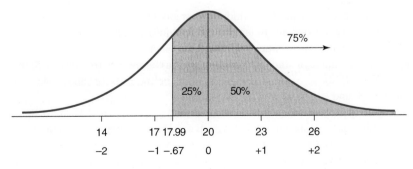

Figure 4–14   Finding the sensitivity to violence raw score for where the top 75% start.

with appropriate numbers and shaded areas marked on it from the relevant question (e.g., the mean, 1 and 2 standard deviations above/below the mean, shaded area for which percentage or Z score is to be determined).

Finding a Probability

A candy dish has four kinds of fruit-flavored candy: 20 apple, 20 strawberry, 5 cherry, and 5 grape. If you close your eyes and pick one piece of candy at random, what is the probability it will be either cherry or grape?

Answer

❶ **Determine the number of possible successful outcomes.** There are 10 possible successful outcomes—5 cherry and 5 grape.

❷ **Determine the number of all possible outcomes.** There are 50 possible outcomes overall: 20 + 20 + 5 + 5 = 50.

❸ **Divide the number of possible successful outcomes (Step ❶) by the number of all possible outcomes (Step ❷).** 10/50 = .2. Thus, the probability of picking either a cherry or grape candy is .2.

Practice Problems

These problems involve figuring. Most real-life statistics problems are done on a computer with special statistical software. Even if you have such software, do these problems by hand to ingrain the method in your mind. In this chapter, in addition, it is important to draw the diagrams for the normal curve problems.

All data are fictional unless an actual citation is given.

Set I (for answers, see p. 440)

1. Suppose the people living in a particular city have a mean score of 40 and a standard deviation of 5 on a measure of concern about the environment. Assume that these concern scores are normally distributed. Using the 50%–34%–14% figures, approximately what percentage of people in this city have a score (a) above 40, (b) above 45, (c) above 30, (d) above 35, (e) below 40, (f) below 45, (g) below 30, (h) below 35?

2. Using the information in problem 1 and the 50%–34%–14% figures, what is the minimum score a person has to have to be in the top (a) 2%, (b) 16%, (c) 50%, (d) 84%, and (e) 98%?

3. An education researcher has been studying test anxiety using a particular measure, which she administers to students prior to midterm exams. On this measure, she has found that the distribution follows a normal curve. Using a normal curve table, what percentage of students have Z scores (a) below 1.5, (b) above 1.5, (c) below −1.5, (d) above −1.5, (e) above 2.10, (f) below 2.10, (g) above .45, (h) below −1.78, and (i) above 1.68?

4. In the previous problem, the measure of test anxiety has a mean of 15 and a standard deviation of 5. Using a normal curve table, what percentage of students have scores (a) above 16, (b) above 17, (c) above 18, (d) below 18, (e) below 14?

5. In the test anxiety example of problems 3 and 4, using a normal curve table, what is the lowest score on the test anxiety measure a person has to have to be in (a) the top 40%, (b) the top 30%, (c) the top 20%?

6. Using a normal curve table, give the percent of scores between the mean and a Z score of (a) .58, (b) .59, (c) 1.46, (d) 1.56, (e) $-.58$.

7. Assuming a normal curve, (a) if a student is in the bottom 30% of the class on Spanish ability, what is the highest Z score this person could have? (b) If the person is in the bottom 3%, what would be the highest Z score this person could have?

8. Assuming a normal curve, (a) if a person is in the top 10% of the country on mathematics ability, what is the lowest Z score this person could have? (b) If the person is in the top 1%, what would be the lowest Z score this person could have?

9. Consider a test of coordination that has a normal distribution, a mean of 50, and a standard deviation of 10. (a) How high a score would a person need to be in the top 5%? (b) Explain your answer to someone who has never had a course in statistics.

10. A research article is concerned with the level of self-esteem of Australian high school students. The methods section emphasizes that a "random sample" of Australian high school students was surveyed. Explain to a person who has never had a course in statistics what this means and why it is important.

11. Altman, Levine, Howard, and Hamilton (1997) conducted a telephone survey of the attitudes of the U.S. adult public toward tobacco farmers. In the method section of their article, they explained that their respondents were "randomly selected from a nationwide list of telephone numbers" (p. 117). Explain to a person who has never had a course in statistics or research methods what this means and why it is important.

12. The following numbers of employees in a company received special assistance from the personnel department last year:

Drug/alcohol	10
Family crisis counseling	20
Other	20
Total	50

If you were to select a score at random from the records for last year, what is the probability that it would be in each of the following categories? (a) drug/alcohol, (b) family, (c) drug/alcohol or family, (d) any category except "Other," (e) any of the three categories? (f) Explain your answer to part (a) to someone who has never had a course in statistics.

Set II

13. Consider a test that has a normal distribution, a mean of 100, and a standard deviation of 14. How high a score would a person need to be in the top (a) 1% and (b) 5%?

14. The length of time it takes to complete a word puzzle is found to be normally distributed with a mean of 80 seconds and a standard deviation of 10 seconds. Using the 50%–34%–14% figures, approximately what percentage of scores (on time to complete the word puzzle) will be (a) above 100, (b) below 100, (c) above 90, (d) below 90, (e) above 80, (f) below 80, (g) above 70, (h) below 70, (i) above 60, and (j) below 60?

15. Using the information in problem 14 and the 50%–34%–14% figures, what is the longest time to complete the word puzzle a person can have and still be in the bottom (a) 2%, (b) 16%, (c) 50%, (d) 84%, and (e) 98%?

16. Suppose that the scores of architects on a particular creativity test are normally distributed. Using a normal curve table, what percentage of architects have Z

scores (a) above .10, (b) below .10, (c) above .20, (d) below .20, (e) above 1.10, (f) below 1.10, (g) above −.10, and (h) below −.10?

17. In the example in problem 16, using a normal curve table, what is the minimum *Z* score an architect can have on the creativity test to be in the (a) top 50%, (b) top 40%, (c) top 60%, (d) top 30%, and (e) top 20%?

18. In the example in problem 16, assume that the mean is 300 and the standard deviation is 25. Using a normal curve table, what scores would be the top and bottom score to find (a) the middle 50% of architects, (b) the middle 90% of architects, and (c) the middle 99% of architects?

19. Suppose that you are designing an instrument panel for a large industrial machine. The machine requires the person using it to reach 2 feet from a particular position. The reach from this position for adult women is known to have a mean of 2.8 feet with a standard deviation of .5. The reach for adult men is known to have a mean of 3.1 feet with a standard deviation of .6. Both women's and men's reach from this position is normally distributed. If this design is implemented, (a) what percentage of women will not be able to work on this instrument panel? (b) What percentage of men will not be able to work on this instrument panel? (c) Explain your answers to a person who has never had a course in statistics.

20. Suppose you want to conduct a survey of the voting preference of undergraduate students. One approach would be to contact every undergraduate student you know and ask them to fill out a questionnaire. (a) What kind of sampling method is this? (b) What is a major limitation of this kind of approach?

21. A large study of how people make future plans and its relation to their life satisfaction (Prenda & Lachman, 2001) recruited participants "through random-digit dialing procedures." These are procedures in which phone numbers to call potential participants are randomly generated by a computer. Explain to a person who has never had a course in statistics (a) why this method of sampling might be used and (b) why it may be a problem if not everyone called agreed to be interviewed.

22. Suppose that you were going to conduct a survey of visitors to your campus. You want the survey to be as representative as possible. (a) How would you select the people to survey? (b) Why would that be your best method?

23. You are conducting a survey at a college with 800 students, 50 faculty members, and 150 administrative staff members. Each of these 1,000 individuals has a single listing in the campus phone directory. Suppose you were to cut up the directory and pull out one listing at random to contact. What is the probability it would be (a) a student, (b) a faculty member, (c) an administrative staff member, (d) a faculty or administrative staff member, and (e) anyone except an administrative staff member? (f) Explain your answer to part (d) to someone who has never had a course in statistics.

24. You apply to 20 graduate programs, 10 of which are in the United States, 5 of which are in Canada, and 5 of which are in Australia. You get a message from home that you have a letter from one of the programs you applied to, but nothing is said about which one. Give the probability it is from (a) a program in the United States, (b) a program in Canada, (c) from any program other than in Australia. (d) Explain your answer to (c) to someone who has never had a course in statistics.

CHAPTER 5

Introduction to Hypothesis Testing

CHAPTER OUTLINE

- A Hypothesis-Testing Example
- The Core Logic of Hypothesis Testing
- The Hypothesis-Testing Process
- One-Tailed and Two-Tailed Hypothesis Tests
- Decision Errors
- Hypothesis Tests as Reported in Research Articles
- Summary
- Key Terms
- Example Worked-Out Problems
- Practice Problems

In Chapter 4, you learned about the normal curve, the difference between a sample and a population, and probability. In this chapter, we introduce the crucial topic of **hypothesis testing.** A **hypothesis** is a prediction about the results of a research study. This prediction may be derived from previous observations or a broader *theory* about what is being studied. You can think of a **theory** as a set of principles that attempt to explain one or more facts, relationships, or events. Any one theory usually gives rise to several (or even more) specific hypotheses that can be tested in research studies. *Hypothesis testing* is a systematic procedure you use for evaluating the results of a research study. In particular, hypothesis testing tests whether the results in the sample you studied support a particular theory or practical innovation that applies to a

hypothesis testing Procedure for deciding whether the outcome of a study (results for a sample) supports a particular theory or practical innovation (which is thought to apply to a population).

hypothesis A prediction about the results of a research study.

theory A set of principles that attempt to explain one or more facts, relationships, or events; behavioral and social scientists often derive specific predictions from theories that are then examined in research studies.

TIP FOR SUCCESS

The material in this chapter builds upon what you learned in Chapter 4 and the chapters it is based upon, particularly the material in Chapter 2 on mean, standard deviation, and *Z* scores. We strongly urge you not to proceed to this chapter until you are confident you have mastered this earlier material.

population. Hypothesis testing is the central theme in the rest of this book, as it is in most behavioral and social science research.

Many students find the most difficult part of the course to be mastering the basic logic of this chapter and the next two. This chapter in particular requires some mental gymnastics. Even if you follow everything the first time through, you will be wise to review the chapter thoroughly. Hypothesis testing involves grasping ideas that make little sense covered separately, so in this chapter you learn several new ideas all at once. However, once you understand the material in this chapter and the two that follow, your mind will be used to this sort of thing, and the rest of the course should seem easier.

At the same time, we have kept this introduction to hypothesis testing as simple as possible, putting off what we could for later chapters. For example, a real-life behavioral and social science research study involves a sample of many individuals. However, to simplify how much you have to learn at one time, the examples in this chapter are about studies in which the sample is a single individual. To do this, we use some odd examples. Just remember that you are building a foundation that will, by Chapter 8, prepare you to understand hypothesis testing as it is actually done in real research.

A Hypothesis-Testing Example

Here is our first necessarily odd example that we made up to keep this introduction to hypothesis testing as straightforward as possible. A large research project has been going on for several years. In this project, new babies are given a special vitamin, and then the research team follows their development during the first two years of life. So far, the vitamin has not speeded up the development of the babies. The ages at which these and all other babies start to walk is shown in Figure 5–1. Notice that the mean is 14 months (Population $M = 14$), the standard deviation is 3 months (Population $SD = 3$), and the ages follow a normal curve. Based on the normal curve percentages, you can figure that less than 2% of babies start walking before 8 months of age; these are the babies who are 2 standard deviations or more below the mean. (This fictional distribution actually is close to the true distribution researchers have found for European babies, although that true distribution is slightly skewed to the right [Hindley, Filliozat, Klackenberg, Nicolet-Meister, & Sand, 1966].)

One of the researchers working on the project has an idea. If the vitamin the babies are taking could be more highly refined, perhaps the effect of the vitamin would be dramatically greater: Babies taking the highly purified version should start walking

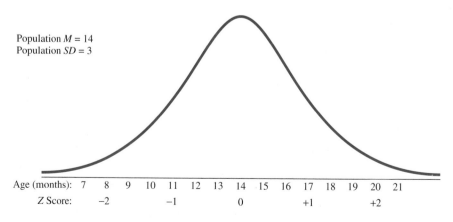

Population $M = 14$
Population $SD = 3$

Age (months): 7   8   9   10   11   12   13   14   15   16   17   18   19   20   21
Z Score: −2   −1   0   +1   +2

Figure 5–1   Distribution of when babies begin to walk (fictional data).

much earlier than other babies. (We will assume that the purification process could not possibly make the vitamin harmful.) However, refining the vitamin in this way is extremely expensive for each dose. Thus, the research team decides to try the procedure with just enough highly purified doses for only one baby. A newborn in the project is then randomly selected to take the highly purified version of the vitamin, and the researchers follow this baby's progress for two years. What kind of result should lead the researchers to conclude that the highly purified vitamin allows babies to walk earlier?

This is a hypothesis-testing problem. The researchers want to draw a conclusion about whether the purified vitamin allows babies *in general* to walk earlier. The conclusion will be about babies in general (a population of babies). However, the conclusion will be based on results of studying a sample. In this example, the sample is of a single baby.

The Core Logic of Hypothesis Testing

There is a standard way researchers approach any hypothesis-testing problem. For this example, it works as follows. Consider first the population of babies that are not given the specially purified vitamin. In this population, the chance of a baby's starting to walk at age 8 months or earlier would be less than 2%. Thus, walking at 8 months or earlier is highly unlikely among such babies. But what if the randomly selected sample of one baby in our study does start walking by 8 months? If the specially purified vitamin had no effect on this particular baby's walking age, this would mean that the baby's walking age should be similar to that of babies that were not given the vitamin. In that case, it is highly unlikely (less than a 2% chance) that the particular baby we selected at random would start walking by 8 months. But what if the baby in our study does in fact start walking by 8 months? If that happened, we could *reject* the idea that the specially purified vitamin has *no* effect. And if we reject the idea that the specially purified vitamin has no effect, then we must also *accept* the idea that the specially purified vitamin *does* have an effect. Using the same reasoning, if the baby starts walking by 8 months, we can reject the idea that this baby comes from a population of babies with a mean walking age of 14 months. We therefore conclude that babies given the specially purified vitamin will start to walk before 14 months. Our explanation for the baby's early walking age in the study would be that the specially purified vitamin speeded up the baby's development.

The researchers first spelled out what would have to happen to conclude that the special purification procedure makes a difference. Having laid this out in advance, the researchers could then go on to carry out their study. In this example, carrying out the study means giving the specially purified vitamin to a randomly selected baby and watching to see how early that baby walks. Suppose the result of the study shows that the baby starts walking before 8 months. The researchers would then conclude that it is unlikely the specially purified vitamin makes *no* difference, and thus also conclude that it *does* make a difference.

This kind of testing the opposite-of-what-you-predict, roundabout reasoning is at the heart of inferential statistics in behavioral and social sciences. It is something like a double negative. One reason for this approach is that we have the information to figure the probability of getting a particular experimental result if the situation of there being no difference is true. In the purified vitamin example, the researchers know what the probabilities are of babies walking at different ages if the specially purified vitamin does not have any effect. It is the probability of babies walking at various ages that is already known from studies of babies in general—that is, babies who have not received the specially purified vitamin. (Suppose the specially purified vitamin has no effect. In that situation, the age at which babies start walking is the same regardless of

research hypothesis In hypothesis testing, statement about the predicted relation between populations (usually a prediction of difference between population means).

whether they receive the specially purified vitamin. Thus, the distribution is that shown in Figure 5–1, based on ages at which babies start walking in general.)

Without such a tortuous way of going at the problem, in most cases you could just not do hypothesis testing at all. In almost all behavioral and social sciences research, whether involving experiments, surveys, or whatever, we base our conclusions on this question: What is the probability of getting our research results if the opposite of what we are predicting were true?

That is, we are usually predicting an effect of some kind. However, we decide on whether there *is* such an effect by seeing if it is unlikely that there is *not* such an effect. If it is highly unlikely that we would get our research results if the opposite of what we are predicting were true, that allows us to reject that opposite prediction. If we reject that opposite prediction, we are able to accept our prediction. However, if it is likely that we would get our research results if the opposite of what we are predicting were true, we are not able to reject that opposite prediction. If we are not able to reject that opposite prediction, we are not able to accept our prediction.

The Hypothesis-Testing Process

Let's look at our example, this time going over each step in some detail. Along the way, we cover the special terminology of hypothesis testing. Most important, we introduce five steps of hypothesis testing you use for the rest of this book.

Step 1: Restate the Question as a Research Hypothesis and a Null Hypothesis about the Populations

Our researchers are interested in the effects on babies in general (not just this particular baby). That is, the purpose of studying samples is to know about populations. Thus, it is useful to restate the research question in terms of populations. In our example, we can think of two populations of babies:

Population 1: Babies who take the specially purified vitamin.
Population 2: Babies who do not take the specially purified vitamin.

Population 1 consists of those who receive the experimental treatment. In our example, we use a sample of one baby to draw a conclusion about the age that babies in Population 1 start to walk. Population 2 is a kind of comparison baseline of what is already known.

The prediction of our research team is that Population 1 babies (those who take the specially purified vitamin) will on the average walk earlier than Population 2 babies (those who do not take the specially purified vitamin). This prediction is based on the researchers' theory of how these vitamins work. A prediction like this about the difference between populations is called a **research hypothesis.** Put more formally, the prediction in this example is that the mean of Population 1 is lower (babies receiving the special vitamin walk earlier) than the mean of Population 2.

The opposite of the research hypothesis is that the populations are not different in the way predicted. Under this scenario, Population 1 babies (those who take the specially purified vitamin) will on the average *not* walk earlier than Population 2 babies (those who do not take the specially purified vitamin). That is, this prediction is that there is no difference in when Population 1 and Population 2 babies start walking. They start at the same time. A statement like this, about a lack of difference between populations, is the crucial *opposite* of the research hypothesis. It is called a

null hypothesis. It has this name because it states the situation in which there is no difference (the difference is "null") between the populations.[1]

The research hypothesis and the null hypothesis are *complete opposites.* If one is true, the other cannot be true. In fact, the research hypothesis is sometimes called the *alternative hypothesis*—that is, it is the alternative to the null hypothesis. This is a bit ironic. As researchers, we care most about the research hypothesis. But when doing the steps of hypothesis testing, we use this roundabout method of seeing whether we can reject the null hypothesis so that we can decide about its alternative (the research hypothesis).

Step 2: Determine the Characteristics of the Comparison Distribution

Recall that the overall logic of hypothesis testing involves figuring out the probability of getting a particular result if the null hypothesis is true. Thus, you need to know about what the situation would be if the null hypothesis were true. In our example, we start out knowing the key information about Population 2 (see Figure 5–1): We know that Population $M = 14$, Population $SD = 3$, and it is normally distributed. (We use the term "Population" before M and SD because we are referring to the mean and standard deviation of a population.) If the null hypothesis is true, Population 1 and Population 2 are the same—in our example, this would mean Populations 1 and 2 both follow a normal curve and have a mean of 14 months and a standard deviation of 3 months.

In the hypothesis-testing process, you want to find out the probability that you could have gotten a sample score as extreme as what you got (say, a baby walking very early) if your sample were from a population with a distribution of the sort you would have if the null hypothesis were true. Thus, in this book we call this distribution a **comparison distribution.** (The comparison distribution is sometimes called a *statistical model* or a *sampling distribution*—an idea we discuss in Chapter 6.) That is, in the hypothesis-testing process, you compare the actual sample's score to this comparison distribution.

In our vitamin example, the null hypothesis is that there is no difference in walking age between babies who take the specially purified vitamin (Population 1) and babies who do not take the specially purified vitamin (Population 2). The comparison distribution is the distribution for Population 2, since this population represents the walking age of babies if the null hypothesis is true. In later chapters, you will learn about different types of comparison distributions, but the same principle applies in all cases: The comparison distribution is the distribution that represents the population situation if the null hypothesis is true.

Step 3: Determine the Cutoff Sample Score on the Comparison Distribution at Which the Null Hypothesis Should Be Rejected

Ideally, before conducting a study, researchers set a target against which they will compare their result—how extreme a sample score they would need to decide against the null hypothesis. That is, how extreme the sample score would have to be for it to

null hypothesis   Statement about a relationship between populations that is the opposite of the research hypothesis; a statement that in the population there is no difference (or a difference opposite to that predicted) between populations; a contrived statement set up to examine whether it can be rejected as part of hypothesis testing.

comparison distribution   Distribution used in hypothesis testing. It represents the population situation if the null hypothesis is true. It is the distribution to which you compare the score based on your sample's results.

---

[1]We are oversimplifying a bit here to make the initial learning easier. The research hypothesis is that one population will walk earlier than the other. Thus, to be precise, its opposite is that the other group will either walk at the same time or walk later. That is, the opposite of the research hypothesis in this example includes both no difference and a difference in the direction opposite to what we predicted. We discuss this issue in some detail later in the chapter.

cutoff sample score In hypothesis testing, the point on the comparison distribution at which, if reached or exceeded by the sample score, you reject the null hypothesis; also called *critical value*.

conventional levels of significance (*p* < .05, *p* < .01) The levels of significance widely used in the behavioral and social sciences.

statistically significant Conclusion that the results of a study would be unlikely if in fact there were no difference in the populations the samples represent; an outcome of hypothesis testing in which the null hypothesis is rejected.

be too unlikely that they could get such an extreme score if the null hypothesis were true. This is called the **cutoff sample score.** The cutoff sample score is also known as the *critical value.*

Consider our purified vitamin example in which the null hypothesis is that walking age is not influenced by whether babies take the specially purified vitamin. The researchers might decide that if the null hypothesis were true, a randomly selected baby walking by 8 months would be very unlikely. With a normal distribution, being 2 or more standard deviations below the mean (walking by 8 months) could occur less than 2% of the time. Thus, based on the comparison distribution, the researchers set their cutoff sample score (or *critical value*) even before doing the study. They decide in advance that *if* the result of their study is a baby who walks by 8 months, they will reject the null hypothesis.

But, what if the baby does not start walking until after 8 months? If that happens, the researchers will not be able to reject the null hypothesis.

When setting in advance how extreme a sample's score needs to be to reject the null hypothesis, researchers use Z scores and percentages. In our purified vitamin example, the researchers might decide that if a result were less likely than 2%, they would reject the null hypothesis. Being in the bottom 2% of a normal curve means having a Z score of about −2 or lower. Thus, the researchers would set −2 as their Z-score cutoff point on the comparison distribution for deciding that a result is extreme enough to reject the null hypothesis. So, if the actual sample Z score is −2 or lower, the researchers will reject the null hypothesis. However, if the actual sample Z score is greater than −2, the researchers will not reject the null hypothesis.

Suppose that the researchers are even more cautious about too easily rejecting the null hypothesis. They might decide that they will reject the null hypothesis only if they get a result that could occur by chance 1% of the time or less. They could then figure out the Z-score cutoff for 1%. Using the normal curve table, to have a score in the lower 1% of a normal curve, you need a Z score of −2.33 or less. (In our example, a Z score of −2.33 means 7 months.) In Figure 5–2, we have shaded the 1% of the comparison distribution in which a sample would be considered so extreme that the possibility that it came from a distribution like this would be rejected. So, now the researchers will only reject the null hypothesis if the actual sample Z score is −2.33 or lower—that is, if it falls in the shaded area in Figure 5–2. If the sample Z score falls outside of the shaded area in Figure 5–2, the researchers will *not* reject the null hypothesis.

In general, behavioral and social science researchers use a cutoff on the comparison distribution with a probability of 5% that a score will be at least that extreme (if the null hypothesis were true). That is, researchers reject the null hypothesis if the probability of getting a sample score this extreme (if the null hypothesis were true) is less than 5%. This probability is usually written as $p < .05$. However, in some areas of research, or when researchers want to be especially cautious, they use a cutoff of 1% ($p < .01$).[2] These are called **conventional levels of significance.** They are described as the *.05 significance level* and the *.01 significance level* (we also refer to them as the 5% significance level and the 1% significance level). When a sample score is so extreme that researchers reject the null hypothesis, the result is said to be **statistically significant** (or *significant,* as it is often abbreviated).

_____

[2]These days, when hypothesis testing is usually done on the computer, you have to decide in advance only on the cutoff probability. The computer prints out the exact probability of getting your result if the null hypothesis were true. You then just compare the printed-out probability to see if it is less than the cutoff probability level you set in advance. However, to *understand* what these probability levels mean, you need to learn the entire process, including how to figure the Z score for a particular cutoff probability.

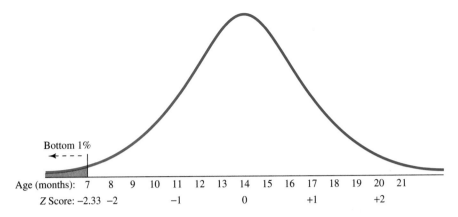

Figure 5-2   Distribution of when babies begin to walk, with bottom 1% shaded (fictional data).

Step 4: Determine Your Sample's Score on the Comparison Distribution

The next step is to carry out the study and get the actual result for your sample. Once you have the results for your sample, you figure the Z score for the sample's raw score. You figure this Z score based on the population mean and standard deviation of the comparison distribution.

Assume that the researchers did the study and the baby who was given the specially purified vitamin started walking at 6 months. The mean of the comparison distribution to which we are comparing these results is 14 months and the standard deviation is 3 months. That is, Population $M = 14$ and Population $SD = 3$. Thus a baby who walks at 6 months is 8 months below the population mean, which puts this baby $2\frac{2}{3}$ standard deviations below the population mean. The Z score for this sample baby on the comparison distribution is thus -2.67 ($Z = [6 - 14]/3$). Figure 5–3 shows the score of our sample baby on the comparison distribution.

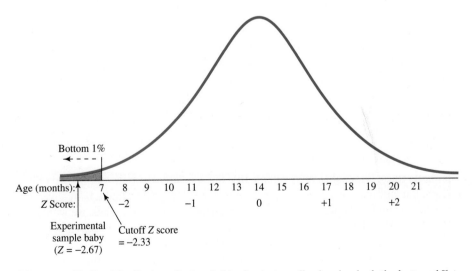

Figure 5-3   Distribution of when babies begin to walk, showing both the bottom 1% and the single baby that is the sample studied (fictional data).

Step 5: Decide Whether to Reject the Null Hypothesis

To decide whether to reject the null hypothesis, you compare your actual sample's Z score (from Step ❹) to the cutoff Z score (from Step ❸). In our example, the actual sample's Z score was -2.67. Let's suppose the researchers had decided in advance that they would reject the null hypothesis if the sample's Z score was below -2. Since -2.67 is below -2, the researchers would reject the null hypothesis.

Or, suppose the researchers had used the more conservative 1% significance level. The needed Z score to reject the null hypothesis would then have been -2.33 or lower. But, again, the actual Z for the randomly selected baby was -2.67 (a more extreme score than -2.33). Thus, even with this more conservative cutoff, they would still reject the null hypothesis. This situation is shown in Figure 5–3. As you can see in the figure, the bottom 1% of the distribution is shaded. We recommend that you always draw such a picture of the distribution. Be sure to shade in the part of the distribution that is *more extreme* (that is, further out in the tail) than the cutoff sample score (critical value). If your actual sample Z score falls within the shaded region, you can reject the null hypothesis. Since the sample Z score (of -2.67) in this example falls within the shaded region, the researchers can reject the null hypothesis.

If the researchers reject the null hypothesis, what remains is the research hypothesis. In this example, the research team can conclude that the results of their study support the research hypothesis, that babies who take the specially purified vitamin begin walking earlier than other babies.

Implications of Rejecting or Failing to Reject the Null Hypothesis

It is important to emphasize two points about the conclusions you can make from the hypothesis-testing process. First, suppose you reject the null hypothesis. Therefore, your results support the research hypothesis (as in our example). You would still not say that the results *prove* the research hypothesis or that the results show that the research hypothesis is *true*. This would be too strong because the results of research studies are based on probabilities. Specifically, they are based on the probability being low of getting your result if the null hypothesis were true. *Proven* and *true* are okay words in logic and mathematics, but to use these words in conclusions from scientific research is inappropriate. (It is okay to use *true* when speaking hypothetically—for example, "*if* this hypothesis *were* true, then . . ."—but not when speaking of conclusions about an actual result.) What you do say when you reject the null hypothesis is that the results are *statistically significant*. You can also say the results *support* or *provide evidence for* the research hypothesis.

Second, when a result is not extreme enough to reject the null hypothesis, you do not say that the result *supports* the null hypothesis. You simply say the result is *not statistically significant*. A result that is not strong enough to reject the null hypothesis means the study was inconclusive. The results may not be extreme enough to reject the null hypothesis, but the null hypothesis might still be false (and the research hypothesis true). Suppose in our example that the specially purified vitamin had only a slight but still real effect. In that case, we would not expect to find a baby given the purified vitamin to be walking a lot earlier than babies in general. Thus, we would not be able to reject the null hypothesis, even though it is false. (You will learn more about such situations in the Decision Errors section later in this chapter.)

Showing the null hypothesis to be true would mean showing that there is absolutely no difference between the populations. It is always possible that there is a difference between the populations, but that the difference is much smaller than what the particular study was able to detect. Therefore, when a result is not extreme enough to reject the null hypothesis, the results are *inconclusive*. Sometimes, however, if studies have been done using large samples and accurate measuring procedures, evidence may build up in support of something close to the null hypothesis—that there is at most very little difference between the populations. (We have more to say on this important issue later in this chapter and in Chapter 7.)

Summary of the Steps of Hypothesis Testing

Here is a summary of the five steps of hypothesis testing:

❶ **Restate the question as a research hypothesis and a null hypothesis about the populations.**
❷ **Determine the characteristics of the comparison distribution.**
❸ **Determine the cutoff sample score on the comparison distribution at which the null hypothesis should be rejected.**
❹ **Determine your sample's score on the comparison distribution.**
❺ **Decide whether to reject the null hypothesis.**

How are you doing?

1. A sample of rats in a laboratory is given an experimental treatment intended to make them learn a maze faster than other rats. State (a) the null hypothesis and (b) the research hypothesis.
2. (a) What is a comparison distribution? (b) What role does it play in hypothesis testing?
3. What is the cutoff sample score?
4. Why do we say that hypothesis testing involves a double negative logic?
5. What can you conclude when (a) a result is so extreme that you reject the null hypothesis, and (b) a result is not very extreme so you cannot reject the null hypothesis?
6. A training program to increase friendliness is tried on one individual randomly selected from the general public. Among the general public (who do not get this training program) the mean on the friendliness measure is 30 with a standard deviation of 4. The researchers want to test their hypothesis at the 5% significance level. After going through the training program, this individual takes the friendliness measure and gets a score of 40. What should the researchers conclude?

Answers

1. (a) The population of rats like those who get the experimental treatment treatment score the same on the time to learn the maze as the population of rats who do not get the experimental treatment. (b) The population of rats like those who get the experimental treatment learn the maze faster than the population of rats who do not get the experimental treatment.
2. (a) A distribution to which you compare the results of your study. (b) In hypothesis testing, the comparison distribution is the distribution for the situation when the null hypothesis is true. To decide whether to reject the null hypothesis, you check how extreme the score of your sample is on this comparison distribution—how likely it would be to get a sample with a score this extreme if your sample came from this comparison distribution.

directional hypothesis Research hypothesis predicting a particular direction of difference between populations—for example, a prediction that one population has a higher mean than the other.

one-tailed test Hypothesis-testing procedure for a directional hypothesis; situation in which the region of the comparison distribution in which the null hypothesis would be rejected is all on one side (tail) of the distribution.

3. The Z score at which, if the sample's Z score is more extreme than it on the comparison distribution, you reject the null hypothesis.

4. Because we are interested in the research hypothesis, but we test whether it is true by seeing if we can reject its opposite, the null hypothesis.

5. (a) The research hypothesis is supported; the result is statistically significant. (b) The result is not statistically significant; the result is inconclusive.

6. The training program increases friendliness. The cutoff sample Z score on the comparison distribution is 1.64. The actual sample's Z score of 2.50 is more extreme (that is, further in the tail) than the cutoff Z score. Therefore, reject the null hypothesis; the research hypothesis is supported; the result is statistically significant.

One-Tailed and Two-Tailed Hypothesis Tests

In the baby-walking example, the researchers were interested in only one direction of result. Specifically, they tested whether babies given the specially purified vitamin would walk *earlier* than babies in general. The researchers in this study were not really interested in the possibility that giving the specially purified vitamins would cause babies to start walking *later*.

Directional Hypotheses and One-Tailed Tests

The baby-walking study is an example of a **directional hypothesis.** The study focused on a specific direction of effect. When a researcher makes a directional hypothesis, the null hypothesis is also, in a sense, directional. Suppose the research hypothesis is that taking the specially purified vitamin will make babies walk earlier. The null hypothesis, then, is that the specially purified vitamin will either have no effect or make babies walk later. Thus, in Figure 5–2, for the null hypothesis to be rejected, the sample had to have a score in one particular tail of the comparison distribution—the lower extreme or tail (in this example, the bottom 1%) of the comparison distribution. (When it comes to rejecting the null hypothesis with a directional hypothesis, a score at the other tail would be the same as a score in the middle of the distribution—that is, it would not allow you to reject the null hypothesis.) For this reason, the test of a directional hypothesis is called a **one-tailed test.** A one-tailed test can be one-tailed in either direction. In this example, the prediction was that the baby given the specially purified vitamin would start walking especially early—a prediction in the direction of a low score on months before walking. Thus, the cutoff region was at the low end (left side) of the comparison distribution. In other research situations with a directional hypothesis, the cutoff may be at the high end (right side) of the comparison distribution. That is, in these situations, the researchers would be predicting that the experimental procedure will produce a high score.

Nondirectional Hypotheses and Two-Tailed Tests

Sometimes, a research hypothesis is that an experimental procedure will have an effect, without saying whether it will produce a very high score or a very low score. Suppose a researcher is interested in whether a new social skills program will affect worker productivity. The program could improve productivity by making the working environment more pleasant. Or, the program could hurt productivity by encouraging people to socialize instead of work. The research hypothesis is that the social skills program *changes* the level of productivity. The null hypothesis is that the program does not change productivity one way or the other.

When a research hypothesis predicts an effect but does not predict a particular direction for the effect, it is called a **nondirectional hypothesis.** To test the significance of a nondirectional hypothesis, you have to consider the possibility that the sample could be extreme at either tail of the comparison distribution. Thus, this is called a **two-tailed test.**

Determining Cutoff Scores with Two-Tailed Tests. There is a special complication in a two-tailed test. You have to divide up the significance percentage between the two tails. For example, with a 5% significance level, you would reject a null hypothesis only if the sample was so extreme that it was in either the top 2.5% or the bottom 2.5% of the comparison distribution. This keeps the overall level of significance at a total of 5%.

Note that a two-tailed test makes the cutoff Z scores for the 5% level +1.96 and −1.96. For a one-tailed test at the 5% level, the cutoff was not so extreme—only +1.64 or −1.64. But with a one-tailed test, only one side of the distribution was considered. These situations are shown in Figure 5–4a.

nondirectional hypothesis Research hypothesis that does not predict a particular direction of difference between populations.

two-tailed test Hypothesis-testing procedure for a nondirectional hypothesis; the situation in which the region of the comparison distribution in which the null hypothesis would be rejected is divided between the two sides (tails) of the distribution.

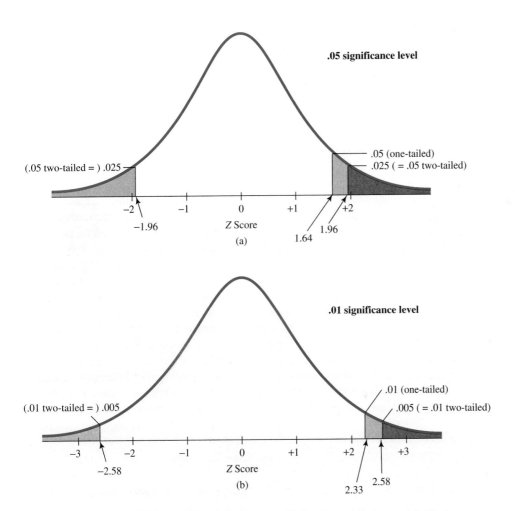

Figure 5–4 Significance level cutoffs for one-tailed and two-tailed tests: (a) .05 significance level; (b) .01 significance level. (The one-tailed tests in these examples assume the prediction was for a high score. You could instead have a one-tailed test where the prediction is for the lower, left tail.)

Table 5-1 One-Tailed and Two-Tailed Cutoff *Z* Scores for the .05 and .01 Significance Levels			
		Type of Test	
		One-Tailed	Two-Tailed
Significance	.05	−1.64 *or* 1.64	−1.96 *and* 1.96
Level	.01	−2.33 *or* 2.33	−2.58 *and* 2.58

Using the 1% significance level, a two-tailed test (.5% at each tail) has cutoffs of +2.58 and −2.58. With a one-tailed test, the cutoff is either +2.33 or −2.33. These situations are shown in Figure 5–4b. The Z score cutoffs for one-tailed and two-tailed tests for the .05 and .01 significance levels are also summarized in Table 5-1.

When to Use One-Tailed or Two-Tailed Tests

If the researcher decides in advance to use a one-tailed test, then the sample's score does not need to be so extreme to be significant compared to what would be needed with a two-tailed test. Yet there is a price. The problem with a one-tailed test is what happens if the result is extreme in the direction opposite to what was predicted. In that case, no matter how extreme, the result cannot be considered statistically significant.

In principle, you plan to use a one-tailed test when you have a clearly directional hypothesis. You plan to use a two-tailed test when you have a clearly nondirectional hypothesis. In practice, it is not so simple. Even when a theory clearly predicts a particular result, the actual result may come out opposite to what you expected. Sometimes, this opposite result may be more interesting than what you had predicted. By using one-tailed tests, we risk having to ignore possibly important results.

For these reasons, researchers disagree about whether one-tailed tests should be used, even when there is a clearly directional hypothesis. To be safe, many researchers use two-tailed tests for both nondirectional and directional hypotheses. If the two-tailed test is significant, then the researcher looks at the result to see the direction and considers the study significant in that direction. In practice, always using two-tailed tests is a conservative procedure. This is because the cutoff scores are more extreme for a two-tailed test, so it is less likely a two-tailed test will give a significant result. Thus, if you do get a significant result with a two-tailed test, you are more confident about the conclusion. In fact, in most behavioral and social sciences research articles, unless the researcher specifically states that a one-tailed test was used, it is assumed that it was a two-tailed test.

In practice, however, it is our experience that most research results are either so extreme that they will be significant whether you use a one-tailed or two-tailed test. Or that they would be so far from extreme that they would not be significant no matter what you use. But what happens when a result is less certain? The researcher's decision about one-tailed or two-tailed tests now can make a big difference. In this situation the researcher tries to use the type of test that will give the most accurate and noncontroversial conclusion. The idea is to let nature—and not a researcher's decisions—determine the conclusion as much as possible. Further, whenever a result is less than completely clear one way or the other, most researchers will not be comfortable drawing strong conclusions until more research is done.

An Example of Hypothesis Testing with a Two-Tailed Test

Here is another made-up example, this time using a two-tailed test. A researcher is interested in the effect of going through a natural disaster on the attitude of police chiefs about the goodness of the people in their city. The researcher believes that after a dis-

BOX 5–1   To Be or Not to Be—But Can Not Being Be?
The Problem of Whether and When to Accept the Null Hypothesis

The null hypothesis states that there is no difference between populations represented by different groups or experimental conditions. As we have seen, the usual rule in statistics is that a study cannot find the null hypothesis to be true. A study can only tell you that you cannot reject the null hypothesis. That is, a study that fails to reject the null hypothesis is simply uninformative. Such studies tend not to be published, obviously. However, much work could be avoided if people knew what interventions, measures, or experiments had not worked. Indeed, Greenwald (1975) reports that sometimes ideas have been assumed too long to be true just because a few studies found results supporting them, while many more, unreported, had not.

Frick (1995) has pointed out that sometimes it may be true that one thing has so little effect on another that it probably represented no real, or at least no important, relationship or difference. The problem is knowing when to conclude that. Frick (1995) gives three criteria. First, the null hypothesis should seem possible. Second, the results in the study should be consistent with the null hypothesis and not easily interpreted any other way. Third, and most important, the researcher has to have made a strong effort to find the effect that he or she wants to conclude is not there. Among other things, this means studying a large sample, and having sensitive measurement, a strong manipulation, and rigorous conditions of testing.

Frick (1995) points out that all of this leaves a subjective element to the acceptance of the null hypothesis. But subjective judgments are a part of science. For example, reviewers of articles submitted for publication in the top scientific journals have to decide if a topic is important enough to compete for limited space in those journals. Furthermore, the null hypothesis is being accepted all the time anyway. (For example, many behavioral and social scientists accept the null hypothesis about the effect of extrasensory perception.) It is better to discuss our basis for accepting the null hypothesis than just to accept it.

aster, the police chief is likely to have a more positive attitude about the people of the city (because the chief will have seen many acts of heroism and helping of neighbors after the event). However, it is also possible that a disaster will lead to police chiefs having more negative attitudes, because there may be looting and other dishonest behavior after the disaster. Thus, the researcher will make a nondirectional hypothesis.

Let us assume that there is lots of previous research on the attitudes of police chiefs about the goodness of the people in their cities. And also let's assume that this previous research shows that on a standard questionnaire, the mean attitude rating is 69.5 with a standard deviation of 14.1, and the attitude scores follow a normal curve. Finally, let's assume that a major earthquake has just occurred in an isolated city, and shortly afterward the researcher is able to give the standard questionnaire to the police chief of that city. Remember that in this chapter we are considering the special situation in which the sample is a single individual. The researchers then carries out the five steps of hypothesis testing.

❶ **Restate the question as a research hypothesis and a null hypothesis about the populations.** There are two populations of interest:

Population 1: Police chiefs whose city has just been through a disaster.
Population 2: Police chiefs in general.

The research hypothesis is that when measured on their attitude toward the goodness of the people of their city, police chiefs whose city has just been through a disaster (Population 1) score differently from police chiefs in general (Population 2). The opposite of the research hypothesis, the null hypothesis, is this: Police chiefs whose city has just been through a disaster have the same attitude as police chiefs in general. That is, the null hypothesis is that the attitudes of Populations 1 and 2 are the same.

TIP FOR SUCCESS

Remember that the research hypothesis and null hypothesis must always be *complete opposites*. Researchers specify the research hypothesis, and this determines what the null hypothesis that goes with it will be.

❷ **Determine the characteristics of the comparison distribution.** If the null hypothesis is true, the distributions of Populations 1 and 2 are the same. We know the distribution of Population 2, so we can use it as our comparison distribution. As noted, it follows a normal curve, with Population $M = 69.5$ and Population $SD = 14.1$.

❸ **Determine the cutoff sample score on the comparison distribution at which the null hypothesis should be rejected.** The researcher selects the 5% significance level. The researcher has made a nondirectional hypothesis and will therefore use a two-tailed test. Thus, the researcher will reject the null hypothesis only if the police chief's attitude score is in either the top or bottom 2.5% of the comparison distribution. In terms of Z scores, these cutoffs are $+1.96$ and -1.96 (see Figure 5–4 and Table 5–1).

❹ **Determine your sample's score on the comparison distribution.** The police chief whose city went through the earthquake took the standard attitude questionnaire and had a score of 41. This corresponds to a Z score on the comparison distribution of -2.02. That is, $Z = (X - M)/SD = (41 - 69.5)/14.1 = -2.02$.

❺ **Decide whether to reject the null hypothesis.** A Z score of -2.02 is slightly more extreme than the Z score of -1.96, which is where the lower 2.5% of the comparison distribution begins. Notice in Figure 5–5 that the Z score of -2.02 falls within the shaded area in the left tail of the comparison distribution. This Z score of -2.02 is a result so extreme that it is unlikely to have occurred if this police chief were from a population no different than Population 2. Therefore, the researcher rejects the null hypothesis. The result is statistically significant. It supports the research hypothesis that going through a disaster does indeed change police chiefs' attitudes toward their city. In this case, the results would mean that the effect is one of making the chief less positive about the city's people. (Remember, however, that this is a fictional study.)

TIP FOR SUCCESS

When carrying out the five steps of hypothesis testing, always draw a figure like Figure 5–5. Be sure to include the cutoff score(s) and shade the appropriate tail(s). If the sample score falls within a shaded tail region, you reject the null hypothesis and the result is statistically significant. If the sample score does not fall within a shaded tail region, you do not reject the null hypothesis.

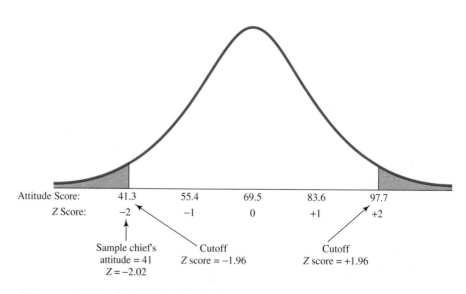

Figure 5–5 Distribution of attitudes of police chiefs toward goodness of people in their cities with upper and lower 2.5% shaded and showing the sample police chief whose city has just been through a disaster (fictional data).

How are you doing?

1. What is a nondirectional hypothesis test?
2. What is a two-tailed test?
3. Why do you use a two-tailed test when testing a nondirectional hypothesis?
4. What is the advantage of using a one-tailed test when your theory predicts a particular direction of result?
5. Why might you use a two-tailed test even when your theory predicts a particular direction of result?
6. A researcher predicts that making people hungry will affect how they do on a coordination test. A randomly selected person is asked not to eat for 24 hours before taking a standard coordination test and gets a score of 400. For people in general of this age group and gender, tested under normal conditions, coordination scores are normally distributed with a mean of 500 and a standard deviation of 40. Using the .01 significance level, what should the researcher conclude?

Answers

1. A nondirectional hypothesis test is a hypothesis test in which you do not predict a particular direction of difference.
2. A two-tailed test is one in which the overall percentage for the cutoff is evenly divided between the two tails of the comparison distribution. A two-tailed test is used to test the significance of a nondirectional hypothesis.
3. You use a two-tailed test when testing a nondirectional hypothesis because an extreme result in either direction would support the research hypothesis.
4. The cutoff for a one-tailed test is not so extreme; thus, if your result comes out in the predicted direction, it is more likely to be significant. The cutoff is not so extreme because the entire percentage (say 5%) is put in one tail instead of being divided between two tails.
5. It lets you count as significant an extreme result in either direction; if you used a one-tailed test and the result came out opposite to the prediction, it could not be called statistically significant.
6. The cutoffs are +2.58 and −2.58. The sample person's Z score is $(400 - 500)/40 = -2.5$. The result is not significant; the study is inconclusive.

Decision Errors

Another crucial topic for making sense of statistical significance is the kind of errors that are possible in the hypothesis-testing process. The kind of errors we consider here are about how, in spite of doing all your figuring correctly, your conclusions from hypothesis testing can still be incorrect. It is *not* about making mistakes in calculations or even about using the wrong procedures. That is, **decision errors** are a situation in which the *right procedures* lead to the *wrong decisions.*

Decision errors are possible in hypothesis testing because you are making decisions about populations based on information in samples. The whole hypothesis-testing process is based on probabilities. The hypothesis-testing process is set up to make the probability of decision errors as small as possible. For example, we only decide to reject the null hypothesis if a sample's mean is so extreme that there is a very small probability (say, less than 5%) that we could have gotten such an extreme sample if the null hypothesis is true. But a very small probability is not the same as a zero probability! Thus, in spite of your best intentions, decision errors are always possible.

Type I error   Rejecting the null hypothesis when in fact it is true; getting a statistically significant result when in fact the research hypothesis is not true.

There are two kinds of decision errors in hypothesis testing: Type I error and Type II error.

Type I Error

You make a **Type I error** if you reject the null hypothesis when in fact the null hypothesis is true. Or, to put it in terms of the research hypothesis, you make a Type I error when you conclude that the study supports the research hypothesis when in reality the research hypothesis is false.

Suppose you did a study in which you had set the significance level cutoff at a very lenient probability level, such as 20%. This would mean that it would not take a very extreme result to reject the null hypothesis. If you did many studies like this, you would often (about 20% of the time) be deciding to consider the research hypothesis supported when you should not. That is, you would have a 20% chance of making a Type I error.

Even when you set the probability at the conventional .05 or .01, you will still make a Type I error sometimes (to be precise, 5% or 1% of the time). Consider again the example of giving a baby a new purified vitamin and examining the age at which the baby starts walking. Suppose the special new vitamin in reality has no effect whatsoever on the age at which babies start walking. However, in randomly picking a sample of one baby to study, the researchers might just happen to pick a baby who will start walking at a very young age, regardless of whether it is given the new vitamin. Randomly selecting a sample baby like this is *unlikely*. But such extreme samples are *possible*. Should this happen, the researchers would reject the null hypothesis and conclude that the new vitamin does make a difference. Their decision to reject the null hypothesis would be wrong—a Type I error. Of course, the researchers could not know they had made a decision error of this kind. What reassures researchers is that they know from the logic of hypothesis testing that the probability of making such a decision error is kept low (less than 5% if you use the .05 significance level).

Still, the fact that Type I errors can happen at all is of serious concern to behavioral and social scientists. It is of serious concern because they might construct entire theories and research programs, not to mention practical applications, based on a conclusion from hypothesis testing that is in fact mistaken. It is because these errors are of such serious concern that they are called Type I.

As we have noted, researchers cannot tell when they have made a Type I error. However, they can try to carry out studies so that the chance of making a Type I error is as small as possible.

What is the chance of making a Type I error? It is the same as the significance level we set. If you set the significance level at $p < .05$, you are saying you will reject the null hypothesis if there is less than a 5% (.05) chance that you could have gotten your result if the null hypothesis were true. When rejecting the null hypothesis in this way, you are allowing up to a 5% chance that you got your results even though the null hypothesis was actually true. That is, you are allowing a 5% chance of a Type I error. (You will sometimes see the significance level, the chance of making a Type I error, referred to as *alpha,* the Greek letter α.)

Again, the significance level is the same as the chance of making a Type I error. Thus, the lower probability we set for the significance level, the smaller the chance of a Type I error. Researchers who do not want to take a lot of risk set the significance level lower than .05, such as $p < .001$. In this way the result of a study has to be very extreme in order for the hypothesis-testing process to reject the null hypothesis.

Using a .001 significance level is like buying insurance against making a Type I error. However, as when buying insurance, the better the protection, the higher the cost. There is a cost in setting the significance level at too extreme a level. We turn to that cost next.

Type II Error

If you set a very stringent significance level, such as .001, you run a different kind of risk. With a very stringent significance level, you may carry out a study in which in reality the research hypothesis is true, but the result does not come out extreme enough to reject the null hypothesis. Thus, the decision error you would make is in *not* rejecting the null hypothesis when in fact the null hypothesis is false. To put this in terms of the research hypothesis, you make this kind of decision error when the hypothesis-testing procedure leads you to decide that the results of the study are inconclusive when in reality the research hypothesis is true. This is called a **Type II error.**

Consider again our example of the new purified vitamin and the age at which babies begin walking. Suppose that, in truth, the new vitamin does cause babies to begin walking at an earlier age than normal. However, in conducting your particular study, the results for the sample baby are not strong enough to allow you to reject the null hypothesis. Perhaps the random sample baby that you selected to try out the new vitamin happened to be a baby who would not respond to the new vitamin. The results would not be significant. Having decided not to reject the null hypothesis, and thus refusing to draw a conclusion, would be a Type II error.

Type II errors especially concern behavioral and social scientists interested in practical applications. This is because a Type II error could mean that a valuable practical procedure is not used.

As with a Type I error, you cannot know when you have made a Type II error. But researchers can try to carry out studies so as to reduce the probability of making one. One way of buying insurance against a Type II error is to set a very lenient significance level, such as $p < .10$ or even $p < .20$. In this way, even if a study results in only a very small effect, the results have a good chance of being significant. There is a cost to this insurance policy too.

Relation of Type I and Type II Errors

When it comes to setting significance levels, protecting against one kind of decision error increases the chance of making the other. The insurance policy against Type I error (setting a significance level of, say, .001) has the cost of increasing the chance of making a Type II error. (This is because with a stringent significance level like .001, even if the research hypothesis is true, the results have to be quite strong to be extreme enough to reject the null hypothesis.) The insurance policy against Type II error (setting a significance level of, say, .20) has the cost that you increase the chance of making a Type I error. (This is because with a level of significance like .20, even if the null hypothesis is true, it is fairly easy to get a significant result just by accidentally getting a sample that is higher or lower than the general population before doing the study.)

The trade-off between these two conflicting concerns usually is worked out by compromise—thus the standard 5% and 1% significance levels.

Summary of Possible Outcomes of Hypothesis Testing

The entire issue of possible correct and mistaken conclusions in hypothesis testing is shown in Table 5–2. Along the top of this table are the two possibilities about whether the null hypothesis or the research hypothesis is really true. (Remember, you never actually know this.) Along the side is whether, after hypothesis testing, you decide that the research hypothesis is supported (reject the null hypothesis) or decide that the

Type II error   Failing to reject the null hypothesis when in fact it is false; failing to get a statistically significant result when in fact the research hypothesis is true.

TIP FOR SUCCESS

It is very easy to get confused between a Type I error and a Type II error. Be sure you understand each type of error (and the difference between them) before reading on in this chapter.

Table 5-2 Possible Correct and Incorrect Decisions in Hypothesis Testing

		Real Situation (in practice, unknown)	
		Null Hypothesis True	Research Hypothesis True
Conclusion Using Hypothesis-testing Procedure	Research hypothesis supported (reject null hypothesis)	Error (Type I)	Correct decision
	Study is inconclusive (do not reject null hypothesis)	Correct decision	Error (Type II)

results are inconclusive (do not reject the null hypothesis). Table 5–2 shows that there are two ways to be correct and two ways to be in error in any hypothesis-testing situation. You will learn more about these possibilities in Chapter 7.

How are you doing?

1. What is a decision error?
2. (a) What is a Type I error? (b) Why is it possible? (c) What is its probability?
3. (a) What is a Type II error? (b) Why is it possible?
4. If you set a lenient significance level (say .25), what is the effect on the probability of (a) Type I error and (b) Type II error?
5. If you set a stringent significance level (say .001), what is the effect on the probability of (a) Type I error and (b) Type II error?

Answers

1. A decision error is a conclusion from hypothesis testing that does not match reality.
2. (a) Rejecting the null hypothesis (and thus supporting the research hypothesis) when the null hypothesis is actually true (and the research hypothesis false) is a Type I error. (b) You reject the null hypothesis when a sample's result is so extreme it is unlikely you would have gotten that result if the null hypothesis is true. However, even though it is unlikely, it is still possible that the null hypothesis is true. (c) Its probability is the significance level (such as .05).
3. (a) Failing to reject the null hypothesis (and thus failing to support the research hypothesis) when the null hypothesis is actually false (and the research hypothesis true) is a Type II error. (b) You reject the null hypothesis when a sample's result is so extreme it is unlikely you would have gotten that result if the null hypothesis is true. However, the null hypothesis could be false, but the sample mean may not be extreme enough to reject the null hypothesis.
4. (a) It is high; (b) it is low.
5. (a) It is low; (b) it is high.

Hypothesis Tests as Reported in Research Articles

In general, hypothesis testing is reported in research articles as part of one of the specific methods you learn in later chapters. For each result of interest, the researcher usually first says whether the result was statistically significant. Next, the researcher usually gives the symbol for the specific method used in figuring the probabilities, such as t, F, or χ^2 (these procedures are covered in Chapters 8 through 11). Finally, there will be an indication of the significance level, such as $p < .05$ or $p < .01$. (The researcher will usually also provide much other information, such as sample means and standard deviations.) For example, Hopkins and colleagues (2005) conducted a study of factors influencing throwing among captive chimpanzees. They used a sample of 262 chimpanzees, 115 of whom had been observed to throw an object at least once in the past and 147 who had never been observed to throw. Hopkins et al. focused on whether there were age differences between chimpanzees with a history of throwing and those with no throwing history. Here is what they reported: ". . . the mean age of throwers ($M = 16.81$, $SD = 16.81$) was significantly younger than the mean age of nonthrowers ($M = 23.56$, $SD = 11.73$), $t(260) = 5.26$, $p < .001$" (p. 365). There is a lot here that you will learn about in later chapters, but the key thing to understand now about this result is the "$p < .001$." This means that the probability of their results if the null hypothesis (of no difference between the populations their groups represent) were true is less than .001 (.1%). Thus it is very highly unlikely in the population at large of captive chimpanzees that throwers and nonthrowers do not differ in age. That is, the results support the research hypothesis that among captive chimpanzees in general, throwers are on the average younger than nonthrowers. Also, since it was not specified as a one-tailed test, you can assume this was a two-tailed test.

When a result is close, but does not reach the significance level chosen, it may be reported as a "near significant trend" or as having "approached significance," with $p < .10$, for example. When a result is not even close to being extreme enough to reject the null hypothesis, it may be reported as "not significant" or the abbreviation ns will be used. Regardless of whether a result is significant, it is increasingly common for researchers to report the exact p level—such as $p = .03$ or $p = .27$ (these are given in computer outputs of statistical tests). In addition, if a one-tailed test was used, that usually will be noted. Again, when reading research articles, assume a two-tailed test if nothing is said otherwise. Even though a researcher has chosen a significance level in advance, such as .05, results that meet more rigorous standards will likely be noted as such. Thus, in the same article you may see some results noted as "$p < .05$," others as "$p < .01$," and still others as "$p < .001$."

Finally, often the outcomes of hypothesis testing are shown simply as asterisks in a table of results. In such tables, a result with an asterisk is significant, while a result without one is not.

In reporting results of significance testing, researchers rarely make explicit the research hypothesis or the null hypothesis, or describe any of the other steps of the process in any detail. It is assumed that the reader understands all of this very well. Decision errors are rarely mentioned in research articles.

Summary

1. Hypothesis testing considers the probability that the result of a study could have come about even if the experimental procedure had no effect. If this probability is low, the scenario of no effect is rejected and the hypothesis behind the experimental procedure is supported.
2. The expectation of an effect is the research hypothesis, and the hypothetical situation of no effect is the null hypothesis.

3. When a result (that is, a sample score) is so extreme that the result would be very unlikely if the null hypothesis were true, the null hypothesis is rejected and the research hypothesis supported. If the result is not that extreme, the study is inconclusive.

4. Behavioral and social scientists usually consider a result too extreme if it is less likely than 5% (that is, a significance level of .05) to have come about if the null hypothesis were true. Sometimes a more stringent 1% (.01 significance level), or even .1% (.001 significance level), cutoff is used.

5. The cutoff percentage is the probability of the result being extreme in a predicted direction in a directional or one-tailed test. The cutoff percentages are the probability of the result being extreme in either direction in a nondirectional or two-tailed test.

6. The five steps of hypothesis testing are:
   ❶ **Restate the question as a research hypothesis and a null hypothesis about the populations.**
   ❷ **Determine the characteristics of the comparison distribution.**
   ❸ **Determine the cutoff sample score on the comparison distribution at which the null hypothesis should be rejected.**
   ❹ **Determine your sample's score on the comparison distribution.**
   ❺ **Decide whether to reject the null hypothesis.**

7. There are two kinds of decision errors one can make in hypothesis testing. A Type I error is when a researcher rejects the null hypothesis, but the null hypothesis is actually true. A Type II error is when a researcher does not reject the null hypothesis, but the null hypothesis is actually false.

8. Research articles typically report the results of hypothesis testing by saying a result was or was not significant and giving the probability level cutoff (usually 5% or 1%) the decision was based on. Research articles rarely mention decision errors.

Key Terms

hypothesis testing (p. 145)
hypothesis (p. 145)
theory (p. 145)
research hypothesis (p. 148)
null hypothesis (p. 149)
comparison distribution (p. 149)

cutoff sample score (p. 150)
conventional levels of significance
    ($p < .05$, $p < .01$) (p. 150)
statistically significant (p. 150)
directional hypothesis (p. 154)
one-tailed test (p. 154)

nondirectional hypothesis (p. 155)
two-tailed test (p. 155)
decision errors (p. 159)
Type I error (p. 160)
Type II error (p. 161)

Example Worked-Out Problems

A randomly selected individual, after going through an experimental treatment, has a score of 27 on a particular measure. The scores of people in general on this measure are normally distributed with a mean of 19 and a standard deviation of 4. The researcher predicts an effect, but does not predict a particular direction of effect. Using the 5% significance level, what should you conclude? Solve this problem explicitly using all five steps of hypothesis testing and illustrate your answer with a sketch showing the comparison distribution, the cutoff (or cutoffs), and the score of the sample on this distribution.

Answer

❶ **Restate the question as a research hypothesis and a null hypothesis about the populations.** There are two populations of interest:

Population 1: People who go through the experimental procedure.
Population 2: People in general (that is, people who do not go through the experimental procedure).

The research hypothesis is that Population 1 will score differently than Population 2 on the particular measure. The null hypothesis is that the two populations are not different on the measure.

❷ **Determine the characteristics of the comparison distribution:** Population $M = 19$, Population $SD = 4$, normally distributed.

❸ **Determine the cutoff sample score on the comparison distribution at which the null hypothesis should be rejected.** For a two-tailed test at the 5% level (2.5% at each tail), the cutoff sample scores are $+1.96$ and -1.96 (see Figure 5–4 or Table 5–1).

❹ **Determine your sample's score on the comparison distribution.** $Z = (27 - 19)/4 = 2$.

❺ **Decide whether to reject the null hypothesis.** A Z score of 2 is more extreme than the cutoff Z of $+1.96$. Reject the null hypothesis; the result is significant. The experimental procedure affects scores on this measure. The diagram is shown in Figure 5–6.

Outline for Writing Essays for Hypothesis-Testing Problems Involving a Single Sample of One Participant and a Known Population

1. Describe the core logic of hypothesis testing. Be sure to explain terminology such as research hypothesis and null hypothesis, and explain the concept of support

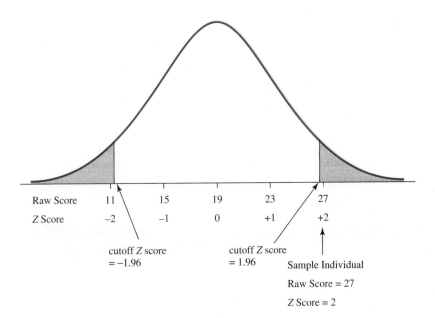

Figure 5–6 Diagram for Example Worked-Out Problem showing comparison distribution, cutoffs (2.5% shaded area in each tail), and sample score.

being provided for the research hypothesis when the study results allow the null hypothesis to be rejected.

2. Explain the concept of the comparison distribution. Be sure to mention that it is the distribution that represents the population situation if the null hypothesis is true. Note that the key characteristics of the comparison distribution are its mean, standard deviation, and shape.

3. Describe the logic and process for determining (using the normal curve) the cut-off sample scores on the comparison distribution at which the null hypothesis should be rejected.

4. Describe how to figure the sample's score on the comparison distribution.

5. Explain how and why the scores from Steps ❸ and ❹ of the hypothesis-testing process are compared. Explain the meaning of the result of this comparison with regard to the specific research and null hypotheses being tested.

Practice Problems

These problems involve figuring. Most real-life statistics problems are done on a computer with special statistical software. Even if you have such software, do these problems by hand to ingrain the method in your mind.

All data are fictional unless an actual citation is given.

Set I (for answers, see pp. 441–442)

1. Define the following terms in your own words: (a) hypothesis-testing procedure, (b) .05 significance level, and (c) two-tailed test.

2. When a result is not extreme enough to reject the null hypothesis, explain why it is wrong to conclude that your result supports the null hypothesis.

3. For each of the following, (a) say what two populations are being compared, (b) state the research hypothesis, (c) state the null hypothesis, and (d) say whether you should use a one-tailed or two-tailed test and why.

   i. Do Canadian children whose parents are librarians score higher than Canadian children in general on reading ability?

   ii. Is the level of income for residents of a particular city different from the level of income for people in the region?

   iii. Do people who have experienced an earthquake have more or less self-confidence than the general population?

4. Based on the information given for each of the following studies, decide whether to reject the null hypothesis. For each, give the Z-score cutoff (or cutoffs) on the comparison distribution at which the null hypothesis should be rejected, the Z score on the comparison distribution for the sample score, and conclusion. Assume that all populations are normally distributed.

	Population				
Study	*M*	*SD*	*Sample Score*	*p*	*Tails of Test*
A	10	2	14	.05	1 (high predicted)
B	10	2	14	.05	2
C	10	2	14	.01	1 (high predicted)
D	10	2	14	.01	2
E	10	4	14	.05	1 (high predicted)

5. Based on the information given for each of the following studies, decide whether to reject the null hypothesis. For each, give the Z-score cutoff (or cutoffs) on the comparison distribution at which the null hypothesis should be rejected, the Z score on the comparison distribution for the sample score, and conclusion. Assume that all populations are normally distributed.

	Population				
Study	M	SD	Sample Score	p	Tails of Test
A	70	4	74	.05	1 (high predicted)
B	70	1	74	.01	2
C	70	2	76	.01	2
D	70	2	77	.01	2
E	70	2	68	.05	1 (high predicted)

6. A researcher studying the senses of taste and smell has carried out many studies in which students are given each of 20 different foods (apricot, chocolate, cherry, coffee, garlic, and so on). She administers each food by dropping a liquid on the tongue. Based on her past research, she knows that for students overall at the university, the mean number of these 20 foods that students can identify correctly is 14, with a standard deviation of 4, and the distribution of scores follows a normal curve. The researcher wants to know whether people's accuracy on this task has more to do with smell than with taste. In other words, she wants to test whether people do *worse* on the task when they are only able to taste the liquid compared to when they can both taste and smell the liquid (note that this is a directional hypothesis). Thus, she sets up special procedures that keep a person from being able to use the sense of smell during the task. The researcher then tries the procedure on one randomly selected student. This student is able to identify only 5 correctly. Using the .05 significance level, what should the researcher conclude? Solve this problem explicitly using all five steps of hypothesis testing and illustrate your answer with a sketch showing the comparison distribution, the cutoff (or cutoffs), and the score of the sample on this distribution. Then explain your answer to someone who has never had a course in statistics (but who is familiar with mean, standard deviation, and Z scores).

7. A nursing researcher is working with people who have had a particular type of major surgery. This researcher proposes that people will recover from the operation more quickly if friends and family are in the room with them for the first 48 hours after the operation. It is known that time to recover from this kind of surgery is normally distributed with a mean of 12 days and a standard deviation of 5 days. The procedure of having friends and family in the room for the period after the surgery is tried with a randomly selected patient. This patient recovers in 18 days. Using the .01 significance level, what should the researcher conclude? Solve this problem explicitly using all five steps of hypothesis testing and illustrate your answer with a sketch showing the comparison distribution, the cutoff (or cutoffs), and the score of the sample on this distribution. Then explain your answer to someone who has never had a course in statistics (but who is familiar with mean, standard deviation, and Z scores).

8. Robins and John (1997) carried out a study on narcissism (self-love), comparing people who scored high versus low on a narcissism questionnaire. (An example item was "If I ruled the world, it would be a better place.") They also had other questionnaires, including one that had an item about how many times the

participant looked in the mirror on a typical day. In their results section, the researchers noted ". . . as predicted, high-narcissism individuals reported looking at themselves in the mirror more frequently than did low narcissism individuals ($Ms = 5.7$ vs. 4.8), . . . $p < .05$" (p. 39). Explain this result to a person who has never had a course in statistics. (Focus on the meaning of this result in terms of the general logic of hypothesis testing and statistical significance.)

9. Reber and Kotovsky (1997), in a study of problem solving, described one of their results comparing a specific group of participants within their overall control condition as follows: "This group took an average of 179 moves to solve the puzzle, whereas the rest of the control participants took an average of 74 moves, $t(19) = 3.31$, $p < .01$" (p. 183). Explain this result to a person who has never had a course in statistics. (Focus on the meaning of this result in terms of the general logic of hypothesis testing and statistical significance.)

10. For each of the following studies, make a chart of the four possible correct and incorrect decisions, and explain what each would mean. (Each chart should be laid out like Table 5–2, but you should put into the boxes the possible results, using the names of the variables involved in the study.)
    (a) A study of whether increasing the amount of recess time improves school-children's in-class behavior.
    (b) A study of whether color-blind individuals can distinguish gray shades better than the population at large.
    (c) A study comparing individuals who have ever been in psychotherapy to the general public to see if they are more tolerant of other people's upsets than is the general population.

11. You conduct a research study. How can you know (a) if you have made a Type I error? and (b) if you have made a Type II error?

Set II

12. List the five steps of hypothesis testing and explain the procedure and logic of each.

13. When a result is significant, explain why is it wrong to say the result "proves" the research hypothesis?

14. For each of the following, (a) say what two populations are being compared, (b) state the research hypothesis, (c) state the null hypothesis, and (d) say whether you should use a one-tailed or two-tailed test and why.
    i. In an experiment, people are told to solve a problem by focusing on the details. Is the speed of solving the problem different for people who get such instructions compared to people who are given no special instructions?
    ii. Based on anthropological reports in which the status of women is scored on a 10-point scale, the mean and standard deviation across many cultures are known. A new culture is found in which there is an unusual family arrangement. The status of women is also rated in this culture. Do cultures with the unusual family arrangement provide higher status to women than cultures in general?
    iii. Do people who live in big cities develop more stress-related conditions than people in general?

15. Based on the information given for each of the following studies, decide whether to reject the null hypothesis. For each, give the Z-score cutoff (or cutoffs) on the comparison distribution at which the null hypothesis should be rejected, the Z score on the comparison distribution for the sample score, and conclusion. Assume that all populations are normally distributed.

	Population				
Study	M	SD	Sample Score	p	Tails of Test
A	5	1	7	.05	1 (high predicted)
B	5	1	7	.05	2
C	5	1	7	.01	1 (high predicted)
D	5	1	7	.01	2

16. Based on the information given for each of the following studies, decide whether to reject the null hypothesis. For each, give the Z-score cutoff (or cutoffs) on the comparison distribution at which the null hypothesis should be rejected, the Z score on the comparison distribution for the sample score, and conclusion. Assume that all populations are normally distributed.

	Population				
Study	M	SD	Sample Score	p	Tails of Test
A	100.0	10.0	80	.05	1 (low predicted)
B	100.0	20.0	80	.01	2
C	74.3	11.8	80	.01	2
D	76.9	1.2	80	.05	1 (low predicted)
E	88.1	12.7	80	.05	2

17. A researcher wants to test whether a certain sound will make rats do worse on learning tasks. It is known that an ordinary rat can learn to run a particular maze correctly in 18 trials, with a standard deviation of 6. (The number of trials to learn this maze is normally distributed. More trials mean worse performance on the task.) The researcher now tries an ordinary rat on the maze, but with the sound. The rat takes 38 trials to learn the maze. Using the .05 level, what should the researcher conclude? Solve this problem explicitly using all five steps of hypothesis testing and illustrate your answer with a sketch showing the comparison distribution, the cutoff (or cutoffs), and the score of the sample on this distribution. Then explain your answer to someone who has never had a course in statistics (but who is familiar with mean, standard deviation, and Z scores).

18. A researcher developed an elaborate training program to reduce the stress of childless men who marry women with adolescent children. It is known from previous research that such men, one month after moving in with their new wife and her children, have a stress level of 85 with a standard deviation of 15, and the stress levels are normally distributed. The training program is tried on one man randomly selected from all those in a particular city who during the preceding month have married a woman with an adolescent child. After the training program, this man's stress level is 60. Using the .05 level, what should the researcher conclude? Solve this problem explicitly using all five steps of hypothesis testing and illustrate your answer with a sketch showing the comparison distribution, the cutoff (or cutoffs), and the score of the sample on this distribution. Then explain your answer to someone who has never had a course in statistics (but who is familiar with mean, standard deviation, and Z scores).

19. A researcher predicts that listening to music while solving math problems will make a particular brain area more active. To test this, a research participant has her brain scanned while listening to music and solving math problems, and the brain area of interest has a percent signal change of 5.8. From many previous studies with this same math-problems procedure (but not listening to music), it

is known that the signal change in this brain area is normally distributed with a mean of 3.5 and a standard deviation of 1.0. Using the .01 level, what should the researcher conclude? Solve this problem explicitly using all five steps of hypothesis testing and illustrate your answer with a sketch showing the comparison distribution, the cutoff (or cutoffs), and the score of the sample on this distribution. Then explain your answer to someone who has never had a course in statistics (but who is familiar with mean, standard deviation, and Z scores).

20. Pecukonis (1990), as part of a larger study, measured ego development (a measure of overall maturity) and ability to empathize with others among a group of 24 aggressive adolescent girls in a residential treatment center. The girls were divided into high and low ego development groups, and the empathy ("cognitive empathy") scores of these two groups were compared. In his results section, Pecukonis reported, "The average score on cognitive empathy for subjects scoring high on ego development was 22.1 as compared with 16.3 for low scorers, . . . p < .005" (p. 68). Explain this result to a person who has never had a course in statistics. (Focus on the meaning of this result in terms of the general logic of hypothesis testing and statistical significance.)

21. In an article about anti-tobacco campaigns, Siegel and Biener (1997) discuss the results of a survey of tobacco usage and attitudes conducted in Massachusetts in 1993 and 1995; Table 5–3 shows the results of this survey. Focusing on just the first line (the percentage smoking >25 cigarettes daily), explain what this result means to a person who has never had a course in statistics. (Focus on the meaning of this result in terms of the general logic of hypothesis testing and statistical significance.)

22. For each of the following studies, make a chart of the four possible correct and incorrect decisions, and explain what each would mean. (Each chart should be laid

Table 5-3 Selected Indicators of Change in Tobacco Use, ETS Exposure, and Public Attitudes toward Tobacco Control Policies—Massachusetts, 1993–1995		
	1993	**1995**
Adult Smoking Behavior		
Percentage smoking >25 cigarettes daily	24	10*
Percentage smoking <15 cigarettes daily	31	49*
Percentage smoking within 30 minutes of waking	54	41
Environmental Tobacco Smoke Exposure		
Percentage of workers reporting a smoke free worksite	53	65*
Mean hours of ETS exposure at work during prior week	4.2	2.3*
Percentage of homes in which smoking is banned	41	51*
Attitudes Toward Tobacco Control Policies		
Percentage supporting further increase in tax on tobacco with funds earmarked for tobacco control	78	81
Percentage believing ETS is harmful	90	84
Percentage supporting ban on vending machines	54	64*
Percentage supporting ban on support of sports and cultural events by tobacco companies	59	53*

*$p < .05$
Source: Siegel, M., & Biener, L. (1997). Evaluating the impact of statewide anti-tobacco campaigns: The Massachusetts and California tobacco control programs. *Journal of Social Issues, 53,* 147–168. Reprinted by permission of Blackwell Publishers Journals.

out like Table 5–2, but put into the boxes the possible results, using the names of the variables involved in the study.)

(a) A study of whether infants born prematurely begin to recognize faces later than do infants in general.

(b) A study of whether high school students who receive an AIDS prevention program in their schools are more likely to practice safe sex than are other high school students.

(c) A study of whether memory for abstract ideas is reduced if the information is presented in distracting colors.

CHAPTER 6

Hypothesis Tests with Means of Samples

CHAPTER OUTLINE

- The Distribution of Means
- Hypothesis Testing with a Distribution of Means: The Z Test
- Hypothesis Tests about Means of Samples (Z Tests) in Research Articles
- Advanced Topic: Estimation and Confidence Intervals
- Advanced Topic: Confidence Intervals in Research Articles
- Summary
- Key Terms
- Example Worked-Out Problems
- Practice Problems

TIP FOR SUCCESS

It is important that you understand Chapter 5 quite solidly before going on to this chapter.

In Chapter 5, we introduced the basic logic of hypothesis testing. The studies we used as examples each had a sample of a single individual. As we noted, however, in actual practice, behavioral and social science research almost always involve a sample of many individuals. In this chapter, we build on what you have learned so far and consider hypothesis testing involving a sample of more than one individual. For example, a team of educational researchers is interested in the effects of different kinds of instructions on timed school achievement tests. These educational researchers have a theory that predicts that people will do better on a test if they are given instructions to answer each question with the first response that comes to mind. To test this theory, the researchers give a standard school achievement test to 64 randomly selected fifth-grade schoolchildren. They give the test in the usual way, except that they add to the instructions a statement that children are to answer each question with the first response that comes to mind. From previous testing, the researchers know the population mean and standard deviation of the test when it is given in the usual way (without any special instructions). In this chapter, you will learn how to test hypotheses in situations like this example: situations in which the population has a *known mean and standard deviation,* and a sample has *more than one individual.* Mainly, this requires examining in some detail a new kind of distribution, called a *distribution of means.* (We will return to the special instructions example later in the chapter.)

distribution of means Distribution of means of samples of a given size from a particular population (also called a sampling distribution of the mean); comparison distribution when testing hypotheses involving a single sample of more than one individual.

The Distribution of Means

Hypothesis testing in the usual research situation, where you are studying a sample of many individuals, is exactly the same as you learned in Chapter 5—with an important exception. When you have more than one person in your sample, there is a special problem with Step ❷, determining the characteristics of the comparison distribution. In each of our examples so far, the comparison distribution has been a distribution of *individual scores* (such as the population of ages when individual babies start walking). The distribution of individual scores has been the correct comparison distribution because we have used examples with a sample of *one individual.* That is, there has been consistency between the type of sample score we have been dealing with (a score from *one individual*) and the comparison distribution (a distribution of *individual scores*).

Now, consider the situation when you have a sample of, say, 64 individuals. You now have a *group of 64 scores.* As you will recall from Chapter 2, the mean is a very useful representative value of a group of scores. Thus, the score you care about when there is more than one individual in your sample is the *mean of the group of scores.* In this example, you would focus on the mean of the 64 individuals. If you were to compare the mean of this sample of 64 individuals to a distribution of a population of individual scores, this would be a mismatch—like comparing apples to oranges. Instead, when you are interested in the mean of a sample of 64 scores you need a comparison distribution that is a distribution of means of samples of 64 scores. We call such a comparison distribution a **distribution of means.** The scores in a distribution of means are *means,* not scores of individuals.

A distribution of means is a distribution of the means of each of lots and lots of samples of the same size, with each sample randomly taken from the same population of individuals. (Statisticians also call this distribution of means a *sampling distribution of the mean.* In this book, however, we use the term *distribution of means* to make it clear that we are talking about populations of *means,* not samples or some kind of distribution of samples.)

The distribution of means is the correct comparison distribution when there is more than one person in a sample. Thus, in most research situations, determining the characteristics of a distribution of means is necessary for Step ❷ of the hypothesis-testing procedure (determining the characteristics of the comparison distribution).

Building a Distribution of Means

To help you understand the idea of a distribution of means, we consider how you could build up such a distribution from an ordinary population distribution of individual scores. Suppose our population of individual scores was the grade levels of the 90,000 elementary and junior-high school children in a particular region. Suppose further (to keep the example simple) that there are exactly 10,000 children at each grade level, from first through ninth grade. This population distribution would be rectangular, with a mean of 5, a variance of 6.67, and a standard deviation of 2.58 (see Figure 6–1).

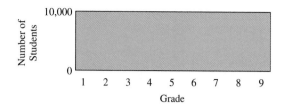

Figure 6-1 Distribution of grade levels among 90,000 school children (fictional data).

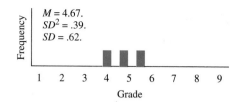

Figure 6-2 Distribution of the means of three randomly taken samples of two schoolchildren's grade levels, each from a population of grade levels of 90,000 schoolchildren (fictional data).

Next, suppose that you wrote each child's grade level on a table tennis ball and put all 90,000 balls into a giant tub. The tub would have 10,000 balls with a 1 on them, 10,000 with a 2 on them, and so forth. Stir up the balls in the tub, and then take two of them out. You have taken a random sample of two balls. Suppose one ball has a 2 on it and the other has a 9 on it. The mean grade level of this sample of two children's grade levels is 5.5, the average of 2 and 9. Now you put the balls back, mix up all the balls, and select two balls again. Maybe this time you get two 4s, making the mean of your second sample 4. Then you try again; this time you get a 2 and a 7, making your mean 4.5. So far you have three means: 5.5, 4, and 4.5.

These three numbers are each a mean of a sample of grade levels of two schoolchildren. And these three means can be thought of as a small distribution in its own right. The mean of this little distribution of means is 4.67 (the sum of 5.5, 4, and 4.5 divided by 3). The variance of this distribution of means is .39 (the variance of 5.5, 4, and 4.5). The standard deviation of this distribution of means is .62 (the square root of .39). A histogram of this distribution of three means is shown in Figure 6–2.

Suppose you continued selecting samples of two balls and taking the mean of the numbers on the two balls. The histogram of means would continue to grow. Figure 6–3 shows examples of distributions of means with just 50 means, up to a distribution of means with 1,000 means (with each mean being of a sample of two randomly drawn balls). (We actually made the histograms shown in Figure 6–3 using a computer to make the random selections instead of using 90,000 table tennis balls and a giant tub.)

As you can imagine, the method we just described is not a practical way of determining the characteristics of a distribution of means. Fortunately, you can figure out the characteristics of a distribution of means directly, using some simple rules, without taking even one sample. The only information you need is (a) the characteristics of the distribution of the population of individuals and (b) the number of scores in each sample. (Don't worry for now about how you could know the characteristics of the population of individuals.) The laborious method of building up a distribution of means in the way we have just considered and the concise method you will learn shortly give the same result. We have had you think of the process in terms of the painstaking method only because it helps you understand the idea of a distribution of means.

Determining the Characteristics of a Distribution of Means

Recall that Step ❷ of hypothesis testing involves determining the characteristics of the comparison distribution. The three characteristics of the comparison distribution that you need are as follows:

1. Its mean
2. Its spread (which you can measure using the variance and standard deviation)
3. Its shape

TIP FOR SUCCESS

Before moving on to later chapters in the book, be sure you fully understand the idea of a distribution of means (and why it is the correct comparison distribution when a sample has more than one individual). Don't worry if you need to go through the chapter a couple of times to master these ideas.

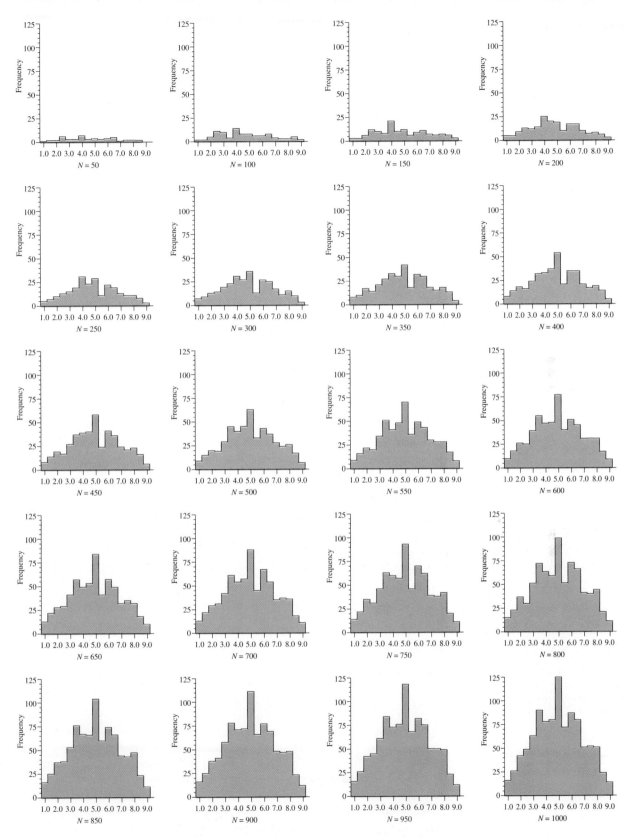

Figure 6-3 Histograms of means of samples of two grade levels randomly selected from a large group of students with equal numbers of grades 1 through 9. Histograms shown are for 50 such means, 100 such means, and so forth, up to 1000 such means. Notice that the histograms become increasingly like a normal curve as the number of means increases.

mean of a distribution of means
The mean of a distribution of means of samples of a given size from a particular population; the same as the mean of the population of individuals.

variance of a distribution of means
Variance of the population divided by the number of scores in each sample.

Notice three things about the distribution of means we built up in our example, as shown in Figure 6–3.

1. The mean of the distribution of means is about the same as the mean of the original population of individuals (both are 5).
2. The spread of the distribution of means is less than the spread of the distribution of the population of individuals.
3. The shape of the distribution of means is approximately normal.

The first two observations, regarding the mean and the spread, are true for all distributions of means. The third, regarding the shape, is true for most distributions of means. These three observations, in fact, illustrate three basic rules that you can use to find the mean, spread, and shape of any distribution of means without having to write on plastic balls and take endless samples.

Now, let's examine the three rules. The first is for the **mean of a distribution of means.**

Rule 1: The mean of a distribution of means is the same as the mean of the population of individuals. Stated as a formula,

$$\text{Population } M_M = \text{Population } M \tag{6-1}$$

Population M_M is the mean of the distribution of means. It uses the word *Population* because the distribution of means is also a kind of population. Population M is the mean of the population of individuals.

Each sample is based on randomly selected individuals from the population of individuals. Thus, the mean of a sample will sometimes be higher and sometimes be lower than the mean of the whole population of individuals. However, because the selection process is random and because we are taking a very large number of samples, eventually the high means and the low means perfectly balance each other out.

In Figure 6–3, as the number of sample means in the distributions of means increase, the mean of the distribution of means becomes more similar to the mean of the population of individuals, which in this example was 5. It can be proven mathematically that if you took an infinite number of samples, the mean of the distribution of means of these samples would come out to be exactly the same as the mean of the distribution of individuals.

The second rule is about spread. This second rule has two parts: the first part, Rule 2a, is for the **variance of a distribution of means.**

Rule 2a: The variance of a distribution of means is the variance of the population of individuals divided by the number of individuals in each sample. A distribution of means will be less spread out than the population of individuals from which the samples are taken. If you are taking a sample of two scores, it is less likely that *both* scores will be extreme. Further, for a particular random sample to have an extreme mean, the two extreme scores would both have to be extreme in the same direction (both very high or both very low). Thus, having more than a single score in each sample has a moderating effect on the mean of such samples. In any one sample, the extremes tend to be balanced out by a middle score or by an extreme in the opposite direction. This makes each sample mean tend toward the middle and away from extreme values. With fewer extreme means, there is less spread, and the variance of the means is less than the variance of the population of individuals.

Consider again our example. There were plenty of 1s and 9s in the population, making a fair amount of spread. That is, about a ninth of the time, if you were taking samples of single scores, you would get a 1, and a ninth of the time you would get a 9.

The mean of the distribution of means is equal to the mean of the population of individuals.

If you are taking samples of two at a time, you would get a sample with a mean of 1 (that is, in which *both* balls were 1s) or a mean of 9 (both balls 9s) much less often. Getting two balls that average out to a middle value such as 5 is much more likely. (This is because several combinations could give this result—a 1 and a 9, a 2 and an 8, a 3 and a 7, a 4 and a 6, or two 5s.)

The more individuals in each sample, the less spread out will be the means of those samples. This is because the more scores in each sample, the rarer it will be for extremes in any particular sample not to be balanced out by middle scores or extremes in the other direction. In terms of the plastic balls in our example, we rarely got a mean of 1 when taking samples of two balls at a time. If we were taking three balls at a time, getting a sample with a mean of 1 (all three balls would have to be 1s) is even less likely. Getting middle values for the means becomes more likely.

Using samples of two balls at a time, the variance of the distribution of means came out to about 3.34. This is half of the variance of the population of individuals, which was 6.67. If we had built up a distribution of means using samples of three balls each, the variance of the distribution of means would have been 2.22. This is one-third of the variance of the population of individuals. Had we randomly selected five balls for each sample, the variance of the distribution of means would have been one-fifth of the variance of the population of individuals.

These examples follow a general rule—our Rule 2a for the distribution of means: The variance of a distribution of means is the variance of the population of individuals divided by the number of individuals in each of the samples. This rule holds in all situations and can be proven mathematically.

Here is Rule 2a stated as a formula:

$$\text{Population } SD_M^2 = \frac{\text{Population } SD^2}{N} \qquad \textbf{(6-2)}$$

Population SD_M^2 is the variance of the distribution of means, Population SD^2 is the variance of the population of individuals, and N is the number of individuals in each sample.

In our example, the variance of the population of individual children's grade levels was 6.67, and there were two children's grade levels in each sample. Thus,

$$\text{Population } SD_M^2 = \frac{\text{Population } SD^2}{N} = \frac{6.67}{2} = 3.34.$$

To use a different example, suppose a population had a variance of 400 and you wanted to know the variance of a distribution of means of 25 individuals each:

$$\text{Population } SD_M^2 = \frac{\text{Population } SD^2}{N} = \frac{400}{25} = 16.$$

The second rule also tells us about the **standard deviation of a distribution of means.**

Rule 2b: The standard deviation of a distribution of means is the square root of the variance of the distribution of means. Stated as a formula,

$$\text{Population } SD_M = \sqrt{\text{Population } SD_M^2} \qquad \textbf{(6-3)}$$

Population SD_M is the standard deviation of the distribution of means.

The standard deviation of the distribution of means also has a special name of its own, the the **standard error (SE)** (or *standard error of the mean,* abbreviated *SEM*). It has this name because it tells you how much the means of samples are typically "in error" as estimates of the mean of the population of individuals. That is, it tells you

standard deviation of a distribution of means (Population SD_M).   Square root of the variance of the distribution of means; same as *standard error (SE).*

standard error (SE)   Same as *standard deviation of a distribution of means;* also called *standard error of the mean.*

> The variance of a distribution of means is the variance of the population of individuals divided by the number of individuals in each sample.

> The standard deviation of a distribution of means is the square root of the variance of the distribution of means.

shape of a distribution of means
Contour of a histogram of a distribution of means, such as whether it follows a normal curve or is skewed; in general, a distribution of means will tend to be unimodal and symmetrical and is often normal.

how much the particular means in the distribution of means deviate from the mean of the population. (We will have more to say about this idea in the Advanced Topic section on confidence intervals later in the chapter.)

Finally, the third rule for finding the characteristics of a distribution of means focuses on its shape.

Rule 3: The shape of a distribution of means is approximately normal if either (a) each sample is of 30 or more individuals or (b) the distribution of the population of individuals is normal. Whatever the shape of the distribution of the population of individuals, the distribution of means tends to be unimodal and symmetrical. In the grade-level example, the population distribution was rectangular. (It had an equal number at each grade level.) However, the **shape of the distribution of means** (Figure 6–3) was roughly that of a bell—unimodal and symmetrical. Had we taken many more than 1,000 samples, the shape would have been even more clearly unimodal and symmetrical.

A distribution of means tends to be unimodal because of the same basic process of extremes balancing each other out that we noted in the discussion of the variance: Middle scores for means are more likely, and extreme means are less likely. A distribution of means tends to be symmetrical because lack of symmetry (skew) is caused by extremes. With fewer extremes, there is less asymmetry. In our grade-level example, the distribution of means we built up also came out so clearly symmetrical because the population distribution of individual grade levels was symmetrical. Had the population distribution of individuals been skewed to one side, the distribution of means would have still been skewed, but not as much.

The more individuals in each sample, the closer the distribution of means will be to a normal curve. In fact, with samples of 30 or more individuals, even with a non-normal population of individuals, the approximation of the distribution of means to a normal curve is very close and the percentages in the normal curve table will be extremely accurate.[1,2] Finally, whenever the population distribution of individuals is normal, the distribution of means will be normal, regardless of the number of individuals in each sample.

Summary of Rules and Formulas for Determining the Characteristics of a Distribution of Means

Rule 1: The mean of a distribution of means is the same as the mean of the population of individuals:

---

[1]We have ignored that a normal curve is a smooth theoretical distribution. However, in most real-life distributions, scores are only at specific numbers, such as a child being in a particular grade and not in a fraction of a grade. So, one difference between our example distribution of means and a normal curve is that the normal curve is smooth. However, in behavioral and social science research, even when our measurements are at specific numbers, we usually assume that the underlying thing being measured is continuous.

[2]We have already considered this principle of a distribution of means tending toward a normal curve in Chapter 4. Though we had not yet discussed the distribution of means, we still used this principle to explain why the distribution of so many things in nature follows a normal curve. In that chapter, we explained it as the various influences balancing each other out, to make an averaged influence come out with most of the scores near the center and a few at each extreme. Now we have made the same point using the terminology of a distribution of means. Think of any distribution of individual scores in nature as about a situation in which each score is actually an average of a random set of influences on that individual. Consider the distribution of weights of pebbles. Each pebble's weight is a kind of average of all the different forces that went into making the pebble have a particular weight. Statisticians refer to this general principle as the Central Limit Theorem.

$$\text{Population } M_M = \text{Population } M$$

Rule 2a: The variance of a distribution of means is the variance of the population of individuals divided by the number of individuals in each sample:

$$\text{Population } SD^2_M = \frac{\text{Population } SD^2}{N}$$

Rule 2b: The standard deviation of a distribution of means is the square root of the variance of the distribution of means:

$$\text{Population } SD_M = \sqrt{\text{Population } SD^2_M}$$

Rule 3: The shape of a distribution of means is approximately normal if either (a) each sample is of 30 or more individuals or (b) the distribution of the population of individuals is normal.

Figure 6–4 shows these three rules graphically.

Example of Determining the Characteristics of a Distribution of Means

Consider the population of scores of students who have taken the Graduate Record Examinations (GREs): Suppose the distribution is approximately normal with a mean of 500 and a standard deviation of 100. What will be the characteristics of the distribution of means of samples of 50 students?

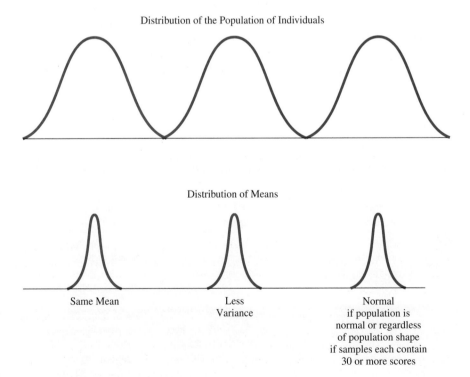

Figure 6–4   Comparing the distribution of the population of individuals (upper curves) and the distribution of means (lower curves).

Rule 1: The mean of a distribution of means is the same as the mean of the population of individuals. The mean of the population is 500. Thus, the mean of the distribution of means will also be 500. That is, Population M_M = Population M = 500.

Rule 2a: The variance of a distribution of means is the variance of the population of individuals divided by the number of individuals in each sample. The standard deviation of the population of individuals is 100; thus, the variance of the population of individuals is 100^2, which is 10,000. The variance of the distribution of means is therefore 10,000 divided by 50 (the size of the sample). This comes out to 200. That is, Population SD_M^2 = Population SD^2/N = 10,000/50 = 200.

Rule 2b: The standard deviation of a distribution of means is the square root of the variance of the distribution of means. The standard deviation of the distribution of means is the square root of 200, which is 14.14. That is, Population SD_M = $\sqrt{\text{Population } SD_M^2}$ = $\sqrt{200}$ = 14.14.

Rule 3: The shape of a distribution of means is approximately normal if either (a) each sample is of 30 or more individuals or (b) the distribution of the population of individuals is normal. Our situation meets both of these conditions—the sample of 50 students is more than 30, and the population of individuals follows a normal distribution. Thus, the distribution of means will follow a normal curve. (It would have been enough even if only one of the two conditions had been met.)

Review of the Three Kinds of Distributions

We have considered three different kinds of distributions: (a) the distribution of a population of individuals, (b) the distribution of a particular sample of individuals taken from that population, and (c) the distribution of means. Figure 6–5 shows these three kinds of distributions graphically and Table 6–1 describes them.

TIP FOR SUCCESS
Be sure you fully understand the different types of distributions shown in Table 6–1 before you move on to later chapters. To check your understanding, cover up portions of the table and then try to recall the information that is covered up.

Table 6–1 Comparison of Three Types of Distributions

	Population's Distribution	Particular Sample's Distribution	Distribution of Means
Content	Scores of all individuals in the population	Scores of the individuals in a single sample	Means of samples randomly taken from the population
Shape	Could be any shape; often normal	Could be any shape	Approximately normal if samples have ≥ 30 individuals in each or if population is normal
Mean	Population M	$M = (\Sigma X)/N$ figured from scores of those in the sample	Population M_M = Population M
Variance	Population SD^2	$SD^2 = [\Sigma(X - M)^2]/N$	Population SD_M^2 = Population SD^2/N
Standard Deviation	Population SD	$SD = \sqrt{SD^2}$	Population SD_M = $\sqrt{\text{Population } SD_M^2}$

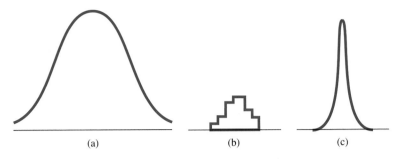

(a)   (b)   (c)

Figure 6-5   Three kinds of distributions: (a) the distribution of a population of individuals, (b) the distribution of a particular sample taken from that population, and (c) the distribution of means.

How are you doing?

1. What is a distribution of means?
2. Explain how you could create a distribution of means by taking a large number of samples of four individuals each.
3. (a) Why is the mean of the distribution of means the same as the mean of the population of individuals? (b) Why is the variance of a distribution of means smaller than the variance of the distribution of the population of individuals?
4. Write the formula for the variance of the distribution of means and define each of the symbols.
5. (a) What is the standard error (SE)? (b) Why does it have this name?
6. A population of individuals has a normal distribution, a mean of 60, and a standard deviation of 10. What are the characteristics of a distribution of means from this population for samples of four each?

Answers

1. It is a distribution of the means of a very large number of samples of the same size randomly taken from the population of individuals.
2. Take a random sample of 4 scores from the population and figure its mean. Repeat this a very large number of times. Make a distribution of these means.
3. (a) With randomly taken samples, some will have higher means and some lower means than the population of individuals; these should balance out. (b) You are less likely to get a sample of several scores with an extreme mean than you are to get a single extreme score. This is because in any random sample it is highly unlikely to get several extremes in the same direction—extreme scores tend to be balanced out by middle scores or extremes in the opposite direction; thus, with fewer extreme scores and more middle scores, there is less variance.
4. Population $SD_M^2 = $ Population SD^2/N. Population SD_M^2 is the variance of the distribution of means; Population SD^2 is the variance of the population of individuals; N is the number of individuals in your sample.
5. (a) The standard deviation of the distribution of means. (b) It tells you about how much means of samples typically (standardly) differ from the population mean, and thus the typical amount that means of samples are in error as estimates of the population mean.
6. Population $M_M = $ Population $M = 60$. Population $SD_M^2 = $ Population SD^2/N $= 10^2/4 = 25$; Population $SD_M = 5$. Shape = normal.

Z test Hypothesis-testing procedure in which there is a single sample and the population variance is known.

Hypothesis Testing with a Distribution of Means: the *Z* Test

Now we are ready to turn to hypothesis testing when there is more than one individual in the study's sample. The hypothesis testing procedure you will learn is called a **Z test** (or a *Z test for a single sample*), because it is the *Z* score that is checked against the normal curve.

The Distribution of Means as the Comparison Distribution in Hypothesis Testing

In the usual research situation in the behavioral and social sciences, a researcher studies a sample of more than one person. In this situation, the distribution of means is the comparison distribution. It is the distribution whose characteristics need to be determined in Step ❷ of the hypothesis-testing process. The distribution of means is the distribution to which you compare your sample's mean to see how likely it is that you could have selected a sample with a mean that extreme *if the null hypothesis were true.*

Figuring the *Z* Score of a Sample's Mean on the Distribution of Means

There can be some confusion in figuring the location of your sample on the comparison distribution in hypothesis testing with a sample of more than one. In this situation, you are finding a *Z* score of your sample's mean on a distribution of means. (Before, you were finding the *Z* score of a single individual on a distribution of a population of single individuals.) The method of changing the sample's mean to a *Z* score is the same as the usual way of changing a raw score to a *Z* score. However, you have to be careful not to get mixed up because more than one mean is involved. It is important to remember that you are treating the sample mean like a single score. Recall that the ordinary formula (from Chapter 2) for changing a raw score to a *Z* score (Formula 2-5) is $Z = (X - M)/SD$. In the present situation, you are actually using the following conceptually identical formula:

> The Z score for the sample's mean on the distribution of means is the sample's mean minus the mean of the distribution of means, divided by the standard deviation of the distribution of means.

(6-4)

$$Z = \frac{(M - \text{Population } M_M)}{\text{Population } SD_M}$$

For example, suppose your sample's mean is 18 and the distribution of means has a mean of 10 and a standard deviation of 4. The *Z* score of this sample mean is +2. Using the formula,

$$Z = \frac{(M - \text{Population } M_M)}{\text{Population } SD_M} = \frac{(18 - 10)}{4} = \frac{8}{4} = 2.$$

This is shown in Figure 6–6.

Example. Let's return to the example at the start of the chapter in which a team of educational researchers is interested in the effects of instructions on timed school achievement tests. The researchers give a standard school achievement test to 64 randomly selected fifth-grade schoolchildren. They give the test in the usual way, except that they add to the instructions a statement that children are to answer each question with the first response that comes to mind. When given in the usual way, the test is

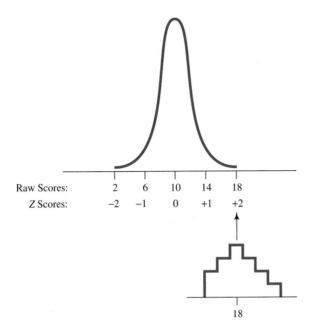

Figure 6-6   *Z* score for the mean of a particular sample on the distribution of means.

known to have a mean of 200, a standard deviation of 48, and an approximately normal distribution. This distribution is shown in Figure 6–7a.

Now let's carry out the *Z* test by following the five steps of hypothesis testing you learned in Chapter 5.

❶ **Restate the question as a research hypothesis and a null hypothesis about the populations.** The two populations are these:

Population 1: Fifth graders who get the special instructions.
Population 2: Fifth graders who do not get the special instructions.

The research hypothesis is that the population of fifth graders who take the test with the special instructions will have a higher mean score on the test than the population of fifth graders who take the test in the normal way. The null hypothesis is that the mean of Population 1's scores will not be higher than the mean of Population 2's scores. Note that these are directional hypotheses. The researchers want to know if their special instructions will increase test scores; results in the opposite direction would not be relevant to the theory the researchers are testing.

❷ **Determine the characteristics of the comparison distribution.** The result of the study will be a mean of a sample of 64 individuals (of fifth graders in this case). Thus, the comparison distribution has to be the distribution of means of samples of 64 individuals each. This comparison distribution of means will have a mean of 200 (the same as the population mean). That is, Population $M_M = 200$. Its variance will be the population variance divided by the number of individuals in the sample. The population variance, Population SD^2, is 2,304 (the population standard deviation of 48 squared); the sample size is 64. Thus, the variance of the distribution of means, Population SD_M^2, will be 36 (that is, 2,304/64). The standard deviation of the distribution of means, Population SD_M, is 6 (the square root of 36). Finally, because there are more than 30 individuals in the sample, the

TIP FOR SUCCESS

As in Chapter 5, Population 2 is the population for the comparison distribution, which is the distribution that represents the population situation if the null hypothesis is true.

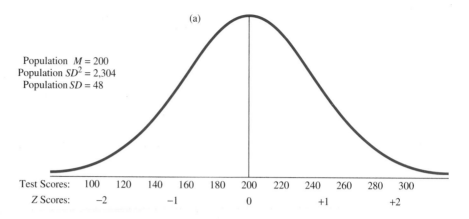

Population $M = 200$
Population $SD^2 = 2{,}304$
Population $SD = 48$

Test Scores:	100	120	140	160	180	200	220	240	260	280	300
Z Scores:		−2			−1		0		+1		+2

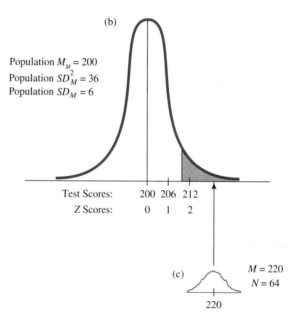

Population $M_M = 200$
Population $SD_M^2 = 36$
Population $SD_M = 6$

Test Scores: 200 206 212
Z Scores: 0 1 2

(c) $M = 220$
$N = 64$
220

Figure 6–7 For the fictional study of performance on a standard school achievement test. (a) the distribution of the population of individuals, (b) the distribution of means (the comparison distribution), and (c) the sample's distribution. The shaded area in the distribution of means is the rejection region—the area in which the null hypothesis will be rejected if the study's sample's mean turns out to be in that area.

shape of the distribution of means will be approximately normal. Figure 6–7b shows this distribution of means.

❸ **Determine the cutoff sample score on the comparison distribution at which the null hypothesis should be rejected.** Let's assume the researchers decide to use the standard 5% significance level. As we noted in Step ❶ , the researchers are making a directional prediction. Hence, the researchers will reject the null hypothesis if the result is in the top 5% of the comparison distribution. The comparison distribution (the distribution of means) is a normal curve. Thus, the top 5% can be found from the normal curve table. It starts at a Z of +1.64 (see also Figure 5–4 and Table 5–1). This top 5% is shown as the shaded area in Figure 6–7b.

❹ **Determine your sample's score on the comparison distribution.** Let's suppose the result of the (fictional) study is that the 64 fifth graders given the special instructions had a mean of 220. (This sample's distribution is shown in Figure 6–7c.) A mean of 220 is 3.33 standard deviations above the mean of the distribution of means:

$$Z = \frac{(M - \text{Population } M_M)}{\text{Population } SD_M} = \frac{(220 - 200)}{6} = \frac{20}{6} = 3.33.$$

❺ **Decide whether to reject the null hypothesis.** We set the minimum Z score to reject the null hypothesis at +1.64. The Z score of the sample's mean is +3.33. Thus, the educational researchers can reject the null hypothesis and conclude that the research hypothesis is supported. To put this another way, the result of the Z test is statistically significant at the $p < .05$ level. You can see this in Figure 6–7b. Note how extreme the sample's mean is on the distribution of means (the distribution that would apply if the null hypothesis were true). The final conclusion is that among fifth graders like those studied, the special instructions do improve test scores.

How are you doing?

1. How is hypothesis testing with a sample of more than one person different from hypothesis testing with a sample of a single person?
2. How do you find the Z score for the sample's mean on the distribution of means?
3. A researcher predicts that showing a certain film will change people's attitudes toward alcohol. The researcher then randomly selects 36 people, shows them the film, and gives them an attitude questionnaire. The mean score on the attitude test for these 36 people is 70. The score for people in general on this test is 75, with a standard deviation of 12. Using the five steps of hypothesis testing and the 5% significance level, carry out a Z test to see if showing the film change people's attitudes toward alcohol.

Answers

1. In hypothesis testing with a sample of more than one person, the comparison distribution is a distribution of means.
2. You use the usual formula for changing a raw score to a Z score, using the mean and standard deviation of the distribution of means. The formula is $Z = (M - \text{Population } M_M)/\text{Population } SD_M$.
3. ❶ **Restate the question as a research hypothesis and a null hypothesis about the populations.** The two populations are these:

   Population 1: People shown the film.
   Population 2: People in general.

   The research hypothesis is that the mean attitude of the population shown the film is different than the mean attitude of the population of people in general; the null hypothesis is that the populations have the same mean attitude score.
   ❷ **Determine the characteristics of the comparison distribution.** Population $M_M = 75$. Population $SD_M^2 = N = \text{Population } SD_M^2/N = 12^2/36 = 4$. Population $SD_M = 2$. Shape is normal.
   ❸ **Determine the cutoff sample score on the comparison distribution at which the null hypothesis should be rejected.** Two-tailed cutoffs, 5% significance level, are +1.96 and −1.96.

pothesis. Seeing the film does change attitudes toward alcohol.

ple's mean is −2.50, which is more extreme than −1.96; reject the null hy-

❺ **Decide whether to reject the null hypothesis.** The *Z* score of the sam-

$Z = (M − \text{Population } M_M)/\text{Population } SD_M = (70 − 75)/2 = −2.50.$

❹ **Determine your sample's score on the comparison distribution.**

Hypothesis Tests About Means of Samples (Z Tests) in Research Articles

As we have noted several times, research in which there is a known population mean and standard deviation is rare in behavioral and social science research. Thus, you will not often see a *Z* test in a research article. We have asked you to learn about this situation mainly as a building block for understanding hypothesis testing in more common research situations. Still, *Z* tests do show up now and then.

Here is an example. As part of a larger study, Wiseman (1997) gave a loneliness test to a group of college students in Israel. As a first step in examining the results, Wiseman checked that the average score on the loneliness test was not significantly different from a known population distribution based on a large U.S. study of university students that had been conducted earlier by other researchers (Russell, Peplau, & Cutrona, 1980). Wiseman reported:

BOX 6–1   **More about Polls: Sampling Errors and Errors in Thinking about Samples**

If you think back to Box 4–1 on surveys and the Gallup poll, you will recall that we left two important questions unanswered about fine print with the results of a poll, saying something like "From a telephone poll of 1,000 American adults taken on June 4 and 5. Sampling error ±3%." First, you might wonder how such small numbers like 1,000 (but rarely much less) can be used to predict the opinion of the entire U.S. population. Second, after working through the material in this chapter on the standard deviation of the distribution of means, you may wonder what a "sampling error" means when a sample is not randomly sampled but rather selected by the complicated probability method used for polls.

Regarding sample size, you know from this chapter that large sample sizes, like 1,000, greatly reduce the standard deviation of the distribution of means. That is, the curve becomes very high and narrow, gathered all around the population mean. The mean of any sample of that size is very close to being the population mean.

When a sample is only a small part of a very large population, the sample's absolute size is the only determiner of accuracy. This absolute size determines the impact of the random errors of measurement and selection. What remains important is reducing bias or systematic error, which can be done only by careful planning.

As for the term *sampling error,* it is worked out according to past experience with the sampling procedures used. It is expressed in tables for different sample sizes (usually below 1,000, because that is where error increases dramatically).

So the number of people polled is not very important, but what matters very much are the methods of sampling and estimating error, which will not be reported in the detail necessary to judge if the results are reliable. If the sampling and error-estimating approach is not revealed at all, be cautious. For more information about how polls are conducted, go to the following website (note that sampling error is referred to as "margin of error" on the website) and click the link "How Polls are Conducted": *http://www.galluppoll.com/help/faq.aspx?ID=249.*

. . .[T]he mean loneliness scores of the current Israeli sample were similar to those of Russell et al.'s (1980) university sample for both males (Israeli: $M = 38.74$, $SD = 9.30$; Russell: $M = 37.06$, $SD = 10.91$; $z = 1.09$, NS) and females (Israeli: $M = 36.39$, $SD = 8.87$; Russell: $M = 36.06$, $SD = 10.11$; $z = .25$, NS). (p. 291)

In this example, the researcher gives the standard deviation for both the sample studied (the Israeli group) and the population (from the Russell et al. study). However, in the steps of figuring each Z (the sample's score on the distribution of means), the researcher would have used the standard deviation only of the population. Notice also that the researcher took the nonsignificance of the difference as support for the sample means being "similar" to the population means. However, the researcher was very careful not to claim that these results showed there was "no difference."

Of the topics we have covered in this chapter, the one you are most likely to see discussed in a research article is the standard deviation of the distribution of means, used to describe the amount of variation that might be expected among means of samples of a given size from this population. In this context, it is usually called the *standard error,* abbreviated *SE* (or *SEM,* for *standard error of the mean*). Standard errors are often shown in research articles as the lines that go above (and sometimes also below) the tops of the bars in a bar graph—these lines are called *error bars.* For example, Stankiewicz and colleagues (2006) examined how limitations in human perception and memory (and other factors) affect people's ability to find their way in indoor spaces. In one of their experiments, eight students used a computer keyboard to move through a virtual indoor space of corridors and hallways shown on a computer monitor. The researchers calculated how efficiently students moved through the space, with efficiency ranging from 0 (extremely inefficient) to 1 (extremely efficient). The researchers compared the efficiency of moving through the space when students had a limited view of the space with when they had a clear (or unlimited) view of the space. The results are shown in Figure 6–8, which includes error bars.

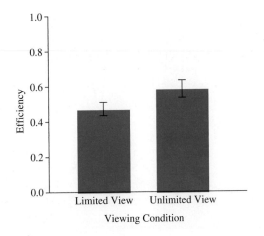

Figure 6–8   The mean navigation efficiency when navigating in the unlimited and limited viewing condition in Experiment 2. In the limited-view condition, visual information was available as far as the next intersection (further details were obscured by "fog"). In the unlimited-view condition, visual information was available to the end of the corridor. Error bars represent 1 standard error of the mean. *Source:* Stankiewicz, B. J., Legge, G. E., Mansfield, J. S., & Schlicht, E. J. (2006). Lost in virtual space: Studies in human and ideal spatial navigation. *Journal of Experimental Psychology: Human Perception and Performance, 32,* 688–704. Copyright © 2006 by the American Psychological Association.

Be careful to read the fine print when you see lines above the tops of bars in a bar graph. Sometimes the bars are not for standard error bars, but instead are standard deviations or confidence intervals (see the Advanced Topic section below)! In Figure 6–8, the note under the figure states that error bars represent 1 standard error of the mean. In some cases you would only know by reading the text of the article what the bars represent.

Advanced Topic: Estimation and Confidence Intervals

Hypothesis testing is our main focus in this book. However, there is another kind of statistical question related to the distribution of means that is also important in the behavioral and social sciences: estimating an unknown population mean based on the scores in a sample. Traditionally, this has been very important in survey research. In recent years it is also becoming important in experimental research and can even serve as an alternative approach to hypothesis testing.

Estimating the Mean: Point Estimates

The best estimate of the population mean is the sample mean. In the study of fifth graders who were given the special instructions, the mean score for the sample of 64 fifth graders was 220. Thus, 220 is the best estimate of the mean for the unknown population of fifth graders who would ever receive the special instructions.

The mean of the sample is the best estimate, because you are more likely to get a sample mean of 220 from a population with a mean of 220 than from a population with any other mean. Consider Figure 6–9. Suppose the true distribution of means

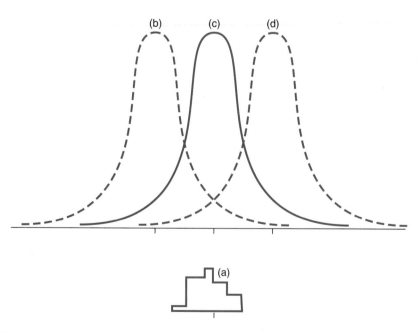

Figure 6–9 A sample and three distributions of sample means. The mean of a particular sample (a) is more likely to have come from a distribution of means with the same mean (c) than from any other distribution of means (such as b and d).

has the same mean as our sample, as would be the case in this figure if the true distribution of means was distribution (c). In this situation, it is very likely that a mean from this distribution of means would be close to our sample's mean. But suppose the true distribution of means was like distribution (d). In this case, many fewer means are near to our sample's mean.

In this example, you are estimating the specific value of the population mean. When you estimate a specific value of a population parameter, it is called a **point estimate.**

The Accuracy of a Point Estimate

How accurate is this point estimate of the mean? A way to get at this question is to ask, How much do means from a distribution of means vary? One indication of such variation, we know, is the standard deviation of the distribution of means. Like any standard deviation, it tells you how much scores in the distribution typically vary. In this case, the "scores" are sample means. Because our interest is in making an estimate of the population mean, any variation is error. Thus, the amount of variation is the amount you can expect means of scores from a population like the one we studied to be in error as an estimate of the true, unknown population mean.[3] As we briefly noted earlier when introducing the standard deviation of the distribution of means, this is why it is also known as the standard error of the mean, or the standard error (*SE*) for short. The accuracy of our estimate of 220 for the mean of the population of fifth graders who get the special instructions would be the standard deviation of the distribution of means, which we figured earlier to be 6.

Interval Estimates

You can also estimate the *range* of possible means that are likely to include the population mean. This is called an **interval estimate.**

Consider our point estimate of 220 with a standard error of 6. It seems reasonable that if you randomly took a mean from the distribution, a mean between 220 and 226 (one standard error above 220) is 34% likely. This is because the distribution of means is a normal curve, the standard error is 1 standard deviation on that curve, and 34% of a normal curve is between the mean and 1 standard deviation above the mean. From this reasoning, we could also figure that another 34% should be between 220 and 214 (1 standard error below 220). Putting this together, we have a region from 214 to 226 that we are 68% confident should include the population mean. (See Figure 6–10a.) This is an example of a **confidence interval (CI).** We would call it the "68% confidence interval." The upper and lower ends of a confidence interval are called **confidence limits.** In this example, the confidence limits for the 68% confidence interval are 214 and 226 (see Figure 6–10a).

Normally, however, you would want to be more than 68% confident about your estimates. Thus, it is standard when figuring confidence intervals to use 95% or even 99% confidence intervals. These are figured based on the distribution of means for the area that includes the middle 95% or middle 99%. For the **95% confidence interval,**

point estimate   Estimate from a sample of the most likely single value of a population parameter (such as the population mean).

interval estimate   Region of scores (that is, the scores between some specified lower and upper value) estimated to include a population parameter such as the population mean; this is in contrast to a *point estimate; a confidence interval* is an example of an interval estimate.

confidence interval   Roughly speaking, the region of scores (that is, the scores between an upper and lower value) that is likely to include the true population mean; more precisely, the range of possible population means from which it is not highly unlikely that you could have obtained your sample mean.

confidence limit   Upper or lower value of a confidence interval.

95% confidence interval   Confidence interval in which roughly speaking, there is a 95% chance that the population mean falls within this interval.

---

[3]You don't know the true distribution of means for the population your sample comes from. But in the examples we have considered in this chapter, you do know the variance and shape of the distribution of means for a similar population (Population 2). It is reasonable to assume that even if the mean is different, the variance and shape of the distribution of the population your sample comes from is the same. Thus, you can use this distribution of means to estimate the amount that a sample mean from any population with the same variance and shape is likely to vary from its population mean.

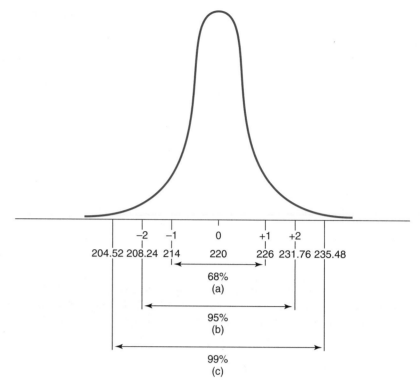

Figure 6–10 A distribution of means and the (a) 68%, (b) 95%, and (c) 99% confidence intervals for fifth graders taking a test with special instructions (fictional data).

you want the area in a normal curve on each side between the mean and the Z score that includes 47.5%. The normal curve table shows this to be 1.96. Thus, in terms of Z scores, the 95% confidence interval is from -1.96 to $+1.96$ on the distribution of means. Changing these Z scores to raw scores for the school achievement test example gives an interval of 208.24 to 231.76 (see Figure 6–10b). That is, for the lower confidence limit, $(-1.96)(6) + 220 = -11.76 + 220 = 208.24$; for the upper confidence limit, $(1.96)(6) + 220 = 11.76 + 220 = 231.76$. In sum, based on the sample of 64 fifth graders who get the special instructions, you can be 95% confident that the true population mean for such fifth graders is between 208.24 and 231.76 (see Figure 6–10b).

For a **99% confidence interval,** you use the Z scores for the middle 99% of the normal curve (the part that includes 49.5% above and below the mean). This comes out to $+2.58$ and -2.58. Changing these Z scores to raw scores, the 99% confidence interval is from 204.52 to 235.48 (see Figure 6–10c).

Notice in Figure 6–10 that the greater the confidence, the broader the confidence interval. In our example, you could be 68% confident that the true population mean is between 214 and 226; but you could be 95% confident that it is between 208.24 and 231.76 and 99% confident it is between 204.52 and 235.48. This is a general principle. It makes sense that you need a wider range of possibility to be more sure you are right.

Steps for Figuring the 95% and 99% Confidence Intervals

Here are three steps for figuring a confidence interval. These steps assume that the distribution of means is approximately a normal distribution.

❶ **Estimate the population mean and figure the standard deviation of the distribution of means.** The best estimate of the population mean is the sample mean. Next, find the variance of the distribution of means in the usual way: Population SD_M^2 = Population SD^2/N. Take the square root of the variance of the distribution of means to find the standard deviation of the distribution of means: Population SD_M = $\sqrt{\text{Population } SD_M^2}$.

❷ **Find the Z scores that go with the confidence interval you want.** For the 95% confidence interval, the Z scores are +1.96 and −1.96. For the 99% confidence interval, the Z scores are +2.58 and −2.58.

❸ **To find the confidence interval, change these Z scores to raw scores.** To find the lower limit, multiply −1.96 (for the 95% confidence interval) or −2.58 (for the 99% confidence interval) by the standard deviation of the distribution of means (Population SD_M) and add this to the population mean. To find the upper limit, multiply +1.96 (for the 95% confidence interval) or +2.58 (for the 99% confidence interval) by the standard deviation of the distribution of means (Population SD_M) and add this to the population mean.

Example.   Let's return again to the study of 64 fifth graders who were given special instructions on a test. Recall that in that example, the test scores of fifth graders who were not given special instructions were normally distributed, with a mean of 200 and a standard deviation of 48. The mean of the sample of 64 fifth graders who were given the special instructions was 220. We figured the 99% confidence limit earlier, but now we are going to do the figuring using the three steps:

❶ **Estimate the population mean and figure the standard deviation of the distribution of means.** The best estimate of the population mean (of fifth graders who take the test with the special instructions) is the sample mean of 220. Population SD_M^2 = Population SD^2/N = $48^2/64$ = 36. Thus, Population SD_M = $\sqrt{\text{Population } SD_M^2}$ = $\sqrt{36}$ = 6.

❷ **Find the Z scores that go with the confidence interval you want.** For the 99% confidence interval, the Z scores are +2.58 and −2.58.

❸ **To find the confidence interval, change these Z scores to raw scores.** Lower confidence limit = (−2.58)(6) + 220 = −15.48 + 220 = 204.52; upper confidence limit = (+2.58)(6) + 220 = 15.48 + 220 = 235.48. The 99% confidence interval is from 204.52 to 235.48. Thus, based on the sample of 64 fifth graders, you can be 99% confident that an interval from 204.52 to 235.48 includes the true population mean of fifth graders who take the test with the special instructions.

Confidence Intervals and Hypothesis Testing

A practical implication of the link of confidence intervals is that you can use confidence intervals to do hypothesis testing! If the confidence interval does not include the mean of the null hypothesis distribution, then the result is significant. For example, in the fifth-grader study, the 99% confidence interval for those who got the special instructions was from 204.52 to 235.48. However, the population that did not get the special instructions had a mean of 200. This population mean is outside the range of the confidence interval. Thus, if you are 99% confident that the true range is 204.52 to 235.48 and the population mean for those who didn't get the special instructions is not in this range, you are 99% confident that that population is not the same as the one your sample came from.

Another way to understand this is in terms of the idea that the confidence limits are the points at which a more extreme true population would not include your sample mean 99% of the time (or 95% of the time for the 95% confidence interval). The population mean for those not getting the special instructions was 200. If this were the true mean also for the group that got the special instructions, 99% of the time it would not produce a sample mean as high as the one we got.

Most behavioral and social science research uses ordinary hypothesis testing. However, sometimes you will see the confidence-interval method used instead. And sometimes you will see both.

How are you doing?

1. (a) What is the best estimate of a population mean, and (b) why?
2. (a) What number is used to indicate the accuracy of an estimate of the population mean, and (b) why?
3. What is a 95% confidence interval?
4. A researcher predicts that showing a certain film will change people's attitudes toward alcohol. The researcher then randomly selects 36 people, shows them the film, and gives them an attitude questionnaire. The mean score on the attitude test for these 36 people is 70. The score for people in general on this test is 75, with a standard deviation of 12. (a) Find the best point estimate of the mean of people who see the film and (b) its 95% confidence interval. (c) Compare this result to the conclusion you drew when you used this example in the "How Are You Doing?" section for hypothesis testing with a distribution of means.

Answers

1. (a) The sample mean. (b) It is more likely to have come from a population with the same mean than from any other population.
2. (a) The standard deviation of the distribution of means. (b) The standard deviation of the distribution of means is roughly the average amount that means vary from the mean of the distribution of means.
3. The range of values that you are 95% confident includes the population mean, estimated based on the scores in a sample.
4. (a) Best estimate is the sample mean: 70.
(b) Population SD_M^2 = Population SD^2/N = $12^2/36$ = 4. Thus, the standard deviation of the distribution of means, Population SD_M = $\sqrt{\text{Population } SD_M^2}$ = $\sqrt{4}$ = 2. Lower confidence limit = $(-1.96)(2) + 70 = -3.92 + 70$ = 66.08; upper confidence limit = $(+1.96)(2) + 70 = 3.92 + 70 = 73.92$. The 95% confidence interval is from 66.08 to 73.92.
(c) The 95% confidence interval does not include the mean of the general population (which was 75). Thus, you can reject the null hypothesis that the two populations are the same. This is the same conclusion as when using this example for hypothesis testing.

Advanced Topic: Confidence Intervals in Research Articles

Confidence intervals (usually abbreviated as CI), while far from standard, are becoming increasingly common in research articles in some fields such as medical research. For example, in an article published in the *Journal of the American Medical*

Association, Hu, Li, Colditz, Willett, and Manson (2003) reported that "Each 1 hour per day of brisk walking was associated with a 24% (95% CI, 19%–29%) reduction in obesity" (p. 1785). This means that we can be 95% confident that the true reduction in obesity was between 19% and 29%. As another example, a researcher might explain that the average amount of overtime hours worked in a particular industry is 3.7 with a 95% confidence interval of 2.5 to 4.9. This would tell you that the true amount of overtime hours is probably somewhere between 2.5 and 4.9.

Summary

1. When studying a sample of more than one individual, the comparison distribution in the hypothesis-testing process is a distribution of means. It can be thought of as what would result from (a) taking a very large number of samples, each of the same number of scores taken randomly from the population of individuals, and then (b) making a distribution of the means of these samples.

2. The distribution of means has the same mean as the corresponding population of individuals. However, it has a smaller variance because the means of samples are less likely to be extreme than individual scores. (In any one sample, extreme scores are likely to be balanced by middle scores or extreme scores in the other direction.) Specifically, the variance of the distribution of means is the variance of the population of individuals divided by the number of individuals in each sample. Its standard deviation is the square root of its variance. The shape of the distribution of means approximates a normal curve if either (a) the samples are each of 30 or more individuals or (b) the population of individuals follows a normal curve.

3. Hypothesis tests with a single sample of more than one individual and a known population are called Z tests and are done in the same way as the hypothesis tests of Chapter 5 (where the studies were of a single individual compared to a population of individual scores). The main exception is that, in a hypothesis test with a single sample of more than one individual and a known population, the comparison distribution is a distribution of means.

4. The kind of hypothesis test described in this chapter (the Z test) is rarely used in research practice; you have learned it as a stepping stone. The standard deviation of the distribution of means (the standard error, SE), is often used to describe the expected variability of means, particularly in bar graphs in which the standard error may be shown as the length of a line above (and sometimes below) the top of each bar.

5. ADVANCED TOPIC: The best point estimate for the population mean is the sample mean. Its accuracy is the standard deviation of the distribution of means (also known as the standard error, SE), which tells you roughly the amount means vary. You can figure an interval estimate of the population mean based on the distribution of means. If we assume the distribution of means follows a normal curve, the 95% confidence interval includes the range from 1.96 standard deviations below the sample mean (the lower confidence limit) to 1.96 standard deviations above the sample mean (the upper confidence limit). The 99% confidence interval includes the range from 2.58 standard deviations below the sample mean (the lower confidence limit) to 2.58 standard deviations above the sample mean (the upper confidence limit). Confidence intervals are sometimes reported in research articles, usually with the abbreviation CI.

Key Terms

distribution of means (p. 173)
mean of a distribution of means
  (Population M_M) (pp. 176)
variance of a distribution of means
  (Population SD_M^2) (p. 176)
standard deviation of a distribution
  of means (Population SD_M)
  (p. 177)

standard error (*SE*) (p. 177–178)
shape of the distribution of means
  (p. 178)
Z test (p. 182)
point estimate (p. 189)
interval estimate (p. 189)
confidence interval (CI) (p. 189)

confidence limits (p. 189)
95% confidence interval
  (p. 189–190)
99% confidence interval (p. 190)

Example Worked-Out Problems

Figure the Standard Deviation of the Distribution of Means

Find the standard deviation of the distribution of means for a population with Population $SD = 13$ and a sample size of 20.

Answer

Using Rules 2a and 2b for the characteristics of a distribution of means: **The variance of a distribution of means is the variance of the population of individuals divided by the number of individuals in each sample; the standard deviation of a distribution of means is the square root of the variance of the distribution of means.** The variance of the population is 169 (that is, 13 squared is 169); 169 divided by 20 gives a variance of the distribution of means of 8.45. The square root of this, 2.91, is the standard deviation of the distribution of means.

Using the formulas, Population SD_M^2 = Population $SD^2/N = 13^2/20 = 8.45$.

$$\text{Population } SD_M = \sqrt{\text{Population } SD_M^2} = \sqrt{8.45} = 2.91.$$

Hypothesis Testing with a Sample of More than One: The *Z* Test

A sample of 75 given an experimental treatment had a mean of 16 on a particular measure. The general population of individuals has a mean of 15 on this measure and a standard deviation of 5. Carry out a *Z* test using the full five steps of hypothesis testing with a two-tailed test at the .05 significance level and make a drawing of the distributions involved.

Answer

❶ **Restate the question as a research hypothesis and a null hypothesis about the populations. The two populations are these:**

Population 1: Those given the experimental treatment.
Population 2: The general population (those not given the experimental treatment).

The research hypothesis is that the population given the experimental treatment will have a different mean on the particular measure than the mean of the population in general (those not given the experimental treatment). The null hypothesis is that the populations have the same mean score on this measure.

❷ **Determine the characteristics of the comparison distribution.** Population M_M = Population M = 15. Population SD_M^2 = Population SD^2/N = $5^2/75$ = .33; Population SD_M = $\sqrt{\text{Population } SD_M^2}$ = $\sqrt{.33}$ = .57; shape is normal (sample size is greater than 30).

❸ **Determine the cutoff sample score on the comparison distribution at which the null hypothesis should be rejected.** Two-tailed cutoffs, .05 significance level, are +1.96 and −1.96.

❹ **Determine your sample's score on the comparison distribution.** Using the formula $Z = (M - \text{Population } M_M)/\text{Population } SD_M$, $Z = (16 - 15)/.57 = 1/.57 = 1.75$.

❺ **Decide whether to reject the null hypothesis.** The sample's Z score of 1.75, is *not* more extreme than the cutoffs of +1.96 and −1.96; do not reject the null hypothesis. The results are inconclusive. The distributions involved are shown in Figure 6–11.

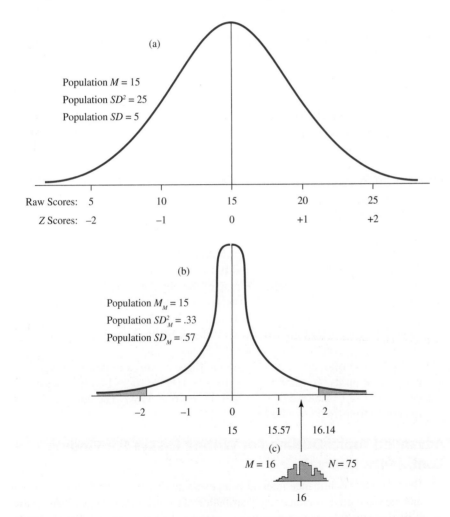

Figure 6–11   Answer to the hypothesis-testing problem in Example Worked-Out Problems: (a) the distribution of the population of individuals, (b) the distribution of means (the comparison distribution), and (c) the sample's distribution.

Outline For Writing Essays For Hypothesis-Testing Problems Involving a Single Sample of More Than One and a Known Population (The *Z* Test)

1. Describe the core logic of hypothesis testing in this situation. Be sure to explain the meaning of the research hypothesis and the null hypothesis in this situation where we focus on the mean of a sample and compare it to a known population mean. Explain the concept of support being provided for the research hypothesis when the study results allow the null hypothesis to be rejected.

2. Explain the concept of the comparison distribution. Be sure to mention that with a sample of more than one, the comparison distribution is a distribution of means because the information from the study is a mean of a sample. Mention that the distribution of means has the same mean as the population mean because there is no reason for random samples in the long run to have a different mean; the distribution of means has a smaller variance (the variance of the population divided by the number in each sample) because it is harder to get extreme means than extreme individual cases by chance, and the larger the samples, the rarer it is to get extreme means.

3. Describe the logic and process for determining (using the normal curve) the cutoff sample score(s) on the comparison distribution at which the null hypothesis should be rejected.

4. Describe why and how you figure the *Z* score of the sample mean on the comparison distribution.

5. Explain how and why the scores from Steps ❸ and ❹ of the hypothesis-testing process are compared. Explain the meaning of the result of this comparison with regard to the specific research and null hypotheses being tested.

Advanced Topic: Finding Confidence Intervals

Find the 99% confidence interval for the sample mean in the study described for the *Z* test Example Worked-Out Problem.

Answer

❶ **Estimate the population mean and figure the standard deviation of the distribution of means.** The best estimate of the population mean in the problem above is the sample mean of 16. The standard deviation of the distribution of means, Population SD_M, in the problem above was .57.

❷ **Find the *Z* scores that go with the confidence interval you want.** For the 99% confidence interval, the *Z* scores are +2.58 and −2.58.

❸ **To find the confidence interval, change these *Z* scores to raw scores.** Lower confidence limit = $(-2.58)(.57) + 16 = -1.47 + 16 = 14.53$; upper confidence limit = $(+2.58)(.57) + 16 = 1.47 + 16 = 17.47$. The 99% confidence interval is from 14.53 to 17.47.

Advanced Topic: Outline For Writing Essays For Finding Confidence Intervals

1. Explain that a confidence interval is an estimate (based on your sample's mean and the standard deviation of the distribution of means) of the range of values that is likely to include the true population mean for the group studied (Population 1). Be sure to mention that the 95% (or 99%) confidence interval is the range of values you are 95% (or 99%) confident include the true population mean.

2. Explain that the first step in figuring a confidence interval is to estimate the population mean (for which the best estimate is the sample mean) and figure the standard deviation of the distribution of means.
3. Mention that you next find the Z scores that go with the confidence interval that you want.
4. Describe how to change the Z scores to raw scores to find the confidence interval.

Practice Problems

These problems involve figuring. Most real-life statistics problems are done on a computer with special statistical software. Even if you have such software, do these problems by hand to ingrain the method in your mind.

All data are fictional unless an actual citation is given.

Set I (for answers, see pp. 442–444)

1. Why is the standard deviation of the distribution of means generally smaller than the standard deviation of the distribution of the population of individuals?
2. For a population that has a standard deviation of 10, figure the standard deviation of the distribution of means for samples of size (a) 2, (b) 3, (c) 4, and (d) 9.
3. For a population that has a standard deviation of 20, figure the standard deviation of the distribution of means for samples of size (a) 2, (b) 3, (c) 4, and (d) 9.
4. ADVANCED TOPIC: Figure the 95% confidence interval (that is, the lower and upper confidence limits) for each part of problem 2. Assume that in each case the researcher's sample has a mean of 100 and that the population of individuals is known to follow a normal curve.
5. ADVANCED TOPIC: Figure the 99% confidence interval (that is, the lower and upper confidence limits) for each part of problem 3. Assume that in each case the researcher's sample has a mean of 10 and that the population of individuals is known to follow a normal curve.
6. For each of the following samples that were given an experimental treatment, test whether they are different from the general population: (a) a sample of 10 with a mean of 44, (b) a sample of 1 with a mean of 48. The general population of individuals has a mean of 40, a standard deviation of 6, and follows a normal curve. For each sample, carry out a Z test using the five steps of hypothesis testing with a two-tailed test at the .05 significance level, and make a drawing of the distributions involved (c) ADVANCED TOPIC: Figure the 95% confidence interval for parts (a) and (b).
7. For each of the following samples that were given an experimental treatment, test whether they scored significantly higher than the general population: (a) a sample of 100 with a mean of 82 and (b) a sample of 10 with a mean of 84. The general population of individuals has a mean of 81, a standard deviation of 8, and follows a normal curve. For each sample, carry out a Z test using the five steps of hypothesis testing with a one-tailed test at the .01 significance level, and make a drawing of the distributions involved. (c) ADVANCED TOPIC: Figure the 99% confidence interval for parts (a) and (b).
8. Twenty-five women between the ages of 70 and 80 were randomly selected from the general population of women their age to take part in a special program to decrease reaction time (speed). After the course, the women had an average reaction time of 1.5 seconds. Assume that the mean reaction time for the general

population of women of this age group is 1.8, with a standard deviation of .5 seconds. (Also assume that the population is approximately normal.) What should you conclude about the effectiveness of the course? (a) Carry out a Z test using the five steps of hypothesis testing (use the .01 significance level). (b) Make a drawing of the distributions involved. (c) Explain your answer to someone who is familiar with the general logic of hypothesis testing, the normal curve, Z scores, and probability, but is not familiar with the idea of a distribution of means. (d) ADVANCED TOPIC: Figure the 99% confidence interval and explain your answer to someone who is familiar with the general logic of hypothesis testing, the normal curve, Z scores, probability, and the idea of a distribution of means, but has not heard of confidence intervals.

9. A large number of people were shown a particular film of an automobile collision between a moving car and a stopped car. Each person then filled out a questionnaire about how likely it was that the driver of the moving car was at fault, on a scale from $0 = not\ at\ fault$ to $10 = completely\ at\ fault$. The distribution of ratings under ordinary conditions follows a normal curve with Population $M = 5.5$ and Population $SD = .8$. Sixteen randomly selected individuals are tested in a condition in which the wording of the question is changed so the question asks, "How likely is it that the driver of the car who crashed into the other was at fault?" (The difference is that in this changed condition, instead of describing the event in a neutral way, the question uses the phrase "crashed into.") Using the changed instructions, these 16 research participants gave a mean at-fault rating of 5.9. Did the changed instructions significantly increase the rating of being at fault? (a) Carry out a Z test using the five steps of hypothesis testing (use the .05 significance level). (b) Make a drawing of the distributions involved. (c) Explain your answer to someone who has never taken statistics. (d) ADVANCED TOPIC: Figure the 95% confidence interval.

10. Lee, Byatt, and Rhodes (2000) tested a theory of the role of distinctiveness in face perception. In their study, participants indicated whether they recognized each of 48 faces of male celebrities when they were shown rapidly on a computer screen. A third of the faces were shown in caricature form, in which facial features were electronically modified so that distinctive features were exaggerated; a third were shown in veridical form, in which the faces were not modified at all; and a third were shown in anticaricature form, in which facial features were modified to be slightly more like the average of the celebrities' faces. The average percent correct across their participants is shown in Figure 6–12. Explain the meaning of the error bars in this figure to a person who understands mean, standard deviation, and variance, but nothing else about statistics.

11. ADVANCED TOPIC: Anderson et al. (2000) studied the rate of HIV testing among adults in the United States and reported one of their findings as follows: "Responses from the NHIS [National Health Interview Survey] indicate that by 1995, 39.7% of adults (95% CI = 38.8%, 40.5%) had been tested at least once . . . ." (p. 1090). Explain what "(95% CI = 38.8%, 40.5%)" means to a person who understands hypothesis testing with the mean of a sample of more than one but has never heard of confidence intervals.

Set II

12. Under what conditions is it reasonable to assume that a distribution of means will follow a normal curve?

13. Indicate the mean and the standard deviation of the distribution of means for each of the following situations.

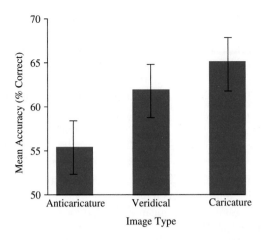

Figure 6–12   Identification accuracy as a function of image type. Standard error bars are shown. *Source:* Lee, K., Byatt, G., & Rhodes, G. (2000). Caricature effects, distinctiveness, and identification: Testing the face-space framework. *Psychological Science, 11,* 381. Copyright © 2000 by Blackwell Publishing. Reprinted by permission of the publisher.

Situation	Population		Sample Size
	M	SD^2	N
(a)	100	40	10
(b)	100	30	10
(c)	100	20	10
(d)	100	10	10
(e)	50	10	10
(f)	100	40	20
(g)	100	10	20

14. Figure the standard deviation of the distribution of means for a population with a standard deviation of 20 and sample sizes of (a) 10, (b) 11, (c) 100, and (d) 101.
15. For each of the following studies, the samples were given an experimental treatment and the researchers compared their results to the general population. (Assume all populations are normally distributed.) For each, carry out a Z test using the five steps of hypothesis testing for a two-tailed test, and make a drawing of the distributions involved. ADVANCED TOPIC: Figure the 95% confidence interval for each study.

Study	Population		Sample Size	Sample Mean	Significance Level
	M	SD	N		
(a)	36	8	16	38	.05
(b)	36	6	16	38	.05
(c)	36	4	16	38	.05
(d)	36	4	16	38	.01
(e)	34	4	16	38	.01

16. For each of the following studies, the samples were given an experimental treatment and the researchers compared their results to the general population. (Assume all populations are normally distributed.) For each, carry out a Z test using the five steps of hypothesis testing for a two-tailed test at the .01 level, and make

a drawing of the distributions involved. ADVANCED TOPIC: Figure the 99% confidence interval for each study.

	Population		Sample Size	Sample Mean
Study	M	SD	N	
(a)	10	2	50	12
(b)	10	2	100	12
(c)	12	4	50	12
(d)	14	4	100	12

17. ADVANCED TOPIC: Figure the 95% confidence interval (that is, the lower and upper confidence limits) for each part of problem 13. Assume that in each case the researcher's sample has a mean of 80 and the population of individuals is known to follow a normal curve.

18. ADVANCED TOPIC: Figure the 99% confidence interval (that is, the lower and upper confidence limits) for each part of problem 14. Assume that in each case the researcher's sample has a mean of 50 and that the population of individuals is known to follow a normal curve.

19. A researcher is interested in whether North Americans are able to identify emotions correctly in people from other cultures. It is known that, using a particular method of measurement, the accuracy ratings of adult North Americans in general are normally distributed with a mean of 82 and a variance of 20. This distribution is based on ratings made of emotions expressed by other North Americans. In the present study, however, the researcher arranges to test 50 adult North Americans rating emotions of individuals from Indonesia. The mean accuracy for these 50 individuals was 78. Using a two-tailed test and the .05 significance level, what should the researcher conclude? (a) Carry out a Z test using the five steps of hypothesis testing. (b) Make a drawing of the distributions involved. (c) Explain your answer to someone who knows about hypothesis testing with a sample of a single individual but knows nothing about hypothesis testing with a sample of more than one individual. (d) ADVANCED TOPIC: Figure the 95% confidence interval and explain your answer to someone who is familiar with the general logic of hypothesis testing, the normal curve, Z scores, probability, and the idea of a distribution of means, but has not heard of confidence intervals.

20. A researcher is interested in the conditions that affect the number of dreams per month that people report in which they are alone. We will assume that based on extensive previous research, it is known that in the general population the number of such dreams per month follows a normal curve, with Population $M = 5$ and Population $SD = 4$. The researcher wants to test the prediction that the number of such dreams will be greater among people who have recently experienced a traumatic event. Thus, the researcher studies 36 individuals who have recently experienced a traumatic event, having them keep a record of their dreams for a month. Their mean number of alone dreams is 8. Should you conclude that people who have recently had a traumatic experience have a significantly different number of dreams in which they are alone? (a) Carry out a Z test using the five steps of hypothesis testing (use the .05 significance level). (b) Make a drawing of the distributions involved. (c) Explain your answer to a person who has never had a course in statistics. (d) ADVANCED TOPIC: Figure the 95% confidence interval.

21. A government-sponsored telephone counseling service for adolescents tested whether the length of calls would be affected by a special telephone system that had a better sound quality. Over the past several years, the lengths of telephone calls (in minutes) were normally distributed with Population $M = 18$ and Pop-

ulation $SD = 8$. They arranged to have the special phone system loaned to them for one day. On that day, the mean length of the 46 calls they received was 21 minutes. Test whether the length of calls has changed using the .05 significance level. (a) Carry out a Z test using the five steps of hypothesis testing. (b) Make a drawing of the distributions involved. (c) Explain your answer to someone who knows about hypothesis testing with a sample of a single individual but knows nothing about hypothesis testing with samples of more than one individual. (d) ADVANCED TOPIC: Figure the 95% confidence interval.

22. Perna et al. (2003) tested whether a stress management intervention could reduce injury and illness among college athletes. In their study, 34 college athletes were randomly assigned to be in one of two groups: (1) a stress management intervention group: This group received a cognitive behavioral stress management (CBSM) intervention during preseason training; (2) a control group: This group did not receive the intervention. At the end of the season, for each athlete, the researchers recorded the number of health center visits (including visits to the athletic training center) and the number of days of illness or injury during the season. The results are shown in Figure 6–13. In the figure caption, Perna et al. note that the figure show shows the "Mean ($+SE$)." This tells you that the line above the top of each bar represents the standard error. Explain what this means, using one of the error bars as an example, to a person who understands mean and standard deviation, but knows nothing else about statistics.

23. ADVANCED TOPIC: Bushman and Anderson (2001) studied news reports of the effects of media violence on aggression over a thirty-year period. Some of their results are shown in Figure 6–14. In the figure caption they note that "Capped vertical bars denote 95% confidence intervals." Explain what this means, using one of the vertical bars as an example, to a person who understands standard error bars but has never heard of confidence intervals.

24. Cut up 90 small slips of paper, and write each number from 1 to 9 on 10 slips each. Put the slips in a large bowl and mix them up. (a) Take out a slip, write down the

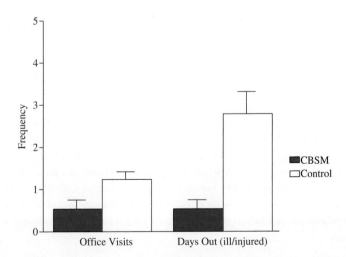

Figure 6–13 Mean ($+SE$) number of accumulated days injured or ill and athletic training room and health center office visits for cognitive behavioral stress management (CBSM) ($n = 18$) and control group ($n = 16$) from study entry to season's end. *Source:* Perna, F. M., Antoni, M. H., Baum, A., Gordon, P., & Schneiderman, N. (2003). Cognitive behavioral stress management effects on injury and illness among competitive athletes: A randomized clinical trial. *Annals of Behavioral Medicine, 25,* 66–73 Copyright © 2003 by Lawrence Erlbaum Associates, Inc. Reprinted by permission.

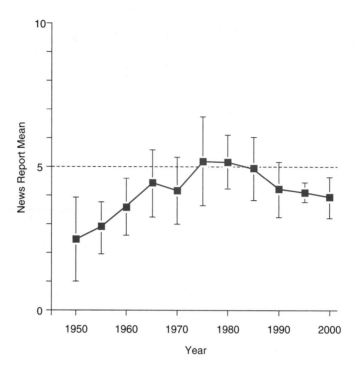

Figure 6-14 News reports of the effect of media violence on aggression. Note: News report means are the average rated conclusions of newspaper and magazine articles. A rating of 0 indicates that the article said there was no relationship between violent media and aggression. A rating of 5 indicates that the article urged parents to discourage their children from consuming violent media. A rating of 10 indicates that the article said that viewing violence caused an increase in aggression. Capped vertical bars denote 95% confidence intervals. *Source:* Bushman, B. J., & Anderson, C. A. (2001). Media violence and the American public: Scientific facts versus media misinformation. *American Psychologist, 56,* 477–489. Copyright © 2001 by American Psychological Association.

number on it, and put it back. Do this 20 times. Make a histogram, and figure the mean and the variance of the result. You should get an approximately rectangular distribution. (b) Take two slips out, figure out their mean, write it down, and put the slips back.[4] Repeat this process 20 times. Make a histogram, then figure the mean and the variance of this distribution of means. The variance should be about half of the variance of this distribution of means. (c) Repeat the process again, this time taking three slips at a time. Again, make a histogram and figure the mean and the variance of the distribution of means. The distribution of means of three slips each should have a variance of about a third of the distribution of samples of one slip each. Also note that as the sample size increases, your distributions are getting closer to normal. (Had you begun with a normally distributed distribution of slips, your distributions of means would have been fairly close to normal regardless of the number of slips in each sample.)

---

[4]Technically, when taking the samples of two slips, this should be done by taking one, writing it down, putting it back, then taking the next, writing it down, and putting it back. You would consider these two scores as one sample for which you figure a mean. The same applies for samples of three slips. This is called sampling with replacement. However, with 90 slips in the bowl, taking two or three slips at a time and putting them back will be a close enough approximation for this exercise and will save you some time.

CHAPTER 7

Making Sense of Statistical Significance

Effect Size and Statistical Power

CHAPTER OUTLINE

- Effect Size
- Statistical Power
- What Determines the Power of a Study?
- The Role of Power When Planning a Study
- The Role of Power When Interpreting the Results of a Study
- Effect Size and Power in Research Articles
- Summary
- Key Terms
- Example Worked-Out Problems
- Practice Problems

Statistical significance is extremely important in behavioral and social science research, but sophisticated researchers and readers of research understand that there is more to the story of a research result than $p < .05$ or *ns* (not significant). This chapter helps you become sophisticated about statistical significance. Gaining this sophistication means learning about two closely interrelated issues: effect size and statistical power.

Effect Size

Consider again the example from Chapter 6 of giving special instructions to fifth graders taking a standard achievement test. In the hypothesis-testing process for this example (the *Z* test), we compared two populations:

Population 1: Fifth graders receiving special instructions.
Population 2: Fifth graders not receiving special instructions.

> **TIP FOR SUCCESS**
>
> This chapter builds directly on Chapters 5 and 6. We do not recommend embarking on this chapter until you have a good understanding of the key material in those chapters, especially hypothesis testing and the distribution of means.

The research hypothesis was that Population 1 would have a higher mean score on the test than Population 2. Population 2 (that is, how fifth graders perform on this test when given in the usual way) is known to have a mean of 200. In the example, we said the researchers found that their sample of 64 fifth graders who were given the special instructions had a mean score on the test of 220. Following the hypothesis-testing procedure, we rejected the null hypothesis that the two populations are the same. This was because it was extremely unlikely that we would get a sample with a score as high as 220 from a population like Population 2 (see Figure 7–1, which is the same as Figure 6–7 from the last chapter). Thus, we could conclude the result is "statistically significant." In this example, our best estimate of the mean of Population 1 is the

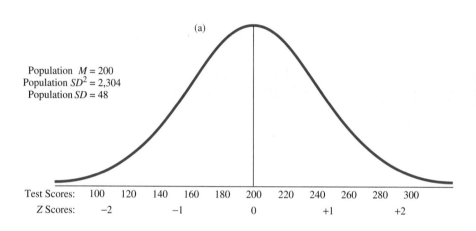

(a)

Population $M = 200$
Population $SD^2 = 2,304$
Population $SD = 48$

Test Scores: 100 120 140 160 180 200 220 240 260 280 300
Z Scores: −2   −1   0   +1   +2

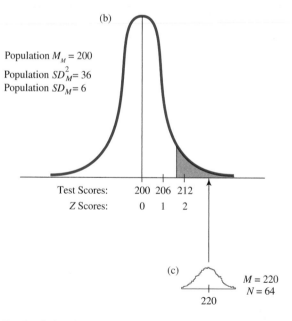

(b)

Population $M_M = 200$

Population $SD^2_M = 36$
Population $SD_M = 6$

Test Scores: 200 206 212
Z Scores: 0   1   2

(c) $M = 220$
      $N = 64$
      220

Figure 7–1   For the fictional study of fifth graders' performance on a standard school achievement test, (a) the distribution of the population of individuals, (b) the distribution of means (the comparison distribution), and (c) the sample's distribution. The shaded area in the distribution of means is the rejection region—the area in which the null hypothesis will be rejected if the study's sample's mean turns out to be in that area. (See discussion in Chapter 6.)

sample's mean, which is 220. Thus, we can estimate that giving the special instructions has an average effect of increasing a fifth grader's score by 20 points.

Now look again at Figure 7–1. Suppose the sample's score had been only 210. This would have had a Z score of 1.67 ([210 − 200]/6 = 1.67). This is more extreme than the cutoff in this example, which was 1.64, so the result would still have been significant. However, in this situation we would estimate that the average effect of the special instructions was only 10 points.

Notice that both results are significant, but in one example the effect is twice as big as in the other example. The point is that knowing statistical significance does not give you much information about the *size* of the effect. Significance tells us that the results of the experiment should convince us that there is an effect (that it is not "due to chance"). But significance does not tell us how *big* this non-chance effect is.

Put another way, **effect size** is a measure of the difference between populations. You can think of effect size as how much something changes after a specific intervention. Effect size indicates the extent to which two populations do *not* overlap—that is, how much they are separated due to the experimental procedure. In the fifth-grader example, Population 2 (the known population) had a mean of 200; based on our original sample's mean of 220, we estimated that Population 1 (those getting the special instructions) would have a mean of 220. The left curve in Figure 7–2 is the distribution (*of individual scores*) for Population 2; the right curve is the distribution for Population 1. Now look at Figure 7–3. Again, the left curve is for Population 2 and is the same as in Figure 7–2. However, this time the right curve for Population 1 is estimated based on a sample (the sample getting the special instructions) with a mean of 210. Here you can see that the effect size is smaller, and the two populations overlap even more. The amount that two populations do not overlap is called the effect size because it is the extent to which the experimental procedure has an *effect* of separating the two populations.

We often very much want to know not only whether a result is significant, but how big the effect is. As we will discuss later, an effect could well be statistically significant, but not of much practical significance. (For example, suppose an increase of only 10 points on the test is not considered important.) Also, as you will see later in

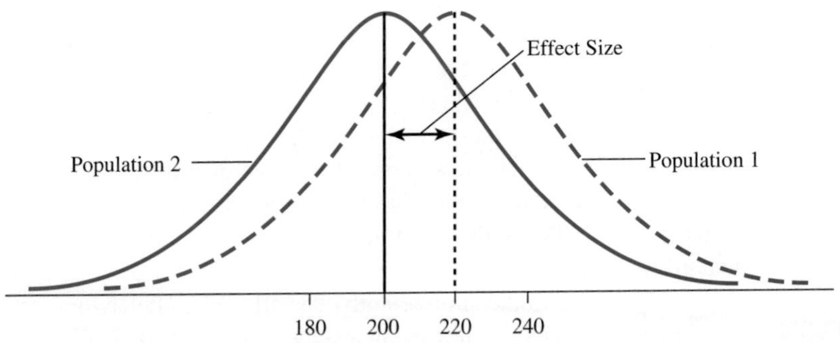

effect size Standardized measure of difference (lack of overlap) between populations. Effect size increases with greater differences between means.

Figure 7–2 For the fictional study of fifth graders' performance on a standard school achievement test, distribution of individuals for Population 1, those given the special instructions (right curve), and for Population 2, those not given special instructions (left curve). Population 1's mean is estimated based on the sample mean of 220, as originally described in Chapter 6; its standard deviation of 48 is assumed to be the same as Population 2's, which is known.

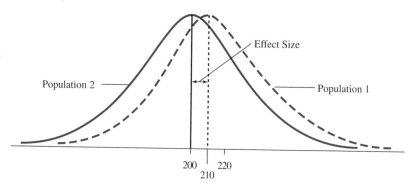

Figure 7–3 For the fictional study of fifth graders' performance on a standard school achievement test, distribution of individuals for Population 1, those given the special instructions (right curve), and for Population 2, those not given special instructions (left curve). Population 1's mean is estimated based on a sample with a mean of 210; its standard deviation of 48 is assumed to be the same as Population 2's, which is known.

the chapter, effect size plays an important role in two other important statistical topics: meta-analysis and power.

Figuring Effect Size

You just learned that effect size is a measure of the difference between two population means. In Figure 7–2, the effect size is shown as the difference between the Population 1 mean and the Population 2 mean, which is 20 (that is, $220 - 200 = 20$). This effect size of 20 is called a *raw score effect size,* because the effect size is given in terms of the raw score on the measure (which, in this case is an achievement test score, from a low of 0 to a high of, say, 300). But what if you want to compare this effect size with the result of a similar study that used a different achievement test? This similar study used a test with possible scores from 0 to 100, and the researchers reported an estimated Population 2 mean of 80, a Population 1 mean of 85 and a population standard deviation of 10? The raw score effect size in this study is 5 (that is, $85 - 80 = 5$). How do we compare this raw score effect size of 5 with the raw score effect size of 20 in our original study? The solution to this problem is to use a *standardized effect size*—that is, to divide the raw score effect size for each study by its respective population standard deviation.

In the original example of giving special instructions to fifth graders taking a standard achievement test, the population standard deviation (of individuals) was 48. Thus, a raw score of effect size of 20 gives a standardized effect size of 20/48, which is .42. That is, the effect of giving the special instructions was to increase test scores by .42 of a standard deviation. The raw score effect size of 5 in the similar study (which had a population standard deviation of 10) is a standardized effect size of $5/10 = .50$. Thus, in this similar study, the effect was to increase the test scores by .50 (half) of a standard deviation. So, in this case the effect size in our original example is smaller than the effect size in the similar study. Usually, when behavioral and social scientists refer to an effect size, they mean a standardized effect size.

Here is the rule for calculating effect size: Divide the predicted difference between the population means by the population standard deviation.[1] Stated as a formula,

---

[1]This procedure gives a measure of effect size called "Cohen's *d.*" It is the preferred method for the kind of hypothesis testing you have learned so far (the Z test). (In later chapters, you learn some additional measures of effect size that are appropriate to particular hypothesis-testing situtations.)

$$\text{Effect Size} = \frac{\text{Population 1 } M - \text{Population 2 } M}{\text{Population } SD} \qquad (7\text{-}1)$$

> Effect size is the difference between the two population means divided by the population's standard deviation.

In this formula, Population 1 M is the mean for the population that receives the experimental manipulation, and Population 2 M is the mean of the known population (the basis for the comparison distribution), and Population SD is the standard deviation of the population of individuals. Notice that when figuring effect size you don't use the standard deviation of the distribution of means. Instead, you use the standard deviation of the population of individuals. Also notice that you are concerned with only one population's SD. This is because in hypothesis testing you usually assume that both populations have the same standard deviation. (We will say more about this in later chapters.)

effect size conventions Standard rules about what to consider a small, medium, and large effect size, based on what is typical in behavioral and social science research; also known as Cohen's conventions.

Consider again the fifth-grader example shown in Figure 7–1. The best estimate of the mean of Population 1 is the sample mean, which was 220. (In hypothesis-testing situations, you don't know the mean of Population 1, so you use an estimated mean; thus, you are actually figuring an *estimated effect size.*) The mean of Population 2 was 200, and the population standard deviation was 48. The difference between the two population means is 20 and the standard deviation of the populations of individuals is 48. Thus, the effect size is 20/48, or .42. In terms of the formula,

$$\text{Effect Size} = \frac{\text{Population 1 } M - \text{Population 2 } M}{\text{Population } SD} = \frac{220 - 200}{48} = \frac{20}{48} = .42$$

For the example in which the sample mean was 210, we would estimate Population 1's mean to be 210. Thus,

$$\text{Effect Size} = \frac{\text{Population 1 } M - \text{Population 2 } M}{\text{Population } SD} = \frac{210 - 200}{48} = \frac{10}{48} = .21$$

In both of these examples, the effect size is positive. If the effect size is negative, it just means that the mean of Population 1 is smaller than the mean of Population 2.

Effect Size Conventions

What should you consider to be a "big" effect, and what is a "small" effect? Jacob Cohen (1988, 1992), a researcher who developed the effect size measure among other major contributions to statistical methods, has helped solve this problem (see Box 7–2). Cohen came up with some **effect size conventions** based on the effects found in many actual studies. Specifically, Cohen recommended that for the kind of situation we are considering in this chapter, we should think of a small effect size as about .20. With an effect size of .20, the populations of individuals have an overlap of about 85%. This small effect size of .20 is, for example, the average difference in height between 15- and 16-year-old girls (see Figure 7–4a), which is about a half-inch difference with a standard deviation of about 2.1 inches. Cohen considered a medium effect size to be .50, which means an overlap of about 67%. This is about the average difference in heights between 14- and 18-year-old girls (see Figure 7–4b). Finally, Cohen defined a large effect size as .80. This is only about a 53% overlap. It is about the average difference in height between 13- and 18-year-old girls (see Figure 7–4c). These three effect size conventions are summarized in Table 7–1. (Note that these effect size conventions apply in the same way to both positive and negative effect sizes. So, −.20 is a small effect size, −.50 is a medium effect size, and −.80 is a large effect size.)

Table 7-1 Summary of Cohen's Effect Size Conventions for Mean Differences

Verbal Description	Effect Size
Small	.20
Medium	.50
Large	.80

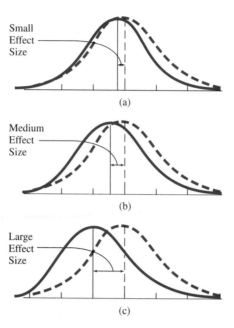

Figure 7–4 Comparisons of pairs of population distributions of individuals showing Cohen's conventions for effect size: (a) small effect size (.20), (b) medium effect size (.50), (c) large effect size (.80).

Consider another example. As we noted earlier in the book, many IQ tests have a standard deviation of 16 points. An experimental procedure with a small effect size would be an increase of 3.2 IQ points. (A difference of 3.2 IQ points between the mean of the population who goes through the experimental procedure and the mean of the population that does not, divided by the population standard deviation of 16, gives an effect size of .20.) An experimental procedure with a medium effect size would increase IQ by 8 points. An experimental procedure with a large effect size would increase IQ by 12.8 points.

A More General Importance of Effect Size

Effect size, as we have seen, is the difference between means divided by the population standard deviation. This division by the population standard deviation standardizes the difference between means, in the same way that a Z score gives a standard for comparison to other scores, even scores on different scales. Especially by using the standard deviation of the population of individuals, we bypass the variation from study to study of different sample sizes, making comparison even easier and effect size even more of a standard.

Knowing the effect size of a study lets you compare results with effect sizes found in other studies, even when the other studies have different sample sizes. Equally important, knowing the effect size lets you compare studies using different measures, even if those measures have different means and variances.

Also, within a particular study, our general knowledge of what is a small or a large effect size helps you evaluate the overall importance of a result. For example, a result may be statistically significant but not very large. Or a result that is not statistically significant (perhaps due to a small sample) may have just as large an effect size as another study (perhaps one with a larger sample) where the result was significant. Knowing the effect sizes of the studies helps us make better sense of such results. We examine both of these important implications of effect size in later sections of this chapter.

An important development in statistics in recent years is a procedure called **meta-analysis.** This procedure combines results from different studies, even results using different methods of measurement. When combining results, the crucial thing combined is the effect sizes. As an example, a sociologist might be interested in the effects of cross-race friendships on prejudice, a topic on which there has been a large number of studies. Using meta-analysis, the sociologist could combine the results of these studies. This would provide an overall average effect size. It would also tell how the average effect sizes differ for studies done in different countries or about prejudice toward different ethnic groups. (For an example of such a study, see Pettigrew & Tropp, 2006.) An educational researcher might be interested in the effects of different educational methods on students' educational achievement. Walberg and Lai (1999) carried out a large meta-analysis on this topic and provided effect size estimates for 275 educational methods and conditions. The effect sizes for selected general educational methods are shown in Table 7–2. As you can see in the table, many of the methods are associated with medium effect sizes and several have large (or very large) effect sizes. For another example of meta-analysis, see Box 7–1.

Reviews of the collection of studies on a particular topic that use meta-analysis are an alternative to the traditional "narrative" literature review article. Such traditional reviews describe and evaluate each study and then attempt to draw some overall conclusion.

meta-analysis Statistical method for combining effect sizes from different studies.

Table 7-2 Effect Sizes of Selected General Educational Methods

Elements of Instruction	
Cues	1.25
Reinforcement	1.17
Corrective feedback	.94
Engagement	.88
Mastery Learning	.73
Computer-Assisted Instruction	
For early elementary students	1.05
For handicapped students	.66
Teaching	
Direct instruction	.71
Comprehension instruction	.55
Teaching Techniques	
Homework with teacher comments	.83
Graded homework	.78
Frequent testing	.49
Pretests	.48
Adjunct questions	.40
Goal setting	.40
Assigned homework	.28
Explanatory Graphics	.75

Source: Adapted from Walberg, H. J., & Lai, J.-S. (1999). Meta-analytic effects for policy. In G. J. Cizek (Ed.). *Handbook of educational policy* (pp. 419–453). San Diego, CA: Academic Press.

1. What does effect size add to just knowing whether a result is significant?
2. Why do researchers usually use a *standardized* effect size?
3. Write the formula for effect size in the situation we have been considering.
4. On a standard test, the population is known to have a mean of 500 and a standard deviation of 100. Those receiving an experimental treatment have a mean of 540. What is the effect size?
5. What are the effect size conventions?
6. (a) What is meta-analysis? (b) What is the role of effect size in a meta-analysis?

Answers

1. A significant result can be just barely big enough to be significant or much bigger than necessary to be significant. Thus, knowing effect size tells you how big the effect is.
2. It makes the results of studies using different measures comparable.
3. Effect Size = (Population 1 M − Population 2 M)/Population SD.
4. Effect Size = (Population 1 M − Population 2 M)/Population SD = (540 − 500)/100 = .40.
5. Small = .20, medium = .50, large = .80.
6. (a) A systematic procedure for combining results of different studies. (b) Meta-analyses usually come up with an average effect size across studies and also sometimes compare average effect sizes for different subgroups of studies.

statistical power Probability that the study will give a significant result if the research hypothesis is true.

Statistical Power

Power is the ability to achieve your goals. A goal of a researcher conducting a study is to get a significant result—but only *if* the research hypothesis really is true. The **statistical power** of a research study is the probability that the study will produce a statistically significant result if the research hypothesis is true. Power is *not* simply the probability that a study will produce a statistically significant result. The power of a study is the probability that it will produce a statistically significant result, but only *if the research hypothesis is true.* If the research hypothesis is false, you do not want to get significant results. (That would be a Type I error, as you learned in Chapter 5.) Remember, however, even if the research hypothesis is true, an experiment will not automatically give a significant result. The particular sample that happens to be selected from the population may not turn out to be extreme enough to reject the null hypothesis.

Statistical power is important for several reasons. As you will learn later in the chapter, figuring power when planning a study helps you determine how many participants you need. Also, understanding power is extremely important when you read a research article, particularly for making sense of results that are not significant or results that are statistically but not practically significant.

Consider once again our example of the effects of giving special instructions to fifth graders taking a standard achievement test. Recall that we compared two populations:

Population 1: Fifth graders receiving special instructions.
Population 2: Fifth graders not receiving special instructions.

BOX 7–1   **Effect Sizes for Relaxation and Meditation: A Restful Meta-Analysis**

In the 1970s and 1980s, the results of research on meditation and relaxation were the subject of considerable controversy. Eppley, Abrams, and Shear (1989) decided to look at the issue systematically by conducting a meta-analysis of the effects of various relaxation techniques on trait anxiety (that is, ongoing anxiety as opposed to a temporary state). Eppley and colleagues chose trait anxiety for their meta-analysis because it is related to many other mental health issues, yet in itself is fairly consistent from test to test.

Following the usual procedure, the researchers searched the scientific literature for studies—not only research journals but also books and unpublished doctoral dissertations. Finding all the relevant research studies is one of the most difficult parts of meta-analysis.

To find the "bottom line," Eppley et al. (1989) compared effect sizes for each of four widely studied methods of meditation and relaxation. The result was that the average effect size for the 35 transcendental meditation (TM) studies was .70 (meaning an average difference of .70 standard deviation in anxiety scores between those who practiced this meditation procedure versus those in the control groups). This effect size was significantly larger than the average effect size of .28 for the 44 studies on all other types of meditation, the average effect size of .38 for the 30 "progressive relaxation" studies (a widely used method by clinical psychologists), and the average effect size of .40 for the 37 studies on other forms of relaxation.

Looking at different populations of research participants, they discovered that people screened to be highly anxious contributed more to the effect size, and prison populations and younger subjects seemed to gain more from TM. There was no impact on effect size of the skill of the instructors, expectations of the subjects or whether subjects had volunteered or been randomly assigned to conditions.

The researchers thought that one clue to TM's high performance might be that techniques involving concentration produced a significantly smaller effect, whereas TM makes a point of teaching an "effortless, spontaneous" method.

Whatever the reasons, Eppley et al. (1989) concluded that there are "grounds for optimism that at least some current treatment procedures can effectively reduce trait anxiety" (p. 973). So if you are prone to worry about matters like statistics exams, consider these results.

Also recall that the research hypothesis was that Population 1 would score higher than Population 2 on the achievement test.

The curve in Figure 7–5 shows the distribution of means for Population 2. (Be careful: When discussing effect size, we showed figures, such as Figures 7–2 and 7–3, for populations of individuals; now we are back to focusing on distributions of means.) This curve is the comparison distribution, the distribution of means that you would expect for both populations if the null hypothesis were true. The mean of this distribution of means is 200 and its standard deviation is 6. In Chapter 6, we found that using the 5% significance level, one-tailed, you need a Z score for the mean of your sample of at least 1.64 to reject the null hypothesis. Using the formula for converting Z scores to raw scores, this comes out to a raw score of 209.84; that is, $(1.64)(6) + 200 = 209.84$. Therefore, we have shaded the tail of this distribution above a raw score of 209.84 (a Z score of 1.64 on this distribution). This is the area where you would reject the null hypothesis if, as a result of your study, the mean of your sample was in this area.

Imagine that the researchers predict that giving students the special instructions will increase students' scores on the achievement test to 208. (This is an increase of 8 points from the mean of 200 when no special instructions are given.) If this prediction is correct, the research hypothesis is true and the mean of Population 1 (the population of students who receive the special instructions) is indeed greater than the

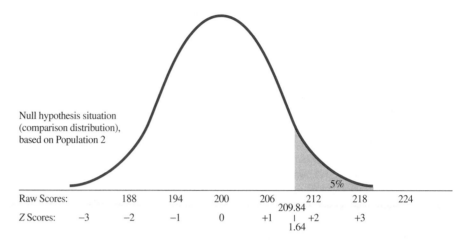

Null hypothesis situation (comparison distribution), based on Population 2

5%

| Raw Scores: | 188 | 194 | 200 | 206 | 212 | 218 | 224 |
| Z Scores: −3 | −2 | −1 | 0 | +1 | +2 | +3 |

209.84

1.64

Figure 7–5 For the fictional study of fifth graders' performance on a standard school achievement test, distribution of means for Population 2 (the comparison distribution), those not given special instructions. Significance cutoff score (209.84) shown for $p < .05$, one-tailed.

mean of Population 2. The distribution of means for Population 1 for this *hypothetical predicted situation* is shown in the top part of Figure 7–6. Notice that the distribution has a mean of 208.

Now take a look at the curve shown in the bottom part of Figure 7–6. This curve is exactly the same as the one shown in Figure 7–5: It is the comparison distribution, the distribution of means for Population 2. Notice that the distribution of means for Population 1 (the top curve) is set off to the right of the distribution of means for Population 2 (the bottom curve). This is because the researchers predict the mean of Population 1 to be higher (a mean of 208) than the mean of Population 2 (which we know is 200). (If Population 1's mean is predicted to be *lower* than Population 2's mean, then Population 1 would be set off to the *left.*) If the null hypothesis is true, the true distribution for Population 1 is the same as the distribution based on Population 2. Thus, the Population 1 distribution would be lined up directly above the Population 2 distribution and would not be set off to the right (or the left).

Recall that the cutoff score for rejecting the null hypothesis in this example is 209.84. Thus, the shaded rejection area for Population 2's distribution of means (shown in the bottom curve in Figure 7–6) starts at 209.84. We can also create a rejection area for the distribution of means for Population 1. This rejection area will also start at 209.84 (see the shaded area in the top curve in Figure 7–6). Remember that, in this example, Population's 1 distribution of means represents the possible sample means we would get if we randomly selected 64 fifth graders from a population of fifth graders with a mean of 208 (and a standard deviation of 48).

Now, suppose the researchers carry out the study. They give the special instructions to a randomly selected group of 64 fifth graders and find their mean score on the achievement test. And suppose this sample's mean turns out to be in the shaded area of the distributions (that is, a mean of 209.84 or higher). If that happens, the researchers will reject the null hypothesis. What Figure 7–6 shows us is that most of the means from Populations 1's distribution of means (assuming that its mean is 208) will not be large enough to reject the null hypothesis. Less than half of the upper distribution is shaded. Put another way, if the research hypothesis is true as the researcher predicts, the sample we study is a random sample from this Population 1 distribution of means.

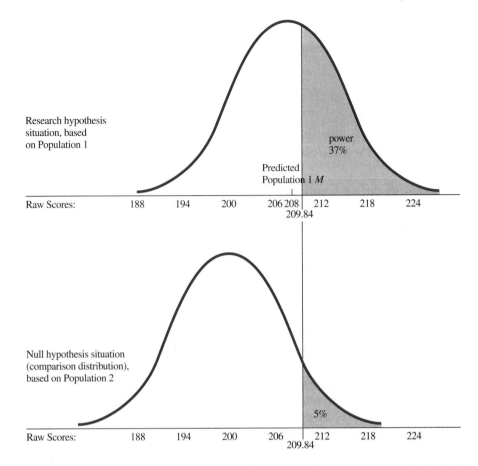

Research hypothesis
situation, based
on Population 1

power
37%

Predicted
Population 1 M

Raw Scores: 188   194   200   206 208 | 212   218   224
                                        209.84

Null hypothesis situation
(comparison distribution),
based on Population 2

5%

Raw Scores: 188   194   200   206 | 212   218   224
                                     209.84

Figure 7–6   For the fictional study of fifth graders' performance on a standard school achievement test, distribution of means for Population 1 based on a predicted population mean of 208 (upper curve), and distribution of means for Population 2 (the comparison distribution) based on a known population mean of 200 (lower curve). Significance cutoff score (209.84) shown for $p < .05$, one-tailed. Shaded sections of both distributions are the area in which the null hypothesis will be rejected. Power $= 37\%$.

However, there is less than a 50–50 chance that the mean of a random sample from this distribution will be in the shaded rejection area.

Recall that the statistical power of a study is the probability that the study will produce a statistically significant result, if the research hypothesis is true. Since we are assuming the research hypothesis is true in this example, the shaded region in the upper distribution represents the power of the study. It turns out that the power for this situation (shown in Figure 7–6) is only 37%. Therefore, assuming the researcher's prediction is correct, the researcher has only a 37% chance that the sample of 64 fifth graders will have a mean high enough to make the result of the study statistically significant.

Suppose that the particular sample of 64 fifth graders studied had a mean of 203.5. Since you would need a mean of at least 209.84 to reject the null hypothesis, the result of this study would not be statistically significant. It would not be significant, even though the research hypothesis really is true. This is how you would come to make a Type II error.

It is entirely possible that the researchers might happen to select a sample from Population 1 with a mean far enough to the right (that is, with a high enough mean

power table Table for a hypothesis-testing procedure showing the statistical power of a study for various effect sizes and sample sizes.

test score) to be in the shaded rejection area. However, given the way we have set up this particular example, there is a better-than-even chance that the study will *not* turn out significant, *even though we know the research hypothesis is true.* (Of course, once again, the researcher would not know this.) When a study like the one in this example has only a small chance of being significant even if the research hypothesis is true, we say the study has *low power.*

Suppose, on the other hand, the situation was one in which the upper curve was expected to be way to the right of the lower curve, so that almost any sample taken from the upper curve would be in the shaded rejection area in the lower curve. In that situation, the study would have high power.

Determining Statistical Power

The statistical power of a study can be figured. In a situation like the fifth-grader-testing example, figuring power involves figuring out the area of the shaded portion of the upper distribution in Figure 7–6. However, the figuring is somewhat laborious. Furthermore, the figuring becomes quite complex once we consider, starting in the next chapter, more realistic hypothesis-testing situations. Thus, researchers do not usually figure power themselves and instead rely on alternate approaches.

Researchers can use a power software package to determine power. There are also power calculators available on the Internet. When using a power software packages or Internet power calculator, the researcher puts in the numbers for the various aspects of the research study (such as the known population mean, the predicted population mean, the population standard deviation, the sample size, the significance level, and whether the test is one-tailed or two-tailed) and the figuring is done automatically. Finally, researchers often find the power of a study using special charts called **power tables.** (Such tables have been prepared by Cohen, 1988, and Kraemer & Thiemann, 1987, among others.) In the following chapters, with each method you learn, we provide basic power tables and discuss how to use them. Table A–5 in the Appendix is an index to these tables.

How are you doing?

1. (a) What is statistical power? (b) How is it different from just the probability of getting a significant result?
2. What is the probability of getting a significant result if the research hypothesis is false?
3. (a) Name three approaches that researchers typically use to determine power. (b) Why do researchers use these approaches, as opposed to figuring power themselves by hand?

Answers

1. (a) Statistical power is the probability of getting a significant result if the research hypothesis is true. (b) It is the probability if the research hypothesis is true.
2. The significance level (that is, the probability of making a Type I error).
3. (a) Power software packages; Internet power calculators; power tables. (b) In common hypothesis-testing situations, figuring power by hand is very complicated.

BOX 7–2   **Jacob Cohen, the Ultimate New Yorker: Funny, Pushy, Brilliant, and Kind**

New Yorkers can be proud of Jacob Cohen, who single-handedly introduced to behavioral and social scientists some of our most important statistical tools, including the main topics of this chapter (power analysis and effect size) as well as many of the sophisticated uses of regression analysis and much more. Never worried about being popular—although he was—he almost single-handedly forced the current debate over significance testing, which he liked to joke was entrenched like a "secular religion." About the asterisk that accompanies a significant result, he said the religion must be "of Judeo-Christian derivation, as it employs as its most powerful icon a six-pointed cross" (1990, p. 1307).

Jacob entered graduate school at New York University in clinical psychology in 1947 and three years later had a masters and a doctorate. He then worked in rather lowly roles for the Veterans Administration, doing research on various practical topics, until he returned to NYU in 1959. There he became a very famous faculty member because of his creative, off-beat ideas about statistics. Amazingly, he made his contributions having no mathematics training beyond high school algebra.

But a lack of formal training may have been Jacob Cohen's advantage, because he emphasized looking at data and thinking about them, not just applying a standard analysis. In particular, he demonstrated that the standard methods were not working very well, especially for "soft" fields of psychology such as clinical, personality, and social psychology, because researchers in these fields had no hope of finding what they were looking for due to a combination of typically small effect sizes of such research and researchers' use of small sample sizes. Entire issues of journals were filled with articles that only had a fifty-fifty chance of finding what their authors were looking for.

His ideas were hailed as a great breakthrough, especially regarding power and effect size. Yet, the all-too-common practice of carrying out studies with inadequate power that he railed against as hindering scientific progress

stubbornly continued. But even after twenty years of this, he was patient, writing that he understood that these things take time. His patience must have been part of why behavioral and social scientists from around the world found him a "joy to work with" (Murphy, 1998). Those around him daily at NYU knew him best; one said Cohen was "warm and engaging . . . renowned for his many jokes, often ribald" (Shrout, 2001, p. 166).

But patient or not, Cohen did not let up on researchers. He wanted them to think more deeply about the standard methods. Starting in the 1990s he really began to force the issue of the mindless use of significance testing. But he still used humor to tease behavioral and social scientists for their failure to see the problems inherent in the arbitrary yes-no decision feature of null hypothesis testing. For example, he liked to remind everyone that significance testing came out of Sir Ronald Fisher's work in agriculture (see Box 10–1), in which the decisions were yes-no matters such as whether a crop needed manure. He pointed out that behavioral and social scientists "do not deal in manure, at least not knowingly" (Cohen, 1990, p. 1307)! He really disliked the fact that Fisher-style decision making is used to determine the fate of not only doctoral dissertations, research funds, publications, and promotions, "but whether to have a baby just now" (1990, p. 1307). And getting more serious, he charged that significance testing's "arbitrary unreasonable tyranny has led to data fudging of varying degrees of subtlety, from grossly altering data to dropping cases where there 'must have been' errors" (p. 1307).

Cohen was active in many social causes, especially desegregation in the schools and fighting discrimination in police departments. He cared passionately about everything he did. He was deeply loved. And he suffered from major depression, becoming incapacitated by it four times in his life.

Got troubles? Got no more math than high school algebra? It doesn't have to stop you from contributing to science.

What Determines the Power of a Study?

It is very important that you understand what power is about. It is especially important to understand the factors that affect the power of a study and how to use power when planning a study and when making sense of a study you read.

The statistical power of a study depends on two main factors: how big an effect (the effect size) the research hypothesis predicts and how many participants are in the study (the sample size). Power is also affected by the significance level chosen, whether a one-tailed or two-tailed test is used, and the kind of hypothesis-testing procedure used.

Effect Size

Figure 7–6 shows the situation in our special test-instructions example in which the researchers had reason to predict that those who got the special instructions (Population 1, the top curve) would have a mean score *8 points higher* than fifth graders in general (Population 2, the bottom curve). Figure 7–7 shows the same study for a situation in which the researchers had reason to expect that Population 1 (those who got the special instructions) would have a mean score *16 points higher* than Population 2 (fifth graders in general). Compare Figure 7–7 to Figure 7–6. You are more likely to

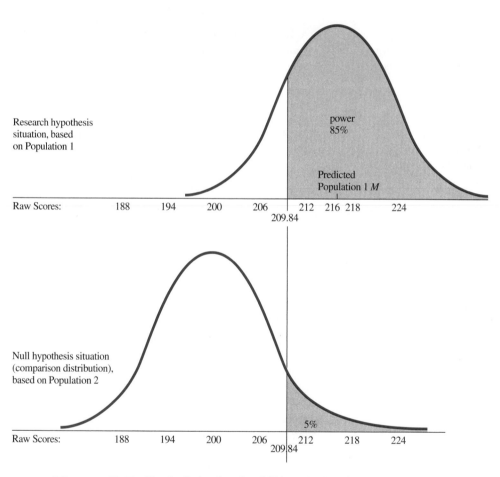

Figure 7–7   For the fictional study of fifth graders' performance on a standard school achievement test, distribution of means for Population 1 based on a predicted population mean of 216 (upper curve), and distribution of means for Population 2 (the comparison distribution) based on a known population mean of 200 (lower curve). Significance cutoff score (209.84) shown for *p* < .05, one-tailed. Power = 85%. Compare with Figure 7–6, in which the predicted population mean was 208 and power was 37%.

get a significant result in the situation shown in Figure 7–7. This is because there is more overlap of the top curve with the shaded area on the comparison distribution. Recall that the probability of getting a significant result (the power) for the situation in Figure 7–6, in which there was a basis for the researchers to predict only a mean of 208, is only 37%. However, for the situation in Figure 7–7, in which the researchers had good reasons to predict a mean of 216, the power is 85%. In any study, the bigger the difference that your theory or previous research says you should expect between the means of the two populations, the more power in the study. That is, if in fact there is a big mean difference in the population, you have more chance of getting a significant result in any given study. So if you predict a bigger mean difference, the power you determine based on that prediction will be greater.

The difference in means between populations we saw earlier is part of what goes into effect size. Thus, the bigger the effect size, the greater the power. The effect size for the situation in Figure 7–6, in which the researchers predicted Population 1 to have a mean of 208, is .17. That is, Effect Size = (Population 1 M − Population 2 M)/Population SD = (208 − 200)/48 = 8/48 = .17. The effect size for the situation in Figure 7–7, in which the researchers predicted Population 1 to have a mean of 216, is .33. That is, Effect Size = (Population 1 M − Population 2 M)/Population SD = (216 − 200)/48 = 16/48 = .33.

Effect size is also affected by the population standard deviation. The smaller the standard deviation, the bigger the effect size. In terms of the effect size formula, this is because if you divide by a smaller number, the result is bigger. In terms of the actual distributions, this is because if two distributions that are separated are narrower, they *overlap less.* Figure 7–8 shows two distributions of means based on the same example. However, this time we have changed the example so that the population standard deviation is exactly half of what it was in Figure 7–6. In this version, the predicted mean is the original 208. However, both distributions of means are much narrower. Therefore, there is much less overlap between the upper curve and the lower curve (the comparison distribution). The result is that the power is 85%, much higher than the power of 37% in the original situation. The idea here is that the smaller the population standard deviation, the greater the power.

Overall, these examples illustrate the general principle that the less overlap between the two distributions, the more likely that a study will give a significant result. Two distributions might have little overlap overall either because there is a large difference between their means (as in Figure 7–7) or because they have such a small standard deviation that even with a small mean difference they do not overlap much (as in Figure 7–8). This principle is summarized more generally in Figure 7–9.

Sample Size

The other major influence on power, besides effect size, is the number of people in the sample that is studied, the sample size. Basically, the more people there are in the study, the more power.

Sample size affects power because the larger the sample size, the smaller the standard deviation of the distribution of means. If these distributions have a smaller standard deviation, they are narrower. And if they are narrower, there is less overlap between them. Figure 7–10 shows the situation for our fifth-grader example if the study included 100 fifth graders instead of the 64 in the original example, with a predicted mean of 208 and a population standard deviation of 48. The power now is 51%.

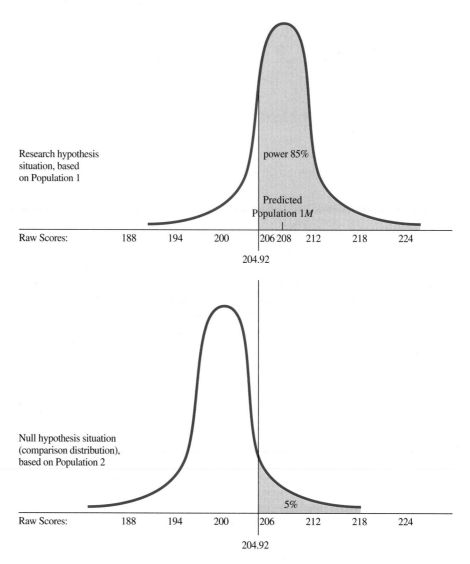

Research hypothesis
situation, based
on Population 1

power 85%

Predicted
Population 1*M*

Raw Scores: 188   194   200   206 208   212   218   224

204.92

Null hypothesis situation
(comparison distribution),
based on Population 2

5%

Raw Scores: 188   194   200   206   212   218   224

204.92

Figure 7–8 For the fictional study of fifth graders' performance on a standard school achievement test, distribution of means for Population 1 based on a predicted population mean of 208 (upper curve), and distribution of means for Population 2 (the comparison distribution) based on a known population mean of 200 (lower curve). Significance cutoff score (209.84) shown for $p < .05$, one-tailed. In this example, the population standard deviation is half as large as that shown for this example in previous figures. Power = 85%. Compare with Figure 7–6, which had the original population standard deviation and power was 37%.

(It was 37% with 64 fifth graders.) With 500 participants in the study, power is 99% (see Figure 7–11).

Don't get mixed up. The distributions of means can be narrow (and thus have less overlap and more power) for two very different reasons. One reason is that the populations of individuals may have small standard deviations. This reason has to do with effect size. The other reason is that the sample size is large. This reason is completely separate. Sample size has nothing to do with effect size. Both effect size and sample size influence power. However, as we will see shortly, these two different influences

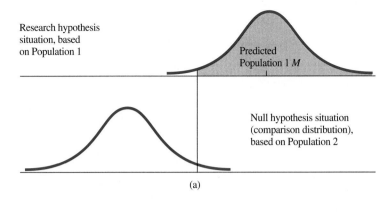

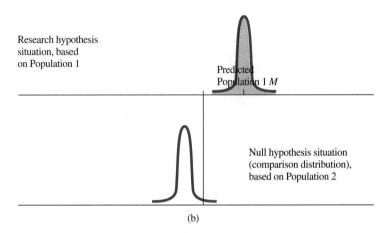

Figure 7–9   The predicted and comparison distributions of means might have little overlap (and thus the study would have high power) because either (a) the two means are very different or (b) the population standard deviation is very small.

on power lead to completely different kinds of practical steps for increasing power when planning a study.

Figuring Needed Sample Size for a Given Level of Power

When planning a study, the main reason researchers consider power is to help decide how many people to include in the study. Sample size has an important influence on power. Thus, a researcher wants to be sure to have enough people in the study for the study to have fairly high power. (Too often, researchers carry out studies in which the power is so low that it is unlikely they will get a significant result even if the research hypothesis is true.)

Suppose the researchers in our fifth-grader example were planning the study and wanted to figure out how many students to include in the sample. Let us presume that based on previous research for a situation like theirs, they predicted a mean difference of 8 and there is a known population standard deviation of 48. In this case, it turns out that the researchers would need 222 fifth graders to have 80% power. In practice,

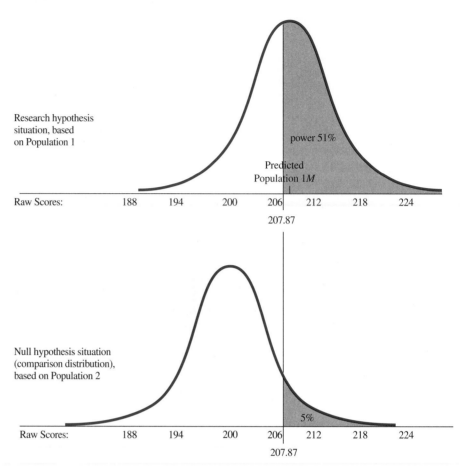

Research hypothesis situation, based on Population 1

power 51%

Predicted Population 1*M*

Raw Scores: 188   194   200   206   212   218   224

207.87

Null hypothesis situation (comparison distribution), based on Population 2

5%

Raw Scores: 188   194   200   206   212   218   224

207.87

Figure 7–10   For the fictional study of fifth graders' performance on a standard school achievement test, distribution of means for Population 1 based on a predicted population mean of 208 (upper curve), and distribution of means for Population 2 (the comparison distribution) based on a known population mean of 200 (lower curve). In this example, the sample size is 100, compared to 64 in the original example. Significance cutoff score (207.87) shown for $p < .05$, one-tailed. Power = 51%. Compare with Figure 7–6, which had the original sample size of 64 fifth graders and power was 37%.

researchers use power software packages, Internet power calculators, or special power tables that tell you how may participants you would need in a study to have a high level of power, given a predicted effect size. We provide simplified versions of power tables for each of the main hypothesis-testing procedures you learn in upcoming chapters.

Other Influences on Power

Three other factors, besides effect size and sample size, affect power:

1. *Significance level.* Less extreme significance levels (such as .10 or .20) mean more power. More extreme significance levels (.01 or .001) mean less power. Less extreme significance levels result in more power because the shaded rejection area on the lower curve is bigger. Thus, more of the area in the upper curve is shaded. More extreme significance levels result in less power because the

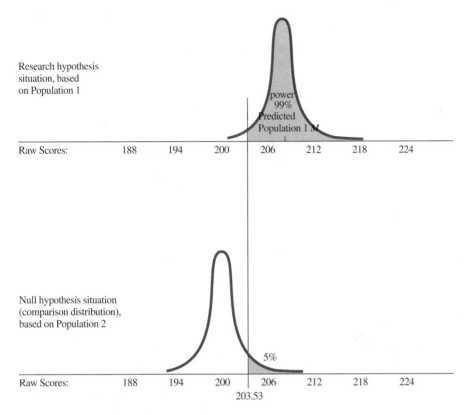

Figure 7–11   For the fictional study of fifth graders' performance on a standard school achievement test, distribution of means for Population 1 based on a predicted population mean of 208 (upper curve), and distribution of means for Population 2 (the comparison distribution) based on a known population mean of 200 (lower curve). In this example, the sample size is 500, compared to 64 in the original example. Significance cutoff score (203.53) shown for $p < .05$, one-tailed. Power = 99%. Compare with Figure 7–6, which had the original sample size of 64 fifth graders and power was 37%, and Figure 7-10, which had a sample size of 100 and a power of 51%.

    shaded rejection region on the lower curve is smaller. Suppose in our original version of the fifth-grader example, we had instead used the .01 significance level. The power would have dropped from 37% to only 16% (see Figure 7–12).

2. *One- versus two-tailed tests.* Using a two-tailed test makes it harder to get significance on any one tail. Thus, keeping everything else the same, power is less with a two-tailed test than with a one-tailed test. Suppose in our fifth-grader testing example we had used a two-tailed test instead of a one-tailed test (but still using the 5% level overall). As shown in Figure 7–13, power would be only 26% (compared to 37% in the original one-tailed version shown in Figure 7–6).

3. *Type of hypothesis-testing procedure.* Sometimes the researcher has a choice of more than one hypothesis-testing procedure to use for a particular study. We have not considered any such situations so far in this book but we will do so in Chapter 11.

Summary of Influences on Power

Table 7–3 summarizes the effects of various factors on the power of a study.

How are you doing?

1. (a) What are the two factors that determine effect size? For each, (b) and (c), explain how and why it affects power.
2. (a) How and (b) why does sample size affect power?
3. (a) How and (b) why does the significance level used affect power?
4. (a) How and (b) why does using a one-tailed versus a two-tailed test affect power?

Answers

1. (a) The two factors are the difference between the population means and the population standard deviation.
(b) The more difference between the population means, the larger the effect size, the more power. This is because it makes the distribution of means further apart and thus have less overlap. Therefore, the area in the predicted distribution more extreme than the cutoff in the known distribution is greater.
(c) The smaller the population standard deviation, the larger the effect size, the more power. This is because it makes the distribution of means narrower and thus have less overlap. Thus, the area in the predicted distribution more extreme than the cutoff in the known distribution is greater.

2. (a) The larger the sample size, the more power. (b) This is because a large sample size makes the distribution of means narrower (because the standard deviation of the distribution of means is the result of dividing the population variance by the sample size) and thus have less overlap, so the area in the predicted distribution more extreme than the cutoff in the known distribution is greater.

3. The more liberal the significance level (for example, .10 versus .05), the more power. (b) This is because it makes the cutoff in the known distribution less extreme, so the corresponding area more extreme than this cutoff in the predicted distribution of means is larger.

4. A study with a one-tailed test has more power (for a result in the predicted direction) than a two-tailed test. (b) This is because with a one-tailed test, the cutoff in the predicted direction in the known distribution is less extreme, so the corresponding area more extreme than this cutoff in the predicted distribution of means is larger. There is an added cutoff in the opposite side with a two-tailed test, but this is so far out on the distribution that it has little effect on power.

The Role of Power When Planning a Study

Determining power is very important when planning a study. If you do a study in which the power is low, even if the research hypothesis is true, the study will probably not give statistically significant results. Thus, the time and expense of carrying out the study, as it is currently planned, would probably not be worthwhile. So when the power of a planned study is found to be low, researchers look for practical ways to increase the power to an acceptable level.

What is an acceptable level of power? A widely used rule is that a study should have 80% power to be worth doing (see Cohen, 1988). Power of 80% means that there is an 80% (8 out of 10) chance that the study will produce a statistically significant result, if the research hypothesis is true. Obviously, the more power the better. How-

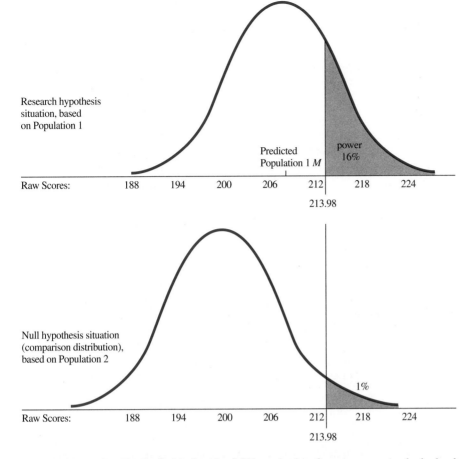

Figure 7–12   For the fictional study of fifth graders' performance on a standard school achievement test, distribution of means for Population 1 based on a predicted population mean of 208 (upper curve), and distribution of means for Population 2 (the comparison distribution) based on a known population mean of 200 (lower curve). Significance cutoff score (213.98) now shown for $p < .01$, one-tailed. Power = 16%. Compare with Figure 7–6, which used a significance level of $p < .05$ and power was 37%.

ever, the costs of greater power, such as studying more people, often make even 80% power beyond your reach.

How can you increase the power of a planned study? In principle, you can increase the power of a planned study by changing any of the factors summarized in Table 7–3. Let's consider each.

1. *Increase the effect size by increasing the predicted difference between population means.* You can't just arbitrarily predict a bigger difference. There has to be a basis for your prediction. Thus, to increase the predicted difference, your method in carrying out the study must make it reasonable to expect a bigger difference. Consider again our example of the experiment about the impact of special instructions on fifth graders' test scores. One way to increase the expected mean difference would be to make the instructions more elaborate, spending more time explaining them, perhaps allowing time for practice, and so forth. In some studies, you may be able to increase the expected mean difference by using a more

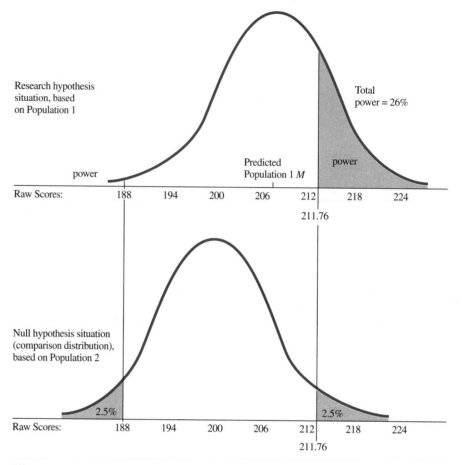

Figure 7–13   For the fictional study of fifth graders' performance on a standard school achievement test, distribution of means for Population 1 based on a predicted population mean of 208 (upper curve), and distribution of means for Population 2 (the comparison distribution) based on a known population mean of 200 (lower curve). Significance cutoff scores (188.24 and 211.76) now shown for $p < .05$, two-tailed. Power = 26%. Compare with Figure 7–6, which used a significance level of $p < .05$, one-tailed, and power was 37%.

Table 7-3   Influences on Power

Feature of the Study	Increases Power	Decreases Power
Effect size	Large	Small
Effect size combines the following two features:		
Predicted difference between population means	Large Differences	Small Differences
Population standard deviation	Small Population *SD*	Large Population *SD*
Sample size (*N*)	Large *N*	Small *N*
Significance level	Lenient (such as .10)	Stringent (such as .01)
One-tailed versus two-tailed test	One-tailed	Two-tailed
Type of hypothesis-testing procedure used	Varies	Varies

intense experimental procedure. A disadvantage of this approach of increasing the impact of the experimental procedure is that you may have to use an experimental procedure that is not like the one to which you want the results of your study to apply. It can also sometimes be difficult or costly.

2. *Increase effect size by decreasing the population standard deviation.* You can decrease the population standard deviation in a planned study in at least two ways. One way is to use a population that has less variation within it than the one originally planned. With the fifth-grader testing example, you might only use fifth graders in a particular suburban school system. The disadvantage is that your results will then apply only to the more limited population.

   Another way to decrease the population standard deviation is to use conditions of testing that are more standardized and measures that are more precise. For example, testing in a controlled laboratory setting usually makes for smaller overall variation among scores in results (meaning a smaller standard deviation). Similarly, using measures and tests with very clear wording also reduces variation. When practical, this is an excellent way to increase power, but often the study is already as rigorous as it can be.

3. *Increase the sample size.* The most straightforward way to increase power in a study is to study more people. Of course, if you are studying astronauts who have walked on the moon, there is a limit to how many are available. Also, using a larger sample size often adds to the time and cost of conducting the research. In most research situations, though, increasing sample size is the main way to change a planned study to raise its power.

4. *Use a less-stringent level of significance.* Ordinarily, the level of significance you use should be the least stringent that reasonably protects against Type I error. Normally, this will be .05. It is rare that much can be done to improve power in this way.

5. *Use a one-tailed test.* Whether you use a one- or a two-tailed test depends on the logic of the hypothesis being studied. As with significance level, it is rare that you have much of a choice about this factor.

6. *Use a more sensitive hypothesis-testing procedure.* This is fine if alternatives are available. We consider some options of this kind in Chapter 11. Usually, however, the researcher begins with the most sensitive method available, so little more can be done.

Table 7–4 summarizes some practical ways to increase the power of a planned experiment.

The Role of Power When Interpreting the Results of a Study

Understanding statistical power and what affects it is very important in drawing conclusions from the results of research.

Role of Power When a Result Is Statistically Significant: Statistical Significance versus Practical Significance

You have learned that a study with a larger effect size is more likely to come out statistically significant. It also is possible for a study with a very small effect size to come out significant. This is likely to happen when a study has high power due to other factors, especially a large sample size. Consider a study in which among all students who take the Scholastic Aptitude Test (SAT) in a particular year, a sample of 10,000 whose first name begins with a particular letter are randomly selected. Suppose

Table 7-4 Summary of Practical Ways of Increasing the Power of a Planned Experiment

Feature of the Study	Practical Way of Raising Power	Disadvantages
Predicted difference between population means	Increase the intensity of experimental procedure.	May not be practical or may distort study's meaning.
Population standard deviation	Use a less diverse population.	May not be available; decreases generalizability.
	Use standardized, controlled circumstances of testing or more precise measurement.	Not always practical.
Sample size (N)	Use a larger sample size.	Not always practical; can be costly.
Significance level	Use a more lenient level of significance (such as .10).	Raises the probability of Type I error.
One-tailed versus two-tailed test	Use a one-tailed test.	May not be appropriate for the logic of the study.
Type of hypothesis-testing procedure	Use a more sensitive procedure.	None may be available or appropriate.

that their mean Verbal SAT is 504, compared to the overall population's mean Verbal SAT of 500 (Population $SD = 100$). This result would be significant at the .001 level. Its effect size is a tiny .04. That is, the significance test tells you that you can be confident there is a real difference—that the population of students whose first name begins with this letter have higher Verbal SAT scores than the general population of students. At the same time, the difference is not very important. The effect size makes it clear that this difference is very small. The distributions of the two populations overlap so much that it would be of little use to know what letter a person's first name begins with.

The message here is that when judging a study's results, there are two questions. First, is the result statistically significant? If it is, you can consider there to be a *real effect*. The next question then is whether the effect size is large enough for the result to be *useful or interesting*. This second question is especially important if the study has practical implications. (Sometimes, in a study testing purely theoretical issues, it may be enough just to be confident there is an effect at all in a particular direction.)

If the sample was small, you can assume that a statistically significant result is probably also practically significant. On the other hand, if the sample size is very large, you must consider the effect size directly, as it is quite possible that the effect size is too small to be useful.

What we just said may seem a bit of a paradox. Most people assume that the more people in the study, the more important its results. In a sense, just the reverse is true. All other things being equal, if a study with only a few participants manages to be significant, that significance must be due to a large effect size. A study with a large number of people in it that is statistically significant may or may not have a large effect size.

Notice that it is not usually a good idea to compare the significance level of two studies to see which has the more important result. For example, a study with a small number of participants that is significant at the .05 level might well have a large effect size. At the same time, a study with a large number of participants that is significant at the .001 level might well have a small effect size.

The most important lesson from all this is that the word *significant* in statistically significant has a very special meaning. It means that you can be pretty confident

Table 7-5   Role of Significance and Sample Size in Interpreting Research Results

Result Statistically Significant	Sample Size	Conclusion
Yes	Small	Important result
Yes	Large	Might or might not have practical importance
No	Small	Inconclusive
No	Large	Research hypothesis probably false

that there is some real effect. But it does *not* mean that the effect is significant in a practical sense, that it is important or noteworthy.

Role of Power When a Result Is Not Statistically Significant

We saw in Chapter 5 that a result that is not statistically significant is inconclusive. Often, however, we really would like to conclude that there is little or no difference between the populations. Can we ever do that?

Consider the relation of power to a nonsignificant result. Suppose you carried out a study that had low power and did not get a significant result. In this situation, the result is entirely inconclusive. Not getting a significant result may have come about because the research hypothesis was false or because the study had too little power (for example, because it had too few participants).

On the other hand, suppose you carried out a study that had high power and you did not get a significant result. In this situation, it seems unlikely that the research hypothesis is true. In this situation (where there is high power), a nonsignificant result is a fairly strong argument against the research hypothesis. This does not mean that all versions of the research hypothesis are false. For example, it is possible that the research hypothesis is true and the populations are only very slightly different (and you figured power based on predicting a large difference).

In sum, a nonsignificant result from a study with low power is truly inconclusive. However, a nonsignificant result from a study with high power does suggest that either the research hypothesis is false or that there is less of an effect than was predicted when figuring power.

Summary of the Role of Significance and Sample Size in Interpreting Research Results

Table 7–5 summarizes the role of significance and sample size in interpreting research results.

How are you doing?

1. (a) What are the two basic ways of increasing the effect size of a planned study? For each, (b) and (c), how can it be done, and what are the disadvantages?
2. What is usually the easiest way to increase the power of a planned study?
3. What are the disadvantages of increasing the power of a planned study by (a) using a more lenient significance level or (b) using a one-tailed test rather than a two-tailed test?
4. Why is statistical significance not the same as practical importance?

5. You are comparing two studies in which one is significant at $p < .01$ and the other is significant at $p < .05$. (a) What can you conclude about the two studies? (b) What can you *not* conclude about the two studies?
6. When a result is significant, what can you conclude about effect size if the study had (a) a very large sample size or (b) a very small sample size?
7. When a result is not significant, what can you conclude about the truth of the research hypothesis if the study had (a) a very large sample size or (b) a very small sample size?

Effect Size and Power in Research Articles

It is increasingly common for articles to mention effect size. For example, Morehouse and Tobler (2000) studied the effectiveness of an intervention program for "high-risk, multiproblem, inner-city, primarily African-American and Latino youth." The authors reported "Youth who received 5–30 hours of intervention ([the high dosage group], $n = 101$) were compared with those who received 1–4 hours (the low-dosage group, $n = 31$). . . . The difference between the groups in terms of reduction in [alcohol and drug] use was highly significant. A between-groups effect size of .68 was achieved for the high-dosage group when compared with the low-dosage group." (Their wording about the study is a bit confusing—they are using "dosage" here to mean the amount of intervention, not the amount of drugs anyone was taking!) The meaning of the .68 effect size is that the group getting 5 to 30 hours of intervention was .68 standard deviations higher in terms of reduction of their drug and alcohol use than the group getting only 1 to 4 hours of the intervention. This is a medium to large effect size. Effect sizes are also almost always reported in meta-analyses, in which results from different articles are being combined and compared (for an example, see Box 7–1 earlier in the chapter).

As was the case with decision errors, you usually think about power when planning research and evaluating the results of a research study. (Power, for example, is often a major topic in grant proposals requesting funding for research and in thesis proposals.) As for research articles, power is sometimes mentioned in the final section of an article where the author discusses the meaning of the results or in discussions of results of other studies. In either situation, the emphasis tends to be on the meaning of nonsignificant results. Also, when power is discussed, it may be explained in some detail. This is because it has been only recently that most behavioral and social scientists have begun to be knowledgeable about power.

For example, Denenberg (1999), in discussing the basis for his own study, makes the following comments about a relevant previous study by Mody, Studdert-Kennedy, and Brady (1997) that had not found significant results.

> [T]hey were confronted with the serious problem of having to accept the null hypothesis. . . . we can view this issue in terms of statistical power. . . . A minimal statistical power of .80 [80%] is required before one can consider the argument that the lack of significance may be interpreted as evidence that Ho [the null hypothesis] is true. To conduct a power analysis, it is necessary to specify an expected mean difference, the alpha [significance] level, and whether a one-tailed or two-tailed test will be used. Given a power requirement of .8, one can then determine the N necessary. Once these conditions are satisfied, if the experiment fails to find a significant difference, then one can make the following kind of a statement: "We have designed an experiment with a .8 probability of finding a significant difference, if such exists in the population. Because we failed to find a significant effect, we think it quite unlikely that one exists. Even if it does exist, its contribution would appear to be minimal. . . ."
>
> Mody et al. never discussed power, even though they interpreted negative findings as evidence for the validity of the null hypothesis in all of their experiments. . . . Because the participants were split in this experiment, the ns [sample sizes] were reduced to 10 per group. Under such conditions one would not expect to find a significant difference, unless the experimental variable was very powerful. In other words it is more difficult to reject the null hypothesis when working with small ns [sample sizes]. The only meaningful conclusion that can be drawn from this study is that no meaningful interpretation can be made of the lack of findings . . . (pp. 380–381).

Summary

1. Effect size is a measure of the differences between population means. You can think of effect size as how much something changes after a specific intervention. The effect size is figured by dividing the difference between population means by the population standard deviation. Cohen's effect size conventions consider a small effect to be .20, a medium effect to be .50, and a large effect to be .80. Effect size is important in its own right in interpreting results of studies. It is also used to compare and combine results of studies, as in meta-analysis, and to compare different results within a study.

2. The statistical power of a study is the probability that it will produce a statistically significant result *if the research hypothesis is true.* Researchers usually figure the power of a study using power software packages, Internet power calculators, or special tables.

3. The larger the effect size, the greater the power. This is because the greater the difference between means or the smaller the population standard deviation (the two ingredients in effect size), the less overlap between the known and predicted populations' distributions of means. Thus, the area in the predicted distribution more extreme than the cutoff in the known distribution is greater.

4. The larger the sample size, the greater the power. This is because the larger the sample, the smaller the variance of the distribution of means. So, for a given effect size, there is less overlap between distributions of means.

5. Power is also affected by significance level (the more extreme, such as .01, the lower the power), by whether a one- or two-tailed test is used (with less power for a two-tailed test), and by the type of hypothesis-testing procedure used (in the occasional situation where there is a choice of procedure).

6. Statistically significant results from a study with high power (such as one with a large sample size) may not have practical importance. Results that are not statistically significant from a study with low power (such as one with a small sample size) leave open the possibility that statistically significant results might show up if power were increased.

7. Research articles increasingly report effect size, and effect sizes are almost always reported in meta-analyses. Research articles sometimes include discussions of power, especially when evaluating nonsignificant results.

Key Terms

effect size (p. 205)
effect size conventions (p. 207)

meta-analysis (p. 209)
statistical power (p. 210)

power tables (p. 214)

Example Worked-Out Problem

In a known population with a normal distribution, Population $M = 40$ and Population $SD = 10$. A sample given an experimental treatment has a mean of 37. What is the effect size? Is this approximately small, medium, or large?

Answer

Effect Size $=$ (Population 1 M $-$ Population 2 M)/Population $SD = (37 - 40)/10 = -3/10 = -.30$. Approximately small.

Outline for Writing Essays on Power and Effect Size for Studies Involving a Single Sample of More than One Individual and a Known Population

1. Explain the idea of power as the probability of getting significant results if the research hypothesis is true. Be sure to mention that the usual minimum acceptable

level of power for a research study is 80%. Explain the role played by power when you are interpreting the results of a study (both when a study is and is not significant), taking into account significance levels and sample size in relation to the likely effect size.

2. Explain the idea of effect size as the degree of overlap between distributions. Note that this overlap is a function of mean difference and population standard deviation (and describe precisely how it is figured and why it is figured that way). If required by the question, discuss the effect size conventions.

3. Explain the relation between effect size and power.

Practice Problems

These problems involve figuring. Most real-life statistics problems are done on a computer with special statistical software. Even if you have such software, do these problems by hand to ingrain the method in your mind.

Set I (for answers, see p. 444)

1. In a completed study, there is a known population with a normal distribution, Population $M = 25$, and Population $SD = 12$. What is the estimated effect size if a sample given an experimental procedure has a mean of (a) 19, (b) 22, (c) 25, (d) 30, and (e) 35? For each part, also indicate whether the effect is approximately small, medium, or large.

2. In a planned study, there is a known population with a normal distribution, Population $M = 50$, and Population $SD = 5$. What is the predicted effect size if the researchers predict that those given an experimental treatment have a mean of (a) 50, (b) 52, (c) 54, (d) 56, and (e) 47? For each part, also indicate whether the effect is approximately small, medium, or large.

3. Here is information about several possible versions of a planned study, each involving a single sample. Figure the predicted effect size for each study:

	Population 2		Predicted
Study	M	SD	Population 1 M
(a)	90	4	91
(b)	90	4	92
(c)	90	4	94
(d)	90	4	86

4. You read a study in which the result is significant (p 6 .05). You then look at the size of the sample. If the sample is very large (rather than very small), how should this affect your interpretation of (a) the probability that the null hypothesis is actually true and (b) the practical importance of the result? (c) Explain your answers to a person who understands hypothesis testing but has never learned about effect size or power.

5. Aron et al. (1997) placed strangers in pairs and asked them to talk together following a series of instructions designed to help them become close. At the end of 45 minutes, individuals privately answered some questions about how close they now felt to their partners. (The researchers combined the answers into a "closeness composite.") One key question was whether closeness would be affected by

either (a) matching strangers based on their attitude agreement or (b) leading participants to believe that they had been put together with someone who would like them. The result for both agreement and expecting to be liked was that "there was no significant differences on the closeness composite" (p. 367). The researchers went on to argue that the results suggested that there was little true effect of these variables on closeness (note that the symbol *d* in the text below means effect size):

> There was about 90% power in this study of achieving significant effects . . . for the two manipulated variables if in fact there were a large effect of this kind (*d* [effect size] = .8). Indeed, the power is about 90% for finding at least a near-significant (*p* < .10) medium-sized effect (*d* [effect size] = .5). Thus, it seems unlikely that we would have obtained the present results if in fact there is more than a small effect. . . . (p. 367).

Explain this result to a person who understands hypothesis testing but has never learned about effect size or power.

6. How does each of the following affect the power of a planned study?
   (a) A larger predicted difference between the means of the populations
   (b) A larger population standard deviation
   (c) A larger sample size
   (d) Using a more stringent significance level (e.g., .01 instead of .05)
   (e) Using a two-tailed test instead of a one-tailed test
7. List two situations in which it is useful to consider power, indicating what the use is for each.

Set II

8. In a completed study, there is a known population with a normal distribution, Population $M = 122$, and Population $SD = 8$. What is the estimated effect size if a sample given an experimental procedure has a mean of (a) 100, (b) 110, (c) 120, (d) 130, and (e) 140? For each part, also indicate whether the effect is approximately small, medium, or large.
9. In a planned study, there is a known population with a normal distribution, Population $M = 0$, and Population $SD = 10$. What is the predicted effect size if the researchers predict that those given an experimental treatment have a mean of (a) −8, (b) −5, (c) −2, (d) 0, and (e) 10? For each part, also indicate whether the effect is approximately small, medium, or large.
10. Here is information about several possible versions of a planned study, each involving a single sample. Figure the predicted effect size for each study:

Study	Population 2 M	SD	Predicted Population 1 M
(a)	90	2	91
(b)	90	1	91
(c)	90	2	92
(d)	90	2	94
(e)	90	2	86

11. What is meant by effect size? (Write your answer for a lay person.)
12. What is meant by the statistical power of an experiment? (Write your answer for a lay person.)

13. You read a study that just barely fails to be significant at the .05 level. That is, the result is not statistically significant. You then look at the size of the sample. If the sample is very large (rather than very small), how should this affect your judgment of (a) the probability that the null hypothesis is actually true and (b) the probability that the null hypothesis is actually false? (c) Explain your answers to a person who understands hypothesis testing but has never learned about power.

14. Caspi et al. (1997) analyzed results from a large-scale longitudinal study of a sample of children born around 1972 in Dunedin, New Zealand. As one part of their study, Caspi et al. compared the 94 in their sample who were, at age 21, alcohol dependent (clearly alcoholic) versus the 863 who were not alcohol dependent. The researchers compared these two groups in terms of personality test scores from when they were 18 years old. After noting that all results were significant, they reported the following results (note that the symbol d in the text below means effect size):

> Young adults who were alcohol dependent at age 21 scored lower at age 18 on Traditionalism ($d = .49$), Harm Avoidance ($d = .44$), Control ($d = .64$), and Social Closeness ($d = .40$), and higher on Aggression ($d = .86$), Alienation ($d = .66$), and Stress Reaction ($d = .50$).

Explain these results, including why it was especially important for the researchers in this study to give effect sizes, to a person who understands hypothesis testing but has never learned about effect size or power.

15. You are planning a study that you determine from a power table as having quite low power. Name six things that you might do to increase power.

CHAPTER 8

Introduction to the *t* Test

Single Sample
and Dependent Means

CHAPTER OUTLINE

- The *t* Test for a Single Sample
- The *t* Test for Dependent Means
- Assumptions of the *t* Test for a Single Sample and *t* Test for Dependent Means
- Effect Size and Power for the *t* test for Dependent Means
- Single-Sample *t* Tests and Dependent Means *t* Tests in Research Articles
- Summary
- Key Terms
- Example Worked-Out Problems
- Practice Problems
- Using SPSS

At this point, you may think you know all about hypothesis testing. Here's a surprise: What you know so far will not help you much as a researcher. Why? The procedures for testing hypotheses described up to this point were, of course, absolutely necessary for what you will now learn. However, these procedures involved comparing a group of scores to a known population. In real research practice, you often compare two or more groups of scores to each other, without any direct information about populations. For example, you may have two scores for each person in a group of people, such as a score on a test of attitudes toward the courts before and after having gone through a law suit. Or you might have one score per person for two groups of people, such as an experimental group and a control group in a study of the effect of a new method of training teachers.

These kinds of research situations are very common in behavioral and social science research, where usually the only information available is from the samples. Nothing is known about the populations that the samples are supposed to come from. In particular, the researcher does not know the variance of the populations involved, which is a crucial ingredient in Step ❷ of the hypothesis-testing process (determining the characteristics of the comparison distribution).

In this chapter, we first look at the solution to the problem of not knowing the population variance by focusing on a special situation: comparing the mean of a single sample to a population with a *known* mean but an *unknown* variance. Then, after describing how to handle this problem of not knowing the population variance, we go on to consider the situation in which there is no known population at all—the situation in which all you have are two scores for each of a number of people.

The hypothesis-testing procedures you learn in this chapter, those in which the population variance is unknown, are examples of what are called ***t* tests.** The *t* test is sometimes called "Student's *t*" because its main principles were originally developed by William S. Gosset, who published his articles anonymously using the name "Student" (see Box 8–1).

The *t* Test for a Single Sample

Let's begin with the following situation. You carry out a study that gives you scores for a sample of people and you want to compare the mean of the scores in this sample to a population for which the mean is known but the variance is unknown. Hypothesis testing in this situation is called a ***t* test for a single sample.** (It is also called a *one-sample t test*.)

The *t* test for a single sample works basically the same way as the procedure you learned in Chapter 6 (the Z test). In the studies we considered in Chapter 6, you had scores for a sample of individuals (such as a group of 64 fifth graders who had taken a standard test with special instructions) and you wanted to compare the mean of this sample to a population (such as fifth graders in general). However, in the studies we considered in Chapter 6, you knew both the mean and variance of the general population to which you were going to compare your sample. In the situations we are now going to consider, everything is the same, but you don't know the population variance. This presents two important new wrinkles having to do with the details of how you carry out two of the steps of the hypothesis-testing process.

The first important new wrinkle is in Step ❷. Because the population variance is not known, you have to estimate it. So the first new wrinkle we consider is how to estimate an unknown population variance. The other important new wrinkle affects both Steps ❷ and ❸. When the population variance has to be estimated, the shape of the comparison distribution is not quite a normal curve. So the second new wrinkle we consider is the shape of the comparison distribution (for Step ❷) and how to use a special table to find the cutoff (Step ❸) on what is a slightly differently shaped distribution.

An Example

Suppose your college newspaper reports an informal survey showing that students at your college study an average of 2.50 hours each day. However, you think that the students in *your* dormitory study much more than that. You randomly pick 16 students from your dormitory and ask them how much they study each day. (We will assume that they are all honest and accurate.) Your result is that these 16 students study an average of 3.20 hours per day. Should you conclude that students in general in your dormitory study more than the college average? Or should you conclude that your results are so close to the college average that the small difference of .70 hours might well

t test Hypothesis-testing procedure in which the population variance is unknown; it compares *t* scores from a sample to a comparison distribution called a *t* distribution.

t test for a single sample Hypothesis-testing procedure in which a sample mean is being compared to a known population mean and the population variance is unknown.

> **TIP FOR SUCCESS**
>
> In order to understand this chapter, you will need to know well the material in Chapters 5, 6, and 7, especially the logic and procedures for hypothesis testing from Chapter 5 and the distribution of means from Chapter 6.

BOX 8–1 William S. Gosset, alias "Student": Not a Mathematician, but a Practical Man

The Granger Collection

William S. Gosset graduated from Oxford University in 1899 with a degree in mathematics and chemistry. It happened that in the same year the Guinness brewers in Dublin, Ireland, were seeking a few young scientists to take a first-ever scientific look at beer making. Gosset took one of these jobs and soon had immersed himself in barley, hops, and vats of brew.

The problem was how to make beer of a consistently high quality. Scientists, such as Gosset, wanted to make the quality of beer less variable and were especially interested in finding the cause of bad batches. A proper scientist would say, "Conduct experiments!" But a business such as a brewery could not afford to waste money on experiments involving large numbers of vats, some of which any brewer worth his hops knew would fail. So Gosset was forced to contemplate the probability of, say, a certain strain of barley producing terrible beer when the experiment could consist of only a few batches of each strain. Adding to the problem was that he had no idea of the variability of a given strain of barley—perhaps some fields planted with the same strain grew better barley. (Does this sound familiar? Poor Gosset, like today's researchers, had no idea of his population's variance.)

Gosset was up to the task, although at the time only he knew that. To his colleagues at the brewery, he was a pro-

fessor of mathematics and not a proper brewer at all. To his statistical colleagues, mainly at the Biometric Laboratory at University College in London, he was a mere brewer and not a proper mathematician.

So Gosset discovered the *t* distribution and invented the *t* test—simplicity itself (compared to most of statistics)—for situations when samples are small and the variability of the larger population is unknown. However, the Guinness brewery did not allow its scientists to publish papers, because one Guinness scientist had revealed brewery secrets. To this day, most statisticians call the *t* distribution "Student's *t*" because Gosset wrote under the anonymous name "Student." A few of his fellow statisticians knew who "Student" was, but meetings with others involved secrecy worthy of a spy novel. The brewery learned of his scientific fame only at his death, when colleagues wanted to honor him.

In spite of his great achievements, Gosset often wrote in letters that his own work provided "only a rough idea of the thing" or so-and-so "really worked out the complete mathematics." He was remembered as a thoughtful, kind, humble man, sensitive to others' feelings. Gosset's friendliness and generosity with his time and ideas also resulted in many students and younger colleagues making major breakthroughs based on his help.

To learn more about William Gosset, go to http://www-history.mcs.st-andrews.ac.uk/Mathematicians/Gosset.html.

Sources: Peters (1987), Salsburg (2001), Stigler (1986), Tankard (1984).

---

be due to your having picked, purely by chance, 16 of the more studious residents of your dormitory?

Step ❶ of the hypothesis-testing process is to restate the problem as hypotheses about populations.

There are two populations:

Population 1: The kind of students who live in your dormitory.
Population 2: The kind of students at your college generally.

The research hypothesis is that Population 1 students study more than Population 2 students; the null hypothesis is that Population 1 students do not study more than Population 2 students. So far the problem is no different from those in Chapter 6.

Step ❷ is to determine the characteristics of the comparison distribution. In this example, its mean will be 2.50, what the survey found for students at your college generally (Population 2).

The next part of Step ❷ is finding the variance of the distribution of means. Now you face a problem. Up to now in this book, you have always known the variance of the population of individuals. Using that variance, you then figured the variance of the distribution of means. However, in the present example, the variance of the number of hours studied for students at your college (the Population 2 students) was not reported in the newspaper article. So you email the paper. Unfortunately, the reporter did not calculate the variance, and the original survey results are no longer available. What to do?

biased estimate Estimate of a population parameter that is likely systematically to overestimate or underestimate the true value of the population parameter. For example, SD^2 would be a biased estimate of the population variance (it would systematically underestimate it).

Basic Principle of the *t* Test: Estimating the Population Variance from the Sample Scores

If you do not know the variance of the population of individuals, you can estimate it from what you do know—the scores of the people in your sample.

In the logic of hypothesis testing, the group of people you study is considered to be a random sample from a particular population. The variance of this sample ought to reflect the variance of that population. If the scores in the population have *a lot* of variation, then the scores in a sample randomly selected from that population should also have *a lot* of variation. If the population has *very little* variation, the scores in samples from that population should also have *very little* variation. Thus, it should be possible to use the variation among the scores in a sample to make an informed guess about the variation of the scores in the population. That is, you could figure the variance of the sample's scores, and that should be similar to the variance of the scores in the population (see Figure 8–1).

There is, however, one small hitch. The variance of a sample will generally be slightly smaller than the variance of the population from which it is taken. For this reason, the variance of the sample is a **biased estimate** of the population variance.[1] It is a *biased estimate* because it consistently *underestimates* the actual variance of the

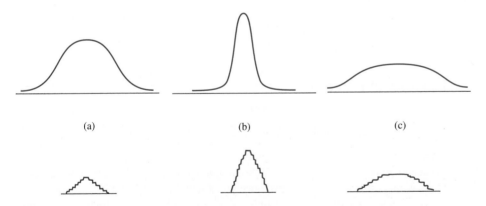

Figure 8–1   The variation in samples (lower distributions) is similar to the variation in the populations they are taken from (upper distributions).

---

[1]A sample's variance is slightly smaller than the population's because it is based on deviations from the sample's mean. A sample's mean is the optimal balance point for its scores. Thus, deviations of a sample's scores from its mean will be smaller than deviations from any other number. The mean of a sample generally is not exactly the same as the mean of the population it comes from. Thus, deviations of a sample's scores from its mean will generally be smaller than deviations of that sample's scores from the population mean.

unbiased estimate of the population variance Estimate of the population variance, based on sample scores, which has been corrected so that it is equally likely to overestimate or underestimate the true population variance; the correction used is dividing the sum of squared deviations by the sample size minus 1, instead of the usual procedure of dividing by the sample size directly.

degrees of freedom (df) Number of scores free to vary when estimating a population parameter; usually part of a formula for making that estimate—for example, in the formula for estimating the population variance from a single sample, the degrees of freedom is the number of scores minus 1.

df Degrees of freedom.

population. If we used a biased estimate of the population variance in our research studies, our results would not be accurate. Therefore, we need to identify an *unbiased estimate* of the population variance.

Fortunately, you can figure an **unbiased estimate of the population variance** by slightly changing the ordinary variance formula. The ordinary variance formula is the sum of the squared deviation scores divided by the number of scores. The changed formula still starts with the sum of the squared deviation scores, but divides this sum by the number of scores *minus 1*. Dividing by a slightly smaller number makes the result slightly larger. Dividing by the number of scores minus 1 makes the resulting variance just enough larger to make it an *unbiased estimate* of the population variance. (This unbiased estimate is our best estimate of the population variance. However, it is still an *estimate*, so it is unlikely to be exactly the same as the true population variance. But, we can be certain that our unbiased estimate of the population variance is equally likely to be too high as it is to be too low. This is what makes the estimate *unbiased.*)

The symbol we will use for the unbiased estimate of the population variance is S^2. The formula is the usual variance formula, but now dividing by $N - 1$ (instead of by N):

> The estimated population variance is the sum of the squared deviation scores divided by the number of scores minus 1.

(8-1)
$$S^2 = \frac{\Sigma(X - M)^2}{N - 1}$$

Let's return to our example of hours spent studying and figure the estimated population variance from the sample's 16 scores. First, you figure the sum of squared deviation scores. (Subtract the mean from each of the scores, square those deviation scores, and add them.) Presume in our example that this comes out to 9.60. To get the estimated population variance, you divide this sum of squared deviation scores by the number of scores minus 1. That is, you divide 9.60 by 16 – 1; 9.60 divided by 15 comes out to .64. In terms of the formula,

$$S^2 = \frac{\Sigma(X - M)^2}{N - 1} = \frac{9.60}{16 - 1} = \frac{9.60}{15} = .64.$$

Degrees of Freedom

The number you divide by (the number of scores minus 1) to get the estimated population variance has a special name. It is called the **degrees of freedom (df).** It has this name because it is the number of scores in a sample that are "free to vary." The idea is that, when figuring the variance, you first have to know the mean. If you know the mean and all but one of the scores in the sample, you can figure out the one you don't know with a little arithmetic. Thus, once you know the mean, one of the scores in the sample is not free to have any possible value. So in this kind of situation the degrees of freedom is the number of scores minus 1. In terms of a formula,

> The degrees of freedom is the number of scores in the sample minus 1.

(8-2)
$$df = N - 1$$

df is the degrees of freedom.

In our example, $df = 16 - 1 = 15$. (In some situations you learn about in later chapters, the degrees of freedom are figured a bit differently. This is because in those situations, the number of scores free to vary is different. For all the situations you learn about in this chapter, $df = N - 1$.) The formula for the estimated population variance is often written using df instead of $N - 1$.

$$S^2 = \frac{\Sigma(X - M)^2}{df} \tag{8-3}$$

t distribution   Mathematically defined curve that is the comparison distribution used in a *t* test.

The Standard Deviation of the Distribution of Means

Once you have figured the estimated population variance, you can figure the standard deviation of the comparison distribution using the same procedures you learned in Chapter 6. As always, when you have a sample of more than one, the comparison distribution is a distribution of means. And the variance of a distribution of means is the variance of the population of individuals divided by the sample size. You have just estimated the variance of the population. Thus, you can estimate the variance of the distribution of means by dividing the estimated population variance by the sample size. The standard deviation of the distribution of means is the square root of its variance. Stated as formulas,

> The estimated population variance is the sum of squared deviation scores divided by the degrees of freedom.

$$S^2_M = \frac{S^2}{N} \tag{8-4}$$

$$S_M = \sqrt{S^2_M} \tag{8-5}$$

> The variance of the distribution of means based on an estimated population variance is the estimated population variance divided by the number of scores in the sample.

Note that with an estimated population variance, the symbols for the variance and standard deviation of the distribution of means use S instead of Population *SD*.

In our example, the sample size was 16 and we worked out the estimated population variance to be .64. The variance of the distribution of means, based on that estimate, will be .04. That is, .64 divided by 16 equals .04. The standard deviation is .20, the square root of .04. In terms of the formulas,

> The standard deviation of the distribution of means based on an estimated population variance is the square root of the variance of the distribution of means based on an estimated population variance.

$$S^2_M = \frac{S^2}{N} = \frac{.64}{16} = .04$$

$$S_M = \sqrt{S^2_M} = \sqrt{.04} = .20.$$

The Shape of the Comparison Distribution When Using an Estimated Population Variance: The *t* Distribution

In Chapter 6 you learned that when the population distribution follows a normal curve, the shape of the distribution of means will also be a normal curve. However, this changes when you do hypothesis testing using an estimated population variance. When you are using an estimated population variance, you have less true information and more room for error. The mathematical effect is that there are likely to be slightly more extreme means than in an exact normal curve. Furthermore, the smaller your sample size, the bigger this tendency. This is because, with a smaller sample size, your estimate of the population variance is based on less information.

The result of all of this is that, when doing hypothesis testing using an estimated variance, your comparison distribution will not be a normal curve. Instead, the comparison distribution will be a slightly different curve, called a **t distribution.**

Actually, there is a whole family of *t* distributions. They vary in shape according to the degrees of freedom in the sample you used to estimate the population variance. However, for any particular degrees of freedom, there is only one *t* distribution.

TIP FOR SUCCESS

Be sure that you fully understand the difference between S^2 and S^2_M. Although S^2 and S^2_M look similar, they are quite different. S^2 is the estimated variance of the population of individuals. S^2_M is the estimated variance of the distribution of means (based on the estimated variance of the population of individuals, S^2).

TIP FOR SUCCESS

Be careful. To find the variance of a distribution of means, you always divide the population variance by the sample size. This is true whether the population's variance is known or estimated. In our example, you divided the population variance, which you had estimated, by 16 (the sample size). It is only when making the estimate of the population variance that you divide by the sample size minus 1. That is, the degrees of freedom are used only when estimating the variance of the population of individuals.

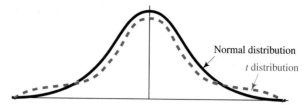

Figure 8–2   A *t* distribution (dashed blue line) compared to the normal curve (solid black line).

Generally, *t* distributions look to the eye like a normal curve—bell-shaped, completely symmetrical, and unimodal. A *t* distribution differs subtly in having higher tails (that is, slightly more scores at the extremes). Figure 8–2 shows the shape of a *t* distribution compared to a normal curve.

This slight difference in shape affects how extreme a score you need to reject the null hypothesis. As always, to reject the null hypothesis, your sample mean has to be in an extreme section of the comparison distribution of means, such as the top 5%. However, if the comparison distribution has more of its means in the tails than a normal curve would have, then the point where the top 5% begins has to be further out on this comparison distribution. The result is that it takes a slightly more extreme sample mean to get a significant result when using a *t* distribution than when using a normal curve.

Just how much the *t* distribution differs from the normal curve depends on the degrees of freedom, the amount of information used in estimating the population variance. The *t* distribution differs most from the normal curve when the degrees of freedom are low (because your estimate of the population variance is based on a very small sample). For example, using the normal curve, you may recall that 1.64 is the cutoff for a one-tailed test at the .05 level. On a *t* distribution with 7 degrees of freedom (that is, with a sample size of 8), the cutoff is 1.895 for a one-tailed test at the .05 level. If the estimate is based on a larger sample, say, a sample of 25 (so that *df* = 24), the cutoff is 1.711, a cutoff much closer to that for the normal curve. If your sample size is infinite, the *t* distribution is the same as the normal curve. (Of course, if your sample size were infinite, it would include the entire population!) But even with sample sizes of 30 or more, the *t* distribution is nearly identical to the normal curve.

Shortly you will learn how to find the cutoff using a *t* distribution, but let's first return briefly to the example of how much students in your dormitory study each night. You finally have everything you need for Step ❷ about the characteristics of the comparison distribution. We have already seen that the distribution of means in this example has a mean of 2.50 hours and a standard deviation of .20. You can now add that the shape of the comparison distribution will be a *t* distribution with 15 degrees of freedom.[2]

---

[2]Statisticians make a subtle distinction in this situation between the comparison distribution and the distribution of means. (We avoid this distinction to simplify your learning of what is already fairly difficult.) The general procedure of hypothesis testing with means of samples, as you learned it in Chapter 6, can be described as figuring a *Z* score for your sample's mean, and then comparing this *Z* score to a cutoff *Z* score from the normal curve table. We described this process as using the distribution of means as your comparison distribution. Statisticians would say that actually you are comparing the *Z* score you figured for your sample mean to a distribution of *Z* scores (which is simply an ordinary normal curve). Similarly, for a *t* test, you will see shortly that we figure what is called a *t* score in the same way as a *Z* score, but using a standard deviation of the distribution of means based on an estimated population variance. You then compare the *t* score you figure for your sample mean to a cutoff *t* score from a *t* distribution table. According to the formal statistical logic, you can think of this process as involving a comparison distribution of *t* scores for means, not of means themselves.

The Cutoff Sample Score for Rejecting the Null Hypothesis: Using the *t* Table

t **table** Table of cutoff scores on the *t* distribution for various degrees of freedom, significance levels, and one- and two-tailed tests.

Step ❸ of hypothesis testing is determining the cutoff for rejecting the null hypothesis. There is a different *t* distribution for any particular degrees of freedom. However, to avoid taking up pages and pages with tables for each different *t* distribution, you use a simplified table that gives only the crucial cutoff points. We have included such a *t* **table** in the Appendix (Table A–2). Just as with the normal curve table, the *t* table only shows positive *t* scores. If you have a one-tailed test, you need to decide if your cutoff score is a positive *t* score or a negative *t* score. If your one-tailed test is testing whether the mean of Population 1 is greater than the mean of Population 2, the cutoff *t* score is positive. However, if your one-tailed test is testing whether the mean of Population 1 is less than the mean of Population 2, the cutoff *t* score is negative.

In the hours-studied example, you have a one-tailed test. (You want to know whether students in your dormitory study *more* than students in general at your college study.) You will probably want to use the 5% significance level because the cost of a Type I error (mistakenly rejecting the null hypothesis) is not great. You have 16 people, making 15 degrees of freedom for your estimate of the population variance.

Table 8–1 shows a portion of the *t* table from Table A–2 in the Appendix. Find the column for the .05 significance level for one-tailed tests and move down to the row for 15 degrees of freedom. The crucial cutoff is 1.753. In this example, you are testing whether students in your dormitory (Population 1) study *more* than students in general at your college (Population 2). In other words, you are testing whether students

Table 8–1   Cutoff Scores for *t* Distributions with 1 Through 17 Degrees of Freedom (Highlighting Cutoff for Hours Studied Example)

	One-Tailed Tests			Two-Tailed Tests		
df	.10	.05	.01	.10	.05	.01
1	3.078	6.314	31.821	6.314	12.706	63.657
2	1.886	2.920	6.965	2.920	4.303	9.925
3	1.638	2.353	4.541	2.353	3.182	5.841
4	1.533	2.132	3.747	2.132	2.776	4.604
5	1.476	2.015	3.365	2.015	2.571	4.032
6	1.440	1.943	3.143	1.943	2.447	3.708
7	1.415	1.895	2.998	1.895	2.365	3.500
8	1.397	1.860	2.897	1.860	2.306	3.356
9	1.383	1.833	2.822	1.833	2.262	3.250
10	1.372	1.813	2.764	1.813	2.228	3.170
11	1.364	1.796	2.718	1.796	2.201	3.106
12	1.356	1.783	2.681	1.783	2.179	3.055
13	1.350	1.771	2.651	1.771	2.161	3.013
14	1.345	1.762	2.625	1.762	2.145	2.977
15	1.341	1.753	2.603	1.753	2.132	2.947
16	1.337	1.746	2.584	1.746	2.120	2.921
17	1.334	1.740	2.567	1.740	2.110	2.898

t score On a *t* distribution, number of standard deviations from the mean (like a *Z* score, but on a *t* distribution).

in your dormitory have a higher *t* score than students in general. This means that the cutoff *t* score is positive. Thus, you will reject the null hypothesis if your sample's mean is 1.753 or more standard deviations above the mean on the comparison distribution. (If you were using a known variance, you would have found your cutoff from a normal curve table. The *Z* score needed to reject the null hypothesis based on the normal curve would have been 1.64.)

One other point about using the *t* table: In the full *t* table in the Appendix, there are rows for each degree of freedom from 1 through 30, then for 35, 40, 45, and so on, up to 100. Suppose your study has degrees of freedom between two of these higher values. To be safe, you should use the nearest degrees of freedom to yours that is given in the table that is *less* than yours. For example, in a study with 43 degrees of freedom, you would use the cutoff for *df* = 40.

The Sample Mean's Score on the Comparison Distribution: The *t* Score

Step ❹ of hypothesis testing is figuring your sample mean's score on the comparison distribution. In Chapter 6, this meant finding the *Z* score on the comparison distribution—the number of standard deviations your sample's mean is from the mean on the comparison distribution. You do exactly the same thing when your comparison distribution is a *t* distribution. The only difference is that, instead of calling this a *Z* score, because it is from a *t* distribution, you call it a **t score.** In terms of a formula,

> The *t* score is your sample's mean minus the population mean, divided by the standard deviation of the distribution of means.

(8-6)
$$t = \frac{M - \text{Population } M}{S_M}$$

In the example, your sample's mean of 3.20 is .70 hours from the mean of the distribution of means, which amounts to 3.50 standard deviations from the mean (.70 hours divided by the standard deviation of .20 hours). That is, the *t* score in the example is 3.50. In terms of the formula,

$$t = \frac{M - \text{Population } M}{S_M} = \frac{3.20 - 2.50}{.20} = \frac{.70}{.20} = 3.50.$$

Deciding Whether to Reject the Null Hypothesis

Step ❺ of hypothesis testing is deciding whether to reject the null hypothesis. This step is exactly the same with a *t* test as it was in those discussed in previous chapters. You compare the cutoff score from Step ❸ with the sample's score on the comparison distribution from Step ❹. In the example, the cutoff *t* score was 1.753 and the actual *t* score for our sample was 3.50. Conclusion: Reject the null hypothesis. The research hypothesis is supported that students in your dormitory study more than students in the college overall. Figure 8–3 shows the various distributions for this example.

Summary of Hypothesis Testing When the Population Variance Is Not Known

Table 8–2 compares the hypothesis-testing procedure we just considered (for a *t* test for a single sample) with the hypothesis testing procedure for a *Z* test from Chapter 6. That is, we are comparing the current situation in which you know the population's mean but not its variance to the Chapter 6 situation where you knew the population's mean *and* variance. Table 8–3 summarizes the steps of hypothesis testing for the *t* test for a single sample.

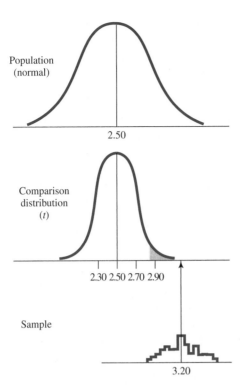

Figure 8-3   Distributions for the hours studied example.

Table 8-2	Hypothesis Testing with a Single Sample Mean When Population Variance Is Unknown (*t* Test for a Single Sample) Compared to When Population Variance Is Known (*Z* Test)	

Steps in Hypothesis Testing	Difference From When Population Variance Is Known
❶ Restate the question as a research hypothesis and a null hypothesis about the populations.	No difference in method.
❷ Determine the characteristics of the comparison distribution:	
Population mean	No difference in method.
Population variance	*Estimate* from the sample.
Standard deviation of the distribution of means	No difference in method (but based on *estimated* population variance).
Shape of the comparison distribution	Use the *t* distribution with $df = N - 1$.
❸ Determine the significance cutoff.	Use the *t* table.
❹ Determine your sample's score on the comparison distribution.	No difference in method (but called a *t* score).
❺ Decide whether to reject the null hypothesis.	No difference in method.

How are you doing?

1. In what sense is a sample's variance a biased estimate of the variance of the population the sample is taken from? That is, in what way does the sample's variance typically differ from the population's?

2. What is the difference between the usual formula for figuring the variance and the formula for estimating a population's variance from the scores in a sample?

3. (a) What are degrees of freedom? (b) How do you figure the degrees of freedom in a t test for a single sample? (c) What do they have to do with estimating the population variance? (d) What do they have to do with the t distribution?

4. (a) How does a t distribution differ from a normal curve? (b) How do degrees of freedom affect this? (c) What is the effect of the difference on hypothesis testing?

5. List three differences in how you do hypothesis testing for a t test for a single sample versus for the Z test you learned in Chapter 6.

6. A population has a mean of 23. A sample of 4 is given an experimental procedure and has scores of 20, 22, 22, and 20. Test the hypothesis that the procedure produces a lower score. Use the .05 significance level. (a) Use the steps of hypothesis testing and (b) make a sketch of the distributions involved.

Answers

1. The sample's variance will in general be smaller than the variance of the population the sample is taken from.

2. In the usual formula you divide by the number of participants (N); in the formula for estimating a population's variance from the scores in a sample, you divide by the number of participants in the sample minus 1 ($N - 1$).

3. (a) The number of scores free to vary. (b) The number of scores in the sample minus 1. (c) In estimating the population variance, the formula is the sum of squared deviations divided by the degrees of freedom. (d) t distributions differ slightly from each other according to the degrees of freedom.

4. (a) It has heavier tails; that is, more scores at the extremes. (b) The more degrees of freedom, the closer the shape (including the tails) to a normal curve. (c) The cutoffs for significance are more extreme for a t distribution than for a normal curve.

5. In the t test you (a) estimate the population variance from the sample (it is not known in advance); (b) you look up the cutoff on a t table in which you also have to take into account the degrees of freedom (you don't use a normal curve table); and (c) your sample's score on the comparison distribution, which is a t distribution (not a normal curve), is a t score (not a Z score).

6. (a) Steps of hypothesis testing:

   ❶ **Restate the question as a research hypothesis and a null hypothesis about the populations.** There are two populations:

   Population 1: People who are given the experimental procedure.
   Population 2: The general population.

   The research hypothesis is that Population 1 will score lower than Population 2.
   The null hypothesis is that Population 1 will not score lower than Population 2.

   ❷ **Determine the characteristics of the comparison distribution.**
   a. The mean of the distribution of means is 23.
   b. The standard deviation is figured as follows:

❶ **Figure the estimated population variance.** You first need to figure the sample mean, which is (20 + 22 + 22 + 20)/4 = 84/4 = 21. The estimated population variance is $S^2 = [\Sigma (X - M)^2]/df = [(20 - 21)^2 + (22 - 21)^2 + (22 - 21)^2 + (20 - 21)^2]/(4 - 1) = (-1^2 + 1^2 + 1^2 + -1^2)/3 = (1 + 1 + 1 + 1)/3 = 4/3 = 1.33$.

❷ **Figure the variance of the distribution of means:**
$S_M^2 = S^2/N = 1.33/4 = .33$.

❸ **Figure the standard deviation of the distribution of means:**
$S_M = \sqrt{S_M^2} = \sqrt{.33} = .57$.

c. The shape of the comparison distribution will be a *t* distribution with *df* = 3.

❸ **Determine the cutoff sample score on the comparison distribution at which the null hypothesis should be rejected.** From Table A-2, the cutoff for a one-tailed *t* test at the .05 level for *df* = 3 is −2.353. The cutoff *t* score is negative, since the research hypothesis is that the procedure produces a *lower* score.

❹ **Determine your sample's score on the comparison distribution.** $t = (M - \text{Population } M)/S_M = (21 - 23)/.57 = -2/.57 = -3.51$.

❺ **Decide whether to reject the null hypothesis.** The *t* of −3.51 is more extreme than the cutoff *t* of −2.353. Therefore, reject the null hypothesis; the research hypothesis is supported.

(b) Sketches of distributions are shown in Figure 8-4.

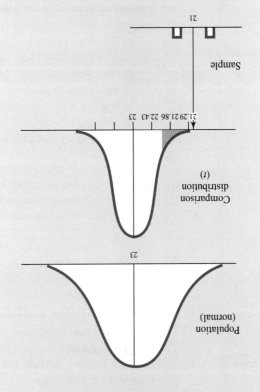

Figure 8-4 Distributions for answer to "How Are You Doing?" question 6b.

Table 8-3 Steps for a t Test for a Single Sample

❶ **Restate the question as a research hypothesis and a null hypothesis about the populations.**

❷ **Determine the characteristics of the comparison distribution.**

   a. The mean is the same as the known population mean.

   b. The standard deviation is figured as follows:

     Ⓐ Figure the estimated population variance: $S^2 = [\Sigma (X - M)^2]/df$

     Ⓑ Figure the variance of the distribution of means: $S_M^2 = S^2/N$

     Ⓒ Figure the standard deviation of the distribution of means: $S_M = \sqrt{S_M^2}$

   c. The shape is a t distribution with $N - 1$ degrees of freedom.

❸ **Determine the cutoff sample score on the comparison distribution at which the null hypothesis should be rejected.**

   a. Decide the significance level and whether to use a one-tailed or a two-tailed test.

   b. Look up the appropriate cutoff in a t table.

❹ **Determine your sample's score on the comparison distribution:** $t = (M - \text{Population } M)/S_M$

❺ **Decide whether to reject the null hypothesis:** Compare the scores from Steps ❸ and ❹

---

repeated-measures design Research strategy in which each person is tested more than once; same as *within-subjects design*.

t test for dependent means Hypothesis-testing procedure in which there are two scores for each person and the population variance is not known; it determines the significance of a hypothesis that is being tested using difference or change scores from a single group of people.

The t Test for Dependent Means

The situation you just learned about (the t test for a single sample) is for when you know the population mean but not its variance, and where you have a single sample of scores. It turns out that in most research you do not even know the population's *mean;* plus, in most research situations, you usually have not one set but *two* sets of scores. These two things, not knowing the population mean and having two sets of scores, almost always go together. This situation is very common.

The rest of this chapter focuses specifically on the important research situation in which you have two scores from each person in your sample. This kind of research situation is called a **repeated-measures design** (also known as a *within-subjects design*). A common example is when you measure the same people before and after some social or psychological intervention. This specific kind of repeated-measures situation is called a *before-after design.* For example, a researcher might measure the quality of men's communication before and after receiving premarital counseling.

The hypothesis-testing procedure for the situation in which each person is measured twice is called a **t test for dependent means.** It has the name *dependent means* because the mean for each group of scores (for example, a group of before-scores and a group of after-scores) are dependent on each other in that they are both from the same people. (In Chapter 9, we consider the situation in which you compare scores from two different groups of people, a research design analyzed by a t test for *independent means.*)

The t test for dependent means is also called a *paired-sample t test,* a *t test for correlated means,* a *t test for matched samples,* and a *t test for matched pairs.* Each of these names comes from the same idea that in this kind of t test you are comparing two sets of scores that are related to each other in a direct way, such as each person being tested before and after some procedure.

You do a t test for dependent means in exactly the same way as a t test for a single sample, except that (a) you use something called *difference scores* and (b) you assume that the population mean (of the difference scores) is 0. We will now consider each of these two aspects.

Difference Scores

With a repeated-measures design, your sample includes two scores for each person instead of just one. The way you handle this is to make the two scores per person into one score per person! You do this magic by creating **difference scores:** For each person, you subtract one score from the other. If the difference is before versus after, difference scores are also called *change scores.*

Consider the example of the quality of men's communication before and after receiving premarital counseling. The researcher subtracts the communication quality score before the counseling from the communication quality score after the counseling. This gives an after-minus-before difference score for each man. When the two scores are a before-score and an after-score, you usually take the after-score minus the before-score to indicate the *change.*

Once you have the difference score for each person in the study, you do the rest of the hypothesis testing with difference scores. That is, you treat the study as if there were a single sample of scores (scores that in this situation happen to be difference scores).[3]

difference score Difference between a person's score on one testing and the same person's score on another testing; often an after score minus a before score, in which case it is also called a *change score.*

Population of Difference Scores with a Mean of 0

So far in the research situations we have considered in this book, you have always known the mean of the population to which you compared your sample's mean. For example, in the college dormitory survey of hours studied, you knew the population mean was 2.50 hours. However, now we are using difference scores, and we usually don't know the mean of the population of difference scores.

Here is the solution. Ordinarily, the null hypothesis in a repeated-measures design is that on the average there is *no difference* between the two groups of scores. For example, the null hypothesis in a study of the quality of men's communication before and after receiving premarital counseling is that on the average there is no difference between communication quality before and after the counseling. What does *no difference* mean? Saying there is on average no difference is the same as saying that the mean of the population of the difference scores is 0. Therefore, when working with difference scores, you are comparing the population of difference scores that your sample of difference scores comes from to a population of difference scores with a mean of 0. In other words, with a *t* test for dependent means, what we call Population 2 will ordinarily have a mean of 0.

Example of a *t* Test for Dependent Means

Olthoff (1989) tested the communication quality of engaged couples three months before and again three months after marriage. One group studied was 19 couples who received ordinary premarital counseling from the ministers who were going to marry them. (To keep the example simple, we will focus on just this one group, and only on the husbands in the group. Scores for wives were similar, though somewhat more varied, making it a more complicated example for learning the *t* test procedure.)

The scores for the 19 husbands are listed in the "Before" and "After" columns in Table 8–4, followed by all the *t* test figuring. The crucial column for starting the

---

[3]You can also use a *t* test for dependent means when you have scores from pairs of research participants. You consider each pair as if it were one person and figure a difference score for each pair. For example, suppose you have 30 married couples and want to test whether husbands are consistently older than wives. You could figure for each couple a difference score of husband's age minus wife's age. The rest of the figuring would then be exactly the same as for an ordinary *t* test for dependent means. When the *t* test for dependent means is used in this way, it is sometimes called a *t test for matched pairs.*

Table 8-4 *t* Test for Communication Quality Scores Before and After Marriage for 19 Husbands Who Received Ordinary Premarital Counseling

Husband	Communication Quality		Difference (After − Before)	Deviation (Difference − *M*)	Squared Deviation
	Before	After			
A	126	115	−11	1.05	1.10
B	133	125	−8	4.05	16.40
C	126	96	−30	−17.95	322.20
D	115	115	0	12.05	145.20
E	108	119	11	23.05	531.30
F	109	82	−27	−14.95	233.50
G	124	93	−31	−18.95	359.10
H	98	109	11	23.05	531.30
I	95	72	−23	−10.95	119.90
J	120	104	−16	−3.95	15.60
K	118	107	−11	1.05	1.10
L	126	118	−8	4.05	16.40
M	121	102	−19	−6.95	48.30
N	116	115	−1	11.05	122.10
O	94	83	−11	1.05	1.10
P	105	87	−18	−5.95	35.40
Q	123	121	−2	10.05	101.00
R	125	100	−25	−12.95	167.70
S	128	118	−10	2.05	4.20
Σ:	2,210	1,981	−229		2,772.90

For difference scores:

$M = -229/19 = -12.05$.

Population $M = 0$ (assumed as a no-change baseline of comparison).

$S^2 = [\Sigma (X - M)^2]/df = 2,772.90/(19 - 1) = 154.05$.

$S_M^2 = S^2/N = 154.05/19 = 8.11$.

$S_M = \sqrt{S_M^2} = \sqrt{8.11} = 2.85$.

t with $df = 18$ needed for 5% level, two-tailed $= \pm 2.101$.

$t = (M - \text{Population } M)/S_M = (-12.05 - 0)/2.85 = -4.23$.

Decision: Reject the null hypothesis.

Source: Data from Olthoff (1989).

analysis is the difference scores. For example, the first husband, whose communication quality was 126 before marriage and 115 after, had a difference of −11. (We figured after minus before, so that an increase is positive and a decrease, as for this husband, is negative.) The mean of the difference scores is −12.05. That is, on the average, these 19 husbands' communication quality decreased by about 12 points.

Is this decrease significant? In other words, how likely is it that this sample of change scores is a random sample from a population of change scores whose mean is 0? Let's carry out the hypothesis-testing procedure. (The distributions involved are shown in Figure 8–5.)

❶ **Restate the question as a research hypothesis and a null hypothesis about the populations.** There are two populations:

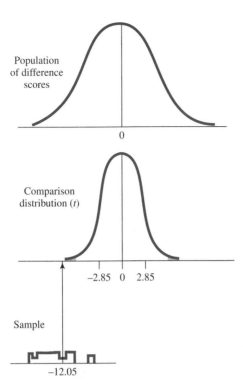

Population
of difference
scores

0

Comparison
distribution (*t*)

−2.85   0   2.85

Sample

−12.05

Figure 8–5   Distributions for the Olthoff (1989) example of a *t* test for dependent means.

Population 1: Husbands who receive ordinary premarital counseling.
Population 2: Husbands whose communication quality does not change from
before to after marriage.

The research hypothesis is that Population 1's mean difference score (communication quality after marriage minus communication quality before marriage)
is different from Population 2's mean difference score. That is, the research hypothesis is that husbands who receive ordinary premarital counseling like the
husbands Olthoff studied *do* change in communication quality from before to
after marriage. The null hypothesis is that the populations are the same. That is,
the null hypothesis is that the husbands who receive ordinary premarital counseling do *not* change in their communication quality from before to after marriage.

Notice that you have no actual information about Population 2 husbands.
The husbands in the study are a sample of Population 1 husbands. In fact, if the
research hypothesis is correct, Population 2 husbands do not even really exist. For
the purposes of hypothesis testing, you set up Population 2 as a kind of straw
man comparison group. That is, for the purpose of the analysis, you set up a comparison group of husbands who, if measured before and after marriage, would on
average show no difference.

❷ **Determine the characteristics of the comparison distribution.** If the null hypothesis is true, the mean of the population of difference scores is 0. The variance
of the population of difference scores can be estimated from the sample of difference scores. As shown in Table 8–4, the sum of squared deviations of the difference scores from the mean of the difference scores is 2,772.90. With 19
husbands in the study, there are 18 degrees of freedom. Dividing the sum of
squared deviation scores by the degrees of freedom gives an estimated population
variance of difference scores of 154.05.

TIP FOR SUCCESS

You now have to deal with some rather complex terms, such as the *standard deviation of the distribution of means of difference scores.* Although these terms are complex, there is good logic behind them. The best way to understand such terms is to break them down into manageable pieces. For example, you will notice that these new terms are the same as the terms for the *t* test for a single sample, with the added phrase "of difference scores." This phrase has been added because all of the figuring for the *t* test for dependent means uses difference scores.

TIP FOR SUCCESS

Step ❷ of hypothesis testing for the *t* test for dependent means is a little trickier than previously. This can make it easy to lose track of the purpose of this step. Step ❷ of hypothesis testing determines the characteristics of the comparison distribution. In the case of the *t* test for dependent means, this comparison distribution is a distribution of means of difference scores. The key characteristics of this distribution are its mean (which is assumed to equal 0), its standard deviation (which is estimated as S_M), and its shape (a *t* distribution with degrees of freedom equal to the sample size minus 1).

The distribution of means of difference scores has a mean of 0, the same as the mean of the population of difference scores. The variance of the distribution of means of difference scores is the estimated population variance of difference scores (154.05) divided by the sample size (19), which gives 8.11. The standard deviation of the distribution of means of difference scores is 2.85, the square root of 8.11.

Because Olthoff was using an estimated population variance, the comparison distribution is a *t* distribution. The estimate of the population variance of difference scores is based on 18 degrees of freedom, so this comparison distribution is a *t* distribution for 18 degrees of freedom.

❸ **Determine the cutoff sample score on the comparison distribution at which the null hypothesis should be rejected.** Olthoff used a two-tailed test to allow for either an increase or a decrease in communication quality. Using the .05 significance level, and 18 degrees of freedom, Table A–2 shows that to reject the null hypothesis you need a *t* score of +2.101 or above, or a *t* score of −2.101 or below.

❹ **Determine your sample's score on the comparison distribution.** Olthoff's sample had a mean difference score of −12.05. That is, the mean was 12.05 points below the mean of 0 on the distribution of means of difference scores. The standard deviation of the distribution of means of difference scores is 2.85. Thus, the mean of the difference scores of −12.05 is 4.23 standard deviations below the mean of the distribution of means of difference scores. So Olthoff's sample of difference scores has a *t* score of −4.23.

❺ **Decide whether to reject the null hypothesis.** The *t* of −4.23 for the sample of difference scores is more extreme than the needed *t* of ± 2.101. Thus, Olthoff could reject the null hypothesis. This suggests that the husbands are from a population in which husbands' communication quality is different after marriage from what it was before (it got lower).

Olthoff's actual study was more complex. You may be interested to know that he found that the wives also showed this decrease in communication quality after marriage. But a group of similar engaged couples who were given special communication-skills training by their ministers (much more than the usual short sessions) had no significant decline in marital communication quality after marriage. In fact, there is a great deal of research showing that relationship quality of all kinds on the average declines from before to after marriage (e.g., Karney & Bradbury, 1997) and that intensive communication skills training can be very helpful in reducing or eliminating this decline (Markman et al., 1993).

Summary of Steps for a *t* Test for Dependent Means

Table 8–5 summarizes the steps for a *t* test for dependent means.[4]

---

[4]The usual steps of carrying out a *t* test for dependent means can be somewhat combined into computational formulas for *S* and *t* based on difference scores. For purposes of learning the ideas, we strongly recommend that you use the regular procedures as we have discussed them in this chapter when doing the practice problems. In a real research situation, the figuring is usually done by computer (see the *Using SPSS* section at the end of this chapter). However, if you ever have to do a *t* test for dependent means for an actual research study by hand (without a computer), you may find these formulas useful.

D in the formulas below is for difference score:

(8-7)
$$S = \sqrt{\frac{\Sigma D^2 - ((\Sigma D)^2/N)}{N-1}}$$

(8-8)
$$t = \frac{\Sigma D/N}{S/\sqrt{N}}$$

Table 8-5   Steps for a *t* Test for Dependent Means
❶ **Restate the question as a research hypothesis and a null hypothesis about the populations.**
❷ **Determine the characteristics of the comparison distribution.**
a. Make each person's two scores into a difference score. Do all the remaining steps using these difference scores.
b. Figure the mean of the difference scores.
c. Assume a mean of the distribution of means of difference scores of 0.
d. The standard deviation of the distribution of means of difference scores is figured as follows:
Ⓐ Figure the estimated population variance of difference scores: $S^2 = [\Sigma (X - M)^2]/df$
Ⓑ Figure the variance of the distribution of means of difference scores: $S_M^2 = S^2/N$
Ⓒ Figure the standard deviation of the distribution of means of difference scores: $S_M = \sqrt{S_M^2}$
e. The shape is a *t* distribution with $N - 1$ degrees of freedom.
❸ **Determine the cutoff sample score on the comparison distribution at which the null hypothesis should be rejected.**
a. Decide the significance level and whether to use a one-tailed or a two-tailed test.
b. Look up the appropriate cutoff in a *t* table.
❹ **Determine your sample's score on the comparison distribution:** $t = (M - \text{Population } M)/S_M$
❺ **Decide whether to reject the null hypothesis:** Compare the scores from Steps ❸ and ❹.

A Second Example of a *t* Test for Dependent Means

Here is another example. A team of researchers examined the brain systems involved in human romantic love (Aron et al., 2005). One issue was whether romantic love engages a part of the brain called the caudate (a brain structure known to become active when people win money in an experimental task, are given cocaine, and other such "reward" situations). Thus, the researchers recruited individuals who had very recently fallen "madly in love." (For example, to be in the study participants had to think about the partner at least 80% of their waking hours.) Participants brought a picture of their beloved with them, plus a picture of a neutral person (someone of the same age and sex as their beloved with whom they were very familiar, but about whom they did not have any particularly strong feelings). Participants then went in to the functional magnetic resonance imaging (fMRI) machine and their brain was scanned while they looked at the two pictures—30 seconds at the neutral person's picture, 30 seconds at their beloved, 30 seconds at the neutral person, and so forth. (Some saw the beloved person's picture first, to be sure that the conditions were equal overall on which was first. This is called *counterbalancing order*.)

Table 8–6 shows average brain activations (mean fMRI scanner values) in the caudate area of interest during the two kinds of pictures. (We have simplfied the example for teaching purposes, including using only 10 participants when the actual study had 17.) It also shows the figuring of the difference scores and all the other figuring for the *t* test for dependent means. (The large differences among participants in the level of the activations are typical of fMRI studies. They are due to such factors as the exact location of a person's head in the machine and differences in basic metabolism. Thus, it is especially important in most fMRI research to use difference scores.) Figure 8–6 shows the distributions involved. Here are the steps of hypothesis testing:

❶ **Restate the question as a research hypothesis and a null hypothesis about the populations.** There are two populations:

Population 1: Individuals like those tested in this study.

Table 8-6 *t* Test for a Study of Romantic Love and Brain Activation in Part of the Caudate

Student	Brain Activation Beloved's photo	Brain Activation Control photo	Difference (Beloved – Control)	Deviation (Difference – *M*)	Squared Deviation
1	1487.8	1487.2	.6	−.800	.640
2	1329.4	1328.1	1.3	−.100	.010
3	1407.9	1405.9	2.0	.600	.360
4	1236.1	1234.0	2.1	.700	.490
5	1299.8	1298.2	1.6	.200	.040
6	1447.2	1444.7	2.5	1.100	1.210
7	1354.1	1354.3	−.2	−1.600	2.560
8	1204.6	1203.7	.9	−.500	.250
9	1322.3	1320.8	1.5	.100	.010
10	1388.5	1386.8	1.7	.300	.090
Σ:	13477.7	13463.7	14.0		5.660

For difference scores:

$M = 14.0/10 = 1.400$.

Population $M = 0$ (assumed as a no-change baseline of comparison).

$S^2 = [\Sigma (X - M)^2]/df = 5.660/(10 - 1) = 5.660/9 = .629$.

$S_M^2 = S^2/N = .629/10 = .063$.

$S_M = \sqrt{S_M^2} = \sqrt{.063} = .251$.

t with $df = 9$ needed for 5% level, one-tailed = 1.833.

$t = (M - \text{Population } M)/S_M = (1.400 - 0)/.251 = 5.58$.

Decision: Reject the null hypothesis.

Source: Data based on Aron et al., 2005.

Population 2: Individuals whose brain activation in the caudate area of interest is the same whether looking at a picture of their beloved or a picture of a neutral person.

The research hypothesis is that Population 1's mean difference score (brain activation when viewing the beloved's picture minus brain activation when viewing the neutral person's picture) is greater than Population 2's mean difference score (of no difference). That is, the research hypothesis is that brain activation in the caudate area of interest is greater when viewing the beloved person's picture than when viewing the neutral person's picture. The null hypothesis is that Population 1's mean difference score is not greater than Population 2's. That is, the null hypothesis is that brain activation in the caudate area of interest is not greater when viewing the beloved person's picture than when viewing the neutral person's picture.

❷ **Determine the characteristics of the comparison distribution.**

a. Make each person's two scores into a difference score. This is shown in the column labeled "Difference" in Table 8–6. You do all the remaining steps using these difference scores.

b. Figure the mean of the difference scores. The sum of the difference scores (14.0) divided by the number of difference scores (10) gives a mean of the difference scores of 1.400. So, $M = 1.400$.

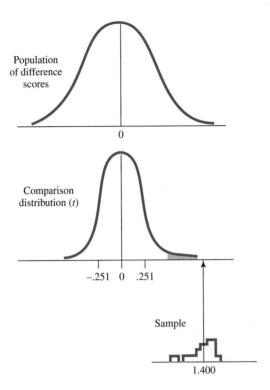

Population
of difference
scores

0

Comparison
distribution (*t*)

−.251 0 .251

Sample

1.400

Figure 8-6   Distributions for the example of romantic love and brain activation in part
of the caudate.

c. Assume a mean of the distribution of means of difference scores of 0: Population $M = 0$.
d. The standard deviation of the distribution of means of difference scores is figured as follows:
   ❹ Figure the estimated population variance of difference scores: $S^2 = [\Sigma (X - M)^2]/df = 5.660/(10 - 1) = .629$.
   ❺ Figure the variance of the distribution of means of difference scores: $S_M^2 = S^2/N = .629/10 = .063$.
   ❻ Figure the standard deviation of the distribution of means of difference scores: $S_M = \sqrt{S_M^2} = \sqrt{.063} = .251$.
e. The shape is a *t* distribution with $df = N - 1$. Therefore, the comparison distribution is a *t* distribution for 9 degrees of freedom. It is a *t* distribution because we figured its variance based on an estimated population variance. It has 9 degrees of freedom because there were 9 degrees of freedom in the estimate of the population variance.

❸ **Determine the cutoff sample score on the comparison distribution at which the null hypothesis should be rejected.**
a. We will use the standard .05 significance level. This is a one-tailed test because the researchers were only interested in a specific direction of difference.
b. Using the .05 significance level with 9 degrees of freedom, Table A–2 shows a cutoff *t* of 1.833. In Table 8–6, the difference score is figured as brain activation when viewing the beloved's picture minus brain activation when viewing

the neutral person's picture. Thus, the research hypothesis predicts a positive difference score, which means that our cutoff is +1.833.

❹ **Determine your sample's score on the comparison distribution.** $t = (M - \text{Population } M)/S_M = (1.400 - 0)/.251 = 5.58$. The sample's mean difference of 1.400 is 5.58 standard deviations (of .251 each) above the mean of 0 on the distribution of means of difference scores.

❺ **Decide whether to reject the null hypothesis.** The sample's t score of 5.58 is more extreme than the cutoff t of 1.833. You can reject the null hypothesis. Brain activation in the caudate area of interest is greater when viewing a beloved's picture than when viewing a neutral person's picture.

How are you doing?

1. Describe the situation in which you would use a t test for dependent means.
2. When doing a t test for dependent means, what do you do with the two scores you have for each participant?
3. In a t test for dependent means, (a) what is usually considered to be the mean of the "known" population (Population 2), and (b) why?
4. Five individuals are tested before and after an experimental procedure; their scores are given below. Test the hypothesis that there is no change, using the .05 significance level. (a) Use the steps of hypothesis testing and (b) sketch the distributions involved.

Person	Before	After
1	20	30
2	30	50
3	20	10
4	40	30
5	30	40

Answers

1. It is used when you are doing hypothesis testing and you have two scores for each participant (such as a before-score and an after-score) and the population variance is unknown.
2. Subtract one from the other to create a difference (or change) score for each person. The t test is then done with these difference (or change) scores.
3. (a) 0. (b) Because you are comparing your sample to a situation in which there is no difference—a population of difference scores in which the average difference is 0.
4. (a) Steps of hypothesis testing (all figuring is shown in Table 8–7):
   ❶ **Restate the question as a research hypothesis and a null hypothesis about the populations.** There are two populations:
   Population 1: People like those tested before and after the experimental procedure.
   Population 2: People whose scores are the same before and after the experimental procedure.
   The research hypothesis is that Population 1's mean change scores (after minus before) are different than Population 2's. The null hypothesis is that Population 1's change is the same as Population 2's.

❷ **Determine the characteristics of the comparison distribution.** The mean of the distribution of means of difference scores (the comparison distribution) is 0. The standard deviation of the distribution of means of difference scores is 0. It is a *t* distribution with 4 degrees of freedom.

❸ **Determine the cutoff sample score on the comparison score at which the null hypothesis should be rejected.** For a two-tailed test at the .05 level, the cutoff sample *t* scores are 2.776 and −2.776.

❹ **Determine your sample's score on the comparison distribution.** *t* = (4 − 0)/6 = .67.

❺ **Decide whether to reject the null hypothesis.** The sample's *t* score of .67 is not more extreme than the cutoff *t* of ± 2.776. Therefore, do *not* reject the null hypothesis.

The distributions are shown in Figure 8-7.

Table 8-7 Figuring for Answer to "How Are You Doing?" Question 4

Person	Score Before	Score After	Difference (After − Before)	Deviation (Difference − M)	Deviation Squared
1	20	30	10	6	36
2	30	50	20	16	256
3	20	10	−10	−14	196
4	40	30	−10	−14	196
5	30	40	10	6	36
Σ:	140	160	20		720

For difference scores:

$M = 20/5 = 4.$

Population $M = 0.$

$S^2 = [\Sigma (X - M)^2]/df = 720/(5 - 1) = 720/4 = 180.$

$S^2_M = S^2/N = 180/5 = 36.$

$S_M = \sqrt{S^2_M} = \sqrt{36} = 6.$

t for *df* = 4 needed for 5% significance level, two-tailed = ± 2.776.

$t = (M - \text{Population } M)/S_M = (4 - 0)/6 = .67$

Decision: Do not reject the null hypothesis.

Assumptions of the *t* Test for a Single Sample and *t* Test for Dependent Means

As you have seen, when using an estimated population variance, the comparison distribution is a *t* distribution. However, the comparison distribution will be exactly a *t* distribution only if the distribution of individuals follows a normal curve. Otherwise, the comparison distribution will follow some other (usually unknown) shape.

Thus, strictly speaking, a normal population is a requirement within the logic and mathematics of the *t* test. A requirement like this for a hypothesis-testing procedure is called an **assumption.** That is, a normal population distribution is one assumption of the *t* test. You can think of an assumption as a requirement that you must meet for the results of a hypothesis testing procedure to be accurate. In this case, the effect of this assumption of a normal population is that if the population distribution

assumption A condition, such as a population's having a normal distribution, required for carrying out a particular hypothesis-testing procedure; a part of the mathematical foundation for the accuracy of the tables used in determining cutoff values.

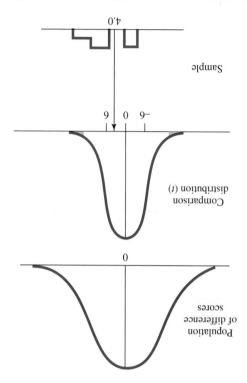

is not normal, the comparison distribution will be some unknown shape other than a *t* distribution—and thus the cutoffs on the *t* table will be incorrect.

Unfortunately, when you do a *t* test, you don't know whether the population is normal. This is because when doing a *t* test, usually all you have are the scores in your sample. Fortunately, however, as you saw in Chapter 4, distributions in the behavioral and social sciences quite often do approximate a normal curve. (This applies to distributions of difference scores too.) Also, statisticians have found that in practice, you get reasonably accurate results with *t* tests even when the population is rather far from normal. The only very common situation in which using a *t* test for dependent means is likely to give a seriously distorted result is when you are using a one-tailed test and the population is highly skewed (that is, it is very asymmetrical, with a much longer tail on one side than the other). Thus, you need to be cautious about your conclusions when doing a one-tailed test if the sample of difference scores is highly skewed, suggesting that the population it comes from is also highly skewed.

Effect Size and Power for the *t* Test for Dependent Means[5]

Effect Size

The estimated effect size for a study using a *t* test for dependent means is the mean of the difference scores divided by the estimated standard deviation of the population of difference scores. In terms of a formula,

$$\text{Estimated Effect Size} = M/S \qquad (8\text{-}9)$$

> The estimated effect size for a study using a *t* test for dependent means is the mean of the difference scores divided by the estimated standard deviation of the population of difference scores.

---

[5]Note that effect size and power for the *t* test for a single sample are determined in the same way as for the *t* test for dependent means.

M is the mean of the difference scores and *S* is the estimated standard deviation of the population of individual difference scores.

This is basically the same as the way you learned to figure effect size in Chapter 7, except that (a) you use the mean of the difference scores instead of the difference of the sample mean from the population mean, and (b) you use an estimated population standard deviation instead of a known population standard deviation.

The conventions for effect size are the same as you learned for the situation we considered in Chapter 7: A small effect size is .20, a medium effect size is .50, and a large effect size is .80.

Consider our first example of a *t* test for dependent means, the study of husbands' change in communication quality. In that study, the mean of the difference scores was -12.05. The estimated population standard deviation of the difference scores would be 12.41. That is, we figured the estimated variance of the difference scores (S^2) to be 154.05 and the square root of 154.05 is 12.41. Therefore, the effect size is -12.05 divided by 12.41, which is $-.97$. This is a very large effect size. (The negative sign for the effect size means that the large effect was a decrease in communication scores.)

Power

Power for a *t* test for dependent means can be determined using a power software package, an Internet power calculator, or a power table. Table 8–8 gives the approximate power at the .05 significance level for small, medium, and large effect sizes and one-tailed and two-tailed tests.

Suppose a researcher plans a study using the .05 significance level, two-tailed, with 20 participants. Based on previous related research, the researcher predicts an effect size of about .50 (a medium effect size). The table shows the study would have a

Table 8-8 Approximate Power for Studies Using the *t* Test for Dependent Means for Testing Hypothesis at the .05 Significance Level

Difference Scores in Sample (*N*)	Effect Size		
	Small (.20)	Medium (.50)	Large (.80)
One-tailed test			
10	.15	.46	.78
20	.22	.71	.96
30	.29	.86	*
40	.35	.93	*
50	.40	.97	*
100	.63	*	*
Two-tailed test			
10	.09	.32	.66
20	.14	.59	.93
30	.19	.77	.99
40	.24	.88	*
50	.29	.94	*
100	.55	*	*

*Power is nearly 1.

Table 8-9	Approximate Number of Research Participants Needed for 80% Power for the *t* Test for Dependent Means in Testing Hypotheses at the .05 Significance Level		
	Effect Size		
	Small (.20)	**Medium (.50)**	**Large (.80)**
One-tailed	156	26	12
Two-tailed	196	33	14

power of .59. This means that, if the research hypothesis is true and has a medium effect size, there is a 59% chance that this study will come out significant.

The power table (Table 8–8) is also useful when you are reading about a nonsignificant result in a published study. Suppose that a study using a *t* test for dependent means has a nonsignificant result. The study tested significance at the .05 level, was two-tailed, and had 10 participants. Should you conclude that there is in fact no difference at all between the populations? Probably not. Even assuming a medium effect size, Table 8–8 shows that there is only a 32% chance of getting a significant result in this study.

Consider another study that was not significant. This study also used the .05 significance level, one-tailed. This study had 100 research participants. Table 8–8 tells you that there would be a 63% chance of the study's coming out significant if there were even a true small effect size in the population. If there were a medium effect size in the population, the table indicates that there is almost a 100% chance that this study would have come out significant. In this study with 100 participants, you could conclude from the results of this study that in the population there is probably at most a small difference.

To keep Table 8–8 simple, we have given power figures for only a few different numbers of participants (10, 20, 30, 40, 50, and 100). This should be adequate for the kinds of rough evaluations you need to make when evaluating results of research articles.[6]

Planning Sample Size

Table 8–9 gives the approximate number of participants needed to have 80% power for a planned study. (Eighty percent is a common figure used by researchers for the minimum power to make a study worth doing.) The table gives the number of participants needed based on predicted small, medium, and large effect sizes, using one- and two-tailed tests, for the .05 significance levels. Suppose you plan a study in which you expect a large effect size and will use the .05 significance level, two-tailed. The table shows that you would need only 14 participants to have 80% power. On the other hand, a study using the same significance level, also two-tailed, but in which you expect only a small effect size, would need 196 participants for 80% power.[7]

---

[6]Cohen (1988, pp. 28–39) provides more detailed tables in terms of numbers of participants, levels of effect size, and significance levels. If you use his tables, note that the *d* referred to is actually based on a *t* test for independent means (the situation we consider in Chapter 9). To use these tables for a *t* test for dependent means, first multiply your effect size by 1.4. For example, if your effect size is .30, for purposes of using Cohen's tables, you would consider it to be .42 (that is, .30 × 1.4 = .42). The only other difference from our table is that Cohen describes the significance level by the letter *a* (for "alpha level"), with a subscript of either 1 or 2, referring to a one-tailed or two-tailed test. For example, a table that refers to "a_1 = .05" at the top means that this is the table for *p* < .05, one-tailed.

[7]More detailed tables, giving needed numbers of participants for levels of power other than 80% (and also for effect sizes other than .20, .50, and .80 and for other significance levels), are provided in Cohen (1988, pp. 54–55). However, see footnote 6 in this chapter about using Cohen's tables for a *t* test for dependent means.

The Power of Studies Using the *t* Test for Dependent Means

Studies using difference scores (that is, studies using a repeated-measures design) often have much larger effect sizes for the same amount of expected difference between means than have other kinds of research designs. That is, testing each of a group of participants twice (once under one condition and once under a different condition) usually produces a high-power type of study. In particular, this kind of study gives more power than dividing the participants up into two groups and testing each group once (one group tested under one condition and the other tested under the other condition). In fact, studies using difference scores usually have even more power than those in which you have twice as many participants, but tested each only once.

Why do repeated-measures designs have so much power? The reason is that the standard deviation of difference scores is usually quite low. (The standard deviation of difference scores is what you divide by to get the effect size when using difference scores.) This produces a larger effect size, which increases the power. In a repeated measures design, the only variation is in the difference scores. Variation among participants on each testing's scores are not part of the variation involved in the analysis. This is because difference scores are all comparing participants to themselves. The effect of all this is that studies using difference scores often have quite large effect sizes (and thus high power) even with a small number of people in the study.

However, although it has advantages from the point of view of power, the kind of repeated-measures study discussed in this chapter (testing a group of people before and after an experimental procedure, without any kind of control group that does not go through the procedure) often has disadvantages from the point of view of the meaning of the results. For example, consider a study where people are tested before and after some experimental procedure. Even if such a study produces a significant difference, it leaves many alternative explanations for that difference. For example, the research participants might have improved during that period anyway, or perhaps other events happened in between, or the participants not getting benefits may have dropped out. It is even possible that the initial test itself caused changes. The limitations of this kind of research are discussed in detail in research methods textbooks.

How are you doing?

1. (a) What is an assumption in hypothesis testing? (b) Describe a specific assumption for a *t* test for dependent means. (c) What is the effect of violating this assumption? (d) When is the *t* test for dependent means likely to give a very distorted result?
2. (a) Write the formula for estimated effect size, and (b) describe each of its terms.
3. You are planning a study in which you predict an effect size of .50. You plan to test significance using a *t* test for dependent means, one-tailed, with an alpha of .05. (a) What is the power of this study if you carry it out with 20 participants? (b) How many participants would you need to have 80% power?
4. (a) Why do repeated-measures designs have so much power? (b) What is the main disadvantage of the kind of repeated-measures study discussed in this chapter?

Answers

1. (a) It is a requirement that you must meet for the results of the hypothesis-testing procedure to be accurate.
(b) The population of individuals' difference scores is assumed to be a normal distribution.

planations for that difference.

(b) Even if a study produces a significant difference, there are alternative ex-
low (which makes the effect size relatively high, thereby increasing power).

4. (a) Because the standard deviation of the difference scores is usually quite

3. (a) .71. (b) 26.

tion of the population of individual difference scores.

(b) *M* is the mean of the difference scores. *S* is the estimated standard devia-

2. (a) Estimated Effect Size = *M/S*

skewed.

(d) When doing a one-tailed test and the population distribution is highly

(c) The significance level cutoff from the *t* table is not accurate.

Single-Sample *t* Tests and Dependent Means *t* Tests in Research Articles

Research articles usually describe *t* tests in a fairly standard format that includes the degrees of freedom, the *t* score, and the significance level. For example, $t(24) = 2.80$, $p < .05$ tells you that the researcher used a *t* test with 24 degrees of freedom, found a *t* score of 2.80, and the result was significant at the .05 level. Whether a one- or two-tailed test was used may also be noted. (If not, assume that it was two-tailed.) Usually the means, and sometimes the standard deviations, are given for each testing. Rarely does an article report the standard deviation of the difference scores.

Had our student in the dormitory example reported the results in a research article, she would have written something like this: "The sample from my dormitory studied a mean of 3.20 hours ($SD = .80$). Based on a *t* test for a single sample, this was significantly different from the known mean of 2.50 for the college as a whole, $t(15) = 3.50$, $p < .01$, one-tailed."

As we noted earlier, behavioral and social scientists only occasionally use the *t* test for a single sample. We introduced it mainly as a stepping stone to the more widely used *t* test for dependent means. Olthoff (1989) might have reported the results of the *t* test for dependent means in his study of husbands' communication quality as follows: "There was a significant decline in communication quality, dropping from a mean of 116.32 before marriage to a mean of 104.26 after marriage, $t(18) = 2.76$, $p < .05$, two-tailed." As another example, Rashotte and Webster (2005) carried out a study about people's general expectations about the abilities of men and women. In the study, the researchers showed 174 college students photos of women and men (referred to as the female and male targets, respectively). The students rated the person in each photo in terms of that person's general abilities (e.g., in terms of their intelligence, abstract abilities, capability at most tasks, and so on). For each participant, these ratings were combined to create a measure of the perceived status of the female targets and the male targets. The researchers then compared the status ratings given for the female targets and male targets. Since each participant in the study rated both the female and the male targets, the researchers compared the status ratings assigned to the female and male targets using a *t* test for dependent means. Table 8–10 shows the results. The row entitled "Whole sample ($N = 174$)" gives the result of the *t* test for all 174 participants and shows that the status rating assigned to the male targets was significantly higher than the rating assigned to the female targets ($t = 3.46$, $p < .001$). As shown in the table, the researchers also conducted two additional *t* tests to see if this effect was the same among the female participants and the male participants.

Table 8-10 Status Scale: Mean (and *SE*) General Expectations for Female and Male Targets

Respondents	Mean score (*SE*)		M − F target difference	*t* (1-tailed *p*)
	Female target	Male target		
Whole sample (*N* = 174)	5.60 (.06)	5.85 (.07)	.25	3.46 (< .001)
Female respondents (*N* = 111)	5.62 (.07)	5.84 (.081)	.22	2.62 (< .05)
Male respondents (*N* = 63)	5.57 (.10)	5.86 (.11)	.29	2.26 (< .05)

Source: Rashotte, L.S., & Webster, M., Jr. (2005). Gender status beliefs. *Social Science Research, 34,* 618–633. Copyright © 2005 by Elsevier. Reprinted by permission of Elsevier.

The results showed that both the female and the male participants assigned higher ratings to the male targets. As with this study, it is common for the results of dependent means *t* tests to be shown in a table. Asterisks will often be used to indicate the level of significance, with a note at the bottom of the table listing the corresponding significance level (although this wasn't the case in Table 8–10). And sometimes the *t* value itself is not given, just the asterisks indicating the significance level.

Summary

1. You use the standard five steps of hypothesis testing even when you don't know the population variance. However, in this situation you have to estimate the population variance from the scores in the sample, using a formula that divides the sum of squared deviation scores by the degrees of freedom ($df = N - 1$).
2. When the population variance is estimated, the comparison distribution of means is a *t* distribution (with cutoffs given in a *t* table). A *t* distribution has slightly heavier tails than a normal curve (just how much heavier depends on how few degrees of freedom). Also, in this situation, a sample's number of standard deviations from the mean of the comparison distribution is called a *t* score.
3. You use a *t* test for a single sample when a sample mean is being compared to a known population mean and the population variance is unknown.
4. You use a *t* test for dependent means in studies where each participant has two scores, such as a before-score and an after-score, or a score in each of two experimental conditions. In this *t* test, you first figure a difference score for each participant, then go through the usual five steps of hypothesis testing with the modifications described in summary points 1 and 2 above and making Population 2 a population of difference scores with a mean of 0 (no difference).
5. An assumption of the *t* test is that the population distribution is a normal curve. However, even when it is not, the *t* test is usually fairly accurate.
6. The effect size of a study using a *t* test for dependent means is the mean of the difference scores divided by the standard deviation of the difference scores. Power and needed sample size for 80% power can be looked up using power software packages, an Internet power calculator, or special tables.
7. The power of studies using difference scores is usually much higher than that of studies using other designs with the same number of participants. However, research using a single group tested before and after some intervening event, without a control group, allows for alternative explanations of any observed changes.
8. *t* tests are reported in research articles using a standard format. For example, "$t(24) = 2.80, p < .05$."

t tests (p. 233)
t test for a single sample (p. 233)
biased estimate (p. 237)
unbiased estimate of the population
    variance (S^2) (p. 238)

degrees of freedom (*df*) (p. 238)
t distribution (p. 239)
t table (p. 241)
t score (p. 242)
repeated-measures design (p. 246)

t test for dependent means (p. 246)
difference scores (p. 247)
assumption (p. 255)

Example Worked-Out Problems

t Test for a Single Sample

Eight participants are tested after being given an experimental procedure. Their scores are 14, 8, 6, 5, 13, 10, 10, and 6. The population (of people not given this procedure) is normally distributed with a mean of 6. Using the .05 level, two-tailed, does the experimental procedure make a difference? (a) Use the five steps of hypothesis testing and (b) sketch the distributions involved.

Answer

(a) Steps of hypothesis testing:

❶ **Restate the question as a research hypothesis and a null hypothesis about the populations.** There are two populations:

Population 1: People who are given the experimental procedure.
Population 2: The general population.

The research hypothesis is that Population 1 will score differently than Population 2. The null hypothesis is that Population 1 will score the same as Population 2.

❷ **Determine the characteristics of the comparison distribution.** The mean of the distribution of means is 6 (the known population mean). To figure the estimated population variance, you first need to figure the sample mean, which is $(14 + 8 + 6 + 5 + 13 + 10 + 10 + 6)/8 = 72/8 = 9$. The estimated population variance is $S^2 = [\Sigma (X - M)^2]/df = 78/7 = 11.14$; the variance of the distribution of means is $S_M^2 = S^2/N = 11.14/8 = 1.39$. The standard deviation of the distribution of means is $S_M = \sqrt{S_M^2} = \sqrt{1.39} = 1.18$. Its shape will be a *t* distribution for $df = 7$.

❸ **Determine the cutoff sample score on the comparison distribution at which the null hypothesis should be rejected.** From Table A–2, the cutoffs for a two-tailed *t* test at the .05 level for $df = 7$ are 2.365 and -2.365.

❹ **Determine your sample's score on the comparison distribution.** $t = (M - \text{Population } M)/S_M = (9 - 6)/1.18 = 3/1.18 = 2.54$.

❺ **Decide whether to reject the null hypothesis.** The *t* of 2.54 is more extreme than the needed *t* of 2.365. Therefore, reject the null hypothesis; the research hypothesis is supported. The experimental procedure does make a difference.

(b) Sketches of distributions are shown in Figure 8–8.

t Test for Dependent Means

A researcher tests 10 individuals before and after an experimental procedure. The results were as follows:

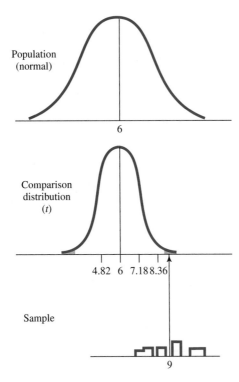

Figure 8–8   Distributions for answer to Example Worked-Out Problem for *t* test for a single sample.

Participant	Before	After
1	10.4	10.8
2	12.6	12.1
3	11.2	12.1
4	10.9	11.4
5	14.3	13.9
6	13.2	13.5
7	9.7	10.9
8	11.5	11.5
9	10.8	10.4
10	13.1	12.5

Test the hypothesis that there is an increase in scores, using the .05 significance level. (a) Use the five steps of hypothesis testing and (b) sketch the distributions involved.

Answer

(a) Table 8–11 shows the results, including the figuring of difference scores and all the other figuring for the *t* test for dependent means. Here are the steps of hypothesis testing:

➀ **Restate the question as a research hypothesis and a null hypothesis about the populations.** There are two populations:

Population 1: People like those who are given the experimental procedure.

Table 8–11 Figuring for Answer to Example Worked-Out Problem for *t* Test for Dependent Means

Participant	Score		Difference (After − Before)	Deviation (Difference − M)	Squared Deviation
	Before	*After*			
1	10.4	10.8	.4	.260	.068
2	12.6	12.1	−.5	−.640	.410
3	11.2	12.1	.9	.760	.578
4	10.9	11.4	.5	.360	.130
5	14.3	13.9	−.4	−.540	.292
6	13.2	13.5	.3	.160	.026
7	9.7	10.9	1.2	1.060	1.124
8	11.5	11.5	0.0	−.140	.020
9	10.8	10.4	−.4	−.540	.292
10	13.1	12.5	−.6	−.740	.548
Σ	117.7	119.1	1.4		3.488

For difference scores:

$M = 1.4/10 = .140.$

Population $M = 0.$

$S^2 = [\Sigma (X - M)^2]/df = 3.488/(10 - 1) = 3.488/9 = .388.$

$S_M^2 = S^2/N = .388/10 = .039.$

$S_M = \sqrt{S_M^2} = \sqrt{.039} = .197.$

t for *df* = 9 needed for 5% significance level, one-tailed = 1.833.

$t = (M - \text{Population } M)/S_M = (.140 - 0)/.197 = .71.$

Decision: Do not reject the null hypothesis.

Population 2: People who show no change from before to after.

The research hypothesis is that Population 1's mean difference score (after minus before) is greater than Population 2's. The null hypothesis is that Population 1's mean difference (after minus before) is not greater than Population 2's.

❷ **Determine the characteristics of the comparison distribution.** Its population mean is 0 difference. The estimated population variance of difference scores is shown in Table 8–11 to be .388. The standard deviation of the distribution of means of difference scores, S_M, is .197. Therefore, the comparison distribution has a mean of 0 and a standard deviation of .197. It will be a *t* distribution for *df* = 9.

❸ **Determine the cutoff sample score on the comparison distribution at which the null hypothesis should be rejected.** For a one-tailed test at the .05 level with *df* = 9, the cutoff is 1.833. (The cutoff is positive because the research hypothesis is that Population 1's mean difference score will be *greater* than Population 2's.)

❹ **Determine your sample's score on the comparison distribution.** The sample's mean difference of .140 is .71 standard deviations (of .197 each) on the distribution of means above that distribution's mean of 0. That is, $t = (M - \text{Population } M)/S_M = (.140 - 0)/.197 = .71.$

❺ **Decide whether to reject the null hypothesis.** The sample's *t* of .71 is less extreme than the needed *t* of 1.833. Thus, you cannot reject the null hypothesis. The study is inconclusive.

(b) Sketches of distributions are shown in Figure 8–9.

Outline for Writing Essays for a *t* Test for a Single Sample

1. Describe the core logic of hypothesis testing in this situation. Be sure to mention that the *t* test for a single sample is used for hypothesis testing when you have scores for a sample of individuals and you want to compare the mean of this sample to a population for which the mean is known but the variance is unknown. Be sure to explain the meaning of the research hypothesis and the null hypothesis in this situation.
2. Outline the logic of estimating the population variance from the sample scores. Explain the idea of biased and unbiased estimates of the population variance, and describe the formula for estimating the population variance and why it is different from the ordinary variance formula.
3. Describe the comparison distribution (the *t* distribution) that is used with a *t* test for a single sample, noting how it is different from a normal curve and why. Explain why a *t* distribution (as opposed to the normal curve) is used as the comparison distribution.
4. Describe the logic and process for determining the cutoff sample score(s) on the comparison distribution at which the null hypothesis should be rejected.
5. Describe why and how you figure the *t* score of the sample mean on the comparison distribution.

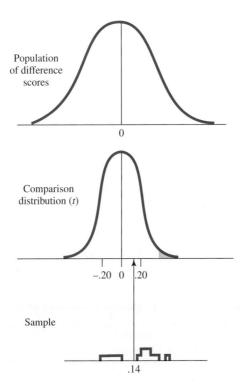

Figure 8–9   Distributions for answer to Example Worked-Out Problem for *t* test for dependent means.

6. Explain how and why the scores from Steps ❸ and ❹ of the hypothesis-testing process are compared. Explain the meaning of the result of this comparison with regard to the specific research and null hypotheses being tested.

Outline for Writing Essays for a *t* Test for Dependent Means

1. Describe the core logic of hypothesis testing in this situation. Be sure to mention that the *t* test for dependent means is used for hypothesis testing when you have two scores from each person in your sample. Be sure to explain the meaning of the research hypothesis and the null hypothesis in this situation. Explain the logic and procedure for creating difference scores.
2. Explain why you use 0 as the mean for the comparison distribution.
3. Outline the logic of estimating the population variance of difference scores from the sample scores. Explain the idea of biased and unbiased estimates of the population variance, and describe the formula for estimating the population variance. Describe how to figure the standard deviation of the distribution of means of difference scores.
4. Describe the comparison distribution (the *t* distribution) that is used with a *t* test for dependent means. Explain why a *t* distribution (as opposed to the normal curve) is used as the comparison distribution.
5. Describe the logic and process for determining the cutoff sample score(s) on the comparison distribution at which the null hypothesis should be rejected.
6. Describe why and how you figure the *t* score of the sample mean on the comparison distribution.
7. Explain how and why the scores from Steps ❸ and ❹ of the hypothesis-testing process are compared. Explain the meaning of the result of this comparison with regard to the specific research and null hypotheses being tested.

Practice Problems

These problems involve figuring. Most real-life statistics problems are done on a computer with special statistical software. Even if you have such software, do these problems by hand to ingrain the method in your mind. To learn how to use a computer to solve statistics problems like those in this chapter, refer to the *Using SPSS* section at the end of this chapter and the *Student's Study Guide and SPSS Workbook* that accompanies this text.

All data are fictional unless an actual citation is given.

Set I (for answers, see pp. 444–447)

1. In each of the following studies, a single sample's mean is being compared to a population with a known mean but an unknown variance. For each study, decide whether the result is significant. (Be sure to show all of your calculations.)

Study	Sample Size (*N*)	Population Mean	Estimated Population Variance (*S²*)	Sample Mean (*M*)	Tails	Significance Level
(a)	64	12.40	9.00	11.00	1 (low predicted)	.05
(b)	49	1,006.35	317.91	1,009.72	2	.01
(c)	400	52.00	7.02	52.41	1 (high predicted)	.01

2. Suppose a candidate running for sheriff claims that she will reduce the average speed of emergency response to less than 30 minutes. (30 minutes is thought to be the average response time with the current sheriff.) There are no past records, so the actual standard deviation of such response times cannot be determined. Thanks to this campaign, she is elected sheriff, and careful records are now kept. The response times for the first month are 26, 30, 28, 29, 25, 28, 32, 35, 24, and 23 minutes.

   Using the .05 significance level, did she keep her promise? (a) Go through the five steps of hypothesis testing. (b) Sketch the distributions involved. (c) Explain your answer to someone who has never taken a course in statistics.

3. A researcher tests five individuals who have seen paid political ads about a particular issue. These individuals take a multiple-choice test about the issue in which people in general (who know nothing about the issue) usually get 40 questions correct. The number correct for these five individuals was 48, 41, 40, 51, and 50.

   Using the .05 level of significance, two-tailed, do people who see the ads do better on this test? (a) Use the steps of hypothesis testing. (b) Sketch the distributions involved. (c) Explain your answer to someone who is familiar with the Z test (from Chapter 6), but is unfamiliar with *t* tests.

4. For each of the following studies using difference scores, test the significance using a *t* test for dependent means. Also, figure the estimated effect size for each study.

Study	Number of Difference Scores in Sample	Mean of Difference Scores in Sample	Estimated Population Variance of Difference Scores	Tails	Significance Level
(a)	20	1.7	8.29	1 (high predicted)	.05
(b)	164	2.3	414.53	2	.05
(c)	15	−2.2	4.00	1 (low predicted)	.01

5. A program to decrease littering was carried out in four cities in California's Central Valley starting in August 2005. The amount of litter in the streets (average pounds of litter collected per block per day) was measured during the July before the program was started and then the next July, after the program had been in effect for a year. The results were as follows:

City	July 2005	July 2006
Fresno	9	2
Merced	10	4
Bakersfield	8	9
Stockton	9	1

   Using the .01 level of significance, was there a significant decrease in the amount of litter? (a) Use the five steps of hypothesis testing. (b) Sketch the distributions involved. (c) Explain your answer to someone who understands mean, standard deviation, and variance, but knows nothing else about statistics.

6. A researcher assesses the level of a particular hormone in the blood in five patients before and after they begin taking a hormone treatment program. Results for the five are as follows:

Patient	Before	After
A	.20	.18
B	.16	.16
C	.24	.20
D	.22	.19
E	.17	.16

Using the .05 level of significance, was there a significant change in the level of this hormone? (a) Use the steps of hypothesis testing. (b) Sketch the distributions involved. (c) Explain your answer to someone who understands the *t* test for a single sample but is unfamiliar with the *t* test for dependent means.

7. Figure the estimated effect size and indicate whether it is approximately small, medium, or large, for each of the following studies:

Study	Mean Change	S
(a)	20	32
(b)	5	10
(c)	.1	.4
(d)	100	500

8. What is the power of each of the following studies, using a *t* test for dependent means (based on the .05 significance level)?

Study	Effect Size	N	Tails
(a)	Small	20	One
(b)	Medium	20	One
(c)	Medium	30	One
(d)	Medium	30	Two
(e)	Large	30	Two

9. About how many participants are needed for 80% power in each of the following planned studies that will use a *t* test for dependent means with $p < .05$?

Study	Predicted Effect Size	Tails
(a)	Medium	Two
(b)	Large	One
(c)	Small	One

10. Weller and Weller (1997) conducted a study of the tendency for the menstrual cycles of women who live together (such as sisters) to become synchronized. For their statistical analysis, they compared scores on a measure of synchronization of pairs of sisters living together versus the degree of synchronization that would be expected by chance (lower scores mean more synchronization). Their key results (reported in a table not reproduced here) were synchrony scores of 6.32 for the 30 roommate sister pairs in their sample compared to an expected synchrony score of 7.76; they then reported a *t* score of 2.27 for this difference. This result is statistically significant at $p < .05$. Explain this result to a person who is familiar with hypothesis testing with a known population variance, but not with the *t* test for a single sample.

11. A researcher conducts a study of perceptual illusions under two different lighting conditions. Twenty participants were each tested under both of the two different conditions. The experimenter reported: "The mean number of effective illusions was 6.72 under the bright conditions and 6.85 under the dimly lit conditions, a difference that was not significant, $t(19) = 1.62$." Explain this result to a person who has never had a course in statistics. Be sure to use sketches of the distributions in your answer.

Set II

12. In each of the following studies, a single sample's mean is being compared to a population with a known mean but an unknown variance. For each study, decide whether the result is significant.

Study	Sample Size (N)	Population Mean	Estimated Population Standard Deviation (S)	Sample Mean (M)	Tails	Significance Level
(a)	16	100.31	2.00	100.98	1 (high predicted)	.05
(b)	16	.47	4.00	.00	2	.05
(c)	16	68.90	9.00	34.00	1 (low predicted)	.01

13. Evolutionary theories often emphasize that humans have adapted to their physical environment. One such theory hypothesizes that people should spontaneously follow a 24-hour cycle of sleeping and waking—even if they are not exposed to the usual pattern of sunlight. To test this notion, eight paid volunteers were placed (individually) in a room in which there was no light from the outside and no clocks or other indications of time. They could turn the lights on and off as they wished. After a month in the room, each individual tended to develop a steady cycle. Their cycles at the end of the study were as follows: 25, 27, 25, 23, 24, 25, 26, and 25.

Using the .05 level of significance, what should we conclude about the theory that 24 hours is the natural cycle? (That is, does the average cycle length under these conditions differ significantly from 24 hours?) (a) Use the steps of hypothesis testing. (b) Sketch the distributions involved. (c) Explain your answer to someone who has never taken a course in statistics.

14. In a particular country, it is known that college seniors report falling in love an average of 2.20 times during their college years. A sample of five seniors, originally from that country but who have spent their entire college career in the United States, were asked how many times they had fallen in love during their college years. Their numbers were 2, 3, 5, 5, and 2. Using the .05 significance level, do students like these who go to college in the United States fall in love more often than those from their country who go to college in their own country? (a) Use the steps of hypothesis testing. (b) Sketch the distributions involved. (c) Explain your answer to someone who is familiar with the *Z* test (from Chapter 6), but is not familiar with the *t* test for a single sample.

15. For each of the following studies using difference scores, test the significance using a *t* test for dependent means.

Study	Number of Difference Scores in Sample	Mean of Difference Scores in Sample	Estimated Population Variance of Difference Scores	Tails	Significance Level
(a)	10	3.8	50	1 (high predicted)	.05
(b)	100	3.8	50	1 (high predicted)	.05
(c)	100	1.9	50	1 (high predicted)	.05
(d)	100	1.9	50	2	.05
(e)	100	1.9	25	2	.05

16. Four individuals with high levels of cholesterol went on a special diet, avoiding high-cholesterol foods and taking special supplements. Their total cholesterol levels before and after the diet were as follows:

Participant	Before	After
J. K.	287	255
L. M. M.	305	269
A. K.	243	245
R. O. S.	309	247

Using the .05 level of significance, was there a significant change in cholesterol level? (a) Use the steps of hypothesis testing. (b) Sketch the distributions involved. (c) Explain your answer to someone who has never taken a course in statistics.

17. Five people who were convicted of speeding were ordered by the court to attend a workshop. A special device put into their cars kept records of their speeds for 2 weeks before and after the workshop. The maximum speeds for each person during the 2 weeks before and the 2 weeks after the workshop follow.

Participant	Before	After
L. B.	65	58
J. K.	62	65
R. C.	60	56
R. T.	70	66
J. M.	68	60

Using the .05 significance level, should we conclude that people are likely to drive more slowly after such a workshop? (a) Use the steps of hypothesis testing. (b) Sketch the distributions involved. (c) Explain your answer to someone who is familiar with hypothesis testing involving known populations, but has never learned anything about *t* tests.

18. Five sophomores were given an English achievement test before and after receiving instruction in basic grammar. Their scores are shown below.

Student	Before	After
A	20	18
B	18	22
C	17	15
D	16	17
E	12	9

Is it reasonable to conclude that future students would show higher scores after instruction? Use the .05 significance level. (a) Use the steps of hypothesis testing. (b) Sketch the distributions involved. (c) Explain your answer to someone who understands mean, standard deviation, and variance, but knows nothing else about statistics.

19. Figure the estimated effect size and indicate whether it is approximately small, medium, or large, for each of the following studies:

Study	Mean Change	S
(a)	8	30
(b)	8	10
(c)	16	30
(d)	16	10

20. What is the power of each of the following studies, using a *t* test for dependent means (based on the .05 significance level)?

Study	Effect Size	N	Tails
(a)	Small	50	Two
(b)	Medium	50	Two
(c)	Large	50	Two
(d)	Small	10	Two
(e)	Small	40	Two
(f)	Small	100	Two
(g)	Small	100	One

21. About how many participants are needed for 80% power in each of the following planned studies that will use a *t* test for dependent means with $p < .05$?

Study	Predicted Effect Size	Tails
(a)	Small	Two
(b)	Medium	One
(c)	Large	Two

22. A study compared union activity of employees in 10 plants during two different decades. The researchers reported "a significant increase in union activity, $t(9) = 3.28, p < .01$." Explain this result to a person who has never had a course in statistics. Be sure to use sketches of the distributions in your answer.

23. Holden, Thompson, Zambarano, and Marshall (1997) compared mothers' reported attitudes toward corporal punishment of their children from before to 3 years after having their first child. "The average change in the women's prior-to-current attitudes was significant, $t(107) = 10.32, p < .001$" (p. 485). (The change was that they felt more negatively about corporal punishment after having their child.) Explain this result to someone who is familiar with the *t* test for a single sample, but not with the *t* test for dependent means.

24. Table 8–12 (reproduced from Table 4 of Larson, Dworkin, & Verma, 2001) shows ratings of various aspects of work and home life of 100 middle-class men in India who were fathers. Pick three rows of interest to you and explain the results to someone who is familiar with the mean, variance, and Z scores, but knows nothing else about statistics.

Table 8–12 Comparison of Fathers' Mean Psychological States in the Job and Home Spheres (*N* = 100)

Scale	Range	Sphere		Work vs. home
		Work	Home	
Important	0–9	5.98	5.06	6.86***
Attention	0–9	6.15	5.13	7.96***
Challenge	0–9	4.11	2.41	11.49***
Choice	0–9	4.28	4.74	−3.38***
Wish doing else	0–9	1.50	1.44	0.61
Hurried	0–3	1.80	1.39	3.21**
Social anxiety	0–3	0.81	0.64	3.17**
Affect	1–7	4.84	4.98	−2.64**
Social climate	1–7	5.64	5.95	4.17***

Note: Values for column 3 are *t* scores; *df* = 99 for all *t* tests.
** $p < .01$. *** $p < .001$.
Source: Larson, R., Dworkin, J., & Verma, S. (2001). Men's work and family lives in India: The daily organization of time and emotions. *Journal of Family Psychology, 15,* 206–224. Copyright © 2001 by the American Psychological Association.

Using SPSS

The ✐ in the steps below indicates a mouse click. (We used SPSS version 13.0 for Windows to carry out these analyses. The steps and output may be slightly different for other versions of SPSS.)

t Test for a Single Sample

❶ Enter the scores from your distribution in one column of the data window.
❷ ✐ *Analyze.*
❸ ✐ *Compare means.*
❹ ✐ *One-sample T test* (this is the name SPSS uses for a *t* test for a single sample).
❺ ✐ on the variable for which you want to carry out the *t* test and then ✐ the arrow.
❻ Enter the population mean in the "Test Value" box.
❼ ✐ *OK.*

Practice the steps above by carrying out a single sample *t* test for the example worked-out problem for a *t* test for a single sample. In that example, eight participants were tested after an experimental procedure. Their scores were 14, 8, 6, 5, 13, 10, 10, and 6. The population of people not given this procedure is normally distributed with a mean of 6. Your SPSS output window should look like Figure 8–10. The first table provides information about the variable: the number of scores ("N"); the mean of the scores ("Mean"); the estimated population standard deviation, *S* ("Std. Deviation"); and the standard deviation of the distribution of means, S_M ("Std. Error Mean"). Check that the values in that table are consistent (allowing for rounding error) with the values in the exampled worked-out problem section. The second table in the SPSS output window gives the outcome of the *t* test. Compare the values of *t* and *df* in that table with the values given in the example worked-out problem section. The exact two-tailed significance level of the *t* test is given in the "Sig. 2-tailed" column. In this study, the researcher was using the .05 significance level. The significance

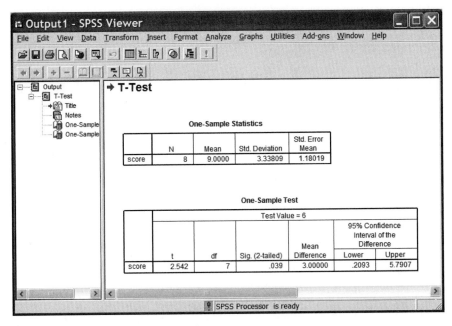

Figure 8-10 Using SPSS to carry out a *t* test for a single sample for the example worked-out problem for a single sample *t* test.

level given by SPSS (.039) is more extreme than .05, which means that the researcher can reject the null hypothesis and the research hypothesis is supported.

t Test for Dependent Means

❶ Enter the first set of scores (for example, the "before" scores) in the first column of the data window. Then enter the second set of scores (for example, the "after" scores) in the second column of the data window. (Be sure to enter the scores in the order they are listed.).

❷ ✑ *Analyze.*

❸ ✑ *Compare means.*

❹ ✑ *Paired-Samples T Test* (this is the name SPSS uses for a *t* test for dependent means).

❺ ✑ on the first variable (this will highlight the variable). ✑ on the second variable (this will highlight the variable). ✑ the arrow. The two variables will now appear in the "Paired Variables" box.

❻ ✑ *OK.*

Practice the steps above by carrying out a *t* test for dependent means for Olthoff's (1989) study of communication quality of 19 men who received ordinary premarital counseling. The scores and figuring for that study are shown in Table 8–4. Your SPSS output window should look like Figure 8–11. The key information is contained in the third table (labeled "Paired Samples Test"). The final three columns of this table give the *t* score (4.240), the degrees of freedom (18), and the two-tailed significance level (.000 in this case) of the *t* test. The significance level is so small that even after rounding to three decimal places, it is less than .001. Since the significance level is more extreme than the .05 significance level we set for this study, you can reject the null hypothesis. By looking at the means for the "before" variable and the "after" variable in

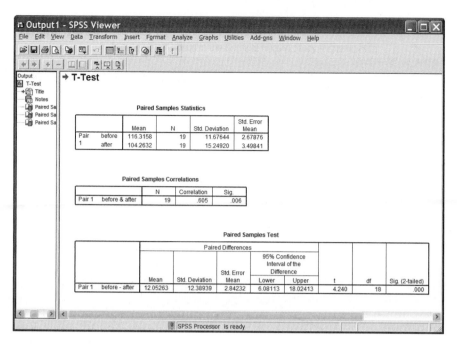

Figure 8–11 Using SPSS to carry out a *t* test for dependent means for Olthoff's (1989) study of communication quality among 19 men who received ordinary premarital counseling.

the first table (labeled "Paired Samples Statistics"), you can see that the husbands' communication quality was lower after marriage (a mean of 104.2632) than before marriage (a mean 116.3158). (Don't worry that the *t* value figured in Table 8–4 was negative, whereas the *t* value in the SPSS output is positive. This happens because the difference score in Table 8–4 was figured as after minus before, but SPSS figured the difference scores as before minus after. Both ways of figuring the difference score are correct and the overall result is the same in each case.)

CHAPTER 9

The *t* Test for Independent Means

CHAPTER OUTLINE

- The Distribution of Differences between Means
- Hypothesis Testing with a *t* Test for Independent Means
- Assumptions of the *t* Test for Independent Means
- Effect Size and Power for the *t* Test for Independent Means
- Review and Comparison of the three Kinds of *t* Tests
- The *t* Tests for Independent Means in Research Articles
- Summary
- Key Terms
- Example Worked-Out Problems
- Practice Problems
- Using SPSS

In the previous chapter, you learned how to use the *t* test for dependent means to compare two groups of scores from a *single group of people* (such as the same men measured on communication before and after premarital counseling). In this chapter, you learn how to compare scores from *two entirely separate groups of people*. This is a very common situation in behavioral and social sciences research. For example, a study may compare the scores from individuals in an experimental group with the scores from individuals in a control group. (Another example is comparing scores from a group of men with scores from a group of women.) The scores of these two groups are independent of each other, so the test you will learn is called a *t* **test for independent means.**

Let's consider an example. A team of researchers is interested in whether writing about thoughts and feelings about traumatic life events can affect physical health. This kind of writing is called expressive writing. Suppose the researchers recruit

***t* test for independent means** Hypothesis-testing procedure in which there are two separate groups of people tested and in which the population variance is not known.

TIP FOR SUCCESS

You should be thoroughly comfortable with the material in Chapter 8, particularly the basic logic and procedures of the *t* test for a single sample, before going on to the material in this chapter.

distribution of differences between means Distribution of differences between means of pairs of samples such that for each pair of means, one is from one population and the other is from a second population; the comparison distribution in a *t* test for independent means.

undergraduate students to take part in a study and then randomly assign them to be in either an expressive writing group or a control group. Students in the expressive writing group are instructed to write four 20-minute essays over four consecutive days about their most traumatic life experiences. Students in the control group write four 20-minute essays over four consecutive days describing their plans for that day. One month later, the researchers ask the students to rate their overall level of physical health (on a scale from 0 = *very poor health* to 100 = *perfect health*). The expressive writing and the control group contain different students. Thus, the researchers need to use a *t* test for independent means to test the effect of expressive writing on physical health. We will return to this example later in the chapter. But first, you will learn about the logic of the *t* test for independent means, which involves learning about a new kind of distribution (called the *distribution of differences between means*).

The Distribution of Differences between Means

In the previous chapter, you learned the logic and figuring for the *t* test for dependent means. In that chapter, the situation was about a single group of people being studied with each person having two scores, such as a before score and an after score. This allowed you to create a difference score for each person. You then carried out the hypothesis-testing procedure using these difference scores. The comparison distribution you used for this hypothesis testing was a *distribution of means of difference scores.*

In the situation you face in this chapter, you have two groups of people but one score per person. So, you don't have any pairs of scores for each person as you did in Chapter 8. Thus, it wouldn't make sense in this new situation to create difference scores, and you can't use difference scores for the hypothesis-testing procedure in this chapter. Instead, when you have one score for each person with two different groups of people, what you can compare is the *mean* of one group to the *mean* of the other group.

So, the key focus in the *t* test for independent means becomes the *difference between the means* of the two groups. The hypothesis-testing procedure, however, works just like the hypothesis-testing procedures you have already learned. Since the focus is now on the difference between means, the comparison distribution is a **distribution of differences between means.**

A distribution of differences between means is, in a sense, two steps removed from the populations of individuals: First, there is a distribution of means from each population of individuals. Second, there is a distribution of differences between pairs of means, one of each pair from each of these distributions of means.

Think of this distribution of differences between means as being built up as follows: (a) Randomly select one mean from the distribution of means for Population 1, (b) randomly select one mean from the distribution of means for Population 2, and (c) subtract. (That is, take the mean from the first distribution of means minus the mean from the second distribution of means.) This gives a difference score between the two selected means. Then repeat the process. This creates a second difference, a difference between the two newly selected means. Repeating this process a large number of times creates a distribution of differences between means. You would never actually create a distribution of differences between means using this lengthy method. But it shows clearly what the distribution is made up of.

The Logic

Figure 9–1 shows the entire logical construction involved in a distribution of differences between means. At the top are the two population distributions. We do not know the characteristics of these population distributions. But we do know that if the null

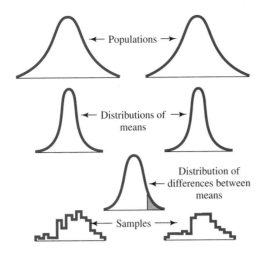

Figure 9–1   A diagram of the logic of a distribution of differences between means.

hypothesis is true, the two population means are the same. That is, the null hypothesis is that Population M_1 = Population M_2. We also can estimate the variance of these populations based on the sample information (these estimated variances will be S_1^2 and S_2^2).

Below each population distribution is the distribution of means for that population. Using the estimated population variance and knowing the size of each sample, you can figure the variance of each distribution of means in the usual way. (It is the estimated variance of its parent population divided by the size of the sample from that population that is being studied.)

Below these two distributions of means, and built from them, is the crucial distribution of differences between means. This distribution's variance is ultimately based on estimated population variances. Thus, we can think of it as a *t* distribution. The goal of a *t* test for independent means is to decide whether the difference between the means of your two actual samples is a more extreme difference than the cutoff difference on this distribution of differences between means. The two actual samples are shown (as histograms) at the bottom.

Remember, this whole procedure is really a kind of complicated castle in the air. It exists only in our minds to help us make decisions based on the results of an actual experiment. The only concrete reality in all of this is the actual scores in the two samples. You estimate the population variances from these sample scores. The variances of the two distributions of means are based entirely on these estimated population variances (and the sample sizes). And, as you will see shortly, the characteristics of the distribution of differences between means is based on these two distributions of means.

Still, the procedure is a powerful one. It has the power of mathematics and logic behind it. It helps you develop general knowledge based on the specifics of a particular study.

With this overview of the basic logic, we now turn to six key details: (1) the mean of the distribution of differences between means, (2) the estimated population variance, (3) the variance of the two distributions of means, (4) the variance and standard deviation of the distribution of differences between means, (5) the shape of the distribution of differences between means, and (6) the *t* score for the difference between the particular two means being compared.

pooled estimate of the population variance (S^2_{Pooled}) In a *t* test for independent means, weighted average of the estimates of the population variance from two samples (each estimate weighted by a proportion consisting of its sample's degrees of freedom divided by the total degrees of freedom for both samples).

weighted average Average in which the scores being averaged do not have equal influence on the total, as in figuring the pooled variance estimate in a *t* test for independent means.

Mean of the Distribution of Differences between Means

In a *t* test for independent means, you are considering two populations—for example, one population from which an experimental group is taken and one population from which a control group is taken. In practice, you don't know the mean of either population. You do know that if the null hypothesis is true, these two populations have equal means. Also, if these two populations have equal means, the two distributions of means have equal means. (This is because each distribution of means has the same mean as its parent population of individuals.) Finally, if you take random samples from two distributions with equal means, the differences between the means of these random samples, in the long run, balance out to 0. The result of all this is the following: Whatever the specifics of the study, the researcher knows that if the null hypothesis is true, the distribution of differences between means has a mean of 0.

Estimating the Population Variance

In Chapter 8, you learned to estimate the population variance from the scores in your sample. It is the sum of squared deviation scores divided by the degrees of freedom (the number in the sample minus 1). To do a *t* test for independent means, it has to be reasonable to assume that the populations the two samples come from have the same variance. (If the null hypothesis is true, they also have the same mean. However, regardless of whether the null hypothesis is true, you must be able to assume the two populations have the same variance.) Therefore, when you estimate the population variance from the scores in either sample, you are getting two separate estimates of what should be the same number. In practice, the two estimates will almost never be exactly identical. Since they are both supposed to be estimating the same thing, the best solution is to average the two estimates to get the best single overall estimate. This is called the **pooled estimate of the population variance** (S^2_{Pooled}).

In making this average, however, you also have to take into account that the two samples may not be the same size. If one sample is larger than the other, the estimate it provides is likely to be more accurate (because it is based on more information). If both samples are exactly the same size, you could just take an ordinary average of the two estimates. On the other hand, when they are not the same size, you need to make some adjustment in the averaging to give more weight to the larger sample. That is, you need a **weighted average,** an average weighted by the amount of information each sample provides.

Also, to be precise, the amount of information each sample provides is not its number of scores but its degrees of freedom (its number of scores minus 1). Thus, your weighted average needs to be based on the degrees of freedom each sample provides. To find the weighted average, you figure out what proportion of the total degrees of freedom each sample contributes and multiply that proportion by the population variance estimate from that sample. Finally, you add up the two results and that is your weighted, pooled estimate. In terms of a formula:

The pooled estimate of the population variance is the degrees of freedom in the first sample divided by the total degrees of freedom (from both samples) multiplied by the population estimate based on the first sample, plus the degrees of freedom in the second sample divided by the total degrees of freedom multiplied by the population estimate based on the second sample.

(9-1)
$$S^2_{Pooled} = \frac{df_1}{df_{Total}}(S^2_1) + \frac{df_2}{df_{Total}}(S^2_2)$$

In this formula, S^2_{Pooled} is the pooled estimate of the population variance. df_1 is the degrees of freedom in the sample for Population 1, and df_2 is the degrees of freedom in the sample for Population 2. (Remember, each sample's *df* is its number of scores minus 1.) df_{Total} is the total degrees of freedom ($df_{Total} = df_1 + df_2$). S^2_1 is the estimate of the population variance based on the scores in the sample from Population 1; S_2^2 is the estimate based on the scores in the sample from Population 2.

Consider a study in which the population variance estimate based on an experimental group of 11 participants is 60, and the population variance estimate based on a control group of 31 participants is 80. The estimate from the experimental group is based on 10 degrees of freedom (11 participants minus 1), and the estimate from the control group is based on 30 degrees of freedom (31 minus 1). The total information on which the estimate is based is the total degrees of freedom—in this example, 40 (10 + 30). Thus, the experimental group provides one-quarter of the information (10/40 = 1/4), and the control group provides three-quarters of the information (30/40 = 3/4).

You then multiply the variance estimate from the experimental group by 1/4, making 15 (that is, 60 × 1/4 = 15). You multiply the estimate from the control group by 3/4, making 60 (that is, 80 × 3/4 = 60). Adding the two, this gives an overall population variance estimate of 15 plus 60, which is 75. Using the formula,

$$S_{Pooled}^2 = \frac{df_1}{df_{Total}}(S_1^2) + \frac{df_2}{df_{Total}}(S_2^2) = \frac{10}{40}(60) + \frac{30}{40}(80)$$

$$= \frac{1}{4}(60) + \frac{3}{4}(80) = 15 + 60 = 75$$

Notice that this procedure does not give the same result as ordinary averaging (without weighting). Ordinary averaging would give an estimate of 70 (that is, [60 + 80]/2 = 70). Your weighted, pooled estimate of the population variance of 75 is closer to the estimate based on the control group alone than to the estimate based on the experimental group alone. This is as it should be, because the control group estimate in this example was based on more information.

Figuring the Variance of Each of the Two Distributions of Means

The pooled estimate of the population variance is the best estimate for both populations. (Remember, to do a *t* test for independent means, you have to be able to assume that the two populations have the same variance.) However, even though the two populations have the same variance, if the samples are not the same size, the distributions of means taken from them do not have the same variance. That is because the variance of a distribution of means is the population variance divided by the sample size. In terms of formulas,

$$S_{M_1}^2 = \frac{S_{Pooled}^2}{N_1} \qquad (9\text{-}2)$$

The variance of the distribution of means for the first population (based on an estimated population variance) is the pooled estimate of the population variance divided by the number of participants in the sample from the first population.

$$S_{M_2}^2 = \frac{S_{Pooled}^2}{N_2} \qquad (9\text{-}3)$$

The variance of the distribution of means for the second population (based on an estimated population variance) is the pooled estimate of the population variance divided by the number of participants in the sample from the second population.

Consider again the study with 11 participants in the experimental group and 31 participants in the control group. We figured the pooled estimate of the population variance to be 75. So for the experimental group, the variance of the distribution of means would be 75/11, which is 6.82. For the control group, the variance would be 75/31, which is 2.42.

The variance of the distribution of differences between means is the variance of the distribution of means for the first population (based on an estimated population variance) plus the variance of the distribution of means for the second population (based on an estimated population variance).

The standard deviation of the distribution of differences between means is the square root of the variance of the distribution of differences between means.

variance of a distribution of differences between means ($S^2_{\text{Difference}}$) One of the numbers figured as part of a *t* test for independent means; it equals the sum of the variances of the distributions of means for each of the two samples.

standard deviation of a distribution of differences between means ($S_{\text{Difference}}$) In a *t* test for independent means, square root of the variance of the distribution of differences between means.

In terms of formulas,

$$S^2_{M_1} = \frac{S^2_{\text{Pooled}}}{N_1} = \frac{75}{11} = 6.82$$

$$S^2_{M_2} = \frac{S^2_{\text{Pooled}}}{N_2} = \frac{75}{31} = 2.42$$

The Variance and Standard Deviation of the Distribution of Differences between Means

The **variance of the distribution of differences between means** ($S^2_{\text{Difference}}$) is the variance of Population 1's distribution of means plus the variance of Population 2's distribution of means. (This is because in a difference between two numbers, the variation in each contributes to the overall variation in their difference. It is like subtracting a moving number from a moving target.) Stated as a formula,

(9-4)
$$S^2_{\text{Difference}} = S^2_{M_1} + S^2_{M_2}$$

The **standard deviation of the distribution of differences between means** ($S_{\text{Difference}}$) is the square root of the variance:

(9-5)
$$S_{\text{Difference}} = \sqrt{S^2_{\text{Difference}}}$$

In the example we have been considering, the variance of the distribution of means for the experimental group was 6.82, and the variance of the distribution of means for the control group was 2.42. The variance of the distribution of the difference between means is thus 6.82 plus 2.42, which is 9.24. This makes the standard deviation of this distribution the square root of 9.24, which is 3.04. In terms of the formulas,

$$S^2_{\text{Difference}} = S^2_{M_1} + S^2_{M_2} = 6.82 + 2.42 = 9.24$$

$$S_{\text{Difference}} = \sqrt{S^2_{\text{Difference}}} = \sqrt{9.24} = 3.04$$

Steps to Find the Standard Deviation of the Distribution of Differences between Means

Ⓐ Figure the estimated population variances based on each sample. That is, figure one estimate for each population using the formula $S^2 = [\Sigma(X - M)^2]/(N - 1)$.

Ⓑ Figure the pooled estimate of the population variance:
$$S^2_{\text{Pooled}} = \frac{df_1}{df_{\text{Total}}}(S^2_1) + \frac{df_2}{df_{\text{Total}}}(S^2_2)$$
$$(df_1 = N_1 - 1 \text{ and } df_2 = N_2 - 1; df_{\text{Total}} = df_1 + df_2)$$

Ⓒ Figure the variance of each distribution of means:
$$S^2_{M_1} = S^2_{\text{Pooled}}/N_1 \text{ and } S^2_{M_2} = S^2_{\text{Pooled}}/N_2$$

Ⓓ Figure the variance of the distribution of differences between means:
$$S^2_{\text{Difference}} = S^2_{M_1} + S^2_{M_2}$$

Ⓔ Figure the standard deviation of the distribution of differences between means:
$$S_{\text{Difference}} = \sqrt{S^2_{\text{Difference}}}$$

The Shape of the Distribution of Differences between Means

The distribution of differences between means is based on estimated population variances. Thus, the distribution of differences between means (the comparison distribution) is a *t* distribution. The variance of this distribution is figured based on population variance estimates from two samples. Therefore, the degrees of freedom for this *t* distribution are the sum of the degrees of freedom of the two samples. In terms of a formula,

$$df_{Total} = df_1 + df_2 \qquad (9\text{-}6)$$

> The total degrees of freedom is the degrees of freedom in the first sample plus the degrees of freedom in the second sample.

In the example we have been considering with an experimental group of 11 participants and a control group of 31 participants, we saw earlier that the total degrees of freedom is 40 ($11 - 1 = 10$; $31 - 1 = 30$; and $10 + 30 = 40$). To determine the *t* score needed for significance, you look up the cutoff point in the *t* table in the row with 40 degrees of freedom. Suppose you were conducting a one-tailed test using the .05 significance level. The *t* table in the Appendix (Table A–2) shows a cutoff of 1.684 for 40 degrees of freedom. That is, for a result to be significant, the difference between the means has to be at least 1.684 standard deviations above the mean difference of 0 on the distribution of differences between means.

The *t* Score for the Difference between the Two Actual Means

Here is how you figure the *t* score for Step ❹ of the hypothesis testing: First, figure the difference between your two samples' means. (That is, subtract one from the other.) Then, figure out where this difference is on the distribution of differences between means. You do this by dividing your difference by the standard deviation of this distribution. In terms of a formula,

$$t = \frac{M_1 - M_2}{S_{Difference}} \qquad (9\text{-}7)$$

> The *t* score is the difference between the two sample means divided by the standard deviation of the distribution of differences between means.

For our example, suppose the mean of the first sample is 198 and the mean of the second sample is 190. The difference between these two means is 8 (that is, $198 - 190 = 8$). Earlier we figured the standard deviation of the distribution of differences between means in this example to be 3.04. That would make a *t* score of 2.63 (that is, $8/3.04 = 2.63$). In other words, in this example the difference between the two means is 2.63 standard deviations above the mean of the distribution of differences between means. In terms of the formula,

$$t = \frac{M_1 - M_2}{S_{Difference}} = \frac{198 - 190}{3.04} = 2.63$$

How are you doing?

1. (a) When would you carry out a *t* test for independent means? (b) How is this different from the situation in which you would carry out a *t* test for dependent means?
2. (a) What is the comparison distribution in a *t* test for independent means? (b) Explain the logic of going from scores in two samples to an estimate of the

variance of this comparison distribution. (c) Illustrate your answer with sketches of the distributions involved. (d) Why is the mean of this distribution 0?

3. Write the formula for each of the following: (a) pooled estimate of the population variance, (b) variance of the distribution of means for the first population, (c) variance of the distribution of differences between means, and (d) t score in a t test for independent means. (e) Define all the symbols used in these formulas.

4. Explain (a) why a t test for independent means uses a single pooled estimate of the population variance, (b) why, and (c) how this estimate is "weighted."

5. For a particular study comparing means of two samples, the first sample has 21 participants and an estimated population variance of 100; the second sample has 31 participants and an estimated population variance of 200. (a) What is the standard deviation of the distribution of differences between means? (b) What is its mean? (c) What will be its shape? (d) Illustrate your answer with sketches of the distributions involved.

Answers

1. (a) When you have done a study in which you have scores from two samples of different individuals and you do not know the population variance. (b) In a t test for dependent means you have two scores from each of several individuals.

2. (a) A distribution of differences between means. (b) You estimate the population variance from each sample's scores. You assume the populations have the same variance, so that both estimates are estimates of the same thing. Thus, you then pool these two estimates (giving proportionately more weight in this averaging to the sample that has more degrees of freedom in its estimate). Using this pooled estimate, you figure the variance of the distribution of means for each sample's population by dividing this pooled estimate by the sample's number of participants. Finally, since your interest is in a difference between means, you create a comparison distribution of differences between means. This comparison distribution will have a variance equal to the sum of the variances of the two distributions of means. (The distribution of differences between means is made up of pairs of means, one taken from each distribution of means. Thus, the variance of both of these distributions of means contribute to the variance of the comparison distribution.) (c) Your sketch should look like Figure 9–1. (d) It will have a mean of zero because if the null hypothesis is true, the two populations have the same mean. So, differences between means would on the average come out to zero.

3. (a) $S_{Pooled}^2 = \frac{df_1}{df_{Total}}(S_1^2) + \frac{df_2}{df_{Total}}(S_2^2)$

(b) $S_{M_1}^2 = \frac{S_{Pooled}^2}{N_1}$

(c) $S_{Difference}^2 = S_{M_1}^2 + S_{M_2}^2$

(d) $t = \frac{M_1 - M_2}{S_{Difference}}$

(e) S_{Pooled}^2 is the pooled estimate of the population variance; df_1 and df_2 are the degrees of freedom of the samples from the first and second populations, respectively; df_{Total} is the total degrees of freedom (the sum of df_1 and df_2); S_1^2 and S_2^2 are the population variance estimates based on the samples from the first and second populations, respectively; $S_{M_1}^2$ is the variance of the distribution of means for the first population based on an estimated variance of the population of individuals; N_1 is the number of participants in the sample from the first population; $S^2_{Difference}$ is the variance of the distribution of differences between means based on estimated variances of the populations of individuals; t is the t score for a t test for independent means (the number of standard deviations from the mean on the distribution of differences between means); M_1 and M_2 are the means of the samples from the first and second populations, respectively; and $S_{Difference}$ is the standard deviation of the distribution of differences between means based on estimated variances of the population of individuals.

4. (a) You assume that both populations have the same variance; thus the estimates from the two samples should be estimates of the same number. (b) We weight (give more influence to) an estimate from a larger sample because, being based on more information, it is likely to be more accurate. (c) The actual weighting is done by multiplying each sample's estimate by the degrees of freedom for that sample divided by the total degrees of freedom; you then sum these two products.

5. (a) $S^2_{Pooled} = (20/50)(100) + (30/50)(200) = 40 + 120 = 160$; $S^2_{M_1} = 160/21 = 7.62$; $S^2_{M_2} = 160/31 = 5.16$; $S^2_{Difference} = 7.62 + 5.16 = 12.78$; $S_{Difference} = \sqrt{12.78} = 3.57$. (b) 0; (c) t distribution with $df = 50$; (d) Should look like Figure 9-1 with numbers written in (see Figure 9-2 for an example).

Hypothesis Testing with a *t* Test for Independent Means

Considering the five steps of hypothesis testing, there are three new wrinkles for a *t* test for independent means: (a) The comparison distribution is now a distribution of differences between means (this affects Step ❷); (b) the degrees of freedom for finding the cutoff on the *t* table is based on two samples (this affects Step ❸); and (c) your sample's score on the comparison distribution is based on the difference between your two means (this affects Step ❹).

Example of a *t* Test for Independent Means

Let's return to the expressive writing study example from the start of the chapter. Twenty students were recruited to take part in the study. The 10 students randomly assigned to the expressive writing group wrote about their thoughts and feelings associated with their most traumatic life events. The 10 students randomly assigned to the control group wrote about their plans for the day. One month later, all of the students rated their overall level of physical health on a scale from $0 = very\ poor\ health$ to $100 = perfect\ health$.

The scores and figuring for the *t* test are shown in Table 9–1. Figure 9–2 shows the distributions involved. Let's go through the five steps of hypothesis testing.

❶ **Restate the question as a research hypothesis and a null hypothesis about the populations.** There are two populations:

Population 1: Students who do expressive writing.
Population 2: Students who write about a neutral topic (their plans for the day).

The researchers were interested in whether there was a positive or a negative health effect of expressive writing. Thus, the research hypothesis was that

Table 9-1 *t* Test for Independent Means for a Fictional Study of the Effect of Expressive Writing on Physical Health

Expressive Writing Group			Control Writing Group		
Score	Deviation from Mean (Score – M)	Squared Deviation from Mean	Score	Deviation from Mean (Score – M)	Squared Deviation from Mean
77	−2	4	87	19	361
88	9	81	77	9	81
77	−2	4	71	3	9
90	11	121	70	2	4
68	−11	121	63	−5	25
74	−5	25	50	−18	324
62	−17	289	58	−10	100
93	14	196	63	−5	25
82	3	9	76	8	64
79	0	0	65	−3	9
Σ: 790		850	680		1002

$M_1 = 79.00; S_1^2 = 850/9 = 94.44; M_2 = 68.00; S_2^2 = 1002/9 = 111.33$

$N_1 = 10; df_1 = N_1 - 1 = 9; N_2 = 10; df_2 = N_2 - 1 = 9$

$df_{Total} = df_1 + df_2 = 9 + 9 = 18$

$S_{Pooled}^2 = \dfrac{df_1}{df_{Total}}(S_1^2) + \dfrac{df_2}{df_{Total}}(S_2^2) = \dfrac{9}{18}(94.44) + \dfrac{9}{18}(111.33) = 47.22 + 55.67 = 102.89$

$S_{M_1}^2 = S_{Pooled}^2 / N_1 = 102.89/10 = 10.29$

$S_{M_2}^2 = S_{Pooled}^2 / N_2 = 102.89/10 = 10.29$

$S_{Difference}^2 = S_{M_1}^2 + S_{M_2}^2 = 10.29 + 10.29 = 20.58$

$S_{Difference} = \sqrt{S_{Difference}^2} = \sqrt{20.58} = 4.54$

Needed *t* with $df = 18$, 5% level, two-tailed $= \pm 2.101$

$t = (M_1 - M_2)/S_{Difference} = (79.00 - 68.00)/4.54 = 2.42$

Decision: Reject the null hypothesis.

Population 1 students would rate their health differently than Population 2 students (a two-tailed test). The null hypothesis was that Population 1 students would rate their health the same as Population 2 students.

❷ **Determine the characteristics of the comparison distribution.** The comparison distribution is a distribution of differences between means. (a) Its mean is 0 (as it almost always is in a *t* test for independent means, because we are interested in whether there is more than 0 difference between the two populations). (b) Regarding its standard deviation,

ⓐ **Figure the estimated population variances based on each sample.** As shown in Table 9–1, S_1^2 comes out to 94.44 and $S_2^2 = 111.33$.

ⓑ **Figure the pooled estimate of the population variance:** As shown in Table 9–1, the figuring for S_{Pooled}^2 gives a result of 102.89.

ⓒ **Figure the variance of each distribution of means:** Dividing S_{Pooled}^2 by the *N* in each sample, as shown in Table 9–1, gives $S_{M_1}^2 = 10.29$ and $S_{M_2}^2 = 10.29$.

ⓓ **Figure the variance of the distribution of differences between means:** Adding up the variances of the two distributions of means, as shown in Table 9–1, comes out to $S_{Difference}^2 = 20.58$.

TIP FOR SUCCESS

In this example, note that the value for $S_{M_1}^2$ is the same as the value for $S_{M_2}^2$. This is because there are the same number of students in the two groups (that is, N_1 was the same as N_2). When the number of individuals in the two groups is not the same, the values for $S_{M_1}^2$ and $S_{M_2}^2$ will be different.

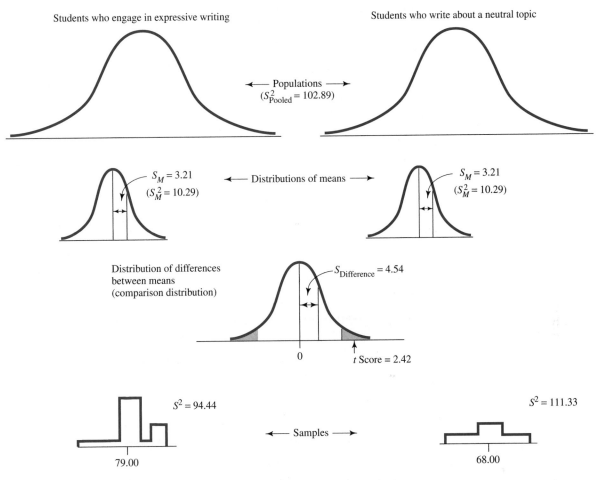

Figure 9-2   The distributions for a *t* test for independent means for the expressive writing example.

❷ **Figure the standard deviation of the distribution of differences between means:** $S_{\text{Difference}} = \sqrt{S^2_{\text{Difference}}} = \sqrt{20.58} = 4.54$.

The shape of this comparison distribution will be a *t* distribution with a total of 18 degrees of freedom.

❸ **Determine the cutoff sample score on the comparison distribution at which the null hypothesis should be rejected.** This requires a two-tailed test because the researchers were interested in an effect in either direction. As shown in Table A–2 (in the Appendix), the cutoff *t* scores at the .05 level are 2.101 and –2.101.

❹ **Determine your sample's score on the comparison distribution.** The *t* score is the difference between the two sample means (79.00 − 68.00, which is 11.00), divided by the standard deviation of the distribution of differences between means (which is 4.54). This comes out to 2.42.

❺ **Decide whether to reject the null hypothesis.** The *t* score of 2.42 for the difference between the two actual means is larger than the cutoff *t* score of 2.101. You can reject the null hypothesis. The research hypothesis is supported: Students who do expressive writing report a higher level of health than students who write about a neutral topic.

The actual numbers in this study were fictional. However, the result are consistent with those from many previous studies that have shown beneficial effects of expressive writing on self-reported health outcomes, as well as on other outcomes, such as psychological well-being (e.g., Pennebaker & Beall, 1986; see also Lepore & Smyth, 2002; Smyth, 1998).

Summary of Steps for Conducting a *t* Test for Independent Means

Table 9–2 summarizes the steps for a *t* test for independent means.[1]

Table 9-2   Steps for a *t* Test for Independent Means

❶ **Restate the question as a research hypothesis and a null hypothesis about the populations.**

❷ **Determine the characteristics of the comparison distribution.**

   a. Its mean will be 0.

   b. Figure its standard deviation.

   Ⓐ Figure the estimated population variances based on each sample. For each population, $S^2 = [\Sigma(X - M)^2]/(N - 1)$.

   Ⓑ Figure the pooled estimate of the population variance:

$$S^2_{\text{Pooled}} = \frac{df_1}{df_{\text{Total}}}(S^2_1) + \frac{df_2}{df_{\text{Total}}}(S^2_2)$$

   $(df_1 = N_1 - 1$ and $df_2 = N_2 - 1; df_{\text{Total}} = df_1 + df_2)$

   Ⓒ Figure the variance of each distribution of means: $S^2_{M_1} = S^2_{\text{Pooled}}/N_1$ and $S^2_{M_2} = S^2_{\text{Pooled}}/N_2$

   Ⓓ Figure the variance of the distribution of differences between means:

$$S^2_{\text{Difference}} = S^2_{M_1} + S^2_{M_2}$$

   Ⓔ Figure the standard deviation of the distribution of differences between means:
$$S_{\text{Difference}} = \sqrt{S^2_{\text{Difference}}}$$

   c. The comparison distribution will be a *t* distribution with df_{Total} degrees of freedom.

❸ **Determine the cutoff sample score on the comparison distribution at which the null hypothesis should be rejected.**

   a. Determine the degrees of freedom (df_{Total}), desired significance level, and tails in the test (one or two).

   b. Look up the appropriate cutoff in a *t* table. If the exact *df* is not given, use the *df* below it.

❹ **Determine your sample's score on the comparison distribution:**

   $t = (M_1 - M_2)/S_{\text{Difference}}$

❺ **Decide whether to reject the null hypothesis:** Compare the scores from Steps ❸ and ❹.

---

[1]The steps of figuring the standard deviation of the distribution of differences between means can be combined into a single overall computational formula:

(9-8)
$$S_{\text{Difference}} = \sqrt{\frac{(N_1 - 1)(S^2_1) + (N_2 - 1)(S^2_2)}{N_1 + N_2 - 2}\left(\frac{1}{N_1} + \frac{1}{N_2}\right)}$$

As usual, we urge you to use the full set of steps and the regular, definitional formulas in your figuring when doing the practice problems in this book. Those steps help you learn the basic principles. However, this computational formula will be useful if statistics software is not available and you have to figure by hand a *t* test for independent means on scores from a real study with many participants in each group.

A Second Example of a *t* Test for Independent Means

Suppose a researcher wants to study the effectiveness of a new job skills training program for people who have not been able to hold a job. Fourteen people who have not been able to hold a job agree to be in the study. The researcher randomly picks 7 of these volunteers to be an experimental group that will go through the special training program. The other 7 volunteers are put in a control group that will go through an ordinary job skills training program. After finishing their training program (of whichever type), all 14 are placed in similar jobs.

A month later, each volunteer's employer is asked to rate how well the new employee is doing using a 9-point scale. The scores and figuring for the *t* test are shown in Table 9–3. The distributions involved are shown in Figure 9–3. Let's carry out the analysis, following the five steps of hypothesis testing.

❶ **Restate the question as a research hypothesis and a null hypothesis about the populations.** There are two populations:

Population 1: Individuals who could not hold a job who then participate in the special job skills program.
Population 2: Individuals who could not hold a job who then participate in an ordinary job skills program.

Table 9-3   Figuring for a *t* Test for Independent Means for the Job Skills Example

Experimental Group (Receiving Special Program)			Control Group (Receiving Ordinary Program)		
Score	Deviation From Mean	Squared Deviation From Mean	Score	Deviation From Mean	Squared Deviation From Mean
6	0	0	6	3	9
4	−2	4	1	−2	4
9	3	9	5	2	4
7	1	1	3	0	0
7	1	1	1	−2	4
3	−3	9	1	−2	4
6	0	0	4	1	1
Σ: 42	0	24	21	0	26

$M_1 = 6$; $S_1^2 = 24/6 = 4$; $M_2 = 3$; $S_2^2 = 26/6 = 4.33$

$N_1 = 7$; $df_1 = N_1 - 1 = 6$; $N_2 = 7$; $df_2 = N_2 - 1 = 6$

$df_{Total} = df_1 + df_2 = 6 + 6 = 12$

$S_{Pooled}^2 = \dfrac{df_1}{df_{Total}}(S_1^2) + \dfrac{df_2}{df_{Total}}(S_2^2) = \dfrac{6}{12}(4) + \dfrac{6}{12}(4.33) = .5(4) + .5(4.33) = 2.00 + 2.17 = 4.17$

$S_{M_1}^2 = S_{Pooled}^2/N_1 = 4.17/7 = .60$

$S_{M_2}^2 = S_{Pooled}^2/N_2 = 4.17/7 = .60$

$S_{Difference}^2 = S_{M_1}^2 + S_{M_2}^2 = .60 + .60 = 1.20$

$S_{Difference} = \sqrt{S_{Difference}^2} = \sqrt{1.20} = 1.10$

Needed *t* with $df = 12$, 5% level, two-tailed $= \pm 2.179$

$t = (M_1 - M_2)/S_{Difference} = (6.00 - 3.00)/1.10 = 3.00/1.10 = 2.73$

Decision: Reject the null hypothesis, the research hypothesis is supported.

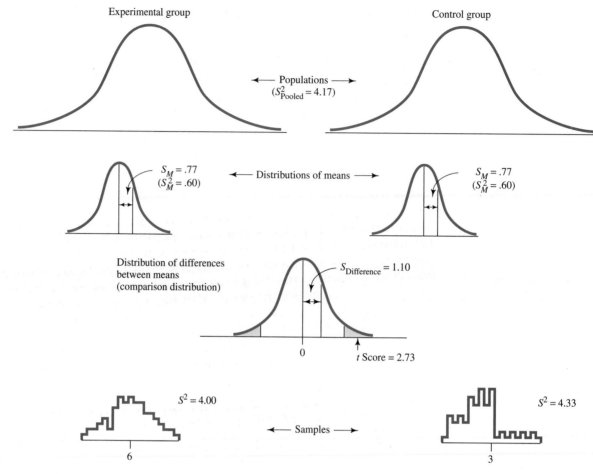

Figure 9-3 The distributions involved in the job skills example of a *t* test for independent means.

It is possible for the special program to have either a positive or a negative effect compared to the ordinary program, and either result would be of interest. Thus, the research hypothesis is that the means of Population 1 and Population 2 are different. This is a nondirectional hypothesis. The null hypothesis is that the means of Population 1 and Population 2 are the same.

❷ **Determine the characteristics of the comparison distribution.**

a. Its mean will be 0.

b. Figure its standard deviation. See Table 9–3 for the figuring for each step below.

   Ⓐ **Figure the estimated population variances based on each sample.** $S_1^2 = 4$ and $S_2^2 = 4.33$.

   Ⓑ **Figure the pooled estimate of the population variance.** $S_{Pooled}^2 = 4.17$.

   Ⓒ **Figure the variance of each distribution of means.** Dividing S_{Pooled}^2 by the N in each sample gives $S_{M_1}^2 = .60$ and $S_{M_2}^2 = .60$.

   Ⓓ **Figure the variance of the distribution of differences between means.** Adding up the variances of the two distribution of means comes out to $S_{Difference}^2 = 1.20$.

❶ **Figure the standard deviation of the distribution of differences between means.** $S_{\text{Difference}} = \sqrt{1.20} = 1.10$.

c. It is a t distribution with $df_{\text{Total}} = 12$.

❸ **Determine the cutoff sample score on the comparison distribution at which the null hypothesis should be rejected.** The cutoff you need is for a two-tailed test (because the research hypothesis is nondirectional) at the usual .05 level, with 12 degrees of freedom. Looking this up on the t table in the Appendix, the cutoff t scores are 2.179 and -2.179.

❹ **Determine your sample's score on the comparison distribution.** The t score is the difference between the two sample means divided by the standard deviation of the distribution of differences between means. This comes out to a t of 2.73. (That is, $t = 3.00/1.10 = 2.73$.)

❺ **Decide whether to reject the null hypothesis.** The t score of 2.73 is more extreme than the cutoff t score of 2.179. Thus, the researchers can reject the null hypothesis. The research hypothesis is supported: The new special job skills program is more effective than the ordinary job skills program.

How are you doing?

1. List the ways in which hypothesis testing for a t test for independent means is different from a t test for dependent means in terms of (a) Step ❷, (b) Step ❸, and (c) Step ❹.

2. Using the .05 significance level, two-tailed, figure a t test for independent means for an experiment in which scores in an experimental condition are predicted to be lower than scores in a control condition. For the experimental condition, with 26 participants, $M = 5$, $S^2 = 10$; for the control condition, with 36 participants, $M = 8$, $S^2 = 12$. (a) Use five the steps of hypothesis testing. (b) Sketch the distributions involved.

Answers

1. (a) The comparison distribution for a t test for independent means is a distribution of differences between means. (b) The degrees of freedom for a t test for independent means is the sum of the degrees of freedom for the two samples. (c) The t score for a t test for independent means is based on differences between means (divided by the standard deviation of the distribution of differences between means).

2. (a) Steps of hypothesis testing:

❶ **Restate the question as a research hypothesis and a null hypothesis about the populations.** There are two populations.

Population 1: People given the experimental procedure.
Population 2: People given the control procedure.

The research hypothesis is that the mean of Population 1 is less than the mean of Population 2. The null hypothesis is that the mean of Population 1 is not less than the mean of Population 2.

❷ **Determine the characteristics of the comparison distribution.**
a. Its mean will be 0.
b. Figure its standard deviation.
❹ **Figure the estimated population variances based on each sample.** $S_1^2 = 10$ and $S_2^2 = 12$.

❶ **Figure the pooled estimate of the population variance.**
$S^2_{Pooled} = (25/60)(10) + (35/60)(12) = 4.17 + 7.00 = 11.17$.

❷ **Figure the variance of each distribution of means.**
$S^2_{M_1} = 11.17/26 = .43$ and $S^2_{M_2} = 11.17/36 = .31$.

❸ **Figure the variance of the distribution of differences between means.** $S^2_{Difference} = .43 + .31 = .74$.

❹ **Figure the standard deviation of the distribution of differences between means.** $S_{Difference} = \sqrt{.74} = .86$.

c. It is a t distribution with $df_{Total} = 60$.

❷ **Determine the cutoff sample score on the comparison distribution at which the null hypothesis should be rejected.** The t cutoff for the .05 level, one-tailed, $df = 60$ is -1.671. (The cutoff is a negative t score, as the research hypothesis is that the mean of Population 1 will be *lower* than the mean of Population 2.)

❸ **Determine your sample's score on the comparison distribution.** $t = (M_1 - M_2)/S_{Difference} = (5 - 8)/.86 = -3.49$.

❺ **Decide whether to reject the null hypothesis.** The t of -3.49 is more extreme than the cutoff t of -1.671. Therefore, reject the null hypothesis.

(b) The distributions involved are shown in Figure 9–4.

Assumptions of the *t* Test for Independent Means

The first assumption for a *t* test for independent means is the same as that for any *t* test: Each of the population distributions is assumed to follow a normal curve. In practice, this is only a problem if you have reason to think that the two populations are dramatically skewed distributions, and in opposite directions. The *t* test holds up well even when the shape of the population distributions is fairly far from normal.

In a *t* test for independent means, you also have to be able to assume that the two populations have the same variance. (You take advantage of this assumption when you average the estimates from each of the two samples.) Once again, however, it turns out that in practice the *t* test gives pretty accurate results even when there are fairly large differences in the population variances, particularly when there are equal or near equal numbers of scores in the two samples.

However, the *t* test can give quite misleading results if (a) the scores in the samples suggest that the populations are very far from normal (highly skewed), (b) the variances are very different, or (c) there are both problems. In these situations, there are alternatives to the ordinary *t* test procedure, some of which we will consider in Chapter 11.

Many computer programs for figuring the *t* test for independent means actually provide two sets of results. One set of results figures the *t* test assuming the population variances are equal. This method is the standard one, the one you have learned in this chapter. A second set of results uses a special alternative procedure that takes into account that the population variances may be unequal. (But it still assumes the populations follow a normal curve.) An example of these two sets of results is shown in the Using SPSS section at the end of this chapter (see Figure 9–8). However, in most situations we can assume that the population variances are equal. Thus, researchers usually use the standard method. Using the special alternative procedure has the advantage that you don't have to worry about whether you met the equal population variance assumption. But it has the disadvantage that if you have met that assumption,

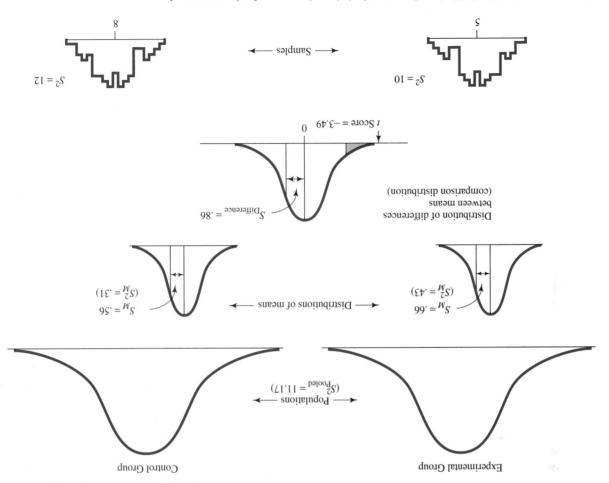

Figure 9–4   The distributions for a *t* test for independent means for the answer to the "How Are You Doing?" question 2.

with this special method you have less statistical power. That is, when you do meet the assumption, you would be less likely to get a significant result if you used the special method.

Effect Size and Power for the *t* Test for Independent Means

Effect Size

The effect size for the *t* test for independent means is the difference between the population means divided by the standard deviation of the population of individuals. When you have results of a completed study, you estimate the effect size as the difference between the sample means divided by the pooled estimate of the population standard deviation. (The pooled estimate of the population standard deviation is the square root of the pooled estimate of the population variance.) Stated as a formula,

$$\text{Estimated Effect Size} = \frac{M_1 - M_2}{S_{\text{Pooled}}} \qquad \textbf{(9-9)}$$

> The estimated effect size for a *t* test for independent means is the difference between the sample means divided by the pooled estimate of the population's standard deviation.

Cohen's (1988) conventions for the *t* test for independent means are the same as in all the situations we have considered so far: .20 for a small effect size, .50 for a medium effect size, and .80 for a large effect size.

Consider our example of the effectiveness of a special job skills program. The mean for the sample of individuals who participated in the special job skills program was 6.00. The mean for the sample of individuals who participated in the ordinary job skills program was 3.00. We figured the pooled estimate of the population variance to be 4.17; the pooled estimate of the population's standard deviation is thus 2.04. The difference in means of 3.00, divided by 2.04, gives an effect size of 1.47. This is a very large effect size. In terms of the formula,

$$\text{Estimated Effect Size} = \frac{M_1 - M_2}{S_{\text{Pooled}}} = \frac{6.00 - 3.00}{2.04} = 1.47$$

Power

Power for a *t* test for independent mean can be determined using a power table, a power software package, or an Internet power calculator. The power table shown in Table 9–4 gives the approximate power for the .05 significance level for small, medium, and large effect sizes, and one-tailed or two-tailed tests.[2]

For example, suppose you have read a study using a *t* test for independent means that had a nonsignificant result using the .05 significance level, two-tailed. There were 40 participants in each group. Should you conclude that there is in fact no difference

Table 9-4 Approximate Power for Studies Using the *t* Test for Independent Means Testing Hypotheses at the .05 Significance Level

Number of Participants in Each Group	Effect Size		
	Small (.20)	Medium (.50)	Large (.80)
One-tailed test			
10	.11	.29	.53
20	.15	.46	.80
30	.19	.61	.92
40	.22	.72	.97
50	.26	.80	.99
100	.41	.97	*
Two-tailed test			
10	.07	.18	.39
20	.09	.33	.69
30	.12	.47	.86
40	.14	.60	.94
50	.17	.70	.98
100	.29	.94	*

*Nearly 1.

[2]Cohen (1988, pp. 28–39) provides more detailed tables in terms of number of participants, levels of effect size, and significance levels. Note that Cohen describes the significance level by the letter *a* (for "alpha level"), with a subscript of either 1 or 2, referring to a one-tailed or two-tailed test. For example, a table that refers to "$a_1 = .05$" at the top means that this is the table for $p < .05$, one-tailed.

BOX 9–1   Two Women Make a Point about Gender and Statistics

One of the most useful advanced statistics books written so far is *Using Multivariate Statistics* by Barbara Tabachnick and Linda Fidell (2007), two experimental psychologists at California State University at Northridge. These two met at a faculty luncheon soon after Tabachnick was hired. Fidell recalls:

I had this enormous data set to analyze, and out came lots of pretty numbers in nice neat little columns, but I was not sure what all of it meant, or even whether my data had violated any critical assumptions. That was in 1975. I had been trained at the University of Michigan; I knew statistics up through the analysis of variance. But none of us were taught the multivariate analysis of variance at that time. Then along came these statistical packages to do it. But how to comprehend them?

Both Fidell and Tabachnick had gone out and learned on their own, taking the necessary courses, reading, asking others who knew the programs better, trying out what would happen if they did this with the data, what would happen if they did that. Now the two women asked each other, why must this be so hard? Were others reinventing this same wheel at the very same time? They decided to put their wheel into a book.

"And so began [many] years of conflict-free collaboration," reports Fidell. (That is something to compare to the feuds recounted in other boxes in this book.) The authors had no trouble finding a publisher, and the book, now in its fifth edition (Tabachnick & Fidell, 2007), has sold "nicely." In Fidell's opinion, statistics is a field in which women seem particularly to excel and feel comfortable.

Source: Personal interview with Linda Fidell.

---

at all in the populations? This conclusion seems quite unjustified. Table 9–4 shows a power of only .14 for a small effect size. This suggests that if such a small effect really exists in the populations, this study would probably not come out significant. Still, we can also conclude that if there is a true difference in the populations, it is probably not large. Table 9–4 shows a power of .94 for a large effect size. This suggests that if a large effect exists, it almost surely would have produced a significant result.

harmonic mean Special average influenced more by smaller numbers; in a *t* test for independent means when the number of scores in the two groups differ, the harmonic mean is used as the equivalent of each group's sample size when determining power.

Power When Sample Sizes Are Not Equal

For a study with any given total number of participants, power is greatest when the participants are divided into two equal groups. Recall the example from the start of this chapter where the 42 participants were divided into 11 in the experimental group and 31 in the control group. This study has much less power than it would have if the researchers had been able to divide their 42 participants into 21 in each group.

There is a practical problem in figuring power from tables when sample sizes are not equal. (Power software packages and Internet power calculators require you to specify the sample sizes, which are then taken into account when they figure power.) Like most power tables, Table 9–4 assumes equal numbers in each of the two groups. What do you do when your two samples have different numbers of people in them? It turns out that in terms of power, the **harmonic mean** of the numbers of participants in two unequal sample sizes gives the equivalent sample size for what you would have with two equal samples. The harmonic mean sample size is given by this formula:

$$\text{Harmonic Mean} = \frac{(2)(N_1)(N_2)}{N_1 + N_2} \tag{9-10}$$

The harmonic mean is two times the first sample size times the second sample size, all divided by the sum of the two sample sizes.

In our example with 11 in one group and 31 in the other, the harmonic mean is 16.24:

Table 9–5 Approximate Number of Participants Needed in Each Group (Assuming Equal Sample Sizes) for 80% Power for the *t* Test for Independent Means, Testing Hypotheses at the .05 Significance Level

	Effect Size		
	Small (.20)	**Medium (.50)**	**Large (.80)**
One-tailed	310	50	20
Two-tailed	393	64	26

$$\text{Harmonic Mean} = \frac{(2)(N_1)(N_2)}{N_1 + N_2} = \frac{(2)(11)(31)}{11 + 31} = \frac{682}{42} = 16.24$$

Thus, even though you have a total of 42 participants, the study has the power of a study with equal sample sizes of only about 16 in each group. (This means that a study with a total of 32 participants divided equally would have had about the same power.)

Planning Sample Size

Table 9–5 gives the approximate number of participants needed for 80% power for estimated small, medium, and large effect sizes, using one-tailed and two-tailed tests, all using the .05 significance level.[3] Suppose you plan a study in which you expect a medium effect size and will use the .05 significance level, one-tailed. Based on Table 9–5, you need 50 people in each group (100 total) to have 80% power. However, if you did a study using the same significance level but expected a large effect size, you would need only 20 people in each group (40 total).

How are you doing?

1. List two assumptions for the *t* test for independent means. For each, give the situations in which violations of these assumptions would be a serious problem.
2. Why do you need to assume the populations have the same variance?
3. What is the predicted effect size for a study in which the sample drawn from Population 1 has a mean of 17, Population 2's sample mean is 25, and the pooled estimate of the population standard deviation is 20?
4. What is the power of a study using a *t* test for independent means, with a two-tailed test at the .05 significance level, in which the researchers predict a large effect size and there are 20 participants in each group?
5. What is the approximate power of a study using a *t* test for independent means, with a two-tailed test at the .05 significance level, in which the researchers predict a large effect size, and there are 6 participants in one group and 34 participants in the other group?

---

[3]Cohen (1988, pp. 54–55) provides fuller tables, indicating needed numbers of participants for levels of power other than 80%; for effect sizes other than .20, .50, and .80; and for other significance levels.

6. How many participants do you need in each group for 80% power in a planned study in which you predict a small effect size and will be using a *t* test for independent means, one-tailed, at the .05 significance level?

Answers

1. One assumption is that the two populations are normally distributed; this is mainly a problem if you have reason to think the two populations are strongly skewed in opposite directions. A second assumption is that the two populations have the same variance; this is mainly a problem if you believe the two distributions have quite different variances *and* the sample sizes are quite different.
2. Because you make a pooled estimate of the population variance. The pooling would not make sense if the estimates from the two samples were for populations with different variances.
3. Predicted effect size = $(17 - 25)/20 = -8/20 = -.40$.
4. .69.
5. Harmonic mean = $(2)(6)(34)/(6 + 34) = 408/40 = 10.2$. Power for a study like this with 10 in each group = .39.
6. 310.

Review and Comparison of the Three Kinds of *t* Tests

You have now learned about three kinds of *t* tests: in Chapter 8, you learned about the *t* test for a single sample and the *t* test for dependent means; in this chapter you learned about the *t* test for independent means. Table 9–6 provides a review and comparison of these three kinds of *t* tests.

TIP FOR SUCCESS
We recommend that you spend some time carefully going through Table 9–6. Test your understanding of the three kinds of *t* tests by covering up portions of the table and trying to recall the hidden information. If you are at all unsure about any information in the table, be sure to review the relevant material in this chapter and in Chapter 8.

Table 9-6   Review of the Three Kinds of *t* Tests

Feature of the *t* Tests	Type of *t* Test		
	Single Sample	**Dependent Means**	**Independent Means**
Population variance is known	No	No	No
Population mean is known	Yes	No	No
Number of scores for each participant	1	2	1
t test carried out on difference scores	No	Yes	No
Shape of comparison distribution	*t* distribution	*t* distribution	*t* distribution
Formula for degrees of freedom	$df = N - 1$	$df = N - 1$	$df_{Total} = df_1 + df_2$ $(df_1 = N_1 - 1; df_2 = N_2 - 1)$
Formula for *t*	$t = (M - \text{Population } M)/S_M$	$t = (M - \text{Population } M)/S_M$	$t = (M_1 - M_2)/S_{Difference}$

The *t* Test for Independent Means in Research Articles

A *t* test for independent means is usually described in research articles by giving the means (and sometimes the standard deviations) of the two samples, plus the usual way of reporting any kind of *t* test—for example, $t(18) = 4.72$, $p < .01$. (Recall that the number in parentheses is the degrees of freedom.) The result of the study of the health effects of expressive writing might be written up as follows: "The mean level of self-reported health in the expressive writing group was 79.00 ($SD = 9.72$), and the mean for the control writing group was 68.00 ($SD = 10.55$), $t(18) = 2.42$, $p < .05$." (In most cases, articles do not say whether a test is two-tailed; they usually only mention tails when it is a one-tailed test.)

Table 9–7 is an example in which the results of several *t* tests are given in a table. This table is taken from a study conducted by Gibbons and colleagues (2006). In that study, 152 college students in Guatemala were surveyed on their beliefs about machismo (a strong sense of masculinity), their attitudes toward women, and their beliefs about adoption. As shown in Table 9–7, the researchers used three *t* tests for independent means to examine whether female and male students differed on these beliefs and attitudes. The scales were scored so that higher scores were for more positive attitudes about machismo, more egalitarian (equal) gender beliefs (which were measured using the Attitudes Towards Women Scale for Adolescents, abbreviated as AWSA in Table 9–7), and more favorable beliefs about adoption. The first line of the table shows that men (with a mean score of 1.32) had more positive attitudes about machismo than women (mean score of 1.17). The *t* score for this comparison was 4.77, and it was statistically significant at $p < .001$. The results in Table 9–7 also show that women had more positive attitudes toward women than men did and that women had more favorable beliefs regarding adoption than men. (The number after each $\pm$ sign is the standard deviation for that particular group.)

Table 9-7 Mean and Standard Deviation of Scores for Women and Men on Measures of Machismo, Attitudes toward Women, and Adoption Beliefs

	Women ($n = 64$)	Men ($n = 88$)	*t*	*p*
Machismo	$1.17 \pm .15$	$1.32 \pm .20$	4.77	<.001
AWSA	$3.26 \pm .31$	$2.98 \pm .35$	5.00	<.001
Adoption	$3.10 \pm .39$	$2.85 \pm .41$	3.07	<.01

Source: Gibbons, J. L., Wilson, S. L., & Rufener, C. A. (2006). Gender attitudes mediate gender differences in attitudes towards adoption in Guatemala. *Sex Roles, 54,* 139–145. Copyright © 2006. Reprinted by permission of Springer Science and Business Media.

Summary

1. A *t* test for independent means is used for hypothesis testing with scores from two entirely separate groups of people. The comparison distribution for a *t* test for independent means is a distribution of differences between means of samples. This distribution can be thought of as being built up in two steps: Each population of individuals produces a distribution of means, and then a new distribution

is created of differences between pairs of means selected from these two distributions of means.

2. The distribution of differences between means has a mean of 0 and is a *t* distribution with the total of the degrees of freedom from the two samples. Its standard deviation is figured in several steps:

   ❹ Figure the estimated population variances based on each sample.
   ❺ Figure the pooled estimate of the population variance.
   ❻ Figure the variance of each distribution of means.
   ❼ Figure the variance of the distribution of differences between means.
   ❽ Figure the standard deviation of the distribution of differences between means.

3. The assumptions of the *t* test for independent means are that the two populations are normally distributed and have the same variance. However, the *t* test gives fairly accurate results when the true situation is moderately different from the assumptions.

4. Estimated effect size for a *t* test for independent means is the difference between the sample means divided by the pooled estimate of the population standard deviation. Power is greatest when the sample sizes of the two groups are equal. When they are not equal, you use the harmonic mean of the two sample sizes when looking up power on a table. Power for a *t* test for independent means can be determined using a table (see Table 9–4), a power software package, or an Internet power calculator.

5. *t* tests for independent means are usually reported in research articles with the means of the two groups plus the degrees of freedom, *t* score, and significance level. Results may also be reported in a table where each significant difference is shown by asterisks.

Key Terms

t test for independent means (p. 275)
distribution of differences between means (p. 276)
pooled estimate of the population variance (S^2_{Pooled}) (p. 278)

weighted average (p. 278)
variance of the distribution of differences between means ($S^2_{Difference}$) (p. 280)

standard deviation of the distribution of differences between means ($S_{Difference}$) (p. 280)
harmonic mean (p. 293)

Example Worked-Out Problems

Figuring the Standard Deviation of the Distribution of Differences between Means

Figure $S_{Difference}$ for the following study: $N_1 = 40$, $S^2_1 = 15$; $N_2 = 60$; $S^2_2 = 12$.

Answer

❹ **Figure the estimated population variances based on each sample:** $S^2_1 = 15$; $S^2_2 = 12$.

ⓑ Figure the pooled estimate of the population variance: $df_1 = N_1 - 1 = 40 - 1 = 39$; $df_2 = N_2 - 1 = 60 - 1 = 59$; $df_{Total} = df_1 + df_2 = 39 + 59 = 98$.

$$S^2_{Pooled} = \frac{df_1}{df_{Total}}(S^2_1) + \frac{df_2}{df_{Total}}(S^2_2) = (39/98)(15) + (59/98)(12)$$

$$= 5.97 + 7.22 = 13.19$$

ⓒ Figure the variance of each distribution of means: $S^2_{M_1} = S^2_{Pooled}/N_1 = 13.19/40 = .33$; $S^2_{M_2} = S^2_{Pooled}/N_2 = 13.19/60 = .22$

ⓓ Figure the variance of the distribution of differences between means: $S^2_{Difference} = S^2_{M_1} + S^2_{M_2} = .33 + .22 = .55$

ⓔ Figure the standard deviation of the distribution of differences between means: $S_{Difference} = \sqrt{S^2_{Difference}} = \sqrt{.55} = .74$

Hypothesis Testing Using the *t* Test for Independent Means

A researcher randomly assigns 5 individuals to receive a new experimental procedure and 5 to a control condition. At the end of the study, all 10 are measured. Scores for those in the experimental group were 7, 6, 9, 7, and 6. Scores for those in the control group were 5, 2, 4, 3, and 6. Carry out a *t* test for independent means using the .05 level of significance, two-tailed. Use the steps of hypothesis testing and sketch the distributions involved.

Answer

The figuring is shown in Table 9–8; the distributions are shown in Figure 9–5. Here are the steps of hypothesis testing.

❶ **Restate the question as a research hypothesis and a null hypothesis about the populations.** There are two populations:

Population 1: People like those who receive the experimental procedure.
Population 2: People like those who receive the control procedure.

The research hypothesis is that the means of the two populations are different. The null hypothesis is that the means of the two populations are the same.

❷ **Determine the characteristics of the comparison distribution.**
 a. The distribution of differences between means has a mean of 0.
 b. Figure its standard deviation.
  ⓐ **Figure the estimated population variances based on each sample:** $S^2_1 = 1.50$; $S^2_2 = 2.50$.
  ⓑ **Figure the pooled estimate of the population variance:** $S^2_{Pooled} = 2.00$.
  ⓒ **Figure the variance of each distribution of means:** $S^2_{M_1} = .40$; $S^2_{M_2} = .40$.
  ⓓ **Figure the variance of the distribution of differences between means:** $S^2_{Difference} = .80$.
  ⓔ **Figure the standard deviation of the distribution of differences between means:** $S_{Difference} = .89$.
 c. The shape of the comparison distribution is a *t* distribution with $df_{Total} = 8$.

❸ **Determine the cutoff sample score on the comparison distribution at which the null hypothesis should be rejected.** With $df_{Total} = 8$, .05 significance level, two-tailed test, the cutoffs are 2.306 and −2.306.

Table 9-8 Figuring for Example Worked-Out Problem for Hypothesis Testing Using the *t* Test Independent Means

Experimental Group			Control Group		
Score	Deviation From Mean	Squared Deviation From Mean	Score	Deviation From Mean	Squared Deviation From Mean
7	0	0	5	1	1
6	−1	1	2	−2	4
9	2	4	4	0	0
7	0	0	3	−1	1
6	−1	1	6	2	4
Σ: 35	0	6	20	0	10

$M_1 = 7$; $S_1^2 = 6/4 = 1.50$; $M_2 = 4$; $S_2^2 = 10/4 = 2.50$

$N_1 = 5$; $df_1 = N_1 - 1 = 4$; $N_2 = 5$; $df_2 = N_2 - 1 = 4$

$df_{Total} = df_1 + df_2 = 4 + 4 = 8$

$S_{Pooled}^2 = \dfrac{df_1}{df_{Total}}(S_1^2) + \dfrac{df_2}{df_{Total}}(S_2^2) = \dfrac{4}{8}(1.50) + \dfrac{4}{8}(2.50) = .75 + 1.25 = 2.00$

$S_{M_1}^2 = S_{Pooled}^2/N_1 = 2.00/5 = .40$

$S_{M_2}^2 = S_{pooled}^2/N_2 = 2.00/5 = .40$

$S_{Difference}^2 = S_{M_1}^2 + S_{M_2}^2 = .40 + .40 = .80$

$S_{Difference} = \sqrt{S_{Difference}^2} = \sqrt{.80} = .89$

Needed *t* with $df = 8$, 5% level, two-tailed $= \pm 2.306$

$t = (M_1 - M_2)/S_{Difference} = (7 - 4)/.89 = 3/.89 = 3.37$

Decision: Reject the null hypothesis; the research hypothesis is supported.

❹ **Determine the sample's score on the comparison distribution.** $t = (7 - 4)/.89 = 3.37$.

❺ **Decide whether to reject the null hypothesis.** The *t* of 3.37 is more extreme than the cutoffs of ± 2.306. Thus, you can reject the null hypothesis. The research hypothesis is supported.

Finding Power When Sample Sizes Are Unequal

A planned study with a predicted small effect size has 22 in one group and 51 in the other. What is the approximate power for a one-tailed test at the .05 significance level?

Answer

$$\text{Harmonic Mean} = \frac{(2)(N_1)(N_2)}{N_1 + N_2} = \frac{(2)(22)(51)}{22 + 51} = \frac{2244}{73} = 30.7$$

From Table 9–4, for a one-tailed test with 30 participants in each group, power for a small effect size is .19.

Outline for Writing Essays for a *t* Test for Independent Means

1. Describe the core logic of hypothesis testing in this situation. Be sure to mention that the *t* test for independent means is used for hypothesis testing when you have

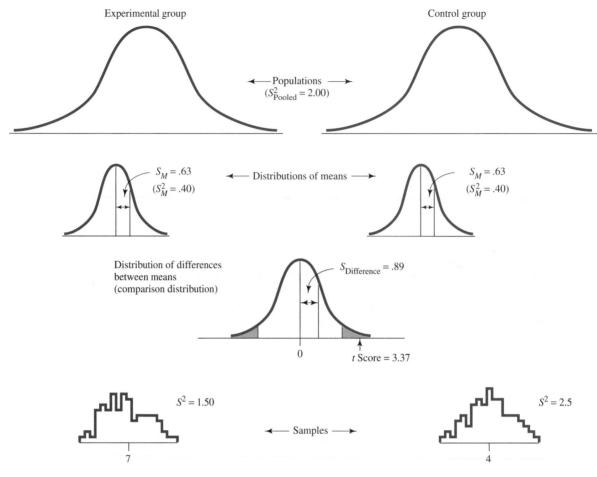

Figure 9-5 The distributions in the Example Worked-Out Problem for hypothesis testing using the *t* test for independent means.

scores from two entirely separate groups of people. Be sure to explain the meaning of the research hypothesis and the null hypothesis in this situation.

2. Explain the entire complex logic of the comparison distribution that is used with a *t* test for independent means (the distribution of differences between means). Be sure to explain why you use 0 as its mean. (This and point 3 will be the longest part of your essay.)

3. Outline the logic of estimating the population variance and the variance of the two distributions of means. Describe how to figure the standard deviation of the distribution of differences between means.

4. Explain why the shape of the comparison distribution that is used with a *t* test for independent means is a *t* distribution (as opposed to the normal curve).

5. Describe the logic and process for determining the cutoff sample score(s) on the comparison distribution at which the null hypothesis should be rejected.

6. Describe why and how you figure the *t* score of the sample mean on the comparison distribution.

7. Explain how and why the scores from Steps ❸ and ❹ of the hypothesis-testing process are compared. Explain the meaning of the result of this comparison with regard to the specific research and null hypotheses being tested.

Practice Problems

These problems involve figuring. Most real-life statistics problems are done on a computer with special statistical software. Even if you have such software, do these problems by hand to ingrain the method in your mind. To learn how to use a computer to solve statistics problems like those in this chapter, refer to the *Using SPSS* section at the end of this chapter and the *Student's Study Guide and SPSS Workbook* that accompanies this text.

All data are fictional unless an actual citation is given.

Set I (for answers, see pp. 447–448)

1. For each of the following studies, say whether you would use a *t* test for dependent means or a *t* test for independent means.
   (a) An education researcher randomly assigns a group of 47 fourth-grade students to receive a new after-school math program and 48 other fourth-grade students to receive the standard after-school math program, and then measures how well they all do on a math test.
   (b) A marketing researcher measures 100 doctors' reports of the number of their patients asking them about a particular drug during the month before and the month after a major advertising campaign.
   (c) A researcher tests reaction time of each of a group of 14 individuals twice, once while in a very hot room and once while in a normal-temperature room.

2. Figure $S_{Difference}$ for each of the following studies:

Study	N_1	S_1^2	N_2	S_2^2
(a)	20	1	20	2
(b)	20	1	40	2
(c)	40	1	20	2
(d)	40	1	40	2
(e)	40	1	40	4

3. For each of the following experiments, decide if the difference between conditions is statistically significant at the .05 level (two-tailed).

	Experimental Group			Control Group		
Study	N	M	S^2	N	M	S^2
(a)	30	12.0	2.4	30	11.1	2.8
(b)	20	12.0	2.4	40	11.1	2.8
(c)	30	12.0	2.2	30	11.1	3.0

4. A communication researcher randomly assigned 82 volunteers to one of two experimental groups. Sixty-one were instructed to get their news for a month only from television, and 21 were instructed to get their news for a month only from the Internet. (Why the researcher didn't assign equal numbers to the two conditions is a mystery!) After the month was up, all participants were tested on their knowledge of several political issues. The researcher did not have a prediction as to which news source would make people more knowledgeable. That is, the researcher simply predicted that there is some kind of difference. These were the results of the study. TV group: $M = 24$, $S^2 = 4$; Internet group: $M = 26$, $S^2 = 6$. Using the .01 level, what should the researcher conclude? (a) Use the steps of hypothesis testing; (b) sketch the distributions involved; and (c) explain your

answers to someone who is familiar with the *t* test for a single sample, but not with the *t* test for independent means.

5. A teacher was interested in whether using a student's own name in a story affected children's attention span while reading. Six children were randomly assigned to read a story under ordinary conditions (using names like Dick and Jane). Five other children read versions of the same story, but with each child's own name substituted for one of the children in the story. The teacher kept a careful measure of how long it took each child to read the story. The results are shown below. Using the .05 level, does including the child's name make any difference? (a) Use the steps of hypothesis testing; (b) sketch the distributions involved; and (c) explain your answers to someone who has never had a course in statistics.

Ordinary Story		Own-Name Story	
Student	Reading Time	Student	Reading Time
A	2	G	4
B	5	H	8
C	7	I	10
D	9	J	9
E	6	K	8
F	7		

6. A developmental researcher compares 4-year-olds and 8-year-olds on their ability to understand the analogies used in stories. The scores for the five 4-year-olds tested were 7, 6, 2, 3, and 8. The scores for the three 8-year-olds tested were 9, 2, and 5. Using the .05 level, do older children do better? (a) Use the steps of hypothesis testing; (b) sketch the distributions involved; and (c) explain your answers to someone who understands the *t* test for a single sample, but does not know anything about the *t* test for independent means.

7. Figure the estimated effect size for problems (a) 4, (b) 5, and (c) 6. (d) Explain what you have done in part (a) to someone who understands the *t* test for independent means but knows nothing about effect size.

8. Figure the approximate power of each of the following planned studies, all using a *t* test for independent means at the .05 significance level, one-tailed, with a predicted small effect size:

Study	N_1	N_2
(a)	3	57
(b)	10	50
(c)	20	40
(d)	30	30

9. What are the approximate numbers of participants needed for each of the following planned studies to have 80% power, assuming equal numbers in the two groups and all using the .05 significance level? (Be sure to give the total number of participants needed, not just the number needed for each group.)

Study	Expected Means		Expected S_{Pooled}	Tails
	M_1	M_2		
(a)	107	149	84	1
(b)	22.5	16.2	31.5	2
(c)	14	12	2.5	1
(d)	480	520	50	2

10. Van Aken and Asendorpf (1997) studied 139 German 12-year-olds. All of the children completed a general self-worth questionnaire and were interviewed about the supportiveness they experienced from their mothers, fathers, and classmates. The researchers then compared the self-worth of those with high and low levels of support of each type. The researchers reported that "lower general self-worth was found for children with a low-supportive mother ($t(137) = 4.52$, $p < .001$, d[effect size] $= 0.78$) and with a low-supportive father ($t(137) = 4.03$, $p < .001$, d[effect size] $= 0.69$). . . . A lower general self-worth was also found for children with only low-supportive classmates ($t(137) = 2.04$, $p < .05$, d[effect size] $= 0.35$)." ("d" in the above is a symbol for effect size.) (a) Explain what these results mean to a person who has never had a course in statistics. (b) Include a discussion of effect size and power. (When figuring power, you can assume that the two groups in each comparison had about equal sample sizes.)

11. Gallagher-Thompson, Dal Canto, Jacob, and Thompson (2001) compared 27 wives who were caring for their husbands who had Alzheimer's disease to 27 wives in which neither partner had Alzheimer's disease. The two groups of wives were otherwise similar in terms of age, number of years married, and social economic status. Table 9–9 (reproduced from their Table 1) shows some of their results. Focusing on the Geriatric Depression Scale (the first row of the table) and the Mutuality Scale for Shared Values (the last row in the table), explain these results to a person who knows about the *t* test for a single sample, but is unfamiliar with the *t* test for independent means.

Set II

12. Make up two examples of studies (not in the book or from your lectures) that would be tested with a *t* test for independent means.

Table 9-9   Comparison of Caregiving and Noncaregiving Wives on Select Psychosocial Variables

	Caregiving Wives (*n* = 27)			Noncaregiving Wives (*n* = 27)				
	M	*SD*	Range	*M*	*SD*	Range	*t*	*p*
Geriatric Depression Scale[a]	9.42	6.59	1–25	2.37	2.54	0–8	5.14	.0001
Perceived Stress Scale[b]	22.29	8.34	6–36	15.33	6.36	7–30	3.44	.001
Hope questionnaire[c]								
Agency	11.88	1.63	9–16	13.23	1.39	10–16	3.20	.002
Resilience	11.89	0.91	10–14	13.08	1.60	10–16	3.31	.002
Total	23.77	2.03	21–29	26.31	2.56	22–31	3.97	.0001
Mutuality Scale[d]								
Closeness	3.51	.81	.33–4	3.70	.41	2.67–4	−1.02	.315
Reciprocity	2.25	1.19	.17–4	3.25	.55	1.67–4	−3.68	.001
Shared pleasures	2.65	1.00	0–4	3.52	.61	1.75–4	−3.66	.001
Shared values	3.15	.89	0–4	3.46	.45	2.4–4	−1.51	.138

Note: For all measures, higher scores indicate more of the construct being measured.
[a]Maximum score is 30.
[b]Maximum score is 56.
[c]Four questions in each subscale, with a maximum total score of 32.
[d]Maximum mean for each subscale is 4.
Source: Gallagher-Thompson, D., Dal Canto, P. G., Jacob, T., & Thompson, L. W. (2001). A comparison of marital interaction patterns between couples in which the husband does or does not have Alzheimer's disease. *The Journals of Gerontology Series B: Psychological Sciences and Social Sciences, 56,* 5140–5150. Copyright © 2001 by the Gerontological Society of America. Reprinted by permission of the publishers.

13. For each of the following studies, say whether you would use a *t* test for dependent means or a *t* test for independent means.
    (a) A researcher measures the heights of 40 college students who are the firstborn in their families and compares the 15 who come from large families to the 25 who come from smaller families.
    (b) A researcher tests performance on a math skills test of each of 250 individuals before and after they complete a one-day seminar on managing test anxiety.
    (c) A researcher compares the resting heart rate of 15 individuals who have been taking a particular drug to the resting heart rate of 48 other individuals who have not been taking this drug.

14. Figure $S_{\text{Difference}}$ for each of the following studies:

Study	N_1	S_1^2	N_2	S_2^2
(a)	30	5	20	4
(b)	30	5	30	4
(c)	30	5	50	4
(d)	20	5	30	4
(e)	30	5	20	2

15. For each of the following experiments, decide if the difference between conditions is statistically significant at the .05 level (two-tailed).

	Experimental Group			Control Group		
Study	N	M	S^2	N	M	S^2
(a)	10	604	60	10	607	50
(b)	40	604	60	40	607	50
(c)	10	604	20	40	607	16

16. A researcher theorized that people can hear better when they have just eaten a large meal. Six individuals were randomly assigned to eat either a large meal or a small meal. After eating the meal, their hearing was tested. The hearing ability scores (high numbers indicate greater ability) are given below. Using the .05 level, do the results support the researcher's theory? (a) Use the steps of hypothesis testing, (b) sketch the distributions involved, and (c) explain your answers to someone who has never had a course in statistics.

Big Meal Group		Small Meal Group	
Subject	Hearing	Subject	Hearing
A	22	D	19
B	25	E	23
C	25	F	21

17. Twenty students randomly assigned to an experimental group receive an instructional program; 30 in a control group do not. After 6 months, both groups are tested on their knowledge. The experimental group has a mean of 38 on the test (with an estimated population standard deviation of 3); the control group has a mean of 35 (with an estimated population standard deviation of 5). Using the .05 level, what should the experimenter conclude? (a) Use the steps of hypothesis testing; (b) sketch the distributions involved; and (c) explain your answer to someone who is familiar with the *t* test for a single sample, but not with the *t* test for independent means.

18. A study of the effects of color on easing anxiety compared anxiety test scores of participants who completed the test printed on either soft yellow paper or on harsh green paper. The scores for five participants who completed the test printed on the yellow paper were 17, 19, 28, 21, and 18. The scores for four participants who completed the test on the green paper were 20, 26, 17, and 24. Using the .05 level, one-tailed (predicting lower anxiety scores for the yellow paper), what should the researcher conclude? (a) Use the steps of hypothesis testing; (b) sketch the distributions involved; and (c) explain your answers to someone who is familiar with the *t* test for a single sample, but not with the *t* test for independent means.

19. Figure the estimated effect size for problems (a) 16, (b) 17, and (c) 18. (d) Explain your answer to part (a) to a person who understands the *t* test for independent means but is unfamiliar with effect size.

20. What is the approximate power of each of the following planned studies, all using a *t* test for independent means at the .05 significance level, two-tailed, with a predicted medium effect size?

Study	N_1	N_2
(a)	90	10
(b)	50	50
(c)	6	34
(d)	20	20

21. What are the approximate numbers of participants needed for each of the following planned studies to have 80% power, assuming equal numbers in the two groups and all using the .05 significance level? (Be sure to give the total number of participants needed, not just the number needed for each group.)

Study	Expected Means M_1	M_2	Expected S_{Pooled}	Tails
(a)	10	15	25	1
(b)	10	30	25	1
(c)	10	30	40	1
(d)	10	15	25	2

22. Escudero, Rogers, and Gutierrez (1997) videotaped 30 couples discussing a marital problem in their laboratory. The videotapes were later systematically rated for various aspects of the couple's communication, such as domineeringness and the positive or negative quality of affect (emotion) expressed between them. A major interest of their study was to compare couples who were having relationship problems with those who were not. The 18 couples in the group having problems were recruited from those who had gone to a marital clinic for help; they were called the Clinic group. The 12 couples in the group not having problems were recruited through advertisements and were called the Nonclinic group. (The two groups in fact had dramatically different scores on a standard test of marital satisfaction.) Table 9–10 presents some of their results. (You can ignore the arrows and plus and minus signs, which have to do with how they rated the interactions. Also, ignore the note at the bottom about "arcsine transformation.") (a) Focusing on Domineeringness and Submissiveness, explain these results to a person who has never had a course in statistics. (b) Include a discussion of effect size and power. (When figuring power, you can assume that the two groups in each comparison had about equal sample sizes.)

23. Jackson, Ervin, Gardner, and Schmitt (2001) gave a questionnaire about Internet usage to college students. Table 9–11 (their Table 1) shows their results comparing

Table 9-10 Base-Rate Differences between Clinic and Nonclinic Couples on Relational Control and Nonverbal Affect Codes Expressed in Proportions (*SD*s in Parentheses)

	Couple Status		Between-Group Differences
	Clinic Mean	**Nonclinic Mean**	***t***
Domineeringness (↑)	.452 (107)	.307 (.152)	3.06*
Levelingness (→)	.305 (.061)	.438 (.065)	5.77**
Submissiveness (↓)	.183 (.097)	.226 (.111)	1.12
Double-codes	.050 (.028)	.024 (.017)	2.92*
Positive affect (+)	.127 (.090)	.280 (.173)	3.22*
Negative affect (−)	.509 (.192)	.127 (.133)	5.38**
Neutral affect (0)	.344 (.110)	.582 (.089)	6.44**
Double-codes (+/−)	.019 (.028)	.008 (.017)	2.96*

Note: Proportions of each control and affect code were converted using arcsine transformation for use in between-group comparisons. *$p < .01$, **$p < .001$, (d.f. = 28).
Source: Escudero, V., Rogers, L. E., & Gutierrez, E. (1997). Patterns of relational control and nonverbal affect in clinic and nonclinic couples. *Journal of Social and Personal Relationships, 14,* 5–29. Copyright © 1997 by Sage Publications, Ltd. Reprinted by permission of Sage Publications, Thousand Oaks, London and New Delhi.

Table 9-11 Gender Differences in Internet Use and Potential Mediators

	Males[a]	**Females[b]**	***t*-value**	***df***	***p*-value**
E-mail use	4.16 (0.66)	4.30 (0.57)	2.81	626	.005
Web use	3.57 (0.67)	3.30 (0.67)	−4.84	627	.000
Overall internet use	3.86 (0.58)	3.80 (0.53)	−1.44	627	.130
Computer anxiety	1.67 (0.56)	1.80 (0.57)	4.03	612	.000
Computer self-efficacy	3.89 (0.52)	3.71 (0.62)	−3.49	608	.001
Loneliness	2.06 (0.64)	1.96 (0.64)	−1.88	607	.061
Depression	1.22 (0.32)	1.28 (0.34)	2.36	609	.019
E-mail privacy	4.04 (0.78)	4.10 (0.69)	−0.97	609	.516
E-mail trust	3.50 (0.77)	3.46 (0.75)	−0.65	610	.516
Web privacy	4.06 (0.74)	4.09 (0.71)	0.62	623	.534
Web trust	3.14 (0.73)	3.12 (0.73)	−0.28	624	.780
Web search success	4.05 (0.85)	4.13 (0.81)	1.12	568	.262
Importance of computer skills	2.54 (1.03)	2.31 (0.90)	−2.57	477	.011
Computers cause health problems	2.67 (1.00)	3.00 (1.08)	3.36	476	.001
Gender stereotypes about computer skills	3.45 (1.15)	4.33 (0.96)	−8.95	476	.000
Racial/ethnic stereotypes about computer skills	3.63 (1.17)	3.99 (1.07)	3.40	477	.001
Computers are taking over	3.08 (1.19)	2.87 (1.08)	−1.89	476	.059

Note: For the attitude items, 1 = strongly agree, 2 = strongly disagree. For gender, 1 = male, 2 = female. Numbers in parentheses are standard deviations.
[a]$n = 227$.
[b]$n = 403$.
Source: Jackson, L. A., Ervin, K. S., Gardner, P. D., & Schmitt, N. (2001). Gender and the Internet: Women communicating and men searching. *Sex Roles, 44,* 363–379. Copyright © 2001. Reprinted by permission of Springer Science and Business Media.

men and women. (a) Select one significant and one nonsignificant result and explain these two results to a person who understands the *t* test for a single sample but does not know anything about the *t* test for independent means. (b) Include a discussion of effect size and power (note that the sample sizes for the male and female groups are shown in the table footnote).

24. Do men or women have longer first names? Take out a phone book and use the following random numbers to select the pages: 12, 79, 10, 97, 53, 74, 15, 55, 41, 128, 57, 93, 94, 31, 68, 516, 60, 56, 7, 93, 43, 91, 57, 58, 38, 120, 14, 38, 57, 223, 98, 199. On the first page (page 12), look for the first clearly female name and write down how many letters it has. Do the same thing (find the page for the number, etc.) 16 times. Then continue, getting lengths for 16 male names. (You will have to exclude names for which you cannot tell the gender.) Carry out a *t* test for independent means using these two samples. (Be sure to note the city and year of the telephone book you used.)

Using SPSS

The ☞ in the steps below indicates a mouse click. (We used SPSS version 13.0 for Windows to carry out these analyses. The steps and output may be slightly different for other versions of SPSS.)

t Test for Independent Means

It is easier to learn these steps using actual numbers, so we will use the expressive writing example from earlier in the chapter. The scores for that example are shown in Table 9–1 on p. 284.

❶ Enter the scores into SPSS. SPSS assumes that all scores in a row are from the same person. In this example, each person is in only one of the two groups (*either* the expressive writing group *or* the control writing group). Thus, in order to tell SPSS which person is in each group, you should enter the numbers as shown in Figure 9–6. In the first column (labeled "group"), we used the number "1" to indicate that a person is in the expressive writing group and the number "2" to indicate that a person is in the control writing group. Each person's score on the health measure is listed in the second column (labeled "health").

❷ ☞ *Analyze.*

❸ ☞ *Compare means.*

❹ ☞ *Independent-Samples T Test* (this is the name SPSS uses for a *t* test for independent means).

❺ ☞ on the variable called "health" and then ☞ the arrow next to the box labeled "Test Variable(s)." This tells SPSS that the *t* test should be carried out on the scores for the "health" variable.

❻ ☞ the variable called "group" and then ☞ the arrow next to the box labeled "Grouping Variable." This tells SPSS that the variable called "group" shows which person is in which group. ☞ *Define Groups.* You now tell SPSS the values you used to label each group. Put "1" in the Group 1 box and put "2" in the Group 2 box. Your screen should now look like Figure 9–7. ☞ *Continue.*

❼ ☞ *OK.* Your SPSS output window should look like Figure 9–8.

The first table in the SPSS output provides information about the two variables. The first column gives the values of the grouping variable (1 and 2, which indicate the expressive

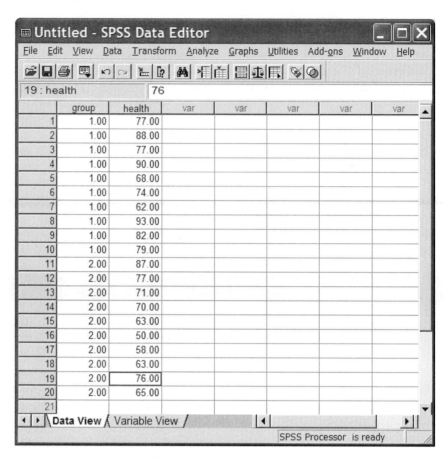

Figure 9–6 SPSS data editor window for the expressive writing example (in which 20 students were randomly assigned to be in an expressive writing group or a control writing group).

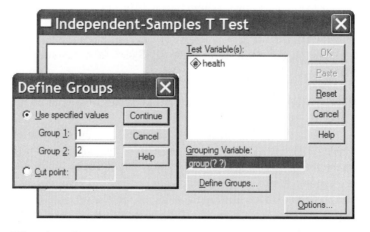

Figure 9–7 SPSS independent means *t* test window for the expressive writing example.

writing group and the control writing group, respectively). The second, third, and fourth columns give, respectively, the number of individuals (*N*), mean (*M*), and estimated population standard deviation (*S*) for each group. The fifth column, labeled "Std. error mean," is the standard deviation of the distribution of means, S_M, for each group. Note that these values for the standard error of the mean are based on each population variance estimate and not on the pooled estimate, so they are not quite the same for each group as the square root of each S_M^2 figured in the text. (See Table 9–1 for the figuring for this example.)

The second table in the SPSS output shows the actual results of the *t* test for independent means. Before the *t* test results, SPSS shows the results of "Levene's Test for Equality of Variances," which is a test of whether the *variances* of the two populations are the same. This test is important mainly as a check on whether you have met the assumption of equal population variances. (Recall the earlier section in this chapter on the Assumptions of the *t* Test for Independent Means.) If Levene's test is significant (that is, if the value in the "Sig." column is less than .05), this assumption of equal population variances is brought into question. However, in this example, the result is clearly not significant (.766 is well above .05), so we have no reason to doubt the assumption of equal population variances. Thus, we can feel more confident that whatever conclusion we draw from the *t* test will be accurate.

The *t* test results begin with the column labeled "t." Note that there are two rows of *t* test results. The first row (a *t* of 2.425, *df* of 18, and so on), labeled "Equal variances assumed" (on the left-hand side of the table), shows the *t* test results assuming the population variances are equal. The second row (a *t* of 2.425, *df* of 17.880, and so on), labeled "Equal variances not assumed," shows the *t* test results if we do not assume that the population variances are equal. In the present example (as in most real-life cases) Levene's test was not significant, so we use the *t* test results assuming equal population variances. Compare the values for "t" (the sample's *t* score), "df" (degrees of freedom), and "Std. Error Difference" (the standard deviation of the distribution of differences between means, $S_{\text{Difference}}$) from Figure 9–8 with their respective values

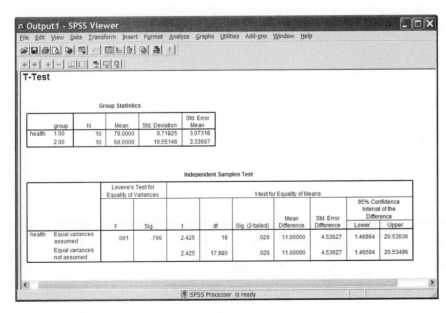

Figure 9–8 SPSS output window for a *t* test for independent means for the expressive writing example.

we figured by hand in Table 9–1. The column labeled "Sig. (2-tailed)" shows the exact significance level of the sample's *t* score. The significance level of .026 is less than our .05 cutoff for this example, which means that you can reject the null hypothesis and the research hypothesis is supported. (You can ignore the final two columns of the table, listed under the heading "95% Confidence Interval of the Difference." These columns refer to the raw scores corresponding to the *t* scores at the bottom 2.5% and the top 2.5% of the *t* distribution.) Note that SPSS does not know if you are doing a one-tailed or a two-tailed test. So it always gives results for a two-tailed test. If you are doing a one-tailed test, the true significance level is exactly half of what is given by SPSS. (For example, if the significance level given were .16, this would be equivalent to .08 for a one-tailed test.)

CHAPTER 10

Introduction to the Analysis of Variance

CHAPTER OUTLINE

- Basic Logic of the Analysis of Variance
- Carrying Out an Analysis of Variance
- Hypothesis Testing with the Analysis of Variance
- Assumptions in the Analysis of Variance
- Comparing Each Group to Each Other Group
- Effect Size and Power for the Analysis of Variance
- Factorial Analysis of Variance
- Recognizing and Interpreting Interaction Effects
- Analyses of Variance in Research Articles
- Summary
- Key Terms
- Example Worked-Out Problems
- Practice Problems
- Using SPSS

In Chapter 9, you learned about the *t* test for independent means, a procedure for comparing *two groups of scores* from *entirely separate groups of people* (such as an experimental group and a control group). In this chapter, you will learn about a procedure for comparing *more than two groups of scores,* each of which is from an *entirely separate group of people.*

We will begin with an example. Cindy Hazan and Phillip Shaver (1987) arranged to have the *Rocky Mountain News,* a large Denver area newspaper, print a mail-in survey. The survey included the question shown in Table 10–1 to measure what is called attachment style. Those who selected the first choice are "secure"; those who selected the second, "avoidant"; and those who selected the third, "anxious-ambivalent." These attachment styles are thought to be different ways of behaving and thinking in close relationships that develop from a person's experience with early caretakers (e.g., Shaver & Mikulincer, in press). Readers also answered questions about various aspects

> **TIP FOR SUCCESS**
>
> This chapter assumes you understand hypothesis testing and the *t* test, particularly the material on the distribution of means. So be sure you understand the relevant material in Chapters 5, 6, 8, and 9, before starting this chapter.

Table 10–1	Question Used in Hazan and Shaver (1987) Newspaper Survey

Which of the following best describes your feelings? [Check One]

[ ] I find it relatively easy to get close to others and am comfortable depending on them and having them depend on me. I don't often worry about being abandoned or about someone getting too close to me.

[ ] I am somewhat uncomfortable being close to others; I find it difficult to trust them completely, difficult to allow myself to depend on them. I am nervous when anyone gets too close, and often, love partners want me to be more intimate than I feel comfortable being.

[ ] I find that others are reluctant to get as close as I would like. I often worry that my partner doesn't really love me or won't want to stay with me. I want to merge completely with another person, and this desire sometimes scares people away.

Source: From Hazan & Shaver (1987), p. 515.

analysis of variance (ANOVA)
Hypothesis-testing procedure for studies with three or more groups.

of love, including amount of jealousy. Hazan and Shaver then compared the amount of jealousy reported by people with the three different attachment styles.

With a *t* test for independent means, Hazan and Shaver could have compared the mean jealousy scores of any two of the attachment styles. Instead, they were interested in differences among all three attachment styles. The statistical procedure for testing variation among the means of *more than two groups* is called the **analysis of variance,** abbreviated as **ANOVA.** (You could use the analysis of variance for a study with only two groups, but the simpler *t* test gives the same result.)

In this chapter, we introduce the analysis of variance, focusing on the fundamental logic, how to carry out an analysis of variance in the most basic situation, and how to make sense of more complicated forms of the analysis of variance when reading about them in research articles.

Basic Logic of the Analysis of Variance

The null hypothesis in an analysis of variance is that the several populations being compared all have the same mean. For example, in the attachment-style example, the null hypothesis is that the populations of secure, avoidant, and anxious-ambivalent people all have the same average degree of jealousy. The research hypothesis would be that the degree of jealousy is not the same among these three populations.

Hypothesis testing in analysis of variance is about whether the means of the samples differ more than you would expect if the null hypothesis were true. This question about *means* is answered, surprisingly, by analyzing *variances* (hence the name *analysis of variance*). Among other reasons, you focus on variances because when you want to know how several means differ, you are asking about the variation among those means.

Thus, to understand the logic of analysis of variance, we consider variances. In particular, we begin by discussing *two different ways* of estimating population variances. As you will see, the analysis of variance is about a comparison of the results of these two different ways of estimating population variances.

Estimating Population Variance from Variation within Each Sample

With the analysis of variance, as with the *t* test, you do not know the true population variances. However, as with the *t* test, you can estimate the variance of each of the populations from the scores in the samples. Also, as with the *t* test, you assume in the analysis of variance that all populations have the *same* variance. This allows you to average the population variance estimates from each sample into a single pooled estimate, called the **within-groups estimate of the population variance.** It is an average of estimates figured entirely from the scores *within* each of the samples.

One of the most important things to remember about this within-groups estimate of the population variance is that it is not affected by whether the null hypothesis is true. This estimate comes out the same whether the means of the populations are all the same (the null hypothesis is true) or whether the means of the populations are not all the same (the null hypothesis is false). This estimate comes out the same because it focuses only on the variation inside of each population. Thus, it doesn't matter how far apart the means of the different populations are.

If the variation in scores within each sample is not affected by whether the null hypothesis is true, what determines the level of within-group variation? The answer is that chance factors (that is, factors that are unknown to the researcher) account for why different people within a sample have different scores. These chance factors include the fact that different people respond differently to the same situation or treatment and that there may be some experimental error associated with the measurement of the variable of interest. Thus, we can think of the within-groups population variance estimate as an estimate based on chance (or unknown) factors that cause different people in a study to have different scores.

within-groups estimate of the population variance (S_{Within}^2) In analysis of variance, estimate of the variance of the distribution of the population of individuals based on the variation among the scores within each of the actual groups studied.

Estimating the Population Variance from Variation Between the Means of the Samples

There is also a second way to estimate the population variance. Each sample's mean is a number in its own right. If there are several samples, there are several such numbers, and these numbers will have some variation among them. The variation among these means gives another way to estimate the variance in the populations that the samples come from. Just how this works is a bit tricky, so follow the next two sections closely.

When the Null Hypothesis Is True.   First, consider the situation in which the null hypothesis is true. In this situation, all samples come from populations that have the *same mean.* Remember, we are always assuming that all populations have the same variance (and also that they are all normal curves). Thus, if the null hypothesis is true, all populations are identical and they have the same mean, variance, and shape.

However, even when the populations are identical (that is, even when the null hypothesis is true), the samples will each be a little different, and the sample means will each be a little different. How different can the sample means be? That depends on how much variation there is within each population. If a population has very little variation in the scores within it, then the means of samples from that population (or any identical population) will tend to be very similar to each other. When the null hypothesis is true, the variability among the sample means is influenced by the same chance (or unknown) factors that influence the variability among the scores within each sample.

What if several identical populations (with the same population mean) have a lot of variation in the scores within each? In that situation, if you take one sample from each population, the means of those samples could easily be very different from each other. Being very different, the variance of these means will be large. The point is that the more variance within each of several identical populations, the more variance there will be among the means of samples when you take a random sample from each population.

between-groups estimate of the population variance In an analysis of variance, estimate of the variance of the population of individuals based on the variation among the means of the groups studied.

Suppose you were studying samples of six children from each of three large playgrounds (the populations in this example). If each playground had children who were all either 7 or 8 years old, the means of your three samples would all be between 7 and 8. Thus, there would not be much variance among those means. However, if each playground had children ranging from 3 to 12 years old, the means of the three samples would probably vary quite a bit. What this shows is that the variation among the means of samples is related directly to the amount of variation within each of the populations from which the samples are taken. The more variation within each population, the more variation among the means of samples taken from those populations.

This principle is shown in Figure 10–1. The three identical populations on the left have small variances and the three identical populations on the right have large variances. In each set of three identical populations, even though the *means of the populations* are exactly the same, the *means of the samples* from those populations are not exactly the same. Most important, the means from the populations with less variance are closer together (have less variance among them). The means from the populations with more variance are more spread out (have more variance among them).

We have now seen that the variation among the means of samples taken from identical populations is related directly to the variation of the scores within each of those populations. This has a very important implication: It should be possible to estimate the variance within each population from the variation among the means of our samples.

Such an estimate is called a **between-groups estimate of the population variance.** (It has this name because it is based on the variation between the means of the samples, the "groups." Grammatically, it ought to be *among* groups; but *between* groups is traditional.) You will learn how to actually figure this estimate later in the chapter.

So far, all of this logic we have considered has assumed that the null hypothesis is true, so that there is no variation among the means of the *populations.* Let's now consider what happens when the null hypothesis is not true, and instead the research hypothesis is true.

When the Null Hypothesis Is Not True. If the null hypothesis is not true (and thus the research hypothesis is true), the populations themselves do not have the same mean. In this situation, variation among means of samples taken from these populations is still caused by the chance factors that cause variation within the populations. So, the larger the variation within the populations, the larger the variation among the means of samples taken from the populations. However, in this situation in which the research hypothesis is true, variation among the means of the samples is *also* caused by the variation among the population means. You can think of this variation among population means as resulting from a *treatment effect*—that is, the different treatment received by the groups (as in an experiment) causes the groups to have different means. So, when the research hypothesis is true, the means of the samples are spread out for two different reasons: (a) because of variation within each of the populations (due to unknown chance factors) and (b) because of variation among the means of the populations (that is, a treatment effect). The left side of Figure 10–2 shows populations with the same means and the means of samples taken from them. (This is the same situation as in both sides of Figure 10–1.) The right side of Figure 10–2 shows three populations with different means and the means of samples taken from them. (This is the situation we have just been discussing.) Notice that the means of the samples are more spread out in the situation on the right side of Figure 10–2. This is true even

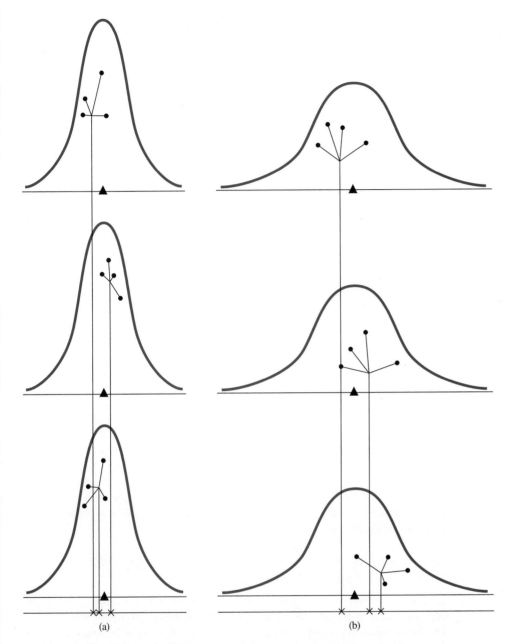

Figure 10-1   Means of samples from identical populations will not be identical. (a) Sample means from populations with less variation will vary less. (b) Sample means from populations with more variation will vary more. (Population means are indicated by a triangle, sample means by an X.)

though the variations within the populations are the same for the situation on both sides of Figure 10–2. The additional spread (variance) for the means on the right side of the figure is due to the populations having different means.

In summary, the between-groups estimate of the population variance is figured based on the variation among the means of the samples. If the null hypothesis is true, this estimate gives an accurate indication of the variation within the populations (that

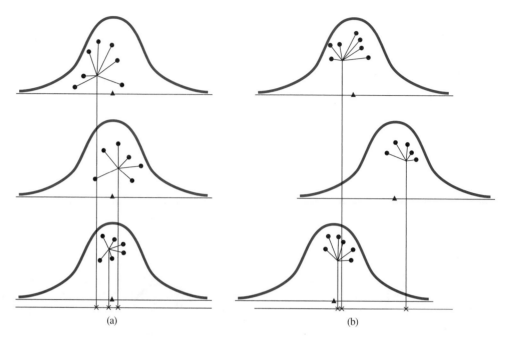

Figure 10–2 Means of samples from populations whose means differ (b) will vary more than sample means taken from populations whose means are the same (a). (Population means are indicated by a triangle, sample means by an X.)

is, the variation due to chance factors). But if the null hypothesis is false, this method of estimating the population variance is influenced both by the variation within the populations (the variation due to chance factors) and the variation among the population means (the variation due to a treatment effect). It will not give an accurate estimate of the variation within the populations, because it also will be affected by the variation among the populations. This difference has important implications. It is what makes the analysis of variance a method of testing hypotheses about whether there is a difference among means of groups.

Comparing the Within-Groups and Between-Groups Estimates of Population Variance

Table 10–2 summarizes what we have seen so far about the within-groups and between-groups estimates of population variance, both when the null hypothesis is true and when the research hypothesis is true. When the null hypothesis is true, the within-groups and between-groups estimates are based on the same thing (that is, the chance variation within populations). Literally, they are estimates of the same population variance. Therefore, when the null hypothesis is true, both estimates should be about the same. (Only *about* the same—these are estimates.) Here is another way of describing this similarity of the between-groups estimate and the within-groups estimate when the null hypothesis is true. In this situation, the ratio of the between-groups estimate to the within-groups estimate should be approximately 1 to 1. For example, if the within-groups estimate is 107.5, the between-groups estimate should be around 107.5, so that the ratio would be about 1. (A ratio is found by dividing one number by the other; thus 107.5/107.5 = 1.)

The situation is quite different when the null hypothesis is not true. As shown in Table 10–2, when the research hypothesis is true, the between-groups estimate is in-

Table 10-2 Sources of Variation in Within-Groups and Between-Groups Variance Estimates

	Variation Within Populations (Due to Chance Factors)	Variation Between Populations (Due to a Treatment Effect)
Null hypothesis is true		
Within-groups estimate reflects	✓	
Between-groups estimate reflects	✓	
Research hypothesis is true		
Within-groups estimate reflects	✓	
Between-groups estimate reflects	✓	✓

TIP FOR SUCCESS

Table 10–2 provides a useful summary of the logic of the analysis of variance. Test your understanding of this logic by trying to explain Table 10–2 without referring to the book. You might try writing your answer down and swapping it with someone else in your class.

fluenced by two sources of variation: (a) the variation of the scores within each population (due to chance factors), and (b) the variation of the means of the populations from each other (due to a treatment effect). Yet even when the research hypothesis is true, the within-groups estimate still is influenced *only* by the variation within the populations. Therefore, when the research hypothesis is true, the between-groups estimate should be *larger* than the within-groups estimate. In this situation, the ratio of the between-groups estimate to the within-groups estimate should be greater than 1. For example, the between-groups estimate might be 638.9 and the within-groups estimate 107.5, making a ratio of 638.9 to 107.5 or 5.94. That is, when we divide the larger, the between-groups estimate, by the smaller, the within-groups estimate, we get not 1 but more than 1 (in the example, $638.9/107.5 = 5.94$). In this example the between-groups estimate is nearly six times bigger (5.94 times to be exact) than the within-groups estimate.

This is the central principle of the analysis of variance: *When the null hypothesis is true, the ratio of the between-groups population variance estimate to the within-groups population variance estimate should be about 1. When the research hypothesis is true, this ratio should be greater than 1.* If you figure this ratio and it comes out much bigger than 1, you can reject the null hypothesis. That is, it is unlikely that the null hypothesis could be true and the between-groups estimate be a lot bigger than the within-groups estimate.

The *F* Ratio

This crucial ratio of the between-groups to the within-groups population variance estimate is called an ***F* ratio.** (The *F* is for Sir Ronald Fisher, an eminent statistician who developed the analysis of variance; see Box 10–1.)

The *F* Distribution and the *F* Table

We have said that if the crucial ratio of between-groups estimate to within-groups estimate (the *F* ratio) is a lot larger than 1, you can reject the null hypothesis. The next question is, just how much bigger than 1?

Statisticians have developed the mathematics of an ***F* distribution** and have prepared tables of *F* ratios. For any given situation, you merely look up in an ***F* table** how extreme an *F* ratio is needed to reject the null hypothesis at, say, the .05 level. (You learn to use the *F* table later in the chapter.)

For an example of an *F* ratio, let's return to the attachment-style study. The results of that study, for jealousy, were as follows: The between-groups population

***F* ratio** In analysis of variance, ratio of the between-groups population variance estimate to the within-groups population variance estimate; score on the comparison distribution (an *F* distribution) in an analysis of variance; also referred to simply as *F*.

***F* distribution** Mathematically defined curve that is the comparison distribution used in an analysis of variance; distribution of *F* ratios when the null hypothesis is true.

***F* table** Table of cutoff scores on the *F* distribution for various degrees of freedom and significance levels.

variance estimate was 23.27 and the within-groups population variance estimate was .53. (You will learn shortly how to figure these estimates on your own.) The ratio of the between-groups to the within-groups variance estimates (23.27/.53) came out to 43.91; that is, $F = 43.91$. This F ratio is considerably larger than 1. The F ratio needed to reject the null hypothesis at the .05 level in this study is only 3.01. Thus, the researchers confidently rejected the null hypothesis and concluded that amount of jealousy is not the same among the three attachment styles. (Mean jealousy ratings were 2.17 for secures, 2.57 for avoidants, and 2.88 for anxious-ambivalents.)

An Analogy

Some students find an analogy helpful in understanding the analysis of variance. The analogy is to what engineers call the signal-to-noise ratio. For example, your ability to make out the words in a staticky cell-phone conversation depends on the strength of the signal versus the amount of random noise. With the F ratio in the analysis of variance, the difference among the means of the samples is like the signal; it is the information of interest. The variation within the samples is like the noise. When the variation among the samples is sufficiently great in comparison to the variation within the samples, you conclude that there is a significant effect.

How are you doing?

1. When do you use an analysis of variance?
2. (a) What is the within-groups population variance estimate based on? (b) How and (c) why is it affected by the null hypothesis being true or not?
3. (a) What is the between-groups population variance estimate based on? (b) How and (c) why is it affected by the null hypothesis being true or not?
4. What are two sources of variation that can contribute to the between-groups population variance estimate?
5. (a) What is the F ratio; (b) why is it usually about 1 when the null hypothesis is true; and (c) why is it usually larger than 1 when the null hypothesis is false?

Answers

1. You use the analysis of variance when you are comparing means of samples from more than two populations.
2. (a) The variation of scores within each of the samples. (b) It is not affected. (c) Whether the null hypothesis is true has to do with whether the means of the populations differ. Thus, the within-groups estimate is not affected by whether the null hypothesis is true. This is because the variation each *within* each population (which is the basis for the variation within each sample) is not affected by whether the population means differ.
3. (a) The variation among the means of the samples. (b) It is larger when the null hypothesis is false. (c) Whether the null hypothesis is true has to do with whether the means of the populations differ. When the null hypothesis is false, the means of the populations differ. Thus, the between-groups estimate is bigger when the null hypothesis is false. This is because the variation among the means of the populations (which is one basis for the variation among the means of the samples) is greater when the population means differ.
4. Variation among the scores within each of the populations (that is, variation due to chance factors) and variation among the means of the populations (that is, variation due to a treatment effect).
5. (a) The ratio of the between-groups population variance estimate to the within-groups population variance estimate. (b) Because both estimates are based entirely on the same source of variation—the variation of the scores within each of the populations (that is due to chance factors). (c) Because the between-groups estimate is also influenced by the variation among the means of the populations (that is, a treatment effect), while the within-groups estimate is not. Thus, when the null hypothesis is false (meaning that the means of the populations are not the same), the between-groups estimate will be bigger than the within-groups estimate.

Carrying Out an Analysis of Variance

Having considered the basic logic of the analysis of variance, we will go through an example to illustrate the details. (We will use a fictional study to keep the numbers simple.)

Suppose a researcher is interested in the influence of knowledge of previous criminal record on juries' perceptions of the guilt or innocence of defendants. The researcher recruits fifteen volunteers who have been selected for jury duty (but have not yet served at a trial). The researcher shows them a videotape of a four-hour trial in which a woman is accused of passing bad checks. Before viewing the tape, however, all of the research participants are given a "background sheet" with age, marital status, education, and other such information about the accused woman. The sheet is the same for all fifteen participants, with one difference. For five of the participants, the last section of the sheet says that the woman has been convicted several times before for passing bad checks—we will call these participants the *Criminal Record Group.* For five other participants, the last section of the sheet says the woman has a completely clean criminal record—the *Clean Record Group.* For the remaining five participants, the sheet does not mention anything about criminal record one way or the other—the *No Information Group.*

The participants are randomly assigned to groups. After viewing the tape of the trial, all fifteen participants make a rating on a 10-point scale, which runs from completely sure she is innocent (1) to completely sure she is guilty (10). The results of this fictional study are shown in Table 10–3. As you can see, the means of the three groups are not the same (8, 4, and 5). Yet there is also quite a bit of variation within each of the three groups. Population variance estimates from the scores within each of these three groups are 4.5, 5.0, and 6.5.

You need to figure three numbers to test the hypothesis that the three populations are different: (a) a population variance estimate based on the variation of the scores within each of the samples, (b) a population variance estimate based on the differences among the group means, and (c) the ratio of the two, the F ratio. (In addition, we need the significance cutoff from an F table.)

Figuring the Within-Groups Estimate of the Population Variance

You can estimate the population variance from any one group (that is, from any one sample) using the usual method of estimating a population variance from a sample. First, you figure the sum of the squared deviation scores. That is, you take the devia-

Table 10-3 Results of the Criminal Record Study (Fictional Data)

	Criminal Record Group			Clean Record Group			No Information Group		
	Rating	Deviation from Mean	Squared Deviation from Mean	Rating	Deviation from Mean	Squared Deviation from Mean	Rating	Deviation from Mean	Squared Deviation from Mean
	10	2	4	5	1	1	4	−1	1
	7	−1	1	1	−3	9	6	1	1
	5	−3	9	3	−1	1	9	4	16
	10	2	4	7	3	9	3	−2	4
	8	0	0	4	0	0	3	−2	4
Σ:	40	0	18	20	0	20	25	0	26

$M = 40/5 = 8.$
$S^2 = 18/4 = 4.5.$

$M = 20/5 = 4.$
$S^2 = 20/4 = 5.0.$

$M = 25/5 = 5.$
$S^2 = 26/4 = 6.5.$

tion of each score from its group's mean, square that deviation score, and sum all the squared deviation scores. Second, you divide that sum of squared deviation scores by that group's degrees of freedom. (The degrees of freedom for a group are the number of scores in the group minus 1.) For the example, as shown in Table 10–3, this gives an estimated population variance of 4.5 based on the Criminal Record Group's scores, an estimate of 5.0 based on the Clean Record Group's scores, and an estimate of 6.5 based on the No Information Group's scores.

Once again, in the analysis of variance, as with the *t* test, we assume that the populations have the same variance. The estimates based on each sample's scores are all estimating the same true population variance. The sample sizes are equal in this example so that the estimate for each group is based on an equal amount of information. Thus, you can pool these variance estimates by straight averaging. This gives an overall estimate of the population variance based on the variation within groups of 5.33 (that is, the sum of 4.5, 5.0, and 6.5, which is 16, divided by 3, the number of groups).

The estimated population variance based on the variation of the scores within each of the groups is the within-groups variance estimate. This is symbolized as S^2_{Within}. In terms of a formula,

$$S^2_{\text{Within}} = \frac{S^2_1 + S^2_2 + \cdots + S^2_{\text{Last}}}{N_{\text{Groups}}} \qquad \text{(10-1)}$$

> The within-groups population variance estimate is the sum of the population variance estimates based on each sample, divided by the number of groups.

In this formula, S^2_1 is the estimated population variance based on the scores in the first group (the group from Population 1), S^2_2 is the estimated population variance based on the scores in the second group, and S^2_{Last} is the estimated population variance based on the scores in the last group. (The dots, or ellipses, in the formula show that you are to fill in a population variance estimate for as many other groups as there are in the analysis.) N_{Groups} is the number of groups. Using this formula for our figuring, we get

$$S^2_{\text{Within}} = \frac{S^2_1 + S^2_2 + \cdots + S^2_{\text{Last}}}{N_{\text{Groups}}} = \frac{4.5 + 5.0 + 6.5}{3} = \frac{16}{3} = 5.33.$$

Figuring the Between-Groups Estimate of the Population Variance

Figuring the between-groups estimate of the population variance involves two steps. You first estimate, from the means of your samples, the variance of a distribution of means. Second, based on the variance of this distribution of means, you figure the variance of the population of individuals. Here are the two steps in more detail:

❹ Estimate the variance of the distribution of means: Add up the sample means' squared deviations from the overall mean (the mean of all the scores) and divide this by the number of means minus 1.

You can think of the means of your samples as taken from a distribution of means. You follow the standard procedure of using the scores in a sample to estimate the variance of the population from which these scores are taken. In this situation, you think of the means of your samples as the scores and the distribution of means as the population from which these scores come. What this all boils down to are the following procedures. You begin by figuring the sum of squared deviations. (You find the mean of your sample means, figure the deviation of each sample mean from this mean of means, square each of these deviations, and then sum these squared deviations.) Then, divide this sum of squared deviations

grand mean (*GM*) In analysis of variance, overall mean of all the scores, regardless of what group they are in; when group sizes are equal, mean of the group means.

Table 10–4 Estimated Variance of the Distribution of Means Based on Means of the Three Experimental Groups in the Criminal Record Study (Fictional Data)

Sample Means	Deviation from Grand Mean	Squared Deviation from Grand Mean
(M)	*(M − GM)*	*(M − GM)²*
4	−1.67	2.79
8	2.33	5.43
5	−.67	.45
Σ 17	−0.01	8.67

$GM = (\Sigma M)/N_{\text{Groups}} = 17/3 = 5.67; S_M^2 = \Sigma(M - GM)^2/df_{\text{Between}} = 8.67/2 = 4.34.$

> The estimated variance of the distribution of means is the sum of each sample mean's squared deviation from the grand mean, divided by the degrees of freedom for the between-groups population variance estimate.

by the degrees of freedom, which is the number of means minus 1. In terms of a formula (when sample sizes are all equal),

(10-2)
$$S_M^2 = \frac{\Sigma(M - GM)^2}{df_{\text{Between}}}$$

In this formula, S_M^2 is the estimated variance of the distribution of means (estimated based on the means of the samples in your study). M is the mean of each of your samples. GM is the **grand mean,** the overall mean of all your scores, which is also the mean of your means. df_{Between} is the degrees of freedom in the between-groups estimate, the number of groups minus 1. Stated as a formula,

> The degrees of freedom for the between-groups population variance estimate is the number of groups minus 1.

(10-3)
$$df_{\text{Between}} = N_{\text{Groups}} - 1$$

In the criminal-record example, the three means are 8, 4, and 5. The figuring of S_M^2 is shown in Table 10–4.

ⓑ **Figure the estimated variance of the population of individual scores:** Multiply the variance of the distribution of means by the number of scores in each group.

What we have just figured in Step **ⓐ**, from a sample of a few means, is the estimated variance of a distribution of means. From this we want to estimate the variance of the population (the distribution of individuals) on which the distribution of means is based. We saw in Chapter 6 that the variance of a distribution of means is smaller than the variance of the population (the distribution of individuals) that it is based on. This is because means are less likely to be extreme than are individual scores (because several scores that are extreme in the same direction are unlikely to be included in any one sample). Specifically, you learned in Chapter 6 that the variance of a distribution of means is the variance of the distribution of individual scores divided by the number of scores in each sample.

Now, however, we are going to reverse what we did in Chapter 6. In Chapter 6 you figured the variance of the distribution of means by *dividing* the variance of the distribution of individuals by the sample size. Now you are going to figure the variance of the distribution of individuals by *multiplying* the variance of the distribution of means by the sample size (see Table 10–5). That is, to come up with the variance of the population of individuals, you multiply your estimate of the variance of the distribution of means by the sample size in each of the groups. The result of all this is the between-groups population variance estimate. Stated as a formula (for when sample sizes are equal),

> The between-groups population variance estimate is the estimated variance of the distribution of means multiplied by the number of scores in each group.

(10-4)
$$S_{\text{Between}}^2 = (S_M^2)(n)$$

Table 10-5   Comparison of Figuring the Variance of a Distribution of Means from the Variance of a Distribution of Individuals, and the Reverse
• From distribution of individuals to distribution of means: $S_M^2 = S^2/N$
• From distribution of means to distribution of individuals: $S^2 = (S_M^2)(N)$

In this formula, $S_{Between}^2$ is the estimate of the population variance based on the variation among the means (the between-groups population variance estimate); n is the number of participants in each sample.

Let's return to our example in which there were five participants in each sample and an estimated variance of the distribution of means of 4.34. In this example, multiplying 4.34 by 5 gives a between-groups population variance estimate of 21.70. In terms of the formula,

$$S_{Between}^2 = (S_M^2)(n) = (4.34)(5) = 21.70.$$

To summarize, the procedure of estimating the population variance based on the differences between group means is (a) figure the estimated variance of the distribution of means and then (b) multiply that estimated variance by the number of scores in each group.

Figuring the *F* Ratio

The *F* ratio is the ratio of the between-groups estimate of the population variance to the within-groups estimate of the population variance. Stated as a formula,

$$F = \frac{S_{Between}^2}{S_{Within}^2} \qquad (10\text{-}5)$$

> The *F* ratio is the between-groups population variance estimate divided by the within-groups population variance estimate.

In the example, the ratio of between and within is 21.70 to 5.33. Carrying out the division gives an *F* ratio of 4.07. In terms of the formula,

$$F = \frac{S_{Between}^2}{S_{Within}^2} = \frac{21.70}{5.33} = 4.07$$

The *F* Distribution

You are not quite done. You still need to find the cutoff for the *F* ratio that is large enough to reject the null hypothesis. This requires a distribution of *F* ratios that you can use to figure out what is an extreme *F* ratio.

In practice, you simply look up the needed cutoff in a table. To understand from where that number in the table comes, you need to understand the *F* distribution. The easiest way to understand this distribution is to think about how you would go about making one.

Start with three identical populations. Next, randomly select five scores from each. Then, on the basis of these three samples (of five scores each), figure the *F* ratio. (That is, you use these scores to make a between-groups estimate and a within-groups estimate and divide the first by the second.) Let's say that you do this and the *F* ratio you come up with is 1.36. Now you select three new random samples of five scores each and figure the *F* ratio using these three samples. Perhaps you get an *F* of 0.93. If you do this whole process many, many times, you will eventually get a lot of

> **TIP FOR SUCCESS**
>
> A very common mistake when figuring the *F* ratio is to turn the formula upside down. Just remember it is as simple as Black and White, so it is Between divided by Within.

between-groups degrees of freedom ($df_{Between}$) Degrees of freedom used in the between-groups estimate of the population variance in an analysis of variance (the numerator of the F ratio); number of scores free to vary (number of means minus 1) in figuring the between-groups estimate of the population variance; same as *numerator degrees of freedom*.

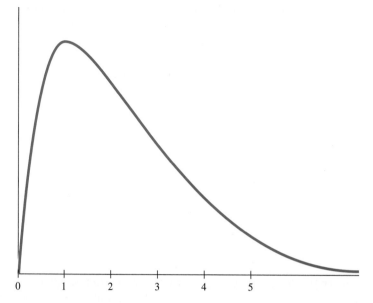

Figure 10–3 An F distribution.

F ratios. The distribution of all possible F ratios figured in this way (from random samples from identical populations) is called the F distribution. Figure 10–3 shows an example of an F distribution. (There are many different F distributions, and each has a slightly different shape. The exact shape depends on how many samples you take each time and how many scores are in each sample. The general shape is like that shown in the figure.)

No one actually goes about making F distributions in this way. It is a mathematical distribution whose exact characteristics can be found from a formula. Statisticians can also prove that if you had the patience to follow this procedure of taking random samples and figuring the F ratio of each for a very long time, you would get the same result.

As you can see in Figure 10–3, the F distribution is not symmetrical, but has a long tail on the right. The reason for this positive skew is that an F distribution is a distribution of ratios of variances. Variances are always positive numbers. (A variance is an average of squared deviations, and anything squared is a positive number.) A ratio of a positive number to a positive number can never be less than 0. Yet there is nothing to stop a ratio from being a very high number. Thus, the F ratios' distribution cannot be lower than 0 and can rise quite high. (Most F ratios pile up near 1, but they spread out more on the positive side, where they have more room to spread out.)

The F Table

The F table is a little more complicated than the t table. This is because there is a different F distribution according to both the degrees of freedom used in the between-groups variance estimate and the degrees of freedom used in the within-groups variance estimate. That is, you have to take into account two different degrees of freedom to look up the needed cutoff. One is the **between-groups degrees of freedom.** It is also called the *numerator degrees of freedom*. This is the degrees of freedom you use in the between-groups variance estimate, the numerator of the F ratio. As shown earlier in Formula 10-3, the degrees of freedom for the between-groups population variance estimate is the number of groups minus 1 ($df_{Between} = N_{Groups} - 1$).

The other type of degrees of freedom is the **within-groups degrees of freedom,** also called the *denominator degrees of freedom*. This is the sum of the degrees of freedom from each sample you use when figuring out the within-groups variance estimate, the denominator of the F ratio. Stated as a formula,

$$df_{Within} = df_1 + df_2 + \ldots + df_{Last} \tag{10-6}$$

In the criminal record study example, the between-groups degrees of freedom is 2. (There are 3 means, minus 1.) In terms of the formula,

$$df_{Between} = N_{Groups} - 1 = 3 - 1 = 2.$$

The within-groups degrees of freedom is 12. This is because each of the groups has 4 degrees of freedom on which the estimate is based (5 scores minus 1) and there are 3 groups overall, making a total of 12 degrees of freedom. In terms of the formula,

$$df_{Within} = df_1 + df_2 + \ldots + df_{Last} = (5-1) + (5-1) + (5-1) = 4 + 4 + 4 = 12.$$

You would look up the cutoff for an F distribution "with 2 and 12" degrees of freedom. As shown in Table 10–6, for the .05 level, you need an F ratio of 3.89 to reject the null hypothesis. (The full F table is Table A–3 in the Appendix.)

> The degrees of freedom for the within-groups population variance estimate is the sum of the degrees of freedom used in making estimates of the population variance from each sample.

within-groups degrees of freedom (df_{Within}) Degrees of freedom used in the within-groups estimate of the population variance in an analysis of variance (the denominator of the F ratio); number of scores free to vary (number of scores in each group minus 1, summed over all the groups) in figuring the within-groups population variance estimate; same as *denominator degrees of freedom*.

Table 10-6 Selected Cutoffs for the F Distribution (with Values Highlighted for the Criminal Record Study)

Denominator Degrees of Freedom	Significance Level	Numerator Degrees of Freedom					
		1	2	3	4	5	6
10	.01	10.05	7.56	6.55	6.00	5.64	5.39
	.05	4.97	4.10	3.71	3.48	3.33	3.22
	.10	3.29	2.93	2.73	2.61	2.52	2.46
11	.01	9.65	7.21	6.22	5.67	5.32	5.07
	.05	4.85	3.98	3.59	3.36	3.20	3.10
	.10	3.23	2.86	2.66	2.54	2.45	2.39
12	.01	9.33	6.93	5.95	5.41	5.07	4.82
	.05	4.75	3.89	3.49	3.26	3.11	3.00
	.10	3.18	2.81	2.61	2.48	2.40	2.33
13	.01	9.07	6.70	5.74	5.21	4.86	4.62
	.05	4.67	3.81	3.41	3.18	3.03	2.92
	.10	3.14	2.76	2.56	2.43	2.35	2.28

Note: Full table is Table A-3 in the Appendix.

How are you doing?

For part (c) of each question, use the following scores involving three samples: The scores in Sample A are 5 and 7 ($M = 6$), the scores in Sample B are 6 and 10 ($M = 8$), and the scores in Sample C are 8 and 9 ($M = 8.5$).

1. (a) Write the formula for the within-groups population variance estimate and (b) define each of the symbols. (c) Figure the within-groups population variance estimate for the above scores.

2. (a) Write the formula for the variance of the distribution of means when using it as part of an analysis of variance and (b) define each of the symbols. (c) Figure the variance of the distribution of means for the above scores.

3. (a) Write the formula for the between-groups population variance estimate based on the variance of the distribution of means and (b) define each of the symbols and explain the logic behind this formula. (c) Figure the between-groups population variance estimate for the above scores.

4. (a) Write the formula for the F ratio and (b) define each of the symbols. (c) Figure the F ratio for the above scores.

5. (a) Write the formulas for the between-groups and within-groups degrees of freedom and (b) define each of the symbols. (c) Figure the between-groups and within-groups degrees of freedom for the above scores.

6. (a) What is the F distribution? (b) Why is it skewed to the right? (c) What is the cutoff F for the above scores for the .05 significance level?

Answers

1. (a) $S^2_{Within} = (S^2_1 + S^2_2 + \cdots + S^2_{Last})/N_{Groups}$.
   (b) S^2_{Within} is the within-groups population variance estimate; S^2_1 is the estimated population variance based on the scores from Population A); S^2_2 is the estimated population variance based on the scores in the second group; S^2_{Last} is the estimated population variance based on the scores in the last group; the dots show that you are to fill in the population variance estimate for as many other groups as there are in the analysis; N_{Groups} is the number of groups.
   (c) $S^2_1 = [(5 - 6)^2 + (7 - 6)^2]/(2 - 1) = (1 + 1)/1 = 2$;
   $S^2_2 = [(6 - 8)^2 + (10 - 8)^2]/(2 - 1) = (4 + 4)/1 = 8$;
   $S^2_3 = [(8 - 8.5)^2 + (9 - 8.5)^2]/(2 - 1) = (.25 + .25)/1 = .5$;
   $S^2_{Within} = (S^2_1 + S^2_2 + \cdots + S^2_{Last})/N_{Groups} = (2 + 8 + .5)/3 = 10.5/3 = 3.5$.

2. (a) $S^2_M = \Sigma(M - GM)^2/df_{Between}$.
   (b) S^2_M is the estimated variance of the distribution of means (estimated based on the means of the samples in your study). M is the mean of each of your samples. GM is the grand mean, the overall mean of all your scores, which is also the mean of your means. $df_{Between}$ is the degrees of freedom in the between-groups estimate, the number of groups minus 1.
   (c) Grand mean (GM) is $(6 + 8 + 8.5)/3 = 7.5$.
   $S^2_M = \Sigma(M - GM)^2/df_{Between}$
   $= ([6 - 7.5]^2 + [8 - 7.5]^2 + [8.5 - 7.5]^2)/(3 - 1)$
   $= (2.25 + .25 + 1)/2 = 3.5/2 = 1.75$.

3. (a) $S^2_{Between} = (S^2_M)(n)$.
   (b) $S^2_{Between}$ is the between-groups population variance estimate; S^2_M is the estimated variance of the distribution of means based on the means

of the samples in your study); n is the number of participants in each sample. The goal is to have a variance of a distribution of individuals based on the variation among the means of the groups. S_M^2 is the estimate of the variance of a distribution of means from the overall population based on the means of the samples. To go from the variance of a distribution of means to the variance of a distribution of individuals, you multiply by the size of each sample. This is because the variance of the distribution of means is always smaller than the distribution of individuals (because means of samples are less likely to be extreme than are individual scores); the exact relation is that the variance of the distribution of means is the variance of the distribution of individuals divided by the sample size; thus you reverse that process here.

(c) $S_{Between}^2 = (S_M^2)(n) = (1.75)(2) = 3.5$.

4. (a) $F = S_{Between}^2/S_{Within}^2$.

(b) F is the ratio; $S_{Between}^2$ is the between-groups population variance estimate; S_{Within}^2 is the within-groups population variance estimate.

(c) $F = S_{Between}^2/S_{Within}^2 = 3.5/3.5 = 1.0$.

5. (a) $df_{Between} = N_{Groups} - 1$ and $df_{Within} = df_1 + df_2 + \cdots + df_{Last}$.

(b) $df_{Between}$ is the between-groups degrees of freedom; N_{Groups} is the number of groups; df_{Within} is the within-groups degrees of freedom; df_1 is the degrees of freedom for the population variance estimate based on the scores in the first sample; df_2 is the degrees of freedom for the population variance estimate based on the scores in the second sample; df_{Last} is the degrees of freedom for the population variance estimate based on the scores in the last sample; the dots show that you are to fill in the population degrees of freedom for as many other samples as there are in the analysis.

(c) $df_{Between} = N_{Groups} - 1 = 3 - 1 = 2$; $df_{Within} = df_1 + df_2 + \cdots + df_{Last} = 1 + 1 + 1 = 3$.

6. (a) The distribution of F ratios you would expect by chance. (b) F ratios are a ratio of variances. Variances, as averages of squared numbers, always have to be positive. F ratios thus are ratios of two positive numbers, which always have to be positive and can't be less than 0. But there is no limit to how high an F ratio can be. The result is that the scores bunch up at the left (near 0) and spread out to the right. (c) 9.55.

Hypothesis Testing with the Analysis of Variance

Here are the five steps of hypothesis testing for the criminal record study.

❶ **Restate the question as a research hypothesis and a null hypothesis about the populations.** There are three populations:

Population 1: Jurors told that the defendant has a criminal record.
Population 2: Jurors told that the defendant has a clean record.
Population 3: Jurors given no information of the defendant's record.

The null hypothesis is that these three populations have the same mean. The research hypothesis is that the populations' means are not the same.

❷ **Determine the characteristics of the comparison distribution.** The comparison distribution is an F distribution with 2 and 12 degrees of freedom.

❸ **Determine the cutoff sample score on the comparison distribution at which the null hypothesis should be rejected.** Using the F table for the .05 significance level, the cutoff F ratio is 3.89.

❹ **Determine your sample's score on the comparison distribution.** In the analysis of variance, the comparison distribution is an F distribution, and the sample's score on that distribution is thus its F ratio. In the example, the F ratio was 4.07.

❺ **Decide whether to reject the null hypothesis.** In the example, the F ratio of 4.07 is more extreme than the .05 significance level cutoff of 3.89. Thus, the researcher would reject the null hypothesis that the three groups come from populations with the same mean. This suggests that they come from populations with different means: that people exposed to different kinds of information (or no information) about the criminal record of a defendant in a situation of this kind will differ in their ratings of the defendant's guilt.

You may be interested to know that several real studies have looked at whether knowing a defendant's prior criminal record affects the likelihood of conviction. The overall conclusion seems to be reasonably consistent with that of the fictional study described here. For a review of such studies, see Dane and Wrightsman (1982). (For an example of a study showing this pattern, see Greene & Dodge, 1995.)

Summary of Steps for Hypothesis Testing Using the Analysis of Variance

Table 10–7 summarizes the steps of an analysis of variance of the kind we have been considering in this chapter.[1]

Assumptions in the Analysis of Variance

The assumptions for the analysis of variance are basically the same as for the t test for independent means. That is, you get strictly accurate results only when the populations follow a normal curve and have equal variances. As with the t test, in practice you get quite acceptable results even when your populations are moderately far from normal

---

[1]There are, as usual, computational formulas that can be used for analysis of variance. They can be used in the unlikely situation in which you have to do an analysis of variance for a real study by hand (without a computer). However, they are also useful in a more common situation. The procedure you have learned to do in the chapter works (without modification) only if you have equal numbers of scores in each group, while the computational formulas below also work when there are unequal numbers of scores in each group. These formulas require that you first figure an intermediary for the two variance estimates, called "sum of squares," or SS for short. For the between-groups estimate, $S^2_{Between} = SS_{Between}/df_{Between}$. The formula for $SS_{Between}$ is as follows:

$$\text{(10-7)} \qquad SS_{Between} = \frac{(\Sigma X_1)^2}{n_1} + \frac{(\Sigma X_2)^2}{n_2} + \cdots + \frac{(\Sigma X_{Last})^2}{n_{Last}} - \frac{(\Sigma X)^2}{N}$$

For the within-groups estimate, $S^2_{Within} = SS_{Within}/df_{Within}$. The formula for SS_{Within} is as follows:

$$\text{(10-8)} \qquad SS_{Within} = \Sigma X^2 - \frac{(\Sigma X)^2}{N} - SS_{Between}$$

However, as usual, we urge you to use the definitional formulas we have presented in the chapter to work out the practice problems. The definitional formulas are closely related to the meaning of the procedures. Using the definitional formulas to work out the problems helps you learn the meaning of the analysis of variance.

Table 10-7 Steps for the Analysis of Variance (When Sample Sizes Are Equal)

❶ **Restate the question as a research hypothesis and a null hypothesis about the populations.**

❷ **Determine the characteristics of the comparison distribution.**

  a. The comparison distribution is an F distribution.

  b. The between-groups degrees of freedom is the number of groups minus 1: $df_{Between} = N_{Groups} - 1$.

  c. The within-groups degrees of freedom is the sum of the degrees of freedom in each group (the number in the group minus 1): $df_{Within} = df_1 + df_2 + \ldots + df_{Last}$.

❸ **Determine the cutoff sample score on the comparison distribution at which the null hypothesis should be rejected.**

  a. Decide the significance level.

  b. Look up the appropriate cutoff in an F table, using the degrees of freedom from Step ❷.

❹ **Determine your sample's score on the comparison distribution.** This will be an F ratio.

  a. Figure the between-groups population variance estimate ($S^2_{Between}$).

    Figure the mean of each group.

   Ⓐ **Estimate the variance of the distribution of means:**

     $S^2_M = \Sigma(M - GM)^2/df_{Between}$.

   Ⓑ **Figure the estimated variance of the population of individual scores:**

     $S^2_{Between} = (S^2_M)(n)$.

  b. Figure the within-groups population variance estimate (S^2_{Within}).

    i. Figure population variance estimates based on each group's scores: For each group,
      $S^2 = \Sigma(X - M)^2/(n - 1)$.

    ii. Average these variance estimates:
      $S^2_{Within} = (S^2_1 + S^2_2 + \cdots + S^2_{Last})/N_{Groups}$.

  c. Figure the F ratio: $F = S^2_{Between}/S^2_{Within}$.

❺ **Decide whether to reject the null hypothesis:** Compare the scores from Steps ❸ and ❹.

and have moderately different variances. As a general rule, if the variance estimate of the group with the largest estimate is no more than 4 or 5 times that of the smallest and the sample sizes are equal, the conclusions using the F distribution should be adequately accurate. In Chapter 11, we consider what to do when your populations are a long way from meeting these assumptions.

Comparing Each Group to Each Other Group

When you reject the null hypothesis in an analysis of variance, this tells you that the population means are not all the same. What is not clear, however, is which population means differ from which. For example, in the criminal record study, the Criminal Record group jurors had the highest ratings for the defendant's guilt ($M = 8$); the No Information group jurors, the second highest ($M = 5$); and the Clean Record group jurors, the lowest ($M = 4$). From the analysis of variance results, we concluded that the true means of the three populations our samples represent are not all the same. (That is, the overall analysis of variance was significant.) However, we do not know which particular populations' means are *significantly different* from each other.

For this reason, researchers often do not stop after getting a significant result with an analysis of variance. Instead, they may go on to compare each population to each other population. For example, with three groups, you would compare group 1 to group 2, group 1 to group 3, and group 2 to group 3. You could do each of these comparisons using ordinary t tests for independent means. However, there is a problem with using ordinary t tests like this. The problem is that you are making three comparisons,

protected *t* tests In analysis of variance, *t* tests among pairs of means after finding that the *F* for the overall difference among the means is significant.

each at the .05 level. The overall chance of at least one of them being significant just by chance is more like .15.

Some statisticians argue that it is all right to do three *t* tests in this situation because we have first checked that the overall analysis of variance is significant. These are called **protected *t* tests.** We are protected from making too big an error by the overall analysis of variance being significant. However, most statisticians believe that the protected *t* test is not enough protection. Advanced statistics texts give procedures that provide even more protection. (Also, most standard statistics software have options as part of the analysis of variance that provide various ways to compare means that provide strong protection of this kind. One widely used method is called *Tukey's HSD* test.)

How are you doing?

1. A study compares the effects of three experimental treatments, A, B, and C, by giving each treatment to sixteen participants and then assessing their performance on a standard measure. The results on the standard measure are, Treatment A group: $M = 20$, $S^2 = 8$; Treatment B group: $M = 22$, $S^2 = 9$; Treatment C group: $M = 18$, $S^2 = 7$. Use the steps of hypothesis testing (with the .01 significance level) to test whether the three experimental treatments create any difference among the populations these groups represent.
2. Give the two main assumptions for the analysis of variance.
3. Why do we need the equal variance assumption?
4. What is the general rule about when violations of the equal variance assumption are likely to lead to serious inaccuracies in results?
5. After getting a significant result with an analysis of variance, why do researchers usually go on to compare each population to each other population?

Answers

1. Steps of hypothesis testing:
   ❶ **Restate the question as a research hypothesis and a null hypothesis about the populations.** There are three populations:

   Population 1: People given experimental treatment A.
   Population 2: People given experimental treatment B.
   Population 3: People given experimental treatment C.

   The null hypothesis is that these three populations have the same mean. The research hypothesis is that their means are not the same.
   ❷ **Determine the characteristics of the comparison distribution.** The comparison distribution will be an *F* distribution. Its degrees of freedom are figured as follows: The between-groups variance estimate is based on three groups, making 2 degrees of freedom. The within-groups estimate is based on 15 degrees of freedom (16 participants) in each of the three groups, making 45 degrees of freedom.
   ❸ **Determine the cutoff sample score on the comparison distribution at which the null hypothesis should be rejected.** Using Table A-3 in the Appendix, the cutoff for $df = 2, 45$ at the .01 level is 5.11.
   ❹ **Determine your sample's score on the comparison distribution.**
   a. Figure the between-groups population variance estimate ($S^2_{Between}$): Figure the mean of each group. The group means are 20, 22, and 18.

proportion of variance accounted for (R^2) Measure of effect size for analysis of variance.

❹ **Estimate the variance of the distribution of means:** Sum the sample means' squared deviations from the grand mean and divide by the number of means minus 1:

$$S^2_M = [(20 - 20)^2 + (22 - 20)^2 + (18 - 20)^2]/(3 - 1)$$
$$= (0 + 4 + 4)/2 = 4.$$

❺ **Figure the estimated variance of the population of individual scores:** Multiply the variance of the distribution of means by the number of scores in each group:

$$S^2_{Between} = (4)(16) = 64.$$

b. **Figure the within-groups population variance estimate ($S^2_{Between}$):**
    i. Figure population variance estimates based on each group's scores. Treatment A group, $S^2 = 8$; Treatment B group, $S^2 = 9$; Treatment C group, $S^2 = 7$.
    ii. Average these variance estimates. $S^2_{Within} = (8 + 9 + 7)/3 = 8$.
    The F ratio is the between-groups estimate divided by the within-groups estimate: $F = 64/8 = 8.00$.

❺ **Decide whether to reject the null hypothesis.** The F of 8.00 is more extreme than the .01 cutoff of 5.11. Therefore, reject the null hypothesis. The research hypothesis is supported; the different experimental treatments do produce different effects on the standard performance measure.

2. The populations are assumed to be normally distributed with equal variances.
3. We need the equal variance assumption in order to be able to justify averaging the estimates from each sample into an overall within-groups population variance estimate.
4. The analysis can lead to inaccurate results when the variance estimate from the group with the largest estimate is more than four or five times the smallest variance estimate.
5. To find out which populations' means are significantly different from each other.

Effect Size and Power for the Analysis of Variance
Effect Size

Effect size for the analysis of variance is a little more complex than for a *t* test. With the *t* test, you took the difference between the two means and divided by the pooled population standard deviation. In the analysis of variance, we have more than two means, so it is not obvious just what is the equivalent to the difference between the means—the numerator in figuring effect size. Thus, in this section we consider a quite different approach to effect size, the **proportion of variance accounted for (R^2).**

To be precise, R^2 is the proportion of the total variation of scores from the grand mean that is accounted for by the variation between the means of the groups. (In other words, you consider how much of the variance in the measured variable—such as ratings of guilt—is accounted for by the variable that divides up the groups—such as what experimental condition one is in.) In terms of a formula,

$$R^2 = \frac{(S^2_{Between})(df_{Between})}{(S^2_{Between})(df_{Between}) + (S^2_{Within})(df_{Within})} \qquad \textbf{(10-9)}$$

The proportion of variance accounted for is the between-groups population variance estimate multiplied by the between-groups degrees of freedom, divided by the sum of the between-groups population variance estimate multiplied by the between-groups degrees of freedom, plus the within-groups population variance estimate multiplied by the within-groups degrees of freedom.

The between- and within-groups degrees of freedom are included in the formula to take into account the number of participants and the number of groups used in the study.

Consider once again the criminal record study. In that example, $S^2_{\text{Between}} = 21.70$, $df_{\text{Between}} = 2$, $S^2_{\text{Within}} = 5.33$, and $df_{\text{Within}} = 12$. Thus, the proportion of the total variation accounted for by the variation between groups is $(21.70)(2)$ / $[(21.70)(2) + (5.33)(12)]$, which is .40 (or 40%). In terms of the formula,

$$R^2 = \frac{(S^2_{\text{Between}})(df_{\text{Between}})}{(S^2_{\text{Between}})(df_{\text{Between}}) + (S^2_{\text{Within}})(df_{\text{Within}})}$$

$$= \frac{(21.70)(2)}{(21.70)(2) + (5.33)(12)} = \frac{43.40}{107.36} = .40$$

The proportion of variance accounted for is a useful measure of effect size because it has the direct meaning suggested by its name. (Further, researchers are familiar with R^2 and its square root R from their use in multiple regression and multiple correlation—see the Advanced Topic section in Chapter 3.) R^2 has a minimum of 0 and a maximum of 1. However, in practice it is rare for an analysis of variance to have an R^2 even as high as .20. Cohen's (1988) conventions for R^2 are .01, a small effect size; .06, a medium effect size; and .14, a large effect size. (You should also know that another common name for this measure of effect size, besides R^2, is η^2, the Greek letter eta squared.)

Power

Table 10–8 shows the approximate power for the .05 significance level for small, medium, and large effect sizes; sample size of 10, 20, 30, 40, 50, and 100 per group; and three, four, and five groups.[2]

Consider a planned study with five groups of 10 participants each and an expected large effect size (.14). Using the .05 significance level, the study would have a power of .56. Thus, even if the research hypothesis is in fact true and has a large effect size, there is only a little greater than even chance (56%) that the study will come out significant.

As we have noted in previous chapters, determining power is especially useful when interpreting the practical implication of a nonsignificant result. For example, suppose that you have read a study using an analysis of variance with four groups of 30 participants each in which the researcher reports a nonsignificant result at the .05 level. Table 10–8 shows a power of only .13 for a small effect size. This suggests that even if such a small effect exists in the population, this study would be very unlikely to have come out significant. But the table shows a power of .96 for a large effect size. This suggests that if a large effect existed in the population, it almost surely would have shown up in that study.

Planning Sample Size

Table 10–9 gives the approximate number of participants you need in each group for 80% power at the .05 significance level for estimated small, medium, and large effect sizes for studies with three, four, and five groups.[3]

---

[2]More detailed tables are provided in Cohen (1988, pp. 289–354). When using these tables, note that the value of u at the top of each table refers to df_{between}, which for a one-way analysis of variance is the number of groups minus 1, not the number of groups as used in our Table 10–8.

[3]More detailed tables are provided in Cohen (1988, pp. 381–389). If you use these, see footnote 2 in this chapter.

Table 10-8   Approximate Power for Studies Using the Analysis of Variance Testing Hypotheses at the .05 Significance Level

Participants per Group (n)	Effect Size		
	Small ($R^2 = .01$)	Medium ($R^2 = .06$)	Large ($R^2 = .14$)
Three groups ($df_{Between} = 2$)			
10	.07	.20	.45
20	.09	.38	.78
30	.12	.55	.93
40	.15	.68	.98
50	.18	.79	.99
100	.32	.98	*
Four groups ($df_{Between} = 3$)			
10	.07	.21	.51
20	.10	.43	.85
30	.13	.61	.96
40	.16	.76	.99
50	.19	.85	*
100	.36	.99	*
Five groups ($df_{Between} = 4$)			
10	.07	.23	.56
20	.10	.47	.90
30	.13	.67	.98
40	.17	.81	*
50	.21	.90	*
100	.40	*	*

* Nearly 1.

For example, suppose you are planning a study involving four groups, and you expect a small effect size (and will use the .05 significance level). For 80% power, you would need 274 participants in each group, a total of 1,096 in all. However, suppose you could adjust the research plan so that it was now reasonable to predict a large effect size (perhaps by using more accurate measures and a more powerful experimental procedure). Now you would need only 18 in each of the four groups, for a total of 72.

Table 10-9   Approximate Number of Participants Needed in Each Group (Assuming Equal Sample Sizes) for 80% Power for the One-Way Analysis of Variance Testing Hypotheses at the .05 Significance Level

	Effect Size		
	Small ($R^2 = .01$)	Medium ($R^2 = .06$)	Large ($R^2 = .14$)
Three groups ($df_{Between} = 2$)	322	52	21
Four groups ($df_{Between} = 3$)	274	45	18
Five groups ($df_{Between} = 4$)	240	39	16

factorial analysis of variance
Analysis of variance for a factorial research design.

How are you doing?

1. (a) Write the formula for effect size in analysis of variance; (b) define each of the symbols; and (c) figure the effect size for a study in which $S^2_{Between} = 12.22$, $S^2_{Within} = 7.20$, $df_{Between} = 2$, and $df_{Within} = 8$.
2. What is the power of a study with four groups of 40 participants each to be tested at the .05 significance level, in which the researchers predict a large effect size?
3. About how many participants do you need in each group for 80% power in a planned study with five groups in which you predict a medium effect size and will be using the .05 significance level?

Answers

1. (a) $R^2 = (S^2_{Between})(df_{Between})/[(S^2_{Between})(df_{Between}) + (S^2_{Within})(df_{Within})]$. (b) R^2 is the proportion of variance accounted for; $S^2_{Between}$ is the between-groups population variance estimate; $df_{Between}$ is the between-groups degrees of freedom (number of groups minus 1); S^2_{Within} is the within-groups population variance estimate; df_{Within} is the within-groups degrees of freedom (the sum of the degrees of freedom for each group's population variance estimate). (c) $R^2 = .30$.

2. .99.

3. 39.

Factorial Analysis of Variance

Factorial analysis of variance is an extension of the procedures you just learned. It is a wonderfully flexible and efficient approach that handles many types of experimental studies. The actual figuring of a factorial analysis of variance is beyond what we can cover in an introductory book. Our goal in this section is to help you understand the basic approach and the terminology so that you can make sense of research articles that use it.

We will introduce factorial analysis of variance with an example. Lambert, Khan, Lickel, and Fricke (1997) were interested in how stereotypes affect the evaluations we make of others. For example, people often use age or gender stereotypes to evaluate whether someone will be successful in a particular job. Lambert et al. were especially interested in how the influence of stereotypes is affected (a) by awareness that a stereotype is inappropriate for a particular circumstance and (b) by mood. They believed that people are less affected by a stereotype when it is inappropriate and are particularly unaffected by stereotypes when in a sad mood.

Thus, Lambert et al. did the following experiment. Participants were asked to put themselves in the position of a job interviewer. Their task was to "form a preliminary evaluation of the suitability of an individual for a particular job" (1997, p. 1010)—which for all participants was that of a flight attendant. The participants were then given a resume of an applicant that included a photo of a very attractive woman. Based on this information, the participants were asked how likely it was they would hire her, using a scale from 0 (not at all) to 10 (extremely). This experiment used the *attractiveness stereotype,* a stereotype that includes the tendency to think that good-looking people are especially competent.

The researchers put half the participants in a sad mood prior to reading the resume, supposedly as part of a separate experiment. These participants were asked to think about "an episode in your life that made you feel very sad and continues to make you sad whenever you think about it, even today" (p. 1004). This was the *Sad Mood* condition. The other half of the participants were not given any particular instructions. This was the *Neutral Mood* condition.

The other influence of interest to the researchers was appropriateness of the stereotype. Participants were given a description of a good flight attendant that differed according to how important attractiveness was for the job. For half the participants in each of the mood groups, the description emphasized the ability "to solve and analyze problems in a rational and analytic fashion" (p. 1010); this was the *Stereotype Inappropriate* condition. For the other participants, the description emphasized passenger satisfaction and how appearance contributed to it; this was the *Stereotype Appropriate* condition.

In sum, there were *two experimental manipulations:* sad mood versus neutral mood and the job description being stereotype appropriate versus stereotype inappropriate.

Lambert and his colleagues could have conducted two studies, one comparing participants put in a sad versus a neutral mood and one comparing participants given the stereotype appropriate versus inappropriate job descriptions. Instead, they studied the effects of both mood and stereotype appropriateness in a single study. They considered four groups of participants (see Table 10–10): (a) those in the sad mood and stereotype-appropriate conditions, (b) those in the sad mood and stereotype-inappropriate conditions, (c) those in the neutral mood and stereotype-appropriate conditions, and (d) those in the neutral mood and stereotype-inappropriate conditions.

Factorial Research Design Defined

The Lambert et al. (1997) study is an example of a **factorial research design** study. In a factorial research design the effect of *two or more variables* are examined at once by making groupings of every combination of the variables. In this example, there are two levels of mood (sad and neutral) and two levels of stereotype appropriateness (appropriate and inappropriate). This allows four possible combinations, and Lambert et al. used all of them in their study.

A factorial research design has a major advantage over doing separate studies of each variable—efficiency. With a factorial design you can study both variables at once, without needing twice as many participants. In the example, Lambert et al. were able to use a single group of participants to study the effects of mood and stereotype appropriateness on ratings of the likelihood of hiring.

Interaction Effects

There is an even more important advantage of a factorial research design. A factorial design lets you study the effects of *combining two or more variables.* In this example, mood and stereotype appropriateness might affect hiring in a simple additive way. By additive, we mean that their combined influence is the sum of their separate influences—if you are more of one and also more of the other, then the overall effect is the total of the two individual effects. For example, suppose being sad makes you more willing to hire someone; similarly, the stereotype being appropriate makes you more willing to hire a person. If these two effects are additive, then participants in the sad, stereotype-appropriate group will be most willing to hire the person; participants in the neutral, stereotype-inappropriate group will be least likely to hire the person; and those in the other two conditions would have an intermediate likelihood of hiring the person.

factorial research design Way of organizing a study in which the influence of two or more variables is studied at once by setting up the situation so that a different group of people are tested for each combination of the levels of the variables.

Table 10–10 Factorial Research Design Employed by Lambert et al. (1997)

		Mood	
		Sad	**Neutral**
Stereotype	**Appropriate**	a	c
	Inappropriate	b	d

interaction effect Situation in a factorial analysis of variance in which the combination of variables has an effect that could not be predicted from the effects of the two variables individually.

two-way analysis of variance Analysis of variance for a two-way factorial research design.

two-way factorial research design Factorial design with two variables that each divide the groups.

grouping variable A variable that separates groups in analysis of variance.

independent variable Variable considered to be a cause, such as what group a person is in in an analysis of variance.

one-way analysis of variance Analysis of variance in which there is only one grouping variable (as distinguished from a factorial analysis of variance).

main effect Difference between groups on one grouping variable in a factorial analysis of variance; result for a variable that divides the groups, averaging across the levels of the other variable that divides the groups.

It could also be that one variable but not the other has an effect. Or perhaps neither variable has any effect. In the additive situation, or the one in which only one variable or neither has an effect, looking at the two variables in combination does not give any interesting additional information.

However, it is also possible that the *combination of the two variables* changes the result. In fact, Lambert et al. (1997) predicted that the effect of stereotype inappropriateness on the likelihood of hiring would be especially strong in the sad mood condition. This prediction was based on the notion that when in a sad mood, we are more willing to revise our initial, unthinking, stereotype-based reactions.

A situation where the *combination* of variables has a special effect is called an **interaction effect.** An interaction effect is an effect in which the impact of one variable (on the measured variable) is different across the levels of the other variable. In the Lambert et al. (1997) study, there was an interaction effect. Look at Table 10–11. The result was that the participants in the Appropriate-Sad group were most likely to hire the applicant, the Inappropriate-Neutral group was the next most likely, and the two other groups were least likely (to about an equal extent). Consider the bottom row of the results, the Inappropriate-Stereotype group. This part of the result supported the researchers' theory that when in a sad mood, people are able to counteract their stereotypes. (What about the Appropriate-Sad being the most likely to hire? The researchers acknowledged that this result was "unexpected and difficult to explain" [p. 1011].)

Suppose the researchers had studied stereotype appropriateness and mood in two separate studies. They would have concluded that each factor had only a slight effect. The average likelihood of hiring for the appropriate is 6.77 (that is, the average of 5.80 and 7.73 comes out to 6.77) and for inappropriate is 6.29. The average likelihood of hiring for those in the sad-mood condition was 6.78 versus 6.28 for those in the neutral-mood condition. Thus, following the approach of two separate studies, they would have completely missed the important result. The most important results had to do with the combination of the two factors.

Some Terminology

The Lambert et al. study would be analyzed with what is called a **two-way analysis of variance** (it uses a **two-way factorial research design**) because it considers the effect of two variables that separate groups. These variables are called **grouping variables,** also known as **independent variables.** By contrast, the situations we considered earlier (such as the attachment style study or the criminal record study) were examples of studies analyzed using a **one-way analysis of variance.** Such studies are called *one-way* because they consider the effect of only one grouping (or independent) variable (such as a person's attachment style or information about a defendant's criminal record).

In a two-way analysis, each grouping (or independent) variable or "way" (each dimension in the diagram) is a possible **main effect.** If the result for a variable, averaging across the other grouping variable, is significant, it is a *main effect.* This is entirely different from an *interaction effect,* which is based on the *combination of grouping variables.* In the two-way Lambert et al. study, there was a possibility of two main effects and one interaction effect. The two possible main effects are one for stereotype appropriateness and one for mood. The possible interaction effect is for the combination of stereotype appropriateness and mood. In a two-way analysis of variance, you are always testing two possible main effects and one possible interaction.

Table 10–11 Mean Likelihood of Hiring in the Lambert et al. (1997) Study

		Mood	
		Sad	**Neutral**
Stereotype	**Appropriate**	7.73	5.80
	Inappropriate	5.83	6.75

Each grouping combination in a factorial design is called a **cell.** The mean of the scores in each grouping is called a **cell mean.** In the Lambert et al. study, there are four cells. Thus, there are four cell means, one for each combination of the levels of stereotype appropriateness and mood. That is, one cell is Stereotype Appropriate and Sad Mood (as shown in Table 10–11, its mean is 7.33); one cell is Stereotype Inappropriate and Sad Mood (5.83); one cell is Stereotype Appropriate and Neutral Mood (5.80); and one cell is Stereotype Inappropriate and Neutral Mood (6.75).

The means of one variable alone are called **marginal means.** For example, in the Lambert et al. study there are four marginal means, one mean for all the stereotype-appropriate participants (as we saw earlier, 6.77), one for all the stereotype-inappropriate participants (6.29), one for all the sad-mood participants (6.78), and one for all the neutral-mood participants (6.28). (Because we were mainly interested in the interaction, we did not show these marginal means in the tables.)

To look at a main effect, you focus on the marginal means. To look at the interaction effect, you focus on the pattern of individual cell means.

The individual cell means and marginal means are means of the variable that is measured in the research study. In the Lambert et al. study, it was ratings of how likely the participant would be to hire the person. A variable like this, which is measured and represents the effect of the experimental procedure, is called a **dependent variable.** It is *dependent* in the sense that any participant's score on this variable depends on what happens in the experiment.

cell   In a factorial research design, a particular combination of levels of the variables that divide the groups.

cell mean   Mean of a particular combination of levels of the variables that divide the groups in a factorial design in analysis of variance.

marginal mean   In a factorial design, mean score for all the participants at a particular level of one of the variables; often shortened to *marginal.*

dependent variable   Variable considered to be an effect; usually a measured variable.

How are you doing?

1. (a) What is a factorial research design? (b) and (c) Give two advantages of a factorial research design over doing two separate experiments.
2. In a factorial research design, (a) what is a main effect, and (b) what is an interaction effect?
3. Below are the means from a study in which participants rated the originality of paintings under various conditions. For each mean, indicate its grouping and whether it is a cell or marginal mean.

	Contemporary	Rennaissance	Overall
Landscape	6.5	5.5	6
Portrait	3.5	2.5	3
Overall	5	4	

4. In each of the following studies, participants' performance on a coordination task was measured under various conditions or compared for different groups. For each study, make a diagram of the research design and indicate whether it is a one-way or two-way design: (a) a study in which people are assigned to either a high-stress condition or a low-stress condition, and within each of these conditions, half are assigned to work alone and half to work in a room with other people; (b) a study comparing students majoring in physics, chemistry, or engineering; (c) a study comparing people doing a task in a hot room versus a cold room, with half in each room doing the task with their right hand and half with their left hand. (Your diagrams for a two-way analysis should look something like the diagram in Table 10–11, but without the means written in; diagrams for a one-way analysis would have just one row with the categories across the top.)

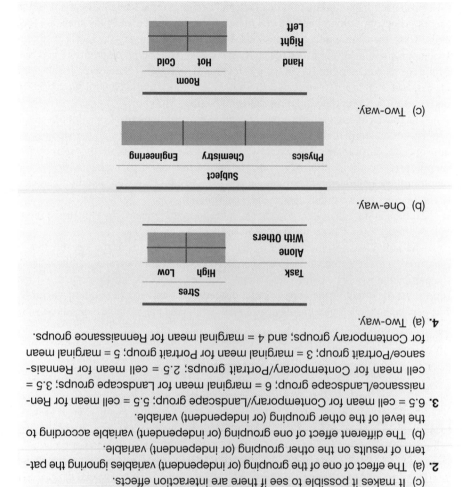

(c) Two-way.

(b) One-way.

4. (a) Two-way.

Answers

1. (a) A research design in which the effect of two or more variables is examined at once by making groupings of every combination of the variables.
   (b) It is more efficient. For example, you can study the effects of two grouping (or independent) variables at once with only a single group of participants.
   (c) It makes it possible to see if there are interaction effects.
2. (a) The effect of one of the grouping (or independent) variables ignoring the pattern of results on the other grouping (or independent) variable.
   (b) The different effect of one grouping (or independent) variable according to the level of the other grouping (or independent) variable.
3. 6.5 = cell mean for Contemporary/Landscape group; 5.5 = cell mean for Renaissance/Landscape group; 6 = marginal mean for Landscape groups; 3.5 = cell mean for Contemporary/Portrait groups; 2.5 = cell mean for Renaissance/Portrait group; 3 = marginal mean for Portrait group; 5 = marginal mean for Contemporary groups; and 4 = marginal mean for Renaissance groups.

Recognizing and Interpreting Interaction Effects

It is very important to understand interaction effects. In many experiments the interaction effect is the main point of the research. As we have seen, an interaction effect is an effect in which the impact of one grouping variable depends on the level of another grouping variable. The Lambert et al. study results (Table 10–11) show an interaction effect. This is because the impact of stereotype appropriateness is different with a sad mood than with a neutral mood. You can think out and describe an interaction effect in three ways: in words, in numbers, or in a graph. Note that in discussing the examples in this section on identifying interaction effects, we will treat all differences that have the pattern of an interaction effect or main effect as if they were statistically significant. (In reality, you would carry out hypothesis testing steps to test whether the patterns were strong enough to be statistically *significant*.) We are taking this approach here to keep the focus on the idea of interaction effects while you are learning this fairly abstract idea.

Identifying Interaction Effects in Words and Numbers

You can think out an interaction effect in words by saying that you have an interaction effect when the effect of one grouping variable varies according to the level of another grouping variable. In the Lambert et al. example, the effect of stereotype appropriateness on the likelihood of hiring varies according to the level of mood. (You can also say that the effect of mood varies according to the level of stereotype appropriateness. Interaction effects are completely symmetrical; you can describe them from the point of view of either variable.) Another way of saying this is that the effect of stereotype appropriateness depends on the level of mood (the impact of stereotype appropriateness is different with a sad mood than with a neutral mood).

You can see an interaction effect numerically by looking at the pattern of cell means. If there is an interaction effect, the *pattern of differences in cell means* across one row will not be the same as the pattern of differences in cell means across another row. Consider the Lambert et al. example. In the Stereotype Appropriate row, the Sad Mood participants' mean rating of how likely they were to hire was 7.33, which is much *higher* than the Neutral Mood participants' mean rating of 5.80. This was a positive difference of 1.93 (that is, $7.73 - 5.80 = 1.93$). However, look at the Stereotype Inappropriate row. Those in a sad mood had a mean rating for their likelihood of hiring of 5.83, which was *lower* than the mean rating of 6.75 for those in the neutral mood. The difference for sad versus neutral mood for stereotype-inappropriate participants was $-.92$.

Table 10–12 gives cell and marginal means for six possible results of a fictional two-way factorial study on the relation of age and education (the grouping or independent variables) to income (the dependent variable). The grouping variable age has two levels (younger, such as 25 to 34, versus older, such as 35 to 44), and the grouping variable education has two levels (high school versus college). These fictional results are exaggerated to make clear when there are interactions and main effects. Before you look at the six possible results, take a minute to think about what kind of results you might expect (and hope!) to see. For example, do you expect that people with a college education will earn less than or more than people with only a high

Table 10-12 Possible Means for Results of a Study of the Relation of Age and Education to Income (in Thousands of Dollars)

	Result A			Result B			Result C		
Age	High School	College	Overall	High School	College	Overall	High School	College	Overall
Younger	40	40	40	60	40	50	20	60	40
Older	40	60	50	40	60	50	40	80	60
Overall	40	50		50	50		30	70	

	Result D			Result E			Result F		
Age	High School	College	Overall	High School	College	Overall	High School	College	Overall
Younger	20	20	20	40	60	50	30	45	37.5
Older	120	120	120	40	80	60	35	60	47.5
Overall	70	70		40	70		32.5	52.5	

school education? Would you expect younger people to earn more or less than older people? Most importantly (since this section focuses on interaction effects), what about the possibility of an interaction effect? Do you think that the effect of education (college versus high school) will be different according to age (younger versus older)? Let's take a look at the six possible results and then we'll tell you what the results of actual research show.

Result A: Interaction. Note that in the Younger row, education makes no difference, but in the Older row, the college cell mean is much higher than the high-school cell mean. One way to say this is that for the younger group, education is unrelated to income; but for the older group, people with a college education earn much more than those with less education. (There are also two main effects: older people earn more than younger people, and people with a college education earn more than those with only a high school education.)

Result B: Interaction. This is because in the Younger row the high-school mean income is higher than the college mean income, but in the Older row the high-school mean income is lower. Put in words, among younger people, those with only a high-school education make more money (perhaps because they entered the workplace earlier or the kinds of jobs they have start out at a higher level); but among older people, those with a college education make more money. (There are no main effects in Result B, since the marginal means for the rows are the same and marginal means for the columns are the same.)

Result C: No interaction. In the Younger row, the high-school mean is 40 lower than the college mean, and the same is true in the Older row. In words, whether young or old, people with college educations earn $40,000 more. (There are also main effects for both age and education.)

Result D: No interaction. There is no difference in the pattern of income between the two rows. Regardless of education, older people earn $100,000 more. (There is also a main effect for age, but no main effect for education.)

Result E: Interaction. In the Younger row, the college mean is 20 higher, but in the Older row, the college mean is 40 higher than the high-school mean. So among young people, college-educated people earn a little more, but among older people, those with a college education earn much more. (There are also main effects for both age and education.)

Result F: Interaction. There is a smaller difference between the high school and college mean in the Younger row than in the Older row. As with Result E, for people with a college education, income increases more with age than it does for those with only a high-school education.[4]

Identifying Interaction Effects Graphically

Another common way of making sense of interaction effects is by graphing the pattern of cell means. This is usually done with a bar graph, although a line graph is sometimes used. Figure 10–4 is reproduced from Lambert et al.'s (1997) article. The

[4]Based on 1990 statistics from the U.S. Department of Education, the actual situation in the United States is closest to Result F (Day & Newberger, 2002). People with a college education earn more than those with only a high-school education in both age groups, but the difference is somewhat greater for the older group. (You may be interested to know that, over a typical working life, people in the United States with a college degree earn an average of 1.8 times more than those with only a high school education [Day & Newberger, 2002]. However, it is important to keep in mind that whether people receive a college education is also related to the social class of their parents and other factors that may affect income as much or more than education does.)

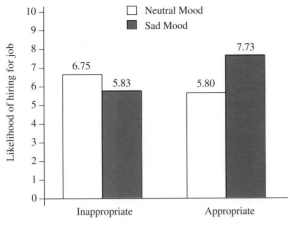

Figure 10–4 Judgments of the physically attractive job candidate as a function of framing attractiveness (inappropriate vs. appropriate) and manipulated mood (sad vs. neutral), Experiment 3. Higher numbers indicate a greater likelihood of hiring the target for the job. *Source:* Lambert, A. J., Khan, S. R., Lickel, B. A., & Fricke, K. (1997). Mood and the correlation of positive versus negative stereotypes. *Journal of Personality and Social Psychology, 72,* 1002-1016. Copyright © 1997 by the American Psychological Association. Reprinted by permission.

graphs in Figure 10–5 show the graphs for the fictional age and education results we just considered (the ones shown in Table 10–12).

One thing to notice about such graphs is this: Whenever there is an interaction, the pattern of bars on one section of the graph is different from the pattern on the other section of the graph. Thus, in Figure 10–4, the pattern for inappropriate is a step down, but the pattern for appropriate is a step up. The bars having a different pattern is just a graphic way of saying that the pattern of differences between the cell means from row to row is not the same.

Consider Figure 10–5. First, look at Results C and D. In Result C the younger and older sets of bars have the same pattern—both step up by 40. In Result D, both are flat. Within both Results C and D, the younger bars and the older bars have the same pattern. These were the examples that *did not have interactions.* All the other results, which did have interactions, have patterns of bars that are not the same for younger and older age groups. For example, in Result A, the two younger bars are flat but the older bars show a step up. In Result B, the younger bars show a step down from high school to college, but the older bars show a step up from high school to college. In Results E and F, both younger and older bars show a step up, but the younger bars show a smaller step up than the older bars.

You can also see *main effects* from these graphs. In Figure 10–5, a main effect for age would be shown by the bars for younger being overall higher or lower than the bars for older. For example, in Result C, the bars for older are clearly higher than the bars for younger. What about the main effect for the bars that are not grouped together—college versus high school in this example? With these bars, you have to see whether the overall step pattern goes up or down. For example, in Result C, there is also a main effect for education, because the general pattern of the bars for high school to college goes up, and it does this for both the younger and older bars. Result D shows a main effect for age (the older bars are higher than the younger bars). But Result D does not show a main effect for education—the pattern is flat for both the older and younger bars.

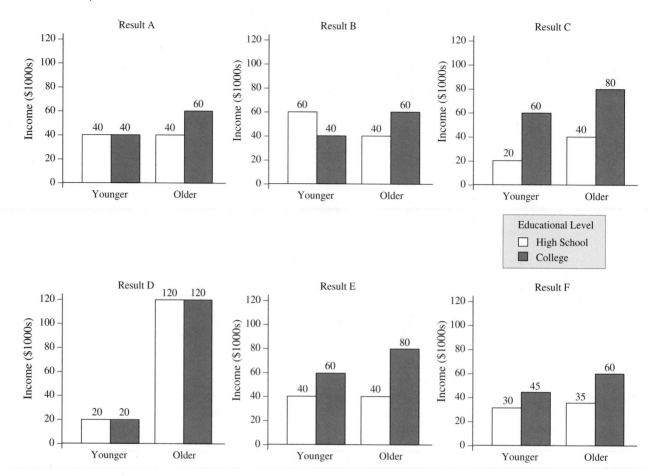

Figure 10–5   Bar graphs of fictional results in Table 10–12.

Relation of Interaction and Main Effects

Any combination of main and interaction effects can be significant. For example, they may all be significant, as in the pattern in Result F of Table 10–12. In this result, as we saw, older students earn more (a main effect for age), college students earn more (a main effect for level of education), and how much more college students earn depends on age (the interaction effect).

There can also be an interaction effect with no main effects. Result B of Table 10–12 is an example. The average level of income is the same for younger and older (no main effect for age), and it is the same for college and high school (no main effect for level of education).

There can also be one main effect significant along with an interaction, one main effect significant by itself, or for there to be no significant main or interaction effects. See how many of these possibilities you can find in the fictional results in Table 10–12.

When there is no interaction, a main effect has a straightforward meaning. However, when there is an interaction along with a main effect, you have to be cautious in drawing conclusions about the main effect. This is because the main effect may be created by just one of the levels of the variable. For example, in Result A the main effect for education (40 vs. 50) is entirely due to the difference for older people. It would be misleading to say that education makes a difference without noting that it really only matters when you are older.

Sometimes the main effect clearly holds up over and above any interaction. For example, in Result F in the age and education example, it seems clear that the main effect for age holds up over and above the interaction. That is, it is true for both people with and without a college education that older people earn more. (There is still an interaction, of course, because how much more older people earn depends on education.)

Extensions and Special Cases of the Factorial Analysis of Variance

Analysis of variance is very versatile. Factorial designs can be extended into three-way and higher designs (in which the effects of three or more grouping variables are examined). There are also procedures to handle situations in which the same participants are tested more than once. This is like the *t* test for dependent means but works with more than two testings. It is called a *repeated measures analysis of variance*.

How are you doing?

Questions 1 to 3 are based on the results shown below of a fictional study of the effects of vividness and length of examples on number of examples recalled.

Example Length	Vividness		
	Low	*High*	*Overall*
Short	5	7	6
Long	3	1	2
Overall	4	4	

1. Describe the pattern of results in words.
2. Explain the pattern in terms of numbers.
3. Make two bar graphs of these results: one graph should show vividness (low and high) on the horizontal axis, with bars for short and long example length; another graph should show example length (short and long) on the horizontal axis, with bars for low and high vividness.
4. For a two-way factorial design, what are the possible combinations of main and interaction effects?
5. When there is both a main and an interaction effect, (a) under what conditions must you be cautious in interpreting the main effect, and (b) under what conditions can you still be confident in the overall main effect?

Answers

1. There is a main effect in which short examples are recalled better and an interaction effect such that there is a bigger advantage of short over long examples when they are highly vivid.
2. The main effect is that on the average people recall six short examples but only two long examples. The interaction effect is that for short examples, people recall two more highly vivid than low vivid; but for long examples, they recall two fewer highly vivid than low vivid.
3. See Figure 10–6.

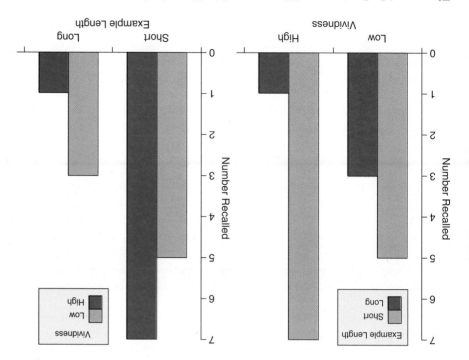

Figure 10–6 Answer to "How are you doing?" question 3.

4. All possible combinations: no main or interaction effects, either main effect only, the interaction only, both main effects but no interaction effect, an interaction effect with either main effect, or an interaction effect with both main effects.
5. (a) When the main effect is found for only one level of the other grouping variable.
(b) When the main effect holds at each level of the other grouping variable.

Analyses of Variance in Research Articles

A one-way analysis of variance is usually described in a research article by giving the *F*, the degrees of freedom, and the significance level. For example, $F(3, 68) = 5.21, p < .01$. The means for the groups usually are given in a table. However, if there are only a few groups and only one or a few measures, the means may be given in the regular text of the article. Returning to the criminal-record study example, we could describe the analysis of variance results this way: "The means for the Criminal Record, Clean Record, and No Information conditions were 7.0, 4.0, and 5.0, respectively, $F(2, 12) = 4.07, p < .05$."

In a factorial analysis of variance, researchers usually give a description in the text plus a table. The text gives the *F* ratio and the information that goes with it for each main and interaction effect. The table gives the cell means and sometimes also the marginal means. If there is an interaction effect, there may also be a graph. For example, Lambert et al. (1997) described the result we used for our example as follows:

Analysis of participants' intention to hire the target revealed only one significant effect, the predicted Mood × Job Type interaction, $F(1, 57) = 11.46$, $p < .001$. Data relevant to this interaction are displayed in Figure [10–4]. (p. 101)

Summary

1. The analysis of variance (ANOVA) is used to test hypotheses based on differences among means of more than two samples. The procedure compares two estimates of population variance. One, the within-groups estimate, is figured by averaging the population variance estimates from each of the samples. The other, the between-groups estimate, is based on the variation among the means of the samples.
2. The F ratio is the between-groups estimate divided by the within-groups estimate. The null hypothesis is that all the samples come from populations with the same mean. If the null hypothesis is true, the F ratio should be about 1. This is because the two population variance estimates are based on the same thing, the variation within each of the populations (due to chance factors). If the research hypothesis is true, so that the samples come from populations with different means, the F ratio should be larger than 1. This is because the between-groups estimate is now influenced by the variation both within the populations (due to chance factors) and among them (due to a treatment effect). But the within-groups estimate is still affected only by the variation within each of the populations.
3. When the samples are of equal size, the within-groups population variance estimate is the ordinary average of the estimates of the population variance figured from each sample. The between-groups population variance estimate is done in two steps. First, you estimate the variance of the distribution of means based on the means of your samples. (This is figured with the usual formula for estimating population variance from sample scores.) Second, you multiply this estimate by the number of participants in each group. This step takes you from the variance of the distribution of means to the variance of the distribution of individual scores.
4. The distribution of F ratios when the null hypothesis is true is a mathematically defined distribution that is skewed to the right. Significance cutoffs are given on an F table according to the degrees of freedom for each population variance estimate: the between-groups (numerator) degrees of freedom is the number of groups minus 1 and the within-groups (denominator) degrees of freedom is the sum of the degrees of freedom within all samples.
5. The assumptions for the analysis of variance are the same as for the t test. The populations must be normally distributed, with equal variances. Like the t test, the analysis of variance is adequately accurate even when there are moderate violations of these assumptions.
6. The proportion of variance accounted for (R^2) (also called eta squared, η^2), is a measure of analysis of variance effect size. The formula for R^2 is: $R^2 = (S^2_{Between})(df_{Between})/[(S^2_{Between})(df_{Between}) + (S^2_{Within})(df_{Within})]$. Power depends on effect size, number of people in the study, significance level, and number of groups.
7. In a factorial research design, participants are put into groupings according to the combinations of the variables whose effects are being studied. In such designs, you can study the effects of two grouping (or independent) variables without needing twice as many participants. Also, such designs allow you to study the effects of combinations of the two grouping variables.

8. An interaction effect is when the impact of one grouping variable varies according to the level of the other grouping variable. A main effect is the impact of one grouping variable, ignoring the effect of the other grouping variable. Interaction effects and main effects can be described verbally, numerically, and graphically (usually on a graph with bars for each combination of the grouping variables, with the height of the bar being the score on the measured or dependent variable).

9. Analysis of variance results are reported in a standard fashion in research articles, such as $F(3, 68) = 5.21$, $p < .01$. In a factorial analysis of variance, there is usually a description in the text plus a table. A graph may also be used to show any significant interactions.

Key Terms

analysis of variance (ANOVA) (p. 312)

within-groups estimate of the population variance (S^2_{Within}) (p. 313)

between-groups estimate of the population variance ($S^2_{Between}$) (p. 314)

F ratio (p. 317)

F distribution (p. 317)

F table (p. 317)

grand mean (GM) (p. 322)

between-groups degrees of freedom ($df_{Between}$) (p. 324)

within-groups degrees of freedom (df_{within}) (p. 325)

protected t tests (p. 330)

proportion of variance accounted for (R^2) (p. 331)

factorial analysis of variance (p. 334)

factorial research design (p. 335)

interaction effect (p. 336)

two-way analysis of variance (p. 336)

two-way factorial research design (p. 336)

grouping variable (p. 336)

independent variable (p. 336)

one-way analysis of variance (p. 336)

main effect (p. 336)

cell (p. 337)

cell mean (p. 337)

marginal means (p. 337)

dependent variable (p. 337)

Example Worked-Out Problems

Overall Analysis of Variance

An experiment compares the effects of four treatments, giving each treatment to 20 participants and then assessing their performance on a standard measure. The results on the standard measure are Treatment 1: $M = 15$, $S^2 = 20$; Treatment 2: $M = 12$, $S^2 = 25$; Treatment 3: $M = 18$, $S^2 = 14$; Treatment 4: $M = 15$, $S^2 = 27$. Use the five steps of hypothesis testing (and the .05 significance level) to determine whether treatment matters.

Answer

Steps of hypothesis testing:

❶ **Restate the question as a research hypothesis and a null hypothesis about the populations.** There are four populations:

Population 1: People given experimental treatment 1.
Population 2: People given experimental treatment 2.
Population 3: People given experimental treatment 3.
Population 4: People given experimental treatment 4.

The null hypothesis is that these four populations have the same mean. The research hypothesis is that the four population means are not the same.

❷ **Determine the characteristics of the comparison distribution.** The comparison distribution will be an F distribution.

$$df_{\text{Between}} = N_{\text{Groups}} - 1 = 4 - 1 = 3;$$
$$df_{\text{Within}} = df_1 + df_2 + \ldots + df_{\text{Last}} = 19 + 19 + 19 + 19 = 76.$$

❸ **Determine the cutoff sample score on the comparison distribution at which the null hypothesis should be rejected.** Using Table A–3 in the Appendix for $df = 3, 75$ (the closest below 3, 76) at the .05 level, the cutoff F is 2.73.

❹ **Determine your sample's score on the comparison distribution.**

a. Figure the between-groups population variance estimate (S^2_{Between}): Figure the mean of each group. The group means are 15, 12, 18, and 15.

   ❹ **Estimate the variance of the distribution of means:** Sum the sample means' squared deviations from the grand mean and divide by the number of means minus 1:

$$GM = (15 + 12 + 18 + 15)/4 = 15.$$
$$S^2_M = \Sigma(M - GM)^2/df_{\text{Between}}$$
$$= ([15 - 15]^2 + [12 - 15]^2 + [18 - 15]^2 + [15 - 15]^2)/(4 - 1)$$
$$= (0 + 9 + 9 + 0)/3 = 18/3 = 6.$$

   ❺ **Figure the estimated variance of the population of individual scores:** Multiply the variance of the distribution of means by the number of scores in each group.

$$S^2_{\text{Between}} = (S^2_M)(n) = (6)(n) = (6)(20) = 120.$$

b. Figure the within-groups population variance estimate (S^2_{Within}):
   i. Figure population variance estimates based on each group's scores. Treatment 1 group, $S^2 = 20$; Treatment 2 group, $S^2 = 25$; Treatment 3 group, $S^2 = 14$; Treatment 4 group, $S^2 = 27$.
   ii. Average these variance estimates.

$$S^2_{\text{Within}} = (20 + 25 + 14 + 27)/4 = 86/4 = 21.5.$$

c. Figure the F ratio:

$$F = S^2_{\text{Between}}/S^2_{\text{Within}} = 120/21.5 = 5.58.$$

❺ **Decide whether to reject the null hypothesis.** The F of 5.58 is more extreme than the .05 cutoff F of 2.73. Therefore, reject the null hypothesis. The research hypothesis is supported; the different experimental treatments do produce different effects on the standard performance measure.

Figuring Effect Size for an Analysis of Variance

Figure the effect size for the analysis of variance question above.

Answer

$$R^2 = (S^2_{\text{Between}})(df_{\text{Between}})/[(S^2_{\text{Between}})(df_{\text{Between}}) + (S^2_{\text{Within}})(df_{\text{Within}})]$$
$$= (120)(3)/[(120)(3) + (21.5)(76)] = (360)/[(360) + (1634)] = .18.$$

Outline for Writing Essays for a One-Way Analysis of Variance

1. Explain that the one-way analysis of variance is used for hypothesis testing when you have scores from three or more entirely separate groups of people. Be sure to explain the meaning of the research hypothesis and the null hypothesis in this situation.
2. Describe the core logic of hypothesis testing in this situation. Be sure to mention that the analysis of variance involves comparing the results of two ways of estimating the population variance. One population variance estimate (the within-groups estimate) is based on the variation within each sample and the other estimate (the between-groups estimate) is based on the variation among the means of the samples. Be sure to describe these estimates in detail (including how they are figured, why they are figured that way, and how each is affected by whether or not the null hypothesis is true) and explain how and why they are used to figure an F ratio.
3. Explain the logic of the comparison distribution that is used with a one-way analysis of variance (the F distribution).
4. Describe the logic and process for determining the cutoff sample F score on the comparison distribution at which the null hypothesis should be rejected.
5. Explain how and why the scores from Steps ❸ and ❹ of the hypothesis-testing process are compared. Explain the meaning of the result of this comparison with regard to the specific research and null hypotheses being tested.

Practice Problems

These problems involve figuring. Most real-life statistics problems are done on a computer with special statistical software. Even if you have such software, do these problems by hand to ingrain the method in your mind. To learn how to use a computer to solve statistics problems like those in this chapter, refer to the *Using SPSS* section at the end of this chapter and the *Student's Study Guide and SPSS Workbook* that accompanies this text.

All data are fictional unless an actual citation is given.

Set I (for answers, see pp. 449–451)

1. For each of the following studies, decide whether you can reject the null hypothesis that the groups come from identical populations. Use the .05 level. In addition, figure the effect size and approximate power for each. Note that studies (b) and (c) provide S, not S^2.

(a)	Group 1	Group 2	Group 3
n	10	10	10
M	7.4	6.8	6.8
S^2	.82	.90	.80

(b)	Group 1	Group 2	Group 3	Group 4
n	25	25	25	25
M	94	101	124	105
S	24	28	31	25

(c)	Group 1	Group 2	Group 3	Group 4	Group 5
n	25	25	25	25	25
M	94	101	124	105	106
S	24	28	31	25	27

2. For each of the following studies, decide whether you can reject the null hypothesis that the groups come from identical populations. Use the .01 level. In addition, figure the effect size for each. (Be sure to show your calculations throughout.)

(a)	Group 1	Group 2	Group 3
	8	6	4
	8	6	4
	7	5	3
	9	7	5

(b)	Group 1	Group 2	Group 3
	12	10	8
	4	2	0
	12	10	8
	4	2	0

3. A social worker at a small mental hospital was asked to determine whether there was any clear difference in the length of stay of patients with different categories of diagnosis. Looking at the last four clients in each of the three major categories, the results (in terms of weeks of stay) were as follows:

Diagnosis Category		
Affective Disorders	Cognitive Disorders	Drug-Related Conditions
8	12	8
6	8	10
4	9	12
6	11	10

(a) Using the .05 level and the five steps of hypothesis testing, determine if there is a significant difference in length of stay among diagnosis categories; (b) figure the effect size for the study; and (c) explain your answer to (a) to someone who understands everything involved in conducting a *t* test for independent means but who is unfamiliar with the analysis of variance.

4. A study compared the felt intensity of unrequited love among three groups: 50 individuals who were currently experiencing unrequited love, who had a mean experienced intensity, $M = 3.5$, $S^2 = 5.2$; 50 who had previously experienced unrequited love and described their experiences retrospectively, $M = 3.2$, $S^2 = 5.8$; and 50 who had never experienced unrequited love but described how they thought they would feel if they were to experience it, $M = 3.8$, $S^2 = 4.8$. (a) Using the .05 level and the five steps of hypothesis testing, determine the significance of the difference among groups; (b) figure the effect size and approximate power; and (c) explain your answer to (a) to someone who has never had a course in statistics.

5. A researcher studying genetic influences on learning compares the maze performance of four genetically different strains of rats, using eight rats per strain. Performance for the four strains were as follows:

Strain	Mean	S
J	41	3.5
M	38	4.6
Q	14	3.8
W	37	4.9

(a) Using the .01 significance level and the five steps of hypothesis testing, is there an overall difference in maze performance among the four strains?; (b) figure the effect size for the study; and (c) explain your answer to (a) to someone who is familiar with hypothesis testing with known populations, but is unfamiliar with the *t* test or the analysis of variance.

6. What is the power of each of the following planned studies, using the analysis of variance with $p < .05$?

	Predicted Effect Size	Number of Groups	Participants in Each Group
(a)	Small	3	20
(b)	Small	3	30
(c)	Small	4	20
(d)	Medium	3	20

7. About how many participants do you need in each group for 80% power in each of the following planned studies, using the analysis of variance with $p < .05$?

	Predicted Effect Size	Number of Groups
(a)	Small	3
(b)	Large	3
(c)	Small	4
(d)	Medium	3

8. Each of the following is a table of means showing results of a study using a factorial design. Assuming that any differences are statistically significant, for each table, (a) and (b) make two bar graphs showing the results (in one graph grouping the bars according to one variable and in the other graph grouping the bars according to the other variable); (c) indicate which effects (main and interaction), if any, are found; and (d) describe the meaning of the pattern of means (that is, any main or interaction effects or the lack thereof) in words.
   i. Measured variable: Income (thousands of dollars)

		Age	
		Young	Old
Class	Lower	20	35
	Upper	25	100

   ii. Measured variable: Grade point average

		Major	
		Science	Arts
College	Community	2.1	2.8
	Liberal Arts	2.8	2.1

iii. Measured variable: Days sick per month

	Gender	
Group	*Females*	*Males*
Exercisers	2.0	2.5
Controls	3.1	3.6

9. Each of the following is a table of means showing results of a study using a factorial design. Assuming that any differences are statistically significant, for each table, (a) and (b) make two bar graphs showing the results (in one graph grouping the bars according to one variable and in the other graph grouping the bars according to the other variable); (c) indicate which effects (main and interaction), if any, are found; and (d) describe the meaning of the pattern of means (that is, any main or interaction effects or the lack thereof) in words.

i. Measured variable: Conversation length

	Topic	
Relationship	*Nonpersonal*	*Personal*
Friend	16	20
Parent	10	6

ii. Measured variable: Rated restaurant quality

	City		
Cost	*New York*	*Chicago*	*Vancouver*
Expensive	9	5	7
Moderate	6	4	6
Inexpensive	4	3	5

iii. Measured variable: Ratings of flavor

	Coffee Brand		
Type	*X*	*Y*	*Z*
Regular	7	4	6
Decaf	5	2	6

10. Grilo, Walker, Becker, Edell, and McGlashan (1997) are researchers interested in the relation of depression and substance use to personality disorders. Personality disorders are persistent, problematic traits and behaviors that exceed the usual range of individual differences. The researchers conducted interviews assessing personality disorders with adolescents who were psychiatric inpatients and had one of three diagnoses: those with major depression, those with substance abuse, and those with both major depression and substance abuse. The mean number of disorders was as follows: major depression, $M = 1.0$; substance abuse, $M = .7$; those with both conditions, $M = 1.9$. The researchers reported, "The three study groups differed in the average number of diagnosed personality disorders, $F(2, 112) = 10.18, p < .0001$." Explain this result to someone who is familiar with hypothesis testing with known populations, but is unfamiliar with the t test or the analysis of variance.

11. A researcher wants to know if the need for health care among prisoners varies according to the different types of prison facilities. The researcher randomly selects 40 prisoners from each of the three main types of prisons in a particular Canadian province and conducts exams to determine their need for health care. In the article describing the results, the researcher reported the means for each

group and then added: "The need for health care among prisoners in the three types of prison systems appeared to be clearly different, $F(2, 117) = 5.62, p < .01$." Explain this result to a person who has never had a course in statistics.

12. Do different types of English words—such as nouns, verbs, and adjectives—vary in length? Go to your dictionary, turn to random pages (using the random numbers listed below), and go down the column until you come to a noun. Note its length (in number of letters). Do this for 10 different nouns. Do the same for 10 verbs and then for 10 adjectives. Using the .05 significance level, carry out an analysis of variance comparing the three types of words. (Be sure also to give the full bibliographic information on your dictionary—authors, title, year published, publisher, city.)

651, 73, 950, 320, 564, 666, 736, 768, 661, 484, 990, 379, 323, 219, 715, 472, 176, 811, 167, 612, 102, 452, 849, 615, 228, 352, 851, 981, 821, 834, 719, 525, 907, 448, 4, 335, 671, 118, 403.

Set II

13. For each of the following studies, decide if you can reject the null hypothesis that the groups come from identical populations. Use the .05 level.

(a)	Group 1	Group 2	Group 3
n	5	5	5
M	10	12	14
S^2	4	6	5

(b)	Group 1	Group 2	Group 3
n	10	10	10
M	10	12	14
S^2	4	6	5

(c)	Group 1	Group 2	Group 3
n	5	5	5
M	10	14	18
S^2	4	6	5

(d)	Group 1	Group 2	Group 3
n	5	5	5
M	10	12	14
S^2	2	3	2.5

14. For each of the following studies, decide whether you can reject the null hypothesis that the groups come from identical populations. Use the .01 level. In addition, figure the effect size for each.

(a)	Group 1	Group 2	Group 3
	1	1	8
	2	2	7
	1	1	8
	2	2	7

(b)	Group 1	Group 2	Group 3
	1	4	8
	2	5	7
	1	4	8
	2	5	7

15. An organizational researcher was interested in whether individuals working in different sectors of a company differed in their attitudes toward the company. The results for the three people surveyed in engineering were 10, 12, and 11; for the three in the marketing department, 6, 6, and 8; for the three in accounting, 7, 4, and 4; and for the three in production, 14, 16, and 13 (higher numbers mean more positive attitudes). Was there a significant difference in attitude toward the company among employees working in different sectors of the company at the .05 level? (a) Carry out the five steps of hypothesis testing; (b) figure the effect size; and (c) explain your answer to (a) to someone who understands everything involved in conducting a t test for independent means, but is unfamiliar with the analysis of variance.

16. Do students at various colleges differ in how sociable they are? Twenty-five students were randomly selected from each of three colleges in a particular region and were asked to report on the amount of time they spent socializing each day with other students. The results for College X was a mean of 5 hours and an estimated population variance of 2 hours; for College Y, $M = 4$, $S^2 = 1.5$; and for College Z, $M = 6$, $S^2 = 2.5$. What should you conclude? Use the .05 level. (a) Use the five steps of hypothesis testing; (b) figure the effect size; and (c) explain your answers to (a) and (b) to someone who understands everything involved in conducting a t test for independent means but who has never heard of the analysis of variance.

17. A researcher studying artistic preference randomly assigns a group of 45 participants to one of three conditions in which they view a series of unfamiliar abstract paintings. The 15 participants in the Famous condition are led to believe that these are each famous paintings; their mean rating for liking the paintings is 6.5 ($S = 3.5$). The 15 in the Critically Acclaimed condition are led to believe that these are paintings that are not famous but are very highly thought of by a group of professional art critics; their mean rating is 8.5 ($S = 4.2$). The 15 in the Control condition are given no special information about the paintings; their mean rating is 3.1 ($S = 2.9$). Does what people are told about paintings make a difference in how well they are liked? Use the .05 level. (a) Use the five steps of hypothesis testing; (b) figure the effect size; and (c) explain your answer to (a) to someone who is familiar with the t test for independent means, but is unfamiliar with analysis of variance.

18. What is the power of each of the following planned studies, using the analysis of variance with $p < .05$?

	Predicted Effect Size	Number of Groups	Participants in Each Group
(a)	Small	4	50
(b)	Medium	4	50
(c)	Large	4	50
(d)	Medium	5	50

19. About how many participants do you need in each group for 80% power in each of the following planned studies, using the analysis of variance with $p < .05$?

	Predicted Effect Size	Number of Groups
(a)	Small	5
(b)	Medium	5
(c)	Large	5
(d)	Medium	3

20. Each of the following is a table of means showing results of a study using a factorial design. Assuming that any differences are statistically significant, for each table (a) and (b), make two bar graphs showing the results (in one graph grouping the bars according to one variable and in the other graph grouping the bars according to the other variable); (c) indicate which effects (main and interaction), if any, are found; and (d) describe the meaning of the pattern of means (that is, any main or interaction effects or the lack thereof) in words.

    i. Measured variable: Degree of envy of another person's success

	Degree of Success	
Status of Other	*Great*	*Small*
Friend	8	5
Stranger	1	4

    ii. Measured variable: Observed engagement in the activity

	Play Activity	
Situation	*Blocks*	*Dress Up*
Alone	4.5	2.5
With playmate	2.5	4.5

    iii. Measured variable: Intensity of attention

	Program	
Type of Balletgoer	*The Nutcracker*	*Modern*
Regular	20	15
Sometime	15	15
Novice	10	5

21. Each of the following is a table of means showing results of a study using a factorial design. Assuming that any differences are statistically significant, for each table (a) and (b), make two bar graphs showing the results (in one graph grouping the bars according to one variable and in the other graph grouping the bars according to the other variable); (c) indicate which effects (main and interaction), if any, are found; and (d) describe the meaning of the pattern of means (that is, any main or interaction effects or the lack thereof) in words.

    i. Measured variable: Right frontal neural activity in brain during memory task

	Items Remembered	
Times Presented	*Words*	*Pictures*
Once	45	68
Twice	30	30

ii. Measured variable: Approval rating of the U.S. president

		Region			
		West	East	Midwest	South
Class	Middle	70	45	55	50
	Lower	50	25	35	30

iii. Measured variable: Satisfaction with education

		Gender	
		Females	Males
Time After Obtaining BA	1 month	3	3
	1 year	4	4
	5 years	9	9

22. An experiment is conducted in which 60 participants each fill out a personality test, but not according to the way the participants see themselves. Instead, 15 are randomly assigned to fill it out according to the way they think their mothers see them (that is, the way they think their mothers would fill it out to describe the participants); 15 as their fathers would fill it out for them; 15 as their best friends would fill it out for them; and 15 as the professors they know best would fill it out for them. The main results appear in Table 10–13. Explain these results to a person who has never had a course in statistics.

23. Sinclair and Kunda (2000) tested the idea that if you want to think well of someone (for example, because they have said positive things about you), you are less influenced by the normal stereotypes when evaluating them. Participants filled out a questionnaire on their social skills and then received feedback from either a male or female "manager in training." The study was rigged so that the managers gave half the participants positive feedback and half negative feedback. The participants then rated the managers for their skill at evaluating them. The question was whether the usual tendency to stereotype women as less skillful managers would be undermined when people got positive ratings. Sinclair and Kunda described their results as follows:

> Participants' ratings of the manager's skill at evaluating them were analyzed with a 2 (feedback) $\times$ 2 (manager gender) [two-way] ANOVA. Managers who had provided positive feedback ($M = 9.08$) were rated more highly than were managers who had provided negative feedback ($M = 7.46$), $F(1,46) = 19.44$, $p < .0001$. However, as may be seen in . . . [Figure 10–7], the effect was qualified by a significant interaction, $F(1, 46) = 4.71$, $p < .05$ . . . (pp. 1335–1336).

Table 10-13 Means for Main Personality Scales for Each Experimental Condition (Fictional Data)

Scale	Mother	Father	Friend	Professor	F(3, 56)
Conformity	24	21	12	16	4.21**
Extroversion	14	13	15	13	2.05
Maturity	15	15	22	19	3.11*
Self-confidence	38	42	27	32	3.58*

*p < .05, **p < .01.

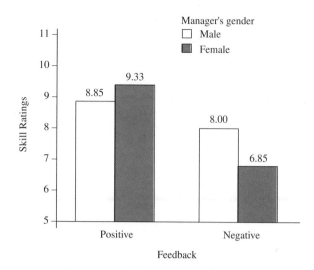

Figure 10–7 Participants' ratings of the manager's skill at evaluating them as a function of feedback favorability and the manager's gender (Study 2). *Source:* Sinclair, L., & Kunda, Z. (2000). Motivated stereotyping of women: She's fine if she praised me but incompetent if she criticized me. *Personality and Social Psychology Bulletin, 26, 11,* 1329–1342. Copyright © 1997 by the Society for Personality and Social Psychology, Inc. Reprinted by permission of Sage Publications, Inc. Journal via Copyright Clearance Center.

Describe the meaning of these results to a person who has never had a course in statistics. (Do not go into the details of the figuring, just the basic logic of the pattern of means, and the meaning of any significant results.)

24. Cut up 100 little pieces of paper of about the same size and write "1" on 16, "2" on 34, "3" on 34, and "4" on 16 of them. (You are creating an approximately normal distribution.) Put the slips into a bowl or hat, mix them up, draw out two, write the numbers on them down, and put them back. Then draw out another two, write down their numbers, and put them back, and finally another two, write down their numbers, and put them back. (Strictly speaking, you should sample "with replacement." That means putting each one, not two, back after writing its number down. But we want to save you a little time, and it should not make much difference in this case.) Figure an analysis of variance for these three randomly selected groups of two each. Write down the F ratio, and repeat the entire drawing process and analysis of variance again. Do this entire process at least 20 times, and make a frequency polygon of your results. You are creating an F distribution for 2 (3 groups − 1) and 3 (2 − 1 in each of three groups) degrees of freedom. At what point do the top 5% of your F scores begin? Compare that to the 5% cutoff given in Table A-3 in the Appendix for 2 and 3 degrees of freedom.

Using SPSS

The ✐ in the steps below indicates a mouse click. (We used SPSS version 13.0 for Windows to carry out these analyses. The steps and output may be slightly different for other versions of SPSS.)

One-Way Analysis of Variance

It is easier to learn these steps using actual numbers, so we will use the criminal record example from earlier in the chapter. The scores for that example are shown in Table 10–3.

❶ Enter the scores into SPSS. SPSS assumes that all scores in a row are from the same person. In this example, each person is in only one of the three groups (the criminal record group, the clean record group, or the no information group). Thus, in order to tell SPSS which person is in each group, you should enter the numbers as shown in Figure 10–8. In the first column (labeled "group"), we used the number "1" to indicate that a person is in the criminal record group, the number "2" to indicate that a person is in the clean record group, and the number "3" to indicate a person is in the no information group.

❷ ✐ *Analyze.*

❸ ✐ *Compare means.*

❹ ✐ *One-Way ANOVA.*

❺ ✐ on the variable called "guilt" and then ✐ the arrow next to the box labeled "Dependent List" (this is the name used by SPSS to refer to the measured variable). This tells SPSS that the analysis of variance should be carried out on the scores for the "guilt" variable.

❻ ✐ the variable called "group" and then ✐ the arrow next to the box labeled "Factor." This tells SPSS that the variable called "group" shows which person is in which group.

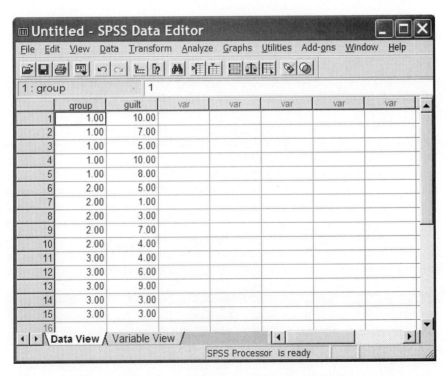

Figure 10–8   SPSS data editor window for the criminal record study example (in which 15 individuals rated the guilt of a defendant after being randomly assigned to one of three groups that were given different information about the defendant's previous criminal record).

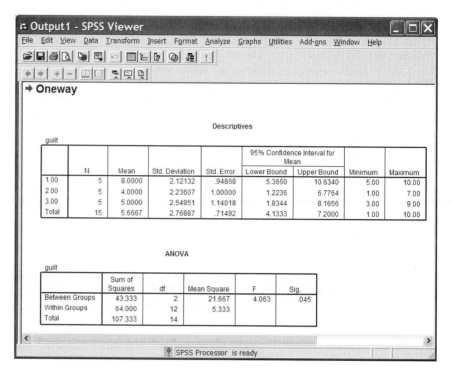

Figure 10–9   SPSS output window for a one-way analysis of variance for the criminal record example.

❼   ✎ *Options.* Click the box labeled *Descriptive* (this checks the box). This tells SPSS to provide descriptive statistics (such as the mean and standard deviation) for each group. ✎ *Continue.* (Step ❼ is optional, but we recommend always requesting descriptive statistics for any hypothesis testing situation.)

❽   ✎ *OK.* Your SPSS output window should look like Figure 10–9.

The first table in the SPSS output provides descriptive statistics (number of individuals, mean, estimated population standard deviation, and other statistics) for the "guilt" scores for each of the three groups.

The second table in the SPSS output shows the actual results of the one-way analysis of variance. The first column lists the types of population variance estimates (between groups and within groups). For our purposes, you can ignore the second column (labeled "Sums of Squares"). The third column, "df," gives the degrees of freedom. In the between groups row, this corresponds to $df_{Between}$; in the within groups row, this corresponds to df_{Within}. The fourth column, labeled "Mean Square," gives the population variance estimates ($S^2_{Between}$ and S^2_{Within}), with the between-groups estimate first and then the within-groups estimate. The next column gives the F ratio for the analysis of variance. Allowing for rounding error, the values for "df," "Mean Square," and "F" are the same as those given earlier in the chapter. The final column, "Sig." shows the exact significance level of the F ratio. The significance level of .045 is less than our .05 cutoff for this example. Thus, you can reject the null hypothesis and the research hypothesis is supported (that is, the result is statistically significant).

CHAPTER 11

Chi-Square Tests and Strategies When Population Distributions Are Not Normal

CHAPTER OUTLINE

- Chi-Square Tests
- The Chi-Square Statistic and the Chi-Square Test for Goodness of Fit
- The Chi-Square Test for Independence
- Assumptions for the Chi-Square Tests
- Effect Size and Power for the Chi-Square Tests for Independence
- Strategies for Hypothesis Testing When Population Distributions Are Not Normal
- Data Transformations
- Rank-Order Tests
- Comparison of Methods
- Chi-Square Tests, Data Transformations, and Rank-Order Tests in Research Articles
- Summary
- Key Terms
- Example Worked-Out Problems
- Practice Problems
- Using SPSS

The hypothesis-testing procedures you have learned in the last few chapters (the *t* test and the analysis of variance) are very versatile, but there are many research situations in which these methods cannot be used. One such situation is hypothesis testing for variables whose values are categories—such as a person's region of the country, religious preference, or hair color.

The *t* test and the analysis of variance all require that the measured variable have scores that are quantitative, such as rating on a 7-point scale or number of years served as mayor. Another research situation in which the ordinary *t* test and analysis of variance do not apply is when the populations do not clearly follow a normal curve.

This chapter examines hypothesis testing in these two situations in which the ordinary hypothesis-testing procedures cannot be used properly. The first half of the chapter focuses on chi-square tests. **Chi-square tests** are used when the variable of interest is a *nominal variable* (that is, a variable with values that are categories). (Chi

chi-square test Hypothesis-testing procedure used when the variables of interest are nominal variables.

TIP FOR SUCCESS

This chapter assumes you have a solid command of hypothesis testing and are familiar with the *t* test and analysis of variance, and in particular the assumptions required for their use. In addition, you should review the Chapter 1 material on kinds of variables and on shapes of distributions.

is the Greek letter χ and is pronounced *ki,* rhyming with *high* and *pie.*) The chi-square test was originally developed by Karl Pearson (see Box 11–1) and is sometimes called the *Pearson chi-square.* The second half of the chapter focuses on strategies for hypothesis testing when you cannot assume that the population distributions are even roughly normal.

Chi-Square Tests

Consider an example. Harter et al. (1997) were interested in three styles of relating to romantic partners: a self-focused autonomy style, an other-focused connection style, and a mutuality style. Harter et al. conducted a newspaper survey that included items about the respondents' relationship styles and also the respondents' perceptions of their partners' styles. One of the researchers' predictions was that men who described

---

BOX 11–1　Karl Pearson: Inventor of Chi-Square and Center of Controversy

Topham/The Image Works

Karl Pearson, sometimes hailed as the founder of the science of statistics, was born in 1857. Both his virtues and vices are revealed in what he reported to his colleague Julia Bell as his earliest memory: He was sitting in his highchair, sucking his thumb, when he was told to stop or his thumb would wither away. Pearson silently thought, "I can't see that the thumb I suck is any smaller than the other. I wonder if she could be lying to me." Here we see Pearson's faith in himself and in observational evidence and his rejection of authority. We also see his tendency to doubt the character of people with whom he disagreed.

Pearson studied mathematics at Cambridge. Soon after he arrived, he requested to be excused from compulsory chapel. As soon as his request was granted, however, he appeared in chapel. The dean summoned him for an explanation, and Pearson declared that he had asked to be excused not from chapel "but from *compulsory* chapel."

After graduation, Pearson studied in Germany, becoming a socialist and a self-described "free-thinker." Returning to England, he changed his name from Carl to Karl (in honor of Karl Marx) and wrote an attack on Christianity under a pen name. In 1885 he founded a "Men and Women's Club" to promote equality between the sexes.

Most of Pearson's research from 1893 to 1901 focused on the laws of heredity, but he needed better statistical methods, leading to his most famous contribution, the chi-square test. Pearson also invented the method of computing correlation used today and coined the terms *histogram, skew,* and *spurious correlation.* When he felt that biology journals failed to appreciate his work, he founded the famous journal *Biometrika.*

Unfortunately, Pearson was a great fan of eugenics, and his work was later used by the Nazis as justification for their treatment of the Jews. Toward the end of his life he wrote a paper using clear logic and data on Jews and Gentiles from all over the world to demonstrate that the Nazis' ideas were sheer nonsense.

Indeed, throughout his life, Pearson's strong opinions led to a long list of enemies, especially as other, younger statisticians passed him by, while he refused to publish their work in *Biometrika.* William S. Gosset (Chapter 8, Box 8–1) was one of his friends. Sir Ronald Fisher (Chapter 10, Box 10–1), was one of Pearson's worst enemies. The kindly Gosset was always trying to smooth matters between them. In 1933, Pearson finally retired, and Fisher, of all persons, took over his chair, the Galton Professorship of Eugenics at University College in London. In 1936, the two entered into their bitterest argument yet; Pearson died the same year.

For more information about Pearson, see http://en.wikipedia.org/wiki/Karl_Pearson and http://human-nature.com/nibbs/03/kpearson.html.

Sources: Peters (1987), Salsburg (2001), Stigler (1986), Tankard (1984).

themselves as having the self-focused autonomy style would be most likely to describe their partners as having the other-focused style. And sure enough, of the 101 self-focused men in their study, 49.5% "reported the predicted pairing, compared to 25.5% who reported self-focused autonomous partners and 24.5% who reported partners displaying mutuality" (p. 156). In terms of raw numbers, of the 101 self-focused men, 50 had other-focused partners, 26 had self-focused partners, and 25 had mutuality-style partners.

Suppose the partners of these 101 self-focused men had been equally likely to be of each of the three relationship styles. If that were the situation, then about 33.66 (1/3 of the 101) of the partners of these men should have been of each style. This information is laid out in the "Observed Frequency" and "Expected Frequency" columns of Table 11–1. The Observed Frequency column shows the breakdown of relationship styles of partners actually *observed*. The Expected Frequency column shows the breakdown you would *expect* if the different partner styles had been exactly equally likely. (Note that it won't always be the case that you expect an *equal breakdown* across the categories. In other situations, the expected frequency for each category may be based on theory, or on a distribution in another study or circumstance.)

Clearly, there is a discrepancy between what was actually observed and the breakdown you would expect if each of the three partner styles were equally likely. The question is this: Should you assume that this discrepancy is no more than what we would expect just by chance for a sample of this size? Suppose that self-focused men in general (the population) are equally likely to have partners of the three styles. Still, in any particular sample from that population, you would not expect a perfectly equal breakdown of partners' styles. But if the breakdown in the sample is a long way from equal, you would doubt that the partner styles in the population really are equal. In other words, we are in a hypothesis-testing situation, much like the ones we have been considering all along. But with a big difference too.

In the situations in previous chapters, the scores have all been *numerical values* on some dimension, such as a score on a standard achievement test, length of time in a relationship, an employer's rating of an employee's job effectiveness on a 9-point scale, and so forth. By contrast, relationship style of a man's partner is an example of what in Chapter 1 we called a *nominal variable* (or a *categorical variable*). A nominal variable is one in which the information is the number of people in each category. These are called nominal variables because the different categories or levels of the variable have names instead of numbers. Hypothesis testing with nominal variables uses what are called *chi-square tests*.

Table 11–1 Observed and Expected Frequencies for Relationship Styles of Partners of Self-Focused Autonomous Men

Partner Style	Observed Frequency[a] (O)	Expected Frequency (E)	Difference $(O - E)$	Difference Squared $(O - E)^2$	Difference Squared Weighted by Expected Frequency $(O - E)^2/E$
Other-Focused Connection	50	33.67	16.33	266.67	7.92
Self-Focused Autonomous	26	33.67	−7.67	58.83	1.75
Mutuality	25	33.67	−8.67	75.17	2.23

[a]Data from Harter et al. (1997).

chi-square test for goodness of fit
Hypothesis-testing procedure that examines how well an observed frequency distribution of a single nominal variable fits some expected pattern of frequencies.

chi-square test for independence
Hypothesis-testing procedure that examines whether the distribution of frequencies over the categories of one nominal variable are unrelated to (independent of) the distribution of frequencies over the categories of a second nominal variable.

observed frequency (O) In a chi-square test, number of individuals actually found in the study to be in a category or cell.

expected frequency (E) In a chi-square test, number of people in a category or cell expected if the null hypothesis were true.

The Chi-Square Statistic and the Chi-Square Test for Goodness of Fit

The basic idea of any chi-square test is that you compare how well an *observed breakdown* of people over various categories fits some *expected breakdown* (such as an equal breakdown). In this chapter, you will learn about two types of chi-square tests. First, you will learn about the **chi-square test for goodness of fit,** which is a chi-square test involving levels of a *single nominal variable.* Later in the chapter, you will learn about the **chi-square test for independence,** which is used when there are *two nominal variables,* each with several categories.

In terms of the relationship style example—in which there is a single nominal variable with three categories—you are comparing the observed breakdown of 50, 26, and 25 to the expected breakdown of about 34 (33.67) for each style. A breakdown of numbers of people expected in each category is actually a frequency distribution, as you learned in Chapter 1. Thus, a chi-square test is more formally described as comparing an **observed frequency** distribution to an **expected frequency** distribution. Overall, what the hypothesis testing involves is first figuring a number for the amount of mismatch between the observed frequencies and the expected frequencies and then seeing whether that number indicates a greater mismatch than you would expect by chance.

Let's start with how you would come up with that mismatch number for the observed versus expected frequencies. The mismatch between observed and expected for any one category is just the observed frequency minus the expected frequency. For example, consider again the Harter et al. (1997) study. For self-focused men with an other-focused partner, the observed frequency of 50 is 16.33 more than the expected frequency of 33.67 (recall the expected frequency is 1/3 of the 101 total). For the second category, the difference is −7.67. For the third, −8.67. These differences are shown in the Difference column of Table 11–1.

You do not use these differences directly. One reason is that some differences are positive and some are negative. Thus, they would cancel each other out. To get around this, you square each difference. (This is the same strategy we used in Chapter 2 to deal with difference scores in figuring the variance.) In the relationship-style example, the squared difference for self-focused men with other-focused partners is 16.33 squared, or 266.67. For those men with self-focused partners, it is 58.83. For those with mutuality-style partners, 75.17. These squared differences are shown in the Difference Squared column of Table 11–1.

In the Harter et al. (1997) example, the expected frequencies are the same in each category. But in other research situations, expected frequencies for the different categories may not be the same. A particular amount of difference between observed and expected has a different importance according to the size of the expected frequency. For example, a difference of eight people between observed and expected is a much bigger mismatch if the expected frequency is 10 than if the expected frequency is 1,000. If the expected frequency is 10, a difference of 8 would mean that the observed frequency was 18 or 2, frequencies that are dramatically different from 10. But if the expected frequency is 1,000, a difference of 8 is only a slight mismatch. This would mean that the observed frequency was 1,008 or 992, frequencies that are only slightly different from 1,000.

How can you adjust the mismatch (the squared difference) between observed and expected for a particular category? What you need to do is adjust or weight the mismatch to take into account the expected frequency for that category. You can do this by dividing your squared difference for a category by the expected frequency for that category. Thus, if the expected frequency for a particular category is 10, you divide the squared difference by 10. If the expected frequency for the category is 1,000, you divide the squared difference by 1,000. In this way, you weight each squared difference by the expected frequency. This weighting puts the squared difference onto a more appropriate scale of comparison.

Let's return to our example. For men with an other-focused partner, you would weight the mismatch by dividing the squared difference of 266.67 by 33.67, giving 7.92. For those with a self-focused partner, 58.83 divided by 33.67 gives 1.75. For those with a mutuality-style partner, 75.17 divided by 33.67 gives 2.23. These adjusted mismatches (squared differences divided by expected frequencies) are shown in the rightmost column of Table 11–1.

What remains is to get an overall number for the mismatch between observed and expected frequencies. This final step is done by adding up the mismatch for all the categories. That is, you take the result of the squared difference divided by the expected frequency for the first category, add the result of the squared difference divided by the expected frequency for the second category, and so on. In the Harter et al. example, this would be 7.92 plus 1.75 plus 2.23, for a total of 11.90. This final number (the sum of the weighted squared differences) is an overall indication of the amount of mismatch between the expected and observed frequencies. It is called the **chi-square statistic.** In terms of a formula,

$$\chi^2 = \Sigma \frac{(O - E)^2}{E} \qquad \textbf{(11-1)}$$

chi-square statistic (χ^2) Statistic that reflects the overall lack of fit between the expected and observed frequencies; the sum, over all the categories, of the squared difference between observed and expected frequencies divided by the expected frequency.

> Chi-square is the sum, over all the categories, of the squared difference between observed and expected frequencies divided by the expected frequency.

In this formula, χ^2 is the chi-square statistic. Σ is the summation sign, telling you to sum over all the different categories. O is the observed frequency for a category (the number of people actually found in that category in the study). E is the expected frequency for a category. (In this example, it is based on what we would expect if there were equal numbers in each category.)

Applying the formula to the Harter et al. example,

$$\chi^2 = \Sigma \frac{(O - E)^2}{E} = \frac{(50 - 33.67)^2}{33.67} + \frac{(26 - 33.67)^2}{33.67} + \frac{(25 - 33.67)^2}{33.67} = 11.90$$

Steps for Figuring the Chi-Square Statistic

Here is a summary of what we've said so far in terms of steps:

Ⓐ Determine the actual, observed frequencies in each category.
Ⓑ Determine the expected frequencies in each category.
Ⓒ In each category, take observed minus expected frequencies.
Ⓓ Square each of these differences.
Ⓔ Divide each squared difference by the expected frequency for its category.
Ⓕ Add up the results of Step Ⓔ for all the categories.

The Chi-Square Distribution

Now we turn to the question of whether the chi-square statistic you have figured is a bigger mismatch than you would expect by chance. To answer that, you need to know how likely it is to get chi-square statistics of various sizes by chance. That is, you need the distribution of chi-square statistics that would arise by chance. As long as you have a reasonable number of people in the study, the distribution of the chi-square

TIP FOR SUCCESS

Notice in the chi-square formula that, for each category, you *first* divide the squared difference between observed and expected frequencies by the expected frequency, and *then* you sum the resulting values for all the categories. This is a slightly different procedure that you are used to from previous chapters (in which you often *first* summed a series of squared values in the numerator and *then* divided by a denominator value). So be sure to follow the formula carefully.

chi-square distribution
Mathematically defined curve used as the comparison distribution in chi-square tests; the distribution of the chi-square statistic.

chi-square table Table of cutoff scores on the chi-square distribution for various degrees of freedom and significance levels.

> The degrees of freedom for the chi-square test for goodness of fit are the number of categories minus 1.

statistic follows quite closely a known mathematical distribution—the **chi-square distribution.**

The exact shape of the chi-square distribution depends on the degrees of freedom. For a chi-square test, the degrees of freedom are the number of categories that are free to vary, given the totals. In the partners' relationship-style example, there are three categories. If you know the total number of people and you know the number in any two categories, you could figure out the number in the third category—so only two are free to vary. That is, in a study like this one (which uses a chi-square test for goodness of fit), if there are three categories, there are two degrees of freedom. In terms of a formula,

(11-2)
$$df = N_{\text{Categories}} - 1$$

Chi-square distributions for several different degrees of freedom are shown in Figure 11–1. Notice that the distributions are all skewed to the right. This is because the chi-square statistic cannot be less than 0 but can have very high values. (Chi-square must be positive because it is figured by adding a group of fractions, in each of which the numerator and denominator both have to be positive. The numerator has to be positive because it is squared. The denominator has to be positive because the number of people expected in a given category can't be a negative number—you can't expect less than no one!)

The Chi-Square Table

Table 11–2 Portion of a Chi-Square Table (with Cutoff Value Highlighted for the Harter et al. Example)

df	Significance Level		
	.10	**.05**	**.01**
1	2.706	3.841	6.635
2	4.605	5.992	9.211
3	6.252	7.815	11.345
4	7.780	9.488	13.277
5	9.237	11.071	15.087

Note: Full table is Table A-4 in the Appendix.

What matters most about the chi-square distribution for hypothesis testing is the cutoff for a chi-square to be extreme enough to reject the null hypothesis. For example, suppose you are using the .05 significance level. In that situation, you want to know the point on the chi-square distribution where 5% of the chi-square statistics are above that point. A **chi-square table** gives the cutoff chi-square for different significance levels and various degrees of freedom. Table 11–2 shows a portion of a chi-square table like the one in the Appendix (Table A–4). For our example, where there were two degrees of freedom, the table shows that the cutoff chi-square for the .05 level is 5.992.

The Chi-Square Test for Goodness of Fit

In the Harter et al. example, we figured a chi-square of 11.90. This is clearly larger than the chi-square cutoff for this example (using the .05 significance level) of 5.992 (see Figure 11–2). Thus, the researchers rejected the null hypothesis. That is, they rejected as too unlikely that the mismatch they observed (between the observed and expected frequencies) could have come about if in the population of self-focused men

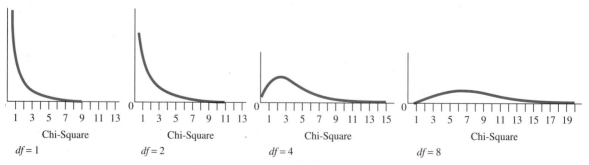

Figure 11–1 Examples of chi-square distributions for different degrees of freedom.

there were an equal number of partners of each relationship style. It seemed more reasonable to conclude that there truly were different proportions of relationship styles of the partners of such men.

We have just carried out a full hypothesis-testing procedure for the Harter et al. example. This example involved differing numbers of people at three levels of a particular nominal variable (the relationship style of partners of self-focused men). As we mentioned earlier, this kind of chi-square test involving levels of a single nominal variable is called a *chi-square test for goodness of fit*.

Steps of Hypothesis Testing

Let us review the chi-square test for goodness of fit. We will use the same example, but this time systematically follow our standard five steps of hypothesis testing. In the process we also consider some fine points.

❶ **Restate the question as a research hypothesis and a null hypothesis about the populations.** There are two populations:

Population 1: Self-focused men like those in the study.
Population 2: Self-focused men whose partners are equally of the three relationship styles.

The research hypothesis is that the distribution of people over categories in the two populations is different; the null hypothesis is that they are the same.

❷ **Determine the characteristics of the comparison distribution.** The comparison distribution here is a chi-square distribution with 2 degrees of freedom. (Once you know the total, there are only two category numbers still free to vary.)

❸ **Determine the cutoff on the comparison distribution at which the null hypothesis should be rejected.** You do this by looking up the cutoff on the chi-square table for your significance level and the study's degrees of freedom. In the present example, we used the .05 significance level, and we determined in Step ❷ that there were 2 degrees of freedom. Based on the chi-square table, this gives a cutoff chi-square of 5.992.

❹ **Determine your sample's score on the comparison distribution.** Your sample's score is the chi-square figured from the sample. In other words, this is where you do all the figuring.

ⓐ **Determine the actual, observed frequencies in each category.** These are shown in the first column of Table 11–1.

ⓑ **Determine the expected frequencies in each category.** We figured these each to be 33.67 based on expecting an equal distribution of the 101 partners.

ⓒ **In each category, take observed minus expected frequencies.** These are shown in the third column of Table 11–1.

ⓓ **Square each of these differences.** These are shown in the fourth column of Table 11–1.

ⓔ **Divide each squared difference by the expected frequency for its category.** These are shown in the fifth column of Table 11–1.

ⓕ **Add up the results of Step ⓔ for all the categories.** The result we figured earlier (11.90) is the chi-square statistic for the sample. It is shown in Figure 11–2.

❺ **Decide whether to reject the null hypothesis.** The chi-square cutoff to reject the null hypothesis (from Step ❸) is 5.992 and the chi-square of the sample (from Step ❹) is 11.90. Thus, you can reject the null hypothesis. The research hypothesis

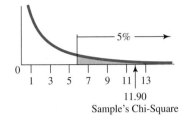

Figure 11–2 For the Harter et al. (1997) example, the chi-square distribution (*df* = 2) showing the cutoff for rejecting the null hypothesis at the .05 level and the sample's chi-square.

that the two populations are different is supported. That is, Harter et al. could conclude that the partners of self-focused men are not equally likely to be of the three relationship styles.

How are you doing?

1. In what situation do you use a chi-square test for goodness of fit?
2. List the steps for figuring the chi-square statistic and explain the logic behind each step.
3. Write the formula for the chi-square statistic and define each of the symbols.
4. (a) What is a chi-square distribution? (b) What is its shape? (c) Why does it have that shape?
5. Use the steps of hypothesis testing to carry out a chi-square test for goodness of fit (using the .05 significance level) for a sample in which one category has 15 people, the other has 35 people, and the categories are expected to have equal frequencies.

Answers

1. When you want to test whether a sample's distribution of people across categories represents a population that is significantly different from a population with an expected distribution of people across categories.

2. ❶ **Determine the actual, observed frequencies in each category.** This is the key information for the sample studied.
   ❷ **Determine the expected frequencies in each category.** Having these numbers makes it possible to make a direct comparison of what is expected to the observed frequencies.
   ❸ **In each category, take observed minus expected frequencies.** This is the direct comparison of the distribution for the sample versus the distribution representing the expected population.
   ❹ **Square each of these differences.** This gets rid of the direction of the difference (since the interest is only in how much difference there is).
   ❺ **Divide each squared difference by the expected frequency for its category.** This adjusts the degree of difference for the absolute size of the expected frequencies.
   ❻ **Add up the results of Step ❺ for all the categories.** This gives you a statistic for the overall degree of discrepancy.

3. $$\chi^2 = \sum \frac{(O - E)^2}{E}$$

   χ^2 is the chi-square statistic; $\sum$ tells you to sum over all the different categories; O is the observed frequency for a category; E is the expected frequency for a category.

4. (a) For any particular number of categories, the distribution you would expect if you figured a very large number of chi-square statistics for samples from a population in which the distribution of people over categories is the expected distribution.
   (b) It is skewed to the right.
   (c) It has this shape because a chi-square statistic can't be less than 0 (since the numerator, a squared score, has to be positive, and its denominator, an expected number of individuals, also has to be positive), but there is no limit to how large it can be.

5. ❶ **Restate the question as a research hypothesis and a null hypothesis about the populations.** There are two populations:

Population 1: People like those in the sample.

Population 2: People who have an equal distribution of the two categories.

The research hypothesis is that the distribution of numbers of people over categories is different in the two populations; the null hypothesis is that it is the same.

❷ **Determine the characteristics of the comparison distribution.** The comparison distribution is a chi-square distribution with 1 degree of freedom (that is, $df = N_{Categories} - 1 = 2 - 1 = 1$).

❸ **Determine the cutoff sample score on the comparison distribution at which the null hypothesis should be rejected.** At the .05 level with $df = 1$, cutoff is 3.841.

❹ **Determine your sample's score on the comparison distribution.**

  ❶ **Determine the actual, observed frequencies in each category.** As given in the problem, these are 15 and 35.

  ❷ **Determine the expected frequencies in each category.** With 50 people total and expecting an even breakdown, the expected frequencies are 25 and 25.

  ❸ **In each category, take observed minus expected frequencies.** These come out to −10 (that is, 15 − 25 = −10) and 10 (that is, 35 − 25 = 10).

  ❹ **Square each of these differences.** Both come out to 100 (that is, $-10^2 = 100$ and $10^2 = 100$).

  ❺ **Divide each squared difference by the expected frequency for its category.** These both come out to 4 (that is, 100/25 = 4).

  ❻ **Add up the results of Step ❺ for all the categories.** 4 + 4 = 8.

❺ **Decide whether to reject the null hypothesis.** The sample's chi-square of 8 is more extreme than the cutoff of 3.841. Reject the null hypothesis; people like those in the sample are different from the expected even breakdown.

The Chi-Square Test for Independence

So far, we have looked at the distribution of *one nominal variable* with several categories, such as the relationship style of men's partners. In fact, this kind of situation is fairly rare in research. We began with an example of this kind mainly as a stepping stone to a more common actual research situation, to which we now turn.

The most common use of chi-square is one in which there are *two nominal variables,* each with several categories. For example, Harter et al. (1997) might have been interested in whether the breakdown of partners of self-focused men was the same as the breakdown of partners of other-focused men. If that were their purpose, we would have had two nominal variables. Relationship style of partners would be the first nominal variable. Men's own relationship style would be the second nominal variable. Hypothesis testing in this kind of situation is called a *chi-square test for independence.* You will learn shortly why it has this name.

Suppose researchers at a large university survey 200 staff members. The staff members are asked about the kind of transportation they use to get to work, as well as whether they are "morning people" (prefer to go to bed early and awaken early) or "night people" (go to bed late and awaken late). Table 11–3 shows the results. Notice

| Table 11-3 | Contingency Table of Observed Frequencies of Morning and Night People Using Different Types of Transportation (Fictional Data) |

		Transportation			Total
		Bus	Carpool	Own Car	
Sleep Tendency	Morning	60	30	30	120 (60%)
	Night	20	20	40	80 (40%)
	Total	80	50	70	200 (100%)

contingency table Two-dimensional chart showing frequencies in each combination of categories of two nominal variables, as in a chi-square test for independence.

independence Situation of no relationship between two variables; term usually used regarding two nominal variables in the chi-square test for independence.

the two nominal variables: *type of transportation* (with three levels) and *sleep tendency* (with two levels).

Contingency Tables

Table 11–3 is a **contingency table**—a table in which the distributions of two nominal variables are set up so that you have the frequencies of their combinations, as well as the totals. Thus, in Table 11–3, the 60 in the Bus/Morning combination is how many morning people ride the bus. (A contingency table is similar to the tables in factorial analysis of variance that you learned about in Chapter 10; but in a contingency table, the number in each cell is a *number of people,* not a *mean.*)

Table 11–3 is called a 3 × 2 contingency table because it has three levels of one variable crossed with two levels of the other (which dimension is named first does not matter). It is also possible to have larger contingency tables, such as a 4 × 7 or a 6 × 18 table. Smaller tables, 2 × 2 contingency tables, are especially common.

Independence

The question in this example is whether there is any relation between the type of transportation people use and whether they are morning or night people. If there is no relation, the *proportion* of morning and night people is the same among bus riders, carpoolers, and those who drive their own cars. Or to put it the other way, if there is no relation, the *proportion* of bus riders, carpoolers, and own car drivers is the same for morning and night people. However you describe it, the situation of no relation between the variables in a contingency table is called **independence.**[1]

Sample and Population

In the observed survey results in the example, the proportions of night and morning people in the sample vary with different types of transportation. For example, the bus riders are split 60–20, so three-fourths of the bus riders are morning people. Among people who drive their own cars, the split is 30–40. Thus, a slight majority are night people. Still, the sample is only of 200. It is possible that in the larger population, the type of transportation a person uses is independent of the person's being a morning or a night person. The big question is whether the lack of independence in the sample is large enough to reject the null hypothesis of independence in the population. That is, you need to do a chi-square test.

---

[1]Independence is usually used to talk about a lack of relation between two nominal variables. However, if you have studied Chapter 3, it may be helpful to think of independence as roughly the same as the situation of no correlation ($r = 0$).

Determining Expected Frequencies

One thing that is new in a chi-square test for independence is that you now have to figure differences between observed and expected for each *combination* of categories—that is, for each **cell** of the contingency table. (When there was only one nominal variable, you figured these differences just for each category of that single nominal variable.) Table 11–4 is the contingency table for the example survey with the expected frequency shown for each cell.

The key consideration in figuring expected frequencies in a contingency table is that "expected" is based on the two variables being independent. If they are independent, then the proportions up and down the cells of each column should be the same. In the example, overall, there are 60% morning people and 40% night people; thus, if transportation method is independent of being a morning or night person, this 60%–40% split should hold for each column (each transportation type). First, the 60%–40% overall split should hold for the bus group. This would make an expected frequency in the bus cell for morning people of 60% of 80, which comes out to 48 people. The expected frequency for the bus riders who are night people is 32 (that is, 40% of 80 is 32). The same principle holds for the other columns: The 50 carpool people should have a 60%–40% split, giving an expected frequency of 30 morning people who carpool (that is, 60% of 50 is 30) and 20 night people who carpool (that is, 40% of 50 is 20), and the 70 own-car people should have a 60%–40% split, giving expected frequencies of 42 and 28.

Summarizing what we have said in terms of steps,

❶ **Find each row's percentage of the total.**
❷ **For each cell, multiply its row's percentage by its column's total.**

Applying these steps to the top left cell (morning persons who ride the bus),

❶ **Find each row's percentage of the total.** The 120 in the morning person row is 60% of the overall total of 200 (that is, 120/200 = 60%).
❷ **For each cell, multiply its row's percentage by its column's total.** The column total for the bus riders is 80; 60% of 80 comes out to 48 (that is, .60 × 80 = 48).

These steps can also be stated as a formula,

$$E = \left(\frac{R}{N}\right)(C) \tag{11-3}$$

cell In chi-square, the particular combination of categories for two variables in a contingency table.

A cell's expected frequency is the number in its row divided by the total number of people, multiplied by the number in its column.

Table 11–4 Contingency Table of Observed (and Expected) Frequencies of Morning and Night People Using Different Types of Transportation (Fictional Data)

		Transportation			Total	
		Bus	Carpool	Own Car		
Sleep Tendency	Morning	60 (48)[a]	30 (30)	30 (42)	120	(60%)
	Night	20 (32)	20 (20)	40 (28)	80	(40%)
	Total	80	50	70	200	(100%)

[a]Expected frequencies are in parentheses.

In this formula, E is the expected frequency for a particular cell, R is the number of people observed in this cell's row, N is the total number of people, and C is the number of people observed in this cell's column. (If you reverse cells and columns, the expected frequency still comes out the same; but it is best to always do it the same way to avoid making mistakes.)

Applying the formula to the same top left cell,

$$E = \left(\frac{R}{N}\right)(C) = \left(\frac{120}{200}\right)(80) = (.60)(80) = 48$$

Looking at the entire Table 11–4, notice that the expected frequencies add up to the same totals as the observed frequencies.

For example, in the first column (bus), the expected frequencies of 32 and 48 add up to 80, just as the observed frequencies in that column of 60 and 20 do. Similarly, in the top row (morning), the expected frequencies of 48, 30, and 42 add up to 120, the same total as for the observed frequencies of 60, 30, and 30.

Figuring Chi-Square

You figure chi-square the same way as in the chi-square test for goodness of fit, except that you now figure the weighted squared difference for each *cell* and add these up. Here is how it works for our survey example:

$$\chi^2 = \Sigma \frac{(O - E)^2}{E} = \frac{(60 - 48)^2}{48} + \frac{(30 - 30)^2}{30}$$

$$+ \frac{(30 - 42)^2}{42} + \frac{(20 - 32)^2}{32} + \frac{(20 - 20)^2}{20} + \frac{(40 - 28)^2}{28}$$

$$= 3 + 0 + 3.43 + 4.50 + 0 + 5.14 = 16.07.$$

Degrees of Freedom

A contingency table with many cells may have relatively few degrees of freedom. In our example, there are six cells but only 2 degrees of freedom. Recall that the degrees of freedom are the number of categories free to vary once the totals are known. With a chi-square test for independence, the number of categories is the number of cells; the totals include the row and column totals—and if you know the row and column totals, you have a lot of information.

Consider the sleep tendency and transportation example. Suppose you know the first two cell frequencies across the top, for example, and all the row and column totals. You could then figure all the other cell frequencies just by subtraction. Table 11–5 shows the contingency table for this example with just the row and column to-

Table 11–5	Contingency Table Showing Marginal and Two Cells' Observed Frequencies to Illustrate Figuring of Degrees of Freedom			
		Transportation		**Total**
	Bus	**Carpool**	**Own Car**	
Morning	60	30	—	120 (60%)
Night	—	—	—	80 (40%)
Total	80	50	70	200 (100%)

(Sleep Tendency — row labels for Morning, Night, Total)

tals and these two cell frequencies. Let's start with the Morning/Own Car cell. There is a total of 120 morning people, and the other two morning-person cells have 90 in them (60 + 30). Thus, only 30 remain for the Morning/Own-Car cell. Now consider the three night person cells. You know the frequencies for all the morning people cells and the column totals for each type of transportation. Thus, each cell frequency for the night people is its column's total minus the morning people in that column. For example, there are 80 bus riders and 60 are morning people. Thus, the remaining 20 must be night people.

What you can see in all this is that with knowledge of only two of the cells, you could figure out the frequencies in each of the other cells. Thus, although there are six cells, there are only 2 degrees of freedom—only two cells whose frequencies are really free to vary once we have all the row and column totals.

However, rather than having to think all this out each time, there is a short cut. In a chi-square test for independence, the degrees of freedom is the number of columns minus 1 multiplied by the number of rows minus 1. Put as a formula,

$$df = (N_{Columns} - 1)(N_{Rows} - 1) \qquad \textbf{(11-4)}$$

> The degrees of freedom for the chi-square test for independence is the number of columns minus 1 multiplied by the number of rows minus 1.

$N_{Columns}$ is the number of columns and N_{Rows} is the number of rows.
Using this formula for our survey example,

$$df = (N_{Columns} - 1)(N_{Rows} - 1) = (3 - 1)(2 - 1) = (2)(1) = 2.$$

With 2 degrees of freedom, Table 11–2 (or Table A–4) shows that the chi-square you need for significance at the .01 level is 9.211. The chi-square of 16.07 for our example is larger than this cutoff. Thus, you can reject the null hypothesis that the two variables are independent in the population.

Steps of Hypothesis Testing

Now let's go through the survey example again, this time following the steps of hypothesis testing.

➊ **Restate the question as a research hypothesis and a null hypothesis about the populations.** There are two populations:

Population 1: People like those surveyed.
Population 2: People for whom being a night or a morning person is independent of the kind of transportation they use to commute to work.

The null hypothesis is that the two populations are the same—that, in general the proportions using different types of transportation are the same for morning and night people. The research hypothesis is that the two populations are different, that among people in general the proportions using different types of transportation are different for morning and night people.

Put another way, the null hypothesis is that the two variables are independent (they are unrelated to each other). The research hypothesis is that they are not independent (that they are related to each other).

➋ **Determine the characteristics of the comparison distribution.** The comparison distribution is a chi-square distribution with 2 degrees of freedom (the number of columns minus 1 multiplied by the number of rows minus 1).

➌ **Determine the cutoff sample score on the comparison distribution at which the null hypothesis should be rejected.** You use the same table as for any chi-square test. In the example, setting a .01 significance level with 2 degrees of freedom, you need a chi-square of 9.211.

❹ **Determine your sample's score on the comparison distribution.**
  ❹ **Determine the actual, observed frequencies in each cell.** These are the results of the survey, as given in Table 11–3.
  ❺ **Determine the expected frequencies in each cell.** These are shown in Table 11–4. For example, for the bottom right cell (Night Person/Own Car cell):
    ❶ **Find each row's percentage of the total.** The 80 people in the night person's row are 40% of the overall total of 200 (that is, 80/200 = 40%).
    ❷ **For each cell, multiply its row's percentage by its column's total.** The column total for those with their own car is 70; 40% of 70 comes out to 28 (that is, .40 × 70 = 28).
  ❻ **In each cell, take observed minus expected frequencies.** For example, for the Night Person/Own Car cell, this comes out to 12 (that is, 40 − 28 = 12).
  ❼ **Square each of these differences.** For example, for the Night Person/Own Car cell, this comes out to 144 (that is, $12^2 = 144$).
  ❽ **Divide each squared difference by the expected frequency for its cell.** For example, for the Night Person/Own Car cell, this comes out to 5.14 (that is, 144/28 = 5.14).
  ❾ **Add up the results of Step ❽ for all the cells.** As we saw, this came out to 16.07.
❺ **Decide whether to reject the null hypothesis.** The chi-square needed to reject the null hypothesis is 9.211 and the chi-square for our sample is 16.07 (see Figure 11–3). Thus, you can reject the null hypothesis. The research hypothesis that the two variables are not independent in the population is supported. That is, the proportions of type of transportation used to commute to work are different for morning and night people.

A Second Example

Riehl (1994) studied the college experience of first-year students who were the first generation in their family to attend college. These students were compared to other students who were not the first generation in their family to go to college. (All students in the study were from Indiana University.) One of the variables Riehl measured was whether students dropped out during their first semester.

Table 11–6 shows the results along with the expected frequencies (shown in parentheses) based on these percentages. Below the contingency table is the figuring for the chi-square test for independence.

❶ **Restate the question as a null hypothesis and a research hypothesis about the populations.** There are two populations:

Population 1: Students like those surveyed.

Figure 11–3 For the sleep tendency and transportation example, chi-square distribution ($df = 2$) showing the cutoff for rejecting the null hypothesis at the .01 level and the sample's chi-square.

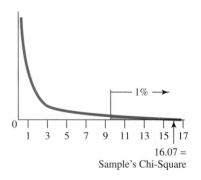

Table 11-6　Results and Figuring of the Chi-Square Test for Independence Comparing Whether First-Generation College Students Differ from Others in First Semester Dropouts

	Generation to Go to College		Total
	First	Other	
	Ⓐ	Ⓑ	
Dropped Out	73 (57.7)	89 (103.9)	162 (7.9%)
Did Not Drop Out	657 (672.3)	1,226 (1,211.1)	1,883 (92.1%)
Total	730	1,315	2,045

$df = (N_{Columns} - 1)(N_{Rows} - 1) = (2 - 1)(2 - 1) = (1)(1) = 1.$ ❷

Chi-square needed, $df = 1$, .01 level: 6.635. ❸

$$\chi^2 = \Sigma \frac{(O - E)^2}{E} = \frac{(73 - 57.7)^2}{57.7} + \frac{(89 - 103.9)^2}{103.9} + \frac{(657 - 672.3)^2}{672.3} + \frac{(1,226 - 1,211.1)^2}{1,211.1}$$
Ⓒ

$$= \frac{15.3^2}{57.7} + \frac{-14.9^2}{103.9} + \frac{-15.3^2}{672.3} + \frac{14.9^2}{1,211.1}$$

Ⓓ
$$= \frac{234.1}{57.7} + \frac{222}{103.9} + \frac{234.1}{672.3} + \frac{222}{1,211.1}$$

Ⓔ
$$= 4.06 + 2.14 + .35 + .18$$

$$= 6.73.$$ Ⓕ

Decision: Reject the null hypothesis. ❺

Notes. 1. With a 2 × 2 analysis, the differences and squared differences (numerators) are the same for all four cells. In this example, the cells are a little different due to rounding error. 2. Data from Riehl (1994). The exact chi-square (6.73) is slightly different from that reported in the article (7.2), due to rounding error.

Population 2: Students whose dropping out or staying in college their first semester is independent of whether they are the first generation in their family to go to college.

　The null hypothesis is that the two populations are the same—that, in general, whether students drop out of college is independent of whether they are the first generation in their family to go to college. The research hypothesis is that the populations are not the same. In other words, the research hypothesis is that students like those surveyed are unlike the hypothetical population in which dropping out is unrelated to whether you are first generation.

❷ **Determine the characteristics of the comparison distribution.** This is a chi-square distribution with 1 degree of freedom.

❸ **Determine the cutoff sample score on the comparison distribution at which the null hypothesis should be rejected.** Using the .01 level and 1 degree of freedom, Table A–4 shows that you need a chi-square for significance of 6.635. This is shown in Figure 11–4.

❹ **Determine your sample's score on the comparison distribution.**

　Ⓐ **Determine the actual, observed frequencies in each cell.** These are the results of the survey, as given in Table 11–6.

　Ⓑ **Determine the expected frequencies in each cell.** These are shown in parentheses in Table 11–6. For example, for the top left cell (First Generation/Dropped Out cell),

　　❶ **Find each row's percentage of the total.** The Dropped Out row's 162 is 7.9% of the overall total of 2,045 (that is, 162/2,045 = 7.9%).

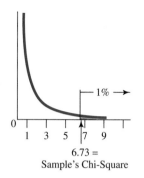

0 1 3 5 7 9

6.73 =
Sample's Chi-Square

Figure 11–4 For the example from Riehl (1994), chi-square distribution (*df* = 1) showing the cutoff for rejecting the null hypothesis at the .01 level and the sample's chi-square.

❻ **For each cell, multiply its row's percentage by its column's total.** The column total for the First Generation students is 730; 7.9% of 730 comes out to 57.7 (that is, .079 × 730 = 57.7).

❼ **In each cell, take observed minus expected frequencies.** These are shown in Table 11–6. For example, for the First Generation/Dropped Out cell, this comes out to 15.3 (that is, 73 − 57.7 = 15.3).

❽ **Square each of these differences.** These are also shown in Table 11–6. For example, for the First Generation/Dropped Out cell, this comes out to 234.1 (that is, $15.3^2 = 234.1$).

❾ **Divide each squared difference by the expected frequency for its cell.** Once again, these are shown in Table 11–6. For example, for the First Generation/Dropped Out cell, this comes out to 4.06 (that is, 234.1/57.7 = 4.06).

❿ **Add up the results of Step ❾ for all the cells.** As shown in Table 11–6, this comes out to 6.73. Its location on the chi-square distribution is shown in Figure 11–4.

❺ **Decide whether to reject the null hypothesis.** Your chi square of 6.73 is larger than the cutoff of 6.635 (see Figure 11–4). Thus, you can reject the null hypothesis. That is, judging from a sample of 2,045 Indiana University students, first-generation students are somewhat more likely to drop out during their first semester than are other students. (Remember, of course, that there could be many reasons for this result.)

How are you doing?

1. (a) In what situation do you use a chi-square test for independence? (b) How is this different from the situation in which you would use a chi-square test for goodness of fit?
2. (a) List the steps for figuring the expected frequencies in a contingency table. (b) Write the formula for expected frequencies in a contingency table and define each of its symbols.
3. (a) Write the formula for figuring degrees of freedom in a chi-square test for independence and define each of its symbols. (b) Explain the logic behind this formula.
4. Use the steps of hypothesis testing to carry out a chi-square test for independence for the observed scores below (using the .05 significance level).

		Nominal Variable A	
		Category 1	**Category 2**
Nominal Variable B	**Category 1**	10	10
	Category 2	50	10

Answers

1. (a) When you have the number of people in each of the various combinations of levels of two nominal variables, and you want to test whether the difference from independence in the sample is sufficiently great to reject the null hypothesis of independence in the population. (b) The focus is on the independence of *two nominal variables;* whereas in a chi-square test for goodness of fit the focus is on the distribution of people over categories of a single *nominal variable.*

2. (a) ❶ Find each row's percentage of the total.
❷ For each cell, multiply its row's percentage by its column's total.

(b) $E = \left(\dfrac{R}{N}\right)(C)$

E is the expected frequency for a particular cell, R is the number of people observed in this cell's row, N is the total number of people, and C is the number of people observed in this cell's column.

3. (a) $df = (N_{Columns} - 1)(N_{Rows} - 1)$.
df are the degrees of freedom, $N_{Columns}$ is the number of columns, and N_{Rows} is the number of rows.

(b) df are the number of cell totals free to vary, given you know the column and row totals. If you know the totals in all the columns but one, you can figure the total in the cells in the remaining column by subtraction. Similarly, if you know the total in all the rows but one, you can figure the total in the cells in the remaining row by subtraction.

4. ❶ Restate the question as a null hypothesis and a research hypothesis about the populations. There are two populations:

Population 1: People like those studied.
Population 2: People whose being in a particular category of Nominal Variable A is independent of their being in a particular category of Nominal Variable B.

The null hypothesis is that the two populations are the same; the research hypothesis is that the populations are not the same.

❷ Determine the characteristics of the comparison distribution. This is a chi-square distribution with 1 degree of freedom. That is, $df = (N_{Columns} - 1)(N_{Rows} - 1) = (2 - 1)(2 - 1) = 1$.

❸ Determine the cutoff score on the comparison distribution at which the null hypothesis should be rejected. From Table A-4, for the .05 significance level and 1 degree of freedom, the needed chi-square is 3.841.

❹ Determine your sample's score on the comparison distribution.
❶ Determine the actual, observed frequencies in each cell. These are shown in the contingency table for the problem.
❷ Determine the expected frequencies in each cell.
❸ Find each row's percentage of the total. For the top row 20/80 = 25%; for the second row, 60/80 = 75%.
❹ For each cell, multiply its row's percentage by its column's total. For the top left cell, 25% × 60 = 15; for the top right cell, 25% × 20 = 5; for the bottom left cell, 75% × 60 = 45; for the bottom right cell, 75% × 20 = 15.
❺ In each cell, take observed minus expected frequencies. For the four cells, 10 − 15 = −5; 50 − 45 = 5; 10 − 5 = 5; 10 − 15 = −5.
❻ Square each of these differences. This is 25 for each cell (that is, $5^2 = 25$ and $-5^2 = 25$).
❼ Divide each squared difference by the expected frequency for its cell. These come out to 25/15 = 1.67, 25/5 = 5, 25/45 = .56, and 25/15 = 1.67.
❽ Add up the results of Step ❼ for all the cells. 1.67 + 5 + .56 + 1.67 = 8.90.
❺ Decide whether to reject the null hypothesis. The sample's chi-square of 8.90 is larger than the cutoff of 3.841. Thus, you can reject the null hypothesis: Which category people are in on Nominal Variable A is not independent of which category they are in on Nominal Variable B.

phi coefficient (φ) Measure of association between two dichotomous nominal variables; square root of division of chi-square statistic by *N;* equivalent to correlation of the two variables if they were each given numerical values (for example, of 1 and 0 for the two categories); effect-size measure for a chi-square test of independence with a 2 × 2 contingency table.

Cramer's phi Effect-size measure for a chi-square test for independence used with a contingency table that is larger than 2 × 2; square root of result of dividing the chi-square statistic by the product of the number of participants times the degrees of freedom of the smaller side of the contingency table; also known as *Cramer's V* and sometimes written as ϕ_c or V_c.

> The phi coefficient (effect size for a chi-square test for independence for a 2 × 2 contingency table) is the square root of the result of dividing the sample's chi-square by the total number of people in the sample.

Assumptions for the Chi-Square Tests

The chi-square tests for goodness of fit and for independence do not require the usual assumptions of normal population variances and such. There is, however, one key assumption: Each score must not have any special relation to any other score. This means that you can't use these chi-square tests if the scores are based on the same people being tested more than once. Consider a study in which 20 people are tested to see if the distribution of their preferred brand of breakfast cereal changed from before to after a recent nutritional campaign. The results of this study could not be tested with the usual chi-square because the distributions of cereal choice before and after are from the same people.

Effect Size and Power for Chi-Square Tests for Independence

Effect Size

In chi-square tests for independence, you can use your sample's chi-square to figure a number that shows the degree of association of the two nominal variables.

With a 2 × 2 contingency table, the measure of association is called the **phi coefficient (φ).** Here is the formula,

(11-5)
$$\phi = \sqrt{\frac{\chi^2}{N}}$$

The phi coefficient has a minimum of 0 and a maximum of 1, and can be considered similar to a correlation coefficient (see Chapter 3).[2] Cohen's (1988) conventions for the phi coefficient are that .10 is a small effect size, .30 is a medium effect size, and .50 is a large effect size (the same as for a correlation coefficient).

For example, in the Riehl (1994) study of first-generation college students, the chi-square we calculated was 6.73 and there were 2,045 people in the study. Applying the formula for the phi coefficient,

$$\phi = \sqrt{\frac{\chi^2}{N}} = \sqrt{\frac{6.73}{2,045}} = \sqrt{.00329} = .06$$

This is a very small effect size. The fact that the chi-square of 6.73 was significant in this study tells you that the greater likelihood of first-generation students dropping out that you saw in the sample is probably not due to the particular people that were randomly recruited to be in this sample. You can thus have some confidence that there is a pattern of this kind in the population. But the small phi coefficient tells you that this true population tendency may not be a very important factor in practice. (See Chapter 7 for a discussion of this kind of situation when a result is statistically significant but has a very small effect size.)

You only use the phi when you have a 2 × 2 situation. **Cramer's phi** is an extension of the ordinary phi coefficient that you can use for contingency tables larger

---

[2]Phi is actually identical to the correlation coefficient. Suppose you were to take the two variables in a 2 × 2 contingency table and arbitrarily make one of the values of each equal to 1 and the other equal to 2 (you could use any two numbers). And suppose you then figured a correlation coefficient between the two variables. The result would be exactly the same as the phi coefficient. (Whether it was a positive or negative correlation, however, would depend on which categories in each variable got the higher number.)

than 2×2. (Cramer's phi is also known as *Cramer's V* and is sometimes written ϕ_C or V_C.) You figure Cramer's phi the same way as the ordinary phi coefficient, except that instead of dividing by N, you divide by N times the degrees of freedom of the smaller side of the table. Stated as a formula,

$$\text{Cramer's } \phi = \sqrt{\frac{\chi^2}{(N)(df_{\text{Smaller}})}} \qquad \textbf{(11-6)}$$

> Cramer's phi coefficient (effect size for a chi-square test for independence) is the square root of the result of dividing the sample's chi-square by the product of the total number of people in the sample times the degrees of freedom for the smaller side of the table.

In this formula, df_{Smaller} is the degrees of freedom for the smaller side of the contingency table.

In the sleep tendency and transportation preference example, the sample's chi-square was 16.07 and the total number of people surveyed was 200. The degrees of freedom for the smaller side of the table (the rows in this example) was 1. Cramer's phi is the square root of what you get when you divide 16.07 by 200 multiplied by 1. This comes out to .28. In terms of the formula,

$$\text{Cramer's } \phi = \sqrt{\frac{\chi^2}{(N)(df_{\text{Smaller}})}} = \sqrt{\frac{16.07}{(200)(1)}} = \sqrt{.08} = .28$$

Cohen's (1988) conventions for effect size for Cramer's phi depend on the degrees of freedom for the smaller side of the table. Table 11–7 shows Cohen's effect size conventions for Cramer's phi for tables in which the smallest side of the table is 2, 3, and 4. Notice that when the smallest side of the table is 2, the degrees of freedom is 1. Thus, the effect sizes in the table for this situation are the same as for the ordinary phi coefficient.

Based on the table, in the transportation example there is an approximately medium effect size (.28), a medium amount of relationship between type of transportation one uses and whether one is a morning or a night person.

Power

Table 11–8 shows the approximate power at the .05 significance level for small, medium, and large effect sizes and total sample sizes of 25, 50, 100, and 200. Power is given for tables with 1, 2, 3, and 4 degrees of freedom.[3]

Consider the power of a planned 2×4 study ($df = 3$) of 50 people with an expected medium effect size (Cramer's $\phi = .30$). The researchers will use the .05 level. From Table 11–8 you can find that this study would have a power of .40. That is, if the research hypothesis is true, and there is a true medium effect size, there is about a 40% chance that the study will come out significant.

Table 11-7 Cohen's Conventions for Cramer's Phi

Smallest Side of Contingency Table	Effect Size		
	Small	Medium	Large
2 ($df_{\text{Smaller}} = 1$)	.10	.30	.50
3 ($df_{\text{Smaller}} = 2$)	.07	.21	.35
4 ($df_{\text{Smaller}} = 3$)	.06	.17	.29

---

[3]Cohen (1988, pp. 228–248) gives more detailed tables. However, Cohen's tables are based on an effect size called w, which is equivalent to phi but not to Cramer's phi. He provides a helpful conversion table of Cramer's phi to w on page 222.

Table 11-8 Approximate Power for the Chi-Square Test for Independence for Testing Hypotheses at the .05 Significance Level

Total *df*	Total *N*	Effect Size		
		Small	Medium	Large
1	25	.08	.32	.70
	50	.11	.56	.94
	100	.17	.85	*
	200	.29	.99	*
2	25	.07	.25	.60
	50	.09	.46	.90
	100	.13	.77	*
	200	.23	.97	*
3	25	.07	.21	.54
	50	.08	.40	.86
	100	.12	.71	.99
	200	.19	.96	*
4	25	.06	.19	.50
	50	.08	.36	.82
	100	.11	.66	.99
	200	.17	.94	*

*Nearly 1.

Needed Sample Size

Table 11–9 gives the approximate total number of participants needed for 80% power with small, medium, and large effect sizes at the .05 significance level for chi-square tests for independence of 2, 3, 4, and 5 degrees of freedom.[4] Suppose you are planning a study with a 3×3 ($df = 4$) contingency table. You expect a large effect size and will use the .05 significance level. According to the table, you would only need 48 participants.

Table 11-9 Approximate Total Number of Participants Needed for 80% Power for the Chi-Square Test of Independence for Testing Hypotheses at the .05 Significance Level

Total *df*	Effect Size		
	Small	Medium	Large
1	785	87	26
2	964	107	39
3	1,090	121	44
4	1,194	133	48

[4]More detailed tables are provided in Cohen (1988, pp. 253–267). When using these tables, see footnote 3. Also, Dunlap and Myers (1997) have shown that with a 2×2 table, the approximate number of participants needed for 80–90% power is $8/\phi^2$.

How are you doing?

1. What are the assumptions for chi-square tests?
2. (a) What is the measure of effect size for a 2×2 chi-square test for independence? (b) Write the formula for this measure of effect size and define each of the symbols. (c) What are Cohen's conventions for small, medium, and large effect sizes? (d) Figure the effect size for a 2×2 chi-square test for independence in which there are a total of 100 participants and the chi-square is 12.
3. (a) What is the measure of effect size for a chi-square test for independence for a contingency table that is larger than 2×2? (b) Write the formula for this measure of effect size and define each of the symbols. (c) What is Cohen's convention for a small effect size for a 4×6 contingency table? (d) Figure the effect size for a 4×6 chi-square test for independence in which there are a total of 200 participants and the chi-square is 20.
4. What is the power of a planned 3×3 chi-square with 50 participants total and a predicted medium effect size?
5. About how many participants do you need for 80% power in a planned 2×2 study in which you predict a medium effect size and will be using the .05 significance level?

Answers

1. The only major assumption is that the numbers in each cell or category are from separate persons.
2. (a) The phi coefficient.
   (b) $\phi = \sqrt{\dfrac{\chi^2}{N}}$. ϕ is the phi coefficient (effect size for a chi-square test for independence with a 2×2 contingency table); χ^2 is the sample's chi-square; and N is the total number of participants in the study.
   (c) .10 is a small effect size, .30 is a medium effect size, and .50 is a large effect size.
   (d) $\phi = \sqrt{(12/100)} = .35$.
3. (a) Cramer's phi.
   (b) Cramer's $\phi = \sqrt{\dfrac{\chi^2}{(N)(df_{smaller})}}$. Cramer's ϕ is Cramer's phi coefficient (effect size for a chi-square test for independence); χ^2 is the sample's chi-square; N is the total number of participants in the study; and $df_{smaller}$ is the degrees of freedom for the smaller side of the contingency table.
   (c) .06.
   (d) $\sqrt{20/[(200)(3)]} = .18$.
4. .36.
5. 87.

Strategies for Hypothesis Testing When Population Distributions Are Not Normal

This second main part of the chapter examines some strategies researchers use when the variables are quantitative, but the assumption of a normal population distribution is clearly violated. (This assumption of normality is part of most ordinary hypothesis-testing procedures, such as the *t* test and the analysis of variance.) First, we briefly review the role of assumptions in the standard hypothesis-testing procedures. Then we examine two approaches researchers use when the assumptions have not been met: data transformations and rank-order tests.

Assumptions in the Standard Hypothesis-Testing Procedures

As we saw in Chapters 8 through 10, you have to meet certain conditions (the assumptions) to get accurate results with a *t* test or an analysis of variance. In these hypothesis-testing procedures, you treat the scores from a study as if they came from some larger, though unknown, populations. One assumption you have to make is that the populations involved follow a normal curve. The other main assumption you have to make is that the populations have equal variances.

You also learned in previous chapters that you get fairly accurate results when a study suggests that the populations even very roughly meet the assumptions of following a normal curve and having equal variances. Our concern here, however, is about the situation where there is strong evidence that the populations are nowhere near normal, or nowhere near having equal variances. In such situations, if you use the ordinary *t* test or analysis of variance, you can get quite incorrect results. For example, you could do all the figuring correctly and decide to reject the null hypothesis based on your results. And yet, if your populations do not meet the assumptions, this result could be wrong—wrong in the sense that instead of there actually being only a 5% chance of getting your results if the null hypothesis is true, in fact there might be a 15% or 20% chance! (It could also be 1% or 2%. The problem is that the usual cutoff can be a long way from accurate and you don't know in what way.)

Remember: Assumptions are about *populations* and not about *samples*. It is quite possible for a sample not to follow a normal curve even though it comes from a population that does follow a normal curve. Figure 11–5 shows histograms for several samples, each taken randomly from a population that follows a normal curve. (Notice that the smaller the sample, the harder it is to see that it came from a normal population.) Of course, it is quite possible for non-normal populations to produce any of these samples as well. Unfortunately, the sample is usually all you have when doing a study. One thing researchers do is to make a histogram for the sample; if it is not drastically different from normal, the researchers assume that the population it came from is normal or at least close enough. When considering normality, most behavioral and social science researchers consider a distribution innocent until proven guilty.

One common situation where you might doubt the assumption that the population follows a normal curve is when there is a *ceiling* or *floor effect* (see Chapter 1). Another common situation that raises such doubts is when the sample has outliers, extreme scores at one or both ends of the sample distribution. Figure 11–6 shows some examples of distributions with outliers. Outliers are a big problem in the statistical methods we ordinarily use. This is because these methods ultimately rely on squared deviations from the mean. Because it is so far from the mean, an outlier has a huge influence when you square its deviation from the mean. The result is that a single outlier, if it is extreme enough, can distort the results of a study. An outlier can cause a statistical test to give a significant result even when all the other scores would not, or in other cases, an outlier can also make a result not significant that would be significant without the outlier.

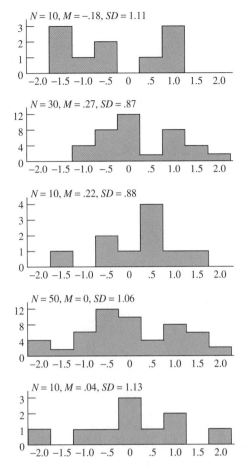

Figure 11–5 Histograms for several random samples, each taken from a normal population with a mean of 0 and a standard deviation of 1.

---

1. What are the two main assumptions for *t* tests and the analysis of variance?
2. (a) How do you check to see if you have met the assumptions? (b) Why is this problematic?
3. (a) What is an outlier? (b) Why are outliers likely to have an especially big distorting effect in most statistical procedures?

Answers

1. The populations are normally distributed and have equal variances.
2. (a) You look at the distributions of the samples. (b) The samples, especially if they are small, can have quite different shapes and variances from the populations.
3. (a) An extreme score. (b) Most procedures are based on squared deviations from the mean. Thus, the extremeness of an outlier is greatly multiplied when its deviation from the mean is squared.

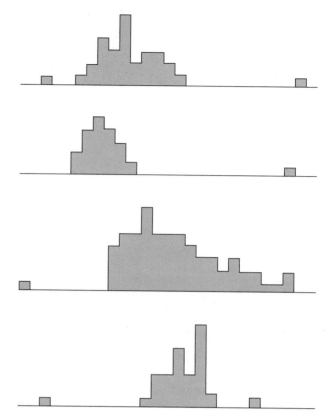

Figure 11–6 Distributions with outliers at one or both ends.

data transformation Mathematical procedure (such as taking the square root) applied to each score in a sample, usually done to make the sample distribution closer to normal.

Data Transformations

One widely used procedure when the scores in the sample do not appear to come from a normal population is to change the scores! Not by fudging—although at first it may sound that way, until we explain. The method is that the researcher applies some mathematical procedure to each score, such as taking its square root. The idea is to make a non-normal distribution closer to normal. (Sometimes this can also make the variances of the groups more similar.) This is called a **data transformation.** Once you have made a data transformation that makes the data appear to meet the normality assumption (and if the other assumptions are met), you can then go ahead with a usual *t* test or analysis of variance.

Data transformation has an important advantage over other procedures of coping with non-normal populations: Once you have made a data transformation, you can use familiar and sophisticated hypothesis-testing procedures.

Consider an example. Measures of reaction time (such as how long it takes a research participant to press a particular key when a light flashes) are usually highly skewed to the right (positively skewed). There are many short (quick) responses, but usually a few quite long (slow) ones. It is unlikely that the reaction times shown in Figure 11–7 come from a population that follows a normal curve. The population of reaction-time scores itself is probably skewed.

However, suppose you take the square root of each reaction time. Most reaction times are affected only a little. A reaction time of 1 second stays 1; a reaction time of 1.5 seconds reduces to 1.22. However, very long reaction times, the ones that create the long tail to the right, are much reduced. For example, a reaction time of 9 seconds is reduced to 3, and a reaction time of 16 seconds (for the person who was really distracted and forgot about the task) reduces to 4. Figure 11–8 shows the result of taking the square root of each score in the skewed distribution shown in Figure 11–7. After a **square-root transformation,** this distribution of scores seems much more likely to have come from a population with a normal distribution (of transformed scores).

square-root transformation Data transformation using the square root of each score.

Legitimacy of Data Transformations

Do you feel that this is somehow cheating? It would be if you did this knowingly in some way to make the result come out more favorable to your predictions. However, in actual research practice, the first step after the data are collected and recorded (and checked for accuracy) is to see if the data suggest that the populations meet assumptions. If the scores in your sample suggest that the populations do not meet assumptions, you do data transformations. Hypothesis testing is done only after this checking and any transformations.

Remember that you must do any transformation for *all* the scores on that variable, not just those in a particular group. Most important, no matter what transformation procedure you use, the order of the scores always stays the same. A person with an actual original score that is between the actual original scores of two other participating people will still have a transformed score between those same two people's transformed scores.

The procedure may seem somehow to distort reality to fit the statistics. In some cases, this is a legitimate concern. Suppose you are looking at the difference in income between two groups of Americans. You probably do not care about how much the two groups differ in the square root of their income. What you care about is the difference in actual dollars.

On the other hand, consider a survey question in which the person rates his or her agreement with the statement "I am satisfied with local law enforcement" on a 7-point rating from 1, strongly disagree, to 7, strongly agree. Higher scores on this scale certainly mean more agreement; lower scores, less agreement. However, each scale-point increase is not necessarily related to an equal amount of increase in an individual's agreement. It is just as likely that the square root of each scale point's increase is directly related to the person's underlying degree of agreement. In many research situations, there may be no strong reason to think that the transformed version is any less accurate a reflection of the reality than the original version. And the transformed version may meet the normality assumption.

Kinds of Data Transformations

There are several types of data transformations. We already have shown a square-root transformation: Instead of using each score, you use the square root of each score. We gave an example in Figures 11–7 and 11–8. The general effect is shown in Figure 11–9. As you can see, a distribution that is skewed to the right (positively skewed) becomes less skewed to the right after square-root transformation. To put it numerically, moderate numbers become only slightly lower and high numbers become much lower. The result is that the right side is pulled in toward the middle. (If the distribution is skewed the other way, you may want to *reflect* all the scores—that is, subtract them all from some high number so that they are now all reversed. Then, using the square root will have the correct effect. However, you then have to remember when looking at the final results that you have reversed the direction of scoring.)

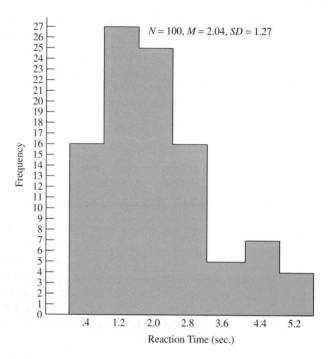

Figure 11–7   Skewed distribution of reaction times (fictional data).

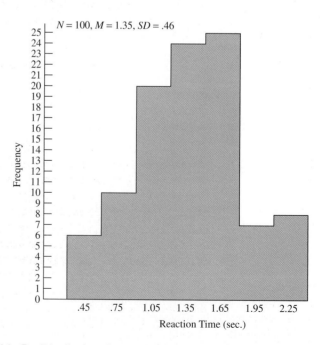

Figure 11–8   Distribution of scores from Figure 11–7 after square-root transformation.

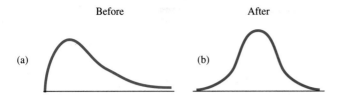

Before   After

(a)   (b)

Figure 11–9   Distribution skewed to the right before (a) and after (b) taking the square root of each score.

There are many other kinds of transformations you will see in behavioral and social science research articles. One common type is called a *log transformation.* Log transformation has the same type of effect as the square root transformation, but the effect is stronger, so it is more suitable for distributions that are very strongly skewed to the right. (In a log transformation, instead of the square root, the researcher takes the logarithm of each score.) Some other transformations you might see are *inverse transformations* and *arcsine transformations.* We will not go into examples of all these kinds of transformations here. Just learning the square-root transformation will help you get the principle. The main thing to remember about other kinds of transformations is that they all use this same principle of taking each score and applying some arithmetic to it to make the set of scores come out more like a normal curve. Once again, whatever transformation you use, a score that is between two other scores always stays between those two other scores.

An Example of a Data Transformation

Consider a fictional study in which four children who score high on a test of being "highly sensitive" are compared on the number of books read in the preceding year to four children who score low on the test. (The general idea of being a highly sensitive person is described in Aron, 1996, 2002; Aron & Aron, 1997.) Based on theory, the researcher predicts that highly sensitive children will read more books. Table 11–10 shows the results.

Ordinarily, in a study like this, involving a comparison of two independent groups, you would use a *t* test for independent means. Yet the *t* test for independent means is like all of the procedures you have learned for hypothesis testing (except chi-square): It requires that the parent populations of scores for each group be normally distributed. In this study, however, the distribution of the sample is strongly skewed to the right—the scores tend to bunch up at the left, leaving a long tail to the right. It thus seems likely that the population of scores of number of books read (for both sensitives and nonsensitives) is also skewed to the right. This shape for the population distribution also seems reasonable in light of what is being measured. A child cannot read fewer than zero books; but once a child starts reading, it is easy to read a lot of books in a year.

Also note that the estimated population variances based on the two samples are dramatically different, 95.58 versus 584.25. This is another reason you would not want to go ahead with an ordinary *t* test.

However, suppose you do a square-root transformation on the scores (Table 11–11). Now both samples are much more like a normal curve—both samples have their middle scores bunch up in the middle (for example, for the Yes group, 6.00 and 6.71) and the more extreme (high and low) scores spread out a little from the mean (4.12 and 8.71). Also, the transformation seems reasonable in terms of the meaning

Table 11–10   Results of a Study Comparing Highly Sensitive and Not Highly Sensitive Children on the Number of Books Read in the Past Year (Fictional Data)

	Highly Sensitive	
	No	**Yes**
	0	17
	3	36
	10	45
	22	75
Σ:	35	173
$M =$	8.75	43.25
$S^2 =$	95.58	584.25

Table 11–11   Square-Root Transformation of the Scores in Table 11-10

Highly Sensitive			
No		**Yes**	
X	$\sqrt{X}$	X	$\sqrt{X}$
0	0.00	17	4.12
3	1.73	36	6.00
10	3.16	45	6.71
22	4.69	75	8.66

Table 11–12 Figuring for a *t* Test for Independent Means Using Square-Root Transformed Scores for the Study of Books Read by Highly Sensitive Versus Not Highly Sensitive Children (Fictional Data)

t needed for .05 significance level, $df = (4 - 1) + (4 - 1) = 6$, one-tailed $= -1.943$.

	Highly Sensitive	
	No	Yes
	0.00	4.12
	1.73	6.00
	3.16	6.71
	4.69	8.66
Σ:	9.58	25.49
$M =$	$9.58/4 = 2.40$	$25.49/4 = 6.37$
$S^2 =$	$12.03/3 = 4.01$	$10.56/3 = 3.52$

$$S^2_{Pooled} = 3.77$$

$S^2_M =$	$3.77/4 = .94$	$3.77/4 = .94$

$$S^2_{Difference} = .94 + .94 = 1.88$$
$$S_{Difference} = \sqrt{1.88} = 1.37$$
$$t = (2.40 - 6.37)/1.37 = -2.90$$

Decision: Reject the null hypothesis.

of the numbers. Number of books read is meant as a measure of interest in things literary. Thus, the difference between 0 and 1 book is a much greater difference than the difference between 20 and 21 books.

Table 11–12 shows the *t* test analysis using the transformed scores.

How are you doing?

1. What is a data transformation?
2. Why is it done?
3. When is this legitimate?
4. Consider the following distribution of scores: 4, 16, 25, 25, 25, 36, 64. (a) Are these scores roughly normally distributed? (b) Why? (c) Carry out a square-root transformation for these scores (that is, list the square-root transformed scores). (d) Are the square-root transformed scores roughly normally distributed? (e) Why?

Answers

1. When each score is changed following some rule (such as take the square root or log).
2. In order to make the distribution more like a normal curve (or to make variances closer to equal across groups).
3. It is legitimate when it is done to all the scores, it is not done to make the results come out to fit the researcher's predictions, and the underlying meaning of the distance between scores is arbitrary.
4. (a) No. (b) They are skewed to the right. (c) 2, 4, 5, 5, 5, 6, 8. (d) Yes. (e) The middle scores are bunched in the middle and the extremes spread out evenly on both sides.

Rank-Order Tests

Another way of coping with non-normal distributions is to transform the scores to ranks. Suppose you have a sample with scores 4, 8, 12, and 64. This would be a rather surprising sample if the population was really normal. A **rank-order transformation** would change the scores to 1, 2, 3, and 4, the 1 referring to the lowest number in the group, the 2 to the second lowest, and so forth. (A complication with a rank-order transformation occurs when you have two or more scores that are tied. The usual solution to ties is to give them each the average rank. For example, the scores 12, 81, 81, 107, and 154 would be ranked 1, 2.5, 2.5, 4, and 5.)

Changing ordinary scores to ranks is a kind of data transformation. But unlike the square-root transformations we just considered, with a rank-order transformation you aren't trying to get a normal distribution. The distribution you get from a rank-order transformation is rectangular, with equal numbers of scores (one) at each value. Ranks have the effect of spreading the scores out evenly.

There are special hypothesis-testing procedures that make use of rank-ordered data, called **rank-order tests.** They also have two other common names. You can transform scores from a population with any shaped distribution into ranks. Thus, these tests are sometimes called **distribution-free tests.** Also, the distribution of rank-order scores is known exactly rather than estimated. Thus, rank-order tests do not require estimating any parameters (population values). For example, there is no need to estimate a population variance because you can determine exactly what it will be if you know that ranks are involved. Hence, hypothesis-testing procedures based on ranks are also called **nonparametric tests.**

The ordinary hypothesis-testing procedures you have learned (t test and analysis of variance) are examples of **parametric tests.** Chi-square, like the rank-order tests, is considered a nonparametric test, but it is distribution-free only in the sense that no assumptions are made about the shape of the population distributions. However, the terms *distribution-free* and *nonparametric* are typically used interchangeably; the subtleties of differences between them are a matter of ongoing debate among statisticians.

Rank-order tests also have the advantage that they can be used where the actual scores in the study are themselves ranks—for example, a study comparing the class standings of two types of graduates.

Overview of Rank-Order Tests

Table 11–13 shows the name of the rank-order test that you would substitute for each of the parametric hypothesis-testing procedures you have learned. (Full procedures for using such tests are given in intermediate statistics texts.) For example, in a situation with three groups, you would normally do a one-way analysis of variance. But if you want to use a rank-order method, you would use the Kruskal-Wallis H test.

rank-order transformation   Changing a set of scores to ranks, so that the highest score is rank 1, the next highest rank 2, and so forth.

rank-order test   Hypothesis-testing procedure designed to use rank-ordered data.

distribution-free test   Hypothesis-testing procedure making no assumptions about the shape of the populations; also called a *nonparametric test.*

nonparametric test   Hypothesis-testing procedure making no assumptions about population parameters; also called a *distribution-free test.*

parametric test   Ordinary hypothesis-testing procedure, such as a t test or an analysis of variance, that requires assumptions about the shape or other parameters (such as the variance) of the populations.

Table 11–13   Major Rank-Order Tests Corresponding to Major Parametric Tests

Ordinary Parametric Test	Corresponding Rank-Order Test
t test for dependent means	Wilcoxon signed-rank test
t test for independent means	Wilcoxon rank-sum test or Mann-Whitney U test
Analysis of variance	Kruskal-Wallis H test

Next, we will describe how such tests are done in a general way, including an example. However, we do not actually provide all the needed information for you to carry them out in practice. We introduce you to these techniques because you may see them used in articles you read and because their logic is the foundation of an alternative procedure that we do teach you to use (shortly). This alternative procedure does roughly the same thing as these rank-order tests and is closer to what you have already learned.

Basic Logic of Rank-Order Tests

Consider a study involving an experimental group and a control group. (This is the kind of situation for which you would use a *t* test for independent means if all the assumptions were met.) If you wanted to use a rank-order test, you would first transform all the scores into ranks, ranking all the scores from lowest to highest, regardless of whether a score was in the experimental or the control group. If the two groups were scores randomly taken from a single population, there should be about equal amounts of high ranks and low ranks in each group. (That is, if the null hypothesis is true, the ranks in the two groups should not differ.) Because the distribution of ranks can be worked out exactly, statisticians can figure the exact probability of getting any particular division of ranks into two groups if in fact the two groups were randomly taken from identical distributions.

The way this actually works is that the researcher converts all the scores to ranks, adds up the total of the ranks in the group with the lower scores, and then compares this total to a cutoff from a special table of significance cutoffs for totals of ranks in this kind of situation. (Also, as with ordinary parametric tests, this can be done automatically with SPSS or other statistical software programs.)

An Example of a Rank-Order Test

Table 11–14 shows the transformation to ranks and the computation of the Wilcoxon rank-sum test for the kind of situation we have just described, using the books read by highly sensitive versus not highly sensitive children example. The logic is a little different from what you are used to, so be patient until we explain it.

Table 11-14 Figuring for a Wilcoxon Rank-Sum Test for the Study of Books Read by Highly Sensitive Versus Not Highly Sensitive Children (Fictional Data)

Cutoff for significance: Maximum sum of ranks in the not highly sensitive group for significance at the .05 level, one-tailed (from a standard table) = 11.

Highly Sensitive

No		Yes	
X	Rank	X	Rank
0	1	17	4
3	2	36	6
10	3	45	7
22	5	75	8
Σ:	11		

Comparison to cutoff: Sum of ranks of group predicted to have lower scores, 11, equals but does not exceed cutoff for significance.

Decision: Reject the null hypothesis.

Notice that we first set the significance cutoff, as you would in any hypothesis-testing procedure. (This cutoff is based on a table you don't have but is available in most intermediate statistics texts.)

The next step is to rank all the scores from lowest to highest, then add up the ranks in the group you expect to have the smaller total. You then compare the smaller total to the cutoff. If this smaller total is less than or equal to the cutoff, you reject the null hypothesis. In the example, the total of the ranks for the lower was actually equal to the cutoff, so the null hypothesis was rejected.

Using Parametric Tests with Rank-Transformed Data

Two statisticians (Conover & Iman, 1981) have shown that instead of using the special procedures for rank-order tests, you get approximately the same results for the *t* test and one-way analysis of variance if you transform the data into ranks and then apply all the usual *t* test or one-way analysis of variance procedures.

The result of using a parametric test with data transformed into ranks will not be quite as accurate as either the ordinary parametric test or the rank-order test. It will not be as accurate as the ordinary parametric test because the assumption of normal distributions is violated. The distribution is, in fact, rectangular when ranks are involved. It will also not be quite as accurate as the rank-order test because the parametric test uses the *t* or *F* distribution instead of the special tables that rank-order tests use, which are based on exact probabilities of getting certain divisions of ranks. However, the approximation seems to be quite close for the *t* test and the analysis of variance.[5]

Table 11–15 shows the figuring for an ordinary *t* test for independent means for the fictional sensitive children data, using each child's rank instead of the child's actual number of books read. Again we get a significant result. (In practice, carrying out an ordinary procedure like a *t* test with scores that have been transformed to ranks is least accurate with a very small sample like this. However, we used the small sample to keep the example simple.)

Comparison of Methods

We have considered two methods of carrying out hypothesis tests when samples appear to come from non-normal populations: data transformation and rank-order tests. How do you decide which to use?

Advantages and Disadvantages

Data transformations have the advantage of allowing you to use the familiar parametric techniques on the transformed scores. Transformations may also come closer to the true meaning of the underlying measurement. But transformations will not always work. That is, there may not be any reasonable transformation that makes the

---

[5]If you want to be very accurate, for a *t* test or one-way analysis of variance, you can convert your result to what is called an *L* statistic and look it up on a chi square table (Puri & Sen, 1985). The *L* statistic for a *t* test is $([N-1]r^2)/(t^2 + [N-2])$ and you use a chi-square distribution with $df = 1$. The *L* statistic for a one-way analysis of variance is $([N-1][df_{Between}]F)/([df_{Between}]F + df_{Within})$, and you use a chi-square distribution with $df = df_{Between}$. The *L* for the significance of a correlation (see Chapter 3 Appendix) is just $(N-1)r^2$ and you use the chi-square table for $df = 1$. It is especially important to use the *L* statistic when using rank-transformed scores for more advanced parametric procedures, such as factorial analysis of variance (Chapter 10) and multiple regression (Chapter 3). Thomas, Nelson, and Thomas (1999) give fully worked-out examples.

Table 11-15 Figuring for a *t* Test for Independent Means Using Ranks Instead of Raw Scores for the Study of Books Read by Highly Sensitive Versus Not Highly Sensitive Children (Fictional Data)

t needed for .05 significance level, $df = (4 - 1) + (4 - 1) = 6$, one-tailed $= -1.943$

	Highly Sensitive	
	No	Yes
	1	4
	2	6
	3	7
	5	8
Σ	11	25
$M =$	$11/4 = 2.75$	$25/4 = 6.25$
$S^2 =$	$8.75/3 = 2.92$	$8.75/3 = 2.92$

$$S^2_{Pooled} = 2.92$$

$S^2_M = \quad 2.92/4 = .73 \qquad 2.92/4 = .73$

$S^2_{Difference} = .73 + .73 = 1.46$

$S_{Difference} = \sqrt{1.46} = 1.21$

$t = (2.75 - 6.25)/1.21 = -2.89$

Decision: Reject the null hypothesis.

scores normal in all groups. Also, transformations may distort the scores in ways that lose the original meaning.

Rank-order methods can be applied regardless of the distributions. They are especially appropriate when the original scores are ranks, and they are also useful when the scores do not clearly follow a simple numeric pattern (such as equal-interval), which some psychologists think is a common situation. Further, the logic of rank-order methods is simple and direct, requiring no elaborate construction of hypothetical distributions or estimated parameters.

However, rank-order methods are not as familiar to readers of research, and rank-order methods have not been developed for many complex situations. Another problem is that the simple logic of rank-order tests breaks down if there are many ties in ranks. Finally, like data transformation methods, rank-order methods distort the original data, losing information. For example, in the same sample, a difference between 6.1 and 6.2 could be one rank, but the difference between 3.4 and 5.8 might also be one rank.

Relative Risk of Type I and Type II Errors

How accurate are the various methods in terms of the 5% significance level really meaning that there is a 5% chance of incorrectly rejecting the null hypothesis (a Type I error)? And how do the different methods affect power?

When the assumptions for parametric tests are met, the parametric tests are as good as or better than any of the alternatives. This is true for protection against both Type I and Type II errors. This would be expected, as these are the conditions for which the parametric tests were designed.

However, when the assumptions for a parametric test are not met, the relative advantages of the possible alternative procedures we have considered are not at all clear. In fact, the relative merits of the various procedures are topics of lively controversy, with many articles appearing in statistics-oriented journals every year.

1. (a) What is a rank-order transformation? (b) Why is it done? (c) What is a rank-order test?
2. Transform the following scores to ranks: 5, 18, 3, 9, 2.
3. (a) If you wanted to use a standard rank-order test instead of at test for independent means, what procedure would you use? (b) What are the steps of doing such a test?
4. (a) What happens if you change your scores to ranks and then figure an ordinary parametric test using the ranks? (b) Why will this not be quite as accurate even assuming the transformation to ranks is appropriate? (c) Why will this result not be quite as accurate using the standard rank-order test?
5. If conditions are not met for a parametric test (a) what are the advantages and (b) disadvantages of data-transformation over rank-order tests, and what are the (c) advantages and (d) disadvantages of rank-order tests over data transformation?

Answers

1. (a) Changing each score to its rank (order from lowest to highest) among all the scores.
   (b) To make the distribution a standard shape.
   (c) A special type of significance testing procedure designed for use with rank-ordered scores.
2. 5 = 3, 18 = 5, 3 = 2, 9 = 4, and 2 = 1.
3. (a) Wilcoxon rank-sum test or Mann-Whitney U test.
   (b) Set the significance cutoff (based on a table) for the maximum sum of ranks for the group predicted to have the lower scores, change all scores to ranks (ignoring what group they are in), add up the ranks in the group predicted to have the lower scores, compare that total to the cutoff.
4. (a) You get fairly similar results to doing the standard parametric test.
   (b) Because the population distribution will be rectangular and not normal (an assumption for the t test).
   (c) Because the rank-order test is based on knowing for sure the shape of the population distribution and using exact probabilities on that basis.
5. (a) You can use the familiar parametric methods and the transformation may come closer to the true meaning of the underlying measurement.
   (b) They will not always work and may distort underlying meaning of the measurement.
   (c) They can be used regardless of the distribution, and rank order may better reflect the true meaning of the measurement.
   (d) They are often unfamiliar and have not been developed for many complex methods; also, ties in ranks (which are common) distort the accuracy of these tests.

Chi-Square Tests, Data Transformations, and Rank-Order Tests in Research Articles
Chi-Square Tests

In research articles, chi-square tests usually include the frequencies in each category or cell, as well as the degrees of freedom, number of participants, the sample's chi-square, and significance level. For example, Harter et al. (1997) reported their finding for the relationship style of the self-focused men as "χ^2 (2, n = 101) = 11.89, p < .005" (p. 156).

Here is another example of a chi-square test for goodness of fit. Sandra Moriarty and Shu-Ling Everett (1994) did a study of television viewing in which graduate students actually went to 55 different homes and observed people watching television for 45-minute sessions. In one part of their results, they compared the number of people they observed who fell into one of four distinct categories:

> Flipping [very rapid channel changing], the category dominated by the most active type of behavior, occurred most frequently, in 33% of the sessions (n = 18). The grazing category [periods of browsing through channels] dominated 24% of the sessions (n = 13), and 22% were found to be in each of the continuous and stretch viewing categories (n = 12). These differences were not statistically significant (χ^2 = 1.79, df = 3, p > .05). (p. 349)

Published reports of chi-square tests for independence provide the same basic chi-square information. For example, Durkin and Barber (2002) studied the relationship between playing computer games and positive development (such as being close to one's family, involved in activities, having positive mental health, and low disobedience to parents) among 16-year-old high school students in Michigan. As part of the study, the researchers tested whether male and female students differed in how often they played computer games. Students indicated how often they played computer games with a 7-point scale, from *never* (1) to *daily* (7). Here is how the researchers reported their results:

> The participants were categorized into three groups based on their frequency of play: "None" included participants who did not use computers at all, as well as those who used computers, but never for computer games; "Low" included participants who checked 2, 3, 4, or 5 for frequency of computer use to play computer games; and "High" included participants who checked 6 or 7 for frequency of computer game play. A chi-square test [for independence] indicated that males and females were not evenly distributed across these three categories [χ^2(2, N = 1043) = 62.39, p < .001]. Girls were overrepresented among the nonusers, with a majority never playing computer games (50.6%), compared to 29.4% of boys who never played. Boys were more than twice as likely (23.8%) as girls (9.9%) to be in the high use group. A substantial number of both girls (39.4%) and boys (46.8%) were in the low use group. (p. 381)

You may be interested to read the researchers' conclusions from the overall study: "No evidence was obtained of negative outcomes among game players. On several measures—including . . . [all of the positive development outcomes mentioned earlier]—game players scored more favorably than did peers who never played computer games. It is concluded that computer games can be a positive feature of a healthy adolescence." (Durkin & Barber, 2002, p. 373)

Durkin and Barber (2002) do not give the effect size for their significant result. However, you can figure it out from the chi-square, number of participants, and design of the study (2 × 3 in this example). Using the formula,

$$\text{Cramer's } \phi = \sqrt{\chi^2/[(N)(df_{\text{Smaller}})]} = \sqrt{62.39/[(1043)(1)]} = \sqrt{.060} = .24.$$

This suggests that there is something close to a moderate effect size.

Data Transformations

Data transformations are usually mentioned in the Results section, just prior to the description of the analysis that uses the data that were transformed. For example, Stake and Malkin (2003) studied students' reports of the quality of their classes on women's and gender studies. Prior to presenting the main results, the researchers noted:

. . . all variables were tested for normality. The following variables were found to be skewed and were logarithmically transformed to normalize the distributions: age, relationship capacity, class expectations, percentage of gender match, percentage of ethnic match, and class experience ratings. All of the above distributions except age were negatively skewed and were therefore reversed [reflected] prior to the log transformation. (p. 178)

Rank-Order Tests

Here is an example of a rank-order test reported in a research study by Rottenstreich and Hsee (2001), focusing on the importance of subjective feeling in making risk-taking decisions. In one of their studies, one group of students was asked how much they would pay for having a 1% chance of winning a $500 coupon toward a European summer vacation. A second group was asked how much they would pay for having a 1% chance of winning a $500 coupon toward their tuition. Here are the results: "Although the two coupons had equivalent redemption value, the median price of the 1% chance of winning the European coupon was $20, whereas the median price of the 1% chance of winning the tuition coupon was only $5 ($p < .05$ by Mann-Whitney test . . .)" (p. 187).

Summary

1. Chi-square tests are used for hypothesis tests with *nominal variables.* A sample's chi-square statistic (χ^2) shows the amount of mismatch between expected and observed frequencies over several categories. It is figured by finding, for each category or combination of categories, the difference between observed frequency and expected frequency, squaring this difference (eliminating positive and negative signs), and dividing by the expected frequency (making the squared differences more proportionate to the numbers involved). The results are then added up for all the categories or combinations of categories. The distribution of the chi-square statistic is known and the cutoffs can be looked up in standard chi-square tables.

2. The chi-square test for goodness of fit is used to test hypotheses about whether a distribution of frequencies over two or more categories of a *single nominal variable* matches an expected distribution. (These expected frequencies are based, for example, on theory or on a distribution in another study or circumstance.) In this test, the expected frequencies are given in advance or are based on some expected percentages (such as equal percentages in all groups). The degrees of freedom are the number of categories minus 1.

3. The chi-square test for independence is used to test hypotheses about the relation between *two nominal variables*—that is, about whether the breakdown over the categories of one variable has the same proportional pattern within each of the categories of the other variable. The frequencies are set up in a contingency table, in which the two variables are crossed and the numbers in each combination are placed in each of the resulting cells. The frequency expected for a cell if the two variables are independent is the percentage of all the people in that cell's row times the total number of people in that cell's column. The degrees of freedom for the chi-square test for independence are the number of columns minus 1 multiplied by the number of rows minus 1.

4. Chi-square tests make no assumptions about normal distributions of their variables, but they do require that no individual be counted in more than one category or cell.

5. The estimated effect size for a chi-square test for independence (that is, the degree of association) for a 2×2 contingency table is the phi coefficient; for larger tables, Cramer's phi. Phi is the square root of the result of dividing your sample's chi-square by the number of persons. Cramer's phi is the square root of the result of dividing your sample's chi-square by the product of the number of persons multiplied by the degrees of freedom in the smaller side of the contingency table. These coefficients range from 0 to 1.

6. The t test, the analysis of variance, and other standard parametric tests all assume that populations follow a normal curve and have equal variances. When samples suggest that the populations are very far from normal (as when they are highly skewed, especially due to outliers), using the ordinary procedures gives incorrect results.

7. One approach when the populations appear to be non-normal is to transform the scores, such as taking the square root of each score so that the distribution of the transformed scores appears to represent a normally distributed population. The ordinary hypothesis-testing procedures can then be used.

8. Another approach is to rank all of the scores in a study. Special rank-order tests (sometimes called nonparametric or distribution-free tests) use basic principles of probability to determine the chance of the ranks being unevenly distributed across groups. However, in many situations, using the rank-transformed scores in an ordinary parametric test gives a good approximation.

9. Data transformations allow you to use the familiar parametric techniques, but cannot always be used and may distort the meaning of the scores. You can use rank-order methods in almost any situation, they are especially appropriate with rank or similar data, and they have a straightforward conceptual foundation. But rank-order methods are not widely familiar and they have not been developed for many complex data analysis situations. As with data transformations, information may be lost or meaning distorted with rank-order methods.

10. Chi-square tests are reported in research articles using a standard format. For example, $\chi^2(3, N = 196) = 9.22$, $p < .05$. Research articles usually describe data transformations just prior to analyses using them. Rank-order methods are described much like any other kind of hypothesis test.

Key Terms

chi-square tests (p. 359)
chi-square test for goodness of fit (p. 362)
chi-square test for independence (p. 362)
observed frequency (p. 362)
expected frequency (p. 362)
chi-square statistic (χ^2) (p. 363)

chi-square distribution (p. 364)
chi-square table (p. 364)
contingency table (p. 368)
independence (p. 368)
cell (p. 369)
phi coefficient (ϕ) (p. 376)
Cramer's phi (p. 376)
data transformation (p. 382)

square-root transformation (p. 384)
rank-order transformation (p. 387)
rank-order tests (p. 387)
distribution-free tests (p. 387)
nonparametric tests (p. 387)
parametric tests (p. 387)

Example Worked-Out Problems

Chi-Square Test for Goodness of Fit

The expected distribution (from previous years) on an exam roughly follows a normal curve in which the highest scoring 2.5% of the students get As; the next highest scoring 14%, Bs; the next 67%, Cs; the next 14%, Ds; and the lowest 2.5%, Fs. A class takes a test using a new grading system and 10 get As, 34 get Bs, 140 get Cs, 10 get Ds, and 6 get Fs. Use the steps of hypothesis testing to decide whether the new system produces a different distribution of grades (using the .01 level).

Answer

Table 11–16 shows the observed and expected frequencies and the figuring for the chi-square test.

❶ **Restate the question as a research hypothesis and a null hypothesis about the populations.** There are two populations:

Population 1: Students graded with the new system.
Population 2: Students graded with the old system.

The research hypothesis is that the populations are different; the null hypothesis is that the populations are the same.

❷ **Determine the characteristics of the comparison distribution.** The comparison distribution is a chi-square distribution with 4 degrees of freedom ($df = N_{\text{Categories}} - 1 = 5 - 1 = 4$).

❸ **Determine the cutoff sample score on the comparison distribution at which the null hypothesis should be rejected.** Using the .01 level and $df = 4$, Table A–4 (in the Appendix) shows a needed chi-square of 13.277.

Table 11–16   Figuring for Chi-Square Test for Goodness of Fit Example Worked-Out Problem

Grade	Observed Ⓐ	Expected Ⓑ
A	10	5 (2.5% × 200)
B	34	28 (14.0% × 200)
C	140	134 (67.0% × 200)
D	10	28 (14.0% × 200)
F	6	5 (2.5% × 200)

Degrees of freedom = $N_{\text{Categories}} - 1 = 5 - 1 = 4$ ❷
Chi-square needed, $df = 4$, .01 level: 13.277 ❸

$$\chi^2 = \Sigma \frac{(O - E)^2}{E} = \frac{(10 - 5)^2}{5} + \frac{(34 - 28)^2}{28} + \frac{(140 - 134)^2}{134} + \frac{(10 - 28)^2}{28}$$

$$+ \frac{(6 - 5)^2}{5}$$

$$= \frac{5^2}{5} + \frac{6^2}{28} + \frac{6^2}{134} + \frac{-18^2\,Ⓒ}{28} + \frac{1^2}{5}$$

$$= \frac{25}{5} + \frac{36}{28} + \frac{36\,Ⓓ}{134} + \frac{324}{28} + \frac{1}{5}$$

$$= 5 + 1.29 + .27 + 11.57 + .20 = 18.33.\,Ⓕ$$
Ⓔ

Decision: Reject the null hypothesis. ❺

❹ **Determine your sample's score on the comparison distribution.** As shown in Table 11–16, this comes out to 18.33.

❺ **Decide whether to reject the null hypothesis.** The sample's chi square of 18.33 is more extreme than the needed chi-square of 13.277. Thus, you can reject the null hypothesis and conclude that the populations are different; the new grading system produces a different distribution of grades than the previous one.

Chi-Square Test for Independence

Steil and Hay (1997) conducted a survey of professionals (lawyers, doctors, bankers, etc.) regarding the people they compare themselves to when they think about their job situation (salary, benefits, responsibility, status, etc.). One question of special interest was how much professionals compare themselves to people of their own sex, the opposite sex, or both. Here are the results:

	Participant Gender	
	Men	**Women**
Comparison		
Same sex	29	17
Opposite sex	4	14
Both sexes	26	28

Use the steps of hypothesis testing to decide if the researchers can conclude that the gender of who people compare themselves to is different depending on their own gender (use the .05 level).

Answer

Table 11–17 shows the figuring for the chi-square test.

Table 11–17 Figuring for Chi-Square Test for Independence Example Worked-Out Problem

Response

		Men	**Women**	**Total**
Comparison	Same sex	29 (23) Ⓐ	17 (23) Ⓑ	46 (39.0%)
	14 (9)	18 (15.3%)		
	Both sexes	26 (27)	28 (27)	54 (45.8%)
	Total	59	59	118

$df = (N_{Columns} - 1)(N_{Rows} - 1) = (2 - 1)(3 - 1) = (1)(2) = 2.$ ❷

Chi-square needed, $df = 2$, .05 level: 5.992. ❸

$$\chi^2 = \Sigma \frac{(O - E)^2}{E} = \frac{(29 - 23)^2}{23} + \frac{(17 - 23)^2}{23} + \frac{(4 - 9)^2}{9} + \frac{(14 - 9)^2}{9} + \frac{(26 - 27)^2}{27} + \frac{(28 - 27)^2}{27}$$

$$= \frac{6^2}{23} + \frac{-6^2}{23} + \frac{-5^2}{9} + \frac{5^2}{9} + \frac{-1^2}{27} + \frac{1^2}{27}$$ Ⓒ

$$= \frac{36}{23} + \frac{36}{23} + \frac{25}{9} + \frac{25}{9} + \frac{1}{27} + \frac{1}{27}$$ Ⓓ

$$= 1.57 + 1.57 + 2.78 + 2.78 + .04 + .04 = 8.78.$$ Ⓕ

Decision: Reject the null hypothesis. ❺

Note. Data from Steil and Hay (1997). The chi-square computed here (8.78) is slightly different from that reported in their article (8.76) due to rounding error.

❶ **Restate the question as a null hypothesis and a research hypothesis about the populations.** There are two populations:

Population 1: Professionals like those surveyed.
Population 2: Professionals for whom own sex is independent of the sex of those to whom they compare their job situations.

      The null hypothesis is that the two populations are the same, that, in general, professional men and women do not differ in the sex of those to whom they compare their job situations. The research hypothesis is that the populations are not the same, that professionals like those surveyed are unlike the hypothetical population in which men and women do not differ in the sex of those to whom they compare their job situations.

❷ **Determine the characteristics of the comparison distribution.** This is a chi-square distribution with 2 degrees of freedom.

❸ **Determine the cutoff sample score on the comparison distribution at which the null hypothesis should be rejected.** Using the .05 level and 2 degrees of freedom, the needed chi-square for significance is 5.992.

❹ **Determine your sample's score on the comparison distribution.** As shown in Table 11–17, this comes out to 8.78.

❺ **Decide whether to reject the null hypothesis.** The chi square of 8.78 is larger than the cutoff of 5.992. Thus you can reject the null hypothesis: The gender of the people with whom professionals compare their job situations is likely to be different for men and women.

Effect Size for a 2 × 2 Chi-Square Test for Independence

Figure the effect size for a study with 85 participants and a chi-square of 14.41.

Answer

$$\phi = \sqrt{\chi^2/N} = \sqrt{14.41/85} = \sqrt{.170} = .41.$$

Effect Size for a Chi-Square Test for Independence with a Contingency Table Greater Than 2 × 2

Figure the effect size for a 3 × 7 study with 135 participants and the chi-square is 18.32.

Answer

$$\text{Cramer's } \phi = \sqrt{\chi^2/[(N)(df_{\text{Smaller}})]} = \sqrt{18.32/[(135)(2)]}$$
$$= \sqrt{18.32/270} = \sqrt{.068} = .26.$$

Outline for Writing Essays for a Chi-Square Test for Goodness of Fit

1. Explain that chi-square tests are used for hypothesis testing with nominal variables. The chi-square test for goodness of fit is used to test hypotheses about whether a distribution of frequencies over two or more categories of a single nominal variable matches an expected distribution. Be sure to explain the meaning of the research hypothesis and the null hypothesis in this situation.

2. Describe the core logic of hypothesis testing in this situation. Be sure to mention that the hypothesis testing involves comparing observed frequencies (that is,

frequencies found in the actual study) with expected frequencies (that is, frequencies that you would expect based on a particular theory or the results of previous research studies). The size of the discrepancy between the observed and expected frequencies determines whether the null hypothesis can be rejected.

3. Explain that the comparison distribution in this situation is a chi-square distribution. Be sure to mention that the shape of the chi-square distribution depends on the number of degrees of freedom. Describe how to determine the degrees of freedom and the cutoff chi-square value.

4. Describe how to figure the chi-square value for the sample. The key idea is to get a single number that indicates the overall discrepancy between what was found in the study and what would be expected based on some null hypothesis idea (such as the groups all being equal). To get this number you figure, for each group, the difference between the observed frequency and the expected frequency, square it (because otherwise the sign of the differences would cancel each other out when you added them up), and divide the squared difference by the expected frequency (to adjust for the size of the numbers involved). You then add up all of the adjusted squared differences to get an overall number. (This should all be explained using the numbers in the study as an example.)

5. Explain how and why the scores from Steps ❸ and ❹ of the hypothesis-testing process are compared. Explain the meaning of the result of this comparison with regard to the specific research and null hypotheses being tested.

Outline for Writing Essays for a Chi-Square Test for Independence

Follow the general outline above for the chi-square test for goodness of fit, noting that the chi-square test for independence is used to test hypotheses about the relation between two nominal variables. Be sure also to explain the concept of independence and how and why you figure the expected frequency for each cell (using the actual numbers in your study as examples).

Square-Root Transformation

Carry out a square-root transformation on the scores below from a study with three groups:

Group A	Group B	Group C
15	21	18
4	16	19
12	49	11
14	17	22

Answer

Group A	Group B	Group C
3.88	4.58	4.24
2	4	4.36
3.46	7	3.32
3.74	4.12	4.69

Rank-Order Transformation

Carry out a rank-order transformation on the same scores you used for the square-root transformation above.

Answer

Group A	Group B	Group C
5	10	8
1	6	9
3	12	2
4	7	11

Practice Problems

These problems involve figuring. Most real-life statistics problems are done on a computer with special statistical software. Even if you have such software, do these problems by hand to ingrain the method in your mind. To learn how to use a computer to solve statistics problems like those in this chapter, refer to the *Using SPSS* section at the end of this chapter and the *Student's Study Guide and SPSS Workbook* that accompanies this text.

All data are fictional unless an actual citation is given.

Set I (for answers, see pp. 451–453)

1. Carry out a chi-square test for goodness of fit for each of the following (use the .05 level for each):

(a)

Category	Expected	Observed
A	20%	19
B	20%	11
C	40%	10
D	10%	5
E	10%	5

(b)

Category	Expected	Observed
I	30%	100
II	50%	100
III	20%	100

(c)

Category	Number in the Past	Observed
1	100	38
2	300	124
3	50	22
4	50	16

2. A director of a social service agency is planning to hire temporary staff to assist with intake. In making plans, the director needs to know whether there is any

difference in the use of the agency at different seasons of the year. Last year there were 28 new clients in the winter, 33 in the spring, 16 in the summer, and 51 in the fall. On the basis of last year's data, should the director conclude that season makes a difference? (Use the .05 level.) (a) Carry out the five steps of hypothesis testing. (b) Explain your answer to a person who has never taken a course in statistics. (This problem is a chi-square for a single nominal variable like the Harter et al. study of relationship styles at the beginning of this chapter. This problem is not a chi-square test for independence and does not involve any contingency tables.)

3. Carry out a chi-square test for independence for each of the following contingency tables (use the .01 level). Also, figure the effect size for each contingency table.

(a)	10	16		(b)	100	106		(c)	100	160
	16	10			106	100			160	100

(d)	10	16	10		(e)	10	16	16		(f)	10	16	10
	16	10	10			16	10	16			16	10	16

4. A political analyst is interested in whether the community in which a person lives is related to that person's opinion on an upcoming water conservation ballot initiative. The analyst surveys 90 people by phone. The results are shown below. Is opinion related to community at the .05 level? (a) Carry out the five steps of hypothesis testing. (b) Compute Cramer's phi and power. (c) Explain your answers to (a) and (b) to a person who has never taken a course in statistics.

	Community A	Community B	Community C
For	12	6	3
Against	18	3	15
No opinion	12	9	12

5. Figure the effect size for the following studies:

	N	Chi-Square	Design
(a)	100	16	2×2
(b)	100	16	2×5
(c)	100	16	3×3
(d)	100	8	2×2
(e)	200	16	2×2

6. What is the power of the following planned studies using a chi-square test for independence with $p < .05$?

	Predicted Effect Size	Design	N
(a)	small	2×2	25
(b)	medium	2×2	25
(c)	small	2×2	50
(d)	small	2×3	25
(e)	small	3×3	25
(f)	small	2×5	25

7. About how many participants do you need for 80% power in each of the following planned studies using a chi-square test for independence with $p < .05$?

	Predicted Effect Size	Design
(a)	medium	2×2
(b)	large	2×2
(c)	medium	2×5
(d)	medium	3×3
(e)	large	2×3

8. Lydon, Pierce, and O'Regan (1997) conducted a study that compared long-distance to local dating relationships. The researchers first administered questionnaires to a group of students one month prior to their leaving home to begin their first semester at McGill University (Time 1). Some of these students had dating partners who lived in the McGill area; others had dating partners who lived a long way from McGill. The researchers contacted the participants again late in the fall semester, asking them about the current status of their original dating relationships (Time 2). Here is how they reported their results:

> Of the 69 participants...55 were involved in long-distance relationships, and 14 were in local relationships (dating partner living within 200 km of them). Consistent with our predictions, 12 of the 14 local relationships were still intact at Time 2 (86%), whereas only 28 of the 55 long-distance relationships were still intact (51%), $\chi^2(1, N = 69) = 5.55, p < .02$. (p. 108)

(a) Figure the chi-square yourself (your results should be the same, within rounding error). (b) Figure the effect size. (c) Explain the results to parts (a) and (b) to a person who has never had a course in statistics.

9. For each of the distributions below, make a square-root transformation:
   (a) 16, 4, 9, 25, 36
   (b) 35, 14.3, 13, 12.9, 18

10. A researcher compares the typical family size in 10 cultures, 5 from Language Group A and 5 from Language Group B. The figures for the Group A cultures are 1.2, 2.5, 4.3, 3.8, and 7.2. The figures for the Group B cultures are 2.1, 9.2, 5.7, 6.7, and 4.8. Based on these 10 cultures, does typical family size differ in cultures with different language groups? Use the .05 level. (a) Carry out a t test for independent means using the actual scores. (b) Carry out a square-root transformation (to keep things simple, round off the transformed scores to one decimal place). (c) Carry out a t test for independent means using the transformed scores. (d) Explain what you have done and why to someone who is familiar with the t test for independent means but not with data transformation.

11. A researcher randomly assigns participants to watch one of three kinds of films: one that tends to make people sad, one that tends to make people exuberant, and one that tends to make people angry. The participants are then asked to rate a series of photos of individuals on how honest they appear. The ratings for the sad-film group were 201, 523, and 614; the ratings for the angry-film group were 136, 340, and 301; and the ratings for the exuberant-film group were 838, 911, and 1,007. (a) Carry out an analysis of variance using the actual scores (use $p < .01$). (b) Carry out a square-root transformation of the scores (to keep things simple, round off the transformed scores to one decimal place). (c) Carry out an analysis of variance using the transformed scores. (d) Explain what you have done and why to someone who is familiar with analysis of variance but not with data transformation.

12. Miller (1997) conducted a study of commitment to a romantic relationship and how much attention a person pays to attractive alternatives. In this study, participants were shown a set of slides of attractive individuals. At the start of the results section, Miller notes, "The self-reports on the Attentiveness to Alternative Index and the time spent actually inspecting the attractive opposite-sex slides . . . were positively skewed, so logarithmic transformations of the data were performed" (p. 760). Explain what is being described here (and why it is being done) to a person who understands ordinary parametric statistics but has never heard of data transformations.

Set II

13. Carry out a chi-square test for goodness of fit for each of the following (use the .01 level for each):

(a)

Category	Expected	Observed
1	2%	5
2	14%	15
3	34%	90
4	34%	120
5	14%	50
6	2%	20

(b)

Category	Proportion Expected	Observed
A	1/3	10
B	1/6	10
C	1/2	10

14. A researcher wants to be sure that the sample in her study is not unrepresentative of the distribution of ethnic groups in her community. Her sample includes 300 whites, 80 African Americans, 100 Latinos, 40 Asians, and 80 others. In her community, according to census records, there are 48% whites, 12% African Americans, 18% Latinos, 9% Asians, and 13% others. Is her sample unrepresentative of the population in her community? (Use the .05 level.) (a) Carry out the steps of hypothesis testing. (b) Explain your answer to a person who has never taken a course in statistics. (This problem is a chi-square for a single nominal variable like the Harter et al. study of relationship styles at the beginning of this chapter. This problem is not a chi-square test for independence and does not involve any contingency tables.)

15. Carry out a chi-square test for independence for each of the following contingency tables (use the .05 level). Also, figure the effect size for each contingency table.

(a)

0	18
18	0

(b)

0	0	18
9	9	0

(c)

0	0	9	9
9	9	0	0

(d)

20	40
0	40

16. Below are results of a survey of a sample of people buying ballet tickets, laid out according to the type of seat they purchased and how regularly they attend. Is there a significant relation? (Use the .05 level.) (a) Carry out the steps of hypothesis testing. (b) Figure the effect size. (c) Explain your answer to parts (a) and (b) to a person who has never taken a course in statistics.

		Attendance	
		Regular	Occasional
Seating Category	Orchestra	20	80
	Dress circle	20	20
	Balcony	40	80

17. Figure the effect size for the following studies:

	N	Chi-Square	Design
(a)	40	10	2 × 2
(b)	400	10	2 × 2
(c)	40	10	4 × 4
(d)	400	10	4 × 4
(e)	40	20	2 × 2

18. What is the power of the following planned studies, using a chi-square test for independence with $p < .05$?

	Predicted Effect Size	Design	N
(a)	medium	2 × 2	100
(b)	medium	2 × 3	100
(c)	large	2 × 2	100
(d)	medium	2 × 2	200
(e)	medium	2 × 3	50
(f)	small	3 × 3	25

19. About how many participants do you need for 80% power in each of the following planned studies, using a chi-square test for independence with $p < .05$?

	Predicted Effect Size	Design
(a)	small	2 × 2
(b)	medium	2 × 2
(c)	large	2 × 2
(d)	small	3 × 3
(e)	medium	3 × 3
(f)	large	3 × 3

20. Everett, Price, Bedell, and Telljohann (1997) mailed a survey to a random sample of physicians. Half were offered $1 if they would return the questionnaire (this was the experimental group); the other half served as a control group. The point of the study was to see if even a small incentive would increase the return rate for physician surveys. Everett et al. report their results as follows:

Of the 300 surveys mailed to the experimental group, 39 were undeliverable, 2 were returned uncompleted, and 164 were returned completed. Thus, the response rate for the experimental group was 63% [164/(300 − 39) = .63]. Of the 300 surveys mailed to the control group, 40 were undeliverable, and 118 were returned completed. Thus, the response rate for the control group was 45% [118/(300 − 40) = .45]. A chi-square test comparing the response rates for the experimental and control groups found the $1 incentive had a statistically significantly improved response rate over the control group [$\chi^2(1, N = 521) = 16.0, p < .001$].

(a) Figure the chi-square yourself (your results should be the same, within rounding error). (b) Figure the effect size. (c) Explain the results to parts (a) and (b) to a person who has never had a course in statistics.

21. For each of the distributions below, make a square-root transformation:
    (a) 100, 1, 64, 81, 121
    (b) 45, 30, 17.4, 16.8, 47

22. A study compares performance on a novel task for fifth-grade students who do the task either alone, in the presence of a stranger, or in the presence of a friend. The scores for the students in the alone condition are 1, 1, and 0; the scores of the participants in the stranger condition are 2, 6, and 1; and the scores for those in the friend condition are 3, 9, and 10. (a) Carry out an analysis of variance using the actual scores ($p < .05$). (b) Carry out a square-root transformation of the scores (to keep things simple, round off the transformed scores to one decimal place). (c) Carry out an analysis of variance using the transformed difference scores. (d) Explain what you have done and why to someone who is familiar with analysis of variance but not with data transformation.

23. A researcher conducted an experiment organized around a major televised address by the U.S. president. Immediately after the address, three participants were randomly assigned to listen to the commentaries provided by the television networks' political commentators. The other three were assigned to spend the same time with the television off, reflecting quietly about the speech. Participants in both groups then completed a questionnaire that assessed how much of the content of the speech they remembered accurately. The group that heard the commentators had scores of 4, 0, and 1. The group that reflected quietly had scores of 9, 3, and 8. Did hearing the commentary affect memory? Use the .05 level, one-tailed, predicting higher scores for the reflected-quietly group. (a) Carry out a *t* test for independent means using the actual scores. (b) Carry out a square-root transformation (to keep things simple, round off the transformed scores to one decimal place). (c) Carry out a *t* test for independent means using the transformed scores. (d) Explain what you have done and why to someone who is familiar with the *t* test for independent means but not with data transformation.

24. June, Curry, and Gear (1990) surveyed black students at a Midwestern university about problems in their use of college services. Surveys were conducted of about 250 students each time at the end of the spring quarter over five different years. The researchers ranked the nine main problem areas for each of the years. One of their analyses then proceeded as follows: "A major question of interest was whether the ranking of most serious problems and use of services varied by years. Thus, a Kruskal-Wallis one-way analysis of variance (ANOVA) was performed on the rankings but was not significant" (p. 180). Explain why the researchers used the Kruskal-Wallis test instead of an ordinary analysis of variance and what conclusions can be drawn from this result.

Using SPSS

The ✍ in the steps below indicates a mouse click. (We used SPSS version 13.0 for Windows to carry out these analyses. The steps and output may be slightly different for other versions of SPSS.)

It is easier to learn the SPSS steps for chi-square tests using actual numbers. As an example, imagine you are a student in a class of 20 students and want to determine if the students in the class are split equally among first- and second-year students (the class is not open to students in other year groups). We will use a chi-square test for goodness of fit to answer this question. Each student's year in college is shown in the first column of Figure 11–10.

Chi-Square Test for Goodness of Fit

❶ Enter the scores into SPSS. As shown in Figure 11–10, the score for each person is listed in a separate row. We labeled the variable "year." (For now, you can ignore the "gender_w1m2" variable.)

❷ ✍ *Analyze.*

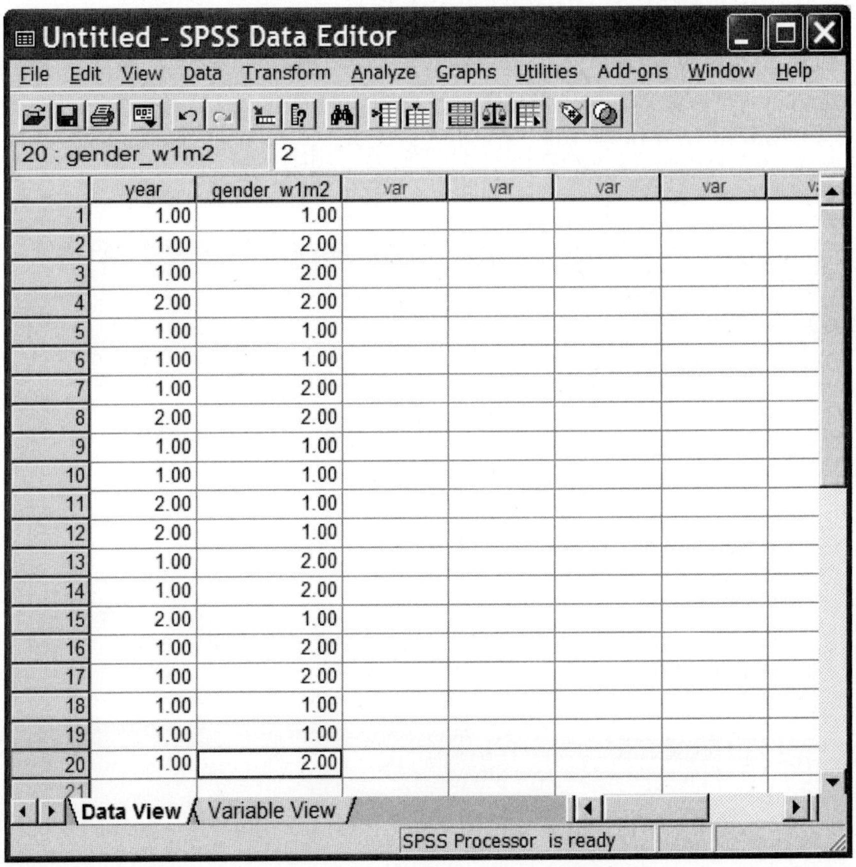

Figure 11–10   SPSS data editor window for a fictional study examining the distribution of first- and second-year college students and gender for a particular class.

❸ 🖰 *Non-Parametric Tests,* 🖰 *Chi-Square.*

❹ 🖰 on the variable called "year" and then 🖰 the arrow next to the box labeled "Test Variable List." This tells SPSS that the chi-square test for goodness of fit should be carried out on the scores for the nominal variable called "year." Notice in the "Expected Values" box that the option "All categories equal" is selected by default. This means that SPSS will carry out the chi-square to compare the observed frequency distribution in your sample with an expected frequency distribution based on an equal spread of scores across the categories. If you wish to use a different expected frequency distribution, select the "Values" option and enter the appropriate expected values.

❺ 🖰 *OK.* Your SPSS output window should look like Figure 11–11.

The first table in the SPSS output gives the observed frequencies, the expected frequencies, and the difference between the observed and expected frequencies (in the "Residual" column). The second table gives the value of chi-square, the degrees of freedom, and the exact significance level. The significance level of .013 (for the chi-square value of 5.00) is less than our .05 cutoff, which means that you can reject the null hypothesis. Thus, you can conclude that the students in the class are not split equally among first- and second-year students.

Chi-Square Test for Independence

Using the same example as for the chi-square test for goodness of fit, let's suppose you are interested in whether the distribution of first- and second-year students in the class is different for male and female students. To answer this question (which involves *two nominal variables*), we will use a chi-square test for independence.

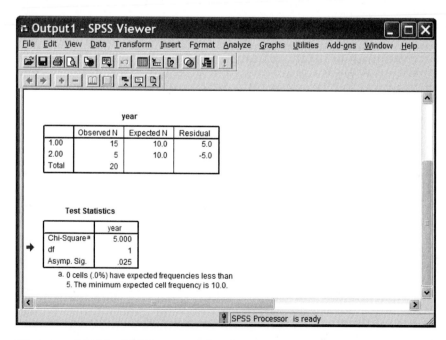

Figure 11–11 SPSS output window for a chi-square test for goodness of fit for a fictional study examining the distribution of first- and second-year college students for a particular class.

❶ Enter the scores into SPSS. As shown in Figure 11–10, the score for each person is listed in a separate row. We labeled the variables "year" and "gender_w1m2." (We assigned women a value of "1" for the gender variable and men a value of "2.")

❷ ✑ *Analyze.*

❸ ✑ *Descriptive Statistics,* ✑ *Crosstabs.*

❹ ✑ on the variable called "gender_w1m2" and then ✑ the arrow next to the box labeled "Row(s)." ✑ on the variable called "year" and then ✑ the arrow next to the box labeled "Column(s)." (It doesn't matter which variable is assigned to rows and which is assigned to columns; the result will be the same.)

❺ ✑ *Statistics.* Click the box labeled *Chi-square* (this checks the box). ✑ *Continue.*

❻ ✑ *OK.* Your SPSS output window should look like Figure 11–12.

The first table in the SPSS output (which is not shown in Figure 11–12) gives the number of individuals for each variable and whether there are any missing scores. The second table (labeled "gender_w1m2 * year Crosstabulation") gives the contingency table of observed values for the two nominal variables ("gender" and "year"). The third table (labeled "Chi-Square Tests") shows the actual result of the chi-square test for independence, as well as the results of other tests. The results of the chi-square test for independence are provided in the first row (labeled "Pearson Chi-Square"), which shows the chi-square value, the degrees of freedom, and the exact significance level. The significance level of .606 (for the chi-square value of 0.267) is greater than

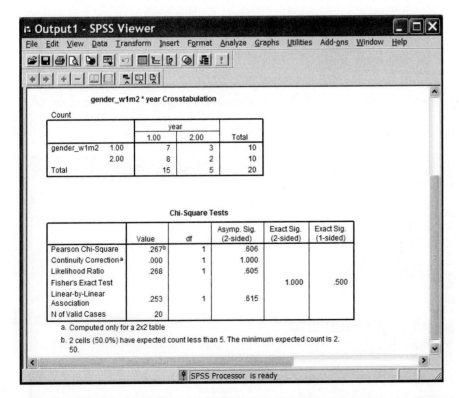

Figure 11–12   SPSS output window for a chi-square test for independence for a fictional study examining the distribution of first- and second-year college students and gender for a particular class.

our .05 cutoff. Thus, you cannot reject the null hypothesis. This means you cannot conclude that the distribution of first- and second-year students year in the class is different for male and female students.

Data Transformations

We will use the example of the square-root transformation of the scores from the study comparing highly sensitive and not highly sensitive children on the number of books read in the past year (see Tables 11–10 and 11–11).

❶ Enter the scores into SPSS. As shown in Figure 11–13, the score for each child is shown in the "books" column. The scores in the "sensitive" column show whether the child was not highly sensitive (a score of "0") or highly sensitive (a score of "1"). Although the "sensitive" scores aren't needed for the data transformation, they are important for figuring a *t* test for independent means on the transformed scores (see Table 11–12).

❷ ☞ *Transform.*

❸ ☞ *Compute.* This will bring up a "Compute Variable" window.

❹ Name the new variable (which will be the square root of the scores for the "books" variable) by typing "sqrtbooks" in the "Target Variable" box. (You could give any name to the new variable, but it is best to give it a name that describes how it was figured, and we recommend keeping your SPSS variable names to 10–12 characters or less.)

❺ Type "sqrt(books)" in the "Numeric Expression" box. This tells SPSS to take the square root of each score for the "books" variable and create a new variable with those transformed scores. The Compute Variable window should now look like Figure 11–14.

❻ ☞ *OK.*

Your SPSS data editor window should now look like Figure 11–15. You can now use the "sqrtbooks" scores in a *t* test for independent means to compare the scores of not highly sensitive and highly sensitive children. In Figure 11–16 we show the SPSS

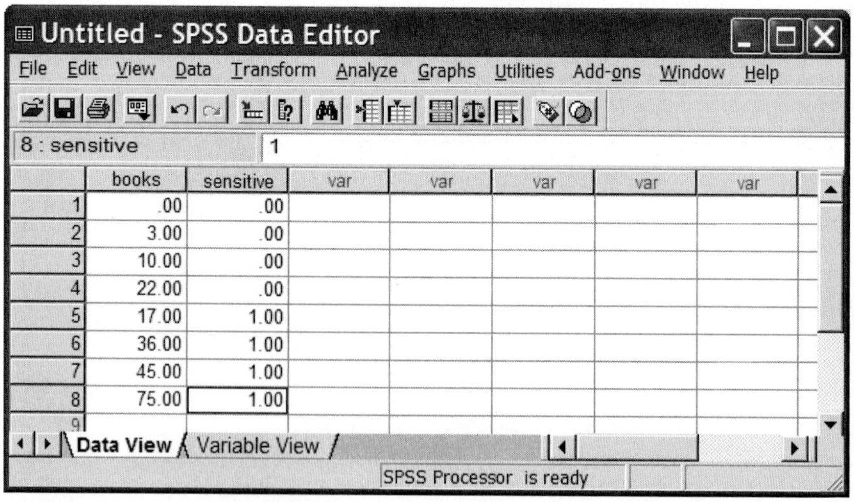

Figure 11–13   SPSS data editor window for the fictional study comparing highly sensitive and not highly sensitive children on the number of books read in the past year.

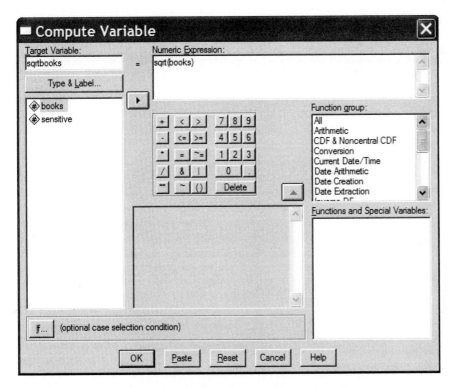

Figure 11–14   SPSS compute variable window for figuring the square root of the books scores for the fictional study comparing highly sensitive and not highly sensitive children on the number of books read in the past year.

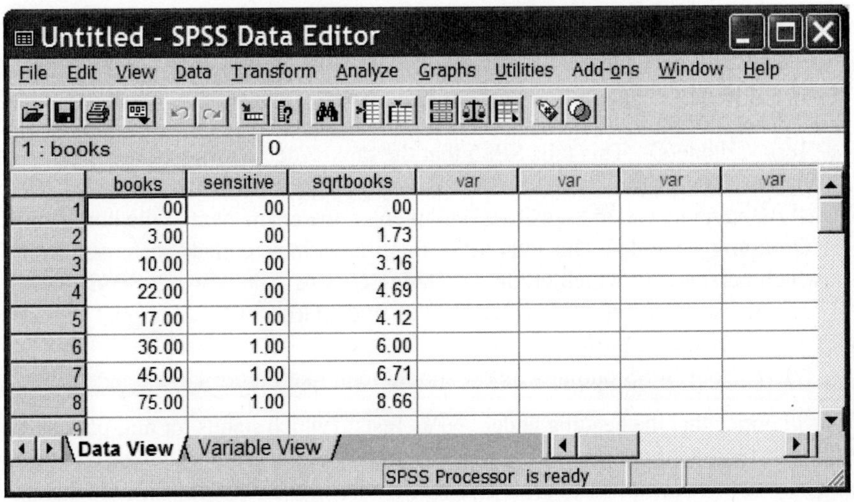

Figure 11–15   SPSS data editor window for the fictional study comparing highly sensitive and not highly sensitive children on the number of books read in the past year, including the scores for the "books" variable after a square root transformation.

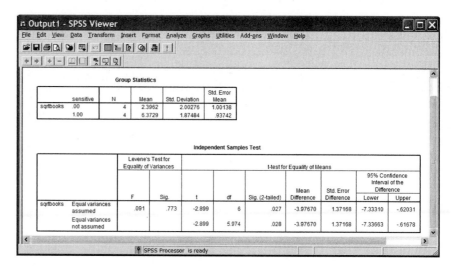

Figure 11–16 SPSS output window for a *t* test for independent means for the square-root transformed book scores from the fictional study comparing highly sensitive and not highly sensitive children on the number of books read in the past year.

output of such a *t* test for independent means. The results of this *t* test are the same (within rounding error) as the results in Table 11–12.

Rank-Order Tests

We will use the example of the Wilcoxon rank-sum test for the scores from the study comparing the highly sensitive and not highly sensitive children on the number of books read in the past year (see Table 11–14).

❶ Enter the scores into SPSS. As shown in Figure 11–13, the score for each child is shown in the "books" column. The scores in the "sensitive" column show whether the child was not highly sensitive (a score of "0") or highly sensitive (a score of "1").

❷ ✍ *Analyze.*

❸ ✍ *Nonparametric tests.*

❹ ✍ *2 Independent Samples.*

❺ ✍ on the variable called "books" and then ✍ the arrow next to the box labeled "Test Variable(s)." This tells SPSS that the rank-order test should be carried out on the scores for the "books" variable.

❻ ✍ the variable called "sensitive" and then ✍ the arrow next to the box labeled "Grouping Variable." This tells SPSS that the variable called "sensitive" shows which person is in which group. ✍ *Define Groups.* You now tell SPSS the values you used to label each group. Put "0" in the Group 1 box and put "1" in the Group 2 box. ✍ *Continue.*

❼ ✍ *OK.* Your SPSS output window should look like Figure 11–17.

You will notice that the heading under "NPar Tests" (which stands for non-parametric tests) is "Mann-Whitney Test." The Mann-Whitney test and the Wilcoxon rank-sum test differ in their computations but give mathematically equivalent final results. (As you will see in the second table in the SPSS output, the significance level is the same for Mann-Whitney and Wilcoxon rank-sum tests.) The first table in the SPSS output (labeled "Ranks") provides information about the two variables. The first column

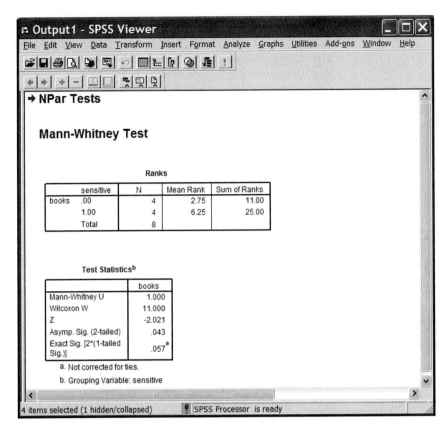

Figure 11–17   SPSS output window for a Wilcoxon rank-sum test for the fictional study comparing highly sensitive and not highly sensitive children on the number of books read in the past year.

gives the levels of the "sensitive" grouping variable (0 and 1, which indicate the not highly sensitive and highly sensitive groups, respectively.) The second, third, and fourth columns give, respectively, the number of individuals (*N*), mean rank, and sum of ranks for each group.

The second table in the SPSS output (labeled "Test Statistics") shows the actual results of the non-parametric rank-ordered tests. We will focus here on the results for the Wilcoxon rank-sum test (but the overall significance level and conclusion is the same, regardless of which test result you consider). Notice that the value of 11.000 is the same as the sum of the ranks for the not highly sensitive group, as shown in Table 11–14. The exact significance level of .043 for this result (shown in the "Asymp. Sig. (2-tailed)" row) is for a two-tailed test. In this example, we were using a one-tailed test, so this two-tailed significance of .043 represents a one-tailed significance of .043/2, which is .0215. This significance level of .0215 is less than our .05 cutoff for this example. This means that you can reject the null hypothesis and the research hypothesis is supported.

CHAPTER 12

Applying Statistical Methods in Your Own Research Project

CHAPTER OUTLINE

- Designing Your Study: Selecting a Statistical Test
- Figuring Power and Needed Sample Size
- Conducting the Study
- Data Screening
- Carrying Out the Major Analyses
- Writing Up Your Results
- In Closing
- Summary
- Key Terms

Welcome to the final chapter of *Statistics for the Behavioral and Social Sciences*. This chapter helps you use what you have learned in the previous chapters to explore an idea in your own research. We have tried to provide a lot of practical advice in this final chapter, while keeping it as brief as possible. (We're sure you will appreciate that after having made it this far through the book!) With that in mind, you won't see some of the familiar sections (such as "How Are You Doing?" and "Practice Problems") that you will be used to from previous chapters.

So you're going to carry out your own research project! You have a fairly clear understanding of the major statistical methods used in behavioral and social sciences and can make sense of them when they are used in a research article. However, it will help to have some additional points to apply this smoothly to your own research. In particular, in this chapter we consider the statistics aspects of designing your study (determining whether there is an appropriate statistical method and determining needed sample size), and conducting the study. We then turn to dealing with the results: entering the scores into the computer, checking for and dealing with missing scores (for example, where a participant did not answer all the questions), checking whether the scores on each variable meet the assumptions for the procedure you want to use (and what to do about it if they don't), carrying out the analyses, and writing up your results. Of course, the focus in all this is on the statistical analysis aspect of your research project. Web Chapter W1 (available at http://www.prenhall.com/aron) has a brief overview of research methods more generally.

TIP FOR SUCCESS:

Before reading this chapter, you should have read as many of the previous chapters as possible. You should also have tackled the Using SPSS sections that are found at the end of several chapters.

Designing Your Study: Selecting a Statistical Test

Once you have a possible idea for a research question, the next step is to develop a specific research plan to address that question—one that does as good a job as possible of approximating the ideal research design in terms of equivalence of experimental and control groups, equivalence of circumstances, generalizability, and measurement (see Web Chapter W1).

Before starting out on a new study, experienced researchers plan what statistical method they will use when the study is done. Otherwise you may find there are no methods available or the ones that are available will be less than ideal for some reason. You also need to decide in advance what statistical test you will use in order to figure out how many participants you will need (sample size) and the power of your planned study.

What Test to Use in the Usual Situation of Equal-Interval Measurement

In the most common research situation, your scores are measured on an approximately equal-interval scale (see Chapter 1 for a discussion of "levels of measurement"). Figure 12–1 shows a decision tree for deciding on an appropriate statistical test in such situations. Answering the questions in the decision tree will guide you to the right statistical test. The first question in the decision tree is: Are you testing the *difference between means* or *the association among variables?* For example, consider a study comparing the effect of different colors of printing on reading time. This study focuses on the mean reading time for each color; thus, this is a study comparing means of

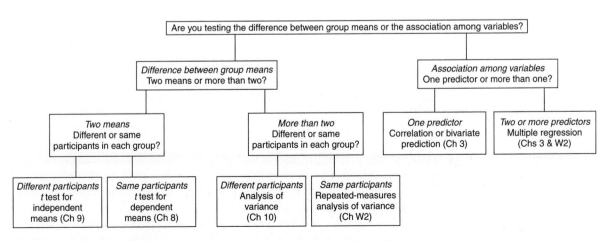

Figure 12–1   Decision tree for identifying statistical tests for studies with an equal-interval criterion or outcome variable.

between-subjects design Research strategy in which each person is tested only once and groups of individuals are compared.

variables. On the other hand, consider a study looking at the relation of mother's age to her oldest child's school grades (or, to put this another way, whether mother's age predicts her oldest child's school grades). This study is about associations among variables.

Suppose your study focuses on *differences between means.* The next question is whether there are two means being compared (for example, if you were looking at red printing vs. black printing) or whether there are three or more means (for example, if you were looking at differences among printing in red, black, green, and blue). You would use a *t* test if you are comparing two means, or an analysis of variance if you are comparing three or more means. Once you have decided on a *t* test or analysis of variance, you have to make another decision. You next must decide whether this is a **between-subjects design** or a repeated-measures design (also called a *within-subjects design,* as we mentioned in Chapter 8). In a between-subjects design, different people are in each group (for example, some participants will read a story in black printing and other participants will read the story in red printing). In a repeated-measures design, the same people will be in each group (for example, each participant will read one story in black printing and another story in red printing).

What if your study focuses on *associations or predictions?* In that case, the next question is whether there is one variable being correlated with or predicting the other (for example, mother's age predicting or associated with her oldest child's school grades) or whether more than one variable is being correlated with or predicting the other (for example, mother's age and father's age predicting or being associated with oldest child's school grades). You use correlation or bivariate prediction when there is one predictor variable. You use multiple regression when there are two or more predictor variables. Notice that in all these situations we are correlating with or predicting about a single variable. In the language of prediction (regression) there is only one criterion variable (in the example, it is oldest child's school grades). We will have more to say about this situation shortly.

The decision tree in Figure 12–1 leads you to the right statistical test to use in each of these situations.

What Test to Use When Your Scores are Categories

Suppose you are testing a hypothesis with a variable whose scores are categories (that is, it is a nominal variable). Examples of categorical variables are which of several candidates a person most favors, or which major a student is taking. The standard chi-square tests for goodness of fit and for independence (see Chapter 11) cover most such situations. However, as noted in Chapter 11, you can only use these tests when each person is in a single category on any one nominal variable. So, for example, you could not use a chi-square test to study the change in distribution of men's and women's preferred brand of shampoo from before to after a new advertising campaign. Also, if you have a three- or more-way contingency table, you need to use procedures that are quite advanced (such as *log-linear chi-square*) and in any case often cannot answer very directly the questions you might pose. Thus, if you have designed a study with a nominal variable and any one person can be in more than one category on a particular nominal variable, or you have more than a two-way table, we strongly urge you to find a way to redesign your study, perhaps by using a measure that is equal-interval instead.

Incidentally, there is a trick you can use when your nominal variable has only two categories, such as male and female (or if you can combine categories so you end up with only two, as in whether various majors are arts or science). In this situation, you can give the two categories any two arbitrary numbers, such as 1 and 2, and then treat the variable as an ordinary equal-interval variable so you can use *t* tests, correlation, and so on. But this does not work for more than two categories; also you should not use this method if the split between the two categories is quite extreme (say more than 80% in one of the groups).

What Test to Use When You Have Rank-Order Scores

Suppose your are interested in carrying out hypothesis testing with scores for a rank-order variable, such as place finished in a race or birth order in one's family. With rank-order scores, you may want to use one of the special rank-order tests discussed briefly in Chapter 11. (You will likely learn more about such tests in intermediate statistics courses.) Most of these are available in SPSS (by selecting *Analyze* and then *Nonparametric Tests*). You can use Figure 12–1 to find what test you would use if you had equal interval scores, and then find the appropriate equivalent rank-order test using Table 11–13. However, as you learned in Chapter 11, in most cases you get reasonably accurate results if you just use the ordinary equal-interval statistical procedures, treating the ranks (1, 2, 3, etc.) as if they were equal-interval scores. If you want to be more accurate you can use the ordinary tests with the adjustment described in Footnote 5 of Chapter 11.

When You Have More Than One Criterion or Outcome Variable

Most behavioral and social science research studies have a single criterion or outcome variable and the standard methods you learned in this book (correlation, regression, *t* test, etc.) are designed for such situations. However, you will sometimes want do to studies that use more than one such variable. For example, an experiment on the effect of color of printing on reading a story might measure both time to read the story and also comprehension of the story. Or a survey might look at how mother's age predicts four criterion variables, her oldest child's grades in elementary school, junior high school, high school, and college. We focus on three potential solutions for handling such research situations; method of separate analyses; method of averaging measures; and multivariate tests.

Method of Separate Analyses.   In studies like these, one solution is to use separate ordinary tests for each variable. Thus, you might run one *t* test comparing the effects of different colors of printing on reading time and another *t* test comparing the effect of the different colors on reading comprehension. Similarly you could conduct one regression analysis with mother's age predicting her oldest child's elementary school grades, another with mother's age predicting her oldest child's junior high school grades, and so on.

Method of Averaging Measures.   Another solution is to combine the several criterion or outcome measures into a single overall measure. (This is particularly appropriate if there are high correlations among the variables being combined.) For example, you could take the average of the four kinds of grades. However, in some situations, it is not so simple. Consider what would happen if you just did a simple average of each participant's reading time and reading comprehension score. One problem is that shorter reading times are better, but higher comprehension scores are

multivariate statistical test
Statistical procedure involving more than
one criterion or outcome variable.

better. So before averaging, you would need to reverse one of them. For example, if reading times go from 200 to 300 seconds, you can subtract each time from 300; then a high score would mean a better time and a low score, a worse reading time. Another problem in this example is that the two variables might be on quite different scales—for example, reading time (after reversing) goes from 0 to 100, comprehension scores might go from 1 to 7. Thus, if you combined them, the reading time would probably have a bigger influence on the mean. A solution to this problem is to convert all the scores on each scale to Z scores, then average the Z scores. (In the reading example, you would still have to reverse one of the measures before figuring the Z scores.) In this way the different measures are put on the same scale.

Multivariate Tests.   Yet another approach would be to carry out an overall analysis that considers all the criterion or outcome variables together. Such procedures are called **multivariate statistical tests** and we describe them briefly in Web Chapter W2 (available at http://www.prenhall.com/aron). After reading that chapter, you should be able to understand what such tests do and make some sense of the results you may read in a research article. You can learn more about multivariate statistical tests in more advanced statistics courses. So, until you take such courses, it is best to use the procedures you know, either doing separate tests for each variable or combining the variables by averaging. (In fact, the general advice even to experienced researchers who are masters of advanced statistical methods is to use the simplest methods available that are reasonably accurate. The idea is that with simpler procedures results will be more understandable to readers; also, the researcher is less likely to make mistakes.)

Figuring Power and Needed Sample Size

As discussed in some detail in Chapter 7, a crucial issue when planning a study is deciding if there is sufficient statistical power. That is, power tells you, if the research hypothesis is true, what is the probability this study will produce a significant result supporting it? To figure the statistical power of a planned study, you first need to decide what statistical test you will use. Then you have to make some estimate of the expected effect size. We discuss estimating effect size in Chapter 7—you may have a rough idea of whether the effect will be small, medium, or large based on previous similar research or a minimum effect size that would be important. If your study will use one of the major procedures we cover (correlation, *t* tests, analysis of variance, chi-square tests) there are power tables in each chapter. (Table A–5 in the Appendix is an index to these power tables.) If you are using a more advanced or unusual procedure that is not covered in the book, you may be able to find the power in Cohen's (1988) book of tables or by using power statistical software or an Internet power calculator. If your planned study has power below about 80%, our Table 7–5 suggests several ways you can alter the study to increase the power—such as by increasing the number of participants.

You can also start with an expected effect size and use one of the tables that tell you how many participants you need for 80% power. (Table A–5 includes an index to such tables.) It often turns out that the number you need is too large to be practical. This is particularly the case since participants are often hard to recruit, not everyone you recruit will qualify, and if you need to test participants on more than one occasion, you are likely to lose many after the first testing. Thus, you may need to use one

BOX 12-1   The Golden Age of Statistics: Four Guys around London

The four most common statistical techniques were created by four Englishmen born within sixty-eight years of each other. Galton, Fisher, and Pearson worked in the vicinity of London, and the fourth, Gosset, stuck at his brewery in Dublin, nevertheless kept in good touch with all that was happening in that city. Clearly, their proximity was important for creating the "critical mass" of minds sometimes associated with a golden age of discovery. And as is often the case with important discoveries, each man faced difficult practical problems or "anomalies" that pushed him to the solution—none simply set out to invent a statistical method in itself.

Also, there was the role of biometrics, which was attempting to test the theory of evolution mathematically. And for the first time, industry and agriculture were hiring university graduates with advanced mathematical training. Most were graduates of Cambridge University, so they could spread out through British industry and still, through their common alma mater, remain in contact and stay up to date with the most recent breakthroughs.

Today is also an interesting time for statistics. After little change for thirty years, the computer made possible all kinds of new statistical methods. The fundamentals developed in the Golden Age are mainly what you have learned in this book. Yet what can be done beyond the fundamentals is changing rapidly and could well revolutionize the research possibilities open to behavioral and social scientists. If we could look back from the future, we would probably say we now live in another Golden Age of Statistics.

Source: Tankard (1984).

Sir Francis Galton
(Corbis/Bettmann)

Sir Ronald Fisher
(Courtesy of the Library of Congress)

Karl Pearson
(Courtesy of the Library of Congress)

William S. Gosset
(The Granger Collection)

of the other methods listed in Table 7–5 to increase power or change the basic study itself.

Conducting the Study

From the point of view of the statistical analyses, there are three main things to keep in mind during the data gathering: (a) When you set up the layout of the questionnaires or data recording sheets, consider how easy it will be to type the scores into the computer; (b) keep all of the questionnaires or data recording sheets in a safe place; and (c) make sure you have recorded everything important on them—such as date and time of the study, experimental condition, and anything else that is not completed by the participants. Now and then a student conducts a study and when it is done discovers that there is no record of which participant was in which experimental condition! It is also important to record anything that happens with a participant that is unusual.

Entering Scores into the Computer

As for entering the scores into a computer, here are some suggestions from our long experience to make the process as straightforward and accurate as possible.

Setting Up the Spreadsheet.　With SPSS and most statistical programs, you type the scores onto a spreadsheet with one line per participant and one column per variable. Give some thought in advance as to how you will set it up. For example, put the columns for the variables in the same order as they are on the questionnaires or data recording sheets that you are typing them in from.

Variable Names.　It is important to type at the top of each column the descriptive name for each variable (rather than leave the variable named by the column number). Use a name that describes the particular variable—for example, "age" and "gender" are better than "variable1" or "question2"! Until a few years ago, SPSS limited variable names to a maximum of eight characters. Recent versions of SPSS allow longer variable names, but we still recommend that you try not to use variable names that are longer than about ten to twelve characters. (Otherwise it gets hard to read the names in the columns and the printouts of results are very lengthy.)

Sums and Codes.　To avoid work and errors, enter the scores directly and let the computer do any needed combining figuring. For example, if you have a ten-item questionnaire, it is better to enter the person's score on each item and let the computer figure the total or average. Similarly, if the computer needs number codes for a variable that was originally entered as words or letters, enter the words or letters—for example, "f" or "m" for gender—and then instruct the computer to make an additional column with number codes it creates for these. That way you will make fewer mistakes. Also you won't forget later which number goes with which letter! Alternatively, you may want to include number codes in your variable name. For example, in the Using SPSS section in Chapter 11, we used the variable name "gender_w1m2." The "w1m2" was a shorthand reminder that women were coded as "1" and men were coded as "2."

Typing in the Scores.　Have all material organized and at hand. If possible, type in all the scores at once. Save often. Keep notes of any irregularities (for example, a participant who answers 8 on a 1 to 7 scale) or any decisions you make (for example, that if a person marks between two scale points, you have decided you will always score it as the higher scale point). When you are done, be sure to save a copy of the data file in more than one location (for example, on the hard drive of your computer and on a CD or memory stick).

Check Your Work.　Accuracy is extremely important. If possible, have someone else double-check the entries for at least a few of your participants.

Data Screening

Experienced researchers resist the urge to jump right into the analysis as soon as all the scores are entered. First, they "screen" the data for accuracy, missing values, and whether the assumptions for the planned statistical tests are met. That way they don't get excited (or depressed) about their conclusions, then find later that all their conclusions had no relation to the real results and it all has to be done again.

Checks for Accuracy

Even after you have double-checked your typing, errors are still common. With so many numbers, it is just too easy to make mistakes (even big ones that drastically change results—such as hitting the 0 key too long so you enter 100 instead of 10!). The most important additional check is based on a listing of each variable's number of cases, mean, standard deviation, and maximum and minimum score. (In SPSS, you can get such a listing by selecting *Analyze, Descriptive Statistics, Descriptives,* then selecting all of your numeric variables and clicking *OK.*) If you have more than one grouping, such as an experimental and a control group, you may want a listing for each group separately. (In SPSS, you can get separate outputs for each grouping by selecting *Data, Split File,* checking "Organize output by groups," selecting the grouping variable and clicking *OK.*)

Once you have this listing, for each variable you look at (a) the number of cases, to be sure that all or most of the participants have scores on the variable; (b) the maximum, to be sure that none of the scores are higher than is possible (such as a 70 on a scale that goes from 1 to 7); (c) the minimum, to be sure that none of the score are lower than possible (such as a minus value for number of children); and (d) the mean and standard deviation, to be sure they seem reasonable in light of other similar variables in your study and what you know about these measures.

If you have any nominal variables, you can do a similar check with a listing for each such variable of how many participants fall into each category. This is also a good idea for numeric variables that have only a few possible whole number values, such as a 1 to 5 scale or number of siblings. (In SPSS, you can get such a listing by selecting *Analyze, Descriptive Statistics, Frequencies,* and then selecting the desired variables and clicking *OK.*) For each variable, check whether the numbers in the different categories seem reasonable.

Missing Values

Often participants don't answer every question on a questionnaire, observers miss a particular behavior, recording devices fail, or a participant's results are lost. These kinds of situations create *missing values.* (When entering your scores, it is usually best to leave the place blank where a missing value would go. If instead you put in some number like 999 or -1, it could end up being included in the figuring later!)

You can tell how many missing values you have from the number of cases for each variable in the variable listing you make for your accuracy check (as described in the previous subsection). It is also a good idea to print out your data file (in SPSS, with the data on the screen, select *File* and then *Print*). You can then see whether any particular participants have most of the missing values or the missing values are spread among different participants.

In general, what you do about missing values depends on whether you think they are missing for some systematic reason or just haphazardly. For example, if the question is about a sensitive topic, those who don't answer might be systematically different in relation to this topic than those who do. In such situations, you have two choices: You can just not do any analyses involving that variable, or you can go ahead with just those participants who answered on it, but keeping in mind that your results only apply to the kinds of people who are likely to answer such questions.

Suppose there are only a few missing values and the pattern seems more or less random. In this situation, a common procedure is to substitute the average of everyone else's score on that variable for each missing value. (If you were just to leave them missing, it could mean that you would exclude any participant who had a missing value on any variable—something SPSS does automatically most of the time—sometimes resulting in losing most of your participants from the analysis!) If the study has groups, you can substitute the value for the average of that group. If a person has a missing value on an item that is part of a multi-item measure (such as one item not answered on a 12-item anxiety questionnaire), you might substitute that person's average on the items that were completed. When substituting missing values, it is a good idea to create a new variable (with its own column on the SPSS spreadsheet) that includes the substituted values, keeping the original variable as it was. That way you don't lose track of exactly when you did and did not substitute.

Checking for Normal Distributions

Most statistical tests require that the variables be normally distributed in the population (see Chapter 11). There are also additional assumptions in many procedures, such as equal population variances, which should be checked before carrying out a particular analysis. But we focus here on normality because it applies to nearly all statistical tests.

Checking for Skewness.   Skewness means a distribution is not normal because it is lopsided with a long tail on one side (see Chapter 1). Thus, as part of data screening, you check each variable for its degree of skewness. First, you figure each variable's numerical skewness value; perfect normality is 0. (In SPSS, you can get skewness by selecting *Analyze, Descriptive Statistics, Descriptives, Options,* checking "Skewness," and then clicking *Continue* followed by *OK.*) Then, for any variable that has a very high or low skewness value—say more extreme than ± 1— you make a histogram and look at it visually to see if it looks seriously skewed. (In SPSS you make a histogram by selecting *Graphs, Histogram,* selecting the variable and clicking *OK.*)

What to Do about Seriously Skewed Distributions.   Presuming skewed distributions are not caused by one or a few very extreme cases (see below), then you can use one of the strategies spelled out in Chapter 11, such as transforming the scores or using a rank-order method.

Checking for Outliers (Extreme Scores).   Most statistical tests still give accurate results as long as skewness is not too extreme. The main cause of extreme skewness are outliers. Outliers are problematic for almost all statistical tests. You check for outliers by looking for *very* high skewness values or for very long tails or separated scores in the histograms. Another method is to figure *Z* scores for your variables. (In SPSS, you can get *Z* scores by selecting *Analyze, Descriptive Statistics, Descriptives,* checking "Save standardized values as variables" and clicking *OK.* This gives for each variable a new column that has the *Z* scores for that variable. (These are not exactly the same as the *Z* scores we figured in Chapter 2 because they use the $N - 1$ formula when figuring the standard deviation. But unless your sample is very small, they are very similar. And for purposes of data screening, they are just fine.) Then you can look down the columns of *Z* scores for any that are extreme—say more than ± 3.

What to Do about Outliers.   If you find an outlier, look at the raw questionnaire or data record to be sure it is not an error in typing in the score. Next consider whether there is something about the participant that might make him or her not part of the population to which you want to apply your results. (For example, in a college student sample, this person might be 45 years old when everyone else is aged 18 to 22.) In that situation you can just exclude the participant from the analysis. If the person really is part of what you consider the relevant population, one option is to use a rank-order test. Another common option is to recode the extreme score so that it is still the most extreme score but just slightly higher than the next highest score. (For example, if this person's reading time was 300 seconds and the next highest was 141 seconds, you could recode the person as 142.) Some researchers simply make it a practice to exclude participants whose scores are very extreme. Whatever solution you adopt, it is very important to include in your research report a description of what you did and why. (One huge advantage of screening data before analyzing results is that you are in a better position to make such decisions without having to worry that you are unconsciously biasing the outcome in your favor.)

Carrying Out the Major Analyses

The most important advice here is, again, be sure you have thoroughly screened your data before you begin! Once you are ready, the next most important advice is to *look* at your data. Look at the means overall and by groups, at the histograms, at scatter diagrams, at patterns of correlations. Get to know your data.

Next, write out a systematic analysis plan—what analyses you are going to carry out and in what order—and follow it. Hopefully you have laid this out in advance when you designed the study. Be sure that your plan focuses first and foremost on the hypotheses or research questions with which you began the study.

When you look at each output, before looking at the results part, be sure that the computer used the variables you intended, that it included all of the participants, and that it did the analysis you intended.

Once you have the major results, then it is a good idea to explore. But even here, it is wise to write out a list of the exploratory analyses you will do. Many of the most important discoveries in behavioral and social sciences came not from what was predicted in advance, but from unexpected findings in these explorations. Remember, however, that findings from exploration are more likely to be chance findings. It is like the problem of too many *t* tests (see Chapter 10). With many tests, a few will come out significant just by chance. Thus, any findings from exploratory analyses need to be labeled as such when you write them up in your report. They need to be taken as very tentative until they are replicated in a new study.

Writing Up Your Results

When you come to write up the results of your research study, it will usually be in the form of a paper or report with the following main sections: Introduction, Methods, Results, Discussion. Some of your results actually go in the Methods section. These would include information on your participants (mean and standard deviations for age and any other relevant background variables, number of each gender, and so on) and any reliability analyses on your measures (see Web Chapter W2). The rest of your results go in the Results section. Usually you begin with descriptive statistics—means and standard deviations of your major variables. Then you describe each analysis in a systematic fashion, starting with those testing your hypotheses and research questions and then turning to exploratory analyses. For each analysis you make clear what hypothesis or research question or exploratory issue it is designed to test; describe the analysis (what kind of analysis it is, such as a correlation or *t* test for independent means, and what variables are involved); and give the results, including means, standard deviations, significance results (with degrees of freedom and *p* values), and effect sizes. Wherever it would make results clearer, use tables and graphs. There are examples of how this is done in the "In Research Articles" sections of each chapter.

After the results section, there is usually a Discussion section where you summarize the key conclusions, describe how your results bear on the larger issues the study was designed to address (that is, how is what we know about what you are studying different now than it was before you did the study and how does this bear on previous research and theory), and note the limitations of your study and anomalous results. Here, it is important not to get bogged down in explaining failures to get significance more than briefly. And remember, a nonsignificant result means "inconclusive," not anything like showing "no difference" (unless you had very high power). Finally, consider the implications for future research. Above all, in the Discussion, it is important to keep to the big picture. You will learn more about writing up your results in research methods courses. We strongly recommend that you take one or more such courses.

In Closing

Congratulations on making it to the final pages of *Statistics for the Behavioral and Social Sciences!* We hope that you have enjoyed this book and your course in general. You have mastered a thorough introduction to a complex topic. That should give you complete confidence that with a little time and attention you can understand anything further in statistics. We hope that you look forward to continuing your learning of statistics in the future. In the meantime, congratulations on your accomplishment.

Summary

1. Before conducting a research study, it is important to plan what statistical method(s) will be used to analyze the results.
2. When scores are measured on an apparently equal-interval scale, you must first decide whether you are testing the difference between means or the association among variables. If the focus is on differences between means, you have to determine whether you are comparing two means (in which case a *t* test is the appropriate test) or three or more means (for which an analysis of variance is the appropriate test). You must also decide whether you have a between-subjects or a repeated-measures (within-subjects) design. If the focus is on the association among variables, you must decide whether there is one variable being correlated with or predicting another variable (in which case correlation or bivariate prediction are appropriate tests) or more than one variable correlated with or predicting another variable (for which multiple regression is the appropriate test).
3. Chi-square tests are used when your scores are categories, but they can only be used when each person is in a single category on any one nominal variable. Special rank-order tests (discussed briefly in Chapter 11) are used when your scores are measured on a rank-order scale.
4. When you have scores on one or more criterion or outcome variables, you can handle this situation using one of three approaches: (a) Conduct separate analyses for

each outcome or criterion variable; (b) create a single measure by averaging the scores across the criterion or outcome variables; (c) use a multivariate test that considers all the criterion or outcome variables together.

5. It is important to estimate the statistical power of a study before carrying out the actual study.

6. There are a number of factors you should consider when entering the scores from your study into the computer, including setting up the spreadsheet carefully, using appropriate variable names, letting the computer do any summing or variable coding, typing in the data accurately, and checking your work.

7. Before carrying out the main statistical analyses, you should screen your data to check for accuracy, to identify and handle missing scores, and to check for normal distributions.

8. After carrying out your plan for the main statistical analyses, you may want to consider conducting some exploratory analyses.

9. When writing up the results of a research study, most of the results of the statistical analyses will go in the Results section of the paper or report, although some information about the study participants is usually given in the Methods section. The implications of the study results and conclusions are described in the Discussion section.

Key Terms

between-subjects design (p. 414)   multivariate statistical tests (p. 416)

Appendix A: Tables

Table A-1 Normal Curve Areas: Percentage of the Normal Curve Between the Mean and the Z Scores Shown and Percentage of Scores in the Tail for the Z Scores Shown

Z	% Mean to Z	% in Tail	Z	% Mean to Z	% in Tail
.00	0.00	50.00	.30	11.79	38.21
.01	0.40	49.60	.31	12.17	37.83
.02	0.80	49.20	.32	12.55	37.45
.03	1.20	48.80	.33	12.93	37.07
.04	1.60	48.40	.34	13.31	36.69
.05	1.99	48.01	.35	13.68	36.32
.06	2.39	47.61	.36	14.06	35.94
.07	2.79	47.21	.37	14.43	35.57
.08	3.19	46.81	.38	14.80	35.20
.09	3.59	46.41	.39	15.17	34.83
.10	3.98	46.02	.40	15.54	34.46
.11	4.38	45.62	.41	15.91	34.09
.12	4.78	45.22	.42	16.28	33.72
.13	5.17	44.83	.43	16.64	33.36
.14	5.57	44.43	.44	17.00	33.00
.15	5.96	44.04	.45	17.36	32.64
.16	6.36	43.64	.46	17.72	32.28
.17	6.75	43.25	.47	18.08	31.92
.18	7.14	42.86	.48	18.44	31.56
.19	7.53	42.47	.49	18.79	31.21
.20	7.93	42.07	.50	19.15	30.85
.21	8.32	41.68	.51	19.50	30.50
.22	8.71	41.29	.52	19.85	30.15
.23	9.10	40.90	.53	20.19	29.81
.24	9.48	40.52	.54	20.54	29.46
.25	9.87	40.13	.55	20.88	29.12
.26	10.26	39.74	.56	21.23	28.77
.27	10.64	39.36	.57	21.57	28.43
.28	11.03	38.97	.58	21.90	28.10
.29	11.41	38.59	.59	22.24	27.76

(continued)

Table A-1 (cont.)

Z	% Mean to Z	% in Tail	Z	% Mean to Z	% in Tail
.60	22.57	27.43	1.03	34.85	15.15
.61	22.91	27.09	1.04	35.08	14.92
.62	23.24	26.76	1.05	35.31	14.69
.63	23.57	26.43	1.06	35.54	14.46
.64	23.89	26.11	1.07	35.77	14.23
.65	24.22	25.78	1.08	35.99	14.01
.66	24.54	25.46	1.09	36.21	13.79
.67	24.86	25.14	1.10	36.43	13.57
.68	25.17	24.83	1.11	36.65	13.35
.69	25.49	24.51	1.12	36.86	13.14
.70	25.80	24.20	1.13	37.08	12.92
.71	26.11	23.89	1.14	37.29	12.71
.72	26.42	23.58	1.15	37.49	12.51
.73	26.73	23.27	1.16	37.70	12.30
.74	27.04	22.96	1.17	37.90	12.10
.75	27.34	22.66	1.18	38.10	11.90
.76	27.64	22.36	1.19	38.30	11.70
.77	27.94	22.06	1.20	38.49	11.51
.78	28.23	21.77	1.21	38.69	11.31
.79	28.52	21.48	1.22	38.88	11.12
.80	28.81	21.19	1.23	39.07	10.93
.81	29.10	20.90	1.24	39.25	10.75
.82	29.39	20.61	1.25	39.44	10.56
.83	29.67	20.33	1.26	39.62	10.38
.84	29.95	20.05	1.27	39.80	10.20
.85	30.23	19.77	1.28	39.97	10.03
.86	30.51	19.49	1.29	40.15	9.85
.87	30.78	19.22	1.30	40.32	9.68
.88	31.06	18.94	1.31	40.49	9.51
.89	31.33	18.67	1.32	40.66	9.34
.90	31.59	18.41	1.33	40.82	9.18
.91	31.86	18.14	1.34	40.99	9.01
.92	32.12	17.88	1.35	41.15	8.85
.93	32.38	17.62	1.36	41.31	8.69
.94	32.64	17.36	1.37	41.47	8.53
.95	32.89	17.11	1.38	41.62	8.38
.96	33.15	16.85	1.39	41.77	8.23
.97	33.40	16.60	1.40	41.92	8.08
.98	33.65	16.35	1.41	42.07	7.93
.99	33.89	16.11	1.42	42.22	7.78
1.00	34.13	15.87	1.43	42.36	7.64
1.01	34.38	15.62	1.44	42.51	7.49
1.02	34.61	15.39	1.45	42.65	7.35

Table A-1 (cont.)

Z	% Mean to Z	% in Tail	Z	% Mean to Z	% in Tail
1.46	42.79	7.21	1.88	46.99	3.01
1.47	42.92	7.08	1.89	47.06	2.94
1.48	43.06	6.94	1.90	47.13	2.87
1.49	43.19	6.81	1.91	47.19	2.81
1.50	43.32	6.68	1.92	47.26	2.74
1.51	43.45	6.55	1.93	47.32	2.68
1.52	43.57	6.43	1.94	47.38	2.62
1.53	43.70	6.30	1.95	47.44	2.56
1.54	43.82	6.18	1.96	47.50	2.50
1.55	43.94	6.06	1.97	47.56	2.44
1.56	44.06	5.94	1.98	47.61	2.39
1.57	44.18	5.82	1.99	47.67	2.33
1.58	44.29	5.71	2.00	47.72	2.28
1.59	44.41	5.59	2.01	47.78	2.22
1.60	44.52	5.48	2.02	47.83	2.17
1.61	44.63	5.37	2.03	47.88	2.12
1.62	44.74	5.26	2.04	47.93	2.07
1.63	44.84	5.16	2.05	47.98	2.02
1.64	44.95	5.05	2.06	48.03	1.97
1.65	45.05	4.95	2.07	48.08	1.92
1.66	45.15	4.85	2.08	48.12	1.88
1.67	45.25	4.75	2.09	48.17	1.83
1.68	45.35	4.65	2.10	48.21	1.79
1.69	45.45	4.55	2.11	48.26	1.74
1.70	45.54	4.46	2.12	48.30	1.70
1.71	45.64	4.36	2.13	48.34	1.66
1.72	45.73	4.27	2.14	48.38	1.62
1.73	45.82	4.18	2.15	48.42	1.58
1.74	45.91	4.09	2.16	48.46	1.54
1.75	45.99	4.01	2.17	48.50	1.50
1.76	46.08	3.92	2.18	48.54	1.46
1.77	46.16	3.84	2.19	48.57	1.43
1.78	46.25	3.75	2.20	48.61	1.39
1.79	46.33	3.67	2.21	48.64	1.36
1.80	46.41	3.59	2.22	48.68	1.32
1.81	46.49	3.51	2.23	48.71	1.29
1.82	46.56	3.44	2.24	48.75	1.25
1.83	46.64	3.36	2.25	48.78	1.22
1.84	46.71	3.29	2.26	48.81	1.19
1.85	46.78	3.22	2.27	48.84	1.16
1.86	46.86	3.14	2.28	48.87	1.13
1.87	46.93	3.07	2.29	48.90	1.10

(continued

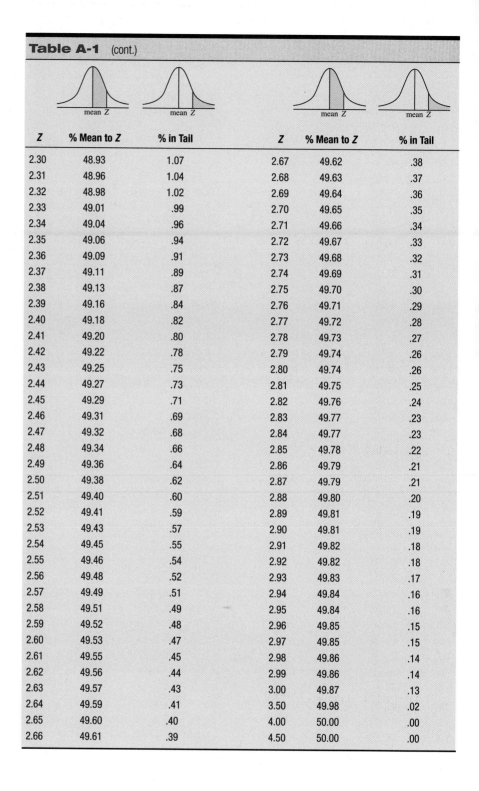

Table A-1 (cont.)

Z	% Mean to Z	% in Tail	Z	% Mean to Z	% in Tail
2.30	48.93	1.07	2.67	49.62	.38
2.31	48.96	1.04	2.68	49.63	.37
2.32	48.98	1.02	2.69	49.64	.36
2.33	49.01	.99	2.70	49.65	.35
2.34	49.04	.96	2.71	49.66	.34
2.35	49.06	.94	2.72	49.67	.33
2.36	49.09	.91	2.73	49.68	.32
2.37	49.11	.89	2.74	49.69	.31
2.38	49.13	.87	2.75	49.70	.30
2.39	49.16	.84	2.76	49.71	.29
2.40	49.18	.82	2.77	49.72	.28
2.41	49.20	.80	2.78	49.73	.27
2.42	49.22	.78	2.79	49.74	.26
2.43	49.25	.75	2.80	49.74	.26
2.44	49.27	.73	2.81	49.75	.25
2.45	49.29	.71	2.82	49.76	.24
2.46	49.31	.69	2.83	49.77	.23
2.47	49.32	.68	2.84	49.77	.23
2.48	49.34	.66	2.85	49.78	.22
2.49	49.36	.64	2.86	49.79	.21
2.50	49.38	.62	2.87	49.79	.21
2.51	49.40	.60	2.88	49.80	.20
2.52	49.41	.59	2.89	49.81	.19
2.53	49.43	.57	2.90	49.81	.19
2.54	49.45	.55	2.91	49.82	.18
2.55	49.46	.54	2.92	49.82	.18
2.56	49.48	.52	2.93	49.83	.17
2.57	49.49	.51	2.94	49.84	.16
2.58	49.51	.49	2.95	49.84	.16
2.59	49.52	.48	2.96	49.85	.15
2.60	49.53	.47	2.97	49.85	.15
2.61	49.55	.45	2.98	49.86	.14
2.62	49.56	.44	2.99	49.86	.14
2.63	49.57	.43	3.00	49.87	.13
2.64	49.59	.41	3.50	49.98	.02
2.65	49.60	.40	4.00	50.00	.00
2.66	49.61	.39	4.50	50.00	.00

| | One-Tailed Tests | | | Two-Tailed Tests | | |

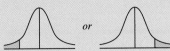

df	.10	.05	.01	.10	.05	.01
1	3.078	6.314	31.821	6.314	12.706	63.657
2	1.886	2.920	6.965	2.920	4.303	9.925
3	1.638	2.353	4.541	2.353	3.182	5.841
4	1.533	2.132	3.747	2.132	2.776	4.604
5	1.476	2.015	3.365	2.015	2.571	4.032
6	1.440	1.943	3.143	1.943	2.447	3.708
7	1.415	1.895	2.998	1.895	2.365	3.500
8	1.397	1.860	2.897	1.860	2.306	3.356
9	1.383	1.833	2.822	1.833	2.262	3.250
10	1.372	1.813	2.764	1.813	2.228	3.170
11	1.364	1.796	2.718	1.796	2.201	3.106
12	1.356	1.783	2.681	1.783	2.179	3.055
13	1.350	1.771	2.651	1.771	2.161	3.013
14	1.345	1.762	2.625	1.762	2.145	2.977
15	1.341	1.753	2.603	1.753	2.132	2.947
16	1.337	1.746	2.584	1.746	2.120	2.921
17	1.334	1.740	2.567	1.740	2.110	2.898
18	1.331	1.734	2.553	1.734	2.101	2.879
19	1.328	1.729	2.540	1.729	2.093	2.861
20	1.326	1.725	2.528	1.725	2.086	2.846
21	1.323	1.721	2.518	1.721	2.080	2.832
22	1.321	1.717	2.509	1.717	2.074	2.819
23	1.320	1.714	2.500	1.714	2.069	2.808
24	1.318	1.711	2.492	1.711	2.064	2.797
25	1.317	1.708	2.485	1.708	2.060	2.788
26	1.315	1.706	2.479	1.706	2.056	2.779
27	1.314	1.704	2.473	1.704	2.052	2.771
28	1.313	1.701	2.467	1.701	2.049	2.764
29	1.312	1.699	2.462	1.699	2.045	2.757
30	1.311	1.698	2.458	1.698	2.043	2.750
35	1.306	1.690	2.438	1.690	2.030	2.724
40	1.303	1.684	2.424	1.684	2.021	2.705
45	1.301	1.680	2.412	1.680	2.014	2.690
50	1.299	1.676	2.404	1.676	2.009	2.678
55	1.297	1.673	2.396	1.673	2.004	2.668
60	1.296	1.671	2.390	1.671	2.001	2.661
65	1.295	1.669	2.385	1.669	1.997	2.654
70	1.294	1.667	2.381	1.667	1.995	2.648
75	1.293	1.666	2.377	1.666	1.992	2.643
80	1.292	1.664	2.374	1.664	1.990	2.639
85	1.292	1.663	2.371	1.663	1.989	2.635
90	1.291	1.662	2.369	1.662	1.987	2.632
95	1.291	1.661	2.366	1.661	1.986	2.629
100	1.290	1.660	2.364	1.660	1.984	2.626
∞	1.282	1.645	2.327	1.645	1.960	2.576

Table A-3 Cutoff Scores for the *F* Distribution

Denominator df	Significance Level	Numerator Degrees of Freedom					
		1	2	3	4	5	6
1	.01	4,052	5,000	5,404	5,625	5,764	5,859
	.05	162	200	216	225	230	234
	.10	39.9	49.5	53.6	55.8	57.2	58.2
2	.01	98.50	99.00	99.17	99.25	99.30	99.33
	.05	18.51	19.00	19.17	19.25	19.30	19.33
	.10	8.53	9.00	9.16	9.24	9.29	9.33
3	.01	34.12	30.82	29.46	28.71	28.24	27.91
	.05	10.13	9.55	9.28	9.12	9.01	8.94
	.10	5.54	5.46	5.39	5.34	5.31	5.28
4	.01	21.20	18.00	16.70	15.98	15.52	15.21
	.05	7.71	6.95	6.59	6.39	6.26	6.16
	.10	4.55	4.33	4.19	4.11	4.05	4.01
5	.01	16.26	13.27	12.06	11.39	10.97	10.67
	.05	6.61	5.79	5.41	5.19	5.05	4.95
	.10	4.06	3.78	3.62	3.52	3.45	3.41
6	.01	13.75	10.93	9.78	9.15	8.75	8.47
	.05	5.99	5.14	4.76	4.53	4.39	4.28
	.10	3.78	3.46	3.29	3.18	3.11	3.06
7	.01	12.25	9.55	8.45	7.85	7.46	7.19
	.05	5.59	4.74	4.35	4.12	3.97	3.87
	.10	3.59	3.26	3.08	2.96	2.88	2.83
8	.01	11.26	8.65	7.59	7.01	6.63	6.37
	.05	5.32	4.46	4.07	3.84	3.69	3.58
	.10	3.46	3.11	2.92	2.81	2.73	2.67
9	.01	10.56	8.02	6.99	6.42	6.06	5.80
	.05	5.12	4.26	3.86	3.63	3.48	3.37
	.10	3.36	3.01	2.81	2.69	2.61	2.55
10	.01	10.05	7.56	6.55	6.00	5.64	5.39
	.05	4.97	4.10	3.71	3.48	3.33	3.22
	.10	3.29	2.93	2.73	2.61	2.52	2.46
11	.01	9.65	7.21	6.22	5.67	5.32	5.07
	.05	4.85	3.98	3.59	3.36	3.20	3.10
	.10	3.23	2.86	2.66	2.54	2.45	2.39
12	.01	9.33	6.93	5.95	5.41	5.07	4.82
	.05	4.75	3.89	3.49	3.26	3.11	3.00
	.10	3.18	2.81	2.61	2.48	2.40	2.33
13	.01	9.07	6.70	5.74	5.21	4.86	4.62
	.05	4.67	3.81	3.41	3.18	3.03	2.92
	.10	3.14	2.76	2.56	2.43	2.35	2.28
14	.01	8.86	6.52	5.56	5.04	4.70	4.46
	.05	4.60	3.74	3.34	3.11	2.96	2.85
	.10	3.10	2.73	2.52	2.40	2.31	2.24

Table A-3 (cont.)

Denom- inator df	Signi- ficance Level	Numerator Degrees of Freedom					
		1	2	3	4	5	6
15	.01	8.68	6.36	5.42	4.89	4.56	4.32
	.05	4.54	3.68	3.29	3.06	2.90	2.79
	.10	3.07	2.70	2.49	2.36	2.27	2.21
16	.01	8.53	6.23	5.29	4.77	4.44	4.20
	.05	4.49	3.63	3.24	3.01	2.85	2.74
	.10	3.05	2.67	2.46	2.33	2.24	2.18
17	.01	8.40	6.11	5.19	4.67	4.34	4.10
	.05	4.45	3.59	3.20	2.97	2.81	2.70
	.10	3.03	2.65	2.44	2.31	2.22	2.15
18	.01	8.29	6.01	5.09	4.58	4.25	4.02
	.05	4.41	3.56	3.16	2.93	2.77	2.66
	.10	3.01	2.62	2.42	2.29	2.20	2.13
19	.01	8.19	5.93	5.01	4.50	4.17	3.94
	.05	4.38	3.52	3.13	2.90	2.74	2.63
	.10	2.99	2.61	2.40	2.27	2.18	2.11
20	.01	8.10	5.85	4.94	4.43	4.10	3.87
	.05	4.35	3.49	3.10	2.87	2.71	2.60
	.10	2.98	2.59	2.38	2.25	2.16	2.09
21	.01	8.02	5.78	4.88	4.37	4.04	3.81
	.05	4.33	3.47	3.07	2.84	2.69	2.57
	.10	2.96	2.58	2.37	2.23	2.14	2.08
22	.01	7.95	5.72	4.82	4.31	3.99	3.76
	.05	4.30	3.44	3.05	2.82	2.66	2.55
	.10	2.95	2.56	2.35	2.22	2.13	2.06
23	.01	7.88	5.66	4.77	4.26	3.94	3.71
	.05	4.28	3.42	3.03	2.80	2.64	2.53
	.10	2.94	2.55	2.34	2.21	2.12	2.05
24	.01	7.82	5.61	4.72	4.22	3.90	3.67
	.05	4.26	3.40	3.01	2.78	2.62	2.51
	.10	2.93	2.54	2.33	2.20	2.10	2.04
25	.01	7.77	5.57	4.68	4.18	3.86	3.63
	.05	4.24	3.39	2.99	2.76	2.60	2.49
	.10	2.92	2.53	2.32	2.19	2.09	2.03
26	.01	7.72	5.53	4.64	4.14	3.82	3.59
	.05	4.23	3.37	2.98	2.74	2.59	2.48
	.10	2.91	2.52	2.31	2.18	2.08	2.01
27	.01	7.68	5.49	4.60	4.11	3.79	3.56
	.05	4.21	3.36	2.96	2.73	2.57	2.46
	.10	2.90	2.51	2.30	2.17	2.07	2.01
28	.01	7.64	5.45	4.57	4.08	3.75	3.53
	.05	4.20	3.34	2.95	2.72	2.56	2.45
	.10	2.89	2.50	2.29	2.16	2.07	2.00

(continued)

Table A-3 (cont.)

Denominator df	Significance Level	Numerator Degrees of Freedom					
		1	2	3	4	5	6
29	.01	7.60	5.42	4.54	4.05	3.73	3.50
	.05	4.18	3.33	2.94	2.70	2.55	2.43
	.10	2.89	2.50	2.28	2.15	2.06	1.99
30	.01	7.56	5.39	4.51	4.02	3.70	3.47
	.05	4.17	3.32	2.92	2.69	2.53	2.42
	.10	2.88	2.49	2.28	2.14	2.05	1.98
35	.01	7.42	5.27	4.40	3.91	3.59	3.37
	.05	4.12	3.27	2.88	2.64	2.49	2.37
	.10	2.86	2.46	2.25	2.11	2.02	1.95
40	.01	7.32	5.18	4.31	3.83	3.51	3.29
	.05	4.09	3.23	2.84	2.61	2.45	2.34
	.10	2.84	2.44	2.23	2.09	2.00	1.93
45	.01	7.23	5.11	4.25	3.77	3.46	3.23
	.05	4.06	3.21	2.81	2.58	2.42	2.31
	.10	2.82	2.43	2.21	2.08	1.98	1.91
50	.01	7.17	5.06	4.20	3.72	3.41	3.19
	.05	4.04	3.18	2.79	2.56	2.40	2.29
	.10	2.81	2.41	2.20	2.06	1.97	1.90
55	.01	7.12	5.01	4.16	3.68	3.37	3.15
	.05	4.02	3.17	2.77	2.54	2.38	2.27
	.10	2.80	2.40	2.19	2.05	1.96	1.89
60	.01	7.08	4.98	4.13	3.65	3.34	3.12
	.05	4.00	3.15	2.76	2.53	2.37	2.26
	.10	2.79	2.39	2.18	2.04	1.95	1.88
65	.01	7.04	4.95	4.10	3.62	3.31	3.09
	.05	3.99	3.14	2.75	2.51	2.36	2.24
	.10	2.79	2.39	2.17	2.03	1.94	1.87
70	.01	7.01	4.92	4.08	3.60	3.29	3.07
	.05	3.98	3.13	2.74	2.50	2.35	2.23
	.10	2.78	2.38	2.16	2.03	1.93	1.86
75	.01	6.99	4.90	4.06	3.58	3.27	3.05
	.05	3.97	3.12	2.73	2.49	2.34	2.22
	.10	2.77	2.38	2.16	2.02	1.93	1.86
80	.01	6.96	4.88	4.04	3.56	3.26	3.04
	.05	3.96	3.11	2.72	2.49	2.33	2.22
	.10	2.77	2.37	2.15	2.02	1.92	1.85
85	.01	6.94	4.86	4.02	3.55	3.24	3.02
	.05	3.95	3.10	2.71	2.48	2.32	2.21
	.10	2.77	2.37	2.15	2.01	1.92	1.85
90	.01	6.93	4.85	4.01	3.54	3.23	3.01
	.05	3.95	3.10	2.71	2.47	2.32	2.20
	.10	2.76	2.36	2.15	2.01	1.91	1.84

Table A-3 (cont.)

Denominator df	Significance Level	Numerator Degrees of Freedom					
		1	**2**	**3**	**4**	**5**	**6**
95	.01	6.91	4.84	4.00	3.52	3.22	3.00
	.05	3.94	3.09	2.70	2.47	2.31	2.20
	.10	2.76	2.36	2.14	2.01	1.91	1.84
100	.01	6.90	4.82	3.98	3.51	3.21	2.99
	.05	3.94	3.09	2.70	2.46	2.31	2.19
	.10	2.76	2.36	2.14	2.00	1.91	1.83
∞	.01	6.64	4.61	3.78	3.32	3.02	2.80
	.05	3.84	3.00	2.61	2.37	2.22	2.10
	.10	2.71	2.30	2.08	1.95	1.85	1.78

Table A-4   Cutoff Scores for the Chi-Square Distribution

df	Significance Level		
	.10	**.05**	**.01**
1	2.706	3.841	6.635
2	4.605	5.992	9.211
3	6.252	7.815	11.345
4	7.780	9.488	13.277
5	9.237	11.071	15.087
6	10.645	12.592	16.812
7	12.017	14.067	18.475
8	13.362	15.507	20.090
9	14.684	16.919	21.666
10	15.987	18.307	23.209

Table A-5   Index to Power Tables and Tables Giving Number of Participants Needed for 80% Power

Hypothesis-Testing Procedure	Chapter	Power Table	Number of Participants Table
Correlation coefficient (r)	3	p. 118	p. 119
t test for dependent means	8	p. 257	p. 258
t test for independent means	9	p. 292	p. 294
One-way analysis of variance	10	p. 333	p. 333
Chi-square test for independence	11	p. 378	p. 378

Appendix B: Answers to Set I Practice Problems

Chapter 1

1. (a) Satisfaction with the vocational counselor; (b) 1, 2, 3, or 4; (c) 3.
2. (a) Likelihood of voting; (b) 1, 2, 3, 4, or 5; (c) 5.
3. (a) Nominal (or categorical); (b) numeric (or quantitative)—more precisely, equal interval; (c) numeric (or quantitative)—more precisely, rank order (or ordinal).
4. (a) Frequency table.

Number of Children	Frequency	Percent
6	1	5
5	0	0
4	1	5
3	2	10
2	7	35
1	5	25
0	4	20

(b) Histogram.

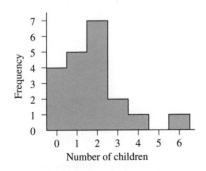

(c) Frequency polygon.

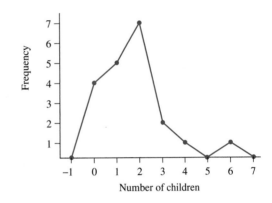

(d) Unimodal, skewed to the right.

5. (a) Frequency table.

Hours	Frequency	Percent	Hours	Frequency	Percent
18	1	2	8	5	10
17	0	0	7	11	22
16	0	0	6	4	8
15	1	2	5	2	4
14	0	0	4	3	6
13	2	4	3	4	8
12	1	2	2	2	4
11	3	6	1	1	2
10	5	10	0	1	2
9	4	8			

(b) and (c) are based on frequency table above. See answer to question 4 for examples.
(d) Approximately unimodal, slightly skewed to the right.
6. (a) Frequency table.

Speed	Frequency	Percent	Speed	Frequency	Percent
52	2	5	33	2	5
51	0	0	32	3	8
50	0	0	31	3	8
49	0	0	30	3	8
48	0	0	29	0	0
47	0	0	28	1	3
46	1	3	27	1	3
45	1	3	26	0	0
44	0	0	25	0	0
43	0	0	24	1	3
42	1	3	23	1	3
41	0	0	22	0	0
40	3	8	21	0	0
39	0	0	20	1	3
38	1	3	19	0	0
37	2	5	18	0	0
36	6	15	17	0	0
35	2	5	16	0	0
34	4	10	15	1	3

(b) and (c) are based on frequency table above. See answer to question 4 for examples. (d) Unimodal, approximately symmetrical.
7. (a) Frequency table.

Score	Frequency	Percent	Score	Frequency	Percent
96	1	4	72	0	0
95	0	0	71	1	4
94	0	0	70	1	4
93	0	0	69	1	4
92	1	4	68	2	8
91	1	4	67	1	4
90	0	0	66	0	0
89	0	0	65	0	0
88	0	0	64	2	8
87	1	4	63	0	0
86	0	0	62	0	0
85	1	4	61	0	0
84	0	0	60	0	0
83	2	8	59	1	4
82	0	0	58	0	0
81	1	4	57	0	0
80	1	4	56	0	0
79	0	0	55	0	0
78	0	0	54	0	0
77	0	0	53	0	0
76	2	8	52	0	0
75	2	8	51	0	0
74	1	4	50	1	4
73	1	4			

(b) Based on frequency table above. See answer to question 4b for an example. (c) Grouped frequency table.

Interval	Frequency	Percent
90–99	3	12
80–89	6	24
70–79	8	32
60–69	6	24
50–59	2	8

(d) Based on frequency table in (c) above. See answer to question 4b for an example. (e) Unimodal, approximately symmetrical (slightly negatively skewed).
8. (a) Similar to 7a above.
(b) Based on frequency table in (a); see answer to question 4c for an example.
(c) Grouped frequency table.

Interval	Frequency	Percent
80–89	10	29.4
70–79	0	0
60–69	5	14.7
50–59	0	0
40–49	5	14.7
30–39	7	20.6
20–29	7	20.6

(d) Histogram.

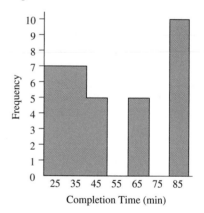

(e) Roughly rectangular.
9. (a) Bimodal; (b) approximately normal (or unimodal or symmetrical); (c) multimodal.
10. (a) A distribution is the way a group of numbers is spread out over the possible values the numbers can have. You can describe such a distribution with a graph, called a histogram—a kind of bar graph with one bar for each possible value with one unit of height for each time its particular value occurs. In a histogram, a symmetrical distribution has a symmetrical shape (the right and left halves are mirror images). A unimodal distribution is one in which this graph has a single high point, with the other values gradually decreasing around it. (b) A negatively skewed unimodal distribution has a single high point, is not symmetrical, and its tail—the long, low side—extends to the left (where the negative scores go on the graph).

11. A ceiling effect describes the situation when many scores pile up at the high end of a distribution because it is not possible to have a higher score. This usually causes the distribution to be negatively skewed (skewed to the left).

12. (a) This is called a frequency table because it lays out how frequently (how many times) each category occurs for nine different categories. A frequency table makes the pattern of numbers easy to see. For example, of the 90 college students in the study, 19 gave bad news about Relationship with family (the first category). The table also gives the percentages. For example, 19 students is 19/90 of the total, or 21.1 percent. (b) The most bad news is given in four of the nine categories: Relationship with family, Relationship with actual/potential girlfriend/boyfriend, Relationship with friends, and Health of family member/friend. All of these categories had to do with family members or friends, most with relationships; there were few cases in the other categories (which had little directly to do with family or friends).

Chapter 2

1. (a) $M = (\Sigma X)/N = 261/9 = 29$; (b) 28; (c) $\Sigma(X - M)^2$
   $= (32 - 29)^2 + (28 - 29)^2 + (24 - 29)^2 + (28 - 29)^2$
   $+ (28 - 29)^2 + (31 - 29)^2 + (35 - 29)^2 + (29 - 29)^2$
   $+ (26 - 29)^2 = 86$; (d) $SD^2 = [\Sigma(X - M)^2]/N = 86/9 = 9.56$;
   (e) $SD = \sqrt{SD^2} = \sqrt{9.56} = 3.09$.
2. (a) 4; (b) 4; (c) 26; (d) 3.25; (e) 1.80.
3. The average temperature, in the sense of adding up the 10 readings and dividing by 10, was −7 degrees Celsius. This is the *mean* (the ordinary average). However, if you line up the temperatures from highest to lowest, the middle two numbers are both −5 degrees. The middle number is the *median*. The specific temperature that came up most often is the *mode*—there are two modes, −1 and −5.

   As for the variation (the amount of variability), one approach is the *variance*—the average of each temperature's squared deviation from the mean temperature, which is 46.8. You get a more direct sense of how much a group of numbers vary among themselves if you take the square root of the variance, which gives the standard deviation—the square root of 46.8 is 6.84. This means, roughly, that on an average day the temperature differs by 6.84 degrees from the average of −7 degrees.
4. (a) .40; (b) .14; (c) similar to 3 above.
5. (a) $Z = (X - M)/SD = (91 - 79)/12 = 1$; (b) −.92; (c) 2.
6. (a) $Z = (X - M)/SD = (-13.12 + 11.46)/2.28 = -.73$; (b) 1.84; (c) .10.
7. (a) $X = (Z)(SD) + M = (0)(19) + 145 = 145$; (b) 172.17; (c) 96.74.
8. Wife: $Z = (X - M)/SD = (63 - 60)/6 = .5$. Husband: $Z = (59 - 55)/4 = 1$. The husband has adjusted better in relation to other divorced men than the wife has adjusted in relation to other divorced women.

   For wives, a score of 63 is 3 points better than the average of 60 for divorced women in general. (The "mean" in the problem is the ordinary average—the sum of the scores divided by the number of scores.) There is, of course, some variation in scores among divorced women. The approximate average amount that women's scores differ from the average

is 6 points—this is the *SD* (standard deviation) referred to in the problem. (*SD* is only approximately the average amount scores differ from the mean. To be precise, *SD* is the square root of the average of the square of the difference of each score from the mean.) Thus, the wife's score is only half as far as above the mean of wives' scores. This gives her what is called a *Z* score of +.5, which gives her location on a scale that compares her score to that of divorced women in general. Using the same logic, the husband's divorce adjustment is as much above the mean as the average amount that men differ from the mean; that is, he has a *Z* score of +1. What this all means is that both have adjusted better than average for their gender, but the husband had adjusted better in relation to other divorced men than the wife has adjusted in relation to other divorced women. Using *Z* scores allowed us to put the raw scores for men and women onto the same scale, which made it easier to compare their scores.

9. The "mean" is the ordinary arithmetic average—add up the total number of nights of too little sleep and divide by the number of students. The average number of nights of too little sleep over the 4-week period was 6.84. The *SD* (standard deviation) describes the variability of the scores. Roughly speaking, the standard deviation is the average amount that the number of nights of too little sleep are spread out from their average—in this case, by 3.18 nights. This is quite a lot of spread. To be more precise, you figure the standard deviation by taking each person's number of nights of too little sleep and subtracting 6.84 from it and squaring this difference; the standard deviation is the square root of the average of these differences.
10. Like the answer to 9 above, focusing on means of 5.02, 5.11, 32.27, and 31.36 and on standard deviations of 2.16, 2.08, 20.36, and 21.08.

Chapter 3

1. (a) Curvilinear; (b) linear, positive, strong; (c) linear, negative, strong; (d) linear, positive, strong; (e) linear, positive, small to moderate; (f) no correlation.
2. Set A:

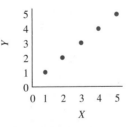

					Cross-Product
	X			**Y**	of **Z** Scores
Raw	Z		Raw	Z	
1	−1.41		1	−1.41	2.0
2	−.71		2	−.71	.5
3	.00		3	.00	0
4	.71		4	.71	.5
5	1.41		5	1.41	2.0
$M = 3$; $SD = 1.41$					5.0
					$r = 5.0/5 = 1.00$

Set B: $r = 4.5/5 = .90$; Set C: $r = -3.0/5 = -.60$; Set D: $r = 3.0/5 = .60$.

3. Possibility A:

Take Drug		Get Cold		Cross-Product of Z Scores
Raw	Z	Raw	Z	
0	−1	1	1	−1
0	−1	1	1	−1
0	−1	1	1	−1
0	−1	1	1	−1
1	1	0	−1	−1
1	1	0	−1	−1
1	1	0	−1	−1
1	1	0	−1	−1
				−8
				$r = -8/8 = -1.00$

Possibility B: $r = -4/8 = -.50$; Possibility C: $r = 0/8 = .00$; Possibility D: $r = -6.2/8 = -.78$.

4. (a) See answer to 2 above for an example; (b) linear, negative, moderate. (c)

Approximate Age (Years)		Number of People Stopping to Look		Cross-Product of Z Scores
X	Z_x	Y	Z_y	$Z_x Z_y$
465	1.39	68	−.69	−.96
515	1.71	71	−.59	−1.01
240	−.09	123	1.19	−.11
107	−.96	112	.82	−.79
376	.80	48	−1.38	−1.10
355	.67	84	−.14	−.09
140	−.75	66	−.76	.57
115	−.91	148	2.05	−1.87
122	−.86	71	−.59	.51
99	−1.01	91	.10	−.10
				−4.95
				$r = -4.95/10 = -.50$

5. (a) See answer to 2 above for an example; (b) linear, no correlation (or very small positive correlation). (c)

Neatness Rating		Achievement Test		Cross-Product of Z Scores
X	Z_x	Y	Z_y	$Z_x Z_y$
18	−.52	60	−.66	.34
24	1.43	58	−1.09	−1.56
14	−1.82	70	1.47	−2.68
19	−.20	58	−1.09	.22
20	.13	66	.62	.08
23	1.11	68	1.04	1.15
20	.13	65	.40	.05
22	.78	68	1.04	.81
15	−1.50	56	−1.51	2.27
21	.46	62	−.23	−.11
				.57
				$r = .57/10 = .06$

6. (a) See answer to 2 above for an example; (b) linear, positive, strong.
(c)

Hours of Violent TV per Week		Number of Violent or Aggressive Acts		Cross-Product of Z Scores
X	Z_x	Y	Z_y	$Z_x Z_y$
14	1.27	9	.97	1.23
8	−.63	6	.00	.00
6	−1.27	1	−1.62	2.06
12	.63	8	.65	.41
$\Sigma = 40$		$\Sigma = 24$		$\Sigma = 3.70$
$M = 10$		$M = 6$		
$SD = 3.16$		$SD = 3.08$		$r = 3.70/4 = .93$

(d) The first thing I did was make a graph, called a scatter diagram, putting one variable on each axis, then putting a dot where each person's pair of scores goes on that graph. This gives a picture of the pattern of relationship between the two variables. In this example, high scores generally go with high scores and lows with lows. The scores going together in a systematic pattern makes this a *correlation;* that highs go with highs and lows with lows makes this correlation *positive;* that dots fall in a roughly straight line pattern makes this positive correlation *linear;* the dots fall very close to a straight line, which makes this a *strong* positive linear correlation.

Next, I figured the *correlation coefficient,* a number describing the degree of linear correlation between weekly viewing of violent TV and the number of violent or aggressive acts toward playmates (in a positive correlation, how consistently highs go with highs and lows with lows). To do this, I changed all the scores to Z scores because Z scores tell you how much a score is low or high relative to the other scores in its distribution. You figure the correlation coefficient by multiplying each person's two Z scores by each other, totaling up these products, then averaging this total over the number of people. This will be a high number if highs go with highs and lows with lows, because with Z scores, highs are always positive and positive times positive is positive, and with Z scores, lows are always negative and negative times negative becomes positive too. Following this procedure, the highest number you can get, if the scores for the two variables are perfectly correlated, is +1. If there were no linear correlation between the two variables, the results would be 0 (because highs would sometimes be multiplied by highs and sometimes by lows, giving a mixture of positive and negative products that would cancel out).

In this example, the products of the Z scores add up to 3.70, which when divided by the number of children is .93. This is called a *Pearson correlation coefficient* (*r*) of .93 and indicates a strong, positive linear correlation between the hours of violent TV watched each week and the number of violent or aggressive acts toward playmates.

(e) Three logically possible directions of causality: (i) Watching violent TV makes children act more aggressively toward playmates; (ii) being aggressive makes children more interested in watching violent TV; (iii) a third factor—such as living in a violent family environment—makes children more interested in watching violent TV and also makes them act aggressively toward playmates.

(f) Formulas: Predicted $Z_Y = (\beta)(Z_X)$; Predicted $Y = (SD_Y)$(Predicted Z_Y) $+ M_Y$

$Z_X = -2$: Predicted $Z_Y = (.93)(-2) = -1.86$; Predicted $Y = (3.08)(-1.86) + 6 = .27$.

$Z_X = -1$: Predicted $Z_Y = (.93)(-1) = -.93$; Predicted $Y = (3.08)(-.93) + 6 = 3.14$.

$Z_X = 0$: Predicted $Z_Y = (.93)(0) = 0$; Predicted $Y = (3.08)(0) + 6 = 6.00$.

$Z_X = +1$: Predicted $Z_Y = (.93)(1) = .93$; Predicted $Y = (3.08)(.93) + 6 = 8.86$.

$Z_X = +2$: Predicted $Z_Y = (.93)(2) = 1.86$; Predicted $Y = (3.08)(1.86) + 6 = 11.73$.

(g) $r^2 = .93^2 = .86$.

7. (a) See answer to 2 above for an example; (b) linear, positive, strong.

(c)

Number of Town-Hall Meetings		Percentage of People Who Can Name Candidate		Cross-Product of Z Scores
X	Z_X	Y	Z_Y	$Z_X Z_Y$
4	.63	70	.36	.23
5	1.26	94	1.45	1.83
2	−.63	36	−1.17	.74
1	−1.26	48	−.63	.79
$\Sigma = 12$		$\Sigma = 248$		$\Sigma = 3.59$
$M = 3$		$M = 62$		
$SD = 1.58$		$SD = 22.14$		$r = 3.59/4 = .90$

(d) See 6d above.

(e) Three logically possible directions of causality: (i) If a candidate has more town-hall meetings, this makes more people become aware of the candidate; (ii) If a candidate is well-known, this causes the candidate to have more town-hall meetings; (iii) A third factor—such as the amount of campaign money the candidate has—means the candidate can afford to hold more town-hall meetings and also causes more people to be aware of the candidate (perhaps because the candidate has been able to afford a large advertising campaign).

(f) Formulas: Predicted $Z_Y = (\beta)(Z_X)$; Predicted $Y = (SD_Y)$(Predicted Z_Y) $+ M_Y$

$Z_X = -2$: Predicted $Z_Y = (.90)(-2) = -1.80$; Predicted $Y = (22.14)(-1.80) + 62 = 22.15$.

$Z_X = -1$: Predicted $Z_Y = (.90)(-1) = -.90$; Predicted $Y = (22.14)(-.90) + 62 = 42.07\%$.

$Z_X = 0$: Predicted $Z_Y = (.90)(0) = 0$; Predicted $Y = (22.14)(0) + 62 = 62.00$.

$Z_X = +1$: Predicted $Z_Y = (.90)(1) = .90$; Predicted $Y = (22.14)(.90) + 62 = 81.93$.

$Z_X = +2$: Predicted $Z_Y = (.90)(2) = 1.80$; Predicted $Y = (22.14)(1.80) + 62 = 101.85$.

(g) $r^2 = .90^2 = .81$.

8. (a) This table shows the degree of association among scores on several measures given to pregnant women and their partners. (Here continue with an explanation of the correlation coefficient like that in 6d above except in this problem you also need to explain the mean, standard deviation, and Z scores—which you do in the same way as in answering the problems in Chapter 2.) For example, the correlation of .17 between women's reports of stress and men's reports of stress indicates that the association between these two measures is quite weak. That is, how much stress a women is under is not highly related to how much stress her partner believes she is under. On the other hand, the correlation of .50 (near the middle of the first column of correlations) tells you that there is a much stronger association between a woman's report of stress and her depressed mood in the second interview. That is, women who report being under stress are also likely to report being depressed, those reporting being under not much stress are likely to report not being very depressed.

(b) In general, the correlations shown in this table are strongest among the stress, support, and mood items; correlations of these variables with demographics (age, ethnicity, etc.) were fairly weak. Partner support seemed to be strongly correlated with stress and mood, and depressed mood at the second testing was particularly related to the other variables.

(c) Just because two variables are correlated, even strongly correlated, does not mean that you can know the particular direction of causality that creates that association. For example, there is a strong negative correlation between partner support at time 1 and depressed mood at time 2. There are three logically possible directions of causality here: (i) Support can be causing lower depression, (ii) lower depression can be causing support, or (iii) some third factor can be causing both. You can rule out the second possibility, since something in the future (low depression) can't cause the past (initial support). However, the other two possibilities remain. It is certainly plausible that having her partner's support helps reduce depression. But it is also possible that a third factor is causing both. For example, consider level of income. Perhaps when a couple has more income, the partner has more time and energy to provide support and the greater comfort of living keeps depression down.

9. (a) Score on knowledge of fitness training principles; (b) number of injuries over subsequent year; (c) .4; (d) Predicted $Z_{Injuries} = (.4)(Z_{Score})$; (e) $(.4)(-2) = -.8$; (f) $-.4$; (g) 0; (h) .4; (i) .8.

10. This study used a statistical procedure called multiple regression. This procedure produces a formula for predicting a person's score on a criterion variable (in this example, third graders' reading comprehension) from his or her scores on a set of predictor variables (in this example, the three specific measures of reading ability). The formula is of the form that you multiply the person's score on each of the predictor variables by some particular number, called a regression coefficient or beta, and then add up the products. The procedure produces the most accurate prediction rule of this kind.

In this example, the prediction rule for the Z score for Reading Comprehension is $-.227$ multiplied by the Z score for Letter-Word Identification, plus .299 multiplied by the Z score for Word Attack, plus .671 multiplied by the Z score for

Oral Reading Fluency. (These are the numbers in the table next to each predictor variable in the Beta column.)

These regression coefficients suggest that reading comprehension is most strongly related to Oral Reading Fluency. Reading comprehension is also somewhat positively related to Word Attack. However, in the context of this prediction equation, reading comprehension is somewhat negatively related to Letter-Word Identification. This means that for any given level of Oral Reading Fluency and Word Attack, the better the child is at Letter-Word Identification, the child will be somewhat *worse* at reading comprehension!

It is important to note, however, that the regression coefficients for each of these predictors reflect what the scores on each predictor contribute to the prediction, over and above what the others contribute. If we were to consider ordinary correlations between each of the predictor variables with the criterion variable, their relative importance could be quite different. (Those correlations, however, were not provided.)

Another important piece of information in this table is R^2. This number tells you the proportion of variance accounted for in the criterion variable by the three predictor variables taken together. That is, 53.4% of the variation in the third graders' reading comprehension is accounted for by these three measures of specific reading abilities. This is equivalent to a correlation between reading comprehension and these three predictor variables of .73 (the square root of .534).

11. (a) Predicted $Z_{\text{Comprehension}} = (-.227)(Z_{\text{Identification}}) + (.299)$ $(Z_{\text{Attack}}) + (.671)(Z_{\text{Fluency}})$ (b) A: Predicted $Z_{\text{Comprehension}} = (-.227)(1) + (.299)(1) + (.671)(1) = .743$; B: Predicted $Z_{\text{Comprehension}} = 0$; C: Predicted $Z_{\text{Comprehension}} = -.743$; D: Predicted $Z_{\text{Comprehension}} = -.227$; E: Predicted $Z_{\text{Comprehension}} = .299$; F: Predicted $Z_{\text{Comprehension}} = .671$; G: Predicted $Z_{\text{Comprehension}} = .289$; H: Predicted $Z_{\text{Comprehension}} = 1.341$; I: Predicted $Z_{\text{Comprehension}} = 1.631$.

Chapter 4

1. (a) 50%; (b) 16%; (c) 98%; (d) 84%; (e) 50%; (f) 84%; (g) 2%; (h) 16%.
2. (a) 50; (b) 45; (c) 40; (d) 35; (e) 30.
3. (a) From the normal curve table, 43.32% (.4332) have Z scores between the mean and 1.5. By definition, 50% have Z scores below the mean. Thus, the total percentage below 1.5 is 50% + 43.32% = 93.32%; (b) 6.68%; (c) 6.68%; (d) 93.32%; (e) 1.79%; (f) 98.21%; (g) 32.64%; (h) 3.75%; (i) 4.65%.
4. (a) $Z = (16 - 15)/5 = .2$; from the normal curve table, percent in the tail for a Z score of .2 = 42.07%; (b) 34.46%; (c) 27.43%; (d) 72.57%; (e) 42.07%.
5. (a) Top 40% means 40% in the tail; the nearest Z score from the normal curve table for 40% in the tail is .25; a Z score of .25 equals a raw score of $(.25)(5) + 15 = 16.25$; (b) 17.6; (c) 19.2.
6. (a) 21.90%; (b) 22.24%; (c) 42.79%; (d) 44.06%; (e) 21.90%.
7. (a) The bottom 30% means 30% in the tail; the nearest Z score from the normal curve table for 30% in the tail is $-.52$; (b) -1.88.
8. (a) The top 10% means 10% in the tail; the nearest Z score for 10% in the tail is 1.28; (b) 2.33.
9. (a) Needed $Z = 1.64$; this corresponds to a raw score of $(1.64)(10) + 50 = 66.4$; (b) The scores for many things you

measure, in nature and the behavioral and social sciences, tend approximately to follow the particular mathematical pattern shown below, called a normal curve. In a normal curve, most of the scores are near the middle, with fewer numbers of scores at each extreme. Because the normal curve is mathematically defined, the precise proportion of scores in any particular section of it can be calculated, and these have been listed in special tables. (Then explain mean, standard deviation, and Z scores as in answers to Chapter 2 problems.) The normal curve table tells the percentage of scores in the normal curve between the mean and any particular Z score; it also tells the percentage of scores in the tail for (that is, more extreme than) any particular Z score.

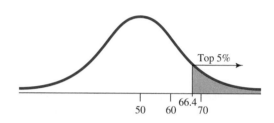

The coordination test scores are known to follow a normal curve. Thus, you can look up in the table the Z score for the point on the normal curve at which 5% of the scores are in the tail. This is a Z score of 1.64 (actually, there is not an exact point on the table for 5% in the tail, so I could have used either 1.64 or 1.65). With a standard deviation of 10, a Z score of 1.64 is 16.4 points above the mean. Adding that to the mean of 50 makes the score needed to be in the top 5% turn out to be 66.4.

10. A *sample* is a group of people studied that represents the entire group to which the results are intended to apply, called the *population*. (In this example, the population is all Australian high school students.) You study a sample because it would be impractical or impossible to test the entire population. One way of ensuring that the sample is not systematically unrepresentative is to select the sample randomly. This does not mean haphazardly. For example, just taking the students who are easily available to test would be haphazard sampling. But this would not be a good method because whatever factors make them easily available—such as living in a nearby town—might make them unrepresentative of the population as a whole. An example of a truly random method would be to acquire a list of all the high school students in Australia, number each student, and then use a table of random numbers to pick as many as are to be surveyed.

11. Similar to 10 above.

12. (a) 10/50: $p = 10/50 = .2$; (b) .4; (c) $(10 + 20)/50 = .6$; (d) .6; (e) 1.

(f) The probability of a particular thing happening is usually defined as the number of possible ways the thing could happen (the number of *possible successful outcomes*) divided by the number of possible ways things like this could happen (the number of *all possible outcomes*). For part (a) there are 10 different drug/alcohol people you might pick out of a total of 50 people you are picking from. Thus, the probability is 10/50 = .2.

Chapter 5

1. (a) The logical, statistical procedure for determining the likelihood of your study having gotten a particular pattern of results if the null hypothesis is true. (b) The situation in hypothesis testing in which you decide to reject the null hypothesis because the probability of getting your particular results if the null hypothesis were true is less than 5%. (c) A procedure used in hypothesis testing when the research hypothesis does not specify a particular direction of difference—it tests for extreme results that are either higher or lower than would be expected by chance.

2. It is possible that the research hypothesis is correct but the result in the particular sample was not extreme enough to be able to reject the null hypothesis.

3. (i) (a) Population 1: Canadian children of librarians; Population 2: All Canadian children. (b) Population 1 children have a higher average reading ability than Population 2 children. (c) Population 1's average reading ability is not higher than Population 2's. (d) One-tailed, because the question is whether they "score higher," so only one direction of difference is of interest.
(ii) (a) Population 1: People who live in a particular city; Population 2: All people who live in the region. (b) Populations 1 and 2 have different mean incomes. (c) Populations 1 and 2 have the same mean income. (d) Two-tailed, because the question is whether the income of the people in the city is "different" from those in the region as a whole, so a difference in either direction would be of interest.
(iii) (a) Population 1: People who have experienced an earthquake; Population 2: People in general. (b) Populations 1 and 2 have different mean levels of self-confidence. (c) Populations 1 and 2 have the same mean level of self-confidence. (d) Two-tailed, because the question specifies "more or less," so a difference in either direction would be of interest.

4.

Study	Cutoff	Z Score on Comparison Distribution	Decision
A	+1.64	2	Reject null hypothesis
B	±1.96	2	Reject null hypothesis
C	+2.33	2	Inconclusive
D	±2.57	2	Inconclusive
E	+1.64	1	Inconclusive

5.

Study	Cutoff	Z Score on the Comparison Distribution	Decision
A	+1.64	1	Inconclusive
B	±2.57	4	Reject null hypothesis
C	±2.57	3	Reject null hypothesis
D	±2.57	3.5	Reject null hypothesis
E	+1.64	−1	Inconclusive

6. ❶ **Restate the question as a research hypothesis and a null hypothesis about the populations.** There are two populations of interest:
Population 1: Students who are prevented from using their sense of smell.
Population 2: Students in general.

The research hypothesis is that students prevented from using their sense of smell (Population 1) will do worse on the taste task than students in general (Population 2). The null hypothesis is that students prevented from using their sense of smell (Population 1) will not do worse on the taste task than students in general (Population 2).
❷ **Determine the characteristics of the comparison distribution.** The comparison distribution will be the same as Population 2. As stated in the problem, Population $M = 14$ and Population $SD = 4$. We assume it follows a normal curve.
❸ **Determine the cutoff sample score on the comparison distribution at which the null hypothesis should be rejected.** For a one-tailed test at the .05 level, the cutoff is -1.64. (The cutoff is a *negative value*, because the research hypothesis is that Population 1 will *do worse* on the task than Population 2—that is, Population 1 will have a *lower score* on the task than Population 2.)
❹ **Determine your sample's score on the comparison distribution.** The sample's score was 5. $Z = (5 - 14)/4 = -2.25$.
❺ **Decide whether to reject the null hypothesis.** A Z score of -2.25 is more extreme than the cutoff of -1.64. Thus, you can reject the null hypothesis. The research hypothesis is supported—not having a sense of smell makes for fewer correct identifications.

Explanation: In brief, you solve this problem by considering the likelihood that being without a sense of smell makes no difference. If the sense of smell made no difference, the probability of the student studied getting any particular number correct is simply the probability of students in general getting any particular number correct. We know the distribution of the number correct that students get in general. Thus, you can figure that probability. It turns out that it would be fairly unlikely to get only 5 correct—so the researcher concludes that not having the sense of smell does make a difference.

To go into the details a bit, the key issue is determining these probabilities. We assumed that the number correct for the students in general follows a normal curve—a specific bell-shaped mathematical pattern in which most of the scores are in the middle and there are fewer scores as the number correct gets higher or lower. There are tables showing exactly what proportions are between the middle and any particular Z score on the normal curve.

When considering what to conclude from a study, researchers often use a convention that if a result could have happened by chance less than 5% of the time under a particular scenario, that scenario will be considered unlikely. The normal curve tables show that the top 5% of the normal curve begins with a Z score of 1.64. The normal curve is completely symmetrical; thus, the bottom 5% includes all Z scores below -1.64. Therefore, the researcher would probably set the following rule: The scenario in which being without the sense of smell makes no difference will be rejected as unlikely if the number correct (converted to a Z score using the mean and standard deviation for students in general) is less than -1.64.

The actual number correct for the student who could not use the sense of smell was 5. The normal curve for students in general had a mean of 14 and a standard deviation of 4. Getting 5 correct is 9 below the mean of 14; in terms of standard deviations of 4 each, it is 9/4 below the mean. A Z score of -2.25 is more extreme than -1.64. Thus, the researcher concludes that the scenario in which being without smell has no effect is unlikely. This is shown below:

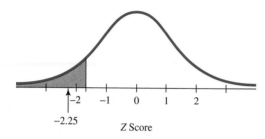

7. Cutoff (.01 level, one-tailed) $= -2.33$; Z score on comparison distribution for patient studied $= 1.2$; the experiment is inconclusive. The hypothesis testing steps, explanation, and sketch are similar to 6 above.

8. The two Ms (5.7 and 4.8) and the $p < .05$ are crucial. M stands for *mean,* the average of the scores in a particular group. The average number of times per day the high-narcissism participants looked in the mirror was 5.7, while the average for the low-narcissism participants was only 4.8. The $p < .05$ tells us that this difference is statistically significant at the .05 level. This means that if a person's level of narcissism made no difference in how often the person looked in the mirror, the chances of getting two groups of participants who were this different on looking in the mirror just by chance would be 5%. Hence, you can reject that possibility as unlikely and conclude that the level of narcissism does make a difference in how often people look in the mirror.

9. Similar to 8 above.

10. (a)

	Real Situation	
Conclusion from Hypothesis Testing	**Null Hypothesis True**	**Research Hypothesis True**
Research Hypothesis Supported (Reject null)	*Type I Error* Decide more recess time improves behavior, but it really doesn't	*Correct Decision* Decide more recess time improves behavior, and it really does
Study Inconclusive (Do not reject null)	*Correct Decision* Decide effect of recess time on behavior is not shown in this study; actually more recess time doesn't improve behavior	*Type II Error* Decide effect of recess time on behavior is not shown in this study; actually more recess time improves behavior

(b) and (c) are similar to (a) above.

11. (a) You can never know for certain if you have made a Type I error. (b) You can never know for certain if you have made a Type II error.

Chapter 6

1. There is less variation among means of samples of more than one score than there are among individual scores. This is because the likelihood of two extreme scores in the same direction randomly ending up in the same sample is less than the probability of each of those extreme scores being chosen individually.

2. (a) Population $SD^2 = 10^2 = 100$; Population $SD_M^2 =$ Population $SD^2/N = 100/2 = 50$; Population $SD_M =$ $\sqrt{\text{Population } SD_M^2} = \sqrt{50} = 7.07$; (b) 5.77; (c) 5; (d) 3.33.

3. (a) Population $SD^2 = 20^2 = 400$; Population $SD_M^2 =$ Population $SD^2/N = 400/2 = 200$; Population $SD_M =$ $\sqrt{\text{Population } SD_M^2} = \sqrt{200} = 14.14$; (b) 11.55; (c) 10; (d) 6.67.

4. (a) The best estimate of the population mean is the sample mean of 100. From question 2a, the standard deviation of the distribution of means (Population SD_M) is 7.07. For the 95% confidence limits, the Z scores you want are -1.96 and $+1.96$. Lower limit $= (-1.96)(7.07) + 100 = 86.14$. Upper limit $= (1.96)(7.07) + 100 = 113.86$; (b) 88.69, 111.31; (c) 90.2, 109.8; (d) 93.47, 106.53.

5. (a) The best estimate of the population mean is the sample mean of 10. From question 3a, the standard deviation of the distribution of means (Population SD_M) is 14.14. For the 99% confidence limits, the Z scores you want are -2.57 and $+2.57$. Lower limit $= (-2.57)(14.14) + 10 = -26.34$; upper limit $= (2.57)(14.14) + 10 = 46.34$; (b) -19.68, 39.68; (c) -15.7, 35.7; (d) -7.14, 27.14.

6. (a)

❶ **Restate the question as a research hypothesis and a null hypothesis about the populations.** There are two populations of interest:

Population 1: People given the experimental treatment.
Population 2: People in general (who do not get the experimental treatment).

The research hypothesis is that the population given the experimental treatment (Population 1) has a different mean score than people in general (Population 2). The null hypothesis is that Population 1's mean is the same as Population 2's.

❷ **Determine the characteristics of the comparison distribution.** Comparison distribution is a distribution of means of samples of 10 taken from the distribution of Population 2. Population $M_M =$ Population $M = 40$; Population $SD_M^2 =$ Population $SD^2/N = 6^2/10 = 3.6$; Population $SD_M = \sqrt{\text{Population } SD_M^2} = \sqrt{3.6} = 1.90$. Because the population is normal, the distribution of means is normal.

❸ **Determine the cutoff sample score on the comparison distribution at which the null hypothesis should be re-**

jected. For a two-tailed test at the .05 level, the cutoffs are −1.96 and 1.96.

❹ **Determine your sample's score on the comparison distribution.** $Z = (44 − 40)/1.90 = 2.11$.

❺ **Decide whether to reject the null hypothesis.** 2.11 is more extreme than 1.96. Thus, you can reject the null hypothesis. The research hypothesis is supported; those who receive the experimental treatment score differently from the general population. The distributions involved are shown below.

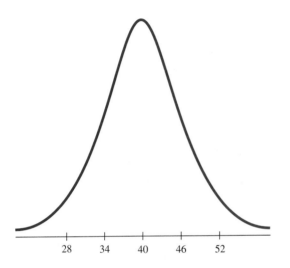

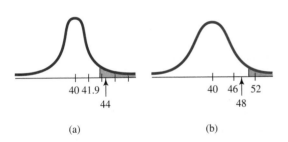

(a)   (b)

(b) Hypothesis-testing steps similar to (a) above. Population $SD_M = 6$; $Z = (48 − 40)/6 = 1.33$; do not reject null hypothesis; study is inconclusive as to whether those who receive the experimental treatment are different from those in the general population.
(c) For part (a), 95% confidence interval: Lower limit = $(−1.96)(1.9) + 44 = 40.28$; Upper limit = $(1.96)(1.9) + 44 = 47.72$ for part (b), 95% confidence interval: 36.24 to 59.76.

7. Hypothesis-testing steps and drawing similar to 6 above.
(a) Population $SD_M = .8$; $Z = (82 − 81)/.8 = 1.25$; do not reject null hypothesis. (b) Population $SD_M = 2.53$; $Z = (84 − 81)/2.53 = 1.19$; do not reject null hypothesis. (c) For part (a), 99% confidence interval: 79.94 to 84.06; for part (b), 99% confidence interval: 77.5 to 90.5.

8. (a) and (b) Hypothesis-testing steps and drawing similar to 6 above. Population $SD_M = .1$; $Z = (1.5 − 1.8)/.1 = −3$; reject the null hypothesis.
(c) This is a standard hypothesis-testing problem, with one exception. You can't compare directly the reaction times for the group of 25 women tested to a distribution of reaction times for individual women. The probability of a group of scores having an extreme mean just by chance is much less than the probability of any one individual having an extreme score just by chance. (When taking a group of scores at random, any extreme individual scores are likely to be balanced out by less extreme or oppositely extreme scores.) Thus, you need to compare the mean of the group of 25 reaction times to a distribution of what would happen if you were to take many random groups of 25 reaction time scores and find the mean of each group of 25 scores.

Such a distribution of many means of samples has the same mean as the original distribution of individual scores (there is no reason for it to be otherwise). However, it is a narrower curve. This is because the chances of extremes are less. In fact, its variance will be exactly the variance of the original distribution of individuals divided by the number of scores in each sample. In this example, this makes a distribution of means with a mean of 1.8 and a standard deviation of .1 (that is, the square root of the result of $.5^2$ divided by 25). This will be a normal distribution because a distribution of many means from a normally distributed population is also normal.

The cutoff for significance, using the .01 level and a one-tailed test, is −2.33. The mean reaction time of the group of 25 women who received the special program, 1.5, was 3 standard deviations below the mean of the distribution of means, making it clearly more extreme than the cutoff. Thus, you can reject the null hypothesis and conclude that the results support the hypothesis that elderly women who take part in the special program have lower reaction times.
(d) 99% confidence interval: 1.24 to 1.76. The confidence interval is an estimate based on your sample's mean and the standard deviation of the distribution of means. What it estimates is the range of values that is likely to include the true population mean for the group studied. (The group studied is Population 1. In this example, the group studied is women who receive the special reaction-time program.) A 99% confidence interval is the range of values you are 99% confident include the true population mean. The lower end of this interval (in this example, 1.24) is the mean of the lowest distribution of means that would have a 99% chance of including this sample mean; its upper end (in this example, 1.76) is the mean of the highest distribution of means that would have a 99% chance of including this sample mean.

To figure the confidence interval, you first consider that the best single point estimate of the mean of Population 1 is the sample's mean (in this case, 1.5). You then assume that the standard deviation of the distribution of means for this population is the same as for the known population (which we figured earlier to be .1). Based on this information, if the true population mean was 1.5, 99% of the time, sample means would fall between a Z score of −2.57 (the point on the normal curve that includes 49.5% of the scores below the mean) and +2.57. In our example, these Z scores correspond to raw scores of 1.24 and 1.76.

It turns out that the values figured in this way are the limits (the upper and lower end) of the confidence interval. Why? Suppose the true population mean was 1.24. In this case, there would be a .5% chance of getting a mean as large as or larger than 1.5. (That is, with a mean of 1.24 and a standard deviation of .1, 1.5 is exactly 2.57 standard deviations above the mean. This is the point that corresponds to the cutoff for the top .5% of this curve.) Similarly, if the true population mean was 1.76, there would only be a .5% chance of getting a mean lower than 1.5.

9. (a) and (b) Hypothesis-testing steps and drawing similar to 6 above. Population $SD_M = .2; Z = (5.9 - 5.5)/.2 = 2$; reject the null hypothesis. (c) Similar to 8c above, plus an explanation of material from previous chapter on hypothesis testing, normal curve, means, and standard deviations. (d) 95% confidence interval; 5.51 to 6.29.

10. The error bars are the lines that go above and below the top of each bar. The error bars show, for each particular group, the standard deviation of the distribution of means for people like those in this group. (Then explain a distribution of means as in 8c above.)

11. Similar to confidence interval part of 8d above.

Chapter 7

1. (a) Effect size = (Population 1 M − Population 2 M)/Population $SD = (19 - 25)/12 = -.50$, medium; (b) −.25, small; (c) 0, no effect; (d) .42, medium; (e) .83, large.
2. (a) Effect size = (Population 1 M − Population 2 M)/Population SD = $(50 - 50)/5 = 0$, no effect; (b) .40, medium; (c) .80, large; (d) 1.20, large; (e) −.60, medium.
3. (a) Predicted effect size = (Population 1 M − Population 2 M)/Population $SD = (91 - 90)/4 = .25$; (b) .50; (c) 1.00; (d) −1.00.
4. (a) Not affected. (b) Possibly of small importance. (c) Regarding situation (a), the significance tells you the probability of getting your results if the null hypothesis is true; sample size is already taken into account in figuring the significance. Regarding situation (b), it is possible to get a significant result with a large sample even when the actual practical effect is slight—such as when the mean of your sample (and this, your best estimate of the mean of the population that gets the experimental treatment) is only slightly higher than the mean of the known population. This is possible because significance is based on the difference between the mean of your sample and the known population mean with this difference then divided by the standard deviation of the distribution of means. If the sample size is very large, then the standard deviation of the distribution of means is very small. (This is because it is figured by taking the square root of the result of dividing the population variance by the sample size.) Thus, even a small difference between the means when divided by a very small denominator can give a large overall result, making the study significant.
5. Power is the chance of rejecting the null hypothesis if the research hypothesis is true. In other words, the power of a study represents the likelihood that you will get a statistically significant result in your study, if in fact the research hypothe-

sis is true. Ideally, a study should have power of 80% or more. If a study has low power and does not get a statistically significant result, the result of the study is entirely inconclusive. This is because it is not clear whether the nonsignificant result is due to the low power of the study or because the research hypothesis is in fact false.

Effect size can be thought of as the degree to which distributions do not overlap. The larger the effect size, the larger the power. As noted in the quotation from the research article, the study had a high level of power (about 90%) for detecting both large and medium-sized effects. Given this high level of power, the researchers were able to conclude that the most likely reason for the nonsignificant study results is that the research hypothesis is in fact false. As the researchers noted, with such a high level of power, it is very unlikely that the results of the study would be nonsignificant if there were in fact a medium-sized or large effect in the population. Since smaller effect sizes are associated with lower power, the researchers were careful not to rule out the possibility that there is in fact a small effect in the population (which may not have been detected in the study due to the lower power for identifying a small effect size).

6. (a) Increases power; (b) decreases power; (c) increases power; (d) decreases power; (e) decreases power.
7. One situation is that when planning an experiment, figuring power gives you the chance to make changes of various kinds (or even abandon the project) if power is too low. (Or if power is higher than reasonably needed, you would then be able to make changes to make the study less costly, for example, by reducing the number of participants.) Another situation is figuring power after a study is done that had nonsignificant results. If you figure that power was high in the study, this means you can be pretty confident that the null hypothesis really is true in the population, in the sense that the true difference in the population is really smaller than the effect size you used to figure power. But if you figure the power of the study was low, this tells you that the result really is ambiguous and that it is still reasonable to think that future research testing this hypothesis might have a chance of being significant. A third possibility is figuring power after a study is done that got a significant result and the researchers do not give the effect size. If the study had high power (as when it used a large sample), this tells you that the effect size could have been small and thus the effect not very important for practical application. But if the study seems to have had low power (as from having a small sample), this tells you that the effect size must have been large for them to get a significant result.

Chapter 8

1. (a) t needed ($df = 63, p < .05$, one-tailed) = −1.671; $S_M^2 = S^2/N = 9/64 = .141$. $S_M = \sqrt{S_M^2} = \sqrt{.141} = .38; t = (M -$ Population $M)/S_M = (11 - 12.40)/.38 = -3.68$; reject null hypothesis. (b) t needed = 2.690; $S_M = 2.55; t = 1.32$; do not reject null hypothesis. (c) t needed = 2.364; $S_M = .13; t = 3.15$; reject null hypothesis.

2. (a)

❶ **Restate the question as a research hypothesis and a null hypothesis about the populations.** There are two populations of interest:

Population 1: Response times under the new sheriff.
Population 2: Response times under the old sheriff.

The research hypothesis is that response times under the new sheriff are lower than response times under the old sheriff. The null hypothesis is that the response times under the new sheriff are not less than under the old sheriff.

❷ **Determine the characteristics of the comparison distribution.** Population 2: shape = assumed normal; Population $M = 30$; The estimated population variance is $S^2 = \Sigma(X - M)^2/df = (124)/(10 - 1) = 13.78$. Distribution of means: shape = $t(df = 9)$; mean of the distribution of means = 30; variance of the distribution of means is $S_M^2 = S^2/N = 13.78/10 = 1.378$; standard deviation of the distribution of means is $S_M = \sqrt{S_M^2} = \sqrt{1.378} = 1.17$.

❸ **Determine the cutoff sample score on the comparison distribution at which the null hypothesis should be rejected.** t needed ($df = 9$, $p < .05$, one-tailed) = -1.833.

❹ **Determine your sample's score on the comparison distribution.** $M = (\Sigma X)/N = 280/10 = 28$; $t = (M - \text{Population } M)/S_M = (28 - 30)/1.17 = -1.71$.

❺ **Decide whether to reject the null hypothesis.** -1.71 is not more extreme than -1.833; do not reject the null hypothesis.

(b)

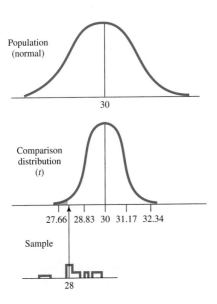

(c) Similar to 5c below, except instead of difference scores, actual scores are used here, and the expected population mean

is the 30 minutes that the sheriff had promised to do better than the current sheriff.

3. (a) and (b) Hypothesis-testing steps and sketch similar to 2a and 2b above; t needed = 2.776; $t = (M - \text{Population } M)/S_M = (46 - 40)/2.3 = 2.61$; do not reject the null hypothesis. (c) Similar to 5c below, except instead of difference scores, actual scores are used here, and the expected population mean is the 40 questions that people usually get correct.

4. (a) t needed ($df = 19$, $p < .05$, one-tailed) = 1.729; $S_M^2 = S^2/N = 8.29/20 = .415$; $S_M = \sqrt{S_M^2} = \sqrt{.415} = .64$; $t = (M - \text{Population } M)/S_M = (1.7 - 0)/.64 = 2.66$; reject null hypothesis. Estimated effect size = $M/S = 1.7/\sqrt{8.29} = .59$.

(b) t needed = -1.984, 1.984; $S_M^2 = S^2/N = 414.53/164 = 2.53$; $S_M = \sqrt{S_M^2} = \sqrt{2.53} = 1.59$; $t = (2.3 - 0)/1.59 = 1.45$; do not reject null hypothesis. Estimated effect size = .10.

(c) t needed = -2.625; $S_M^2 = S^2/N = 4/15 = .27$; $S_M = \sqrt{S_M^2} = \sqrt{.27} = .52$; $t = -4.23$; reject null hypothesis. Estimated effect size = -1.10.

5. (a)

❶ **Restate the question as a research hypothesis and a null hypothesis about the populations.** There are two populations of interest:

Population 1: Cities like those who participated in the anti-littering program.
Population 2: Cities that do not change in the amount of litter over a 1-year period.

The research hypothesis is that Population 1 has a greater mean decrease in litter than Population 2. The null hypothesis is that Population 1 doesn't have a greater mean decrease in litter than Population 2.

❷ **Determine the characteristics of the comparison distribution.** Population 2: shape = assumed normal; Population $M = 0$; The estimated population variance is $S^2 = \Sigma(X - M)^2/df = (50)/(4 - 1) = 16.67$. Distribution of means: shape = $t(df = 3)$; mean of the distribution of means of difference scores = 0; variance of the distribution of means of difference scores is $S_M^2 = S^2/N = 16.67/4 = 4.17$; standard deviation of the distribution of means of difference scores is $S_M = \sqrt{S_M^2} = \sqrt{4.17} = 2.04$.

❸ **Determine the cutoff sample score on the comparison distribution at which the null hypothesis should be rejected.** t needed ($df = 3$, $p < .01$, one-tailed) = -4.541. (The cutoff score is negative, because we will figure changes scores as July 2006 litter minus July 2005 litter. Thus, negative change scores will be in the same direction as the hypothesized *decrease* in litter.)

❹ **Determine your sample's score on the comparison distribution.**
Change scores = $-7, -6, 1, -8$; $M = -20/4 = -5$; $t = (M - \text{Population } M)/S_M = (-5 - 0)/2.04 = -2.45$.

❺ **Decide whether to reject the null hypothesis.** -2.45 (from Step ❹) is not more extreme than the cutoff of -4.541 (from Step ❸); do not reject the null hypothesis.

(b)

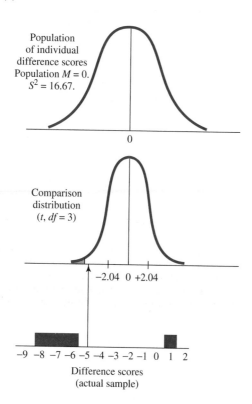

Population
of individual
difference scores
Population $M = 0$.
$S^2 = 16.67$.

0

Comparison
distribution
(t, $df = 3$)

−2.04 0 +2.04

−9 −8 −7 −6 −5 −4 −3 −2 −1 0   1   2

Difference scores
(actual sample)

(c) In this situation, I am using a t test for dependent means to test whether the amount of litter in four cities changes from before to after the introduction of a program to decrease littering. The first thing I did was to simplify things by converting the numbers to change scores—postprogram (2006) litter minus preprogram (2005) litter for each city. Then I found the mean of these difference scores, which was −5. That is, there is an average decrease of 5 pounds of litter per block per day.

The next step was to see whether this result, found in these four cities, indicates some more general, real difference due to being in this program. The alternative is the possibility that this much change could have happened in four randomly selected cities just by chance, even if in general the program would have no real effect. That is, we imagine that the average change for cities in general that would do this program would actually be 0, and maybe this study just happened to pick four cities that would have decreased this much anyway.

I then considered just how much a group of four cities would have to change before I could conclude that they have changed too much to chalk it up to chance. This required figuring out the characteristics of this imagined population of cities in which, on the average, there is no change. An average of no change is the same as saying there is a mean of 0 change. Therefore, I used 0 as the mean of the comparison distribution. Since I didn't know the variance of this hypothetical distribution of cities that don't change, I estimated it from the information in the sample of four cities. If the sample cities were drawn at chance from the hypothetical distribution of no change, the variance of these cities should reflect the variance of this hypothetical distribution (which would be

the distribution they come from). However, the variance figured from a particular group (sample) from a larger population will in general be slightly smaller than the true population's variance. In other words, it will be a biased estimate of the population variance. Thus, I had to modify the variance formula to take this into account: Instead of dividing the sum of the squared deviations by the number of scores (the usual method), I divided it instead by the "degrees of freedom." The degrees of freedom is the number of scores minus 1—in this case, $4 − 1 = 3$. (This adjustment exactly accounts for the tendency of the variance in the sample to underestimate the true population variance and results in an unbiased estimate of the population variance.) As shown in the calculations in the steps of hypothesis testing, this gave an estimated population variance (S^2) of 16.67.

I was interested not in individual cities but in a group of four. Thus, what I really needed to know was the characteristics of a distribution of means of samples of four taken from this hypothetical population of individual city difference scores. Such a distribution of means will have the same mean of 0. (This is because there is no reason to expect the means of such groups of four drawn randomly to be systematically higher or lower than the population's mean of 0.) However, such a distribution will have a much smaller variance than the variance of the population it comes from. (This is because the average of a group of four scores is a lot less likely to be extreme than any individual score.) Fortunately, it is known (and can be proved mathematically) that the variance of a distribution of means is the variance of the distribution of individuals, divided by the number of individuals in each sample. In our example, this works out to 16.67 divided by 4, which is 4.17. The standard deviation of this distribution is thus the square root of 4.17, or 2.04.

It also turns out that if we assume that the hypothetical population of individual cities' difference scores is normally distributed (and we have no reason to think otherwise), the distribution of means of samples from that distribution can be thought of as having a precise known shape, called a t distribution. (A t distribution is similar to a normal curve, but has slightly thicker tails). Thus, I looked in a table for a t distribution for the situation in which 3 degrees of freedom are used to estimate the population variance. The table shows that there is less than a 1% chance of getting a score that is −4.541 standard deviations from the mean of this distribution.

The mean difference score for the sample of four cities was −5, which is 2.45 (that is, −5/2.04) standard deviations below the mean of 0 change on this distribution of means of difference scores. This is not as extreme as −4.541. Thus, there is more than a 1% chance that these results could have come from a hypothetical distribution with no change. Therefore, the researcher would not rule out that possibility, and the experiment would be considered inconclusive.

6. (a), (b), and (c). Hypothesis-testing steps, sketch, and explanation similar to 5 above. t needed = −2.776, 2.776; $t = (M − \text{Population } M)/S_M = (−.02 − 0)/.007 = −2.86$; reject the null hypothesis.

7. (a) Estimated effect size = $M/S = 20/32 = .63$, medium effect size; (b) .50, medium; (c) .25, small; (d) .20, small.

8. From Table 8–8: (a) .22; (b) .71; (c) .86; (d) .77; (e) .99.

9. From Table 8–9: (a) 33; (b) 12; (c) 156.

10. Similar to 5c above except focusing on this study and the simpler situation involving just a single sample. Also, you do not

need to explain the basic logic of hypothesis testing (only what is added when you have an unknown population variance).

11. Similar to 5b and 5c above, except your explanation should focus on this study and you should add material on mean, standard deviation, and variance, as in the answers to Chapter 2 problems.

Chapter 9

1. (a) Independent; (b) dependent; (c) dependent.
2. (a) $S^2_{Pooled} = (df_1/df_{Total})(S^2_1) + (df_2/df_{Total})(S^2_2) = (19/38)(1) + (19/38)(2) = 1.5;$
   $S^2_{M_1} = S^2_{Pooled}/N_1 = 1.5/20 = .075; S^2_{M_2} = .075;$
   $S^2_{Difference} = S^2_{M_1} + S^2_{M_2} = .075 + .075 = .15;$
   $S_{Difference} = .39.$
   (b) .35; (c) .32; (d) .27; (e) .35.
3. (a) t needed $(df = 58, p < .05, \text{two-tailed}) = -2.004, 2.004;$
   $S^2_{Pooled} = (df_1/df_{Total})(S^2_1) + (df_2/df_{Total})(S^2_2) = (29/58)(2.4) + (29/58)(2.8) = 2.6;$
   $S^2_{M_1} = S^2_{Pooled}/N_1 = 2.6/30 = .087;$
   $S^2_{M_2} = .087; S^2_{Difference} = S^2_{M_1} + S^2_{M_2} = .087 + .087 = .174.$
   $S_{Difference} = .417;$
   $t = (M_1 - M_2)/S_{Difference} = (12 - 11.1)/.417 = 2.16.$
   Conclusion: Reject the null hypothesis. The difference is significant. (b) $S^2_{Pooled} = 2.67; S_{Difference} = .45; t = 2.00;$ do not reject the null hypothesis. (c) $S^2_{Pooled} = 2.6;$ $S_{Difference} = .416; t = 2.16;$ reject the null hypothesis.

4. (a)
   ❶ **Restate the question as a research hypothesis and a null hypothesis about the populations.** There are two populations of interest:

   Population 1: People who get their news from TV.
   Population 2: People who get their news from the Internet.

   The research hypothesis is that the two populations have different means. The null hypothesis is that the two populations have the same mean.
   ❷ **Determine the characteristics of the comparison distribution.**
   $S^2_{Pooled} = (60/80)(4) + (20/80)(6) = 4.5;$ comparison distribution (distribution of differences between means): $M = 0; S_{Difference} = .54;$ shape $= t(df = 80).$
   ❸ **Determine the cutoff sample score on the comparison distribution at which the null hypothesis should be rejected.** t needed $(df = 80, p < .01, \text{two-tailed}) t = -2.639, 2.639.$
   ❹ **Determine your sample's score on the comparison distribution.** $t = (24 - 26)/.54 = -3.70.$
   ❺ **Decide whether to reject the null hypothesis.** -3.70 is more extreme than -2.639; reject the null hypothesis; the prediction that there will be some difference is supported by the experiment.

   (b) See figure below.
   (c) In this situation, I am testing whether the two samples come from identical populations. I have two estimates of

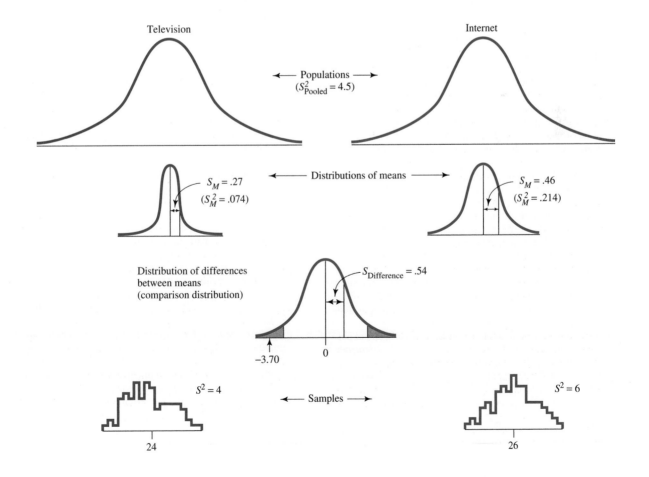

Television

Internet

Populations
($S^2_{Pooled} = 4.5$)

Distributions of means

$S_M = .27$
($S^2_M = .074$)

$S_M = .46$
($S^2_M = .214$)

Distribution of differences
between means
(comparison distribution)

$S_{Difference} = .54$

-3.70 0

Samples

$S^2 = 4$

$S^2 = 6$

24

26

those identical populations, one from each sample. Thus, to get the most accurate overall estimate of the population variance, I can average the two estimates of the population variance. In order to give more weight to the estimate based on the larger degrees of freedom, I figure a weighted average, multiplying each estimate by its proportion of the total degrees of freedom, then adding up the results. This pooled estimate of the population variance comes out to 4.5.

I was interested not in individual scores but in the difference between the mean of a group of 61 and the mean of another group of 21. Thus, I needed to figure out what would be the characteristics of a distribution of differences between means, specifically a distribution of differences between means of groups of 61 and 21 that are randomly taken from the two identical populations whose variance I just estimated. This required two steps. First, I figured the characteristics of the distribution of means in the usual way for the population associated with each sample, but using my pooled estimate for the variance of each population of individuals. This came out to .074 for the TV group and .214 for the Internet group. The second step is directly about the distribution of differences between means. It is like a distribution you would get if you took a mean from the distribution of means for the TV group and took one from the distribution of means for the Internet group and figured the difference between these two means. After doing this many times, the distribution of these differences between two means would make up a new distribution, called a distribution of differences between means. This distribution is the comparison distribution in a t test for independent means. We are assuming (if Internet versus TV made no difference) that the two original populations have the same means. Thus, on average, the difference between a mean taken from the TV group and a mean taken from the Internet group should come out to 0. (This is because sometimes one will be bigger and sometimes the other, but in the long run these random fluctuations should balance out.) The variance of this distribution of differences between means is affected by the variation in both distributions of means. In fact, it is just the sum of the two. Thus, its variance is .074 plus .214, or .288. Its square root, the standard deviation of the distribution of differences between means, is .54.

Because this whole process is based on estimated variances, the distribution of means is a t distribution. Specifically, it will be a t distribution with degrees of freedom equal to the total number of degrees of freedom that went into the two estimates. In this example, $df = 80$. Looking this up on the t table for .01 two-tailed gives a cutoff needed of ± 2.639. The t for my sample is the particular difference between the means of my two groups, divided by the standard deviation of the distribution of differences between means This comes out to $(24 - 26)/.54 = -3.70$. This is more extreme than the cutoff, so I can reject the null hypothesis.

5. (a), (b), and (c). Hypothesis-testing steps, sketch, and explanation similar to 4 above (except for c you also need to include basic material as in the answers to previous chapters' problems). t needed $= -2.262, 2.262$; $S^2_{Pooled} = (5/9)(5.60) + (4/9)(5.20) = 5.42$; $S^2_{Difference} = .90 + 1.08 = 1.98$; $S_{Difference} = 1.41$; $t = (6 - 7.8)/1.41 = -1.28$. Do not reject the null hypothesis; the experiment is inconclusive as to whether including the child's name makes a difference.

6. (a), (b), and (c). Hypothesis-testing steps, sketch, and explanation similar to 4 above. t needed $= 1.943$; $S^2_{Pooled} = (4/6)(6.7) + (2/6)(12.33) = 8.58$; $S^2_{Difference} = 2.86 + 1.72 = 4.58$; $S_{Difference} = 2.14$; $t = (5.33 - 5.2)/2.14 = .06$. Do not reject the null hypothesis; the experiment is inconclusive as to whether older children do better.

7. (a) Estimated effect size $= (M_1 - M_2)/S_{Pooled} = (24 - 26)/\sqrt{4.5} = -.94$; (b) $-.77$; (c) .04. (d) Effect size represents the degree to which two populations do not overlap. The less that two populations overlap, the larger the effect size. In the behavioral and social sciences, we often want to know not just if a result is significant, but how big the effect is. Effect size gives you a measure of how big the effect is. Effect size for the t test for independent means is the difference between the population means, divided by the standard deviation of the population of individuals. However, you do not know the population means. Thus, you estimate them using the sample means. You also do not know the standard deviation of the population of individuals Thus, you have to estimate it too. You do this by using the pooled estimate of the population standard deviation. So, in part (a), the effect size was the difference between the sample means (24 minus 26, which gives -2), divided by the pooled estimate of the population standard deviation (which was the square root of 4.5, or 2.12). This gave an estimated effect size of $-.94$, which is a large effect size according to Cohen's effect size conventions for the t test for independent means.

8. (a) Harmonic mean $= 2(N_1)(N_2)/(N_1 + N_2) = (2)(3)(57)/(3 + 57) = 5.7$; from Table 9–4 approximate power $= .11$; (b) harmonic mean $= 16.7$, power $= .15$; (c) harmonic mean $= 26.7$, power $= .19$; (d) power $= .19$.

9. (a) Estimated effect size $= (M_1 - M_2)/S_{Pooled} = (107 - 149)/84 = -.50$, medium effect size; needed N from Table 9–5 $= 50$ per group, 100 total. (b) Estimated effect size $= .20$; needed $N = 393$ per group, 786 total. (c) Estimated effect size $= .80$; needed $N = 20$ per group, 40 total. (d) Estimated effect size $= -.80$; needed $N = 26$ per group, 52 total.

10. (Along with the following, include a full explanation of all terms and concepts as in 4c and the answers to previous chapters' explanation problems.) (a) and (b) This study shows that using a conventional .05 significance level, German children who receive low levels of support—whether from their mother, father, or classmates—showed lower levels of self-worth. Furthermore, the effect sizes were fairly large (.78 and .69) with regard to support from mother or father; however, the effect size was only small to moderate (.35) with regard to support from classmates. This would seem to imply that support from parents is more important than support from classmates in terms of a child's feeling of self-worth. The power of the study for a large effect size is .98. (This assumes there were about equal numbers of children in the high and low support groups, that the test is two-tailed, and uses the figure for 50 in each group.) The power for a medium effect size is .70. Because we already know that the results are significant and we know the effect sizes, the power calculations are not very important.

11. Similar to 4c above, but focusing on the results of this study.

Chapter 10

1. (a) F needed $(df = 2, 27; p < .05) = 3.36$; $S_M^2 = \Sigma(M - GM)^2/df_{\text{Between}} = [(7.4 - 7)^2 + (6.8 - 7)^2 + (6.8 - 7)^2]/2 = .12$; $S_{\text{Between}}^2 = (S_M^2)(n) = (.12)(10) = 1.2$; $S_{\text{Within}}^2 = (S_1^2 + S_2^2 + \cdots + S_{\text{Last}}^2)/N_{\text{Groups}} = (.82 + .90 + (.82 + .90 + 80)/3 = .84$; $F = 1.2/.84 = 1.43$; do not reject the null hypothesis; effect size, $R^2 = (S_{\text{Between}}^2) (df_{\text{Between}})/[(S_{\text{Between}}^2) (df_{\text{Between}}) + (S_{\text{Within}}^2)(df_{\text{Within}})] = (1.2)(2)/[(1.2)(2) + (.84)(27)] = .10)$; from Table 10–8, approximate power = between .20 and .45.
(b) F needed $(df = 3, 96; p < .05) = 2.70$ (actually using $df = 3, (95)$; $S_M^2 = 164.67$; $S_{\text{Between}}^2 = (164.67)(25) = 4116.75$; 4116.75; $S_{\text{Within}}^2 = 736.5$; $F = 5.59$; reject the null hypothesis; effect size, $R^2 = .15$; approximate power = between .85 and .96.
(c) F needed $(df = 4, 120; p < .05) = 2.46$ (actually using $4, 100$); $S_M^2 = 123.5$; $S_{\text{Between}}^2 = (123.5)(25) = 3087.5$; $S_{\text{Within}}^2 = 735$; $F = 4.20$; reject the null hypothesis; effect size, $R^2 = .12$; approximate power = between .90 and .98 (using the values for $R^2 = .14$ from Table 10–8).

2. (a) F needed $(df = 2, 9; p < .01) = 8.02$; Group 1: $M = 8, S^2 = .67$; Group 2: $M = 6, S^2 = .67$; Group 3: $M = 4, S^2 = .67$; $S_{\text{Between}}^2 = (4)(4) = 16$; $S_{\text{Within}}^2 = .67$; $F = 16/.67 = 23.88$; reject the null hypothesis; effect size, $R^2 = .84$.
(b) F needed $(df = 2, 9; p < .01) = 8.02$; Group 1: $M = 8, S^2 = 21.33$; Group 2: $M = 6, S^2 = 21.33$; Group 3: $M = 4, S^2 = 21.33$; $S_{\text{Between}}^2 = (4)(4) = 16$; $S_{\text{Within}}^2 = 2.133$; $F = 16/21.33 = .75$; do not reject the null hypothesis; effect size, $R^2 = .14$.

3. (a)
❶ **Restate the question as a research hypothesis and a null hypothesis about the populations.** There are three populations of interest:

Population 1: Patients with affective disorders.
Population 2: Patients with cognitive disorders.
Population 3: Patients with drug-related conditions.

The null hypothesis is that the three populations have the same mean. The research hypothesis is that the three populations do not have the same mean.
❷ **Determine the characteristics of the comparison distribution.** F distribution with 2 and 9 degrees of freedom.
❸ **Determine the cutoff sample score on the comparison distribution at which the null hypothesis should be rejected.** 5% level, $F(2, 9)$ needed $= 4.26$.
❹ **Determine your sample's score on the comparison distribution.** $S_{\text{Between}}^2 = (5.33)(4) = 21.32$; $S_{\text{Within}}^2 = (2.67 + 3.33 + 2.67)/3 = 2.89$; $F = 21.32/2.89 = 7.38$.
❺ **Decide whether to reject the null hypothesis.** F from Step ❹ (7.38) is more extreme than cutoff F from Step ❸ (4.26); reject the null hypothesis.
(b) Effect size, $R^2 = (S_{\text{Between}}^2)(df_{\text{Between}})/[(S_{\text{Between}}^2) (df_{\text{Between}}) + (S_{\text{Between}}^2)(df_{\text{Within}})] = .62$.
(c) The scores in this study are from three entirely separate groups of people. An analysis of variance is the appropriate analysis in this situation. The null hypothesis is that the three groups are from populations of length-of-stay scores with equal means. Also, as with a t test, we must be able to assume that they have equal variances. If this null hypothesis is true, then you can estimate the variance of these equal populations in two ways:
(i) You can estimate from the variation within each of the three groups and then average them. (This is just what you would do in a t test for independent means, except now you are averaging three instead of just two. Also in a t test you would weight these variances according to the degrees of freedom they contribute to the overall estimate. However, because all three groups have equal numbers, you can simply average them—in effect weighting them equally.) In this example, the three variance estimates were 2.67, 3.33, and 2.67, which gave a pooled estimate of 2.89. This is called the within-groups estimate of the population variance.
(ii) You can estimate the variance using the three means. If we assume the null hypothesis is true, then the means of the three groups are based on samples taken from identical populations. Each of these identical populations will have an identical distribution of means of samples taken from that population. The means of our three samples are all from identical populations, which is the same as if they were all from the same population. Thus, the amount of variation among our three means should reflect the variation in the distribution of means that they can be thought of as coming from. As a result, I can use these three means (6, 10, and 10) to estimate the variance in this distribution of means. Using the usual formula for estimating a population variance, I get 5.33.

However, what we want is the variance of a distribution of individuals. So the question is this: What would be the distribution of individuals that would produce a distribution of means (of four scores each) with a variance of 5.33? To find the distribution of means from a distribution of individuals, you divide the variance of the distribution of individuals by the size of the samples. However, in our present situation, you want to do the reverse. Thus, you multiply the variance of the distribution of means by the size of the samples to get the variance of the distribution of individuals. This comes out to 5.33 times 4, or 21.32. This is called the between-groups estimate of the population variance.

If the null hypothesis is true, the within-groups and between-groups estimates of the population variance should be about the same. This is because they are estimates of the same thing, the variance of any of the populations (which are all assumed to be the same). This means that the ratio of the between-groups estimate divided by the within-groups estimate should be about 1.

However, suppose the null hypothesis is false so that the three populations from which these groups come in fact have different means. In that situation, the estimate based on the variation among the group means will be bigger than the estimate based on the variation within the groups. The reason it will be bigger is as follows: If the null hypothesis is true, the only reason that the means of our groups vary is because of the variance inside of each of the three identical distributions of means. But if the null hypothesis is false, each of those distributions of means also has a different mean. Thus, the variation in our means is due to *both* the variation inside of each of these now *not* identical distributions of means and also to the differences in the means of these distributions of means. Thus, there is an additional source of variation in the means of our groups. If you estimate the variance of the population using these three means, it will be larger than if the null hypothesis were true. At the same time, however, the within-groups variance is not affected by whether the three groups have different means. This is because the within-groups variance considers variation only within each of the groups. The within-groups variance thus does not get any bigger if the null hypothesis is false. The result of all this is that when the null hypothesis is false, the ratio of the between-groups variance to the within-groups variance will be more than 1.

The ratio of the between-groups estimate to the within-groups estimate is called an *F* ratio. In this example, our *F* ratio is 21.32 to 2.89: 21.32/2.89 = 7.38.

Statisticians have made tables of what happens when you figure *F* ratios based on the situation in which you randomly take a group of four scores from each of three identical populations. This is the situation in which the null hypothesis is true. Looking at these tables, it turns out that there is less than a 5% chance of getting an *F* ratio larger than 4.26. Because our actual *F* ratio is bigger than this, we can reject the null hypothesis.

4. (a), (b), and (c). Hypothesis-testing steps, estimated effect size, and explanation similar to 3 above (except for part c you need to include material similar to the explanations from earlier chapters' practice problems). *F* needed ($df = 2, 147$; $p < .05$) = 3.09 (actually using $df = 2, 100$); $S^2_{Between} = (.09)(50) = 4.5$; $S^2_{Within} = (5.2 + 5.8 + 4.8)/3 = 5.27$; $F = .85$; do not reject the null hypothesis. Effect size, $R^2 = .01$.

5. (a), (b), and (c). Hypothesis-testing steps and explanation similar to 3 above (except for part c you need to include material similar to the explanations from earlier chapters' practice problems). *F* needed ($df = 3, 28$; $p < .01$) = 4.57; $S^2_{Between} = (155)(8) = 1240$; $S^2_{Within} = (3.5^2 + 4.6^2 + 3.8^2 + 3.8^2 + 4.9^2)/4 = 17.97$; $F = 69.0$; reject the null hypothesis. Effect size, $R^2 = .88$.

6. From Table 10–8: (a) .09; (b) .12; (c) .10; (d) .38.

7. From Table 10–9: (a) 322; (b) 21; (c) 274; (d) 52.

8. (i) (a) and (b)

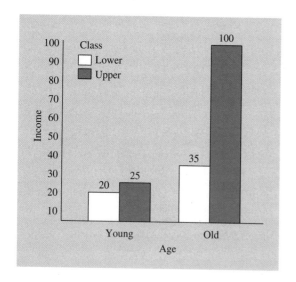

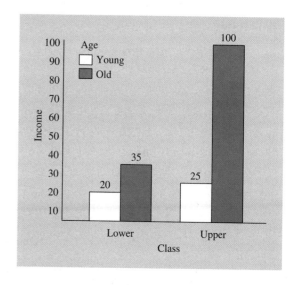

(c) Main effects for class and age, interaction effect; (d) income is greater in general for upper-class and for older individuals, but the combination of older and upper class has a higher income than would be expected just from the effects of either variable alone.

(ii) (a) and (b) Graphs of the same kind as in (i) (a) and (b) above; (c) no main effects, interaction effect; (d) neither type of college nor type of major, by itself, predicts grades, but there is a clear pattern if one considers the combinations: Grades are highest for community college arts majors and for liberal arts college science majors.

(iii) (a) and (b) Graphs of the same kind as in (i) (a) and (b) above; (c) both main effects significant; no interaction; (d) females miss fewer days per month than males; those who exercise miss fewer days per month than controls. Each combination misses the number of days you would expect knowing their level of each variable separately.

9. (i) (a) and (b) Graphs of the same kind as in 8 (i) (a) and (b) above; (c) main effect for relationship and an interaction; (d) conversations are longer with friends; but the difference is much greater for personal than for nonpersonal topics.

(ii) (a) and (b) Graphs of the same kind as in 8 (i) (a) and (b) above; (c) main effect for city and cost, plus an interaction; (d) restaurant quality is different in different cities, with New York highest and Chicago lowest. Restaurant quality is different in different price ranges, with expensive the best and inexpensive the least. The two factors do not simply combine, however, as price makes more difference in New York than in other cities.

(iii) (a) and (b) Graphs of the same kind as in 8 (i) (a) and (b) above; (c) main effects for brand and type and an interaction; (d) flavor is rated on the average more positively for regular than decaf and brands Z and X are rated more favorably than Y. However, there is an interaction in which there is no difference between regular and decaf for brand Z, but for brands Z and Y, regular is rated 2 points higher.

10. Similar to 3c (and also including material from Chapter 9) but focusing on this study's results.
11. Similar to 3c (and also including material from previous chapters) but focusing on this study's results.

Chapter 11

1. (a) χ^2 needed ($df = 5 - 1 = 4$, .05 level) $= 9.488$.

Category	O	Expected	O − E	(O − E)²	(O − E)²/E
A	19	(.2)(50) = 10	9	81	8.10
B	11	(.2)(50) = 10	1	1	.10
C	10	(.4)(50) = 20	−10	100	5.00
D	5	(.1)(50) = 5	0	0	0.00
E	5	(.1)(50) = 5	0	0	0.00
Total	50		50	0	χ^2 = 13.20

Conclusion: Reject the null hypothesis

(b) χ^2 needed $= 5.992$; $\chi^2 = 44.45$, reject the null hypothesis; (c) χ^2 needed $= 7.815$; $\chi^2 = 1.23$, do not reject the null hypothesis.

2. (a)

❶ **Restate the question as a research hypothesis and a null hypothesis about the populations.** There are two populations of interest:

Population 1: Clients like those of this social service agency.
Population 2: Clients for whom season makes no difference in when they use the social service agency.

The research hypothesis is that the distribution over seasons of when clients use the social service agency is different between the two populations. The null hypothesis is that the distributions over seasons of when clients use the social service agency is not different between the two populations.
❷ **Determine the characteristics of the comparison distribution.** Chi-square distribution with 3 degrees of freedom ($df = N_{\text{Categories}} - 1 = 4 - 1 = 3$).
❸ **Determine the cutoff sample score on the comparison distribution at which the null hypothesis should be rejected.** .05 level, $df = 3$: χ^2 needed $= 7.815$.
❹ **Determine your sample's score on the comparison distribution.**

Season	O	Expected	O − E	(O − E)²	$\frac{(O - E)^2}{E}$
Winter	28	(1/4)(128) = 32	−4	16	.50
Spring	33	(1/4)(128) = 32	1	1	.03
Summer	16	(1/4)(128) = 32	−16	256	8.00
Fall	51	(1/4)(128) = 32	19	361	11.28
Total	128		0		χ^2 = 19.81

❺ **Decide whether to reject the null hypothesis.** 19.81 is larger than 7.815; reject the null hypothesis; the research hypothesis is supported.
(b) In this study, the hypothesis testing involves a single nominal variable (that is, a variable with values that are categories). The appropriate statistical test in this situation is a chi-square test for goodness of fit. In this example, this will test whether the number of clients visiting the social service agency is equal across each of the four seasons of the year. The research hypothesis here is that the distribution over seasons of when clients use the social service agency is different for the two populations. (Population 1 is clients like those of this social service agency and Population 2 is clients for whom season makes no difference in when they use the social service agency.) The null hypothesis is that the distributions over seasons of when clients use the social service agency is not different between the two populations. If the season makes no difference, you would expect about 25% of clients to use the social service agency each season. (Last year there were 128 clients, so if season made no difference, we would expect 25% of 128, or 32 to use it each season.) Last year's actual numbers in each season (28, 33, 16, and 51) were clearly different from these expectations of 32 each season. But were they so different from these expectations that you should conclude that, in general, the numbers of new clients are not equally distributed over the seasons? The chi-square statistic reflects the discrepancy between observed (the actual numbers seen in the study) and the expected numbers. These numbers are called frequencies because they refer to how often or how frequently something happens (for example, an observed frequency of 28 clients last winter). For each category (such as the four seasons), you figure that observed minus expected discrepancy, square it, and divide by the expected frequency; then you add up the results. Chi-square uses squared discrepancies so that the result is not affected by the directions of the differences. You divide by the expected number to reduce the impact of the raw number of cases on the result. Applying this method to the present example, for the winter, 28 less than 32 is −4; −4 squared is 16; 16 divided by 32 is .50. Doing the same for the other three seasons, and then adding up the four, gives a total chi-square of 19.81.

Statisticians have determined mathematically what would happen if you took an infinite number of samples from a population with a fixed proportion of cases in each category and figured chi-square for each sample. This distribution depends only on how many categories are free to take on different expected values. (The total number expected is the total number of cases; thus, if you know the expected for any three categories, you can just subtract to get the number expected for the fourth.) A table of the chi-square distribution when three categories are free to vary shows that if the null hypothesis were true, there would be only a 5% chance of getting a chi-square of 7.815 or greater. Because our chi-square is larger than this, the observed result differs from the expected more than you would reasonably expect by chance. Thus, the number of new clients, in the long run, is probably not equal over the four seasons.

3. For (a), (b), and (c): $df = (N_{\text{Columns}} - 1)(N_{\text{Rows}} - 1) = (2 - 1)(2 - 1) = 1$; χ^2 needed $= 6.635$.
(a)

10 (13)	16 (13)	26 (50%)
16 (13)	10 (13)	26 (50%)
26	26	52

$\chi^2 = (10 - 13)^2/13 + (16 - 13)^2/13 + (16 - 13)^2/13 + (10 - 13)^2/13 = 2.77$. Do not reject the null hypothesis. Effect size, $\phi = \sqrt{\chi^2/N} = \sqrt{2.77/52} = \sqrt{.053} = .23$.

(b) $\chi^2 = .36$, do not reject the null hypothesis; Effect size, $\phi = .03$. (c) $\chi^2 = 27.68$, reject the null hypothesis. Effect size, $\phi = .23$.

For (d), (e), and (f): $df = (N_{\text{Columns}} - 1)(N_{\text{Rows}} - 1) = (3 - 1)(2 - 1) = 2$; χ^2 needed $= 9.211$.

(d) $\chi^2 = 2.76$, do not reject the null hypothesis; Effect size, Cramer's $\phi = \sqrt{\chi^2/[(N)(df_{\text{Smaller}})]} = \sqrt{2.76/[(72)(1)]} = \sqrt{.0383} = .20$. (e) $\chi^2 = 2.76$, do not reject the null hypothesis; Effect size, Cramer's $\phi = .18$. (f) $\chi^2 = 3.71$, do not reject the null hypothesis. Effect size, Cramer's $\phi = .22$.

4. (a)

❶ **Restate the question as a research hypothesis and a null hypothesis about the populations.** There are two populations of interest:

Population 1: People like those surveyed.
Population 2: People for whom the community they live in is independent of their opinion on the upcoming ballot initiative.

The research hypothesis is that the two populations are different (the community people live in is not independent of their opinions on the upcoming ballot initiative.) The null hypothesis is that the two populations are the same (the community people live in is independent of their opinions on the upcoming ballot imitative).

❷ **Determine the characteristics of the comparison distribution.** Chi-square distribution with four degrees of freedom. $df = (N_{\text{Columns}} - 1)(N_{\text{Rows}} - 1) = (3 - 1)(3 - 1) = 4$.

❸ **Determine the cutoff sample score on the comparison distribution at which the null hypothesis should be rejected.** .05 level, $df = 4$: χ^2 needed $= 9.488$.

❹ **Determine your sample's score on the comparison distribution.**

	Community			
	A	**B**	**C**	**Total**
For	12 (9.8)	6 (4.2)	3 (7)	21 (23.33%)
Against	18 (16.8)	3 (7.2)	15 (12)	36 (40.00%)
No opinion	12 (15.4)	9 (6.6)	12 (11)	33 (36.67%)
Total	42	18	30	90

$\chi^2 = (12 - 9.8)^2/9.8 + (6 - 4.2)^2/4.2 + (3 - 7)^2/7 + (18 - 16.8)^2/16.8 + (3 - 7.2)^2/7.2 + (15 - 12)^2/12 + (12 - 15.4)^2/15.4 + (9 - 6.6)^2/6.6 + (12 - 11)^2/11 = .49 + .77 + 2.29 + .09 + 2.45 + .75 + .75 + .87 + .09 = 8.55$.

❺ **Decide whether to reject the null hypothesis.** χ^2 in Step ❹ (8.55) is less extreme than Step ❸ cutoff (9.488). Therefore, do not reject the null hypothesis; the study is inconclusive.

(b) Cramer's $\phi = \sqrt{[8.55/(90)(2)]} = \sqrt{[8.55/180]} = \sqrt{.05} = .22$. From Table 11–8, approximate power for a medium effect size and total $N = 100$ (the closest to the $N = 90$ in the study) is .66.

(c) In this study, we are testing a hypothesis with two nominal variables (that is, variables with values that are categories). The appropriate statistical test in this situation is a chi-square test for independence. This test will examine whether the community that people live in is related to their opinions on the upcoming ballot inititative. The research hypothesis in this situation is that the community people live in is not independent of their opinions about the ballot initiaive. The null hypothesis is that the community people live in is independent of their opinions about the ballet initiative. In this example, 23.33% of all survey respondents were for the ballot initiative. Thus, if community is not related to opinion, 23.33% of the people in each community should be for the initiative. For example, you'd expect 9.8 of the 42 people surveyed in Community C to be for the initiative. Are the survey results so discrepant from these expectations that we should conclude that the community people live in is related to their opinion on the upcoming ballot initiative?

Chi-square is a measure of the degree of difference between observed and expected results. For each combination of the 3 × 3 arrangement, you figure that discrepancy between observed and expected, square it, and divide by the expected number; then you add up the results. In the For–Community A combination, 12 minus 9.8 is 2.2, squared is 4.84, divided by 9.8 is .49 (rounded off). Doing the same for the other eight combinations and adding them all up gives 8.55.

Chi-square uses squared discrepancies so that the result is not affected by the directions of the differences. It is divided by the expected number to adjust for the relatively different numbers expected in the combinations.

Statisticians have determined mathematically what would happen if you took an infinite number of samples from a population with a fixed proportion of people in each of several groupings and figured the chi-square for each such sample. The distribution of such chi-squares depends only on the number of groupings free to take on different expected values. We always presume you know the row and column totals. Thus, for each community, if you know the numbers For and Against, you can figure out how many have no opinion. Furthermore, you need to know only two of the communities—say A and B—for any particular opinion, and you can figure out the third by subtracting these from the total of that row. So only four combinations—say For and Against for Communities A and B—are "free to vary."

A table of the chi-square distribution when four groupings are free to vary shows that there is only a 5% chance of getting a chi-square of 9.488 or greater if the null hypothesis is true. Because our chi-square is smaller than this, the observed numbers in each category differ from the expected numbers less than they would need to before we would be willing to reject the null hypothesis that that a person's opinion is unrelated to his or her community. The survey is inconclusive.

We can, however, estimate the actual degree of linkage in this group surveyed between community and opinion. The procedure is called "Cramer's phi," figured by dividing your chi-square by the number of people included in the analysis times the sample side at the table less one, then taking the square root of the results. In this example, this comes out to .22.

This statistic ranges from 0 (no relationship) to 1 (a perfect relationship—knowing a person's status on one of the dimensions, such as what community they are from, would let you perfectly predict their status on the other dimension, such as their opinion). Thus, .22 is a fairly low figure, although given the amount of other things that affect any relationship, by the standards of social and behavorial science research, a Cramer's phi of .22 would be considered a medium-sized relation. (To be exact, a Cramer's phi of .21 is the number given for a medium effect size.)

Looking at this another way, we can ask, if there really is a moderate relationship between opinion and community in the population, what is the chance that this whole process would have led to a positive conclusion? Statisticians have provided tables that give this probability. In this situation, it turns out that there would be about a 66% chance. If there were truly a large effect in the population (which would be a Cramer's phi of about .35), there is a 99% chance we would have come to a positive conclusion. Thus, given the result of this study, if any relationship exists, it is almost surely not a large one.

5. (a) $\phi = \sqrt{\chi^2/N} = \sqrt{16/100} = .40$;

(b) Cramer's $\phi = \sqrt{\chi^2/[(N)(df_{Smaller})]} = \sqrt{16/[(100)(1)]} = .40$;

(c) Cramer's $\phi = .28$;

(d) $\phi = .28$;

(e) $\phi = .28$.

6. From Table 11–8: (a) .08; (b) .32; (c) .11; (d) .07; (e) .06; (f) .06.

7. From Table 11–9: (a) 87; (b) 26; (c) 133; (d) 133; (e) 39.

8. (a) You should get the same results within rounding error. (b) $\phi = \sqrt{\chi^2/N} = \sqrt{5.55/69} = .28$; (c) Similar to 4c but focusing on this study's results.

9. (a) 4, 2, 3, 5, 6; (b) 5.92; 3.78, 3.61, 3.59, 4.24.

10. (a) t needed $(df = 8, p < .05, \text{two-tailed}) = -2.306$, 2.306; Group A: $M = 3.8$, $S^2 = 5.06$; Group B: $M = 5.7$, $S^2 = 6.76$; $S^2_{Pooled} = 5.91$; $S_{Difference} = 1.54$; $t = -1.23$; do not reject the null hypothesis. (b) Group A: 1.1, 1.6, 2.1, 1.9, 2.7; Group B: 1.4, 3.0, 2.4, 2.6, 2.2. (c) t needed $= -2.306$, 2.306; Group A: $M = 1.88$, $S^2 = .35$; Group B: $M = 2.32$, $S^2 = .35$; $S^2_{Pooled} = .35$; $S_{Difference} = .37$; $t = -1.19$; do not reject the null hypothesis. (d) It would not have been correct to carry out a t test on the numbers as they were (without transforming them). This is because the distributions of the

samples were very skewed for both language groups. Thus, it seemed likely that the population distributions were also seriously skewed. That would clearly violate the assumption for a t test that the underlying population distributions are normal. Thus, I took the square root of each score. This had the advantage of making the sample distributions much closer to normal. This suggests that the population distributions of square roots of family sizes are probably nearly normally distributed. I realize that taking the square root of each family size distorts its straightforward meaning. However, the impact for the individuals in the family of each additional child is probably not equal. That is, going from no children to 1 child has a huge impact. Going from 1 to 2 has less, and going from 7 to 8 probably makes much less difference for the family.

In any case, having taken the square root of each score, I then carried out an ordinary t test for independent means using these square-root transformed scores. As with the original t test, the result was inconclusive (the null hypothesis could not be rejected)—but at least I could be confident that I had done the analysis correctly.

11. (a) F needed $(df = 2, 6; p < .01) = 10.93$; Sad: $M = 446$, $S^2 = 47,089$; Angry: $M = 259$, $S^2 = 11,727$; Exuberant: $M = 918.67$, $S^2 = 7,184$; $S^2_{Between} = 346,775.22$; $S^2_{Within} = 22,000$; $F = 15.76$; reject the null hypothesis. (b) 14.2, 22.9, 24.8; 11.7, 18.4, 17.3; 28.9, 30.2, 31.7. (c) $M = 20.63$, $S^2 = 31.94$; $M = 15.8$, $S^2 = 12.91$; $M = 30.27$, $S^2 = 1.96$; $M = 30.27$, $S^2 = 1.96$; $S^2_{Between} = 162.82$; $S^2_{Within} = 15.60$; $F = 10.44$; do not reject the null hypothesis. (d) Similar to 10d above, except note that the square root transformation does *not* solve the problem of skew and that it also creates distributions very likely to violate the assumption of equal population variances.

12. Miller wanted to examine the relationships among the variables he was studying, probably including various parametric hypothesis-testing techniques such as the t test or an analysis of variance. Such procedures are based on the assumption that the distributions of the variables in the population follow a normal curve. However, Miller first checked the distributions of the variables he was studying and found that the scores on two key measures were skewed, suggesting that the population distributions for these variables probably violated the normal distribution assumption. (The rest of your answer should be similar to 10d above.)

Glossary

Numbers in parentheses refer to chapters in which the term is introduced or substantially discussed.

Alpha (α).   Probability of a Type I error; same as *significance level*. (7)

Analysis of variance (ANOVA).   Hypothesis-testing procedure for studies with three or more groups. (10)

Assumption.   A condition, such as a population's having a normal distribution, required for carrying out a particular hypothesis-testing procedure; a part of the mathematical foundation for the accuracy of the tables used in determining cutoff values. (8–11)

Beta β.   Same as *standardized regression coefficient*. (3)

Between-groups degrees of freedom ($df_{Between}$).   Degrees of freedom used in the between-groups estimate of the population variance in an analysis of variance (the numerator of the F ratio); number of scores free to vary (number of means minus 1) in figuring the between-groups estimate of the population variance; same as *numerator degrees of freedom*. (10)

Between-groups estimate of the population variance ($S^2_{Between}$).   In an analysis of variance, estimate of the variance of the population of individuals based on the variation among the means of the groups studied. (10)

Between-subjects design.   Research strategy in which each person is tested only once and groups of individuals are compared as, for example, in a *t* test for independent means. (12)

Biased estimate.   Estimate of a population parameter that is likely systematically to overestimate or underestimate the true value of the population parameter. For example, SD^2 would be a biased estimate of the population variance (it would systematically underestimate it). (8)

Bimodal distribution.   Frequency distribution with two approximately equal frequencies, each clearly larger than any of the others. (1)

Categorical variable.   Same as *nominal variable*. (1, 11)

Ceiling effect.   Situation in which many scores pile up at the high end of a distribution (creating skewness) because it is not possible to have a higher score. (1, 11)

Cell.   In a factorial research design, a particular combination of levels of the variables that divide the groups. (10) In chi-square, the particular combination of categories for two variables in a contingency table. (11)

Cell mean.   Mean of a particular combination of levels of the variables that divide the groups in a factorial design in analysis of variance. (10)

Central limit theorem.   Mathematical principle that the distribution of the sums (or means) of scores taken at random from any distribution of individuals will tend to form a normal curve. (4, 6)

Central tendency.   Typical or most representative value of a group of scores, such as the mean, median, or mode. (2)

Change score.   After score minus before score. A kind of *difference score*. (8)

Chi-square distribution.   Mathematically defined curve used as the comparison distribution in chi-square tests; the distribution of the chi-square statistic. (11)

Chi-square statistic (χ^2).   Statistic that reflects the overall lack of fit between the expected and observed frequencies; the sum, over all the categories or cells, of the squared difference between observed and expected frequencies divided by the expected frequency. (11)

Chi-square table.   Table of cutoff scores on the chi-square distribution for various degrees of freedom and significance levels. (11)

Chi-square test.   Hypothesis-testing procedure that uses the chi-square distribution as the comparison distribution. (11)

Chi-square test for goodness of fit.   Hypothesis-testing procedure that examines how well an observed frequency distribution of a single nominal variable fits some expected pattern of frequencies. (11)

Chi-square test for independence.   Hypothesis-testing procedure that examines whether the distribution of frequencies over the categories of one nominal variable are unrelated to (independent of) the distribution of frequencies over the categories of a second nominal variable. (11)

Comparison distribution.   Distribution used in hypothesis testing. It represents the population situation if the null hypothesis is true. It is the distribution to which you compare the score based on your sample's results. It is made up of the same kinds of numbers as those of the sample's results (such as a sample mean, a difference between sample means, F ratios, or chi-squares). (5)

Computational formula.   Equation mathematically equivalent to the definitional formula. It is easier to use when figuring by hand, but does not directly show the meaning of the procedure. (2)

Confidence interval.   Roughly speaking, the region of scores (that is, the scores between an upper and lower value) that is likely to include the true population mean; more precisely, the range of possible population means from which it is not highly unlikely that you could have obtained your sample mean. (6)

Confidence limit.   Upper or lower value of a confidence interval. (6)

Contingency table.   Two-dimensional chart showing frequencies in each combination of categories of two nominal variables, as in a chi-square test for independence. (11)

Conventional levels of significance ($p < .05, p < .01$).   The levels of significance widely used in the behavioral and social sciences. (5, 7)

Correlation.   Association between scores on two equal-interval numeric variables. (3)

Correlation coefficient (r).   Measure of the degree of linear correlation between two variables, ranging from -1 (a perfect negative linear correlation) through 0 (no correlation) to $+1$ (a perfect positive linear correlation); average of the cross-products of Z scores of two variables; square root of the proportion of variance accounted for. (3)

Correlation matrix.   Common way of reporting the correlation coefficients among several variables in a research article; table in which the variables are named on the top and along the side and the correlations among them are all shown (only half of the resulting square, above or below the diagonal, is usually filled in, the other half being redundant). (3)

Cramer's phi.   Measure of association between two nominal variables; effect-size measure for a chi-square test for independence used with a contingency table that is larger than 2×2; square root of result of dividing the chi-square statistic by the product of the number of participants multiplied by the degrees of freedom of the smaller side of the contingency table; also known as *Cramer's V* and sometimes written as ϕ_c or V_c. (11)

Criterion variable (usually Y).   In prediction (regression), a variable that is predicted; sometimes called *dependent variable*. (3)

Cross-product of Z scores.   The result of multiplying a person's Z score on one variable by the person's Z score on another variable; for a group of individuals, the average of the cross-products of Z scores between two variables is the correlation coefficient for those two variables. (3)

Curvilinear correlation.   Relationship between two variables that shows up on a scatter diagram as dots following a systematic pattern that is not a straight line; any association between two variables other than a linear correlation. (3)

Cutoff sample score.   In hypothesis testing, the point on the comparison distribution at which, if reached or exceeded by the sample score, you reject the null hypothesis; sometimes called *critical value*. (5)

Data transformation.   Mathematical procedure (such as taking the square root) applied to each score in a sample, usually done to make the sample distribution closer to normal. (11)

Decision error.   Incorrect conclusion in hypothesis testing in relation to the real (but unknown) situation, such as deciding the null hypothesis is false when it is really true. (5)

Definitional formula.   Equation for a statistical procedure directly showing the meaning of the procedure. (2)

Degrees of freedom (df).   Number of scores free to vary when estimating a population parameter; usually part of a formula for making that estimate—for example, in the formula for estimating the population variance from a single sample, the degrees of freedom is the number of scores minus 1. (8–11)

Denominator degrees of freedom (df_{Within}).   Same as *within-groups degrees of freedom*. (10)

Dependent variable.   Variable considered to be an effect; usually a measured variable. (10)

Descriptive statistics.   Procedures for summarizing a group of scores or otherwise making them more comprehensible. (1)

Deviation score.   Score minus the mean. (2)

Difference score.   Difference between a person's score on one testing and the same person's score on another testing; often an after score minus a before score, in which case it is also called a *change score*. (8)

Dimension.   In a factorial design, one of the grouping variables that is crossed with another grouping variable; in a contingency table, one of the nominal variables. (10, 11)

Direction of causality.   Path of causal effect; if X is thought to cause Y, then the direction of causality is from X to Y. (3)

Directional hypothesis.   Research hypothesis predicting a particular direction of difference between populations—for example, a prediction that one population has a higher mean than the other. (5)

Distribution-free test.   Hypothesis-testing procedure making no assumptions about the shape of the populations; approximately the same as a *nonparametric test*. (11)

Distribution of differences between means.   Distribution of differences between means of pairs of samples such that for each pair of means, one is from one population and the other is from a second population; the comparison distribution in a t test for independent means. (9)

Distribution of means.   Distribution of means of samples of a given size from a particular population (also called a sampling distribution of the mean); comparison distribution when testing hypotheses involving a single sample of more than one individual. (6–10)

Effect size.   In studies involving means of one or two groups, measure of difference (lack of overlap) between populations; the usual standardized effect size measure used in the behavioral and social sciences increases with greater differences between means and decreases with greater standard deviations in the populations, but it is not affected by sample size. There are also conventional effect size measures for other kinds of studies (correlations, analysis of variance and chi-square test situations); these describe the standardized degree of association in the population. (7)

Effect size conventions. Standard rules about what to consider a small, medium, and large effect size, based on what is typical in behavioral and social science research; also known as Cohen's conventions. (7)

Equal-interval variable. A variable in which the numbers stand for about equal amounts of what is being measured. (1)

Expected frequency (*E*). In a chi-square test, number of people in a category or cell expected if the null hypothesis were true. (11)

Expected relative frequency. In figuring probabilities, number of successful outcomes divided by the number of total outcomes you would expect to get if you repeated an experiment a large number of times. (4)

***F* distribution.** Mathematically defined curve that is the comparison distribution used in an analysis of variance; distribution of *F* ratios when the null hypothesis is true. (10)

***F* ratio.** In analysis of variance, ratio of the between-groups population variance estimate to the within-groups population variance estimate; score on the comparison distribution (an *F* distribution) in an analysis of variance; also referred to simply as *F*. (10)

***F* table.** Table of cutoff scores on the *F* distribution for various degrees of freedom and significance levels. (10)

Factorial analysis of variance. Analysis of variance for a factorial research design. (10)

Factorial research design. Way of organizing a study in which the influence of two or more variables is studied at once by setting up the situation so that a different group of people are tested for each combination of the levels of the variables; for example, in a 2×2 factorial research design there would be four groups, those high on variable 1 and high on variable 2, those high on variable 1 but low on variable 2, those high on variable 2 but low on variable 1, and those low on variable 1 and low on variable 2. (10)

Floor effect. Situation in which many scores pile up at the low end of a distribution (creating skewness) because it is not possible to have any lower score. (1)

Frequency distribution. Pattern of frequencies over the various values; what a frequency table, histogram, or frequency polygon describes. (1)

Frequency polygon. Line graph of a distribution in which the values are plotted along the horizontal axis and the height of each point is the frequency of that value; the line begins and ends at the horizontal axis, and the graph resembles a mountainous skyline. (1)

Frequency table. Listing of the number of individuals having each of the different values for a particular variable. (1)

Grand mean (*GM*). In analysis of variance, overall mean of all the scores, regardless of what group they are in; when group sizes are equal, mean of the group means. (10)

Grouped frequency table. Frequency table in which the number of individuals (frequency) is given for each interval of values. (1)

Grouping variable. A variable that separates groups in analysis of variance (and *t* tests); also see *independent variable*. (10)

Haphazard selection. Procedure of selecting a sample of individuals to study by taking whoever is available or happens to be first on a list; should not be confused with true random selection. (4)

Harmonic mean. Special average influenced more by smaller numbers; in a *t* test for independent means when the number of scores in the two groups differ, the harmonic mean is used as the equivalent of each group's sample size when determining power. (9)

Heavy-tailed distribution. Distribution that differs from a normal curve by being too spread out so that a histogram of the distribution would have too many scores at each of the two extremes ("tails"). (1)

Histogram. Barlike graph of a frequency distribution in which the values are plotted along the horizontal axis and the height of each bar is the frequency of that value; the bars are usually placed next to each other without spaces, giving the appearance of a city skyline. (1)

Hypothesis. A prediction about the results of a research study. (5)

Hypothesis testing. Procedure for deciding whether the outcome of a study (results for a sample) support a particular theory or practical innovation (which is thought to apply to a population). (5)

Independence. Situation of no relationship between two variables; term usually used regarding two nominal variables in the chi-square test for independence. (11)

Independent variable. Variable considered to be a cause, such as what group a person is in in a *t* test or analysis of variance; also see *grouping variable*. (10)

Inferential statistics. Procedures for drawing conclusions based on the scores collected in a research study (sample scores) but going beyond them (to conclusions about a population). (1, 4)

Interaction effect. Situation in a factorial analysis of variance in which the combination of variables has an effect that could not be predicted from the effects of the two variables individually; the effect of one grouping variable depends on the level of the other grouping variable. (10)

Interval. In a grouped frequency table, the range of values that are grouped together. (For example, if the interval size was 10, one of the intervals might be from 10 to 19.) (1)

Interval estimate. Region of scores (that is, the scores between some specified lower and upper value) estimated to include a population parameter such as the population mean; this is in contrast to a *point estimate; a confidence interval* is an example of an interval estimate. (6)

Interval size. In a grouped frequency table, difference between the start of one interval and the start of the next. (1)

Inverse transformation. Data transformation using the inverse (1 divided by the number) of each score. (11)

Level of significance. Same as *significance level*. (5, 7)

Level of measurement. Type of underlying numerical information provided by a measure, such as equal-interval, rank-order, and nominal (categorical). (1, 11, 12)

Light-tailed distribution. Distribution that differs from a normal curve by being too peaked or pinched so that a histogram of the distribution would have too few scores at each of the two extremes ("tails"). (1)

Linear correlation.   Relationship between two variables that shows up on a scatter diagram as the dots roughly following a straight line; a correlation coefficient (r) unequal to 0. (3)

Log transformation.   Data transformation using the logarithm of each score. (11)

Longitudinal study.   A study where people are measured at two or more points in time. (3)

Long-run relative-frequency interpretation of probability. Understanding of probability as the proportion of a particular outcome that you would get if the experiment were repeated many times. (4)

Main effect.   Difference between groups on one grouping variable in a factorial analysis of variance; result for a variable that divides the groups, averaging across the levels of the other variable that divides the groups (sometimes used only for significant differences). (10)

Marginal mean.   In a factorial analysis of variance, mean score for all the participants at a particular level of one of the grouping variables; often shortened to *marginal*. (10)

Mean (M).   Arithmetic average of a group of scores; sum of the scores divided by the number of scores. (2)

Mean of a distribution of means (Population M_M).   The mean of a distribution of means of samples of a given size from a particular population; the same as the mean of the population of individuals. (6)

Median.   Middle score when all the scores in a distribution are arranged from highest to lowest. (2)

Meta-analysis.   Statistical method for combining effect sizes from different studies. (7)

Mode.   Value with the greatest frequency in a distribution. (2)

Multimodal distribution.   Frequency distribution with two or more high frequencies separated by a lower frequency; a bimodal distribution is the special case of two high frequencies. (1)

Multiple correlation.   Correlation of a criterion variable with two or more predictor variables. (3)

Multiple correlation coefficient (R).   Measure of degree of multiple correlation; positive square root of the proportion of variance accounted for in a multiple regression analysis. (3)

Multiple regression.   Procedure for predicting scores on a criterion variable from scores on two or more predictor variables. (3)

Multivariate statistical test.   Statistical procedure involving more than one criterion or outcome variable. (12)

Negative correlation.   Relation between two variables in which high scores on one go with low scores on the other, mediums with mediums, and lows with highs; on a scatter diagram, the dots roughly follow a straight line sloping down and to the right; a correlation coefficient (r) less than 0. (3)

95% confidence interval.   Confidence interval in which, roughly speaking, there is a 95% chance that the population mean falls within this interval. (6)

99% confidence interval.   Confidence interval in which, roughly speaking, there is a 99% chance that the population mean falls within this interval. (6)

No correlation.   No systematic relationship between two variables; also used for correlation coefficient (r) equal to 0. (3)

Nominal variable.   Variable with values that are categories (that is, they are names rather than numbers); same as *categorical variable*. (1, 11)

Nondirectional hypothesis.   Research hypothesis that does not predict a particular direction of difference between populations. (5)

Nonparametric test.   Hypothesis-testing procedure making no assumptions about population parameters; approximately the same as *distribution-free test*. (11)

Normal curve.   Specific, mathematically defined, bell-shaped frequency distribution that is symmetrical and unimodal; distributions observed in nature and in research commonly approximate it. (1, 4)

Normal curve table.   Table showing percentages of scores associated with the normal curve; the table usually includes percentages of scores between the mean and various numbers of standard deviations above the mean and percentages of scores more positive than various numbers of standard deviations above the mean. (4)

Normal distribution.   Frequency distribution following a normal curve. (4)

Null hypothesis.   Statement about a relation between populations that is the opposite of the research hypothesis; a statement that in the population there is no difference (or a difference opposite to that predicted) between populations; a contrived statement set up to examine whether it can be rejected as part of hypothesis testing. (5)

Numerator degrees of freedom ($df_{Between}$).   Same as *between-groups degrees of freedom*. (10)

Numeric variable.   Variable whose values are numbers (as opposed to a nominal variable). (1)

Observed frequency (O).   In a chi-square test, number of individuals actually found in the study to be in a category or cell. (11)

One-tailed test.   Hypothesis-testing procedure for a directional hypothesis; situation in which the region of the comparison distribution in which the null hypothesis would be rejected is all on one side ("tail") of the distribution. (5)

One-way analysis of variance.   Analysis of variance in which there is only one grouping variable (as distinguished from a factorial analysis of variance, such as a two-way or three-way analysis of variance). (10)

Ordinal variable.   Same as *rank-order variable*. (1, 11)

Outcome.   Term used in discussing probability for the result of an experiment (or almost any event, such as a coin coming up heads or raining tomorrow). (4)

Outlier.   Score with an extreme value (very high or very low) in relation to the other scores in the distribution. (2, 11)

Parametric test.   Ordinary hypothesis-testing procedure, such as a *t* test or an analysis of variance, that requires assumptions about the shape or other parameters (such as the variance) of the populations. (11)

Perfect correlation. Relationship between two variables that shows up on a scatter diagram as the dots exactly following a straight line; correlation of $r = 1$ or $r = -1$; situation in which each person's Z score on one variable is exactly the same as that person's Z score on the other variable. (3)

Phi coefficient (ϕ). Measure of association between two dichotomous nominal variables; square root of division of chi-square statistic by N; equivalent to correlation of the two variables if they were each given numerical values (for example, of 1 and 0 for the two categories); effect-size measure for a chi-square test for independence with a 2×2 contingency table. (11)

Point estimate. Estimate from a sample of the most likely single value of a population parameter (such as the population mean). (6)

Pooled estimate of the population variance (S^2_{Pooled}) In a t test for independent means, weighted average of the estimates of the population variance from two samples (each estimate weighted by a proportion consisting of its sample's degrees of freedom divided by the total degrees of freedom for both samples). (9)

Population. Entire group of people to which a researcher intends the results of a study to apply; the larger group to which inferences are made on the basis of the particular set of people (sample) studied. (4)

Population mean. Mean of the population (usually not known). (4)

Population parameter. Actual value of the mean, standard deviation, and so on, for the population (usually population parameters are not known, though often they are estimated based on information in samples). (4)

Population standard deviation. Standard deviation of the population (usually not known). (4)

Population variance. Variance of the population (usually not known). (4)

Positive correlation. Relation between two variables in which high scores on one go with high scores on the other, mediums with mediums, and lows with lows; on a scatter diagram, the dots roughly follow a straight line sloping up and to the right; a correlation coefficient (r) greater than 0. (3)

Power. Same as *statistical power.* (7)

Power table. Table for a hypothesis-testing procedure showing the statistical power of a study for various effect sizes and sample sizes. (7–11)

Prediction model. Formula for making predictions; that is, formula for predicting a person's score on a criterion variable based on the person's score on one or more predictor variables. (3)

Predictor variable (usually X). In prediction (regression), variable that is used to predict scores of individuals on another variable. (3)

Probability (p). Expected relative frequency of a particular outcome; the proportion of successful outcomes to all outcomes. (4)

Proportion of variance accounted for (r^2 or R^2). Measure of association between variables used when comparing associations

found in different studies or with different variables; correlation coefficient squared or multiple correlation coefficient squared; in the context of correlation it represents the proportion of the total variance in one variable that can be explained by the other variable; measure of effect size for analysis of variance. (3, 10)

Protected t tests. In analysis of variance, t tests among pairs of means after finding that the F for the overall difference among the means is significant. (10)

Quantitative variable. Same as *numeric variable.* (1)

Random selection. Method for selecting a sample that uses truly random procedures (usually meaning that each person in the population has an equal chance of being selected); one procedure is for the researcher to begin with a complete list of all the people in the population and select a group of them to study using a table of random numbers; should not be confused with haphazard selection. (4)

Rank-order test. Hypothesis-testing procedure designed to use rank-ordered data. (11)

Rank-order transformation. Changing a set of scores to ranks, so that the highest score is rank 1, the next highest rank 2, and so forth. (11)

Rank-order variable. Numeric variable in which the values are ranks, such as class standing or place finished in a race; also called *ordinal variable.* (1, 11)

Raw score. Ordinary score (or any other number in a distribution before it has been made into a Z score or otherwise transformed). (2)

Rectangular distribution. Frequency distribution in which all values have approximately the same frequency. (1)

Regression coefficient. Number multiplied by a person's score on the predictor variable as part of a prediction model. (3)

Repeated measures analysis of variance. Analysis of variance in which each individual is tested more than once so that the levels of the grouping variable(s) are different times or types of testing for the same people. (10)

Repeated-measures design. Research strategy in which each person is tested more than once; same as *within-subjects design.* (8)

Research hypothesis. In hypothesis testing, statement about the predicted relation between populations (usually a prediction of difference between population means). (5)

Sample. Scores of the particular group of people studied; usually considered to be representative of the scores in some larger population. (4)

Sample statistic. Descriptive statistic, such as the mean or standard deviation, figured from the scores in a particular group of people studied. (4)

Scatter diagram. Graph showing the relationship between two variables: the values of one variable (often the predictor variable) are along the horizontal axis and the values of the other variable (often the criterion variable) are along the vertical axis; each score is shown as a dot in this two-dimensional space; also called *scatterplot* or *scattergram* (3)

Scatterplot. Same as *scatter diagram.* (3)

Score.   Particular person's value on a variable. (1)

Shape of a distribution of means.   Contour of a histogram of a distribution of means, such as whether it follows a normal curve or is skewed; in general, a distribution of means will tend to be unimodal and symmetrical and is often normal. (6)

Significance level.   Probability of getting statistical significance if the null hypothesis is actually true; probability of a Type I error. (5)

Skew.   Extent to which a frequency distribution has more scores on one side of the middle as opposed to being perfectly symmetrical. (1)

Skewed distribution.   Distribution in which the scores pile up on one side of the middle and are spread out on the other side; distribution that is not symmetrical. (1, 11)

Square-root transformation.   Data transformation using the square root of each score. (11)

Squared deviation score.   Square of the difference between a score and the mean. (2)

Standard deviation (*SD*).   Square root of the average of the squared deviations from the mean; the most common descriptive statistic for variation; approximately the average amount that scores in a distribution vary from the mean. (2)

Standard deviation of a distribution of differences between means ($S_{\text{Difference}}$).   In a *t* test for independent means, square root of the variance of the distribution of differences between means. (9)

Standard deviation of a distribution of mean differences (S_M).   In a *t* test for dependent means, square root of the variance of the distribution of mean differences. (8)

Standard deviation of a distribution of means (Population SD_M, S_M).   Square root of the variance of the distribution of means; same as *standard error (SE)*. (6)

Standard error (*SE*).   Same as *standard deviation of a distribution of means;* also called *standard error of the mean.* (6)

Standard score.   *Z* score in a distribution that follows a normal curve; sometimes refers to any *Z* score. (3)

Standardized regression coefficient (beta, β).   Regression coefficient in a prediction model using *Z* scores. (3)

Statistical power.   Probability that the study will give a significant result if the research hypothesis is true. (7)

Statistically significant.   Conclusion that the results of a study would be unlikely if in fact there were no difference in the populations the samples represent; an outcome of hypothesis testing in which the null hypothesis is rejected. (3, 5)

Statistics.   A branch of mathematics that focuses on the organization, analysis, and interpretation of a group of numbers. (1)

Sum of squared deviations.   Total, over all the scores, of each score's squared difference from the mean. (2)

Symmetrical distribution.   Distribution in which the pattern of frequencies on the left and right side are mirror images of each other. (1)

***t* distribution.**   Mathematically defined curve that is the comparison distribution used in a *t* test. (8)

***t* score.**   On a *t* distribution, number of standard deviations from the mean (like a *Z* score, but on a *t* distribution). (8)

***t* table.**   Table of cutoff scores on the *t* distribution for various degrees of freedom, significance levels, and one- and two-tailed tests. (8)

***t* test.**   Hypothesis-testing procedure in which the population variance is unknown; it compares *t* scores from a sample to a comparison distribution called a *t* distribution. (8, 9, 11)

***t* test for a single sample.**   Hypothesis-testing procedure in which a sample mean is being compared to a known population mean and the population variance is unknown. (8)

***t* test for dependent means.**   Hypothesis-testing procedure in which there are two scores for each person and the population variance is not known; it determines the significance of a hypothesis that is being tested using difference or change scores from a single group of people; also called paired sample *t* test, *t* test for correlated means, *t* test for matched samples, and *t* test for matched pairs. (8)

***t* test for independent means.**   Hypothesis-testing procedure in which there are two separate groups of people tested and in which the population variance is not known. (9)

Theory.   A set of principles that attempt to explain one or more facts, relationships, or events; behavioral and social scientists often derive specific predictions from theories that are then examined in research studies. (5)

True experiment.   A study in which participants are randomly assigned (say, by flipping a coin) to a particular level of a grouping or predictor variable and then measured on another variable. (3)

Two-tailed test.   Hypothesis-testing procedure for a nondirectional hypothesis; the situation in which the region of the comparison distribution in which the null hypothesis would be rejected is divided between the two sides ("tails") of the distribution. (5)

Two-way analysis of variance.   Analysis of variance for a two-way factorial research design. (10)

Two-way factorial research design.   Factorial design with two variables that each divide the groups. (10)

Type I error.   Rejecting the null hypothesis when in fact it is true; getting a statistically significant result when in fact the research hypothesis is not true. (5)

Type II error.   Failing to reject the null hypothesis when in fact it is false; failing to get a statistically significant result when in fact the research hypothesis is true. (5)

Unbiased estimate of the population variance (S^2).   Estimate of the population variance, based on sample scores, which has been corrected so that it is equally likely to overestimate or underestimate the true population variance; the correction used is dividing the sum of squared deviations by the sample size minus 1, instead of the usual procedure of dividing by the sample size directly. (2, 8)

Unimodal distribution.   Frequency distribution with one value clearly having a larger frequency than any other. (1)

Value.   Number or category that a score can have. (1)

Variable.   Characteristic that can have different values. (1)

Variance (SD^2). Measure of how spread out a set of scores are; average of the squared deviations from the mean; standard deviation squared. (2)

Variance of a distribution of differences between means ($S^2_{Difference}$). One of the numbers figured as part of a t test for independent means; it equals the sum of the variances of the distributions of means for each of the two samples. (9)

Variance of a distribution of means of difference scores (S^2_M). One of the numbers figured as part of a t test for dependent means; it equals the estimated population variance of differences scores divided by the sample size. (8)

Variance of a distribution of means (Population SD^2_M, S^2_M). Variance of the population divided by the number of scores in each sample. (6)

Weighted average. Average in which the scores being averaged do not have equal influence on the total, as in figuring the pooled variance estimate in a t test for independent means. (9)

Within-groups degrees of freedom (df_{Within}). Degrees of freedom used in the within-groups estimate of the population variance in an analysis of variance (the denominator of the F ratio); number of scores free to vary (number of scores in each group minus 1, summed over all the groups) in figuring the within-groups population variance estimate; same as *denominator degrees of freedom*. (10)

Within-groups estimate of the population variance (S^2_{Within}). In analysis of variance, estimate of the variance of the distribution of the population of individuals based on the variation among the scores within each of the actual groups studied. (10)

Within-subject design. Same as *repeated-measures design*. (8)

Z score. Number of standard deviations a score is above (or below, if it is negative) the mean of its distribution; it is thus an ordinary score transformed so that it better describes that score's location in a distribution. (2)

Z test. Hypothesis-testing procedure in which there is a single sample and the population variance is known. (6)

Glossary of Symbols

α Significance level, such as .05 or .01; probability of a Type I error. (5)

β Standardized regression coefficient. (3)

Σ Sum of; add up all the scores following. (2)

ϕ Phi coefficient; effect size in a chi-square test for independence with a 2×2 contingency table. (11)

ϕ_c Cramer's phi, effect size in chi-square test for independence with a contingency table larger than 2×2. (11)

χ^2 Chi-square statistic. (11)

df Degrees of freedom. (8–11).

$df_1, df_2,$ **and so on.**   Degrees of freedom for the first group, second group, and so on. (9, 10)

$df_{Between}$ Between-groups (numerator) degrees of freedom in analysis of variance. (10)

$df_{Smaller}$ Degrees of freedom for the nominal variable (the row or column in the contingency table) with the smaller number of categories in a chi-square test for independence. (11)

df_{Total} Total degrees of freedom over all groups. (9, 10)

df_{Within} Within-groups (denominator) degrees of freedom in analysis of variance. (10)

F **ratio**   In an analysis of variance, ratio of the between-groups population variance estimate to the within-groups population variance estimate. (10)

GM Grand mean; mean of all scores in the analysis of variance. (10)

M Mean. (2)

$M_1, M_2,$ **and so on.**   Mean of the first group, second group, and so on. (9, 10)

n Number of scores within each group in analysis of variance. (10)

N Total number of scores. (2)

$N_1, N_2,$ **and so on.**   Number of scores in the first group, second group, and so on. (9, 10)

$N_{Categories}$ Number of categories in a chi-square test for goodness of fit. (11)

$N_{Columns}$ Number of columns in a contingency table. (11)

N_{Groups} Number of groups in an analysis of variance. (11)

N_{Rows} Number of rows in a contingency table. (11)

p Probability. (4)

r Correlation coefficient. (3)

r^2, R^2 Proportion of variance accounted for. (3, 10)

R Multiple correlation coefficient. (3, 12)

S Unbiased estimate of the population standard deviation. (2, 8)

S^2 Unbiased estimate of the population variance. (2, 8)

$S_1^2, S_2^2,$ **and so on.**   Unbiased estimate of the population variance based on scores in the first sample, second sample, and so on. (9, 10)

$S_{Between}^2$ Between-groups estimate of the population variance. (10)

$S_{Difference}$ Standard deviation of the distribution of differences between means. (9)

$S_{Difference}^2$ Variance of the distribution of differences between means. (9)

SE Standard error (standard deviation of the distribution of means, S_M). (6)

S_M Standard deviation of the distribution of means based on an estimated population variance, same as standard error (SE). (8)

S_M^2 Variance of a distribution of means based on an estimated population variance in a t test or as estimated from the variation among means of groups in the analysis of variance. (8, 10)

$S_{M_1}^2, S_{M_2}^2,$ **and so on.**   Variance of the distribution of means based on a pooled population variance estimate, corresponding to the first sample, second sample, and so on. (9)

S_{Pooled} Pooled estimate of the population standard deviation. (9)

S_{Pooled}^2 Pooled estimate of the population variance. (9)

S_{Within}^2 Within-groups estimate of the population variance. (10)

SD Standard deviation. (2)

SD^2 Variance. (2)

t **score**   Number of standard deviations from the mean on a *t* distribution. (8)

X   Score on a particular variable; in prediction (regression), *X* is usually the predictor variable. (1–3)

$X_1, X_2,$ *and so on.*   First predictor variable, second predictor variable, and so on. (3)

Y   Score on a particular variable; in prediction (regression), *Y* is usually the criterion variable. (3)

Z   Number of standard deviations from the mean. (2)

Z_X Z score for variable X. (3)

Z_Y Z score for variable Y. (3)

References

Altman, D. G., Levine, D. W., Howard, G., & Hamilton, H. (1997). Tobacco farming and public health: Attitudes of the general public and farmers. *Journal of Social Issues, 53,* 113–128.

Anderson, J. E., Carey, J. W., & Taveras, S. (2000). HIV testing among the general U.S. population and persons at increased risk: Information from national surveys, 1987–1996. *American Journal of Public Health, 90,* 1089–1095,

Aron, A., Aron, E. N., & Smollan, D. (1992). Inclusion of Other in the Self Scale and the structure of interpersonal closeness. *Journal of Personality and Social Psychology, 63,* 596–612.

Aron, A., Fisher, H. E., Mashek, D. J., Strong, S., Li, H.-F., & Brown, L. L. (2005). Reward, motivation and emotion systems associated with early-stage intense romantic love. *Journal of Neurophysiology, 94,* 327–337.

Aron, A., Melinat, E., Aron, E. N., Vallone, R., & Bator, R. (1997). The experimental generation of interpersonal closeness: A procedure and some preliminary findings. *Personality and Social Psychology Bulletin, 23,* 363–377.

Aron, A., Norman, C. C., Aron, E. N., McKenna, C., Heyman, R. E. (2000). Couples' shared participation in novel and arousing activities and experienced relationship quality. *Journal of Personality and Social Psychology, 78,* 273–284.

Aron, A., Paris, M., & Aron, E. N. (1995). Falling in love: Prospective studies of self-concept change. *Journal of Personality and Social Psychology, 69,* 1102–1112.

Aron, E. N. (1996). *The highly sensitive person: How to thrive when the world overwhelms you.* New York: Birch/Lane.

Aron, E. N. (2002). *The highly sensitive child.* New York: Broadway Books.

Aron, E. N., & Aron, A. (1997). Sensory processing sensitivity and its relation to introversion and emotionality. *Journal of Personality and Social Psychology, 73,* 345–368.

Block, N. (1995). How heritability misleads about race. *Cognition, 56,* 99–128.

Bolognesi, M., Nigg, C. R., Massarini, M., & Lippke, S. (2006). Reducing obesity indicators through brief physical activity counseling (PACE) in Italian primary care settings. *Annals of Behavioral Medicine, 31,* 179–185.

Buboltz, W. C., Jr., Johnson, P., & Woller, K. M. P. (2003). Psychological reactance in college students: Family-of-origin predictors. *Journal of Counseling and Development, 81,* 311–317.

Bushman, B. J., & Anderson, C. A. (2001). Media violence and the American public: Scientific facts versus media misinformation. *American Psychologist, 56,* 477–489.

Caspi, A., Begg, D., Dickson, N., Harrington, H., Langley, J., Moffitt, T. E., & Silva, P. A. (1997). Personality differences predict health-risk behaviors in young adulthood: Evidence from a longitudinal study. *Journal of Personality and Social Psychology, 73,* 1052–1063.

Chapman, H. A., Hobfoll, S. E., & Ritter, C. (1997). Partners' stress underestimations lead to women's distress: A study of pregnant inner-city women. *Journal of Personality and Social Psychology, 73,* 418–425.

Cohen, J. (1988). *Statistical power analysis for the behavioral sciences.* Hillsdale, NJ: Lawrence Erlbaum Associates.

Cohen, J. (1990). Things I have learned (so far). *American Psychologist, 45,* 1304–1312.

Cohen, J. (1992). A power primer. *Psychological Bulletin, 112,* 155–159.

Conover, W., & Iman, R. L. (1981). Rank transformations as a bridge between parametric and nonparametric statistics. *American Statistician, 35,* 124–129.

Cooper, S. E., & Robinson, D. A. G. (1989). The influence of gender and anxiety on mathematics performance. *Journal of College Student Development, 30,* 459–461.

Dane, F. C., & Wrightsman, L. S. (1982). Effects of defendants' and victims' characteristics on jurors' verdicts. In N. L. Kerr & R. M. Bray (Eds.), *The psychology of the courtroom* (pp. 83–115). Orlando, FL: Academic Press.

Day, J. C., & Newberger E. C. (2002). The big payoff: Educational attainment and synthetic estimates of work-life earnings. *Current Population Reports,* Series P23-210. Washington, DC: U.S. Printing Office. Available at http://www.census.gov/prod/2002pubs/p23-210.pdf.

DeCarlo, L. T. (1997). On the meaning and use of kurtosis. *Psychological Methods, 2,* 292–307.

Denenberg, V. H. (1999). A critique of Mody, Studdert-Kennedy, and Brady's "Speech perception deficits in poor readers: Auditory processing or phonological coding?" *Journal of Learning Disabilities, 32,* 379–383.

Dunlap, W. P., & Myers, L. (1997). Approximating power for significance tests with one degree of freedom. *Psychological Methods, 2,* 186–191.

Durkin, K., & Barber, B. (2003). Not so doomed: Computer game play and positive adolescent development. *Applied Developmental Psychology, 23,* 373–392.

Dwinell, P. E., & Higbee, J. L. (1991). Affective variables related to mathematics achievement among high-risk college freshmen. *Psychological Reports, 69,* 399–403.

Elsesser, K., Sartory, G., & Tackenberg, A. (2004) Attention, heart rate, and startle response during exposure to trauma-relevant pictures: A comparison of recent trauma victims and patients with posttraumatic stress disorder. *Journal of Abnormal Psychology, 113,* 289–301.

Eppley, K. R., Abrams, A. I., & Shear, J. (1989). Differential effects of relaxation techniques on trait anxiety: A meta-analysis. *Journal of Clinical Psychology, 45,* 957–974.

Escudero, V., Rogers, L. E., & Gutierrez, E. (1997). Patterns of relational control and nonverbal affect in clinic and nonclinic couples. *Journal of Social and Personal Relationships, 14,* 5–29.

Everett, S. A., Price, J. H., Bedell, A. W., & Telljohann, S. K. (1997). The effect of a monetary incentive in increasing the return rate of a survey to family physicians. *Evaluation and the Health Professions, 20,* 207–214.

Eysenck, H. J. (1981). *A model for personality.* Berlin: Springer-Verlag.

Fiske, S. T. (1998). Stereotyping, prejudice, and discrimination. In D. T. Gilbert, S. T. Fiske, & G. Lindzey (Eds.), *The handbook of social psychology* (4th ed., pp. 357–411). New York: McGraw-Hill.

Frick, R. W. (1995). Accepting the null hypothesis. *Memory and Cognition, 23,* 132–138.

Gable, S., & Lutz, S. (2000). Household, parent, and child contributions to childhood obesity. *Family Relations, 49,* 293–300.

Gallagher-Thompson, D., Dal Canto, P. G., Jacob, T., & Thompson, L. W. (2001). A comparison of marital interaction patterns between couples in which the husband does or does not have Alzheimer's disease. *The Journals of Gerontology Series B: Psychological Sciences and Social Sciences, 56,* S140–S150.

Gallup, D. G. H. (1972). *The Gallup poll: Public opinion, 1935–1971.* New York: Random House.

Gibbons, J. L., Wilson, S. L., & Rufener, C. A. (2006). Gender attitudes mediate gender differences in attitudes towards adoption in Guatemala. *Sex Roles, 54,* 139–145.

Goidel, H. K., & Langley, R. E. (1995). Media coverage of the economy and aggregate economic evaluations: Uncovering evidence of indirect media effects. *Political Research Quarterly, 48,* 313–328.

Gonzaga, G. C., Keltner, D., Londahl, E. A., & Smith, M. D. (2001). Love and the commitment problem in romantic relations and friendship. *Journal of Personality and Social Psychology, 81,* 247–262.

Graham, S., Weiner, B., & Zucker, G. S. (1997). An attributional analysis of punishment goals and public reactions to O. J. Simpson. *Personality and Social Psychology Bulletin, 23,* 331–346.

Greene, E., & Dodge, M. (1995). The influence of prior record evidence on juror decision making. *Law and Human Behavior, 19,* 67–78

Greenwald, A. G. (1975). Consequences of prejudice against the null hypothesis. *Psychological Bulletin, 82,* 1–19.

Grilo, C. M., Walker, M. L., Becker, D. F., Edell, W. S., & McGlashan, T. H. (1997). Personality disorders in adolescents with major depression, substance use disorders, and coexisting major depression and substance use disorders. *Journal of Consulting and Clinical Psychology, 65,* 328–332.

Gunn, B., Biglan, A., Smolkowski, K, & Ary, D. (2000). The efficacy of supplemental instruction in decoding skills for Hispanic and non-Hispanic students in early elementary school. *Journal of Special Education, 34,* 90–103.

Harter, S., Waters, P. L., Pettitt, L. M., Whitesell, N., Kofkin, J., & Jordan, J. (1997). Autonomy and connectedness as dimensions of relationship styles in men and women. *Journal of Social and Personal Relationships, 14,* 147–164.

Hazan, C., & Shaver, P. (1987). Romantic love conceptualized as an attachment process. *Journal of Personality and Social Psychology, 52,* 511–524.

Hindley, C., Filliozat, A., Klackenberg, G., Nicolet-Meister, D., & Sand, E. (1966). Differences in age of walking in five European longitudinal samples. *Human Biology, 38,* 364–379.

Holden, G. W., Thompson, E. E., Zambarano, R. J., & Marshall, L. A. (1997). Child effects as a source of change in maternal attitudes. *Journal of Social and Personal Relationships, 14,* 481–490.

Hopkins W. D., Russell, J. L., Cantalupo, C., Freeman, H., & Schapiro, S. J. (2005). Factors influencing the prevalence and handedness for throwing in captive chimpanzees (Pan troglodytes). *Journal of Comparative Psychology, 119,* 363–370.

Hu, F. B., Li, T. Y., Colditz, G. A., Willett, W. C., & Manson, J. E. (2003). Television watching and other sedentary behaviors in relation to risk of obesity and type 2 diabetes mellitus in women. *Journal of the American Medical Association, 289,* 1785–1791.

Jackson, L. A., Ervin, K. S., Gardner, P. D., & Schmitt, N. (2001). Gender and the Internet: Women communicating and men searching. *Sex Roles, 44,* 363–379.

June, L. N., Curry, B. P., & Gear, C. L. (1990). An 11-year analysis of black students' experience of problems and use of services: Implications for counseling professionals. *Journal of Counseling Psychology, 37,* 178–184.

Kagan, J. (1994). *Galen's prophecy: Temperament in human nature.* New York: Basic Books.

Karney, B. R., & Bradbury, T. N. (1997). Neuroticism, marital interaction, and the trajectory of marital satisfaction. *Journal of Personality and Social Psychology, 72,* 1075–1092.

Kraemer, H. C., & Thiemann, S. (1987). *How many subjects? Statistical power analysis in research.* Newbury Park, CA: Sage.

Lambert, A. J., Khan, S. R., Lickel, B. A., & Fricke, K. (1997). Mood and the correction of positive versus negative stereotypes. *Journal of Personality and Social Psychology, 72,* 1002–1016.

Larson, R., Dworkin, J., & Verma, S. (2001). Men's work and family lives in India: The daily organization of time and emotions. *Journal of Family Psychology, 15,* 206–224.

Lee, K., Byatt, G., & Rhodes, G. (2000). Caricature effects, distinctiveness, and identification: Testing the face-space framework. *Psychological Science, 11,* 379–385.

Lepore, S. J., & Smyth, J. M. (Eds). (2002). *The writing cure: How expressive writing promotes health and emotional well-being.* Washington, DC: American Psychological Association.

Li, N. P., Bailey, J. M. Kenrick, D. T., & Linsenmeier, J. A. W. (2002). The necessities and luxuries of mate preferences: Testing the tradeoffs. *Journal of Personality and Social Psychology, 82,* 947–955.

Lydon, J., Pierce, T., & O'Regan, S. (1997). Coping with moral commitment to long-distance dating relationships. *Journal of Personality and Social Psychology, 73,* 104–113.

Markman, H. J., Renick, M. J., Floyd, F. J., Stanley, S. M., & Clements, M. (1993). Preventing marital distress through communication and conflict management training: A 4- and 5-year follow-up. *Journal of Consulting and Clinical Psychology, 61,* 70–77.

McCracken, G. (1988). *The long interview.* London: Sage.

McKee, T. L. E., & Ptacek, J. T. (2001). I'm afraid I have something bad to tell you: Breaking bad news from the perspective of the giver. *Journal of Applied Social Psychology, 31,* 246–273.

McLaughlin-Volpe, T., Aron, A., & Reis, H. T. (2001, February). *Closeness during interethnic social interactions and prejudice: A diary study.* Paper presented at the Annual Meeting of the Society for Personality and Social Psychology, San Antonio, TX.

Miller, R. S. (1997). Inattentive and contented: Relationship commitment and attention to alternatives. *Journal of Personality and Social Psychology, 73,* 758–766.

Mirvis, P., & Lawler, E. (1977). Measuring the financial impact of employee attitudes. *Journal of Applied Psychology, 62,* 1–8.

Misra, R., & Castillo, L. G. (2004). Academic stress among college students: Comparison of American and international students. *International Journal of Stress Management, 11,* 132–148.

Mody, M., Studdert-Kennedy, M., & Brady, S. (1997). Speech perception deficits in poor readers: Auditory processing or phonological coding? *Journal of Experimental Child Psychology, 64,* 1–33.

Morehouse, E., & Tobler, N. S. (2000). Preventing and reducing substance use among institutionalized adolescents. *Adolescence, 35,* 1–28.

Moriarty, S. E., & Everett, S-L. (1994). Commercial breaks: A viewing behavior study. *Journalism Quarterly, 71,* 346–355.

Mouradian, V. E. (2001). Applying schema theory to intimate aggression: Individual and gender differences in representation of contexts and goals. *Journal of Applied Social Psychology, 31,* 376–408.

Murphy, K. R. (1998). Obituary. The passing of giants: Raymond B. Cattell and Jacob Cohen. *The Industrial-Organizational Psychologist, 35*(4). Available online: http://siop.org/tip/backissues/TIPApril98/obituary.aspx.

Norcross, J. C., Kohout, J. L., & Wicherski, M. (2005). Graduate study in psychology: 1971 to 2004. *American Psychologist, 60,* 959–975.

Nownes, A. J. (2000). Policy conflict and the structure of interest communities: A comparative state analysis. *American Politics Quarterly, 28,* 309–327.

Olthoff, R. K. (1989). *The effectiveness of premarital communication training.* Unpublished doctoral dissertation, California Graduate School of Family Psychology, San Francisco.

Pecukonis, E. V. (1990). A cognitive/affective empathy training program as a function of ego development in aggressive adolescent females. *Adolescence, 25,* 59–76.

Pennebaker, J. W., & Beall, S. K. (1986). Confronting a traumatic event: Towards an understanding of inhibition and disease. *Journal of Abnormal Psychology, 95,* 274–281.

Perna, F. M., Antoni, M. H., Baum, A., Gordon, P., & Schneiderman, N. (2003). Cognitive behavioral stress management effects on injury and illness among competitive athletes: A randomized clinical trial. *Annals of Behavioral Medicine, 25,* 66–73.

Peters, W. S. (1987). *Counting for something: Statistical principles and personalities.* New York: Springer-Verlag.

Pettigrew, T. F., & Tropp, L. R. (2006). A meta-analytic test of intergroup contact theory. *Journal of Personality and Social Psychology, 90,* 751–783.

Prenda, K. M., & Lachman, M. E. (2001). Planning for the future: A life management strategy for increasing control and life satisfaction in adulthood. *Psychology and Aging, 16,* 207.

Puri, M. L., & Sen, P. K. (1985). *Nonparametric methods in general linear models.* New York: Wiley.

Rashotte, L. S., & Webster, M., Jr. (2005). Gender status beliefs. *Social Science Research, 34,* 618–633.

Reber, P. J., & Kotovsky, K. (1997). Implicit learning in problem solving: The role of working memory capacity. *Journal of Experimental Psychology: General, 126,* 178–203.

Riehl, R. J. (1994). Academic preparation, aspirations, and first-year performance of first-generation students. *College and University, 70,* 14–19.

Robins, R. W., & John, O. P. (1997). Effects of visual perspective and narcissism on self-perception: Is seeing believing? *Psychological Science, 8,* 37–42.

Rottenstreich, Y., & Hsee, C. K. (2001). Money, kisses, and electric shocks: On the affective psychology of risk. *Psychological Science, 12,* 185–190.

Russell, D., Peplau, L. A., & Cutrona, C. E. (1980). The revised UCLA Loneliness Scale: Concurrent and discriminant validity evidence. *Journal of Personality and Social Psychology, 39,* 472–480.

Salsburg, D. (2001). *The lady tasting tea: How statistics revolutionized science in the twentieth century.* New York: Freeman.

Schram, C. M. (1996). A meta-analysis of gender differences in applied statistics achievement. *Journal of Educational and Behavioral Statistics, 21,* 55–70.

Schuster, M. A., Stein, B. D., Jaycox, L. H., Collins, R. L., Marshall, G. N., Elliott, M. N., Zhou, A. J., Kanouse, D. E., Morrison, J. L., & Berry, S. H. (2001). A national survey of stress reactions after the September 11, 2001, terrorist attacks. *New England Journal of Medicine, 345,* 1507–1512.

Shaver, P. R., & Mikulincer, M. (in press). Attachment theory and research: Core concepts, basic principles, conceptual bridges. In A. Kruglanski & E. T. Higgins (Eds.), *Social psychology: Handbook of basic principles* (2nd ed.). New York: Guilford.

Shrout, P. E. (2001). Jacob Cohen (1923–1998). *American Psychologist, 56,* 166.

Siegel, M., & Biener, L. (1997). Evaluating the impact of statewide anti-tobacco campaigns: The Massachusetts and California Tobacco Control Programs. *Journal of Social Issues, 53,* 147–168.

Sinclair, L., & Kunda, Z. (2000). Motivated stereotyping of women: She's fine if she praised me but incompetent if she criticized me. *Personality and Social Psychology Bulletin, 26,* 1329–1342.

Skinner, B. F. (1956). A case history in scientific method. *American Psychologist, 11,* 221–233.

Smyth, J. M. (1998). Written emotional expression: Effect sizes, outcome types, and moderating variables. *Journal of Consulting and Clinical Psychology, 66,* 174–184.

Speed, A., & Gangestad, S. W. (1997). Romantic popularity and mate preferences: A peer-nomination study. *Personality and Social Psychology Bulletin, 23,* 928–937.

Spencer, S. J., Steele, C. M., & Quinn, D. M. (1999). Stereotype threat and women's math performance. *Journal of Experimental Social Psychology, 35,* 4–28.

Stake, J. E., & Malkin, C. (2003). Students' quality of experience and perceptions of intolerance and bias in the women's and gender studies classroom. *Psychology of Women Quarterly, 27,* 174–185.

Stankiewicz, B. J., Legge, G. E., Mansfield, J. S., & Schlicht, E. J. (2006). Lost in virtual space: Studies in human and ideal spatial navigation. *Journal of Experimental Psychology: Human Perception and Performance, 32,* 688–704.

Steele, C. M. (1997). A threat in the air: How stereotypes shape intellectual identity and performance. *American Psychologist, 52,* 613–629.

Steen, L. A. (1987). Foreword. In S. Tobias, *Succeed with math: Every student's guide to conquering math anxiety* (pp. xvii–xviii). New York: College Entrance Examination Board.

Steil, J. M., & Hay, J. L. (1997). Social comparison in the work place: A study of 60 dual-career couples. *Personality and Social Psychology Bulletin, 23,* 427–438.

Stigler, S. M. (1986). *The history of statistics.* Cambridge, MA: Belknap Press.

Tabachnick, B. G., & Fidell, L. S. (2007). *Using multivariate statistics* (5th ed.). Boston: Allyn and Bacon.

Tankard, J., Jr. (1984). *The statistical pioneers.* Cambridge, MA: Schenkman.

Thomas, J. R., Nelson, J. K., & Thomas, K. T. (1999). A generalized rank-order method for nonparametric analysis of data from exercise science: A tutorial. *Research Quarterly for Exercise and Sport, 70,* 11–27.

Tobias, S. (1982, January). Sexist equations. *Psychology Today,* pp. 14–17.

Tobias, S. (1987). *Succeed with math: Every student's guide to conquering math anxiety.* New York: College Entrance Examination Board.

Tobias, S. (1995). *Overcoming math anxiety.* New York: W. W. Norton.

Valenzuela, M. (1997). Maternal sensitivity in a developing society: The context of urban poverty and infant chronic undernutrition. *Developmental Psychology, 33,* 845–855.

Van Aken, M. A. G., & Asendorpf, J. B. (1997). Support by parents, classmates, friends, and siblings in preadolescence: Covariation and compensation across relationships. *Journal of Social and Personal Relationships, 14,* 79–93.

Viswanath, K., Breen, N., Meissner, H., Moser, R. P., Hesse, B., Randolph Steele, W., & Rakowski, W. (2006). Cancer knowledge and disparities in the information age. *Journal of Health Communication, 11,* 1–17.

Von Franz, M. L. (1979). *The problem of puer aeternus.* New York: Springer-Verlag.

Walberg, H. J., & Lai, J.-S. (1999). Meta-analytic effects for policy. In G. J. Cizek (Ed.), *Handbook of educational policy* (pp. 419–453). San Diego, CA: Academic Press.

Weller, A., & Weller, L. (1997). Menstrual synchrony under optimal conditions: Bedouin families. *Journal of Comparative Psychology, 111,* 143–151.

Wiseman, H. (1997). Interpersonal relatedness and self-definition in the experience of loneliness during the transition to university. *Personal Relationships, 4,* 285–299.

Zeidner, M. (1991). Statistics and mathematics anxiety in social science students: Some interesting parallels. *British Journal of Education, 61,* 319–329.

Index

Note: Page numbers followed by an *f* indicate figures; those followed by a *t* indicate tables.

A

Abrams, A. L., 211
Altman, D. C., 143
Analysis of variance
  one-way, 336
  in research articles, 344–45
  steps for, 329*t*
  two-way, 336
Analysis of variance (ANOVA), 312
  assumptions, 328–29
  effect size, 331–32
  factorial (*See* Factorial analysis of variance)
  figuring, 319–27
  hypothesis testing, 327–28
  logic of, 312–19
  power, 332
  sample size, 332–33
Anderson, C. A., 201, 202
Anderson, J. E., 198
Antoni, M. H., 201
Arcsine transformation, 385
Aron, A., 4, 7, 8, 9, 12, 13, 29, 30, 31, 35, 36, 43, 44, 51, 67, 72, 74, 86, 231, 251, 252, 385
Aron, E. N., 4, 7, 8, 9, 13, 36, 51, 67, 72, 74, 86, 231, 251, 385
Asendorpf, J. B., 303
Assumption, 255

B

Bailey, J. M., 72
Barber, B., 392
Baum, A., 201
Beall, S. K., 286
Becker, D. E., 351
Bedell, A. W., 403

Begg, D., 233
Between-groups degrees of freedom, 324
Between-groups estimate of the population variance, 314
  figuring, 321–23
Between-subjects design, 414
Biased estimate, 237
Biener, L., 170
Biglan, A., 108, 109
Bimodal distribution, 16
Block, N., 19, 20
Bolognesi, M., 21, 22
Bradbury, T. N., 250
Brady, S., 229
Breen, N., 138
Buboltz Jr., W. C., 98
Bushman, B. J., 201, 202
Byatt, G., 198, 199

C

Carey, J. W., 198
Caspi, A., 233
Castillo, L. G., 53
Categorical variables, 5
Causality
  correlation coefficient and, 84–86
  direction of, 84, 85–86
Ceiling effect, 18, 380
Cell, 337, 369
  mean, 337
Chapman, H. A., 107, 108
Chi-square test for independence, 396–97
  defined, 367–68
  degrees of freedom, 370–71
  effect size, 376–77, 397
  example, 372–74

Chi-square test for independence (*cont.*)
  figuring, 370
  hypothesis testing, 371–72
  population, 368
  power, 377
  sample size, 368, 378
Chi-square tests
  assumptions, 376
  defined, 359
  distribution, 363–64
  for goodness of fit, 362–66, 364–65, 395
  hypothesis testing and, 365–66
  for independence (*See* Chi-square test for independence)
  in research articles, 391–92
  statistic, 363
  table, 364
Cohen, J., 207, 214, 215, 222, 258, 292, 294, 377, 378, 416
Colditz, G. A., 193
Comparison distribution, 149, 239–40
Computational formulas, 43
Confidence interval (CI), 189
  defined, 189
  figuring, 190–91, 196
  hypothesis testing and, 191–92
  in research articles, 192–93
Confidence limits, 189
Contingency tables, 368, 369*t*
Conventional levels of significance, 150
Cooper, S. E., 3
Correlation
  curvilinear, 71
  defined, 68
  graphing, 68–71
  identifying, 75
  linear, 71, 75–79
  matrix, 94
  multiple, 95–97
  negative, 74
  no correlation, 73
  patterns, 71–76
  perfect, 78
  positive, 74
  in research articles, 93–95
  strength of, 74–75
Correlation coefficient
  causality and, 84–86
  defined, 79
  effect size, 119

  example, 80–84
  figuring, 75–79, 80
  formula, 79
  multiple, 97
  proportion of variance and, 92
  significance of, 117–19
  statistical significance of, 86–87
Cramer's phi, 376
  Cohen's conventions for, 377*t*
Criterion variables, 88
Cross product of Z scores, 76
Curry, B. P., 404
Curvilinear correlation
  defined, 71
  example, 73*f*
Cutoff scores
  determining with two-tailed tests, 155–56
  sample, 150, 241–42
Cutrona, C. E., 180

D

Dal Canto, P. G., 303
Dane, F. C., 328
Data transformation
  comparison with rank-order tests, 389–90
  defined, 382–86
  example, 385
  legitimacy of, 383
  in research articles, 392–93
  types of, 383, 385
Decision errors, 159–62
  relation of Type I and II, 161
  Type I, 160–61
  Type II, 161
Definitional formulas, 44
Degrees of freedom (*df*), 238–39
  between-groups, 324
  chi-square test for independence, 370–71
  within-groups, 325
Denenberg, V. H., 229
Dependent means, *t* tests, 246–54
Dependent variables, 337
Descriptive statistics, 2
Dickson, N., 233
Difference scores, 247
Directional hypothesis
  defined, 154
  one-tailed test and, 154
Direction of causality, 84

Distribution-free tests, 387
Distribution of means, 173–81, 213*f*
    defined, 173
    determining characteristics of, 174–78
    example, 174*f*, 179*f*, 190*f*
    figuring, 173–74, 194
    formulas for, 178–80
    hypothesis testing, 182–85
    mean of, 176
    sampling, 173
    standard deviation of, 239
    variance of, 176
Distributions
    bimodal, 16
    chi-square, 363–64
    comparison, 149
    of differences between means, 276–81
    heavy-tailed, 18, 21
    light-tailed, 18, 21
    multimodal, 16
    normal curve, 18, 21, 121
    rectangular, 16
    skewed, 16–18, 420
    symmetrical, 16–18
    types of, 180*t*, 181*f*
    unimodal, 16
Dodge, M., 328
Dunlap, W. P., 378
Durkin, K., 392
Dwinell, P. E., 3
Dworkin, J., 271, 272

E

Effect size, 203–9
    analysis of variance, 331–32
    chi-square test for independence, 376–77
    Cohen's conventions for, 208
    conventions, 207–8
    of correlation coefficient, 119
    defined, 205
    example, 207*t*, 208*f*, 211
    figuring, 206–7, 347
    formula for, 207
    importance of, 208–9
    power of study, 216–17
    raw score, 206
    in research articles, 228–29
    standardized, 206
    t tests, 256–57, 291–92

Elsesser, K., 93, 94
Eppley, K. R., 211
Equal-interval variables, 5, 413
Ervin, K. S., 305, 306
Escudero, V., 305, 306
Estimates
    between-group of population variance, 314
    biased, 237
    interval, 189–90
    point, 188–89
    within-group of population variance, 313
Everett, S. A., 403
Everett, S. L., 392
Expected frequency, 362, 369–70
Expected relative frequency, 135
Eysenck, H. J., 4

F

Factorial analysis of variance, 334–36
    extensions of, 343
Factorial research design, 335
    interaction effects, 335–36
    two-way, 336
F distribution, 317–18
    cutoff for, 323, 325*t*
    example, 324*f*
Fidell, L. S., 293
Filliozat, A., 146
Fisher, H. E., 252
Fisher, R. A., 318, 417
Fiske, S. T., 20
Floor effect, 18, 380
Floyd, F. J., 250
Formulas
    computational, 43
    for correlation coefficient, 79
    definitional, 44
    for effect size, 207
    for mean, 34–35
    for prediction model, 88–89
    for standard deviation, 42, 43–45
    for *Z* scores, 50–51
F ratio, 317–19
    figuring, 323
Frequency distributions
    bimodal, 16
    example, 136*f*
    heavy-tailed, 18, 21
    light-tailed, 18, 21

Frequency distributions (*cont.*)
  normal curve, 18, 21
  skewed, 16–18
  symmetrical, 16–18
  unimodal, 16
Frequency graphs, 10–12
Frequency polygons, 13–15
  in research articles, 21
Frequency tables, 6–10
  constructing, 7–8, 29–30
  defined, 7
  grouped, 9–10
  for nominal variables, 8
  in research articles, 21
Frick, R. W., 157
F table, 317–18, 324–25

G

Gable, S., 111
Gallagher-Thompson, D., 303
Gallup, D. G. H., 134
Galton, F., 81, 417
Gangestad, S. W., 111
Gardner, P. D., 305, 306
Gear, C. L., 404
Gibbons, J. L., 296
Goidel, H. K., 61
Gonzaga, G. C., 59
Gosset, W. S., 236, 417
Graham, S., 112, 113
Grand mean, 322
Graphs, frequency, 10–12
Greene, E., 328
Greenwald, A. G., 157
Grilo, C. M., 351
Grouped frequency tables, 9–10
Grouping variables, 336
Gunn, B., 108, 109
Gutierrez, E., 305, 306

H

Haphazard selection, 131
Harmonic mean, 293
Harter, S., 360, 361, 362, 367, 391
Hay, J. L., 396
Hazan, C., 311, 312
Heavy-tailed distributions, 18, 21
Higbee, J. L., 3
Hindley, C., 146

Histograms, 10–12
  constructing, 11*f*, 12*f*, 30–31
  example, 175*f*, 381*f*
  in research articles, 21
Hobfoll, S. E., 107, 108
Holden, G. W., 271
Howard, G., 143
Hsee, C. K., 393
Hu, F. B., 193
Hypothesis, 145
  directional, 154
  nondirectional, 154–56
  null, 148–49
  research, 148
Hypothesis testing, 117, 137
  with analysis of variance, 327–28
  assumptions, 380
  for chi-square test for independence, 371–72
  confidence interval and, 191–92
  core logic of, 147–48
  defined, 145
  example, 146–47
  null hypothesis (*See* Null hypothesis)
  one-tailed, 154
  process, 148–53
  in research articles, 162–63
  steps of, 365–66
  strategies for, 379–81
  with *t* test for independent means, 281, 298
  two-tailed, 154
  with unknown population variance, 242, 243*f*
  Z test, 182–85

I

Independence, 368
Independent variables, 336
Inferential statistics, 2, 134
Interaction effects, 335–36
  interpreting, 338–42
  main effects and, 342–43
Interval, 9
  confidence, 189
  estimates, 189–90
Inverse transformation, 385

J

Jackson, L. A., 305, 306
Jacob, T., 303

Jaycox, L. H., 139
John, O. P., 167
Johnson, P., 98
June, L. N., 404

K

Kagan, J., 4
Karney, B. R., 250
Keltner, D., 59
Kenrick, D. T., 72
Khan, S. R., 334, 335, 336, 340, 341, 344
Klackenberg, G., 146
Kotovsky, K., 168
Kraemer, H. C., 214
Kunda, Z., 355, 356
Kurtosis, 18

L

Lambert, A. J., 334, 335, 336, 340, 341, 344
Langley, R. E., 61
Larson, R., 271, 272
Lawler, E., 74
Lee, K., 198, 199
Legge, G. E., 180, 187
Lepore, S. J., 286
Levels of measurement, 6
Levine, D. W., 143
Li, N., 72
Li, T. Y., 193
Lickel, B. A., 334, 335, 336, 340, 341, 344
Light-tailed distributions, 18, 21
Linear correlation. *See* Correlation
Log transformation, 385
Londahl, E. A., 59
Long-run relative-frequency interpretation of probability.
    See Probability
Lui, J. S., 209
Lutz, S., 111
Lydon, J., 401

M

Main effect, 336
    interaction effects and, 342–43
Malkin, C., 392
Mansfield, J. S., 180, 187
Marginal means, 337
Markman, H. J., 250
Mashek, D. J., 252

Massarini, M., 21, 22
Math anxiety, 3–4
Math performance, gender, ethnicity and, 19–20
Matrix, correlation, 94
McKee, T. L. E., 26
McLaughlin-Volpe, T., 8, 9, 12, 29, 30, 31, 35, 36, 43, 44
Mean, 33–36
    cell, 337
    defined, 33
    distribution of, 173–81
    distribution of differences between, 276–81
    estimating, 188–89
    example, 33*f*, 34*f*, 36*f*, 53*t*
    figuring, 35
    formula, 34–35
    grand, 322
    harmonic, 293
    marginal, 337
    of samples, 315*f*, 316*f*
    standard error of, 177, 187
    statistical symbols, 34–35
Mean of a distribution of means, 176
Measurement, levels of, 6
Median, 38–39
    defined, 38
    finding, 38–39
Meissner, H., 138
Meta-analysis, 209, 211
Miller, R. S., 402
Mirvis, P., 74
Misra, R., 53
Mode, 36–38
    defined, 36
    examples of, 36*f*, 37*f*
Mody, M., 229
Morehouse, E., 228
Moriarty, S. E., 392
Mouradian, V. E., 28
Multimodal distribution, 16
Multiple correlation
    coefficient, 97
    defined, 95
    in research articles, 98–99
Multiple regression
    defined, 95
    predictions, 96, 97
    in research articles, 98–99
Multivariate statistical tests, 416
Murphy, K. R., 215
Myers, L., 378

N

Negative correlation, 74
Nigg, C. R., 21, 22
Nominal variables, 5, 361, 367
   frequency tables for, 8
Nondirectional hypothesis, two-tailed test and, 154–56
Nonparametric tests, 387
Norcross, J. C., 53, 54
Normal curve, 121–30
   checking for, 420–21
   defined, 121
   distributions, 18, 21
   example, 122*f*, 123*f*, 125*f*, 126*f*, 128*f*, 129*f*
   figuring percentage of scores with, 122–23, 125–27
   occurrence in nature, 121
   probability and, 136–37
   in research articles, 138–39
   table, 123*t*–130*t*
   Z scores, 123*t*–130*t*, 127–30
Norman, C. C., 67, 72, 74, 86
Nownes, A. J., 28
Null hypothesis, 148–49, 314–16, 372
   accepting, 157
   rejecting, 152–53, 241–42
Numeric variables, 5

O

Observed frequency, 362
Olthoff, R. K., 248, 249, 260, 273, 274
One-tailed hypothesis testing, 154
   example, 155*f*
   power and, 221
One-way analysis of variance, 336
Ordinal variables, 5
O'Regan, S., 401
Outcome, 135
Outliers, 38, 420

P

Parametric tests, 387, 389
Paris, M., 4, 7, 9, 13, 36, 51, 251
Pearson, K., 360, 417
Pecukonis, E. V., 170
Pennebaker, J. W., 286
Peplau, L. A., 180
Perfect correlation, 78
Perna, F. M., 201
Peters, W. S., 81, 236, 318, 360

Pettigrew, T. F., 209
Pettitt, L. M., 360, 361, 362, 367, 391
Phi coefficient, 376
Pierce, T., 401
Point estimates, 188–89
   accuracy of, 189
   defined, 189
Polls, 134, 186
Pooled estimate of the population variance, 278
Population
   chi-square test for independence, 368
   defined, 130
   of difference scores, 247
   estimating variance, 278–79
   example, 132*f*
   parameters, 133
   in research articles, 138–39
   versus sample, 131
Population variance
   between-groups estimate of, 314
   comparing estimates of, 316–17
   estimating, 312–13, 313–16
   within-groups estimate of, 313
Positive correlation, 74
Power
   analysis of variance, 332
   chi-square test for independence, 377
   figuring, 416
   increasing, 226*t*
   influences on, 220–21, 224*t*
   in research articles, 228–29
   statistical significance, 225–27
   t tests, 257–58, 292–93
Power of study
   determining, 215–21
   effect size, 215–21
   example, 218*f*, 219*f*, 220*f*
   role of, when planning, 222–25
   sample size, 217–19
   for *t* tests for dependent means, 259
Power tables, 214
Prediction, 87–92
   formula for model, 88–89
   model, 88–89
   models, 96
   using raw scores, 91–92
   as regression, 90
   in research articles, 93–95
   using Z scores, 88
Predictor variables, 88

Price, J. H., 403
Probability, 133–38
    defined, 135
    figuring, 135–36
    long-run relative-frequency interpretation of, 135
    range of, 136
    in research articles, 138–39
    symbols, 136
    Z scores and normal distribution, 136–37
Proportion of variance accounted for (R^2), 331
    correlation coefficient and, 92
Protected t tests, 330
Ptacek, J. T., 26

Q

Quantitative variables, 5
Quinn, D. M., 19

R

Random selection, 131
Range, 40
Rank-order tests, 387–89
    comparison with data transformation, 389–90
    defined, 387
    example, 388–89
    logic of, 388
    in research articles, 393
Rank-order variables, 5
Rashotte, L. S., 260
Raw score, 47
    changing to Z score, 50
    effect size, 206
    prediction, 91–92
Reber, P. J., 168
Rectangular distribution, 16
Regression. *See* Multiple regression; Prediction
Reis, H. T., 8, 9, 12, 29, 30, 31, 35, 36, 43, 44
Renick, M. J., 250
Repeated-measures design, 246
Representative values, 35–39
Research articles
    analysis of variance in, 344–45
    chi-square tests in, 391–92
    confidence intervals in, 192–93
    correlation and prediction in, 93–95
    data transformation in, 392–93
    effect size in, 228–29
    frequency polygons in, 21
    frequency tables in, 21

histograms in, 21
hypothesis tests in, 162–63
mean in, 52–53
multiple correlation in, 98–99
multiple regression in, 98–99
normal curve in, 138–39
power in, 228–29
probability in, 138–39
rank-order tests, 393
sample and population in, 138–39
standard deviation in, 52–53
t tests in, 260–61
variance in, 52–53
Z scores in, 52–53
Z tests in, 186–88
Research hypothesis, 148, 372
Research study, designing, 413–16
    accuracy checks, 419
    analysis in, 421
    conducting, 417–18
    data screening, 418–20
    normal curve, checking for, 420–21
    result write-up, 421–22
    test selection, 413–16
    values, missing, 419–20
Rhodes, G., 198, 199
Ritter, C., 107, 108
Robins, R. W., 167
Robinson, D. A. G., 3
Rogers, L. E., 305, 306
Rottenstreich, Y., 393
Rufener, C. A., 296
Russell, D., 180

S

Salsburg, D., 81, 236, 318, 360
Sample
    defined, 130
    errors in, 186
    example, 132f
    methods of, 131–33
    versus population, 131
    in research articles, 138–39
    statistics, 133
Sample size, 217–19
    chi-square test for independence, 368
    figuring, 219–20
    planning, 258, 294, 332–33, 416
    power in, 293

Sartory, G., 93, 94
Scatter diagram, 68–71
  constructing, 68–71
  defined, 68
Scatter diagram (*cont.*)
  example, 67*f*, 70*f*, 71*f*, 72*f*, 74*f*, 77*f*, 78*f*, 80*f*, 83*f*, 94*f*
Schram, C. M., 20
Schuster, M. A., 139
Score, 4
  cutoff sample, 150
  difference, 247
  raw, 47
Shaver, P., 311, 312
Shear, J., 211
Shrout, P. E., 215
Siegel, M., 170
Significance, levels of, 150, 220–21
Sinclair, L., 355, 356
Skewed distributions, 16–18, 420
Skinner, B. F., 48
Smolkowski, K., 108, 109
Smollan, D., 8
Smyth, J. M., 286
Speed, A., 111
Spencer, S. J., 19
Square-root transformation, 383, 384*f*, 385*t*
Stake, J. E., 392
Standard deviation
  computing, 194
  defined, 41
  of distribution of differences between means, 280, 297–98
  of distribution of means, 239
  example, 42*t*, 43*t*
  figuring, 42–43
  formula for, 42, 43–45
Standard error (*SE*), 177, 187
Standardized regression coefficient, 88, 89–90
Stankiewicz, B. J., 180, 187
Statistical power, 210–14
  defined, 210
  determining, 214
Statistical significance, 86–87, 150
  role of power and, 225–27
Statistics
  branches of, 2, 4
  defined, 2
  descriptive, 2
  example of, 293
  inferential, 2, 134
  psychology of, 48

sample, 133
Steele, C. M., 19
Steil, J. M., 396
Stein, B. D., 139
Stigler, S. M., 236, 318, 360
Studdert-Kennedy, M., 229
Sum of squared deviations, 45
Surveys, 134
Symmetrical distribution, 16–18

T

Tabachnick, B. G., 293
Tables
  chi-square, 364
  contingency, 368
  frequency, 6–10
  normal curve, 123–30
  power, 214
Tackenberg, A., 93, 94
Tankard Jr., J., 81, 236, 318, 360, 417
Taveras, S., 198
t distribution, 239–40
Testing hypothesis
  directional (*See* Directional hypothesis)
  nondirectional (*See* Nondirectional hypothesis)
Theory, 145
Thiemann, S., 214
Thompson, E. E., 271
Tobias, S., 3, 20
Tobler, N. S., 228
Transformation, data. *See* Data transformation
Treatment effect, 314
Tropp, L. R., 209
t score, 242, 281
t table
  defined, 241
  rejecting null hypothesis, 241–42
t test for dependent means
  assumptions of, 255–56
  defined, 246
  difference scores, 247
  effect size, 256–57
  example, 247–50, 251–54, 262–65
  power for, 257–58
  power of study using, 259
  in research articles, 260–61
  sample size, planning, 258
t test for independent means
  assumptions, 290–91
  defined, 275

effect size, 291–92
example, 283–89, 291*f*
hypothesis testing with, 281
power, 292–94
in research articles, 296
sample size, 294
steps for, 286*t*
t tests
assumptions of, 255–56
basic principle, 237–38
comparing types of, 295*t*
example, 235–37
protected, 330
in research articles, 260–61
single sample, 235, 262
Two-tailed hypothesis testing, 154–58
example, 155*f*, 156–58
power and, 221
Two-way analysis of variance, 336
Two-way factorial research design, 336
Type I error, 160–61
relation to Type II, 161
risk of, 390
Type II error, 161
relation to Type I, 161
risk of, 390

U

Unbiased estimate of the population variance, 238
Unimodal distribution, 16

V

Values, 4
representative, 35–39
Van Aken, M. A. G., 303
Variability, 39–41
importance of, 45
Variables
categorical, 5
criterion, 88
defined, 4
dependent, 337
equal-interval, 5, 413
grouping, 336
independent, 336
nominal, 5, 361, 367
numeric, 5
ordinal, 5
predictor, 88
rank-order, 5

types of, 5–6
Variance
computing, 40
defined, 40
of distribution of differences between means, 280
distribution of means, 176, 279–80
example, 42*t*, 43*t*
figuring, 42–43
$N - 1$ approach, 45
population, 242
Verma, S., 271, 272
Viswanath, K., 138
Von Franz, M. L., 48

W

Walberg, H. J., 209
Walker, M. I., 351
Waters, P. L., 360, 361, 362, 367, 391
Webster Jr., M., 260
Weighted average, 278
Weiner, B., 112, 113
Weller, A., 268
Weller, L., 268
Wicherski, M., 53, 54
Wilson, S. L., 296
Wiseman, H., 186
Within-groups degrees of freedom, 325
Within-groups estimate of the population variance, 313
figuring, 320–21
Woller, K. M. P., 98
Wrightsman, L. S., 328

Z

Zambarano, R. J., 271
Zeidner, M., 3
Z scores, 46–51, 182–85
cross product of, 76–77
defined, 47
example, 183*f*
figuring, 127–30
figuring from percentages, 140–41
formulas, 50–51
normal table curve and, 123–30
prediction using, 88
probability and, 136–37
as scale, 47–49
as standard of comparison, 49
Z tests, 182–85, 194
in research articles, 186–88
Zucker, G. S., 112, 113

Steps of Hypothesis Testing for Major Procedures

	Z test (Ch. 6)	t test for a single sample (Ch. 8)	t test for dependent means (Ch. 8)	t test for independent means (Ch. 9)
❶	Restate the question as a research hypothesis and a null hypothesis about the populations.	Restate the question as a research hypothesis and a null hypothesis about the populations.	Restate the question as a research hypothesis and a null hypothesis about the populations.	Restate the question as a research hypothesis and a null hypothesis about the populations.
❷	Determine the characteristics of the comparison distribution. Population M_M = Population M; Population SD_M^2 = Population SD^2/N; Population $SD_M = \sqrt{\text{Population } SD_M^2}$; approximately normal if population normal or $N > 30$.	Determine the characteristics of the comparison distribution. (a) The mean of the distribution of means is the same as the population mean. (b) Figure its standard deviation: Ⓐ $S^2 = \Sigma(X - M)^2/(df)$ Ⓑ $S_M^2 = S^2/N$ Ⓒ $S_M = \sqrt{S_M^2}$ (c) t distribution, $df = N - 1$.	Determine the characteristics of the comparison distribution. (a) All based on difference scores. (b) Figure mean of the difference scores. (c) Mean of distribution of means of difference scores = 0. (d) Figure its standard deviation: Ⓐ $S^2 = \Sigma(X - M)^2/(df)$ Ⓑ $S_M^2 = S^2/N$ Ⓒ $S_M = \sqrt{S_M^2}$ (c) t distribution, $df = N - 1$.	Determine the characteristics of the comparison distribution. (a) Its mean will be 0. (b) Figure its standard deviation: Ⓐ For each population, $S^2 = \Sigma(X - M)^2/(N - 1)$ Ⓑ $S_{Pooled}^2 = (df_1/df_{Total})(S_1^2) + (df_2/df_{Total})(S_2^2)$; $df_1 = N_1 - 1$ and $df_2 = N_2 - 1$; $df_{Total} = df_1 + df_2$. Ⓒ $S_{M_1}^2 = S_{Pooled}^2/N_1$; $S_{M_2}^2 = S_{Pooled}^2/N_2$ Ⓓ $S_{Difference}^2 = S_{M_1}^2 + S_{M_2}^2$ Ⓔ $S_{Difference} = \sqrt{S_{Difference}^2}$ (c) t distribution, degrees of freedom = df_{Total}
❸	Determine the cutoff sample score on the comparison distribution at which the null hypothesis should be rejected. Use normal curve table.	Determine the cutoff sample score on the comparison distribution at which the null hypothesis should be rejected. Use t table.	Determine the cutoff sample score on the comparison distribution at which the null hypothesis should be rejected. Use t table.	Determine the cutoff sample score on the comparison distribution at which the null hypothesis should be rejected. Use t table.
❹	Determine your sample's score on the comparison distribution. $Z = (M - \text{Population } M_M)/\text{Population } SD_M$	Determine your sample's score on the comparison distribution. $t = (M - \text{Population } M)/S_M$	Determine your sample's score on the comparison distribution. $t = (M - \text{Population } M)/S_M$	Determine your sample's score on the comparison distribution. $t = (M_1 - M_2)/S_{Difference}$
❺	Decide whether to reject the null hypothesis. Compare scores from Steps ❸ and ❹.	Decide whether to reject the null hypothesis. Compare scores from Steps ❸ and ❹.	Decide whether to reject the null hypothesis. Compare scores from Steps ❸ and ❹.	Decide whether to reject the null hypothesis. Compare scores from Steps ❸ and ❹.